'The presuppositions and contradictions of Analytical Marxism resulted in a movement away from Marxism and towards liberal political philosophy. But what if its originators understood the German idealist tradition and what if their philological skills were as good as their analytic ones? Furner's book marvelously answers this question, staking out a tenable Marxian position within the landscape of contemporary political philosophy.'
–*William S. Lewis, Professor of Philosophy, Skidmore College*

'An important contribution to the vexed debate about Marx and justice.'
–*Jan Kandiyali, Assistant Professor in Philosophy, Istanbul Technical University*

Marx on Capitalism

Historical Materialism
Book Series

The titles published in this series are listed at *brill.com/hm*

Marx on Capitalism

The Interaction-Recognition-Antinomy Thesis

By

James Furner

BRILL

LEIDEN | BOSTON

Library of Congress Cataloging-in-Publication Data

Names: Furner, James, author.
Title: Marx on capitalism : the interaction-recognition-antinomy thesis / by James
    Furner.
Description: Leiden ; Boston : Brill, [2018] | Series: Historical materialism book
    series, ISSN 1570-1522 ; Volume 168 | Includes bibliographical references and
    index.
Identifiers: LCCN 2018035508 (print) | LCCN 2018037720 (ebook) |
    ISBN 9789004384804 (ebook) | ISBN 9789004323315 (hardback : alk. paper)
Subjects: LCSH: Marx, Karl, 1818-1883. | Capitalism–Philosophy.
Classification: LCC HX39.5 (ebook) | LCC HX39.5 .F86 2018 (print) |
    DDC 335.4/12–dc23
LC record available at https://lccn.loc.gov/2018035508

Typeface for the Latin, Greek, and Cyrillic scripts: "Brill". See and download: brill.com/brill-typeface.

ISSN 1570-1522
ISBN 978-90-04-32331-5 (hardback)
ISBN 978-90-04-38480-4 (e-book)

Contents

Acknowledgements

The completion of this book project was made possible by a postdoctoral research fellowship in the School of Social Sciences, University of the Witwatersrand. I would like to thank Mary Carman, Lawrence Hamilton, Peter Hudson, Jan Kandiyali, William Lewis, Thad Metz, Komnas Poriazis, Jürgen Ritsert and one anonymous referee for their comments on various parts of the manuscript.

The book includes revised or expanded versions of arguments first presented in:

'Schütz and Marx on Action', *South African Journal of Philosophy*, 30, 2: 15–27. © The Philosophical Society of South Africa, 2011.

'Marx's Sketch of Communist Society in *The German Ideology* and the Problems of Occupational Identity and Occupational Confinement', *Philosophy and Social Criticism*, 37, 2: 189–215. © SAGE Publications Ltd, 2011.

'Marx with Kant on Exploitation', *Contemporary Political Theory*, 14, 1: 23–44. © Palgrave Macmillan, 2015.

References and Abbreviations

References to works originally written in German, French or classical languages are first to an original language edition and then, if available, to a published translation; for example,

> Menger 1968, p. 86; Menger 2007, p. 120.

Marx's writings are referenced by volume, page number, using the abbreviations:

MECW   *Marx/Engels Collected Works*
MEGA   *Marx-Engels-Gesamtausgabe*
MEJ   *Marx-Engels-Jahrbuch*
MEW   *Marx-Engels-Werke*

If more than one published translation is referenced, the additional translation(s) will follow the reference to MECW. For example,

> *MEW*, 23, p. 12; *MECW*, 35, p. 8; Marx 1976, p. 90.

refers first to volume 23 of the *Marx Engels Werke*, then to volume 35 of the *Marx Engels Collected Works*, then to another translation published in 1976.

The MEGA is a more scholarly edition of Marx's works than the MEW. However, the MEGA is currently incomplete and unevenly distributed. (At present, no copy is registered as held by a library in Africa). Hard copies of the MEW are more widely distributed, and the entire MEW is available online. It is more helpful, therefore, for readers who wish to investigate the context of a citation, or to evaluate a translation, to supply a reference to the MEW. For a book that aims to retranslate Marx's texts transparently, this advantage is decisive. So, if possible, references to a German language edition are to the MEW. As the MEW edition of *The German Ideology* edits the order of the text, references are also provided to the part of *The German Ideology* that appears in the 2003 volume of the MEJ, which is also available online. (At the time of writing, the MEGA edition of *The German Ideology* is still forthcoming).

Kant's writings are referenced by volume: page number in *Kants gesammelte Schriften*, Berlin: de Gruyter, or *Akademie* (*Ak.*) edition, except for *Critique of Pure Reason*, which is cited by A/B pagination. As all the translations of Kant's writings cited here include these paginations, we have a single reference; for example,

Kant 2014, 4: 428.

where 2014 gives the date of publication of an English translation.

The policy of translation is outlined in the appendix to chapter 1.

The Interaction-Recognition-Antinomy Thesis

Books that begin 'Why another book on Karl Marx?' indulge a misconception. It is a misconception that there are many books on Karl Marx. There is a vast literature of second-hand commentary on the official translations of Marx's writings. But those translations do not render central passages unobjectionably. They conceal the substantive philosophical thesis about capitalism defended in this book.

The thesis about capitalism defended here, and which the official translations conceal, is one that connects the capitalist economic structure with the state and classes. The question as to whether Marx's writings contain an overarching thesis connecting these topics, which transcend a single specialism, deserves study in its own right. It goes to the core of how one might think about capitalism. It also raises the most fundamental question of Marxism: is there a plausible thesis in Marx's writings that connects the capitalist economic structure with the state and classes so as to suggest that socialism is both possible and desirable?

The reader will be relieved that the thesis advanced here does not attempt to cover all of what could be said in Marx's name on these topics. Rather, it says just enough about them to connect them through a conception of interaction, recognition and antinomy. The thesis is that the most minimal description of the capitalist economic structure is a description of two types of interaction, which explain the existence of two forms of recognition, and two antinomies. More specifically, the interactions of purchase and sale and capitalist labour-exploitation are said to explain the recognition of personhood, and a recognition-based form of bureaucratic domination; as well as an antinomy between natural rights and popular authorisation, and a rights-antinomy in capitalist production. This thesis is called the *interaction-recognition-antinomy thesis*. An antinomy, the least familiar of these terms, here denotes an oscillation of thought or will between two incompatible assertions that leave no middle ground and appear to be valid, although both rest on the same premises, at least one of which is false.[1]

The interaction-recognition-antinomy thesis is a new thesis. But it is offered in the spirit of an old project, associated with the philosophers Georg Lukács

---

1 See ch. 3, sec. 6.

© KONINKLIJKE BRILL NV, LEIDEN, 2019 | DOI:10.1163/9789004384804_002

(1885–1971) and Theodor Adorno (1903–69). For both Lukács and Adorno, Marx's analysis of the commodity as a general form of wealth, or commodity form, provides the basis for a supra-disciplinary critical theory of capitalism. The research project to explore the supra-disciplinary significance of an analysis of the commodity form may be termed *commodity form philosophy*. The interaction-recognition-antinomy thesis is a thesis in the spirit of commodity form philosophy.

The interaction-recognition-antinomy thesis is defended both as a reconstruction of Marx's writings, and as a substantive thesis. As a substantive thesis, it can be assessed without any special interest in Marx, and/or the development of Marx's thought. The texts of a great thinker can command the attention of non-specialists because they broach topics that are common themes in broader traditions of thought. The aspects of Marx's writings that support the interaction-recognition-antinomy thesis can interest a non-specialist, for they address broader problems in social and political philosophy as various as what social relations are, whether a principle of autonomy can condemn capitalism, how domination or recognition may be conceived, and whether there can be antinomies in the social world. Marx's relation to thinkers in traditions of thought that articulate these concerns is more evident when, as here, passages from across the range of his writings are systematically retranslated.

As a reconstruction of Marx's writings, the interaction-recognition-antinomy thesis places Marx in the post-Kantian tradition. Its conceptions of exploitation and antinomy engage critically with Kant, while recognition is a Hegelian motif. The interaction-recognition-antinomy thesis also bears out the German Marxist Hans-Georg Backhaus's claim that there is 'striking continuity in Marx's thought from 1843 to 1880'[2] on account of the supra-disciplinary significance of Marx's critique of the value form of wealth (commodities, money and capital) over this period.

One of the more controversial features of the interaction-recognition-antinomy thesis is that it challenges the view, advanced by scholars as diverse as Backhaus,[3] Michael Heinrich[4] and G.A. Cohen,[5] that Marx (or at least the mature Marx, or at least the mature and self-aware Marx) offers a critique of capitalism that avoids any normative commitment. The interaction-recognition-antinomy thesis holds that Marx's account of capitalism, in the *Grundrisse* (1857–58) and *Capital* Volume I (1867) in particular, sustains a normative cri-

---

2   Backhaus 1999, p. 107.
3   Backhaus 2011, p. 409.
4   Heinrich 2005, p. 33; Heinrich 2012, p. 36.
5   Cohen 2001, p. 64.

tique. It seeks to testify to the capacity of commodity form philosophy to combine explanatory social theory with normative political philosophy. As the thought that a Marxist project can join both of these concerns is acknowledged as controversial enough to be likened to 'having your cake and eating it'[6] even by its advocates, its basis is best outlined at the start, to bring out the significance of the connection to be established between the three components of the thesis.

Marx's mature account of capitalism sustains a normative critique, for it can be read to honour Marx's declaration of 1843, in his *Letters from the Deutsch-Französische Jahrbücher*, to 'develop new principles for the world out of the world's own principles ... We merely show the world why [*warum*] it is really struggling, and that consciousness is something it *must* acquire, even if it does not want to'.[7] The approach Marx declares here is that of showing how social conflicts imbued with principles belonging to the world as it is can be more decisively prosecuted only if participants adopt new, normatively superior principles, which those conflicts put them in a position to adopt. Marx's mature account of capitalism honours this approach, for *Capital* Volume I identifies a rights-antinomy in capitalist production that rests on a normative premise, the recognition of self-ownership. This rights-antinomy explains the formation of a working-class movement to limit the working day that gives its participants the chance to adopt a normatively superior principle, superior in that it rejects a premise of the rights-antinomy, and would better satisfy the need for recognition expressed in the form of this premise. This superior principle is a system universalisability principle of justice. Marx hints at this principle when, in the *Grundrisse*, he submits money maximisation to a universalisability test. If this principle is superior, condemns capitalism, and could be applied in socialism, the interaction-recognition-antinomy thesis offers a new argument for socialism.

From this angle, we see the relevance of a suggestion made by Allen Wood, that John Stuart Mill and Immanuel Kant adopt the same kind of argumentative strategy as one another in arguing for an ultimate value (the principle of utility and humanity in a person, respectively).[8] The argumentative strategy is

---

6 Callinicos 2001, p. 170.
7 *MEW*, 1, p. 345; *MECW*, 3, p. 144. It is best to translate '*warum*' literally, as 'why'. *MECW* has: 'what it is really fighting for'. If Marx had wished to say 'what ... for', he could have used '*wofür*'. The correction supports my claim. *Capital*'s explanation of why there arises a class struggle for a limited working day rests on its discovery of a rights-antinomy in 'the world's own principles'. A need for 'new principles' relates directly to the cause of this struggle, the rights-antinomy, rather than to the law for which this struggle is fought; see ch. 12.
8 See Mill 1962, p. 32; and Kant 2014, 4: 428–9.

one that 'shows this value to be one we already acknowledge both in theory and in practice'.[9] The strategy is to start from something that can be taken as given, something we do of necessity, and then to argue that we thereby acknowledge the value. The argument is to show 'that this claim about ultimate value is a reasonable interpretation of what we are committed to in our thinking and doing'.[10] The interaction-recognition-antinomy thesis shows that a version of this strategy is open to commodity form philosophy.

In *Capital* Chapter Two, Marx argues that commodity exchange, in which all actors in capitalism necessarily engage, is accompanied by a form of recognition. Then, later on in *Capital* Volume I, Marx identifies a rights-antinomy in capitalist production that problematises this form of recognition. No form of recognition can be satisfactory if it is encumbered by an antinomy. If it can be shown that this rights-antinomy is a necessary result of certain fundamental features of capitalism; that this antinomy produces practical responses that, while problematic, give a type of actor the chance to affirm a principle with which to resolve it; and that this principle rests on an ultimate value; then this ultimate value is one to which we are committed. What is distinctive about this version of the argumentative strategy is that its starting point is a socially anchored defect. A commitment to what Marx's *Theses on Feuerbach* term 'human society, or social humanity'[11] arises from the rational requirement to address a socially anchored defect (an antinomy) by adopting a principle that is available to a type of actor in the class struggle that this antinomy prompts, and which rests on this value.[12]

The author who has carried out the most sustained reconstructive work on the official translations of Marx's writings is the late Oxford philosopher G.A. Cohen, first in *Karl Marx's Theory of History: a Defence* (1978), and followed up by, among others, *History, Labour and Freedom* (1988), and *Self-Ownership, Freedom and Equality* (1995). Insofar as Cohen's critique of Rawlsian liberal thought in *Rescuing Justice and Equality* (2008) is 'Marx-inspired', it, too, must be factored in.[13] Whatever one's judgement of the project of Analytical Marxism, for which Cohen was a leading advocate, one may admire Cohen's commit-

---

9   Wood 2008, p. 89.

10   Ibid.

11   *MEW*, 3, p. 7; *MECW*, 5, p. 5. The Tenth Thesis says: '[t]he standpoint of the old materialism is civil society; the standpoint of the new is human society, or social humanity'.

12   Even if Marx rejected eternal truths (as claimed in Wood 1972, p. 270 and Wood 2004, pp. 130–1; compare *MEW*, 4, p. 480; *MECW*, 6, p. 504), that is, principles whose validity is grounded independently of facts about specific forms of society, this argumentative strategy is consistent with that rejection.

13   Cohen 2008, p. 2. See also Cohen 2001; Cohen 2009; and Cohen 2011, Part Two.

ment to offer a coherent reconstruction, which Marx's voluminous but diverse and incomplete set of writings cry out for. It is on account of Cohen's commitment to reconstruction and the resulting influence of his work[14] that many of the arguments in this book for the interaction-recognition-antinomy thesis defend it either from objections implicitly raised by Cohen's reconstruction, or as a better reconstruction. Even if Analytical Marxism has long ceased to be a live movement,[15] no reconstruction is more widely known among analytic philosophers with a current interest in Marx than Cohen's.

Even on broader terms, there is a reason why Cohen's reconstruction remains the one to better. Systematic accounts of Marx's mature writings since Cohen's do not tend to defend a substantive thesis linking the capitalist economic structure with the state and classes. For example, Moishe Postone's *Time, Labor, and Social Domination* (1993) theorises the dynamics of capitalist production. But it does not seek to advance a substantive thesis based on Marx's writings linking the capitalist economic structure with the state and classes. Nor do the commentaries on Marx's *Capital* that have appeared since the publication of Postone's study explicitly offer such a thesis.[16] The reason for this is simple. To offer such a thesis, it is necessary to argue that the *Grundrisse* and *Capital* allow some of the insights of Marx's earlier writings from the 1840s to come into their own. As this argument exceeds the bounds of a commentary on *Capital*, and *Capital* has absorbed the larger part of recent interest in Marx, it is still Cohen's reconstruction that remains the one to better.

The positive aim of this book is to support the project of commodity form philosophy by reconstructing a thesis from Marx's original texts, unavailable to readers of the official translations, connecting the capitalist economic structure, the state and classes. Its arguments are part interpretive, part linguistic, and part substantive. The interpretive part of the argument is that the interaction-recognition-antinomy thesis is a thesis about capitalism that can be reconstructed from the best translation of Marx's texts. The linguistic argument is that the translations offered here are superior to the official ones, which are often inadequate. On the substantive side, three sorts of argument are advanced: arguments for the project of commodity form philosophy; arguments for a specific conception of interaction, recognition and antinomy; and arguments for the interaction-recognition-antinomy thesis.

---

14   Evident in the debate on Marx and justice (ch. 8, sec. 13) or over the problem of legality (ch. 5).

15   On Analytical Marxism's disappearance, see Conclusion, sec 2.

16   Including Callinicos 2014; Harvey 2010; Heinrich 2005; Jameson 2011; Roberts 2017.

It could, of course, be doubted whether there is *any* defensible overarching thesis about capitalism to be reconstructed from Marx's writings. Insofar as this sceptic is not an *a priori* sceptic – a mirror image of the Stalinist apparatchik who maintained at all costs that Marx and Engels's writings provide the answer for every problem – their scepticism may rest on one of two challengeable beliefs. A sceptic might believe that there is no overarching thesis about capitalism to reconstruct from Marx's writings because Marx's writings are valuable only for their individual insights, or because Marx was an inconsistent thinker. These are different grounds of scepticism, although both appear conjoined in Agnes Heller's claim that Marx's 'many-sided search for truth' resulted in a 'brilliant lack of coherence'.[17]

The only way to overcome the first of these two challengeable forms of scepticism is to go ahead and defend an overarching thesis. Even if this sceptic remains unmoved, they might still adopt one or other aspect of the thesis. The second form of scepticism requires further distinction. If the claim is that Marx is a less than perfectly consistent thinker, then the claim is neither possible to disprove (there being too much potential evidence to retranslate and sift through), nor necessary to disprove, to establish the interpretive part of the argument. If the claim is instead that Marx's writings support different and incompatible overarching theses, the claim is possible to disprove but, again, not necessary to disprove. If, finally, the claim is that a defensible overarching thesis about capitalism based on Marx's writings is condemned to rely on isolated and unrepresentative passages, the claim is possible to disprove and actually disproved, if the argument in this book is accepted. The passages central for the argument of each chapter include some passages that are already prominent in existing interpretations, from which it may be presumed that they are not unrepresentative.

The bulk of the rest of this chapter situates the interaction-recognition-antinomy thesis in relation to existing debates. It does not seek to elaborate the full version of the argument for any particular aspect of the thesis. The full version will be elaborated in later chapters. Rather, it indicates how the thesis would shift or advance some live or influential debates in the Anglophone and German language receptions of, or critical reactions to, Marx's writings. Readers seeking a chapter-by-chapter outline of the argument may turn to section 5.

Section 1 situates the interaction component of the thesis in relation to (among others) Cohen's and Postone's readings of Marx. Section 2 situates its

---

17   Heller 1976, p. 88.

recognition component in relation to rational-choice theory, and Axel Honneth's recognition-based social theory. Section 3 relates the antinomy between natural rights and popular authorisation to the Russian legal theorist Evgeny Pashukanis's *General Theory of Law and Marxism*, and the West German state debate. Section 4 situates the rights-antinomy in capitalist production in relation to what Lukács calls the 'standpoint of the proletariat',[18] and Lenin's thesis of political awareness in *What is to be Done?*

The appended 'Note on Translation', which follows the chapter-by-chapter outline in section 5, documents some prominent errors in the official translations of Marx's writings, and outlines the policy adopted for identifying when and explaining how the official translations have been improved.

1   The Interaction Component

The interaction component of the thesis offers a solution to the problem of how, by virtue of an analysis of the commodity form, capitalist production can be characterised as exploitative. The background to the problem is as follows.

In the Preface to the First Edition of *Capital*, Marx indicates that his analysis will begin with 'the commodity form of the product of labour'.[19] 'The commodity', Marx writes in *Capital*, is a 'unity of use-value and value'.[20] Roughly, 'use-value' is anything that can be used as a means to satisfy a human want, while 'value' is the power of general exchangeability of a product produced for exchange. After arguing that commodities, as a general form of wealth, presuppose money, and wage-labour, Marx characterises capitalist production by a 'degree of exploitation'.[21] The question is: leaving aside quantitative matters of degree, how does a characterisation of capitalist production as exploitative relate to an analysis of the commodity form? How can capitalist production be conceived as exploitative by applying that characterisation to a description of it that follows purely from what the commodity form presupposes? Only then can Marx take capitalism to be inherently exploitative.

The problem of how to link capitalist exploitation to the commodity form is one that philosophically-informed scholarship on Marx has bequeathed, rather than solved. Much work falls into one of two categories. On the one hand,

---

18   Lukács 1977, p. 331; Lukács 1968, p. 149.
19   *MEW*, 23, p. 12; *MECW*, 35, p. 8; Marx 1976, p. 90.
20   *MEW*, 23, p. 201; *MECW*, 35, p. 196; Marx 1976, p. 293; compare *MEW*, 23, p. 119; *MECW*, 35, p. 114; Marx 1976, p. 199.
21   *MEW*, 23, p. 232; *MECW*, 35, p. 227; Marx 1976, p. 326.

the project of Analytical Marxism originated in annual meetings of Anglophone Marxists over the period 1979 to 1981, 'all of whom', Cohen reports, 'were working on the concept of exploitation'.[22] The trend among this group of theorists has been to place the concept of exploitation self-consciously on general foundations that do not relate capitalist exploitation to the commodity form (more on which below).[23] On the other hand, the studies of Isaak Rubin, Helmut Reichelt, Hans-Georg Backhaus and Moishe Postone on the group of terms 'abstract labour', 'commodity' and 'money' that now shape philologically-informed scholarship on Marx more than Analytical Marxism offer no analysis of exploitation.[24] Postone's *Time, Labor, and Social Domination* explicitly downplays the importance of exploitation for Marx's mature critique of capitalism.[25] While the first group does not seek to relate capitalist exploitation to the commodity form, the second has not taken any positive steps towards doing so.

Other accounts of capitalist exploitation do seek to relate it to the commodity form. However, these accounts end up relying on conditions or facts that are not strictly related to the commodity form.

One proposal, by Allen Wood, is to conceive exploitation as a beneficial 'playing on some weakness or vulnerability'.[26] Wood interprets Marx in this light. In a discussion of Marx's account of capitalist exploitation, Wood says: 'the basic vulnerability of workers to capital, as Marx presents it, consists in the fact that if they are going to live, they have no choice but to sell their labor power to capitalists'.[27] Marx can use this vulnerability conception of exploitation to characterise capitalist production as exploitative on the basis of an analysis of the commodity form if the commodity form presupposes that those who sell their labour power to a capitalist have 'no choice' but to do so 'if they are going to live'. The commodity form does not presuppose this, however. Wage-labour can be presumed to be available for hire if those who perform it lack any better or equal option. But that is not to say that they lack any other life-preserving option.[28] Revealingly, Wood no longer repeats his claim (of 2004) that 'the secret of surplus value' is 'due to the vulnerability of labor to capital'.[29] Wood now says that it 'makes sense to think of Marx' as using this vulnerability

---

22   Cohen 2000, p. xix.
23   See Cohen 1988; Cohen 1995; Cohen 2011; Elster 1985; Roemer 1982a; Roemer 1994; Wright 1985.
24   See Backhaus 1999; Backhaus 2011; Postone 1993; Reichelt 2001; Rubin 1973; Rubin 2012.
25   Postone 1993, p. 282; see below.
26   Wood 1995, p. 147.
27   Wood 2004, p. 252; see, similarly, Wood 2017, p. 643.
28   See Furner 2015, pp. 9–10.
29   Wood 2004, p. 251.

conception of exploitation once we avoid Marx's own 'technical notion' for its 'obfuscation'.[30] If vulnerability is conceived of (following Nicholas Vrousalis) as susceptibility to 'a substantial risk of a significant loss',[31] a similar objection applies. Wage-labour can be presumed to be available for hire if those who perform it lack a better or equal option, even if they have a slightly worse option. The common point is this: if capitalist exploitation is taken to rest on a quality of an exploitee's choice situation, rather than on the nature of the option they choose in being played by the exploiter; then, as this option may be chosen in a non-vulnerable choice situation, it is possible to conceive of capitalist production without exploitation.

A different proposal, by William Clare Roberts, is to say that capitalist production is exploitative, for Marx, because it is 'an unnatural use of labor power'.[32] The use of labour power by capitalists is said to be 'unnatural' because it is 'oriented toward accumulation, toward a purpose that could not possibly spring from human deliberation among the workers themselves'.[33] For Roberts, Marx's characterisation of capitalist production as exploitative rests on the counterfactual claim: accumulation is a purpose that workers themselves, after human deliberation, could not possibly adopt. Roberts's arguments for this counterfactual claim relate to the quantity of labour that producers would commit themselves to performing if they were to adopt accumulation as their purpose.

In one argument, Roberts refers to 'surplus labor, labor that continues beyond the point at which it has reproduced its wage' as an 'extension [that] can only come about by somehow getting the laborers to work longer than they would if they were under their own direction'.[34] This argument is not convincing, however; what is sometimes called 'market socialism' is not impossible. Producer cooperatives could deliberate to compete for custom on the market and to require their members to perform a quantity of labour sufficient not only to reproduce their 'wage', but also to reproduce means of life for those unable to work. Roberts suggests a second line of argument, however: to adopt accumulation as a purpose is to be committed to perform an amount of labour for which 'there is no limit to the demand for *more*'.[35] By adopting accumulation as a purpose, producers would impose on themselves an unlimited demand for

---

30   Wood 2017, pp. 642–3.
31   Vrousalis 2013, p. 133.
32   Roberts 2017, p. 108.
33   Roberts 2017, p. 139; see also Sensat 1984, p. 37.
34   Roberts 2017, p. 139.
35   Ibid.

more labour; knowing this, Roberts says, they could not possibly deliberate to adopt this purpose. This deliberative result is not impossible, however, if the members of market-oriented producer cooperatives thought that they could thereby maximise their monetary wealth, and/or their power of investment. As this deliberative result is not impossible, Roberts's premises do not support the judgement that 'accumulation' is unnatural and thus exploitative when a separate class imposes it.

Lastly, Chris Arthur offers an inversion account of capitalist exploitation. Arthur insists that capitalist exploitation has 'to be explicated within an account of specifically capitalist forms',[36] and adds that it is 'the concept of abstract labour, which is a determination of *social form*'.[37] This leads one to expect Arthur to offer an account of capitalist exploitation characterised by an 'abstraction in the constitution of labour in the capital relation'.[38] For, as Arthur says, 'industrial capital treats all labours as identical because it has an equal interest in exploiting them regardless of their concrete specificity'.[39] Yet Arthur goes on to define capitalistically exploited labour as labour subject to 'an *inversion* of subject and object' in which capital and not labour 'sets the agenda', 'direct[s]', 'organises', 'enforces' and 'command[s]'.[40] This inversion of subject and object is an inversion of concretely specific functions, however. If, as Arthur says, capital treats 'all labours as identical' for the purpose of 'exploiting' labour, capitalist exploitation must involve treating labour subject to inversion and labour not subject to inversion (labour performed on a producer's own initiative) as identical. But if so, capitalist exploitation is defined by a feature of social form that pertains regardless of inversion; namely, 'the real object aimed at ... money returns'.[41] We need an account of capitalist production in terms of accumulation on which it is exploitative in virtue of the kind of purpose accumulation is.

This is where the interaction component of the thesis comes in. There is a connection and a similarity between the argument for why generalised production for exchange presupposes money, and the argument for why generalised production with wage-labour for money maximisation is exploitative. In *The*

---

36   Arthur 2002, p. 39. The phrase 'social form of exploitation [*gesellschaftliche Exploitations-form*]' is used by Marx in *Capital* at *MEW*, 23, p. 452; *MECW*, 35, p. 432; Marx 1976, p. 555. *MECW* renders '*Exploitationsform*' as 'mode' (which would be: '*Weise*'), while Marx 1976 renders it as 'form of society' (which would be: '*Gesellschaftsform*').

37   Arthur 2002, p. 44.

38   Arthur 2002, p. 42.

39   Ibid.

40   Arthur 2002, p. 47, p. 50, p. 52, p. 56.

41   Arthur 2002, p. 44.

Dialectic of the Value Form, Backhaus remarks that a 'pre-monetary value-form' has 'an aporetic, self-abolishing structure'; generalised production for exchange 'cannot be thought' without money.[42] The interaction-recognition-antinomy thesis goes a step further. A society in which everyone maximises their monetary wealth also cannot be thought. The very thought contains a logical contradiction, or is contradictory in conception; and that is what justifies a characterisation of capitalist production as exploitative. Capitalist labour-exploitation is an instance of self-seeking action that fails a system-level universalisability test. This test, an anthropological and system-level version of the contradiction in conception test (CC test) belonging to Kant's Formula of the Law of Nature in the *Groundwork to the Metaphysics of Morals*, tests whether or not a maxim reinforced by a system can be acted on successfully by everyone when it is a universal law of human nature. The key passage of text for this argument is provided by Marx's counterfactual thought experiment in the *Grundrisse*.[43]

If capitalist exploitation, on the system universalisability conception, can be linked to an analysis of the commodity form, theorists critical of commodification and instrumental reason have a reason to take an interest in exploitation; while egalitarians have a reason not to ignore the value form of wealth (commodities, money and capital). Further, by conceiving exploitation as self-seeking action that fails a system-level universalisability test, the interaction-recognition-antinomy thesis facilitates a solution to what is here called the *capitalism, rights and injustice problem*. The capitalism, rights and injustice problem is: how is it possible to hold that capitalism is unjust without appeal to rights?

The capitalism, rights and injustice problem has two premises. It arises if one holds that (i) capitalism is unjust, and that (ii) capitalism is not to be condemned by appeal to rights.[44] If it is possible to condemn capitalism as unjust without appeal to rights, then John Rawls's claim that people cannot 'suffer from a greater liberty'[45] must be rejected. If it is possible to do so by laying a charge of exploitation against capitalism, Axel Honneth's claim that 'if "exploitation" becomes a common accusation, then workers must implicitly be legally entitled to the product of their labour',[46] must also be rejected.

---

42   Backhaus 2011, p. 32; compare p. 285.
43   See ch. 8, sec. 10. Carol Gould claims: '[a]lthough Marx offers no explicit discussion of the concept of justice in the *Grundrisse*, this work provides the basis for reconstructing such a conception' (Gould 1978, p. 129). The interaction-recognition-antinomy thesis supports this claim, albeit with a different argument and principle of justice.
44   On Marx's critique of rights, see ch. 8, sec. 13, and ch. 11, sec. 2.
45   Rawls 1971, p. 143.
46   Honneth 2011, p. 420; Honneth 2014, p. 227.

To pose the capitalism, rights and injustice problem is to be committed to a critique of the entire Anglophone debate on Marx and justice. The usual approach to Marx and justice within this debate is to ask whether Marx (consistently) thought that capitalism was unjust on grounds of distributive justice. Its three positions are articulated by Allen Wood, Gary Young and G.A. Cohen. According to Wood, Marx 'never' based his critique of capitalism on 'right' or 'justice', but on other values.[47] According to Young, Marx did consistently think that capitalism is unjust because it violates the rights of workers, and any contradiction is merely apparent.[48] According to Cohen, 'Marx did not always realize that he thought capitalism was unjust'.[49] It is argued here that these three positions share more than their advocates let on. They all rest on the same false interpretive premise that capitalist exploitation belongs to the dimension of value or product, and on the same false substantive premise that questions of justice are reducible to questions of rights.[50] If one or more false premises are common to all of the above positions, they will not exhaust all of the possibilities. It will be possible to propose a *fourth* position, namely: Marx condemned the use of labour in capitalism as unjust, but did not condemn capitalism by appeal to right, and simply by virtue of this, Marx is not inconsistent or suffering from deficient self-understanding.

If the interaction-recognition-antinomy thesis is to allow commodity form philosophy to solve the capitalism, rights and injustice problem, then that can only be because the system-level universalisability test that informs its conception of exploitation suggests a value by which to condemn capitalism that is not the value of freedom of choice. If the value that underpins this condemnation is not freedom of choice, then it need not be enforced in a form that gives effect to individual preferences. The form of guarantee that gives effect to individual preferences is the guarantee of rights.[51] So, if the value underpinning a normative charge of exploitation based on the system universalisability conception of exploitation is not the value of freedom of choice, exploitation need not be overcome by bestowing rights. It need not be condemned by appeal to a right.

Consider a relevantly analogous case. It is possible to believe that public access to court proceedings ought to be enforced, on the grounds of public education in the court process, and public scrutiny. But as public access to

---

47   Wood 2004, p. 129; see, more recently, Wood 2017.
48   Young 1978.
49   Cohen 1983a, p. 444; see also Cohen 2013, p. 12.
50   See ch. 3, sec. 4, and ch. 8, sec. 13.
51   See ch. 11, secs 1–2.

court proceedings is not grounded on the value of freedom of choice, it is not enforced in the form of rights. Although an official is placed under a duty to facilitate public access to court proceedings, no individual has a right to enter the public gallery.[52] If the gallery is full, the official may prohibit a newcomer from entering. The advantage acquired by any given individual, in virtue of the duty on the official, is conditional. A may lose their opportunity to enter a public gallery in virtue of action by an independent individual, B, who turns up before A and takes the last available seat. A conditional advantage is thus a wholly different kind of legal advantage to a right. A right is a type of legal advantage that can only be waived on its holder's say so. Only a rights-holder (or their designated representative) can waive a right. If c has, say, a right against D for payment of damages that occurred in D's performance of a contract, then only c (or c's designated representative) may release D from that liability. By contrast, the reason A is prevented by an official from entering the public gallery of a court is not that A has waived a right; A does not have a right to waive.

The analogous point to make about a condemnation of capitalist exploitation is this. If exploitation is defined by a system-level universalisability test, it is defined by a test that facilitates a normative charge that rests on a prohibition, or duty not to x. As is illustrated by the duty to facilitate public access to court proceedings, an enforceable duty need not create a right. If, like public access to court proceedings, a prohibition on exploitation is underpinned by a value other than freedom of choice, then exploitation, like an official's refusal to admit individuals into an empty public gallery, may be condemned by a principle of justice (a principle that ought to be enforced impartially, now if not forever), without being condemned by appeal to a right.

According to the interaction-recognition-antinomy thesis, the commodity form and capitalist exploitation are intimately related. Both are central to a Marxist acount of capitalism. As Cohen rejects the former claim, while Postone rejects the latter claim, it strengthens the case for these claims to show how both rejections come at a cost.

Cohen's attempt to separate the concept of capitalist exploitation from the commodity form has a positive side and a negative side. Positively, Cohen formulates a product-based charge of exploitation that eschews claims about value, and which, he says, is 'the argument which really moves Marxists politically'.[53] Negatively, Cohen argues that Marx's theory of value is irrelevant to

52   See Jellinik 1919, pp. 73–4.

53   Cohen 1988, p. 229.

the charge that capitalism is exploitative. 'The labour theory of value is not a suitable basis for the charge of exploitation directed by Marxists against capitalism'.[54]

Consider, first, the positive side of this attempt. Cohen's charge of exploitation against capitalism is that capitalism is wrong in virtue of the fact that 'proletarians produce all of the products in capitalist society, but capitalists appropriate some of them'.[55] The charge is a product-based charge, if the wrong relating to this fact is identified without advancing a claim about value.

To 'really mov[e] Marxists politically',[56] a charge of exploitation must support the judgement that capitalism is inherently bad. The attractiveness, for anti-capitalists, of Cohen's product-based charge of exploitation is diminished, therefore, if this charge cannot support the judgement that capitalism is inherently bad. To show that this is indeed the case, it is not necessary to dispute the implicit assumption that capitalism is defined by non-capitalist proletarians and non-proletarian capitalists. This idea could be disputed, on the basis that a form of production dominated by money-maximising cooperatives is a form of capitalist production. Here it is granted[57] that, if non-proletarian capitalists' appropriation of some of the product is always wrong, then capitalism is inherently bad. What will be disputed, however, is that any one of Cohen's three versions of the product-based charge of exploitation can establish that non-proletarian capitalists' appropriation of some of the product is always wrong. Each version only supports the conclusion that non-proletarian capitalists' appropriation of some of the product is sometimes wrong. No version (or combination of versions) supports a charge of exploitation against capitalism as such.

The crucial point is this. If a charge of exploitation eschews claims about value, and hence the value form of wealth, it cannot refer to a capitalist's end, continuous money maximisation.[58] If it cannot refer to the capitalist's end, it cannot, by directly condemning that end, discount the non-producing activities that capitalists perform to that end (such as investment decisions) as a ground for them to appropriate any part of the product. It can only discount the capitalist's non-producing activities as a ground for appropriation *indirectly*, by condemning their conditions, and/or by condemning these activities by reference to a counterfactual outcome. Yet an indirect condemnation of capitalists'

---

54   Cohen 1988, p. 209.
55   Cohen 1988, p. 232.
56   Cohen 1988, p. 229.
57   Compare Cohen 1978, pp. 313–15.
58   See ch. 12, sec. 1.

non-producing activities will not imply that capitalists always have no right to appropriate any part of the product. So, the charge will be unable to condemn all possible capitalisms.

On a product-based charge of exploitation, the capitalist's non-producing activities can be discounted as a ground for appropriation for one of two reasons. One reason is to hold that differential ownership of means of production is 'morally illegitimate',[59] and so the appropriation-facilitating non-producing activities that capitalists perform are not activities they ought to be in a position to perform. That is the normatively fundamental reason in both the autonomy version and the luck egalitarianism version of the charge. But another reason to discount the non-producing activities that capitalists perform as a ground for appropriation is if they lead to unreciprocated product transfers that are unjust because they do not accord with 'need'.[60] That is the 'normatively fundamental'[61] reason in the needs version of the charge. On the needs version of the charge, an unreciprocated product transfer 'is wrong because of what it is, and not because it inherits the wrong of something else'.[62]

Consider, first, the autonomy version of the charge, which has echoes in charges of exploitation grounded on vulnerability-based or force-based conceptions of exploitation.[63] On the autonomy version, capitalist exploitation is an unjust unreciprocated product transfer that inherits its injustice from the fact that workers 'are *forced* to work for some or other person or group'.[64] On this version of the charge, unequal enjoyment of the power 'matching' the right 'to work for no one' is 'the heart of the socialist objection' to capitalism.[65]

The limitation of the autonomy version of the charge is that it would not condemn capitalisms with a sufficient unconditional basic income. An unconditional basic income could give each the power not to work for anyone. But it need not remove the difference between what producers can produce in a

---

59   Cohen 1988, p. 235.
60   Cohen 1988, p. 230.
61   Cohen 1995, p. 199.
62   Ibid.
63   Such as in Arneson 1981, p. 213, p. 226; Buchanan 1979, p. 124; Buchanan 1982, p. 48; Peffer 1990, pp. 144–5; Reiman 1987, p. 3; Schwartz 1995a, pp. 277–9; Schwartz 1995b, p. 159; Wildt 1997, pp. 221–2; Wood 2004, p. 248; Gilabert 2017, p. 566. For some interpreters (Wood, Schwartz), the reason that capitalist exploitation is bad (for Marx) is not that it is unjust. Despite this difference in the nature of the charge, there is a similarity in its condition: in each case, it is a premise that the wage-labourer has no (acceptable) option but to perform labour for a capitalist (that they would prefer not to perform).
64   Cohen 1995, p. 34.
65   Ibid.

given period, and what is required, in terms of commodities, to maintain their capacities to produce over that period. Accordingly, those in a position to hire could still seek to maximise that difference for private gain. An autonomy version of the charge is consistent with support for a reformed capitalism. It does not force a choice between capitalism with a sufficient unconditional basic income, and socialism.

Now consider the luck egalitarianism version of the charge. On this version, capitalist exploitation is an unjust unreciprocated product transfer that inherits its injustice from an ownership structure that is unjust because it arises from unchosen disadvantage. 'Unchosen' disadvantage is 'disadvantage for which the sufferer cannot be held responsible, since it does not appropriately reflect choices that he has made or is making or would make'.[66]

The limitation of the luck egalitarianism version of the charge is that it would not condemn capitalisms that arise from an initial egalitarian distribution of external resources and natural talent. For a luck egalitarian, a distribution of external resources and natural talent is just if the distribution of the former compensates for differentials in the latter. As the luck egalitarian aim is to establish a level playing field for individuals to exercise 'responsibility',[67] luck egalitarianism provides no grounds for regulating the effects of differential preferences on what people do with their shares of wealth. If a distribution of wealth that is just by luck egalitarian standards can give rise to a capitalist ownership structure, then the luck egalitarian version of the charge could not condemn a capitalism that arose from this level playing field.

Imagine, for simplicity's sake, that all individuals are equally talented.[68] Once each is given their per capita share of society's assets, luck egalitarianism amounts to laissez-faire transactional justice. Yet laissez-faire transactional justice facilitates capitalist wage-labour, for two reasons. First, voluntary independent contracting presupposes possession over the items to be transferred; generalised possession generates money, and money generates acquisitiveness.[69] Second, voluntary independent contracting can make wage-labour instrumentally rational, that is, a suitable means to satisfy given desires, in virtue of differential preferences for, or random variations in the success of,

---

66   Cohen 2011, p. 13.

67   Cohen 2011, p. 19.

68   If expensive tastes are a normatively relevant unchosen disadvantage, as argued in Cohen 2011, pp. 9–20, it may also be imagined that individuals have equally expensive tastes. Whether or not expensive tastes are a normatively relevant unchosen disadvantage makes no difference here.

69   See ch. 7, secs 3–4, and ch. 9, sec. 5.

acquiring and using acquired skills ('distance-travelled' or 'being in the right place at the right time'). Producers can be hired for an income higher than they would otherwise receive, and still yield a benefit for their hirer, provided the working day is sufficiently long. A hirer can reap a benefit without a relatively long working day if, as a result of the labour they hire, productive power expands. For example, lone speculative provision for a new need permits an initial monopoly price; discovery of a new patentable technology provides a competitive advantage; or a minority buy-out with borrowed funds can merge resources to give greater economies of scale. Such scenarios permit capital accumulation, even with relatively attractive wages. Over time, capital accumulation can proceed to the point where hirers engulf all branches of production. Production is then capitalist, notwithstanding the fact that it began from a luck egalitarian distribution. A luck egalitarian version of the charge is therefore consistent with support for a 'cleanly generated'[70] capitalism.

Consider, finally, the needs version of the charge. On this version, capitalist exploitation is an unjust unreciprocated product transfer that is unjust *if* it arises from an ownership structure that '*tends*'[71] to produce unreciprocated product transfers that are not needs-oriented, *and because* the transfer is unreciprocated and not needs-oriented.

The needs version of the charge implies that, if an unreciprocated product transfer overrides mere preferences that are not needs to provide for needs (or that this is a result that the ownership structure tends to effect), it is not exploitative. It cannot be denied, however, that capitalists and proletarians both have needs. Hence, the needs version of the charge fails to condemn any capitalism in which, when capitalists' and workers' needs are similar, the private income of capitalists and workers tends to be similar; or, if they are not similar, any capitalism in which the private income of capitalists does not exceed the money they require to purchase what they need. Cohen writes:

> Think of a worker who very much enjoys both his work and the wages it brings him and who works for a wholly infirm neighbour who leads a miserable life but who, unlike the worker, has managed to possess himself of a stock of capital. This infirm capitalist lops off just enough of the worker's product so that he, the capitalist, can stay alive. We can suppose that, if something like the stated capital imbalance did not obtain, then

---

70   Cohen 1995, p. 161.
71   Cohen 1995, p. 199.

the worker would produce for himself alone and callously let his infirm neighbour die. And we can also suppose that it was because he knew that he would die without the power over the worker that capital would give him that the infirm man decided to acquire and exercise that power ... There is, *ex hypothesi*, no unfairness in the distribution of benefits and burdens which would show that the exchange is unjust.[72]

If a progressive tax system ensured that all but the part of the product required by capitalists to meet their needs was re-distributed to non-capitalists, capitalism is no longer vulnerable to the needs-based version of the charge. Once again, therefore, the charge is consistent with support for a reformed capitalism. It does not force a choice between capitalism with an effective 100% income tax band set at the right level, and socialism.

Suppose that Cohen were to concede that none of the above versions of the product-based charge of exploitation support the judgement that capitalism is inherently bad. Cohen might then shift to the position that what *ought* to move Marxists politically is a disposition to revise judgements (such as the judgement that all capitalisms are bad) in light of counterexamples. If capitalism with a sufficient unconditional basic income, a clean history or a 100% tax band is not unjust on grounds of exploitation, so be it, Cohen might say. The problem with this imagined reply is that it passes over a whole area of concern. Capitalism is defined by a societal dynamic of capital accumulation.[73] It is possible to question the desirability of this dynamic directly; that is, the desirability of mere after-the-fact regulation of the effect of competing money-maximising agents' choices over what and how to produce. None of the above versions of the product-based charge of exploitation are directed at the dynamic of accumulation that such choices bring about, however. So, none of the counterfactual conditions on which the above product-based charges cease to condemn capitalism need persuade a Marxist to revise their judgement of capitalism's inherently exploitative character, if the latter is understood as a characterisation of an aspect of this dynamic.

---

72   Cohen 1995, pp. 149–50. The sketch illustrates why Cohen did not raise a (fourth) product-based charge along the lines declined at Cohen 1988, p. 235, and indicates Cohen's rejection of Nancy Holmstrom's view that it is 'the fact that the income is derived through forced, unpaid, surplus labor ... which makes it exploitative' (Holmstrom 1977, p. 359). ('Force', for Holmstrom, denotes a lack of control over what is produced, and how production is organised).

73   A positional conception of the capitalist economic structure (such as Cohen affirms) only encourages passing over this area of concern; see ch. 6, sec. 1.

If Marxists need not be moved politically by product-based charges of capitalist exploitation, there is all the more reason to question the negative side of Cohen's attempt to separate the concept of capitalist exploitation from Marx's value theory. Cohen's claim that Marx's value theory is irrelevant to the charge that capitalism is exploitative has two premises. One premise is that use of the term 'exploitation' carries a normative charge. Its use 'denotes a kind of injustice'.[74] The second premise is that statements about what determines a commodity's value have no normative significance. Cohen says of products of labour: 'what matters, normatively, is what creates that thing, or so transforms it that it has (more) value, not what makes things of its sort have the amount of value they do'.[75] Strictly speaking, only the final clause of this sentence defends the second premise. (As we shall see, the claim advanced in the first part of the sentence is false. That it is labour by producers that creates the product is not what matters, normatively, in the charge of capitalist exploitation. No creation claim underpins this charge).

Cohen's denial that any 'claim to value'[76] redounds to that which determines value, because it determines value, is granted. But it may still be denied that the two above premises support Cohen's irrelevance claim. A statement about value may support a non-normative premise in an argument to the conclusion that capitalism is bad. As Cohen, in another context, acknowledges, 'conceptual claims are sometimes key premises in arguments with normative conclusions'.[77] The argument to be made here is: capitalism is exploitative (non-normatively defined); exploitation (as non-normatively defined) is bad; therefore, capitalism is bad. In this argument, the first premise is non-normative. Accordingly, if a statement about value can support it, a statement about value *is* relevant to an exploitation-based normative critique of capitalism.

If, therefore, the capitalist economic structure reinforces the pursuit of a maxim that cannot be universalised; *if* submitting it to a system-level universalisability test rests on a statement about value, either because the maxim is described with reference to value, or because a statement about value explains why the maxim fails the test, or both;[78] and *if* systems that fail this test are bad; then both the concept and the normative charge of capitalist labour-

---

74   Cohen 1988, p. 212.
75   Cohen 1988, p. 229.
76   Cohen 1988, p. 230.
77   Cohen 2011, p. 186.
78   I will argue both: the end of the maxim is to maximise monetary wealth; and the distinction between use-value and value explains why, in a hypothetical world in which the

exploitation are related to Marx's value theory. Further, *if* this system may be judged bad from a standpoint that an actor in capitalism can adopt, an elaboration of this judgement may belong to an account of capitalism.

What this survey of Cohen's attempt to separate the concept of capitalist exploitation from the commodity form has revealed is the following. First, there is no product-based charge of exploitation against capitalism as such. It is false advertising to claim that purist anti-capitalists can or ought to be moved by it. Second, it is not without hope to examine whether there is a commodity-form-based conception and charge of exploitation that can be directed at capitalism and that can move purist anti-capitalists.

According to Postone's *Time, Labor and Social Domination* (*TLSD*), however, the concept of exploitation does not occupy a central place in Marx's theory of capitalism. The reason for this, according to *TLSD*, is that exploitation is a phenomenon of distribution, and thus distinct from the dynamic of production that was Marx's chief concern.

The response to *TLSD* proceeds in three steps. First, *TLSD*'s direct remarks on exploitation are challenged. Second, one of *TLSD*'s general lines of argument is presented. Finally, it is argued that *TLSD*'s direct remarks on exploitation may be withdrawn, at no cost to that general line of argument. Indeed, the extent to which Marx's writings can be used to advance this general line of argument is expanded if *TLSD*'s direct remarks on exploitation are withdrawn.

Postone remarks in *TLSD*: 'the Marxian critique is a critique of labor in capitalism, rather than merely a critique of labor's exploitation'.[79] Similarly: '[t]he Marxian theory does, of course, include an analysis of class exploitation and domination, but it goes beyond investigating the unequal distribution of wealth and power'.[80] More fully:

> Marx's ... critique should not be understood as one of exploitation alone. In other words, his investigation of the source of the surplus is not of the creation by 'labor' of a surplus of material wealth, whereby he criticizes the appropriation of that surplus by the capitalist class. Relatedly, Marx does not consider the process of production in capitalism to be a labor process controlled extrinsically by the capitalist class for its own benefit, which, in socialism, would be used for the benefit of all. Such interpretations overlook the implications of both the value form of wealth and

---

money-maximising maxim is a universal law of human nature, it cannot be adopted successfully by performing wage-labour.

79   Postone 1993, p. 124.
80   Postone 1993, p. 153.

Marx's analysis of the twofold nature of the production process in capital-ism – that is, of its intrinsically capitalist (capital-determined) character. Capitalist production, according to Marx, is characterized not only by class exploitation but also by a peculiar dynamic, rooted in the constant expansion of value.[81]

In these remarks, TLSD suggests that exploitation in capitalism is a charac-teristic of the unequal distribution of the value form of wealth. Exploitation is of secondary importance, on the reconstruction offered in TLSD, because exploitation, as a feature of the unequal distribution of income, presupposes a capital-determined process of production which imposes specific character-istics on labour that cannot be reduced to class exploitation.

Postone is right that the value-based dynamics which shape the use of total social time as labour time and subject it to a capital-determined discipline are analytically and normatively important in and of themselves. If exploitation were merely a concept of distribution, it would be subordinate to an account of these dynamics. But exploitation is not a concept of distribution. As it char-acterises the use of labour in the pursuit of money maximisation, it contributes to an analysis of labour as it is shaped by the capitalist process of production.

Cohen describes a scheme that illustrates the claim that capitalist exploita-tion is irreducible to an inequality of income distribution. Capitalist exploita-tion, on the system universalisability conception, does not require inequality in the distribution of income. Capitalist exploitation remains in a scheme that Cohen, consistent with a needs version of the product-based charge of exploit-ation, suggests is 'amply worth refining',[82] where

> a standard capitalist market organizes economic activity, but the tax sys-tem cancels the disequalizing results of that market by redistributing income to complete equality. There are (pretax) profit-seeking capitalists, and workers who own no capital, *but* people acknowledge an obligation to serve others, and the extent to which they discharge that obligation is measured by how close their pretax income is to what it would be in the most remunerative (and therefore, on standard assumptions, the most socially contributing) activity available to them, while taxation effects a fully egalitarian posttax distribution of income.[83]

---

81   Postone 1993, p. 282.
82   Cohen 2009, p. 65.
83   Cohen 2009, pp. 63–4; see also Cohen 2008, p. 190.

Postone could, moreover, withdraw his direct remarks on exploitation at no expense to *TLSD*'s general argument. One of *TLSD*'s general lines of argument can be stated as follows:

(1)   In capitalism, labour is alienated[84]
(2)   Therefore, a free society must overcome labour as it exists in capitalism
(3)   A 'theory with emancipatory intent'[85] articulates the conditions for freedom
(4)   'Traditional Marxism' analyses capitalism 'from the standpoint of labor'[86] in capitalism
(5)   Therefore, traditional Marxism is not an emancipatory theory

TLSD argues that, since the qualities of labour as it exists in capitalism are not the qualities of a free activity, labour in capitalism does not exhibit qualities that an emancipatory theory can affirm. To set its qualities free is not to realise freedom.

By implication, an emancipatory theory cannot simply seek to uphold the claims of producers that arise from a positive evaluation of the contribution that producers make to capitalist society by performing labour as it exists in capitalism. No emancipatory theory can culminate in the assertion of a right that presupposes the continued performance of labour as it exists in capitalism, for a society that institutes such a right contains labour that is not free but alienated. A free society must transform labour as it exists in capitalism.

Accordingly, no concept or normative charge of exploitation that implies a right connected to the continued performance of labour as it exists in capitalism can assume a central place in a theory with emancipatory intent. If a concept rests on a premise about the creation of value or product by labour as it exists in capitalism, and if a related normative charge seeks to vindicate what is created to its creator and/or to deny what is created to non-creators, no such concept or charge can assume a central place in an emancipatory Marxist theory. If a theory with emancipatory intent is 'one that criticizes what is on the basis of what could be',[87] and what there are good grounds for wanting to be, then, to assume a central place in such a theory, the concept of exploitation must identify a *frustrated potential*; and a normative charge must condemn the frustration of that potential.

The condition *TLSD*'s critique of traditional Marxism places on any central normative charge of an emancipatory theory is one that the interaction-

---

84   Postone 1993, p. 32.
85   Postone 1993, p. 16.
86   Postone 1993, p. 7.
87   Postone 1993, p. 64.

recognition-antinomy thesis says a charge of exploitation can satisfy. The conception of exploitation as self-seeking action that fails the system-level universalisability test locates exploitation in production, and identifies a frustrated potential for a societal version of autonomy called self-legislative human community. Its related normative charge condemns the frustration of self-legislative human community. The central place that capitalist exploitation has in the interaction-recognition-antinomy thesis is no concession to traditional Marxism, therefore. It is a basis for its critique. *TLSD*'s direct remarks on exploitation's secondary importance can be withdrawn at no cost to *TLSD*'s general line of argument against traditional Marxism.

Indeed, *TLSD*'s direct remarks on capitalist exploitation serve to obscure the extent to which other concepts that presuppose a concept of capitalist exploitation eschew the assumptions of traditional Marxism. Traditional Marxism theorises capitalism from the position of labour as it exists in capitalism. To this end, it must twist Marx's account of capitalist exploitation into a concept of distribution, to be able to raise a normative charge of exploitation against capitalism. Rather than challenge this move, *TLSD*'s direct remarks on exploitation reflect an acceptance of it. This has a problematic upshot, for *TLSD* rightly connects classes to exploitation. If one connects classes to exploitation, but locates exploitation in distribution, one ends up with a distribution-based view of classes. As *TLSD* holds a distribution-based view of classes, what *TLSD* says of the proletariat is similar to what Honneth says of *Capital*: it is tainted by a utilitarian model of social conflict for material resources.[88] *TLSD* claims: 'the universality represented by the proletariat ultimately is that of value'.[89] Postone's claim, no less than Honneth's, reflects a failure to question the pedigree of traditional Marxism. The conception of capitalist exploitation elaborated in chapter 8, in conjunction with the analysis of the rights-antinomy offered in chapter 12, overturns both these views.

2 The Recognition Component

The interaction-recognition-antinomy thesis says that the interactions of purchase and sale and capitalist labour-exploitation are each accompanied by a kind of recognition. Purchase and sale is accompanied by the recognition of personhood, while capitalist labour-exploitation is accompanied by the recog-

---

88   Honneth 2003, p. 238, p. 265; Honneth 1995, p. 149, p. 165.
89   Postone 1993, p. 368.

nition of bureaucratic commands. The recognition component of the thesis provides a critical account of capitalism's social norms with advantages over rational-choice theory, and Honneth's recognition-based theory of capitalism.

A social norm is a practical principle with social validity and existence. A practical principle has social validity and existence if it is possible for actors to believe that everyone has a reason to accept it, and it is actually observed (for whatever reason). On this definition, the judgement 'x is a social norm' implies no commitment to x. It does not imply that everyone ought to observe x: the explanation for why it is possible for actors to believe that everyone has a reason to accept it may cite factors other than the use of fora of rational deliberation, such as illusion-generating social conditions, or the prevalence of a type of oppression.

Social norms mark a limit of rational-choice theory. Rational-choice theory offers a particular kind of intentional explanation of action. An intentional explanation of action is an explanation of action by an agent's intention to bring about a goal. 'A rational-choice explanation of action', Elster writes,

> involves showing that the action was rational and was performed because it was rational. That the action is rational means that given the beliefs of the agent, the action was the best way for him to realize his plans or desires. Hence rationality goes together with some form of maximizing behaviour.[90]

The *explanans* of a rational-choice explanation comprises three properties on the part of the agent: a belief, in light of the agent's desires, that an action is 'the best' or optimal thing for them to do if they are to satisfy their desires; a disposition to act on beliefs about what the optimal thing to do is, to satisfy one's desires; and the exercise of that disposition, leading to a fully formed intention to perform the action. (The beliefs of the agent need not be true). What the optimal thing for an agent to do is in one context of action will depend, however, on the agent's overall plan. Accordingly, a rational-choice explanation assumes that agents have a certain type of personality structure. Agents are assumed to have a complete preference order, in which all their various goals are ranked by the respective strengths of their desires; and a disposition to maximise preference satisfaction.

By virtue of its assumption that agents have this personality structure, rational-choice theory cannot register social norms. The social validity of social

---

90   Elster 1985, p. 9.

norms implies that actors can experience imperatives (not) to perform certain types of action as binding, in spite of any preference order they may have
in which desires to the contrary are ranked higher than desires in line with
those imperatives. Rational-choice theory does not admit any such experience,
however. Relatedly, rational-choice theory does not allow social norms to operate even as constraints on agents' choice of means to given ends. It presupposes,
rather, that agents are not disposed to revise what they do in light of social
norms or other practical principles. As rational choosers, agents will only act in
accordance with principles if they have a sufficiently weighty desire that happens to accord with them. For example, they will keep their promises only if
they know that they will feel rotten if they break them,[91] or that they have more
to gain by keeping them. Rational-choice theory does not register an agent's
experience, on account of a belief that everyone has a reason to keep their
promises, that they ought to keep a promise even when it would not maximise the satisfaction of their preferences to do so. Nor can rational-choice theory
conceive of agents acting to keep their promises in such cases. To the extent
that agents believe in or act on practical principles, including social norms,
rational-choice theory cannot theorise their behaviour.

The inability of the rational-choice strand of Analytical Marxism to register
practical principles manifests itself, in John Roemer's work, in the following
incoherence. In *A General Theory of Exploitation and Class*, Roemer elucid-
ates a game-theoretic account of exploitation through a series of models that
postulate preference maximisation by agents endowed with different types
of assets. Roemer asks whether, with a certain distribution of assets, a given
coalition of agents will receive less in exchange, and its complementary coalition more, than each would receive in a specific alternative arrangement.[92] To
describe that alternative arrangement, Roemer refers to 'withdrawal rules' that
give coalitions a 'right to withdraw' from the society of a given model with their
'entitlements'.[93] Yet preference-maximising agents cannot experience a normative rule or a right or an entitlement. They cannot conceivably act as Roemer's
account of exploitation requires them to be able to act. Roemer's account inter-
nalises a problem Marx identified in his *Economic and Philosophic Manuscripts
of 1844*: 'each sphere applies to me a different and opposed standard – morality
one, and national economy another'.[94]

---

91   Hollis 1994, p. 136.
92   Roemer 1982a, p. 20.
93   Roemer 1982a, p. 196, p. 211, p. 227, p. 283.
94   *MEW*, 40, p. 551; *MECW*, 3, p. 310.

The blindness of rational-choice theory to practical principles is inhibiting, if the very domains of action that rational-choice theory seeks to analyse with the aid of models that postulate preference maximisation create a dynamic by which actors develop a type of freedom of will. That is the significance of generalised purchase and sale. By virtue of the recognition of personhood that accompanies it, actors are able to develop a type of freedom of will. Rational-choice theory is unable to explain the phenomena for which the capitalist economic structure is just one part of the *explanans*, together with this freedom of will; namely, the state of capitalist society, and class struggle.

One aim of Honneth's recognition-based theory of capitalism in *Freedom's Right*, on the other hand, is to improve on what Honneth sees as Marx's failure to examine the normative underpinnings of economic activity. Insofar as Marx fails (according to Honneth) to examine these normative underpinnings, Marx ignores the possibility for social groups to embrace values that allow them to affirm modern capitalist society as a potentially free society. As capitalism could not reproduce itself without the existence of certain shared values, this oversight also leads Honneth to criticise Marx for offering an inadequate account of social reproduction.

Three features of Honneth's recognition-based theory of capitalism sustain this critique of Marx. The first is Honneth's claim that social norms, of a legal, moral and ethical character, enable social reproduction.[95] The second is Honneth's account of recognition, on which recognition presupposes social norms. Social norms provide the context in which subjects learn to formulate plans whose realisation is 'complementary' for others' pursuit of their plans.[96] The third is Honneth's defence of the forms of mutual recognition permitted by the social norms that enable social reproduction in capitalist society as, at least potentially, forms of social freedom.[97]

One problem with this critique, however, relates to the fact that it may not be possible for actors, in pursuing the plans they identify themselves with, and that serve to enable the plans of others, to assume that others value their plans. It is one thing for *Freedom's Right* to hold that market transactions could be regulated by government so that each party can view the transaction as enabling for the plans of both; or that fora of public debate could be arranged so that each participant can view their exchanges as enabling all participants to exercise their capacities to offer and evaluate public claims. It is quite another to

---

95   Honneth 2011, p. 346; Honneth 2014, p. 191.
96   Honneth 2011, p. 85, pp. 92–3; Honneth 2014, p. 44, pp. 48–9.
97   Honneth 2011, pp. 317–624; Honneth 2014, pp. 176–335.

hold out the hope that it will be possible for A to assume that an end for which B conducts market transactions with A, or an end for which B offers claims in public debate with A, is to enable A's plans. If B's end is to maximise B's monetary wealth, or to offer a powerful representative a convenient pretext to protect it, the means B pursues to that end may enable A to take part in a transaction or debate with B in which A counts as B's equal in some respect. Yet A's value to B may remain purely instrumental. If A cannot assume that B's action may be informed by the judgement that A ought to be enabled in the pursuit of A's plans; if A must rather assume that A has a purely instrumental status in B's end; then A is not recognised by B. If a learning process set in train by social norms that allows agents to formulate and pursue plans that enable those of others does *not* suffice for recognition, *Freedom's Right* has yet to show that modern capitalism can potentially exhibit forms of mutual recognition.

This problem threatens to up-end the critique that *Freedom's Right* directs at Marx for ignoring the possibility for social groups to embrace values by which they can affirm modern capitalist society. An account of modern capitalism as a potentially free society cannot proceed from the value that actors bestow on forms of mutual recognition in the market (or in fora of public debate) if there is no warrant to hold that such activities provide a form of mutual recognition. Nor can it be argued that Marx's account of social reproduction is inadequate on account of ignoring the contribution of certain shared values to social reproduction when actors' judgement of recognitionless activity by those values need not be positive.[98] If forms of recognition in capitalism are to provide a basis for its judgement, or to contribute to an explanation for its social reproduction, further argument is required, beyond what *Freedom's Right* offers, just to show that they are in fact present.

The interaction-recognition-antinomy thesis holds that this argument can proceed – to adapt a formulation from Pashukanis – from the notion of as-if recognition.[99] On the pragmatic conception of recognition elaborated in chapter 9, recognition requires that a recognisee is able to interpret the recogniser's behaviour as extending a positive evaluation to them. As-if recognition occurs where an actor must take themselves to have a purely instrumental status in the other's end, because a relevant change in the 'stock of experi-

---

98   For further criticisms of Honneth's view of the potential for freedom in markets, see Jütten 2015.

99   Paschukanis 2003, p. 162; Paschukanis 2002, p. 162; see also Chitty 1998, p. 82; Lohmann 1991, pp. 275–6.

ences'[100] of the as-if recognisee would first have to take place for the other's action to provide genuine recognition.

On this construal, as-if recognition does not presuppose social norms. So, if a type of interaction belonging to the capitalist economic structure is accompanied by a form of as-if recognition, both together may explain a social norm, rather than presuppose it.

In fact, a further element is required, to explain a social norm. A type of generalised interaction and an accompanying form of as-if recognition is insufficient. It may be natural to value the qualities that are objects of esteem for others in the respect in which one holds them in esteem. But as-if recognition does not allow actors to learn to affirm the value of one or more qualities in this way. If A must assume that A's status in B's end is purely instrumental, A has no reason to believe that A is an object of B's esteem; and if B has a purely instrumental status in A's end, A does not hold B in esteem. Since as-if recognition cannot lead an actor to identify themselves with their qualities, it cannot directly explain social norms.

To explain social norms, it is also necessary to identify a *social interest*. An interest is what an actor can believe they have a reason to do or to favour. A social interest is an interest common to all individuals of a group which is *either* such that (i) no one member satisfies it without all other members satisfying it (for example, a common interest in the passage of a law), *or* such that (ii) each member only tends to satisfy it under conditions that promote its satisfaction by all other members (for example, a common interest in not being a victim of crime in a public place). The conditions referred to in describing a type (ii) social interest must be beyond any individual's (or any subgroup's) exclusive disposal. Otherwise, that individual (or subgroup) could withhold them from others (subject to individual payment), which would preclude the common interest. To the extent that some people can rely on personal bodyguards to avoid crime in public places at an insignificant cost, and no matter how bad crime gets for others, such people do not belong to the group of people with a social interest in avoiding crime in public places. Their avoidance of crime in public places is not dependent on the maintenance of a low crime rate, which is the condition that gives rise to others' social interest in the avoidance of crime in public places.

The immediate significance of a social interest is that it encourages the articulation of a practical principle that upholds it. Even self-interested actors have a reason to articulate a principle that upholds a social interest they have. Even

---

100   Schütz 2004, p. 187; Schütz 1992, p. 80. On this concept, see ch. 4, sec. 5.

self-interested actors with a social interest in avoiding crime in public places have a reason to articulate a principle not to commit crime in public places. For if actors articulate a principle that upholds a social interest, they can hope that future incidents of disruption to that interest will not be committed by those who conform (even if only because conformity is in their self-interest) to the principles they know others believe in.

Once a social-interest-upholding principle is articulated, however, actors may be able to identify themselves with their qualities. If it is natural to value the qualities that are objects of esteem for others in the respect in which one holds them in esteem, each articulator of a generally articulated practical principle has a reason to value the qualities that that articulated principle urges people to respect. This quality is the *same* quality that is the object of as-if recognition, if the social-interest-upholding principle upholds a type (ii) social interest whose condition is the general non-disruption of the type of interaction accompanied by the as-if recognition. If a low rate of theft is a type (ii) social interest, whose condition is the general non-disruption of purchase and sale, the principle that upholds a low rate of theft, 'respect people's possessions', has as its object, possession, the object of as-if recognition in purchase and sale. Hence, if mutual recognition in market transactions would enable a type of freedom of will if it were genuine (which there is reason to doubt), then there may be a recognition-based explanation for this type of freedom of will that does not require mutual recognition in market transactions to be genuine. As-if recognition can give rise to a social norm indirectly, in conjunction with a social interest; its articulation as a principle may then generate genuine recognition leading to a type of freedom of will.

The claim that the interaction-recognition-antinomy thesis offers a critical account of capitalism's social norms rests on a further concept: real abstraction. On the Adorno-inspired[101] account of real abstraction outlined in chapter 3, a type of interaction exhibits a real abstraction if it requires at least one actor to treat another as if x is the case; and yet, by virtue of that very interaction, it belongs to their stock of experiences that x is not the case. If a type of interaction exhibiting such a real abstraction has a generalised existence and self-reinforcing dynamic, what an actor can learn from it will conflict with how they must continue to act. If so, the social norm that an actor observes in that type of interaction, as well as the system which reinforces its observance, may appear problematic. By observing social norms, actors act as if they make a kind of evaluative judgement. But if actors observe a social norm in a type of

---

101   Adorno 1974, p. 215; Adorno 2010, pp. 159–60.

interaction defined by a real abstraction, their observation of it simultaneously creates the chance of their becoming aware of a fact that invites a distance towards it. The interaction-recognition-antinomy thesis offers an explanation of capitalism's social norms that is critical in the same sense as its conception of capitalist exploitation is critical: it identifies the frustration of a potential. It identifies a frustrated potential in what an actor can learn about a social norm from the type of interaction in which they observe it.

3   The First Antinomy

One of two antinomies identified by the interaction-recognition-antinomy thesis is the antinomy of natural rights and popular authorisation in the state of capitalist society. There is a logical contradiction in asserting both that government action is only justified if and because it guarantees natural rights, and that government action is only justified if and because it is authorised by a decision of the people for equal liberty. There is a difference between acting only if certain conditions are met, and using all means to an authorised end. Yet capitalism necessarily generates both assertions. (A justification is asserted even when its assertion is merely implied by conduct whose main purpose is practical). On the premise, sustained by the recognition of personhood that accompanies purchase and sale, that each individual has by nature property in their parts and capacities, there is an ambiguity between the subjectivity of self-ownership as the unconditional recipient of legal protection, and as the unconditioned author of the law. The antinomy of natural rights and popular authorisation in the state of capitalist society is a result of this ambiguity.

Through its account of this antinomy, the interaction-recognition-antinomy thesis offers a variant of state derivation theory. This statement requires some clarification. The phrase 'state derivation theory' is associated with the West German state debate begun in the 1970s.[102] The Marxist use of the term 'derivation' did not originate in West Germany, however. The interaction-recognition-antinomy thesis variant of state derivation theory is closer to Pashukanis's and Lukács's interpretation of Marx than to the West German state debate.

In what is the most comprehensive survey of the West German state debate, Ingo Elbe argues that this debate is defined by the question of 'why a coercive force existing "apart from" and "over" the economy is necessary in capitalism;

---

102   One collection in English is Holloway and Picciotto 1978.

and, to be precise, in the form of a rule of law state'.[103] According to Elbe, contributions to this debate are defined by an argument of the form: in light of such and such a feature of the capitalist economy, it is necessary for there to be a separate coercive force based on the rule of law, if capitalism is to be maintained. If Elbe is right, the West German state debate shares a point of departure with Nicos Poulantzas's account of the modern state in *Political Power and Social Classes*. In *Political Power and Social Classes*, Poulantzas argues that the 'separation of the direct producer from the means of production in the relation of real appropriation ... determines a specific autonomy of the political and the economic'.[104] If 'determines' here means 'has as its necessary condition', the approach in both cases is somewhat similar.

Yet the type of argument by which Elbe characterises the West German state debate is not one that would suffice to explain the state, either by functional explanation, or by intentional explanation. Having argued this point, and endorsed intentional explanation, a conception of derivation is proposed.

To identify a function of x for y (such as: a rule of law state helps maintain a capitalist economy) is not to assert a functional explanation of x by y.[105] In a functional explanation, what is supposed to be explanatory is a dispositional fact, that is, a fact of hypothetical conditional form 'if e, then f'. Cohen's preferred term for a functional explanation is thus '*explanation by disposition*'.[106] An adherent of functional explanation, or explanation by disposition, is someone who holds that there is 'good reason for thinking' that a dispositional fact is explanatory if the statement of a law incorporating it (a consequence law) is empirically confirmed, even 'in the absence of a theory as to *how* the dispositional property figures in the explanation of what it explains'.[107] To assert that the rule of law state is functionally explained by the capitalist economy, it would be necessary to hold that empirical confirmation of the law

> IF it is the case that if a rule of law state were to exist at t_1,
> then it would help maintain a capitalist economy at t_2,
> THEN a rule of law state exists at t_3[108]

103   Elbe 2008, p. 319; compare von Flatow and Huisken 1973, p. 119; Müller and Neusüss 1971, p. 49; Preuß 1973, p. 59; Tuschling 1976, p. 9.
104   Poulantzas 1982, p. 30; Poulantzas 1978, p. 32.
105   Cohen 1981b, p. 131.
106   Cohen 1986, p. 225.
107   Cohen 1978, p. 266.
108   Amending Cohen 1978, p. 260.

justifies a belief that the rule of law state is explained by the dispositional fact that, were a rule of law state to exist, it would help maintain a capitalist economy. Contributions to the West German state debate stop short of any such reflection.

Secondly, the type of argument by which Elbe characterises the West German state debate does not suffice for an intentional explanation. For an intentional explanation, the function of a rule of law state in maintaining a capitalist economy would have to be accounted for as an intended or unintended consequence of action. Again, no such reflection is in evidence. On Elbe's characterisation, the West German state debate both stops short of offering an explanation of the state of capitalist society, *and* stops short of offering an explicit argument for or against a particular type of explanation of that state.

Elbe claims that the 'type of Marxist state theory worked out in the context of the West German discussion' has a 'predecessor' in the work of 'Eugen Pashukanis'.[109] But Pashukanis's *General Theory of Law and Marxism* is arguably more advanced than this claim implies. In places, it favours a particular type of explanation of the rule of law state by the capitalist economy.

True, one passage in Pashukanis's *General Theory of Law and Marxism* is of a piece with Elbe's characterisation of the West German state debate:

> Exchange-value ceases to be exchange-value, the commodity ceases to be a commodity, if exchange ratios are determined by an authority situated outside of the internal laws of the market. Coercion as the imperative addressed by one person to another, and backed up by force, contradicts the fundamental precondition for dealings between commodity possessors ... That is also why coercion ... has to appear rather as coercion emanating from an abstract collective person.[110]

Here, Pashukanis claims that a capitalist economy is defined by the exchange of commodities at ratios determined by market laws. Pashukanis infers that the economy is no longer capitalist if particular individuals determine exchange ratios at will. Pashukanis then claims that, if commodity exchangers had direct access to a coercive force sufficient to guarantee market exchange, its wielders would have the bargaining power to manipulate exchange ratios. Pashukanis therefore concludes that, for the economy to be capitalist, any coercive force that is necessary must be wielded by a separate entity. As, for Pashukanis, a

---

109   Elbe 2008, p. 366.

110   Paschukanis 2003, pp. 142–3; Pashukanis 2002, p. 143; compare Dimoulis and Milios 1999, p. 22; Elbe 2008, p. 382.

coercive force is necessary to guarantee market exchange on account of commodity exchangers' conflict of interests,[111] Pashukanis concludes that a capitalist economy requires a separate coercive force to which all commodity exchangers can be non-arbitrarily subject. It requires coercive force to be wielded by a rule of law state.

This type of argument stops short both of offering an explanation of the state of capitalist society, and of offering an argument for or against a particular type of explanation of that state. Earlier in the same chapter, however, Pashukanis appears to favour an intentional explanation of a rule of law state:

> Why is the apparatus of state coercion not created as the private apparatus of the ruling class; why does it detach itself from the ruling class, and assume the form of an impersonal apparatus of public power, separate from society? We cannot confine ourselves to pointing out that it is *advantageous* for the ruling class to erect an ideological smokescreen, and to conceal its class rule behind the screen of the state. For although such an elucidation is undoubtedly correct, it does not explain how such an ideology could arise, nor, therefore, why the ruling class can make use of it.[112]

Pashukanis suggests that, to answer the question of why the state of capitalist society has the form of a rule of law state, it does not suffice to identify its advantage or function for those who benefit from it. It is necessary to offer an account of 'how' the 'form' of a state with this function can arise; that is, how an 'impersonal apparatus of public power, separate from society' can be 'created' by a 'class' that owes its power to the laws of commodity production. If it is only when this how-question is answered that an explanation is given, then Pashukanis is committed to an intentional explanation of the state of capitalist society.

It is this course that is pursued here. To offer an explanation of *x* is to say why *x* had to happen (or was likely to happen) by citing the presence of a powerful particular or particulars, and the enabling conditions for the exercise of their powers.[113] To say that *A* has the power to *p* is to say that *A* can do *p*, in the

111   Paschukanis 2003, p. 79; Pashukanis 2002, p. 81.

112   Paschukanis 2003, pp. 139–40; Pashukanis 2002, pp. 139–40.

113   Here I follow the 'realistic ontology' of Harré and Madden (1975, p. 138). For related arguments that neither generalisations of consequence-explanatory form nor covering laws are required for causal explanation, see Hollis 1994, pp. 40–50, pp. 92–3 and Sayer 1987, pp. 113–25.

appropriate conditions, in virtue of its intrinsic nature.[114] As the description of a power is distinct from a dispositional fact, so an intentional explanation, whose powerful particulars include (groups of) intentional agents, is distinct from an elaboration of a functional explanation, which is supposedly an elaboration of how a dispositional fact is explanatory.

The interaction-recognition-antinomy thesis offers an intentional explanation of the state of capitalist society. It advances claims about the capitalist economic structure that allow it to ascribe actors with a goal, stock of experiences and capacities, and then to imagine how these actors could be led to institute a rule of law state.

The term 'derivation' is reserved for a specific type of explanation. An explanation is a derivation only if it reveals the genesis of something that may otherwise appear to be unquestionably given. This idea of derivation is loosely inspired by Lukács's use of the term 'derivation' in *History and Class Consciousness*.[115] Lukács says that, if something cannot be derived, then it is a 'facticity' or something simply given;[116] that the objects of derivation are 'fetishistic forms';[117] and that Ludwig 'Feuerbach's "anthropological" critique'[118] strikes a blow at a problem that appears incapable of derivation. In *The Essence of Christianity*, Feuerbach describes his method as 'genetic-critical' because it 'destroys' an 'illusion'.[119] These various uses suggest that a derivation is an explanation that reveals an illusion.

Proposal: a derivation of x is an explanation of x that shows that x must register its cause as just one of the phenomena that are subject to its logic. To show that x must register its cause as just one phenomenon among others subject to its logic is to reveal an illusion, for, once x exists, it will seem absurd to suggest that it could be explained by anything its own logic subsumes as a particular case; just as, for a believer, it must appear absurd to suggest that God is a product of just one of his many creations, human beings. The juridical logic of freedom of choice, or the political logic of representation, can be derived, *if* that logic registers its cause as just one of the phenomena that are subject to it. The interaction-recognition-antinomy thesis offers a specific variant of state

---

114 Harré and Madden 1975, p. 86.
115 Lukács's use of the term does not appear to be remarked upon in the West German state debate; see, for example, Kuhlen 1975, pp. 312–37.
116 Lukács 1977, p. 295, p. 298; Lukács 1968, p. 117, p. 120.
117 Lukács 1977, p. 371; Lukács 1968, p. 185.
118 Lukács 1977, p. 381; Lukács 1968, p. 194.
119 Feuerbach 1984, pp. 105–6; Feuerbach 1989, p. 52. The phrases are translated from Feuerbach 1984, which reproduces the text of the First Edition of *The Essence of Christianity*. Feuerbach 1989 is a translation of a later edition.

derivation theory, on this conception of derivation, for (i) its explanation of the antinomy of natural rights and popular authorisation relies on a derivation of the juridical logic of freedom of choice from personhood; and (ii) this antinomy is an influence on the political logic of representation, which is derived from the popular mandate given to a constitution-making power that must be brought into being if a capitalist economic structure encounters monarchical sovereignty.

In sum, the interaction-recognition-antinomy thesis variant of state derivation theory

(1)   advances claims about the capitalist economic structure;
(2)   ascribes goals, (normative) beliefs and capacities to its actors;
(3)   imagines how they would respond to a sovereign monarch;
(4)   derives one or more logics in the state of capitalist society;
(5)   identifies one or more antinomies in the state of capitalist society.

(1) and the non-bracketed part of (2) are implications of the interaction component of the thesis. The inclusion of normative beliefs in (2) is an implication of its recognition component. (3) rests on the claims that capitalist production is just one of the 'modes of production'[120] in history; and that popular sovereignty is incompatible with a pre-capitalist mode of production. (4) qualifies an explanation of the state as state *derivation* theory. (5) is an implication of the antinomy component of the thesis.

To clarify *what* state the interaction-recognition-antinomy thesis derives, a distinction may be drawn between common features, necessary features and essential features. Common features are features found in all (or in a critical mass of) entities of a given type. Necessary features are features without which an entity would not be an entity of a given type. Essential features, on a developmental conception of essence, are features that make entities of a given type developed entities of that type. Non-developed entities of a given type are those which merely possess the potential to develop its essential features, or else those which merely possess some of the features that it would be necessary for a developed entity of that type to possess. A developed human being has the ability to organise and communicate their thoughts while a newborn baby or someone with a severe mental impairment may not. If for some reason over half of the world's population consisted of newborn babies, the ability to communicate one's thoughts would be neither a common feature of the majority of human beings, nor a necessary feature of a human being. But it would remain an essential feature.

---

120   *MEW*, 13, p. 9; *MECW*, 29, p. 263.

Marx shows an interest in more than just the common features of states accompanying capitalist production in his *Critique of the Gotha Programme* (1875), which asserts that, where 'capitalist society' is 'more or less developed', states have 'certain essential characteristics in common'.[121] This statement presupposes a reference point on which certain common features of individual nineteenth-century states may be deemed 'essential', rather than merely common. Likewise, Marx's analysis of the modern state in *On the Jewish Question* (1843) extends beyond an analysis of what is common to existing states. In 1843, not a single state in the world institutionalised the kind of political emancipation that *On the Jewish Question* deems compatible with capitalism, but criticises as limited.[122] Its subject matter cannot be the common features of existing states, or the necessary features of any state that accompanies capitalist production. It must be the essential features of such states. Again, Marx argues in *On Friedrich List's Book* (1845):

> That every people goes through this development [industry – JF] within itself would be as foolish a view as that every people should have to go through France's political development or Germany's philosophical development. What nations have done as nations, they have done for human society.[123]

Marx implies that the kind of 'political development' to which capitalism necessarily leads need not be replicated in every state in a global capitalist economy. What the aforementioned statements require, therefore, is a concept for the most developed state accompanying capitalist production. The term 'state of capitalist society' is used to denote this state.

Use of this term marks a further difference with the West German state debate. As noted above, contributions to this debate offer an argument of the form: in light of such and such a feature of the capitalist economy, it is necessary for there to be a separate coercive force based on the rule of law, if capitalism is to be maintained. To focus on what form of state must exist, if capitalism is to be maintained, is to focus on necessary features, rather than essential features. One objection raised against some contributions to the West German state debate was that certain features that they sought to explain, such as democratic structures, are not necessary for a capitalist economy to be guaranteed

---

121   *MEW*, 19, p. 28; *MECW*, 24, pp. 94–5.
122   *MEW*, 1, p. 356; *MECW*, 3, p. 155.
123   Marx 1982, p. 463; *MECW*, 4, p. 281.

by a rule of law state.[124] There can be no objection, by contrast, to explaining democratic structures in the context of an account of the state of capitalist society.

The interaction-recognition-antinomy thesis variant of state derivation theory is in keeping with the spirit of Marx's claim in his *Letters from the Deutsch-Französische Jahrbücher* that 'reason has always existed, just not always in rational form'.[125] If it can show that a form of state would arise by steps that it is conceivable for actors to take, so as to realise what they regard as their freedom, it can explain why that form of state can appear to be justified ('reason has always existed'). If, moreover, it can also show that that state can be found wanting on other criteria of freedom that actors can come to affirm within, and in part by virtue of, this state, it can also show that social transformation beyond capitalism is possible and desirable ('just not always in rational form'). This again presupposes that the state of capitalist society is the object. Even if a claim about the potential for actors to develop subversive beliefs were added to an argument of the form that only a rule of law state can maintain a capitalist economy, that addition need not identify beliefs that had outstripped the most developed type of state that capitalist production permits.

4   The Second Antinomy

In *Capital* Volume I, Marx identifies an 'antinomy' of 'right against right, both equally licenced by the law of commodity exchange'.[126] The capitalist economic structure is said to sustain, with equal justification, the assertion of a right to an unlimited working day, and the assertion of a right to a limited working day. One of the premises of this rights-antinomy is that commodity exchangers are to recognise one another as self-owners. The premise that each individual has an exclusive claim to their parts and capacities is thus a common premise of both antinomies.

The significance of the rights-antinomy is that it grounds the existence of what Lukács calls a 'standpoint of the proletariat',[127] that is, the standpoint of a participant in a working-class movement. One suggestion in Marx's claim, in his *Letters from the Deutsch-Französische Jahrbücher*, that 'philosophical consciousness itself has been drawn into the torment of the struggle not merely

---

124   Gerstenberger 1975, pp. 9–10.
125   *MEW*, 1, p. 345; *MECW*, 3, p. 143.
126   *MEW*, 23, p. 249; *MECW*, 35, p. 243; Marx 1976, p. 344.
127   Lukács 1977, p. 331; Lukács 1968, p. 149.

externally, but intrinsically',[128] is the idea that social struggle can give rise to a standpoint. The outcome of a struggle between two types of actor is of intrinsic philosophical importance if one of those types of actor occupies a standpoint by virtue of that struggle.

A standpoint may be characterised by *interest* privilege in respect of the good society, and *capacity* privilege in respect of its achievement. Elizabeth Anderson writes: 'Marxism offers the classic model of a standpoint theory, claiming an epistemic privilege ... on behalf of the standpoint of the proletariat'.[129] The terms 'interest privilege' and 'capacity privilege' are preferred here over 'epistemic privilege', because the antinomies identified by the interaction-recognition-antinomy thesis are premised on one or more practical principles. Insofar as these antinomies ground a standpoint, the main issue is what different types of actors can (or cannot) come to will and can (or cannot) bring about, rather than what they can (or cannot) come to believe.

A type of actor has interest privilege if they can will a principle that there is an impartial reason to apply; while at least one other type of actor in the same society cannot will it. Types of actor are distinguished by the goals they pursue in generalised interactions, such as: hiring wage-labour to produce for money maximisation; or: working for a wage in order to live. A type of actor can will a principle, therefore, if the pursuit of such a goal can lead them to will it. The pursuit of a goal can lead a type of actor to will a principle if its pursuit can lead them to formulate the principle, and to develop an interest that, in their judgement, would be promoted by the principle's application. For this to amount to interest privilege, it must also be the case that at least one other type of actor in their society cannot will the principle because it is incompatible with their goal and/or any interests they can develop in its pursuit. It is contradictory for them to will to pursue their goal and/or the interests developed in its pursuit, and to will the principle.

There is an impartial reason to apply a principle if it is possible to give a reason for why it should be applied that everyone affected could accept. There is an impartial reason to apply the principle: antinomies in the social world ought to be resolved, if it is a rational interest to live in a social world not characterised by antinomies. If practical principles are to guide action, any form of society that sustains practical principles that generate an antinomy is in one way defective. An antinomy-generating form of society is worse than a form of society that does not generate antinomies, other things being equal. (As we will

---

128   *MEW*, 1, p. 344; *MECW*, 3, p. 142.
129   Anderson 2012, p. 18.

see, the most resistance to the view that Marx offers any impartial arguments comes from those who ascribe to Marx a conception of justice that is incompatible with *Capital*'s identification of a rights-antinomy in capitalist production; and who either do not remark on this rights-antinomy, or whose remarks are inadequate).[130]

In the Preface to the First Edition of *Capital*, Marx says of his position that it is 'the last to make the individual responsible for relations whose creature they socially remain'.[131] Relatedly, much earlier in 1843, Marx says of Hegel's *Elements of the Philosophy of Right* that, by presenting 'modern morality' as a 'presupposition' of the modern state, Hegel has grasped its 'true position' in the modern state; but that, such a state is not 'the real idea of ethical life'.[132] Marx is here distinguishing between individual morality and social ethics, and thus between moral impartiality and ethical impartiality. If the application of a principle is to give effect to a type of property that individuals possess and are to exercise in their own name, then the principle is a moral principle. The principle that consent must be ongoing throughout sex is a moral principle, because it is a principle about how to treat a capacity (a capacity to consent to sex) that individuals exercise in their own name. By contrast, if the application of a principle is to give effect to a property of a society, whose valuing is owed to all its members, the principle is an ethical principle. The principle that any member of the public may sit in on court proceedings is an ethical principle, because it is a principle in respect of a property of a society, court proceedings, that judges oversee as public office holders. If what Marx says of his position in the Preface to the First Edition of *Capital* is consistent with a social ethics, it is consistent with interpreting *Capital*'s antinomy passage in light of the ethical principle that antinomies in the social world ought to be resolved.

An *antinomy*-based defence of interest privilege has two characteristics. One is that it holds that the learning process that leads one type of actor to be able to will a principle that another type of actor cannot will is shaped by one or more antinomies. Second, it holds that the criterion for whether there is an impartial reason to apply this principle is that of whether it resolves one or more antinomies; that is, rejects one or more of its premises while better satisfying any need separable from the form of its articulation in a rejected premise. The first characteristic relates to the fact that an antinomy is comprised of proofs for two incompatible claims. The difference between one proof and the other, together with the difference between actors' initial goals and capacities, may

---

130   See ch. 12, sec. 4.
131   *MEW*, 23, p. 16; *MECW*, 35, p. 10; Marx 1976, p. 92.
132   *MEW*, 1, p. 313; *MECW*, 3, p. 108.

yield distinctive learning processes for different types of actor, and so allow one type of actor, but not another, to be able to will a given principle. The second characteristic relates to the fact that it is a rational requirement to resolve an antinomy in 'the world's own principles'.[133] As an antinomy rests on the acceptance of one or more false premises, a principle resolves an antinomy only if it implies a rejection of an antinomy's false premise(s). It is nonetheless possible that a false premise articulates a need that remains even once it is no longer expressed in the form of this premise. If so, a principle resolves an antinomy only by better satisfying it.

Capacity privilege rests on a claim about group capacities, which interest privilege by itself does not require. A type of actor has capacity privilege if, by virtue of the pursuit of their initial goal, actors of their type can develop the capacity to bring about a society in which a principle that there is an impartial reason to uphold is applied, without entering into coalition with one or more other types of actor; while the latter type(s) of actor cannot bring about such a society without entering into a coalition that includes the first. For the interaction-recognition-antinomy thesis, interest privilege is the focus. If claims about likelihood are put to one side, it is not in dispute that a socialist society could be brought about by a coalition of agents none of whom are capitalists, but could not be brought about by a coalition of agents none of whom are workers. To the end of defending the merit of what capacity privilege is in this case a privilege to achieve, it is sufficient to defend a claim of interest privilege.

By virtue of this second antinomy, the interaction-recognition-antinomy thesis relates Marxist theory and practice. Marxist theory is a theory that, among other things, gives reasons for holding that socialism is a better form of society than capitalism. If the principle by which the rights-antinomy is resolved, and the value underpinning this principle, can be realised in socialism but not in capitalism, that is one reason for regarding socialism as superior to capitalism. Hence, an antinomy-based argument can belong to Marxist theory. But an account of this antinomy also serves another purpose. Insofar as it serves in an argument for the interest privilege and/or capacity privilege of participants in a working-class movement, it contributes to explaining the centrality of such movements to the achievement of socialism.

The relation of Marxist theory to working-class movements is itself a question for Marxist theory. The question presents a challenge, for Marxist theory acknowledges a tension in this relation, but rejects the idea that the relation

---

133   *MEW*, 1, p. 345; *MECW*, 3, p. 144.

is one of mutual indifference. Marxist theory acknowledges this tension inso-far as it theorises the irreconcilability of social antagonism within capitalism, but grants that working-class movements are not animated by an awareness of this irreconcilability. Marxist theory also rejects the idea that the relation is one of mutual indifference, by professing to be an emancipatory theory. On Marx's conception of freedom, freedom includes the exercise of the capacity to reflect on and realise freedom. This view of freedom informs Marx's claim, in the Pro-visional Rules for the International Workingmen's Association (1864), that 'the emancipation of the working classes must be conquered by the working classes themselves'.[134] It follows that, if Marxist theory is to be an emancipatory the-ory, it must enable the people who, it says, can reflect on and realise freedom, to reflect on and realise freedom, in virtue of its articulating their reflection. So if, as the interaction-recognition-antinomy thesis says, a participant in a working-class movement to limit the working day has interest privilege, this thesis must locate the possibility of Marxist theory within such a movement. The challenge is to identify a potential for an awareness of the irreconcilability between the interests of working-class movements and capital in working-class movements that are not animated by this awareness. An antinomy-based response is to trace this potential to a learning process that results from workers' position in, and practical response to, an antinomy.

This response relates the interaction-recognition-antinomy thesis to recent discussion of Lenin's thesis of political awareness from without in *What is to be Done?* As Alan Shandro and Lars Lih both emphasise, Lenin's thesis of polit-ical awareness from without is a thesis about the relation of Marxist theory to working-class movements, as distinct from a thesis about the relation between intellectuals and workers. For Shandro, Lenin's thesis of political awareness from without concerns the relation of 'Marxist theory' to 'the spontaneous workers' movement';[135] or as Lih describes Lenin's thesis: 'Marx's scientific socialism ... brings the message of socialism to the worker movement "from without"'.[136]

In *What is to be Done?*, Lenin defines 'political awareness' as a readiness 'to respond to *each* and *every* occurrence of abuse of power and oppression, viol-ence and malfeasance, *no matter which class* is affected; – and, in so doing, respond precisely with a Social-Democratic point of view and no other'.[137] Political awareness consists, for Lenin, in the comprehensive awareness of all

---

134   *MECW*, 20, p. 14; see *MEW*, 19, p. 165; *MECW*, 24, p. 269.
135   Shandro 1995, p. 273, p. 279; compare Shandro 2014, pp. 115–48.
136   Lih 2006, p. 649.
137   Lenin 2006, p. 737.

bads from 'a Social-Democratic point of view', that is, from the point of view
of 'the world-historical significance of the liberation struggle of the proletariat'.[138] Thus, Lenin uses the term 'class political awareness'[139] interchangeably with (Social-Democratic) political awareness. We can suppose that the
'world-historical significance' of this liberation struggle is revealed, for Lenin,
by Marxist theory. So, in discussing the relation of Social-Democratic political
awareness or class political awareness to a certain sphere of activity, Lenin is
discussing the relation of a readiness to act steeped in Marxist theory to that
sphere of activity. The point to emphasise here is the comprehensiveness of
Social-Democratic political awareness. Social-Democratic political awareness,
according to Lenin, is a comprehensive awareness of all bads. To respond only
to certain types of bad, or only to those bads that affect a particular class, is to
display a lack of Social-Democratic political awareness.

Having defined Social-Democratic political awareness in these terms, Lenin
argues:

> The economic struggle 'pushes the workers to face' only issues about the
> relation of the government to the worker class ... Class political awareness
> can be brought to the worker *only from without*, that is to say from outside
> the economic struggle, from outside the sphere of the relations of work-
> ers to owners. The only area from which this knowledge can be taken is
> the area of the relations of *all* classes and [social] strata to the state and to
> the government – the area of the interrelations between *all* classes ... In
> a word, any secretary of a *tred-iunion* conducts and helps others conduct
> the 'economic struggle with the owners and the government'. We cannot
> insist too strongly that this is *not yet* Social Democratism and that the
> ideal of the Social-Democrat should ... [be] a *people's tribune* who can
> respond to each and every manifestation of abuse of power and oppres-
> sion, wherever it occurs, whatever stratum or class it concerns, who can
> generalise all these manifestations into one big picture.[140]

One preliminary issue here is to clarify the nature of the struggle or sphere to
which, Lenin claims, Social-Democratic political awareness must be brought
'from without'. Is the thesis of political awareness from without the thesis that
Social-Democratic political awareness must be brought from without (i) to

---

138   Lenin 2006, p. 746.
139   Lenin 2006, p. 745.
140   Lenin 2006, pp. 745–6.

struggles between individual workforces and their employers; or (ii) to all struggles between workers and capitalists, even when the latter develop to the point of demanding that a government pass (or not pass) a general law affecting all members of society? Marx would only call the former an *economic* struggle.[141] By contrast, the italics on '*all*' and '*not yet*' suggest that Lenin's thesis of political awareness from without is a thesis about the awareness that must be brought from without to all movements to improve workers' terms of employment. Let us sketch a straightforward argument for this thesis.

To know what policies or actions deserve a show of opposition, one must have some understanding of the conditions of life of those who perform them, and/or those they affect. It is only possible to judge whether a given policy or action is a type of bad in light of that understanding. For only then can its aims be ascertained, its likely effects noted, and the available alternatives assessed. However, any group can be affected by, or perform, policies and/or actions. So, a readiness to publicly oppose every single bad policy or action requires an understanding of the conditions of life of every social group. Yet, just by virtue of movements to improve their terms of employment, workers cannot be motivated to acquire such understanding. Such movements would only motivate workers to acquire this understanding if it was necessary for their success that workers be able to condemn all bads. But this is not necessary. Not all bads are bad terms of employment, or have a deleterious effect on terms of employment, or have a deleterious effect on movements to improve them. Thus, the limited goals of workers' movements to improve their terms of employment cannot motivate their participants to reflect on all the conditions of life that they would need to understand to publicly oppose every single bad. A worker may have, say, the concept of negligence, and know why negligence is bad, but be unaware of the facts needed to condemn every case (or cause) of negligence; and movements to improve their terms of employment will not by themselves motivate them to acquire the knowledge that this requires. Such movements therefore cannot lead workers to acquire the comprehensive awareness that defines Social-Democratic 'political awareness'. Workers can acquire such political awareness '*only from without*' these movements.

What complicates this straightforward argument for the thesis of political awareness from without is Lenin's claim that Social-Democratic political awareness rests on the theorisation of all bads into 'one big picture', so as to come at them from a single 'point of view'. This claim is uncontroversial: a public response to any given bad will only tend to be adequate if it

---

141   *MEW*, 33, pp. 332–3; *MECW*, 44, p. 258. For further comment, see ch. 12, sec. 8.

is informed by an assessment of its relative severity vis-à-vis other bads, in virtue of an ordering of the principles each bad exhibits. This claim is of a different sort, however, to that made in the straightforward argument for the thesis of political awareness from without. The straightforward argument rests on the idea that movements to improve terms of employment cannot motivate workers to acquire all the factual knowledge they require to condemn every bad, even supposing that they knew which principles of action were bad, and by what degree. Lenin's further claim asserts that the identification of bad principles and their ordering from a Social-Democratic point of view is *also* acquired by workers only from without. The straightforward argument concerns the interest to acquire the knowledge needed to spot all the actions and policies that *apply* bad principles; the further claim concerns the identification and ordering of practical principles by their lack of *justification*.[142]

In virtue of these two different types of claim, there are two possible versions of the thesis of political awareness from without. The strong version of the thesis holds that (a) the sociological understanding required for the comprehensive context-dependent judgement of bads, *and* (b) the capacity to identify and order bad principles from a revolutionary socialist point of view, can only be acquired by workers from without the movements to improve their terms of employment. The weak version of the thesis merely holds that the sociological understanding required for the comprehensive context-dependent judgement of bads can only be acquired by workers from without such movements.

The straightforward argument for the thesis of political awareness from without only supports the weak version of the thesis. It does not support the strong version of the thesis, because it does not follow from: 'the goal of a movement to improve workers' terms of employment cannot motivate a worker to acquire the sociological understanding that they would need to identify and thus oppose the various bads of capitalism'; that 'the goal of a movement to improve workers' terms of employment cannot disclose a principle whose underlying value can be used to condemn various bads of capitalism'.

An antinomy-based defence of interest privilege reveals an objection to the strong version of the thesis of political awareness from without. If it is possible for a participant in a working-class movement to limit the working day to conceive of and will a principle that would resolve one or more antinomies gener-

---

142   Discourse of justification/discourse of application are distinguished in Günther 1989, pp. 157–60.

ated by capitalist production, then it is possible for them to adopt its underlying value to identify, from a Marxist point of view, capitalism's various types of bad, if the application of this principle would abolish capital. They need not acquire all the conditions for class political awareness '*only from without*'.

5   An Outline of the Argument

Chapters 2–3 discuss two projects that claim inspiration from Marx's writings: 'Analytical Marxism' and 'commodity form philosophy'. Analytical Marxism is the most influential reconstructive Marxist project in Anglophone philosophy over the last 40 years; commodity form philosophy is the project to which the interaction-recognition-antinomy thesis belongs. Although Analytical Marxism has ceased to be a live movement for some time, there has been less reflection on what kind of Marxist project could take its place than there has been on what alternative reading of Marx's *Capital* is the best. That justifies a reconsideration of the project. Commodity form philosophy is then proposed as a more promising alternative.

Chapters 4–5 offer a particular conception of action and of a social relation, to underpin the interaction-recognition-antinomy thesis. The Austrian phenomenologist Alfred Schütz's *Phenomenology of the Social World* is used to frame Marx's asides on action and social relations in social phenomenological terms. Chapter 4 outlines Schütz's conception of action as antecedently projected behaviour, and uses this conception of action to connect Marx's description of the antecedently projected form of human labour in *Capital* to his aside, in the *Economic Manuscripts of 1861–63*, that the existence of social relations presupposes a 'capacity for abstraction from sensible singularity and contingency'.[143] This remark then serves as a starting point, in chapter 5, for outlining an interactional conception of a social relation as a relation of mutual affecting. An interactional conception of a social relation is the best fit with Marx's general remarks on social relations, and social relations of production. It also permits solutions to the problems of normativity and legality that are, respectively, more far-reaching and direct than Cohen's. The problem, in each case, is that of how to distinguish social relations of production from norms or legal property relations.

Aided by these general accounts of action and social relation, the rest of the book examines some of the determinate phenomena that define capital-

---

143   *MEW*, 43, p. 226; *MECW*, 30, p. 232.

ism, on a commodity form based account. Chapter 6 defends a *generalised interactions* conception of the capitalist economic structure. The capitalist economic structure is not a distribution of positions, but a combination of types of generalised interactions. The interconnection between these generalised interactions marks it out, more particularly, as a system, in which actors are bearers. To say that actors are bearers is to say that actors in each token interaction treat one another as if they did not have an end beyond it that they have. If actors are bearers of interactions, then the latter exhibit a potential for real abstraction.

Chapters 7–8 elaborate the interaction component of the interaction-recognition-antinomy thesis. Its first part is an account of purchase and sale. An interactional account of purchase and sale must explain why generalised production for exchange generates money. To this end, exchange is first distinguished from reciprocity, and possession, a presupposition of independent exchange, is analysed. Possession has two conditions: detention and *animus domini*. The subjectivity of possession then forms the basis of an argument that generalised production for exchange requires one type of commodity to serve as a universal equivalent and as a general means of exchange.

Chapter 8 argues that production with wage-labour for money maximisation can be characterised as a kind of exploitation: capitalist labour-exploitation. The general notion of exploitation, from its Saint-Simonian origins, is that of instrumentalisation, or benefitting from another's harm. *The Grundrisse* suggests a particular conception of this notion. Exploitation, it is argued here, is self-seeking action whose maxim fails a system-level universalisability test. This system universalisability conception of exploitation facilitates a solution to three problems: the exploitation and need problem (how to condemn exploitation while defending support for needy non-producers); the agency problem (how a group within capitalism can have an interest that can lead it to seek to overcome value production); and the capitalism, rights and injustice problem (how to condemn capitalism as unjust without appeal to rights).

Chapters 9–10 defend the recognition component of the thesis. Chapter 9 reconstructs Marx's suggestion that commodity exchange exhibits a kind of mutual recognition by elaborating a pragmatic conception of recognition. On a pragmatic conception of recognition, a recognisee's interpretive perspective is key to determining what counts as genuine recognition. The passages in which Marx suggests that commodity exchange exhibits a kind of mutual recognition are then analysed and developed with the aid of Marx's claim that security is a social concept. The as-if mutual recognition of personhood, and a social interest in security, combine to explain why commodity exchangers can be led to articulate a principle of self-ownership. Its articulation, and not any genuine recognition in the sphere of circulation, can account for why commodity exchangers develop the freedom of will of persons and private property owners.

Chapter 10 outlines a recognition-based conception of domination on which bureaucratic domination tends to accompany production with wage-labour for money maximisation. The general notion of domination is that of an asymmetrical power relation. Marx adopts a recognition-based conception of domination, as the command of an alien will. In capitalist production, domination is differently conditioned by the formal subsumption and the real subsumption of labour under capital. While formal subsumption facilitates a belief in individual responsibility as the source of legitimacy of a capitalist firm's commands, real subsumption generates a belief in administrative expertise as a second source of legitimacy for its commands. Occupational identity helps to explain why wage-labourers can be assumed to recognise a capitalist firm's commands on account of a belief in administrators' administrative expertise.

Chapters 11–12 present the antinomy component of the thesis. The first part is to explain the antinomy of natural rights and popular authorisation. An explanation for the legal order of capitalism can begin from the freedom of will established by generalised purchase and sale. Persons have a guarantee related and a recognition related reason to institute norms of private property ownership and self-ownership, which award innate absolute rights. Marx's illusion-based critique of innate absolute rights is that they must appear as natural rights. Yet natural rights are not the only source of supra-legal legitimacy for government action. The obstacle that any sovereign monarch poses for the system of capitalist production leads to an appeal to popular sovereignty, institutionalised by a constitution-making power. As its mandate is to uphold equal liberty, the natural rights justification and the popular authorisation justification for government action both rest on the same premise, that individuals have an exclusive claim to their parts and capacities. If a representative law-making power, within a separation of powers, is the form of law-making power that accommodates the values of freedom of choice and popular sovereignty, this antinomy also shapes the conflict between its public discussion, and the authority of a state bureaucracy.

Chapter 12 analyses the conditions, form and function of a second antinomy, the rights-antinomy in capitalist production. Its significance for taking a micro-level conflict in capitalist production to the macro-level is explored with the aid of an antagonistic interdependency conception of classes. Antagonism between capitalists and wage-labourers is first expressed in the assertion of rights that form an antinomy, because commodity exchange leads both capitalists and wage-labourers to conceive themselves as self-owners. An antinomy arises, because there cannot both be a right to an unlimited working day, and a right to a limited working day, even if both assertions appear equally justified. Yet, as a wage-labourer's position in this rights-antinomy exhibits what Lukács calls *'the self-consciousness of the commodity'*,[144] the antinomy is productive. Implicit in workers' practical response, which establishes new forms of recognition, is the possibility of affirming a system universalisability principle of justice, a kind of duty to the whole, as normatively more fundamental than rights. Through its affirmation, a participant in a working-class movement can resolve both antinomies.

Appendix: a Note on Translation

If Marx's writings are retranslated, it is possible to reconstruct a plausible thesis about capitalism that is otherwise not visible. Some questions cannot be raised by appeal to the official translations; other questions, distinct from Marx's, suggest themselves; and the opportunities for linking Marx's various claims are distorted. Without a return to the original texts, arguments germane to interaction, recognition and antinomy will escape Marx scholarship. In respect of passages central for the argument of every chapter from chapter 4 onwards, if what Marx writes in German is true, then what the official translations state in his name is false.

This is a strong claim. In this note, five examples are used to illustrate how errors of translation vitiate even some of Marx's 'famous quotations' and concepts. If even some of Marx's 'famous quotations' and concepts are vitiated by errors of translation, then the philological problem is acute, and an explicit strategy will be required to address it. The purpose of these examples, then, is to convince the reader of the need to outline and follow certain rules of translation, which are set out thereafter. It is only if some rules are made explicit and can be seen to be followed that the strong claim is defensible. The reader is then in a position to judge the extent to which the linguistic argument of the book is successful.

Example 1
In *Critique of the Gotha Programme*, Marx suggests that a developed communist society could surpass 'the narrow, bourgeois horizon of right [*der enge bürgerliche Rechtshorizont*]'.[145]

---

144   Lukács 1977, p. 352; Lukács 1968, p. 168.
145   *MEW*, 19, p. 21.

Two official translations of this phrase render it as 'the narrow horizon of bourgeois right',[146] and in another it is rendered as 'the limited horizon of bourgeois right'.[147] According to all official translations, it is the narrow or limited 'horizon of bourgeois right' that developed communism, in Marx's view, can surpass. Why is that a mistake,[148] and why does it matter?

'Rechtshorizont' is a nominal compound of the kind in which the first component or 'determining word' ('Recht-') modifies the second component or 'basis word' ('-horizont').[149] With compounds of this kind, any attributive adjective 'always relates in the first instance to the basis word and thereby, in the second instance, to the entire compound'.[150] Thus, in English, a red table lamp is a red lamp suitable for use on a table; it is not a lamp designed for use on red tables. Likewise, a clean dish cloth is a clean cloth for wiping dishes; it is not a cloth for wiping clean dishes. Similarly, 'enge bürgerliche Rechtshorizont' is a narrow and bourgeois horizon of right, not a horizon of narrow bourgeois right, or a narrow horizon of bourgeois right.[151] The syntax of Marx's German phrase leaves no room to doubt that in Marx's vision 'Recht' does not occupy a fundamental place in developed communism. It is not merely a bourgeois version of 'Recht' that ceases to occupy a fundamental place.

The mistake matters, because it matters, for an understanding of Marx's vision of the good society, what developed communism is said to surpass. Anglophone debate is characterised by claims which are undermined by Marx's phrase. A few examples:

---

146   *MECW*, 24, p. 87; Marx 1974, p. 347.

147   Marx 1996, p. 215.

148   The mistake is noted at Furner 2011, p. 213. For a sample of Marx's uses of the more general term 'bourgeois horizon' in other contexts, see Murray 2016, pp. 4–8.

149   Engel 1996, p. 580.

150   Engel 1996, p. 587.

151   The same error spoils other phrases. The phrase '*gesellschaftliche Bewußtseinsformen*', which Marx uses in his Preface to *A Contribution to a Critique of Political Economy* (*MEW*, 13, p. 8) should be translated as 'social forms of consciousness', and not, as in the official translations, as 'forms of social consciousness' (*MECW*, 29, p. 263; Marx 1975a, p. 425; Marx 1996, p. 160). Social consciousness, insofar as it consists of beliefs, singles out just those beliefs that are 'beliefs about society' (Wetherly 2005, p. 42). Accordingly, 'forms of social consciousness' denotes forms of belief about society. But the beliefs that '*gesellschaftliche Bewußtseinsformen*' include are not limited to forms of belief about society. That a belief is a belief about society is not a condition for its belonging to a social form of consciousness. See, for example, Marx's remark in his Letter to Engels, dated 18 June 1862: 'with Darwin, the animal kingdom figures as bourgeois society' (*MEW*, 30, p. 249; *MECW*, 41, p. 381). From the phrase 'forms of social consciousness', one would not know that Marx's remark is directed at an instance of a '*gesellschaftliche Bewußtseinsform*'.

if Marx's words are taken literally, it is only the horizon of bourgeois right, not that of rights *überhaupt*, that is superseded in the transition to the higher stage[152]

The natural way to interpret this is not that right is abolished in the communist phase, but that right becomes adequately realized or realized in a developed form[153]

that when Marx said 'the narrow horizon of bourgeois right can be crossed in its entirety' he really meant 'the horizon of right can be crossed in its entirety' is debatable.[154]

In this connection, it is worth mentioning the amusing fact that a German professor who rejected the interpretive claim that Marx's vision of developed communism lacks the form of right[155] *misquotes* Marx's German phrase, replacing it with a phrase that the official English translations would correctly translate. Gustav Radbruch misquotes the above phrase as '"*engen Horizont des bürgerlichen Rechtes*"'.[156]

Marx's characterisation of '*Recht*' as a fundamentally narrow and bourgeois horizon is not without ambiguity, of course, because the term '*Recht*' is not unambiguous, and because what it means to overstep a horizon is not unambiguous (must '*Recht*' cease to exist, or merely cease to fulfil a normatively fundamental function?) But the point of offering and defending new translations is not to try to settle all textual ambiguity. It is sufficient to alter the terrain of reasonable ambiguity. In this case, it shows that one widespread interpretation is not a reasonable interpretation.

Example 2
For a second example, we simply expand Marx's claim in *Critique of the Gotha Programme*. Marx says of developed communism that, once 'all the fountains of communal wealth flow more fully [*voller fließen*] – only then can the narrow, bourgeois horizon of right be completely overstepped'.[157]

Arneson 1981, p. 216. Geras 1985, p. 60, van de Veer 1973, p. 374, and Waldron 1987, p. 135, are similarly mistaken.
153   Green 1983, p. 442.
154   Torrance 1995, pp. 294–5.
155   Radbruch 1987, p. 555.
156   Radbruch 1993a, p. 483.
157   *MEW*, 19, p. 21.

In the *MECW* translation, the first clause of Marx's statement is instead rendered: 'all the springs of common wealth flow more abundantly'.[158] Two other translations render the same clause similarly as: 'all the springs of cooperative wealth flow more abundantly'.[159] What mistake do these translations share, and why does it matter?

The strange phrase 'more abundantly' is a mistake, because Marx does not refer to abundance. Marx does not use a phrase like '*im Überfluss* (in abundance)'. He uses a comparative adjective '*voller* (more fully)'. To say that wealth flows 'more fully' in society x than in society y is not to imply that the level of wealth in society x is abundant. The latter is an absolute judgement: to say that wealth is abundant is to say that it is in excess of current requirements. But there may be improvement from one type or stage of society to the next without this improvement effecting a transition to a level of wealth in excess of requirements.[160]

The mistake matters, because it matters, for an understanding of Marx's vision of the good society, what level of wealth Marx envisions developed communism to exhibit, and what Marx foresees as putting developed communism in a position to surpass the horizon of right.

In *Self-Ownership, Freedom and Equality*, Cohen offers a particular answer to these questions, while repeating the terms 'abundance' or 'abundantly' over 50 times. The only evidence Cohen offers in this work for holding that Marx used either term is the aforecited passage.[161] The repetition is designed to ram home Cohen's claim that Marx sidestepped questions of justice because Marx assumed that developed communism would achieve a level of wealth so abundant that it would make justice unnecessary: 'the "Marxist technological fix" has served as a means of avoiding questions of justice'.[162] Cohen then counters:

> The 'springs of co-operative wealth' will probably never 'flow' so 'abundantly' that no one will be under the necessity of abandoning or revising what he wants, because of the wants of other people. The problem of justice will not go away.[163]

---

158 *MECW*, 24, p. 87.
159 Marx 1974, p. 347; Marx 1996, p. 215.
160 Nor does Marx's vision of developed communism in *Critique of the Gotha Programme* as a society that implements the principle 'from each according to their ability, to each according to their needs!' (*MEW*, 19, p. 21; *MECW*, 24, p. 87) imply that it has the means to implement this principle so as to supply 'what everyone needs' (Cohen 2001, p. 114).
161 Cited at Cohen 1995, p. 126.
162 Cohen 1995, p. 116.
163 Cohen 1995, pp. 127–8; see also pp. 132–3, p. 136, pp. 139–43. Cohen says elsewhere: 'Marx-

Cohen here repeats a theme of Carl Menger's *Principles of Economics*. In Menger's view, a lack of abundance of goods is what makes a coercive legal order necessary. If goods are not abundant, maximising agents, who put their own want-satisfaction above that of others, will compete for, and may be tempted to seize possession of, others' goods.[164] If goods are abundant, by contrast, maximising agents will not be led by their egoism to use violence against others to obtain the goods they want. Cohen's claim of a '"Marxist technological fix"'[165] relates to this theme, for if an abundance of goods ensures that there is no need for a coercive legal order to prevent human egoism from leading to violent conflicts over goods, abundance ensures that there is no need for principles of (distributive) justice. In Cohen's view, Marx avoided questions of justice because Marx accepted what an *economist* can say about the need for a coercive legal order. Will Kymlicka and others agree: 'post-juridical life apparently is impossible without abundance, and is guaranteed by abundance'.[166]

It is crucial, therefore, to the claim of a '"Marxist technological fix"' that there should be evidence that Marx used a term such as 'abundantly' to describe the wealth of developed communism. Only a term such as 'abundantly' would prove that Marx believed that goods in developed communism would be available in excess of human requirements, and thereby support the interpretation that Marx thought that principles of justice would become unnecessary in a future of abundant wealth.

Once the aforecited clause is translated aright, the evidence that Cohen presents is discredited. As Marx does not characterise developed communism by abundance, he cannot be charged with appealing to abundance to avoid questions of justice. To the question: what feature(s) of developed communism and 'Recht' ensure that, in Marx's view, developed communism can surpass the horizon of 'Recht', it is unwarranted to answer: developed communism displays an abundance that makes a coercive legal order unnecessary.[167]

---

ism thought that equality would be delivered to us, by abundance, but we have to seek equality for a context of scarcity' (Cohen 2001, p. 115). By 'abundance', Cohen has in mind a state of affairs in which 'anything anyone needed for a richly fulfilling life could be taken from the common store at no cost to anyone' (Cohen 2001, p. 104; compare Cohen 2008, p. 333).

164   Menger 1968, pp. 55–6; Menger 2007, p. 97; compare Cohen 2008, p. 333.
165   Cohen 1995, p. 116.
166   Kymlicka 1989, p. 119; Buchanan 1979, p. 139; Geras 1985, pp. 82–3.
167   For an alternative answer, see ch. 3, sec. 4.

Example 3

The German Ideology contains the following outline of its conception of history:

> This conception of history rests on elaborating the real production process, by beginning from the material production of immediate life; grasping the form of commerce tied to and generated from this mode of production, i.e. civil society in its various stages, as the foundation of all history; and presenting it in its action as the state, as well as explaining the various different theoretical artefacts and forms of consciousness, religion, philosophy, morality, etc., etc., from it, and tracing its process of emergence out of them [*und ihren Entstehungsprozeß aus ihnen zu verfolgen*]; at which point the matter can naturally then be presented in its totality (and so, too, the interaction of these various sides on one another).[168]

The *MECW* translation of the bracketed German clause instead reads: 'and tracing the process of their formation from that basis'.

I say that what undergoes a process of emergence, according to *The German Ideology*, is 'civil society in its various stages', and that what this process emerges out of are 'theoretical artefacts and forms of consciousness'. The *MECW* translation has things the other way around.

The *MECW* translation is in error, for it cannot account for Marx's use of '*ihnen*'. '*Ihnen*' is a plural pronoun, and so refers to a plural noun or nouns. Hence, it cannot refer to the *singular* 'civil society in its various stages'. It cannot, therefore, be translated as 'that basis', where 'that basis' refers to 'civil society in its various stages'. As '*ihnen*' refers to a plural noun or nouns, it must refer to 'theoretical artefacts and forms of consciousness'. It is best rendered as 'them'.

What *The German Ideology* is claiming, with this bracketed German clause, is that 'theoretical artefacts and forms of consciousness' help to explain the emergence of a stage of civil society. An account of this causality is a part of an account of history 'in its totality', complementing an account of the causality described in the immediately prior clauses. Correcting the translation so that it preserves this point is important in order to resist confirming the hearsay view of Marx as an economic historian; a view expressed in Roemer's claim that 'from a materialist viewpoint ... the answer to "why" should be economic

---

168   *MEJ*, 2003, pp. 28–9; *MEW*, 3, pp. 37–8; *MECW*, 5, p. 53.

ones'.[169] The *MECW* translation encourages this hearsay view, for on its version, the bracketed German clause offers a redundant repetition of the immediately preceding clause. What could be more reassuring for the hearsay view of Marx as an economic historian than if Marx, in stressing the causal weight of civil society, should go to the lengths of redundantly repeating himself!

There is no obvious explanation for the mistake, other than that translators are so blinded by the hearsay view of Marx as to be prepared to ignore a grammatical rule to confirm it.[170] Certainly, the error is not explained by familiarity with Marx's writings. *On the Jewish Question* asserts: '[o]nly under the rule of Christianity, which makes *all* national, natural, ethical and theoretical relations *external* to man, could civil society completely separate itself from state life'.[171] Marx's *Grundrisse* claims that certain conceptual features of Roman private law 'had to be enforced [*geltend gemacht werden musste*] vis-à-vis the Middle Ages as the right of emerging bourgeois society'.[172] These claims are *heretical*, if read in light of the above *MECW* translation. Once the translation is corrected, however, they exemplify it.

Example 4

Marx's *Critique of Hegel's Doctrine of the State* states: '[t]hat the rational is actual is proven by the *contradiction* of *irrational reality*'.[173] In German: '[d]ass das Vernünftige wirklich ist, beweist sich eben im *Widerspruch* der *unvernünftigen Wirklichkeit*'.

One translation instead renders Marx's statement as follows: '[t]he claim that the rational is actual is contradicted precisely by an irrational actuality'.[174]

---

169 Roemer 1982a, pp. 5–6; compare Weber 1988, pp. 161–6; Weber 2012, pp. 108–11.
170 A different translation renders the bracketed German clause as: 'and to trace civil society's process of generation out of its various stages and together with these forms and creations' (Marx 1994, p. 137). This is inadequate for a different reason: it is not reasonable to render '*aus ihnen*' as 'out of its various stages and together with these forms and creations'. The effect is similar: in virtue of twisting a single claim (*x* emerges from *y*) into two different claims (*x* emerges from *x*'s various stages and *x* emerges together with *y*), the causality that *The German Ideology*'s conception of history incorporates (that a stage of civil society emerges from theoretical artefacts and forms of consciousness) is lost.
171 *MEW*, 1, p. 376; *MECW*, 3, p. 173.
172 *MEW*, 42, p. 171; *MECW*, 28, p. 177; Marx 1973a, p. 246. *MECW* says that certain conceptual features of Roman private law 'could be upheld as the law of emerging bourgeois society as against the Middle Ages'. But '*musste*', from '*müssen* (must/have to)' is not '*konnte*', from '*können* (can/could)'. The Marx 1973a translation of this phrase is better.
173 *MEW*, 1, p. 266.
174 Marx 1970b, p. 64.

Another translation is similar: 'that the rational is real is *contradicted* by *the irrational reality*'.[175] What mistake do these translations share, and why does it matter?

The common mistake is that both translations omit to render the verb '*sich beweisen* (to be proven, to be demonstrated)', and instead verbalise the noun '*Widerspruch* (contradiction)'.[176]

The mistake transforms Marx's claim. Marx's claim has the form: x 'is proven by' y. Marx is *affirming* that the rational is actual on particular grounds. To say that x 'is contradicted by' y is one way of saying that x is disproven by y. Both of the aforecited translations imply that Marx is *rejecting* the idea that 'the rational is actual/real'. They represent Marx as denying the claim he is asserting.

Marx's statement continues to be understood along the lines of these official translations. Robert Fine claims: 'Marx argued that the rationality Hegel attributed to the state is contradicted at every point by its irrational reality'.[177] Joseph McCarney claims that Marx's remark is a badly formulated criticism of Hegel's account of the estates as one of the 'irrationalities of mere existence'.[178] Neither of these claims acknowledges that Marx is affirming that the rational is actual.

For Marx to assert that the rational is actual is for him to take the position that human reason is historically active. Human reason is historically active by virtue of a contradiction in an irrational reality if this contradiction cannot exist without being noticed and without troubling a type of actor capable of transforming the reality that gives rise to it, to resolve it. Marx's view of the transformation of irrational reality is not that it is itself a part of a reality whose irrationality proves that the rational is not actual; rather, the transformation of irrational reality is rational.

Example 5

For decades, Marx used the term '*Produktivkräfte*'. '*Produktivkräfte*' is standardly translated as 'productive forces', rather than, as it should be, as 'productive powers'.

---

175 Marx 1975a, p. 127.

176 The less frequently cited Milligan and Ruhemann translation for *MECW* avoids this mistake: 'that the rational is actual is proved precisely in the *contradiction* of irrational actuality' (*MECW*, 3, p. 63).

177 Fine 2009, p. 106.

178 McCarney 2009, p. 20. McCarney uses his own translation: 'that the rational is actual proves itself to be in *contradiction* with the *irrational actuality*'. But this translation is defective in the same way: to say x 'proves itself to be in contradiction with' y is to say that y counts as evidence against x.

One problem with rendering 'Produktivkräfte' as 'productive forces' is that it is at odds with Marx's own practice when writing in English for publication. Wal Suchting first drew attention to the fact that 'when he is writing in English', Marx 'invariably' uses a powers phrase, and not a forces phrase.[179] Marx's first use of the English phrase 'productive forces' in print occurs in the first published piece of writing by Marx in English to refer to what, in German, he would term 'Produktivkräfte'.[180] Besides this use, there is only one other isolated occasion in print where Marx uses the English phrase 'productive forces'.[181] Overwhelmingly, Marx uses the English phrase 'productive power(s) (of labour)'.[182] If 'Produktivkräfte' is to be translated to accord with Marx's preferred phrase, it must be rendered as 'productive powers'.

A second problem is that 'productive forces' is at odds with the meaning of 'Kraft'. Just as a power can be thought apart from its application or effect, and may exist without taking effect; so a type of 'Kraft' can be thought apart from its 'Anwendung' or 'Wirkung'. 'Produktivkräfte' may exist without being applied. The phrase 'productive forces' obscures this, because 'forces' suggests a non-deliberate effect or motion, as in phrases such as 'market forces', 'gale force' or 'force of a wave'. The English phrase 'to come into force' just is a synonym for 'to take effect'. It is said to be part of a realist ontology that '[b]ehind the forces directly manifested in action are powers'.[183] If a 'Kraft' or power, unlike an elemental force, can exist without being applied, then 'Produktivkräfte' must be rendered as 'productive powers'.

Marx's practice when writing in English for publication may reflect this view of 'Kraft', for Marx claims that it is a non-contingent fact that 'Produktivkräfte' exist without being applied. *The German Ideology* remarks: 'productive powers [*Produktivkräfte*] receive, under private property, a merely one-sided development ... and a number of these powers [*Kräfte*] cannot, with private property, be applied at all'.[184] Marx had a reason to abandon the term 'productive forces' when writing in English: 'productive powers' does more to encourage critical thinking about types of social relation in which possible valuable uses of 'Produktivkräfte' are frustrated.

---

179   Suchting 1982, p. 175.
180   *MECW*, 11, p. 531.
181   *MECW*, 15, p. 141.
182   *MECW*, 11, pp. 530–1; *MECW*, 12, p. 219, pp. 221–2; *MECW*, 14, p. 656; *MECW*, 20, p. 9, p. 104, p. 106, p. 108, p. 110, pp. 124–5, pp. 138–40, p. 143, p. 147.
183   Harré and Madden 1975, p. 167.
184   *MEJ*, 2003, p. 66; *MEW*, 3, p. 60; *MECW*, 5, p. 73.

Translating '*Produktivkräfte*' as 'productive powers' alters the terrain of reasonable ambiguity. In *Dialectical and Historical Materialism*, Joseph Stalin asserts: '[b]ut the productive forces are only one aspect of production, only one aspect of the mode of production'.[185] Similarly, Étienne Balibar claims in *Reading Capital*: 'the "productive forces", too, are a connexion of a certain type within the mode of production'.[186] Both of these claims are undermined by the translation of '*Produktivkräfte*' as 'productive powers'. As productive powers may exist without being applied, productive powers are not an 'aspect' or 'connexion' of a type of activity. Postone writes: '[t]*he dialectic of the forces and relations of production ... is, then, a dialectic of two dimensions of capital* rather than of capital and forces extrinsic to it'.[187] This claim, too, is hard to defend, if 'forces' and 'forces of production' are replaced with 'powers' and 'powers of production'. As productive powers may exist without being applied, the productive powers that exist in capitalism are not, in and of themselves, a dimension of capital accumulation.

Rules of Translation

The examples discussed above show that some of Marx's important claims – about communism, social transformation, the terms and nature of his conception of history – cannot be understood solely from the official translations. The above mistakes can be described without reference to a special theory of translation, an intricate account of Marx's project, or an elaborate understanding of the context. They fail to respect basic rules of grammar or everyday meanings of terms.

If these examples are representative of the kind of mistakes that need fixing, it must be possible to specify generally acceptable rules for drawing attention to where and explaining how the official translations of Marx's writings are to be corrected so that, if these rules are successfully followed, the correction stands a chance of general acceptance. It is also *necessary* to formulate and to be seen to follow some rules, for 'in the context of a tradition ... all readers inevitably have sets of expectations formed by previous, related renderings'.[188] The versions of Marx's claims that appear in the official translations have been interpreted and repeated. In this intellectual context, readers must be persuaded

---

185   Stalin 1977, p. 28.
186   Althusser and Balibar 1969, p. 126; Althusser and Balibar 1975, p. 235; see, similarly, Poulantzas 1982, pp. 23–4; Poulantzas 1978, pp. 26–7.
187   Postone 1993, p. 351.
188   Geraets and Harris 1991, p. xxviii.

to adopt a rendering that departs from the old. To this end, the new rendering must be seen to follow from a transparent and systematic process of reasoning. Little can be expected to be gained from silently modifying a translation without any explanation for the change if the existing translation has since become a basis of established debate.

Three rules will therefore be observed. The rules do not depend on acceptance of the interaction-recognition-antinomy thesis. In principle, any study of Marx could adopt them.

> (1) Foreign phrases will be bracketed within citations if and only if it is relevant for an argument advanced in this book to know what phrase is used.

It will count as a sufficient mark of relevance if (a) an argument is not supported as strongly, or at all, by a different rendering of the bracketed phrase in an official translation of that passage in common use; *or* if (b) the foreign phrase and/or cognate phrases also appear in other passages cited in this book, and the multiple usage strengthens the argument, whether or not it is necessary to depart from an official translation; *or*, less commonly, if (c) it strengthens the argument to know that a foreign phrase is not the different foreign phrase that appears in several other passages. When (b) is the cause of relevance, reference to other passages is supplied, usually on first report of the foreign phrase. It will not count as a sufficient mark of relevance if the translation offered here differs only stylistically from an official translation, or if a non-stylistic difference has no particular bearing on the argument.

> (2) All and only all the relevant differences between the translations of bracketed foreign phrases, and the official translation(s) referred to in the footnotes, will be noted and explained in the footnote, or, if especially pertinent, in the main text.

The criteria of relevance are the same as for rule (1). But there will be no note or explanation if there is no departure from the official translation; and explanations will not be repeated. A difference counts as especially pertinent if it bears on the judgement of an entire tradition of interpretation.

> (3) For all translations explained in accordance with (2), if the official translation would more correctly translate a different foreign phrase, that phrase is provided in a footnote, for comparison.

Many but not all foreign phrases explained in accordance with rule (2) will meet the condition in rule (3). The condition may not be met, because various English phrases may be candidates for translating the same foreign phrase (although one of these various phrases is better in a given context); or the official translation may have omitted to render the phrase.

By following these rules, it may be hoped that curious readers will be able to identify the relevant differences between the translations offered here, and the official translations in common use; and be in a position to assess whether or not the translations used here are an improvement and ought to be generally adopted.

CHAPTER 2

Analytical Marxism

The most authoritative statement of Analytical Marxism is Cohen's 'Introduction to the 2000 Edition' of his *Karl Marx's Theory of History* (*KMTH*).[1] Alongside Jon Elster and John Roemer, Cohen was a leading advocate of Analytical Marxism. *KMTH*, first published in 1978, is widely regarded as having initiated the project.[2] Cohen's statement in this Introduction, subtitled 'Reflections on Analytical Marxism', guides the following assessment.

Cohen's Introduction has more than authority on its side. For one, it self-consciously defines the project of Analytical Marxism independently of its founders' theses. That is appropriate, because Analytical Marxists liken Marxism to physics, insofar as 'no one expects it to *preserve* the theses of its founders'.[3] The same must apply to Analytical Marxism. The theses of its founders may be rejected, to the advancement of Analytical Marxism, if they are rejected by arguments of an Analytical Marxist kind. Another reason to distinguish the project of Analytical Marxism from the theses of particular Analytical Marxists is that not every thesis advanced by an author who self-identifies as an Analytical Marxist is guaranteed to satisfy its criteria. For example, Cohen's meta-ethical thesis that 'the principles at the summit of our conviction are grounded in no facts whatsoever'[4] does not belong to Analytical Marxism, if, as Cohen's Introduction says, Analytical Marxism addresses the problems of socialist 'design, justification, and strategy'.[5] The aim in this chapter is to offer a critical assessment of the project of Analytical Marxism. Particular theses are only discussed to this end.

A further reason to focus on Cohen's Introduction is that it succeeds in identifying the character of Analytical Marxism. The two 'analytical standards'[6] by which it defines Analytical Marxism are a variation on the theme of Descartes' first two laws in *Discourse on the Method*: accept only what is presented 'clearly' and 'distinctly'; and 'divide' any difficulties into 'as many parts as

---

1 Cohen 2000, pp. xvii–xxviii.
2 Elster 1985, p. xiv; Callinicos 1987, pp. 3–4; Carver and Thomas 1995, p. 1; Bertram 2010, p. 31. Mayer suggests earlier forerunners (Mayer 1994, pp. 4–5).
3 Cohen 2000, p. xxvii.
4 Cohen 2008, p. 229.
5 Cohen 2000, p. xxv.
6 Cohen 2000, p. xxiv.

© KONINKLIJKE BRILL NV, LEIDEN, 2019 | DOI:10.1163/9789004384804_003

possible and as may be required'.[7] Not all accounts of Analytical Marxism are as successful in this respect. Consider Erik Olin Wright's criteria for what makes 'Analytical Marxism distinctive':

(1)   A commitment to *conventional scientific norms* ...
(2)   An emphasis on the importance of *systematic conceptualization* ...
(3)   A concern with a relatively *fine-grained specification of the steps in the theoretical arguments linking concepts* ...
(4)   The importance accorded to *the intentional action of individuals*[8]

Wright's criteria are too broad. Adorno is a Marxist who is not an Analytical Marxist; and yet the premise of Adorno's critical engagement with Weber is that, while Weber's concept of an ideal type is an 'attempt to survive without a system ... his concept of understanding', designed to grasp meaningful action, is 'an anti-positivistic concept'.[9] In other words, Adorno affirms (2) and (4). (1) is also misleading. According to Adorno, 'non-dialectical scientistic [*szientifischen*] thinking' cannot provide 'scientific knowledge [*wissenschaftliche Erkenntnis*]'.[10] But if the latter became conventional, Adorno would be committed to '*conventional scientific norms*'. He would not have become an Analytical Marxist, however. A critical engagement with Cohen's Introduction reveals why.

1   The Project of Analytical Marxism

Most simply, Analytical Marxism offers a 'reconstruction'[11] of Marxism. It seeks to defend Marxism in a form suited to the achievement of its aims. That is not to say that the need for reconstruction has a complex explanation. Marx's ideas are 'untidy', *KMTH* says, because 'he did not have the time, or the will, or the academic peace, to straighten them out'.[12]

Analytical Marxism takes a particular view of Marxism's aims, and the intellectual form suited to them. The three key problems bequeathed to contemporary Marxist theorists are those of 'design, justification, and strategy'.[13] Marxism

---

7   Descartes 1990, p. 30; Descartes 1988, p. 29.
8   Wright 1995, p. 14.
9   Adorno 2010, p. 238.
10   Adorno 2010, p. 288, p. 297. On '*Wissenschaft*', see ch. 3.
11   Cohen 2000, p. xxiv.
12   Cohen 2000, p. ix.
13   Cohen 2000, p. xxv; recapitulating Cohen 1988, p. xii.

requires a vision of future socialist institutions; an analysis of the values that recommend them over capitalism; and a strategy to achieve that vision. In its approach to these problems, the 'analytical Marxist impetus' is to defend or else revise inherited theory so that it may 'measure up to analytical standards of criticism'.[14] Cohen distinguishes two sorts of 'analytical standards', and each is described in positive as well as contrastive terms.

Firstly, Analytical Marxism uses 'techniques ... commonly styled "analytical", in a broad sense, because their use requires and facilitates precision of statement on the one hand and rigour of argument on the other'.[15] Statements are precise if their intended force is clear.[16] An argument is rigorous, on the other hand, if it is compelling. One way to be compelling, Cohen says, is 'to assemble premises which even opponents will not want to deny, and by dint of skill at inference, to derive results which opponents will indeed want to deny but which, having granted the premises, they will be hard pressed to deny'.[17]

Cohen adds, contrastively, that analysis in this 'broad sense' (analysis-BS) is 'opposed to so-called "dialectical" thinking'.[18] '[S]o-called "dialectical" thinking', Cohen believes, remains caught up in the suggestiveness of the vague notions that analysis-BS untangles. It is inherently 'unthought through and/or obscure'.[19] Its semblance of justification vanishes with the application of analysis-BS.

As Cohen reads Hegel in *KMTH*, dialectical thinking attempts to grasp entities in their 'differentiated unity', guided by the metaphor of 'mutually sustaining parts in a properly functioning organism'.[20] (Consider Chris Arthur's recent remark: 'systematic dialectic explores the "inneraction" of an organic whole').[21] For Cohen, analysis-BS extracts what is rational from this suggestive metaphor, by its use of functional explanation.[22] What is held to be explanatory, in a functional explanation, is a dispositional fact of hypothetical conditional form: 'if e, then f'. For Cohen, the distinct core features of all the forms of society that Marxism explains can be unified in a series of functional explanations in which the effected entity in the dispositional fact of one functional explanation is the effecting entity in the dispositional fact of another. If functional explanations

---

14   Cohen 2000, p. xxiv.
15   Cohen 2000, p. xviii.
16   Cohen 2011, pp. 225–6.
17   Cohen 1995, p. 112.
18   Cohen 2000, p. xvii.
19   Cohen 2000, p. xxvi.
20   Cohen 1978, pp. 20–1.
21   Arthur 2002, p. 74; see also Wood 2004, p. 216.
22   Cohen 1978, p. 156, p. 233.

are sound, a premise that 'so-called "dialectical" thinking'[23] will not want to deny, the premise that societies can be likened to organic totalities, can be separated from any need for 'so-called "dialectical" thinking'.

Adopting a similar tack, Jon Elster writes: 'the dialectical method can be stated in ordinary "analytical" language'.[24] Marx's contribution to modern social science, Elster argues, is '"a theory of social contradictions"'.[25] The theory of social contradictions examines the unintended consequences of actions that proceed on false assumptions about others' relevant behaviour. Actors' 'beliefs about each other ... are such that, although any one of them may well be true, it is logically impossible that they all be'.[26] Accordingly, if 'all act as if they were true, their action will come to grief through the mechanism of unintended consequences'.[27] If, for example, 'each capitalist acts on an assumption – that only *his* workers should save or accept lower wages – which as a matter of logic cannot be true for all',[28] then demand will fall, and capitalists will not make the profits they hoped for. If false assumptions of this kind, together with the ensuing actions, and subsequent attempts to counteract their effects, explain the outcomes of class conflicts, Marxism, Elster claims, can assign social contradictions explanatory weight without any residue of 'Hegelian contradiction'. The latter is largely 'a source of confusion' on account of violating the formal law of non-contradiction.[29]

Cohen says that a second, 'narrower sense' in which Analytical Marxism is analytical (analysis-NS),

> is its disposition to explain molar phenomena by reference to the micro-constituents and micro-mechanisms that respectively compose the entities and underlie the processes which occur at a grosser level of resolution ... Insofar as analytical Marxists are analytical in this narrower sense, they reject the point of view in which social formations and classes are depicted as entities obeying laws of behaviour that are not a function of the behaviours of their constituent individuals.[30]

23 Cohen 2000, p. xvii.
24 Elster 1985, p. 37; see also Elster 1970, pp. 65–6.
25 Elster 1985, p. 48; endorsed by Leopold 2008, p. 125.
26 Elster 1985, p. 44.
27 Ibid.
28 Elster 1985, p. 26.
29 Elster 1985, p. 43, following Popper 1940, p. 411, p. 418.
30 Cohen 2000, p. xxiii; see, similarly, Roemer 1981, p. 7.

Analysis-NS is an individual-based social ontology and explanatory programme that conjoins two thoughts. Not only are the causal powers of 'molar
level entities' (such as classes) to be derived from their 'fundamental constituents';[31] these fundamental constituents are individuals. To explain the causal
powers of 'molar level entities' is 'to know *how* and *why* ... behaviours of individuals lead to that result'.[32] To reconstruct Marxism by analysis-NS is to require
all the concepts Marxism uses to describe the causal powers of 'molar level
entities' to be underpinned by explanations of these powers in which the fundamental constituents of the entities are individuals.

Elster and Cohen contrast 'methodological individualism' or analysis-NS
to 'methodological collectivism'[33] or '"holism"'[34] respectively. Those contrastive terms (collectivism and holism) are a hangover from an earlier contrast,
however, and they conceal the real issue. In *The Open Society and its Enemies*,
Karl Popper contrasts '"methodological individualism"' to 'collectivism and
holism' on the grounds that the former 'rightly insists that the "behavior" and
the "actions" of collectives, such as states or social groups, must be reduced to
the behavior and to the actions of human individuals'.[35] By this Popper means
to say that individuals alone have mental states, and a capacity for action; there
is no supra-individual subject with a 'group mind'.[36] Elster's and Cohen's contrast of analysis-NS to collectivism or holism conceals the real issue, therefore,
for analysis-NS is more than just a denial that there are group minds with causal
efficacy. Analysis-NS denies that the fundamental constituents of collective
entities are anything but individuals. By implication, it denies that one or more
collective entities have constituent *relations*. The latter denial can be clarified
using the notion of a 'relational' property, which both Cohen and Elster adopt.[37]

According to G.E. Moore, who coined the term, a relational property is a
property of an individual whose description requires reference to at least one
other individual.[38] For Moore, a relational property is a token-term: 'if C is a different child from B, then the property of being father of C is a different relational
property from that of being father of B'.[39] In *KMTH*, Cohen silently departs
from Moore's use. *KMTH* refers to 'being a husband', which is a type-term, as

---

31   Cohen 2000, p. xxiv.
32   Ibid.
33   Elster 1985, pp. 5–6.
34   Cohen 2000, p. xxiii.
35   Popper 1950, p. 284.
36   Ibid.
37   Cohen 1978, p. 90; Elster 1985, p. 6, p. 94.
38   Moore 1919–20, pp. 44–5.
39   Moore 1919–20, p. 45.

an example of a relational property.[40] But however that may be, analysis-NS only allows individual behaviours to be described by (token or type) relational properties up to a certain point. To uphold analysis-NS, the description of an *explanans* cannot include a description of any two individuals' behaviour such that a property (= x) of A's behaviour is described with reference to a property of B's behaviour that must itself be described with reference to x (or to a type of property of which x is a token).[41] Otherwise, the entity whose causal power is explained will owe (part of) its causal power to constituent relations.

To illustrate the boundary of analysis-NS, let us consider *KMTH*'s effective control conception of positions in the economic structure. An effective control conception of positions in the economic structure, while by no means an example of what Popper calls 'collectivism and holism',[42] is incompatible with analysis-NS. On the effective control conception, an economic structure consists in the number of tokens, in a given area, of various types of economic position, where an economic position is defined by specific types of '*effective control*'[43] over persons or productive powers. (Productive powers are, roughly, labour power and means of production). On this conception, some types of effective control may presuppose other types of effective control that define distinct types of economic position, and so two types of economic position may presuppose one another. For example, *KMTH* says that a human being is a slave 'in virtue of its relation to' a 'slaveholder'.[44] The lack of effective control over one's own being that helps define the economic position of slave must be explicated by reference to the effective control over another being that helps define the economic position of slaveholder; and vice versa. On *KMTH*'s effective control conception of positions in the economic structure, a slave-based economic structure owes part of its causal power to constituent relations.

One account of economic structure more in line with analysis-NS is an optimising modal relational properties conception (OMRP conception). Although the OMRP conception is developed by Roemer and Elster,[45] its modal and relational features are suggested by Cohen in *KMTH*.[46] An optimising

---

40   Cohen 1978, p. 90.
41   The unqualified statement that 'methodological individualism accepts the explanatory relevance of relational properties' (Wright, Levine and Sober 1992, p. 111) is false in respect of analysis-NS. Analysis-NS does not permit every kind of relational property an explanatory role.
42   Popper 1950, p. 284.
43   Cohen 1978, p. 35.
44   Cohen 1978, p. 90.
45   Roemer 1982a, p. 14, p. 77; Elster 1985, p. 174.
46   Cohen 1978, pp. 72–3; see also Cohen 2001, p. 108. The heading '*Redefining the Proletarian*'

modal relational property is a fact about what an individual must do in order to optimise with respect to a stated goal, and whose explication requires 'reference to other people'.[47] To define a type of economic position by facts about what an individual must do to optimise, whose explication requires reference to facts about others, is not to define it by facts about what others must do to optimise. On the OMRP conception, therefore, all positions in the economic structure may be defined independently of one another. A wage-labourer, for example, is someone who must hire themselves out to optimise the bundle of commodities they can purchase.[48] The actions that a wage-labourer must perform, in order to optimise, must be explicated by reference to another person who hires labour power. But they need not be explicated by reference to a capitalist, that is, someone who '*must* hire labour in order to optimize'[49] net revenue. Thus, on the OMRP conception, the positions of wage-labourer and capitalist do not presuppose one another. On the OMRP conception, all economic structures can be represented entirely in terms of constituent individuals. Judged by the criterion of analysis-NS, the OMRP conception of positions in the economic structure, but not the effective control conception, belongs to the project of Analytical Marxism.

A final point about analysis-NS is that analysis-NS encompasses, but cannot be reduced to, rational-choice theory. Analysis-NS encompasses rational-choice theory, because rational-choice theory assumes that agents are optimisers, and optimising behaviours can be described independently of one another. However, rational-choice theory is only ever a part of, and in any case unnecessary for, analysis-NS. (It is also unnecessary for analysis-BS). Rational-choice theory is only ever a part of analysis-NS, because any given rational-choice explanation presupposes an agent with given beliefs and desires; analysis-NS requires those beliefs and desires to be explained; and agents cannot rationally choose all their beliefs and desires. If agents were to choose some beliefs or desires, that choice, if it is a rational choice, must itself reflect pre-

---

(Cohen 1978, p. 70) indicates Cohen's awareness that a modal relational properties conception of a position differs from an effective control conception; and at 2000, p. 72, Cohen says that the former conception of the proletarian's position is 'better'. The two conceptions differ, as (1) no 'must' is used to represent any relation of effective control (see Cohen 1978, p. 35); and (2) on the effective control conception, a relation 'only' binds persons and productive forces, and 'at most one productive force(s)-term' (Cohen 1978, pp. 31–2). *KMTH*'s redefinition of a proletarian as someone who '*must sell his labour power in order to obtain his means of life*' (Cohen 1978, p. 72) does not meet this condition.

47   Elster 1985, p. 94.
48   Elster 1985, p. 174.
49   Ibid.

existing beliefs and desires. So however far back in the chain of rational-choice explanations one goes, some beliefs and desires must be presupposed for that chain to get off the ground, calling for an explanation of a different kind. Analysis-NS does not imply a commitment to rational-choice theory, moreover, for analysis-NS need not assume that agents seek to maximise preference satisfaction. An advocate of analysis-NS could describe optimising or satisficing behaviours independently of one another while explicating optimising or satisficing in respect of something more than just an agent's given desires. It is one-sided, therefore, to characterise the project of Analytical Marxism, as distinct from the theses of two of its founders (Elster and Roemer), by use of 'the methodological tools of modern neo-classical economics'.[50] Objections to rational-choice Marxism are not fatal to the project of Analytical Marxism. They are consistent with its reform.

2 Dialectical Contradiction

To reconstruct Marxism by analysis-BS is to reconstruct it by using techniques that serve to make Marxist arguments precise and compelling, and by undermining 'so-called "dialectical" thinking'.[51] Analysis-BS is rejected, therefore, by describing clearly one (or more) dialectical argumentative figure(s) that can guide theory construction, empirical analysis and/or normative argument relevant to the problems of Marxism.

To this end, it is neither sufficient nor necessary to dispute Cohen's different claim that Marxism possesses no 'distinctive and valuable *method*'.[52] It is not sufficient, for it would not be relevant to show that Marxism possessed a distinctive and valuable method that was not dialectical. Nor is it necessary. To reject analysis-BS, it is necessary to show that there is such a thing as dialectical thinking. It is not necessary to show either that its use constitutes a method, or that the dialectical thinking that Marxism employs is distinct from the dialectical thinking employed by Hegelians, or by any other non-Marxists.

For the sake of argument, let Cohen's description of Analytical Marxism in terms of the contrastive analysis-BS claim be put aside. What reason is left for holding that the contrastive analysis-BS claim, rather than the distinctiveness claim, is the claim that defines Analytical Marxism? David Leopold has argued

---

50   Rosenthal 1998, p. viii.
51   Cohen 2000, p. xvii.
52   Ibid.

that it is 'a misleading and unfortunate commonplace that Analytical Marxists shun the notion of dialectic'.[53] Leopold has a particular counterexample in mind, which we examine below: Elster's account of real and social contradiction.[54] In Leopold's view, it is the distinctiveness claim, not the contrastive analysis-BS claim, that defines Analytical Marxism.[55] Before offering two reasons for holding that Cohen's Introduction does not mislead when it defines Analytical Marxism by the contrastive analysis-BS claim, let us modify the distinctiveness claim in the spirit of analysis-BS.

In Cohen's version, the distinctiveness claim bundles too much together. It bundles a distinctiveness claim up with a characterisation of dialectic as a *method*. These two thoughts should be separated, for together, they produce a distinctiveness claim that it too conditional. Cohen's version of the distinctiveness claim denies that dialectic (or a version of dialectic) is distinctive of Marxism only insofar as dialectic is regarded as a method. Yet not all dialecticians regard dialectic as a method. William Maker, who takes ' "method" to denote a specific and specifiable set of rules of procedure as operational or cognitive principles for the consideration of a given subject matter', goes on to claim: 'insofar as method is that which can – even if only in principle – be justified, formulated or learned in abstraction from the subject matter to which it is to be applied, Hegel does not have a method'.[56] Stephen Houlgate concurs: 'Hegel does not have a dialectical or speculative method'.[57] If one were to adopt Cohen's version of the distinctiveness claim as a standard for defining Analytical Marxism, one would have to say that Analytical Marxism distinguishes itself only from those who disagree with Maker and Houlgate about dialectic. Yet those who agree with them could still believe that (a version of) a dialectical argumentative figure that does not amount to a method is distinctive of and valuable for Marxism. This belief is surely one that anyone who defines Analytical Marxism by a distinctiveness claim would want to say Analytical Marxism denies. Let the distinctiveness claim therefore be revised to: Marxism makes no distinctive and valuable use of dialectic. This revision of the distinctiveness claim is in the spirit of analysis-BS; it separates what ought not to be bundled together. Yet there are still two reasons to say that the contrastive analysis-BS claim defines Analytical Marxism even when it is compared to this revised distinctiveness claim: historical opposition; and ultimate aim.

---

53   Leopold 2008, p. 121.
54   Leopold 2008, pp. 124–5.
55   Leopold 2008, p. 121.
56   Maker 1994, p. 99.
57   Houlgate 2006, p. 33.

'[T]o be analytical', Cohen says, 'is to be opposed to a form of thinking traditionally thought integral to Marxism'.[58] The form of thinking in question is widely seen to be epitomised by the opening lines of Georg Lukács's famous essay, 'What is Orthodox Marxism?'[59] In these opening lines, Lukács claims that 'orthodoxy in questions of Marxism [*in Fragen des Marxismus*] instead relates exclusively to method'; more particularly, to the method of 'dialectical Marxism'.[60] One criterion for deciding whether a claim defines Analytical Marxism is whether it ensures that Analytical Marxism is defined in opposition to Lukács's claim.

Lukács's claim must first be clarified. Christopher Bertram interprets Lukács's claim incorrectly in commenting: '[i]f Lukács had famously asserted that Marxism was to be distinguished not by its empirical claims but by its method, Cohen forthrightly took the directly opposite view'.[61] Lukács's question is: what is orthodox Marxism? To ask this question is to ask: what is essential to Marxism? It is not to ask: by what is Marxism distinguished? Knowing by what Marxism is distinguished only invites the further question as to what essential feature about Marxism it is that leads it to be so distinguished. Lukács does not here deny that, for example, orthodox Hegelianism is defined by the use of dialectic to address questions of Hegelianism. But that is just what Lukács could be expected to deny if Lukács's question was: by what is Marxism distinguished? What Lukács in fact denies is that it is essential for a Marxist to accept the 'results'[62] of Marx's studies. Leopold interprets Lukács's claim correctly and differently from Bertram when Leopold says that, for Lukács, dialectic (rather than the results of Marx's studies) is at 'the fundamental core of Marxism'.[63]

If these opening lines of Lukács's 'What is Orthodox Marxism?' are anything to go by, the form of thinking in Marxism to which Analytical Marxism is opposed is one that says: dialectic is fundamental or essential to Marxism. But if Analytical Marxism is opposed to *this* thought, it is not to be defined by the distinctiveness claim. For the distinctiveness claim does not deny that the

---

58   Cohen 2000, p. xvii; compare Elster 1985, p. 3.
59   Lukács 1977, p. 171; Lukács 1968, p. 1.
60   Lukács 1977, p. 171; Lukács 1968, p. 1. Lukács 1968 omits to translate '*in Fragen des Marxismus*', producing a less qualified claim. Unlike the English translation, the German text does not appear to deny that Marxism is in part defined by its asking certain questions. To assert that dialectical Marxism applies solely to the history of art does not qualify as orthodox Marxism.
61   Bertram 2008, p. 124.
62   Lukács 1977, p. 171; Lukács 1968, p. 1.
63   Leopold 2008, p. 109.

use of dialectic in questions of Marxism is fundamental to Marxism. It is the contrastive analysis-BS claim that denies this.

Secondly, the distinctiveness claim mistakes a secondary aim for an ultimate aim. If one adopts mainstream economic techniques (game theory, say) *and* one wishes to insist that one's research is Marxist, then it is necessary to argue that Marxism possesses no distinctive and valuable form of thinking. But the ultimate aim of Analytical Marxism is not to have its findings recognised as Marxist; its ultimate aim is to get at the truth. Otherwise, Cohen could not complain that to ask '"Is analytical Marxism *Marxist*?"' is to ask an 'unproductive question';[64] or say that while Analytical Marxism allows many theses of Marxism to be 'dropped', it never relaxes 'the rule of reason'.[65] If the ultimate aim of Analytical Marxism is to get at the truth, rather than to have its findings recognised as Marxist, then a definition of Analytical Marxism must uphold this priority. It must relate reason to analytical thinking and then relate inherited Marxist theory to its use. The distinctiveness claim, which is solely a claim *about Marxism*, fails to do this. It is Cohen's positive and contrastive description of analysis-BS that does this.

One view that defines the project of Analytical Marxism, then, is that analytical thinking reveals that there is no such thing as dialectical thinking. Accordingly, to reject Analytical Marxism on the grounds of its commitment to analysis-BS, it is necessary and sufficient to describe clearly one dialectical argumentative figure. This task represents a problem that Marx poses rather than solves, however. While *Capital* calls 'Hegelian "contradiction", the source of all dialectic',[66] Marx never followed through on the 'desire' he expressed in a letter to Friedrich Engels dated 16 January 1858 'to make accessible to common understanding, in two or three printer's sheets, what is *rational* in the method that Hegel discovered, but simultaneously mystified'.[67] To defeat analysis-BS, it is necessary to go beyond Marx's texts, if only to formulate what they practice.

One approach, taking its cue from Adorno, is provided by Jürgen Ritsert's claim that dialectical contradiction exhibits the structure of a 'logical simultaneity of relations of inclusion and exclusion/opposition'.[68] The same conditions that establish a relation of exclusion or opposition also establish, by virtue of it, a relation of inclusion. During a lecture series delivered in 1962–63 entitled *Philosophische Terminologie*, Adorno says:

---

64   Cohen 2000, p. xxvii.
65   Cohen 2000, p. xxv.
66   *MEW*, 23, p. 623; *MECW*, 35, p. 592; Marx 1976, p. 744.
67   *MEW*, 29, p. 260; *MECW*, 40, p. 249. A printer's sheet contains 16 pages.
68   Ritsert 1997, p. 101; see also Knoll and Ritsert 2004.

inner mediation ... does not consist in the fact that both of the moments that are opposed to one another each refer to one another; but rather in the fact that the analysis of each refers, in itself, to that which is opposed to it as a sense-implicate. One might call that the principle of dialectic.[69]

Suppose that, when a practice is viewed in light of a broader context that it is taken to presuppose, it assumes a characteristic of its opposite. What Adorno calls 'inner mediation' is present if the same can be said, in light of the same broader context, for a second practice that is the contradictory opposite of the first. As an illustration, consider Marx's account of freedom of religion in *On the Jewish Question*.[70]

In *On the Jewish Question*, Marx argues that freedom of religion is not possible in a non-secular state. A theocratic state based on the codes of a particular religion cannot grant the same freedoms to those who choose to practice a non-official religion, or no religion at all, as it grants to those who practice the religion of that state (for example, the same freedom to hold public office). Freedom of religion presupposes a secular state.

In a secular state, freedom of religion has a particular form. It takes the form of an equal liberty to practice a religion of one's choice, including no religion at all, in a private capacity, without discriminatory consequences. In a secular state, the head of state and other high-ranking public functionaries are not at liberty to choose whether or not to perform their public functions in a religious form. As a secular state consigns the practice of freedom of religion to the private sphere, it establishes the separation of religious practice and irreligious practice. Religious practice is no longer directly tied up with the conduct of the human beings who constitute the political state. There is a relation of exclusion between religious practice and irreligious practice.

Now consider, on the one hand, the situation of a believer in a secular state. To enjoy freedom of religion as a believer in a secular state, it is necessary to conform one's religious practice to the laws of a state whose official end is profane. A believer who conforms their religious practice to the laws of a secular state recognises a profane duty that constrains that practice, and hence, in that sense, is higher than it. Yet to believe in a religion just is to believe that one's highest duty is a duty to God. If, therefore, a secular state is a condition for the separation of religious practice and irreligious practice, then the condition for

---

69   Adorno 1974, p. 142. Adorno takes the term 'sense-implicate' from Husserl 1929, p. 184; Husserl 1969, p. 208.

70   *MEW*, 1, pp. 353–5; *MECW*, 3, pp. 152–4.

this separation simultaneously ensures that a believer's religious practice must assume an irreligious character.

Consider, on the other hand, the situation of a non-believer in a secular state. To choose to practise no religion at all is to act as if one believes that the qualities that believers worship as God's gift to man are qualities that human beings owe to no one but themselves. For a non-believer, a favourable response to treatment for an illness is not cause to thank God, but only cause to thank the human provision of health care; to reap a harvest is not cause to thank God, but only cause to thank the invention of fertiliser; and so on. For the non-believer, those who do the former are merely doing the latter in an eccentric, roundabout way: 'religion is precisely the recognition of the human being by a circuitous path'.[71]

One aspect of a non-believer's freedom of religion, as an equal liberty to practice no religion at all, is non-interference from others. Freedom of religion includes non-interference from those who put their private interests above the common good and seek to coerce others to adhere to the codes of a particular religion. In a secular state, that non-interference is guaranteed by the government. To provide that guarantee, a government must separate itself from the private interests of society. It must attempt to immunise its operations from the religious beliefs its officials are at liberty to hold in their private life. But if a non-believer's freedom of religion rests on protection by a government that is separated from society; and if religion is 'the recognition of the human being by a circuitous path';[72] then the condition for the separation of religious practice and irreligious practice simultaneously ensures that a non-believer's practice must assume a religious character.

In short: it is *both* the case that freedom of religion in the secular state is the condition for the separation of religious practice and irreligious practice (relation of exclusion); *and* the case that freedom of religion in the secular state ensures that the practice of a believer has an irreligious character, and the practice of a non-believer has a religious character (relation of inclusion). Marx's account of freedom of religion in the secular state illustrates the conception of dialectical contradiction outlined by Adorno and Ritsert, about which Analytical Marxism has said nothing.

Three distinguishing points can now be made. First, dialectical contradiction is not the thought of polar opposites.[73] John Rosenthal, a critic of anything

---

71   *MEW*, 1, p. 353; *MECW*, 3, p. 152.

72   Ibid.

73   Ritsert 1997, p. 45. Nor is it the thought of two opposed entities that interact/influence one another.

calling itself dialectical thinking,[74] claims that Hegel's appeal to 'polar opposites' as evidence of dialectical contradiction has had an 'intellectually crippling effect in the Marxist tradition'.[75] The first clause in Adorno's statement of 'inner mediation', together with the above illustration of the rest of it, shows that, *even if* Rosenthal's historical claim were true,[76] it would not be a reason to reject the argumentative figure of dialectical contradiction.

Second, the terms with which Cohen and Elster contrast analytical reasoning to dialectical thinking are inaccurate or confused. Although *KMTH* supposes that the key to dialectical thinking is a metaphor of 'mutually sustaining parts in a properly functioning organism',[77] this is inadequate. It is possible to liken a society to a functioning organism without affirming (and even while denying) that it is characterised by dialectical contradiction. It is also confused to contrast analytical reasoning with dialectical thinking on the basis that dialectical contradiction violates the formal law of non-contradiction.[78] The formal law of non-contradiction says that a proposition and its negation cannot both be true of the same entity at one and the same time, and in one and the same respect. That law does not preclude an entity from having different, opposed characteristics in different respects.[79] As the argumentative figure of dialectical contradiction is employed by ascribing opposed characteristics to one and the same entity in different respects, its use does not violate the formal law of non-contradiction.

Third, the conception of dialectical contradiction defended here differs from Bertell Ollman's conception of contradiction.[80] Ollman writes: '[c]ontradic-

---

74 Rosenthal 1998, p. x.

75 Rosenthal 1998, p. 125.

76 Max Adler, for example, likens 'Marx's dialectic' to 'the inseparable polarity of opposites' (compare Adler 1925, p. 100 and p. 106), but as part of an attempt to relate Marx back to Kant.

77 Cohen 1978, pp. 20–1. Elsewhere Cohen writes: the 'dialectical idea' is that 'every living thing ... develops by unfolding its inner nature in outward forms and, when it has fully elaborated that nature, it dies, disappears, is transformed into a successor form' (Cohen 2001, p. 46). This is, again, a 'dialectical idea' without dialectical contradiction.

78 Elster 1985, p. 43, following Popper 1940, p. 411, p. 418; see also Peffer 1990, p. 17; Rosenthal 1998, p. 93, p. 175.

79 Ritsert 1997, p. 109, p. 205.

80 It also differs from Guglielmo Carchedi's conception, on which '*a dialectical contradiction is a contradiction between what has become and what can become, as contradictory to what has become*' (Carchedi 2011, p. 41). For on the view defended here, (i) some dialectical contradictions can be described without reference to past or future; (ii) dialectical contradictions exhibit necessity; and (iii) *if* a dialectical contradiction concerns an entity's future transformation, this transformation will involve the assumption of a character-

tion is understood here as the incompatible development of different elements within the same relation, which is to say between elements that are also dependent on one another'.[81] On this conception of contradiction, it follows that, say, a relation of husband and wife where each can only flourish in their careers by shifting domestic chores onto the other, is a case of contradiction. Yet this case exemplifies a type of antagonism, not a dialectical contradiction. The features of Ollman's conception of contradiction are not sufficient or necessary for dialectical contradiction. They are not sufficient, because neither of its 'elements' need exhibit a characteristic of its opposite. They are not necessary, for two opposites may each exhibit a characteristic of the other without having incompatible paths of development, as when (to borrow an example from one of the founders of critical pedagogy, Paolo Freire) a mutually fruitful teacher-student relation is based on the perception that 'the teacher is no longer merely the-one-who-teaches, but one who is himself taught in dialogue with the students, who in turn while being taught also teach'.[82]

Using square brackets to denote a relation of inclusion, what Adorno calls 'inner mediation' has the form:

$$[B] A \leftarrow excludes \rightarrow B [A]^{83}$$

This figure also fits *The German Ideology*'s reference to an 'absolute dialectic' in which each of two aspects 'is in itself its opposite [*an sich selbst ihr Gegenteil ist*]'.[84]

Suppose, however, that the structure of 'absolute' dialectical contradiction is relaxed, on two counts. Suppose, on a first relaxation, that it sufficed to show that at least one side of an opposition includes a characteristic of its opposite (in the above illustration: that it sufficed to show, in addition to the relation of exclusion, *either* that religious practice has an irreligious character *or* that irreligious practice has a religious character).[85] Second, suppose that it is permitted for such a characteristic to arise only after a passage of time. On these two relax-

---

istic of its opposite, not merely a transformation into something 'different' (Carchedi 2011, p. 41).

81   Ollman 1993, p. 15. Ritsert 1997, pp. 126–37 offers a more extensive critique.

82   Freire 2000, p. 80.

83   See Ritsert 1997, p. 155.

84   *MEW*, 3, p. 236; *MECW*, 5, p. 253. The *MECW* translation of '*an sich selbst ihr Gegenteil ist*', 'is the opposite of itself', would correctly translate: '*Gegenteil ihrer selbst ist*'. It fails to do justice to the first part of the phrase, '*an sich selbst*'. It is less suggestive of what Adorno calls 'inner mediation'.

85   Compare Marx and Engels's judgement in *The German Ideology* in speaking of conquest

ations, Marx's claim, in his Preface to *A Contribution to a Critique of Political Economy* ('*1859 Preface*'), that 'from forms of development of productive power, these relations [existing relations of production – JF] are transformed into their fetters',[86] can be understood as asserting a less 'absolute' form of dialectical contradiction. The level of development of productive power determines that certain types of relation of production are development-enabling and others are development-fettering; and also determines that some types of relation of production that are development-enabling must become, just by virtue of the development they enable, development-fettering. The interaction-recognition-antinomy thesis also makes use of a version of this argumentative figure of dialectical contradiction in its account of real abstraction,[87] the dialectic of non-recognition and recognition,[88] and the derivation of political represent-ation.[89]

On the present account, the argumentative figure of dialectical contradic-tion requires that the conditions that establish a relation of exclusion also establish, *by virtue of this relation of exclusion* (or, in the case of a historical dia-lectic, *by virtue of its unfolding*) a relation of inclusion. To highlight the import of the italicised clauses, compare the following two remarks. The first is from Marx's aforementioned letter to Engels dated 16 January 1858, while the second is from Charles Fourier's description of 'the Little Hordes', the groups of young children who do the tasks that other members of a Phalanx community shun:

> If ever the time comes around again for such work, I would greatly desire to make accessible to common understanding, in two or three printer's sheets, what is *rational* in the method that Hegel discovered, but simul-taneously mystified.[90]

> Let us analyze the sources of their virtues. They are four in number, and all of them are condemned by morality. They are the penchant for dirt, and the feelings of pride, impudence and insubordination. It is by abandon-ing themselves to these so-called vices that the Little Hordes will become virtuous.[91]

---

that 'the slave was the master, and the conquerors quickly assumed language, culture and customs from the conquered' (*MEJ*, 2003, p. 86; *MEW*, 3, p. 64; *MECW*, 5, p. 85).

86   *MEW*, 13, p. 9; *MECW*, 29, p. 263.
87   See ch. 3, sec. 5 and ch. 12, sec. 7.
88   See ch. 9, secs 2–5, and ch. 12, sec. 9.
89   See ch. 11, sec. 5.
90   *MEW*, 29, p. 260; *MECW*, 40, p. 249.
91   Fourier 2015, p. 173; Beecher and Bienvenu 1971, p. 319.

Marx's claim that there is a method 'Hegel discovered, but simultaneously mystified' does not assert a dialectical contradiction. It does not assert that the conditions that led Hegel into mystification also allowed Hegel, by virtue of that, to make a discovery. The mystification and the discovery are simultaneous, but they are not traced to the same conditions, and neither is said to have enabled the other. Fourier's claim, by contrast, does assert a dialectical contradiction. The Little Hordes develop virtue by giving themselves up to 'so-called vices'.

The above defence of dialectical contradiction is in one way akin to Elster's defence of social contradiction. It is possible to describe an argumentative figure of dialectical contradiction specific to society and to illustrate its use by Marx without examining a text that adopts a particular method of exposition. To defend a dialectic in Marx, it is mistaken to suppose[92] that one must either construe dialectic in terms of general laws equally verifiable in nature and society (as suggested by Engels);[93] or confine it to a form of exposition such as is exhibited by Marx's *Capital*.

What distinguishes dialectical contradiction from Elster's (non-dialectical) account of social contradiction is a form of necessity. A dialectical contradiction is tied to a claim of the form: given the nature of a thing, and the broader context it presupposes, there is no alternative but P.[94] The above conception of dialectical contradiction satisfies this requirement, for its application rests on the idea that the same conditions that establish a relation of exclusion also establish, by virtue of it (or else by virtue of its unfolding) a relation of inclusion. In terms of the above illustration: in the broader context that the separation of religious practice and irreligious practice presupposes, religious practice and irreligious practice must both assume a characteristic of their opposite.

To illuminate this point through a contrast, consider Popper's argument in 'What is Dialectic?' Popper asserts that one application of dialectic that (unlike dialectical contradiction) respects the formal law of non-contradiction is its use to describe 'developments of ideas' in the terminology of 'a thesis and its antithesis'.[95] An initial position or thesis 'will arouse opposition', and so lead

---

92   As at Heinrich 2005, pp. 34–6; Heinrich 2012, pp. 37–8.

93   *MEW*, 19, p. 205; *MECW*, 24, p. 301.

94   On the centrality of claims of natural necessity to science, see Harré and Madden 1975, p. 19, pp. 44–8, pp. 79–80, pp. 118–39. Insofar as some thinkers within the Analytical tradition (Hume) deny claims of natural necessity, the gulf that separates some analytical thinking from dialectical thinking would survive greater acquaintance with the latter than Analytical Marxists display.

95   Popper 1940, p. 405.

to 'a new antithesis'.[96] Yet Popper does not require the causes of opposition to the 'thesis' that lead to the 'antithesis' to be explained as effects of the pronouncement of the thesis. Popper rejects 'the dialectical saying that the thesis "produces" its antithesis' on the grounds that 'it is only our critical attitude which produces the antithesis';[97] and the conditions of this 'critical attitude' are left unspecified. Popper believes that a development from one position to another position that may be aroused by intervening circumstances unrelated to the conditions or unveiling of the first position can be dialectical. On the conception of dialectical contradiction defended here, a relation of inclusion must be identified by reflection that is possible by virtue of the conditions that give rise to the relation of exclusion (or by its unfolding).

A social contradiction, on Elster's account, lacks this quality of necessity. Its contradictoriness does not rest on a claim of the form: given the nature of a thing, and the broader context it presupposes, there is no alternative but P. Elster's account of social contradiction rests on the disparity between the potential truth of each one of a class of beliefs held by different actors, and the impossibility of them all being true. Yet the reason that it is impossible for all of them to be true is that that would exhibit a logical contradiction; that they are not all true is 'a matter of logic'.[98] This precludes a claim of the form: the fact that each of a number of actors believes that x is true only for them (that it is possible for 'only *his* workers'[99] to accept lower wages, for example) presupposes certain social conditions, which also ensure that not all of these beliefs can be true. If the impossibility of all of the beliefs being true is 'a matter of logic', it is not social conditions that ensure that not all of them can be true. *In all possible worlds*, not all of them can be true. The only notion of necessity in Elster's account of social contradiction is *logical* necessity. As Elster's account of social contradiction does not tie a contradiction to a claim of natural necessity, it is not an account of dialectical contradiction.[100]

---

96 Ibid.
97 Popper 1940, p. 406.
98 Elster 1985, p. 26.
99 Ibid.
100 In *Logic and Society*, Elster offers his account of social contradiction as part of a broader conception of 'real contradiction' as 'situations in reality that can only be described by means of the concept of a logical contradiction' (Elster 1970, p. 70). What is said here of Elster's account of social contradiction also applies more generally to Elster's conception of 'real contradiction'.

3   Intrastructuration

To reconstruct Marxism by the second of Analytical Marxism's analytical standards, analysis-NS, is to require all the concepts Marxism uses to describe the
causal powers of social entities to be supported by explanations of those
powers in which individuals are their fundamental constituents. To reject
analysis-NS, it is necessary and sufficient to argue that at least one collective
entity whose causal power is of relevance to Marxism owes (part of) that power
to constituent relations. In fact, a vast number of social entities owe some of
their causal power to constituent relations. This is because – to adopt a term
used in the literature on the theory of emergence – a vast number of social
entities are characterised by 'intrastructuration'.[101]

'An emergent property' of an entity, according to Dave Elder-Vass, 'is one that
is not possessed by any of the parts individually and that would not be possessed by the full set of parts in the absence of a structuring set of relations
between them'.[102] I shall use the term 'intrastructuration' to denote any such
'structuring set of relations between' the intentional actions that provide the
parts of a social entity. 'Intrastructuration', so defined, is the name for a mechanism that produces emergent properties in social entities. Although Elder-
Vass does not define 'intrastructuration' in this way (Elder-Vass does not offer a
definition of intrastructuration), the definition is in keeping with Elder-Vass's
view that 'when we postulate emergent causal powers, we must identify … the
mechanisms that produce them'.[103]

Intentional action is liable to intrastructuration, because any given individual's action is liable to be affected in advance by what others' behaviour
permits that individual to believe about others' actions, desires or beliefs. The
intentional action of a number of individuals is intrastructured if the description of each action refers to a property of action by another that must itself be
described with reference to the self-same action of the first (or with reference
to a type of action of which it is a token). The respect in which any one individual's action is conditioned by those of others is then also a respect in which
that individual's action conditions theirs. None of the actions can be described
without at least implicitly referring to the whole of which it is a part. The relations between individual actions make the entity what it is and give it (part of)
its causal power, in the form of emergent properties.

---

101   Elder-Vass 2010, pp. 26–7; compare Bhaskar 2008, p. 45.
102   Elder-Vass 2010, p. 17.
103   Elder-Vass 2010, p. 8.

Intrastructuration occurs in normative and non-normative contexts, in situations of cooperation or competition. Take, first, the case of intrastructuration by cooperation, which includes what Marx called 'combined labour'.[104] You and I cooperate to do x if the content of the intention I act on is to do x with the aid of action by you that I interpret as you seeking, with me, to bring about x; and the content of the intention you act on is to do x with the aid of action by me that you interpret as me seeking, with you, to bring about x. The respect in which your action enables mine (it enables mine to be an action of bringing about x together with you) is also the respect in which your action is enabled by mine (my action of bringing about x together with you enables your action to be an action of bringing about x together with me). The causal power to bring about x by cooperation is a causal power of a group (the group of you and me). The group's power to cooperate to do x cannot be attributed to either one of us without implicitly referring to us both in the respect in which we each contribute to bring x about.

A second type of case is intrastructuration by convention. In *Economy and Society*, Weber defines 'convention' as 'a "custom" regarded as "valid" *by a circle of people*, and guaranteed against deviations by disapproval'.[105] On one interpretation of this definition, a convention exists if (i) each of a number of individuals believes that it is considered appropriate, in situations of type y, to do x; (ii) that belief can be expected, by those individuals, to lead to a show of disapproval towards behavior that deviates from x in situations of type y, with the effect of inducing conformity; and (iii) the conformity-inducing effects of disapproval do not depend on persons specifically and identifiably charged with enforcing the rule. For Weber, (iii) helps to distinguish a convention from a law.

To adapt an example from Elder-Vass,[106] the rule of 'first come, first served' is a convention of queuing, on Weber's definition, if each of a number of individuals believes that, in a queue, it is considered appropriate to wait one's turn; and each can expect behaviour which deviates from this rule to encounter a conformity-inducing show of disapproval, even without the presence of a security guard. Thus, if the rule of 'first come, first served' is a convention of queuing, each can believe that, were they to show their disapproval of an instance of deviant behaviour, others, for whom the rule is a convention, will be likely to back it up. Each show of disapproval can proceed with the assurance that it is likely to be backed up by others acting with the same assurance, sustained by actions like the first show of disapproval. Shows of disapproval

---

104	*MEW*, 23, p. 345; *MECW*, 35, p. 331; Marx 1976, p. 443.
105	Weber 2005, p. 24; Weber 1978, p. 34.
106	Elder-Vass 2010, p. 146.

which proceed *with this assurance* are a means by which the convention is maintained. The ability to show disapproval of deviant behaviour with assurance, and thus the greater power to induce conformity that comes with that ability, are emergent properties of the group.

A third type of case is intrastructuration by standardisation.[107] Some types of action are known to depend for their success on their being correctly understood by another. Intrastructuration by standardisation occurs if a standard form (a buzzword, for example) comes to be used to give off a certain impression in virtue of the fact that others can be anticipated to use it in anticipation of others using it. Each use of this standard form, which proceeds with the assurance that it provides a safe way to give off a certain impression in virtue of an assumption about others' use of it, is the means by which it is confirmed as the standard form for others to use with the same assurance of being correctly understood. The ability to safely communicate a certain impression of a particular type of goal, and thus the greater power to be understood, are here emergent group properties.

Consider, finally, intrastructuration by competition. Take John Maynard Keynes's analogy for speculative investment:

> professional investment may be likened to those newspaper competitions in which the competitors have to pick out the six prettiest faces from a hundred photographs, the prize being awarded to the competitor whose choice most nearly corresponds to the average preferences of the competitors as a whole; so that each competitor has to pick, not those faces which he himself finds prettiest, but those which he thinks likeliest to catch the fancy of the other competitors, all of whom are looking at the problem from the same point of view. It is not a case of choosing those which, to the best of one's judgment, are really the prettiest, nor even those which average opinion genuinely thinks the prettiest.[108]

Keynes's point is that, when investing, it is necessary to anticipate what every other investor is likely to do, each having themselves anticipated other investors' behaviour, and all the while including in any projection the effect of what is commonly known to be misinformation. Each investment decision, in virtue of its response to conditions of success anticipated as bearing upon itself, including those conditions that arise from behaviour based on what is com-

---

107   Compare Schütz 2004, pp. 362–3; Schütz 1967, pp. 197–8.
108   Keynes 1939, p. 156.

monly known to be misinformation, helps to impose the same conditions of success on every other investment decision. Intrastructuration by competition gives rise to an incapacity to make investment decisions based on the objective situation (in the analogy: an incapacity to judge by criteria of beauty), alongside a vulnerability to panic, as an emergent property of the group of investors.

Intrastructuration may or may not have unintended consequences. Intrastructuration has unintended consequences, if those who perform the actions that are intrastructured do not intend for the other actions that are intrastructured to have the form they are lent by intrastructuration, and hence do not control the emergent properties of the group to which they belong. In the case of intrastructuration by cooperation, each actor does intend for their fellow collaborator to perform an action with a form it owes to intrastructuration. I intend for you to seek to act to bring about x together with me. With intrastructuration by convention or by standardisation, each actor may or may not intend for some portion of the other actions that are intrastructured to have the form that intrastructuration gives them. I may show my disapproval of deviant behaviour not only to stop a particular instance of deviant behaviour from succeeding, but also to strengthen others' beliefs that they can show their disapproval with assurance. On any given occasion of showing disapproval, the latter might be more important to me than the former. Similarly, I may or may not observe a certain standard in order to perpetuate its use as a standard. In neither type of case, however, is the actor in control of the causal power of the group to which they belong. Finally, in the case of intrastructuration by competition, it is *not* an actor's intention that others' actions should take the form they owe to intrastructuration. The totality of actions is a power over each, in virtue of what each anticipates, and the absence of cooperation.

As no form of society can exist without either competition or cooperation, no vision of future socialist institutions can afford to misidentify the effects of intrastructuration. By implication, no socialist theory can afford to affirm analysis-NS. The effects of intrastructuration are not more fundamentally understood, but evaporate, if one attempts to reduce all causal powers of social entities to the causal powers of constituent individuals; just as one would not have understood, but mangled, the law of evidence, if one were to suppose that the degree of doubt a defence must cast on the prosecution's case had to be established not in relation to their case as a whole, but in respect of every isolated component of their case.

It would be mistaken to argue (what is in any case unnecessary for its rebuttal) that analysis-NS cannot grasp any aspect of the powers of social entities. Social entities need not possess all their causal powers by virtue of intrastructuration. They can also possess causal power as a result of the aggregation of actions understood in isolation. Take, for example, Philip Pettit's account of 'premise-centered' decision-making.[109] Suppose that the pursuit of a course of action, c, is rational if and only if a and b. Now suppose that three or more individuals take a majority vote on whether or not to do c not by voting on c directly, but by voting yes/no on a, yes/no on b, and pursuing c if and only if there is a majority yes-vote for both a and b. Such 'premise-centered' decision-making yields a different outcome to a direct majority vote 'wherever a majority in the group supports each of the premises, different majorities support different premises, and the intersection or overlap of those majorities is not itself a majority'.[110] A group (such as a three-judge court) that adopts 'premise-centered' decision-making can therefore have a causal effect on its members. But the effect of the group on its members occurs through a procedure of aggregating votes. The causal power of the group is of the kind to which the advocates of analysis-NS illicitly assimilate all the causal powers of social entities.

Revealingly, Cohen's work does not consistently observe the stricture of analysis-NS. One example (besides the effective control conception of positions in the economic structure) is the application of the concept of '*collective unfreedom*'[111] to the situation of the proletariat. Freedom, for Cohen, denotes ability. A is free to x if A is able to x. Cohen adds: 'a group suffers collective unfreedom with respect to a given type of action x if and only if performance of x by all members of the group is impossible'.[112] Interesting cases of collective unfreedom arise if it is possible for *some* members of the group to x. This is the case, according to Cohen, for members of the proletariat, in respect of climbing the class structure. Each member of the proletariat, Cohen says, is free to rise from his or her class position '*only on condition that the others do not exercise their similarly conditional freedom*'.[113]

By virtue of the phrase '*similarly conditional*', the proletariat's situation of collective unfreedom is defined by constituent *relations*. Let A, B, C, D, E and F denote representative members of the proletariat, and let x denote 'rise up the class structure'. Supposing that one sixth of the proletariat would be able to rise up the class structure if it tried to do so, the form of A's freedom is: A can x only on condition that B, C, D, E and F, each of whom can x only on condition that no one else among them x's, do not x. As A's freedom is described with reference

---

109   Pettit 2003, p. 168.
110   Pettit 2003, p. 169.
111   Cohen 1988, p. 269.
112   Cohen 1988, p. 268. I have altered 'A' to 'x'.
113   Cohen 1988, p. 263; Cohen 2011, p. 161.

to the freedom of *B*, *C*, *D*, *E* and *F* to *x*, each of whose freedom is described with reference to *A*'s self-same freedom ('no one else among them'), proletarian collective unfreedom has constituent relations. It is an emergent property of the proletariat as a collective entity. To apply the concept of 'collective unfreedom' to the proletariat is to abandon analysis-NS.

Cohen also offers an example of intrastructuration by convention, in a discussion of the 'sexist and unjust' expectations that lie on husband and wife if 'they direct the woman in a family where both spouses work outside the home to carry a greater burden of domestic tasks'.[114] Such expectations 'need not be supported by the law', Cohen says, if they possess 'informal' weight that exerts itself *'through the choices people make in response to the stated expectations, which are, in turn, sustained by those choices'.*[115] The word *'those'* here has the same consequence for an account of expectations over domestic chores as the phrase *'similarly conditional'* has for an account of proletarian collective unfreedom. Informal pressures on women to carry out a greater burden of domestic tasks are sustained by choices that members of families make in response to (rather than independently of) those very pressures. Shows of disapproval of attempts to shift some of that unequal burden onto the male spouse can proceed with the assurance that they are likely to be supported by others acting with the same assurance sustained by shows of disapproval like the first. The male spouse's ability to induce the female spouse's conformity to this expectation is an emergent property.

4   Conclusion

Analytical Marxism is an ambitious project to reconstruct Marxism on 'analytical' foundations. It has two basic commitments: analysis-BS and analysis-NS. Analytical Marxism is, and must be, absolutist on both counts. Just as it opposes analysis-BS to all dialectical thinking, so it opposes analysis-NS to the view that there are any collective entities whose fundamental constituents are not individuals.

According to the above critique, Analytical Marxism is stillborn and misguided. The project of Analytical Marxism is stillborn, for analysis-BS is supposed, in contrast to dialectical thinking, to be marked by precision of statement and rigour of argument; and yet the contrastive analysis-BS claim cannot

---

114   Cohen 2008, p. 137.
115   Ibid.

stand up to rigorous argument. It cannot be said that Analytical Marxists have understood what they purport to reject. Neither the metaphor of mutually sustaining parts in a properly functioning organism (Cohen) nor violation of the formal law of non-contradiction (Elster) captures the nature of the argumentative figure of dialectical contradiction. Analytical Marxism is also misguided, moreover, for a commitment to analysis-NS is debilitating, and would seal Marxism off from broader trends in social theory that advocates of Analytical Marxism regard their project as uniquely placed (among socialist projects) to tap. Notwithstanding the fact that the interpretation of Marx's writings 'demands, to the highest degree, the style of analytical philosophy, its conceptual resourcefulness, clarity and tolerance for detail',[116] socialism can only be defended by an alternative project to Analytical Marxism.

---

116   Miller 1984, p. 172.

CHAPTER 3

Commodity Form Philosophy

Commodity form philosophy is the name given here to research that proceeds on the basis that an analysis of the commodity as a general form of wealth has supra-disciplinary significance. Two major historical figures to assert the supra-disciplinary significance of Marx's analysis of the commodity form in *Capital* are Georg Lukács and Theodor Adorno. Their reading of Marx has influenced the *Neue Marx-Lektüre* (New Reading of Marx) of Helmut Reichelt[1] and Hans-Georg Backhaus,[2] as well as Moishe Postone's *Time, Labor and Social Domination*,[3] among others.

Commodity form philosophy is inspired by a broad view of the project to which *Capital. A Critique of Political Economy* aims to contribute. Even if Marx had seen all the projected volumes of *Capital* through to publication, he would still not have realised his plan of 1844. In 1844, Marx also planned to publish, separately, a 'critique of law, morality, politics, etc.', as well as a 'critique of the speculative appropriation of that material'.[4] Commodity form philosophy treats Marx's critique of political economy as one critique in a larger project of critiques, all related to the commodity form.

For consider the explanation that Marx offers for why his studies came to focus on the critique of political economy. Marx explains the focus of his later writings on the critique of political economy as his drawing the consequence from his philosophical radicalism. In the words of Marx's *Contribution to the Critique of Hegel's Philosophy of Right. Introduction*, published in 1844, 'to be radical is to grasp the matter at its root [*Wurzel*]'.[5] In Marx's autobiographical sketch in the *1859 Preface*, Marx refers to this *Introduction* by name, and reports the assessment he arrived at as a result of his studies in this period: 'legal relations, like forms of state, are ... rooted [*wurzeln*] in the material conditions of life' whose 'anatomy is to be sought in political economy'.[6] An approach cannot claim to be uncompromising unless it goes to the root of the matter. As, in

---

1 Reichelt 2001, p. 12.
2 Backhaus 2006, p. 13; Backhaus 2011, p. 435.
3 Postone 1993, p. 15.
4 *MEW*, 40, p. 467; *MECW*, 3, p. 231.
5 *MEW*, 1, p. 385; *MECW*, 3, p. 182.
6 *MEW*, 13, p. 8; *MECW*, 29, p. 262. The *MECW* rendering of '*wurzeln*' as 'originate' loses the association with the previous quote.

© KONINKLIJKE BRILL NV, LEIDEN, 2019 | DOI:10.1163/9789004384804_004

Marx's judgement, moneymaking was the fundamental feature of the modern world, Marx had to begin what his *Letters from the Deutsch-Französische Jahrbücher* announce as an *'intransigent* [rücksichtslos] *critique of all existence'*[7] with a critique of political economy.

This explanation for the focus of Marx's later writings is salutary in respect of how to reconstruct them. If Marx's later writings focus on the critique of political economy because Marx was a radical who could not but begin an *'intransigent critique of all existence'* at what he took to be its root, *Capital* ought to be interpreted and evaluated within the wider (if largely unrealised) project of which it is a part: an *'intransigent critique of all existence'*. If Marx's project is a critique of all existence; and if all the other critiques of Marx's plan of 1844 rest on a critique of political economy, and thereby on an analysis of the commodity form, with which *Capital* begins; then the intellectual project to which *Capital* aims to contribute may be termed: commodity form philosophy.

'Commodity form' is a term that refers to commodities insofar as they constitute a general form of wealth. 'Philosophy' is not appended merely to indicate a project that 'respect[s] no boundaries of discipline or research tradition'.[8] This is too thin a notion of philosophy. For all it requires, a thinker's achievements are philosophical even if the results of their following the evidence wherever it may lead have little or nothing do with one another. A batch of discipline-transcending achievements can only be considered philosophical if it exhibits an underlying unity. To call Marx's intellectual project a philosophy in this thicker sense is to claim that its discipline-transcending achievements are to exhibit some discernible unity. To describe it, more particularly, as commodity form philosophy, is to say that this unity is to be supplied by an analysis of the commodity form.

One way to conceive of how an analysis of the commodity form can supply this unity is to hold that it provides a basis for explaining the existence of various distinct sorts of inquiry. In *Phenomenology of the Social World*, Alfred Schütz undertakes to explain the existence of various distinct sorts of inquiry from a single starting point through a phenomenological account of the gen-

---

7 *MEW*, 1, p. 344; *MECW*, 3, p. 142. *MECW* renders 'rücksichtslos' as *'ruthless'* in its oft-cited phrase: *'ruthless criticism of all that exists'*. Yet ruthlessness suggests a lack of principle; even a compromise can be ruthless. Thus, *'ruthless'* is not apt given Marx's judgement (of 1843) that the existing world is itself 'spiritless' (*MEW*, 1, p. 378; *MECW*, 3, p. 175). It is more fitting to translate *'rücksichtslos'* as 'intransigent' or 'implacable'. Compare Goethe's reflection on Laurence Sterne: 'by a process of continual conflict he distinguished truth from falsehood, clung to the former and was intransigent [*rücksichtslos*] against the latter' (Goethe 1833, p. 125; Goethe 1998, p. 105).
8 Wood 2004, pp. xi–xii.

esis of ideal types in everyday life.[9] But a different version of the same sort of philosophical ambition would be to use an analysis of the commodity form to *derive* the various autonomous logics studied by distinct sorts of inquiry. This connects to Friedrich Engels's remark about philosophy in *The Development of Socialism from Utopia to Science*. Engels claims that 'as soon as each special science is required to become aware of its position in the overall context of things and of our knowledge of things', philosophy is reduced to 'formal logic and the dialectic'.[10] If, however, the basic concepts of various distinct types of inquiry can be derived from the commodity form; and if, as a result of the fact that their basic concepts are derived, these types of inquiry lack an awareness of their place within a developed commodity-form-based society; then, by Engels's own criterion, philosophy cannot be so reduced, at least for as long as society is structured by the commodity form.

A derivation of x is an explanation of x that shows that x must register its cause as just one of the phenomena subject to its logic. A project based on the commodity form permits derivations in which the commodity form, or something explained by the commodity form, is the starting point. (It also permits explanations that are not derivations, but in which something derived from or explained by the commodity form has explanatory power). If a commodity form based approach can explain the fundamental concepts of various distinct sorts of inquiry from a single starting point, it can be considered a type of philosophy. If it can derive these fundamental concepts, it can be considered a type of critical philosophy. Any derivation of the fundamental concept of a distinct sort of inquiry has a critical implication for that inquiry. It implies that its fundamental concept does not make its own explanation apparent. That, in turn, implies that the inquiry's place and its object's place within social life as a whole will not be apparent to that inquiry. Insofar as Marx's writings can be reconstructed as a commodity form philosophy employing this notion of derivation, they can, in principle, offer an '*intransigent critique of all existence*'.

Commodity form philosophy has two core features. One is that all its theses rest on an analysis of the commodity form. Lukács's *History and Class Consciousness*, which declares 'no greater ambition than an *interpretation*, an exposition of Marx's theory *as Marx understood it*',[11] argues in this vein that 'the problem of the commodity' is 'the central structural problem of capitalist society in all its expressions of life'.[12] For Adorno, likewise, 'Marx's entire analysis of

---

9   Schütz 2004, pp. 406–7; Schütz 1967, pp. 223–4.
10   *MEW*, 19, p. 207; *MECW*, 24, p. 303.
11   Lukács 1977, p. 164; Lukács 1968, p. xliii.
12   Lukács 1977, p. 257; Lukács 1968, p. 83.

modern society proceeds from an analysis of the commodity form of the object of exchange'.[13] For both Lukács and Adorno, there is no thesis touching on any feature of social life in modern capitalism that is both Marxist and unconnected to the commodity form. To practice commodity form philosophy is to seek to support this claim.

Second, commodity form philosophy seeks to explain the fundamental concepts of individual disciplines, whose status as autonomous disciplines appears to render commodity form philosophy implausible. While Lukács claims that it is imperative 'to reveal the grounds, genesis and necessity of this formalism [of individual sciences – JF]',[14] Adorno says: 'philosophy ... revokes a kind of second nature of thought' in which it is 'as if the individual sphere, with its conceptual apparatus, is an existence in itself'.[15] Both Lukács and Adorno are agreed that there is a philosophical task to perform, of explaining the existence of individual disciplines of the social sciences, and that its execution will render these disciplines problematic to some extent. Commodity form philosophy assumes this task.

The conception of derivation proposed here is offered in this spirit. To derive a basic concept of a type of inquiry is to explain it and render it problematic. A concept can be considered basic to a type of inquiry if it implies a distinct type of subjectivity and object domain that are reproduced in a fully developed commodity form based society. It is argued below (in section 3) that the concept of an economic good implies a subjectivity defined by the rationality of preference maximisation in respect of possessions. The basic concepts of other types of inquiry, too, have their own subjectivity and object domain. Political representation implies a distinct type of subjectivity (a representative's success in offering an image of the people to the people to accept) and object domain (the public existence of the people of a given territory). The same goes for the sociological concept of a social role (the expected use of positional powers vis-à-vis other role occupants) and the juridical concept of freedom of choice (a capacity to voluntarily conclude enforceable agreements in respect of what it is permissible or impermissible to agree). In chapter 11, the juridical logic of freedom of choice and the political logic of representation are derived from the commodity form. While the sociological concept of a social role is not derived, it is explained by appeal to the concept of an economic good, which can be derived.[16]

---

13   Adorno 1974, p. 272; compare Adorno 1974, p. 259.
14   Lukács 1977, p. 285; Lukács 1968, p. 109.
15   Adorno 2010, p. 295; compare Adorno 1973b, p. 9; Adorno 2010, p. 180.
16   See ch. 6, sec. 2.

The project of commodity form philosophy can incorporate findings of Marxists other than Lukács and Adorno, moreover. Evgeny Pashukanis's *A General Theory of Law and Marxism* (1924) aims, more particularly, '"to approximate the legal form to the commodity form"'.[17] Alfred Sohn-Rethel, in *Commodity Form and Thought Form* (*Warenform und Denkform*) (1961), claims that 'the analysis of the commodity at the beginning of *Capital* occupies a very special place in Marx's work'.[18] 'It is no accident that the programmatic formulation of this method [the historical-materialist method – JF] is found in an introduction to the work in which Marx, in 1859, first published his analysis of the commodity and money'.[19] More recently, Postone reaffirms the aim, 'proceeding from the category of the commodity ... to unfold from it the overarching structure of capitalist society as a totality'.[20]

Given this list of authors, it might be asked why 'commodity form philosophy' is preferred over the more familiar label 'Hegelian Marxism'. There are three reasons for this choice.

Firstly, the backwards-looking nature of the label 'Hegelian Marxism' creates a false impression. It draws attention to the author whom Marx, in *Capital*, identified as the source of his understanding of dialectical contradiction.[21] By contrast, 'commodity form philosophy' stresses that which sustains a commitment to it.[22] A commitment to the argumentative figure of dialectical contradiction is not conditional on acceptance of the interpretative claims that that figure is essential to or distinctive of Hegel's philosophy, or that Hegel's arguments are convincing. The label 'Hegelian Marxism' suggests that Marxists could not or ought not to invoke the argumentative figure of dialectical contradiction were these claims unsustainable. But only substantive claims, related to the commodity form, can settle this question.

Secondly, a commodity form based project can incorporate insights from thinkers other than Hegel. Not only does the label 'Hegelian Marxism' discourage such moves; it is incongruent with existing practice. Lukács, Adorno, Sohn-Rethel, Backhaus and Postone all repeatedly invoke the concept of 'antinomy', which goes back to Kant. On the evidence presented in chapter 12, no one in the history of Marxism apart from Lukács can claim to have grasped the significance of *Capital*'s antinomy passage or even just to have analysed

---

17   Paschukanis 2003, p. 36; Pashukanis 2002, p. 38.

18   Sohn-Rethel 1971, p. 103.

19   Ibid.

20   Postone 1993, p. 139; see also p. 48, p. 79.

21   *MEW*, 23, p. 623; *MECW*, 35, p. 592; Marx 1976, p. 744.

22   See sec. 5 below.

the thesis and antithesis of the rights-antinomy it presents such that they form an antinomy. There are insights to unearth from Marx's writings that the label 'Hegelian Marxism' need not promote.

Thirdly, 'commodity form philosophy' has the advantage over 'Hegelian Marxism' of directly suggesting a substantive position. No one can expect an intellectual project to preserve all of its founder's theses.[23] An intellectual project must strive to offer compelling arguments, and avoid faulty ones, even if their soundness or fault was not, or could not have been, detected originally or previously. But if so, a name for *any* intellectual project that refers to a founder is inapt. In connection with this point, consider Lukács's claim in *History and Class Consciousness*:

> For supposing – what is not granted – that later research had incontestably proven the objective incorrectness of all of Marx's individual propositions, every serious 'orthodox' Marxist could acknowledge all of these new results unconditionally, and reject all of Marx's individual theses, without for a minute giving up his Marxist orthodoxy.[24]

Lukács's claim is sometimes greeted with incredulity, but it is impeccable. It would not be inconsistent to believe both that Marx had founded a worthwhile project, and that later research had disproved all of 'Marx's individual propositions'. The latter does not imply the different belief that later research has disproved all of *Marxism*'s individual propositions. Lukács is not claiming that no substantive thesis requiring empirical support, or that is otherwise challengeable, belongs, at a given point in time, to the project Marx founded. Any acknowledged 'new results' belong to it. So, Lukács does not imply that the project Marx founded, in its current guise, cannot be challenged. The semblance of absurdity in Lukács's claim vanishes if ' "orthodox" Marxist' and 'his Marxist orthodoxy' in this sentence are replaced with 'proponent of commodity form philosophy' and 'commodity form philosophy' respectively.

Finally, a name for a Marxist project does best to avoid the English term 'science' and its cognates, such as 'scientific socialism'.[25] '*Wissenschaftlicher Sozialismus*' is a term used by Engels in *The Development of Socialism from Utopia to Science*.[26] But in English, 'science' is understood in contrast to ethics. Consider

23   Lukács 1977, p. 171; Lukács 1968, p. 1; see, similarly, Cohen 2000, p. xxvii.
24   Lukács 1977, p. 171; Lukács 1968, p. 1.
25   Endorsed at Cohen 2000, p. xxvii.
26   *MEW*, 19, p. 187, p. 228; *MECW*, 24, p. 458, p. 325.

Cohen's claim that '[s]cientific socialism offers no ideals or values to the prolet-ariat'.[27] Whatever one thinks of this claim, it enjoys a firmer ring of assurance than the claim that *Marxism* offers no ideals or values to the proletariat. Insofar as a Marxist project is comprised of critiques, and a critique reveals a frus-trated potential in an object that ought to be realised, it incorporates normative argument. It incorporates an argument for the value of realising that potential, which must do something besides marshal empirical facts in the manner of a science.

This is not to deny that Marx used the German term '*Wissenschaft*' to de-scribe his work. But as Patrick Murray notes, '*Wissenschaft*' has a 'more gener-ous, less technical sense' than the English term science as 'reflective, method-ically disciplined knowledge'.[28] Both Hegel's *Science of Logic* (*Wissenschaft der Logik*) and literary studies (*Literaturwissenschaft*) are a form of '*Wissenschaft*'. The neo-Kantian socialist Karl Vorländer could complain that Eduard Bern-stein and others 'restrict the name and concept of science [*Wissenschaft*] one-sidedly to causal explanation'.[29] The qualifications in Marx's use of this term indicate that the fact that his works aspire to '*Wissenschaft*' is no reason to suppose that they are defined, as a social science is defined, by the study of empirical fact. In letters to Ferdinand Lassalle and Friedrich Engels, Marx billed his then future work, *Capital*, as 'science in the German sense [*Wis-senschaft im deutschen Sinn*]',[30] and 'a triumph of German science [*deutschen Wissenschaft*]'.[31] Remarks like these are intended to emphasise *Capital*'s sys-tematic presentation, and/or its use of dialectic. They are not intended to emphasise its study of empirical fact. As *Capital* is not science in the English sense, or a triumph of English science, there is little warrant to describe Marx's project as 'scientific socialism'.[32]

Having defended 'commodity form philosophy' as a name for a Marxist pro-ject, the remainder of this chapter examines Marx's analysis of the commodity form, with a view to establishing the plausibility of commodity form philo-sophy. Sections 1–2 consider the two aspects of a commodity, use-value and value. Section 3 distinguishes a commodity from a good. Section 4 argues that the concept of use-value allows commodity form philosophy to appeal to a dis-tinctive type of principle called a duty to the whole. Finally, sections 5–6 argue

---

27   Cohen 2001, p. 64.
28   Murray 1988, p. 235.
29   Vorländer 1911, p. 187.
30   *MEW*, 29, p. 567; *MECW*, 40, p. 355.
31   *MEW*, 31, p. 183; *MECW*, 42, p. 232.
32   Cohen 2000, p. xxvii.

that commodity form philosophy can employ the argumentative figures of dialectical contradiction and antinomy.

1   Use-Value

Capital begins with an analysis of use-value. *Capital* Chapter One states: '[t]he
usefulness [*Nützlichkeit*] of a thing makes it a use-value'.[33] It adds: 'use-value
is only realised in use, or consumption'.[34] Use-value is thus distinct from that
which can yield a beneficial effect. Imagine two species of wild animal, one of
which is harmful to human existence, and the prey of the non-harmful species. The power of the non-harmful wild species to prey on the harmful species
does not by itself make its members a use-value, despite their beneficial effect
for human existence. They are not the object of a use, or act of human consumption.

    Use-value is that which can be used as a means to satisfy a human want.
More fully: an object is a use-value if a human want can be (*not*: is) satisfied
with it by applying know-how in order to satisfy the want, so that the want is
satisfied in virtue of the anticipated causal connection between the application
of the know-how, and the satisfaction of the want. The want may be a want for a
material thing (bread) or activity (a concert); a want for the means with which
to produce items of consumption (a machine to make bread); a want for the
means to produce those means (a machine to make machine parts); and so on.

    It could be claimed that *Capital* should not refer to anything as 'a use-value'[35]
on the grounds that use-value is not a physical property, but an expression for
a relation between an object and a subject's want.[36] It is permissible to refer
to objects as use-values, however. If an actor regards something as a means to
satisfy a want of theirs, that is not because they identify it as a unique object
capable of satisfying just their want. They identify it as a type of object, permit-
ting a certain type of use, suited to satisfying a certain type of want they identify
in themselves. When I note how useful a particular lift is, I do not suppose that
there could be nothing else like it, or that I am the only one who can use it to
go up and down. For I am aware of situations in which it is a practically valid

---

33   *MEW*, 23, p. 50; *MECW*, 35, p. 46; Marx 1976, p. 126. On '*Nützlichkeit*', compare Marx's claim
        in the *Economic and Philosophic Manuscripts of 1844* cited below.
34   *MEW*, 23, p. 50; *MECW*, 35, p. 46; Marx 1976, p. 126.
35   *MEW*, 23, p. 50; *MECW*, 35, p. 46; Marx 1976, p. 126.
36   See Menger 1968, p. 3; Menger 2007, p. 52.

assumption that it is a type of thing that is generally known to be able to be put to certain types of use in order to satisfy certain types of want. An assumption is practically valid if others are likely to behave in such a way that action informed by the assumption has no reason to fail in virtue of it. It is a practically valid assumption of arranging meetings in an office on the fifth floor that others are able to use a lift to go up and down. It is permissible to refer to objects as use-values, then, because the relation of a particular user to a particular useful object is mediated by their awareness that it is a type of object that is generally known to be able to be put to certain types of use that can satisfy certain types of want; and because the user is aware that this fact is independent of their particular want for the object.

Importantly, the concept of use-value does not presuppose the concept of possession, roughly, control by someone who asserts an exclusive claim.[37] The concept of use-value does not presuppose the concept of possession, because the knowledge that and how an object can be used as a means to satisfy a human want is sufficient. An object is a use-value just in case this knowledge exists. As the conditions or consequences of the form in which objects are distributed is irrelevant to their status as use-values, it is irrelevant for the status of an object as a use-value whether or not someone who is in the position of being able to use it controls it and asserts an exclusive claim to it.

The fact that *Capital* employs a concept, use-value, which abstracts from possession, despite the fact that possession is an aspect of the prevailing form of distribution in capitalism, illustrates Marx's claim, in his Preface to the First Edition of *Capital*, that the 'analysis of economic forms' employs the 'power of abstraction'.[38] As use-values must exist in all forms of human society, *Capital's* concept of use-value is an example of what Murray calls a transhistorical or general abstraction.[39]

Indeed, by virtue of this concept of use-value, *Capital* incorporates an insight from Marx's earlier *Economic and Philosophic Manuscripts of 1844*. In the latter, Marx claims that, although 'industry is the *open* book of *human essential powers*', it has 'not been grasped in its connection with human *essence*, but only ever in an external relation of utility [*äußeren Nützlichkeitsbeziehung*]'.[40] The means and results of productive activity are grasped from the perspective of an external relation of utility, these *Manuscripts* suggest, if their usefulness is con-

37   For a more detailed analysis of possession, see ch. 7, sec. 3.
38   *MEW*, 23, p. 12; *MECW*, 35, p. 8; Marx 1976, p. 90.
39   Murray 1988, pp. 121–2.
40   *MEW*, 40, p. 542; *MECW*, 3, p. 302.

founded with 'the sense of *having*'.[41] Usefulness is confounded with 'the sense of *having*' if usefulness is only conceived insofar as it is related to the will of a possessor. The conceptual separation of usefulness from 'the sense of *having*' is achieved by means of *Capital*'s concept of use-value. Use-value abstracts from possession. By virtue of its concept of use-value, which abstracts from possession, *Capital* suggests a perspective from beyond that of an 'external relation of utility' (more on which below).

One point in favour of *Capital*'s concept of use-value is that it attends to a condition for freedom. In *Capital*, Marx advocates a 'higher form of society whose foundational principle is the full and free development of each'.[42] According to *Capital*, freedom has a development component, consisting in the 'development' of one's abilities; and an awareness component, consisting in the awareness that this development is a 'principle' of society, and so enjoyed by all. A world of things that can yield beneficial effects is insufficient for freedom, therefore. The development of one's abilities as an end in itself requires the deliberate use of means to this end. A world of possessed utility is also insufficient, moreover. Possession is exclusive, and at least some types of use-value (for example, bits of land and infrastructure used to satisfy the need for mobility) may not be possessed, if development is to be enjoyed by all.

Capital's concept of use-value has a further nuance. A thing is a use-value just in case some people know that and how it can be used, and that use would satisfy a want. Use-value abstracts from the conditions and consequences of the form of distribution. But this raises the question as to whether it also abstracts from *wants* for means to engage in forms of distribution. In the statement 'use-value is that which can be used as a means to satisfy a human want', will any want suffice, or must this want also be describable without reference to forms of distribution?

At one point in *A Contribution to the Critique of Political Economy*, Marx calls the money commodity a 'universal use-value'.[43] That designation seems to imply that the concept of use-value does not abstract from wants for means to engage in forms of distribution. For it implies that the power to satisfy a want for a means to engage in commodity exchange can qualify something as a use-value. Yet Marx denies this implication earlier in the same text when he says that 'use-value, as use-value, lies beyond political economy's sphere of investigation'.[44] The power to satisfy a want for a means to engage in commod-

---

41   *MEW*, 40, p. 540; *MECW*, 3, p. 300.

42   *MEW*, 23, p. 618; *MECW*, 35, p. 588; Marx 1976, p. 739.

43   *MEW*, 13, p. 34; *MECW*, 29, p. 288.

44   *MEW*, 13, p. 16; *MECW*, 29, p. 270.

ity exchange cannot qualify something as a use-value if use-value lies beyond political economy's sphere of investigation.

There is a reason to follow the latter, more general of these judgements and adopt a concept of use-value that abstracts from wants for means to engage in forms of distribution. In the Preface to the same publication, Marx claims that the level of development of productive power sets limits to the types of social relations of production that are feasible in a given historical period. Relations of production have a certain level of development of productive power as their 'material conditions of existence'.[45] To determine whether an existing level of productive power is materially sufficient for a new type of relation of production, it is not necessary to factor in the time required to produce any means specific to the existing form of distribution, if this form of distribution is to be replaced. To consider whether the level of productive power under capitalism is sufficient to sustain post-capitalist relations of production, it is not necessary to factor in the time required to advertise a product so that a certain quantity of it can circulate as a commodity. At least one measure of the level of productive power relevant to a Marxist theory of history is thus conceptually distinct from the existing form of distribution. But if a measure of the level of productive power abstracts from the existing form of distribution, the same must go for the wants that its products satisfy. The conditioning role of productive power in Marx's theory of history presupposes a concept of use-value that abstracts from wants for means to engage in forms of distribution.

Accordingly, a human want in the statement 'use-value is that which can be used as a means to satisfy a human want' is a want of a human being that can be described without reference to a form of distribution. This has an important consequence: the want for an object that can be used to acquire other use-values of one's choice in exchange does not count in this context as a human want. An object with the power to acquire other use-values of choice in exchange is not, on account of that power, a use-value. Hence, neither value nor exchange-value is a species of use-value.

Contrast this conclusion with Cohen's elaboration of the statement: 'the use-value of a thing is its power to satisfy, directly or indirectly, a human desire'.[46] On Cohen's elaboration, an object has a power to satisfy human desire 'indirectly when it is used in the production or acquisition of another use-value'.[47]

45   *MEW*, 13, p. 9; *MECW*, 29, p. 263.
46   Cohen 1978, p. 345.
47   Ibid.

Or again: 'the power of exchanging against commodities serves indirectly to sat-isfy human desire'.[48] Cohen therefore concludes: 'exchange-value is a species of use-value'.[49]

It is one of the most fundamental points to grasp about Marx's concept of use-value that value and exchange-value are not a species of it. As Marx writes in the First Edition of *Capital*, at the end of Chapter One: '[t]he commodity is an *immediate unity of use-value and exchange-value,* hence of two oppos-ites'.[50] Exchange-value cannot be a species of use-value if it is its opposite. We are now able to articulate the premise of this claim. Marx's claim that use-value and exchange-value are opposites rests on the premise that use-value abstracts from possession, and from any want for a means to acquire posses-sion in exchange. By contrast, exchange-value presupposes possession, and is necessarily related to the want to acquire possession in exchange. In the absence of possession, or wants to acquire possession in exchange, there is no exchange-value. Exchange-value is the opposite of use-value *in respect of pos-session. Capital*'s concept of the commodity as a '*unity of ...* opposites' draws on Marx's rejection of the 'external relation of utility'[51] in 1844. Some further consequences of this move are explored in sections 3–4.

2   Value

Marx introduces the concept of exchange-value in Chapter One of *Capital* with the remark: '[i]n the form of society we are to study, they [use-values – JF] also constitute the material bearers – of exchange-value'.[52] A page later, 'exchange-value' is referred to as a 'mode of expression'[53] of something distinct from

---

48   Cohen 1978, p. 348.

49   Ibid.

50   *MEGA*, II, 5, p. 51; Marx 1967, p. 40.

51   *MEW*, 40, p. 542; *MECW*, 3, p. 302.

52   *MEW*, 23, p. 50; *MECW*, 35, p. 46; Marx 1976, p. 126.

53   *MEW*, 23, p. 51; *MECW*, 35, p. 47; Marx 1976, p. 127. Marx uses this phrase in the course of his 'third thing argument' for the view that exchange-value expresses value. I rejected this argument in Furner 2004. Patrick Murray then replied in its defence in Murray 2006, reprinted in Murray 2016, pp. 465–83. Furner 2004 had argued that, while Marx's critique of Samuel Bailey may be convincing in respect of money and capital, it is not convincing at the level of the commodity, because *Capital*'s third thing argument is not convincing. One 'problem' Murray raised in reply was: if Marx's third thing argument is rejected, 'one wants to know with what justification Furner introduces Marx's theory of value ... Fur-ner provides no alternative line of argument' (Murray 2016, p. 483). This section, and the test that concludes the next one, attempt to provide such argument. (Both Furner 2004

that expression. Just going by this evidence, exchange-value, for Marx, is the expression of a use-value's power of general exchangeability in terms of some other use-value. Value can then be distinguished both from use-value and from exchange-value by being defined as a use-value's power of general exchangeability itself.

Yet, as the first of these quotes indicates, *Capital* is a study of a 'form of society'. A 'form of society' is, among other things, a type of society that has certain generalised features, and is able to reproduce itself non-contingently in virtue of these features. Its capacity for reproduction is not thought to depend on the coalescence of independent flukes. Thus, if *Capital* is a study of a form of society, it ignores possibilities that rest on supposing that its object is held together by fluke. Weird counterexamples of the kind that may serve to highlight an analytical problem in the different context of an analysis of individual behaviour are out of place. Rules that admit exceptions may be assumed to have no exceptions.

These general remarks on what it is to study a form of society, together with the fact that *Capital* is a study of the capitalist form of society, carry certain implications for its concepts of exchange-value and value. If *Capital* is a study of the capitalist form of society, its concepts of exchange-value and value may reflect the assumption that use-values with the power of general exchangeability *non-contingently* define this form. The above statements of exchange-value and value may be modified, therefore, if it can be shown that use-values with the power of general exchangeability can only non-contingently provide a form of wealth on certain further conditions, and these further conditions require the initial statements of these concepts to be modified if an account of capitalism is to take on greater detail.

One such further condition is: it is necessary that all use-values that are products are produced for exchange. If use-values were not produced, because all objects of human want were always already there in abundance, it could only be by fluke that use-values were generally exchanged, rather than directly appropriated. So, if use-values with the power of general exchangeability are a form of wealth, use-values must be produced. Further, while use-values that are products could still have the power of general exchangeability even if only a few were actually exchanged (as long as it was permissible to exchange them all),

---

and Murray 2006 tend to assume that *either* the third thing argument can be defended, *or* an alternative argument must be reconstructed entirely at a later level; see the use of 'instead' at Furner 2004, p. 90, and 'since' at Murray 2016, p. 467. This assumption is rejected here).

use-values' power of general exchangeability only serves to reproduce a society if it is realised, in exchange. Thus, use-values that are products are assumed to be exchanged. But if this is assumed, use-values that are products must be assumed to be produced for exchange. If all the use-values that are products were not produced for exchange, they could still all be exchanged, but only as a result of a mass of ongoing unforeseen contingencies, which a study of a form of society may ignore. Moreover, for use-values with the power of general exchangeability to provide a general form of wealth, it is sufficient that all products are produced for exchange, and that no non-products are useful and alienable (for example, that there is no useful and alienable uncultivated land).

If use-values with the power of general exchangeability are only a form of wealth if products are produced for exchange; and if they remain a form of wealth even in the absence of useful and alienable non-products; then value and exchange-value may be redefined. Value may be redefined as the power of general exchangeability of a *product produced for exchange*. Exchange-value may be redefined as an expression of the power of general exchangeability of a product produced for exchange. These redefinitions are *permissible*, in light of the necessary and sufficient conditions for use-values with the power of general exchangeability to provide a form of wealth.

What *motivates* the redefinitions is a belief that products are valid objects of inquiry independently of non-products. Products are valid objects of inquiry in and of themselves, for, unlike non-products, time must be devoted to their production, and decisions taken to produce them. These differences are relevant from the perspective of the development and awareness components of *Capital*'s conception of freedom. An evidently universal development of ability is consistent only with certain uses and distributions of time as labour time, and only with certain decision-making procedures for what to produce. To motivate these redefinitions by appeal to this conception of freedom is not to motivate them by a standard external to the object of *Capital*, if *Capital* is able to show that capitalism makes such freedom possible and of value to a type of actor within it.

If the above redefinitions are motivated on this basis, then the point of studying the capitalist form of wealth with their aid is to examine how this form of wealth shapes the use and distribution of total social time as labour time, and decision-making about this use and distribution. A theoretical interest in the use and exchange of non-products is not precluded. But it is qualified. It is of theoretical interest primarily on account of its effect on the use and distribution of total social time as labour time, and the associated decision-making; an effect that is to be studied through the effect of the use and exchange of non-products on the use and distribution of value.

We can now appreciate why the concepts of Marx's theory of value are not ultimately designed to explain price. One typical complaint among critics of *Capital* is that its theory of value is a contorted and unsuccessful attempt to explain price.[54] The response to these unimaginative critics can be brief: at no stage of *Capital* – neither in Volume I nor in Volume III – is price the main issue. *Capital's* main concern is with the effect of the capitalist form of wealth on the use and distribution of total social time as labour time (and on decision-making about this use and distribution).[55] As a rule of thumb: if a critic of *Capital* objects that it is contorted and unsuccessful as a general price theory, transform the question. Turn the question into that of how a commodity form based study of the capitalist form of wealth can theorise the impact of the factor behind the charge of contortion or failure (be it the difference in organic composition of capital, turnover time, non-reproducibility, monopolies, or something else) on the use and distribution of total social time as labour time.

On the above elaboration, the plausibility of *Capital's* concept of value as the power of general exchangeability of a product produced for exchange rests on the premises that a form of society can be based on generalised production for exchange; and that the impact of this form on the use and distribution of total social time as labour time is of theoretical interest in its own right. Before examining *Capital's* claim about the determination (as distinct from the concept) of value, we may respond to the view of Carl Menger that economic 'value' is 'nothing inhering in goods'.[56]

For Menger, a founding figure of marginalist economics, value denotes a relation between an object, and a subject's want. A relation between an object and a subject's want is not a physical property of the object. Hence it is misleading, Menger concludes, to speak of objects as being or having value, as if value were a physical property of the object. 'That which exists objectively are only ever the things, or rather quantities of things'.[57]

For Menger, the exchange-value of *x* is the value to its possessor of what they would have to do without, were they to be denied what *x* is in fact exchangeable for.[58] Where there is even a once-off opportunity for an exchange, there is exchange-value. For even where there is a once-off opportunity for exchange, it is possible to estimate what a possessor would be denied were the exchange to be prevented. Exchange-value, on Menger's account, is an implication of the

---

54   See, for example, Gordon 1991, pp. 14–16.
55   From now on the bracketed phrase is not repeated.
56   Menger 1968, p. 86; Menger 2007, p. 120.
57   Menger 1968, p. 86; Menger 2007, p. 121.
58   Menger 1968, p. 214; Menger 2007, p. 228.

very possibility of exchange. It presupposes nothing more than two possessors who esteem each other's objects sufficiently to offer something agreeable in return.[59]

Capital's claim that commodities 'are values'[60] assumes a different context: a form of society in which generalised production for exchange is an anticipated reality. The reason why a commodity is a value is of a piece with the argument for why an object is a use-value. A commodity is a value, because its possessor's relation to it as something that can serve them as a means to acquire whatever they want to acquire is mediated by their awareness that it is a type of commodity generally known to be able to be used as a means by any possessor of it to acquire whatever type of commodity they want to acquire; and by their awareness that this fact is independent of their particular desire to exchange it.

Capital offers not just a concept of value, however, but also a claim about its determination. This claim, like the concept of value, must not only be permitted by its object of study. It must serve to add detail to an account of how the capitalist form of wealth shapes the use and distribution of total social time as labour time. As a claim about the determination of value comes on the back of the above arguments for redefining value, this claim must have some validity for a form of society described simply as generalised production for exchange; and add detail to an account of how generalised production for exchange shapes the use and distribution of total social time as labour time.

Capital Chapter One states: 'the value of a commodity is determined by ... socially necessary labour-time', that is, the 'labour-time required to produce any use-value in the available, socially normal conditions of production and with the socially average degree of skill and intensity of labour'.[61] Going by this statement, one commodity of a given type has the same value as any other identical commodity of its type, as determined by the socially average conditions for reproducing commodities of this type. Different types of commodity have the same value if the same amount of labour time is required to produce them in socially average conditions.

To support this claim about the determination of value, it is necessary to identify premises that can be taken as given if one assumes nothing more about a form of society than that it is defined by generalised production for exchange; and to show that, on these premises, there is a connection between the socially

---

59   Menger 1968, p. 158; Menger 2007, p. 179.
60   *MEW*, 23, p. 52; *MECW*, 35, p. 48; Marx 1976, p. 128.
61   *MEW*, 23, p. 53; *MECW*, 35, p. 49; Marx 1976, p. 129.

necessary labour time that commodities represent, and the ratios in which they can be thought to exchange. Consider the following premises:

(1)   products are means for possessors to acquire whatever they want to acquire

(2)   labour is only performed in order to possess means of acquisition

(3)   people are at liberty to choose what type of product to produce

(1)–(3) can be taken as given, provided one assumes nothing more about a form of society than that it is defined by generalised production for exchange. (1) is a direct result of generalised production for exchange. (2) can be taken as given, for if labour is assumed to be performed for a reason other than to possess means of acquisition, then that could only limit generalised production for exchange; and there is as yet no reason to introduce such a limit. (3) can be taken as given, for limits on the types of labour people may perform could only limit generalised production for exchange, by limiting the production of products for which demand has risen. Again, there is as yet no reason to introduce such a limit.

Premises (1)–(3) support an 'allocation of labor'[62] defence of the relation between value, as just determined, and exchange-value. A labour allocation defence says that there will be an impetus towards greater proportionality between values and prices after fluctuations caused by changes in demand and supply, because these fluctuations will encourage a transfer of labour into branches of production producing commodities with inflated exchange-values and out of branches producing commodities with deflated exchange-values. For in this way, the labour that actors must perform is minimised, relative to the acquisition of given means of acquisition. At this point, this is far from being an objective law,[63] for (1)–(3) do not entail value-maximising behaviour. But what matters here is that there is *an* impetus for labour to be reallocated, one that can become more law-like in virtue of features of the capitalist form of wealth that can be developed from its initial description as generalised production for exchange.[64]

---

62   Rubin 1973, p. 105. Unlike Rubin 1973, however, the argument is not presented to hold for a 'simple commodity economy' (Rubin 1973, p. 105); that is, a type of society distinct from capitalism, in which producers own means of production and produce for exchange to satisfy their needs, and on which capitalist social relations are thought of as 'impinging' (Meek 1956, p. 303). The argument at this point is to establish a connection between value and exchange-value, not a 'law' (Rubin 1973, p. 105).

63   See Arthur 1997, pp. 14–15.

64   For instance, in *Results of the Immediate Process of Production*, Marx argues that it is 'the wage-labourer' who, in pursuit of 'money', is 'completely indifferent' to the particular type

What Marx's claim about the determination of value adds to an account of how the capitalist form of wealth shapes the use and distribution to total social time as labour time is this. Insofar as a development of productive power establishes more advanced socially average conditions for producing a certain type of commodity, the effect of this development is to establish a higher norm of output per time unit worked that each unit of production in that branch must strive to match, to command as much value as before.

Accordingly, it is a mistake to suppose that, if the determination of value by socially necessary labour time is not meant to explain equilibrium price in actual economies, it is a stipulation with no clear purpose.[65] The claim that value is determined by socially necessary labour time is neither a stipulation, nor an attempt to explain equilibrium price in actual economies. The claim that value is determined by socially necessary labour time is not a stipulation, for it is connected at a certain level of abstraction to a claim about exchange-value through premises that are given at that level of abstraction. It has a purpose, for it adds detail to an account of how the capitalist form of wealth shapes the use and distribution of total social time as labour time. That is not to say that more complex features of the capitalist form of wealth that ensure that commodities do not exchange in proportion to value in actual capitalist economies (such as differences in the 'composition of capital',[66] roughly, the degree to which a branch of production is capital intensive) are of no interest. Rather, they are of interest through their impact on the use and distribution of total social time as labour time, by virtue of their effect on the use and distribution of value, as determined by socially necessary labour time.

3   Commodities and Goods

Capital Chapter One twice uses the phrase 'use-value or good'.[67] On one reading of this phrase, 'good' is a superfluous alternative expression for use-value. After all, in *Capital* the dominant term of the two is 'use-value'. Marx does not use 'good' in his own name in *Capital* Volume I unless preceded by 'use-value or'.

---

of their productive activity (*MEGA*, II, 4.1, pp. 103–4; *MECW*, 34, pp. 437–8; Marx 1976, pp. 1033–4).

65   As supposed by Cohen 1988, p. 224.

66   *MEW*, 23, p. 640; *MECW*, 35, pp. 607–8; Marx 1976, p. 762.

67   *MEW*, 23, p. 50, p. 53; *MECW*, 35, p. 46, p. 48; Marx 1976, p. 126, p. 129; compare *MEW*, 23, p. 192; *MECW*, 35, p. 187; Marx 1976, p. 283.

It is also as alternative expressions for use-value that the terms 'goods', or 'goods and services', are used in recent Marxist works. Chris Arthur writes: '[o]ur problem is to determine the conditions of existence of a system in which goods take the form of commodities offered for exchange on the market'.[68] Tony Smith remarks: there are 'goods and services in *all* forms of social production'.[69] Given the use of these terms by economists, however, the concept of a good (or goods and services) is not a suitable alternative expression or substitute for Marx's concept of use-value.

One indication of the difference between Marx's concept of use-value and the concept of a good used by economists is evident from the passage in Adam Smith's *Wealth of Nations* (1776) that is cited by David Ricardo at the start of his *Principles of Political Economy* (1817):

> It has been observed by Adam Smith, that 'the word Value has two different meanings, and sometimes expresses the utility of some particular object, and sometimes the power of purchasing other goods which the possession of that object conveys. The one may be called *value in use*; the other *value in exchange*'.[70]

On the evidence of this passage, a good, for Smith and Ricardo, is a particular object of utility over which a subject has 'possession'. Lorenz von Stein's *System der Staatswissenschaft* (1852), which Marx refers to in *A Contribution to a Critique of Political Economy*,[71] likewise states: 'there are no goods that are not in legal possession [*Besitz*]'.[72] Already in Marx's sources, therefore, the concept of a good as used by economists differs from Marx's concept of use-value by virtue of the fact that a good is a possession. If a good is a possession and political economy is concerned with goods, then 'use-value, as use-value, lies beyond political economy's sphere of investigation'.[73]

The connection between the concept of a good and the concept of possession assumes systematic importance in Carl Menger's *Principles of Economics* (1871). Menger begins by listing 'four prerequisites' for an object to acquire 'goods-character':

---

68   Arthur 2002, p. 88.
69   Smith 1990, pp. 69–70; see also Murray 2016, p. 159, p. 497.
70   Ricardo 1821, I.I.2.
71   'German compilers love to discuss use-value, under the label of "good"' (*MEW*, 13, p. 16; *MECW*, 29, p. 270).
72   Stein 1852, p. 161. On possession, see ch. 7, sec. 3.
73   *MEW*, 13, p. 16; *MECW*, 29, p. 270.

1.   a human need.
2.   such qualities of a thing that suit it to being placed in a causal connection with the satisfaction of this need.
3.   human knowledge of this causal connection.
4.   command over this thing such that it can in fact be employed to satisfy that need.[74]

For Menger, an object has 'goods-character' if it is known to be able to serve a causal role in satisfying a want of an existing human being, and it is subject to 'command'. In other words, a subject must be able to regard action on any decision they take to satisfy a want with it that it can satisfy as the necessary and sufficient condition of its satisfaction. Thus, a good must be able to satisfy a want of the subject who commands it. Although one subject can reserve an object for another, the other could always independently decide not to satisfy the want of theirs that that object can satisfy.

The command by which Menger defines goods presupposes a subject with the will of a possessor. For a subject to regard action on any decision they take to satisfy a want with an object that can satisfy that want as the necessary and sufficient condition of its satisfaction, they must regard their decision as independent of anyone else's permission or instruction, and regard themselves as entitled to prevent anyone else from taking or depleting it. In other words, they must take themselves to have an exclusive claim to it. To assert an exclusive claim to an object is to have the will characteristic of a possessor. Hence, on Menger's account, the concept of a good presupposes the concept of a subject with the will of a possessor.

Menger draws a further distinction between economic goods and non-economic goods. 'Economic' goods, Menger says, are those goods whose available quantities fall short of requirements.[75] A shortfall gives subjects cause to 'make a choice'[76] as to which of their wants to satisfy, and which of their wants to leave unsatisfied. As the quantities of an economic good fall short of requirements, all subjects, insofar as they behave economically, will want to appropriate any available quantity of it, if only to exchange it. Thus, no subject can be certain that they can satisfy a want that only an economic good can satisfy, if it is available for anyone to appropriate. If a subject has yet to appropriate it, others can be expected to want to do so first, to their exclusion. A subject can only be certain that they can satisfy a want with an economic good once they possess a

---

74   Menger 1968, p. 3; Menger 2007, p. 52.
75   Menger 1968, p. 53; Menger 2007, p. 96.
76   Menger 1968, p. 52; Menger 2007, p. 95.

sufficient quantity of it. It is only once a subject possesses an economic good, that is, appropriates it and asserts an exclusive claim to it, that they command it.

'Non-economic' goods, by contrast, are those goods that are available in amounts that exceed everyone's want for them,[77] due to natural abundance (water from a spring) or endless immaterial copying (open access software). As non-economic goods are abundant, each of an indefinite number of subjects may be certain that they can satisfy a want with a non-economic good even before each has possession of a sufficient quantity of it. Each of an indefinite number of subjects can be certain that they can satisfy a want with a non-economic good provided each is able, at will, to *take* possession of an amount that each regards as entirely sufficient for their wants. The amount that each subject can, at will, possess, must be entirely sufficient, Menger says. Otherwise, 'human egoism', anticipating seizure and hoarding by others, will lead each to seize and hoard 'to the exclusion of others' through 'possession [*Besitz*]',[78] turning the good into an economic good. But if a type of good is a non-economic good, it is available for anyone to appropriate in sufficient amounts. Its abundance ensures that each of an indefinite number of subjects is the sole decider of whether or not to satisfy a want of theirs that it can satisfy even before each possesses some sufficient amount of it.

In sum: an economic good is a possession, because the conditions of its command are the conditions of possession. By contrast, a non-economic good need not exist as a possession. It is sufficient that it is available, and that there is a subject with the will to take possession of it. A non-economic good must at some point become a possession in the respect in which it is to be consumed, to be consumed as a good. But a non-economic good may exist as a good before it is possessed. The difference between an economic good and a non-economic good is that only the former presupposes that the object in question is already in a phase of possession.

'Good' is not a suitable alternative expression or substitute for Marx's concept of use-value, therefore. Marx's concept of use-value, unlike the concept of a good, does not presuppose that a useful object is ever in any respect in a phase of possession. Visitors to a public gallery consume its works as use-values by viewing them. But they do not act as if they did not require anyone else's permission to view them. They do not treat them as goods. If a 'monk' regards their eating a particular portion of food as 'conditional on no starving person

---

77   Menger 1968, pp. 57–9; Menger 2007, pp. 98–9.
78   Menger 1968, pp. 55–6; Menger 2007, p. 97.

happening along who just now needs that food for immediate survival',[79] then, when they eat it, they consume it as a use-value, but not as a good. Even if it is true that there are 'goods and services in *all* forms of social production',[80] it is not true that all means of production and all means of consumption in all forms of production are goods. It is not 'goods' that 'take the form of commodities offered for exchange on the market',[81] but use-values.

Indeed, Menger's *Principles of Economics* has no equivalent term for Marx's concept of use-value. For Menger, 'use-value' is a species of 'value', a subject's esteem for an economic good.[82] For Menger, use-value and exchange-value express, respectively, a subject's esteem for an economic good in regard to its consumption or exchange.[83] Going by Menger's *Principles of Economics*, the discipline of economics takes no interest in what *Capital* calls use-value. It studies possessed wealth only. Relatedly, if economics takes no interest in what *Capital* calls use-value, it can take no interest in any further concept that incorporates this concept. It can take no interest in Marx's concept of the commodity, if a commodity is a use-value produced for exchange in a form of society characterised by generalised production for exchange, and whose value is determined by socially necessary labour time; and it can take no interest in Marx's concept of money or capital, if these concepts presuppose Marx's concept of the commodity.[84]

The commodity form can, however, be used to explain the attraction of the concept of an economic good, if the commodity form can explain money, and money generates acquisitiveness.[85] Two objects, each of which can be used to obtain the same value in exchange, are equally good from the point of view of acquisition. Accordingly, a product and a non-product, a reproducible and a non-reproducible, are all equally good from the point of view of acquisition, just in case they can all be used to obtain the same value in exchange. Acquisitiveness must therefore encourage any economic good, a product or a non-product, a reproducible or a non-reproducible, to be traded. If, by explain-

---

79   Cohen 1998, p. 62.

80   Smith 1990, pp. 69–70.

81   Arthur 2002, p. 88.

82   Menger 1968, p. 83; Menger 2007, p. 118.

83   Menger 1968, p. 216; Menger 2007, p. 228.

84   Patrick Murray claims both that (i) Marx criticises economics for its 'failure to make specific social forms' such as commodities, money and capital 'ingredient to its basic concepts' (Murray 2016, p. 2); and that (ii) 'all that remains is bare use value' or the 'category of wealth' (Murray 2016, p. 190). Yet (ii) does not follow from (i). Economic goods are units of possessed wealth.

85   See ch. 7, sec. 4, and ch. 9, sec. 5 respectively.

ing money, the commodity form can explain acquisitiveness, it can explain the attraction of a concept designed to capture all expressions of acquisitiveness, whether they take the form of trading a product or a non-product, a reproducible or a non-reproducible. It can therefore explain the attraction of the concept of an economic good. The concept of an economic good allows maximising behaviour to be postulated on the part of individual agents at the same time as it satisfies what Lukács calls the 'abstract-formal'[86] need to subsume all possible objects of exchange under a single term.

Suppose that the commodity form can explain the attraction of the concept of an economic good in the manner just outlined; and that economics can take no interest in Marx's concept of the commodity, because economics lacks the concept of use-value. If economics lacks the concept of the commodity, which, as a general form of wealth, explains the attraction of its most fundamental concept, economics cannot comprehend the conditions of applicability of its concepts to capitalism. Indeed, even if economics could take an interest in Marx's concept of the commodity, a commodity would appear as one just type of economic good among others, and so as incapable of explaining the phenomenon of economic goods in general. This derivation of the concept of an economic good from the commodity form is one example consistent with Lukács's broader claim that, in respect of each individual social science in modern capitalism, 'its own concrete underlying reality lies methodologically and in principle outside its grasp'.[87]

The derivation of the concept of an economic good from the commodity form also provides an opportunity to correct the characterisation of commodity form philosophy in the remark: 'economism (understanding capitalism entirely from the commodity form)'.[88] In Reading Capital, Étienne Balibar describes '"economism"' as a type of approach 'which claims precisely to reduce all the non-economic instances of the social structure purely and simply to reflections, transpositions of phenomena of the economic base'.[89] Commodity form philosophy is not a type of 'economism', for it does not claim that the unity of its explanations is provided by an 'economic base'. It is committed to denying that an 'economic base' could serve as a unifying explanans for various non-economic spheres. If capitalism and its discipline of economics are understood 'entirely from the commodity form', then this understanding cannot be

86   Lukács 1977, p. 280; Lukács 1968, p. 104.
87   Ibid.
88   Read 2003, p. 33.
89   Althusser and Balibar 1969, p. 223; Althusser and Balibar 1975, p. 306.

provided by anything aptly termed 'economism'. The questions of economics, posed with the aid of the concept of an economic good, are not the questions posed by commodity form philosophy.

Having distinguished Marx's concept of the commodity (use-value with the power of general exchangeability determined by socially necessary labour time) from the concept of an economic good (a possessed object of esteem that is only available in quantities that fall short of requirements), it is possibly, finally, to say why the former must provide the most basic concept of a study of capitalism that proceeds from the view that generalised production for exchange is the simplest feature of the capitalist form of wealth. The test is: which conception of the total social product ensures that the presuppositions of generalised production for exchange are satisfied – a total social product of commodities, or a total social product of economic goods?

One presupposition of generalised production for exchange is that different types of product are produced. There would be no cause to exchange products if they were all of the same type. By implication, a further presupposition is that human beings have wants for different types of product. There would be no cause to exchange any type of product if human beings had no want for it. This further presupposition is well-founded, both because human beings cannot even meet all their vital needs (eating, drinking, shelter from the elements, etc.) with the same type of use-value; and because the exchange of use-values itself leads wants to expand. Thus, a conception of the total social product only ensures that the presuppositions of generalised production for exchange are met if it presupposes subjects who have wants for different types of product. How, then, do the conceptions of a total social product in terms of commodities or economic goods fare by this criterion?

To say that the total social product is comprised of commodities is to presuppose that it is all exchangeable. A commodity is defined by the power of general exchangeability. Products are not generally exchangeable, however, if they are all use-values of the same type. So, if the total social product is comprised of commodities, we must suppose that it is comprised of different types of commodities, that answer to different wants. To conceive of the total social product as comprised of commodities is adequate to generalised production for exchange, because both total commodification of the social product and generalised production for exchange presuppose subjects who have wants for different types of product.

Now imagine that the total social product is comprised of economic goods. Economic goods are goods that economic subjects compete to possess, and use economically. Accordingly, if the labour of producing a type of economic good is undesirable, the total social product could have economic goods-character despite consisting entirely of one type of product.[90] All economic subjects would still compete for its possession, and use it economically, because no economic subject passes up the chance to avoid the toil of producing it. But if so, a total social product of economic goods does not ensure that the presuppositions of generalised production for exchange are met. It does not presuppose subjects who have wants for different types of product.

By focussing on the *total* social product, it is possible to show why Marx's concept of the commodity, and not the concept of an economic good, is fit for use as the most basic concept in a study of the capitalist form of wealth.

4   Use-Values, Goods and Duties to the Whole

A *duty to the whole* is the name given here to a principle that establishes a duty but no right. A proponent of commodity form philosophy can appeal to duties to the whole, and, *inter alia*, enforceable duties to the whole; while an economist cannot. Before defending these claims, and offering some evidence for thinking that Marx appealed to duties to the whole, and that it is permissible for a Marxist project to do so, it is necessary to give a fuller account of a duty to the whole.

A duty to the whole is a duty underpinned by the value of a property of a group or society, which does not give any individual member an unconditional advantage, and is owed to all members in good standing.[91] Some examples of possible duties to the whole are: a duty to ensure access to the workings of government institutions;[92] a duty to ensure access to public facilities; a duty to preserve cultural relics; a duty to protect endangered species; a policy of solidarity; and a duty not to act on maxims reinforced by systems that fail a system-level universalisability test. If the name for a society in which individuals have no rights is 'Nowheresville',[93] duties to the whole can exist in Nowheresville. But they can also exist in a society whose legal code includes rights.

---

90   For an illustration, see ch. 6, sec. 1.
91   A 'society' is the living together of individuals in a certain space. For a definition of a 'group', see ch. 12, sec. 1. As it is possible for there to be a group of societies, it is possible for there to be global, societal-level duties to the whole that bind all societies, without giving any individual member society an unconditional advantage; for example, a duty of unilateral nuclear disarmament. For simplicity, the analysis in this section assumes that duties to the whole apply within a single society, whose members are individual human beings.
92   See ch. 1, sec. 1.
93   Feinberg 1970, p. 243.

Duties that are not owed to a particular individual are sometimes called 'impersonal duties'.[94] The term 'duties to the whole' is preferred here, for two reasons. First, the term 'impersonal duty' does not make it clear that an impersonal duty is impersonal in virtue of whom it is owed *to*. Second, it is better, if possible, to describe those to whom a duty is owed in positive terms. The term 'duty to the whole' indicates that the duty is owed to all members of a whole, rather than simply denying that it is owed to a particular individual, which would be consistent with thinking it was owed to a god.

To say that a duty is underpinned by the value of a property of a group or society is to deny that it is underpinned by the value of a property of an individual. A whole may possess a property not possessed by any of its parts taken individually. The valuing of that property is then irreducible to the valuing of a property of an individual. It is valued as an aspect of the group or society, or perhaps even as an aspect of the human species.

One implication of being underpinned by the value of a property of a whole is that an enforceable duty to the whole may be claimed by any member. To claim a right or duty is to report an instance of its violation to a competent legal instance, such as a court, with the power of ordering or applying coercive sanctions. While only the allegedly defamed individual can bring a claim of defamation before a court; any member of society in which there is, say, an enforceable duty to the whole not to make law inconsistent with the constitution, may bring the matter of the constitutionality of a law before a court.[95]

To say that a duty to the whole gives no individual an unconditional advantage is to say that it gives no individual an advantage that can only be waived or withdrawn on their say so (or on the say so of their designated representative). An unconditional advantage may consist of the enjoyment of a right to a thing, as when *A* has a right of private property; an owed obligation, as when *A* is owed a service by *B*; or a capacity to create a new legal relation, as when *A* is entitled to marry. The concept of a duty to the whole is not exhausted by the criterion of the lack of an unconditional advantage, however. It is necessary but not sufficient. *B*'s obligation to perform a service gives *A* an unconditional advantage if *B*'s service is owed to *A*, and only *A* can release *B* from that obligation. But if even *A* cannot release *B*, *B*'s duty is not just for that reason a duty to the whole. If *B* has a moral duty to care for a sick relative who is not morally permitted to release *B* from that duty, *B*'s duty is not just for that reason a duty to the whole. It has yet to be shown that *B*'s duty is underpinned by the value of a property of a whole.

---

94   Vallentyne 2012, p. 153.

95   See Jellinik 1919, p. 72.

Finally, to say that a duty to the whole is owed to all members in good standing is just to say that it is owed to all members of the whole who abide by it and
who are not implicated in its violation. A thief, or someone who puts others
up to stealing, may not complain if others steal; and those who commit acts
of terror, or who bear some responsibility for causing others' acts of terror by
unjustifiable actions of their own, may not complain if others commit acts of
terror.[96] The same applies in the case of the violation of a duty to the whole. As
it is the value of a property of a whole that is contravened, all members of this
whole are initially counted in as members to whom a duty is owed; members
not in good standing are then discounted.

The slippery language of 'special' and 'general' grievance[97] is hereby avoided.
A special grievance is a grievance specific to a particular individual; a general
grievance is a grievance not specific to a particular individual. 'Special grievance' can describe a grievance of a particular individual resulting from a violation of their unconditional advantage *regardless* of how they behave. But by
the above criterion of lack of hypocrisy as a condition for being counted in as
a member to whom a duty to the whole is owed, theft of public property in a
world in which only one individual does not steal public property would *also*
(if this language were adopted) have to be taken to generate a special grievance, despite the fact that no unconditional advantage need be violated by the
act of stealing public property. Avoidance of the language of 'special' and 'general' grievance helps to preserve the distinction between these two issues: the
absence of an unconditional advantage, and the lack of hypocrisy as a condition for being counted in as a member to whom a duty is owed.

We now defend the claim that commodity form philosophy, unlike economic thought, can appeal to a duty to the whole. What needs to be shown is
that the concept of use-value enables appeal to a duty to the whole, while the
concept of an economic good cannot underpin such appeal. Consider, first, the
relation of private property rights to the concept of an economic good.

If A is the private property owner of x, A is entitled to use x as A pleases, so
long as A's use of x does not interfere with others' rights, or the conditions of
public order; and others have a duty not to interfere. A's liberty to use x subject to these constraints cannot be diminished without A's say so; and no one
other than A can waive A's claim against others who interfere. A private property owner of a car is entitled to drive it on the roads, but not to run someone
over; and they may be required by officials and in certain circumstances to

---

96   Cohen 2013, pp. 121–8.
97   Cohen 2008, p. 288.

produce a driver's licence as a condition. No one may stop them driving it at a certain time, unless they have hired it out to someone else; and no one but them can release another from a liability to pay damages if they slash its tyres.

If A is the private property owner of x, A is thereby entitled to treat x as an (economic) good. A is entitled to treat their will to use x to satisfy a want of theirs as the necessary and sufficient condition of its satisfaction, for any want whose satisfaction does not interfere with others' rights, or the conditions of public order. A private property owner of a car is entitled to treat their will to use it to drive about as the necessary and sufficient condition of the satisfaction of their want to drive about.

By contrast, someone under a duty in respect of an object is not thereby entitled to treat it as a good. To abide by a duty in respect of an object is to abide by a prohibition to treat it (or not to treat it) in some way, and hence not to satisfy a want with it, just as and when one decides. So, if all subjects have nothing but duties in respect of an object (for example, nothing but a duty to preserve a provision to ameliorate a natural disaster predicted to affect a future generation), that object lacks goods-character. No subject commands it.

In sum: if the total social product is conceived of as entirely comprised of economic goods, the only arguments that can be advanced about duties in respect of products are arguments about duties with correlative rights.

Now consider the relation between duty and use-value. If the total social product is conceived of as entirely comprised of use-values, it is possible to imagine that everyone has nothing but a duty in respect of some use-values; for example, nothing but a duty to preserve provisions to ameliorate future natural disasters, or nothing but a duty to preserve any means of consumption held in a public fund awaiting distribution in accordance with a principle. Such objects are use-values, that is, means to satisfy human wants, even though they are not goods, at least during a certain phase of their existence, as no subject is in command of them. If the total social product is conceived of as entirely comprised of use-values, it is possible to advance arguments that appeal to duties to the whole in respect of products.

Commodity form philosophy, by distinguishing use-value from value, and attending solely to use-value, has the conceptual means to propose a duty-to-the-whole-based principle. Economic thought, by contrast, founded on the concept of an economic good, does not. One feature of commodity form philosophy, as opposed to economic thought, is that it can conceive of duties to the whole.

If commodity form philosophy can conceive of duties to the whole, it can conceive of a society whose *fundamental* principle is a duty to the whole.

Marx's *Critique of the Gotha Programme* refers to a 'narrow, bourgeois horizon of right'.[98] In some contexts, to refer to a 'narrow, bourgeois horizon of right' might simply be to say that rights are not sufficient for a good life, as when it is said that the poor, or the illiterate, who have the same rights as everyone else, but little power to exercise them, cannot enjoy the good life. Marx's *Critique of the Gotha Programme* is not one of these contexts, however. Its use of the phrase follows a criticism of the 'principle' of right, or what right is in its 'nature'.[99] To refer to a 'narrow, bourgeois horizon of right' following a criticism of the principle or nature of right is to say that the good society will adopt a non-rights-based principle as a more fundamental principle than any principle of right it may retain. For in the company of a more fundamental non-rights-based principle, a non-fundamental role for a principle of right cannot prejudice the claim that the horizon of right has been surpassed.

This suggestion is supported by the fact that Marx's reference to a 'narrow, bourgeois horizon of right' occurs in the course of envisioning a developed communist society defined by a policy of solidarity, which is a duty to the whole. The fundamental principle of developed communism is: 'from each according to their abilities, to each according to their needs!'[100] Only a fundamental principle would be rounded off with an exclamation mark, or introduced as a principle that communist society will 'write on its flag'.[101] In content, it is a principle of solidarity in respect of need. The concept of solidarity originates from the Roman legal concept of *obligation in solidum*: 'everyone assumes responsibility for anyone who cannot pay his debt, and he is conversely responsible for everyone else'.[102] If x = a disadvantage, and y = action to redress that disadvantage, the principle of solidarity is: if any member of a group acquires x, each member has a duty to perform y (if they can assist). All we then need to add, to get to the fundamental principle of developed communism, is to assume that non-satisfaction of a need is a disadvantage. The corresponding principle of solidarity in respect of need says: if any member of society has an unsatisfied need, each member has a duty to produce its object (if they can). But that is precisely what the principle 'from each according to their abilities, to each according to their needs!' dictates. In Marx's

---

98   *MEW*, 19, p. 21; *MECW*, 24, p. 87. On the translation of this phrase, see ch. 1, appendix.
99   *MEW*, 19, pp. 20–1; *MECW*, 24, pp. 86–7.
100 *MEW*, 19, p. 21; *MECW*, 24, p. 87; compare the passage in *The German Ideology* at *MEW*, 3, p. 528; *MECW*, 5, p. 537, authored (according to *MECW*, 5, p. 586) by Moses Hess. The principle appears earlier in Becker 1844, p. 34, and later in Blanc 1851, p. 92.
101 *MEW*, 19, p. 21; *MECW*, 24, p. 87.
102 Brunkhorst 2002, p. 10; Brunkhorst 2005, p. 2.

vision, the basic principle of developed communism is a principle of solidarity in respect of need.[103]

A duty of solidarity (in respect of need) is a duty to the whole if (i) the value of acting in solidarity rests in part on a decision by the whole to adopt it as a policy; and (ii) the redress of severe disadvantage has priority over the redress of less severe disadvantage. For if (i) is true, the value of acting in solidarity to redress a disadvantage rests in part on the value of a property of society: that a decision has been made to adopt a policy of solidarity (in respect of need). Further, if (ii) is true, the redress of a disadvantage suffered by any one individual is *conditional* on the non-exhaustion of society's capacity to redress more severe disadvantages. If A is stricken with an extremely pressing need, then, by (ii), A's need enters the queue of needs-to-be-satisfied ahead of B's less pressing need – which might, depending on material conditions, go unmet (for a while) as a consequence.

As the fundamental principle of developed communism is a duty of solidarity in respect of need, which is a duty to the whole, Marx has a good reason, in this context, to suggest that developed communism surpasses the horizon of right. Developed communism surpasses the horizon of right, because its fundamental principle is a duty to the whole. Any principle of right that remains cannot prejudice the claim that the horizon of right has been surpassed.[104] In Marx's vision of the good society, the horizon of '*Recht*' is surpassed because a growth in productive power *and* the transformation of productive activity into 'the prime need of life'[105] allows a duty to the whole to be adopted as the fundamental principle.

Nor is a policy of solidarity in respect of need the only duty to the whole that Marx affirms. Having condemned the alliance of anarchists in the International Working Men's Association on the grounds that 'to achieve its ends, it does not recoil from any means', Marx adds: 'to combat all these intrigues, there is just

---

103   Allen Wood suggests that the 'source' of the principle of Marx's vision of developed communism may be 'the New Testament: "And all that believed were together, and had all things common; and sold their possessions and goods, and parted them to all men, as every man had need" (Acts 2:44–5)' (Wood 2014, p. 259). This suggestion is not plausible, however; the quote does not imply the first part of the principle, 'from each according to their abilities'. The Roman law concept of solidarity is a sufficient source of the principle.

104   If a policy of solidarity in respect of need cannot and/or ought not to be implemented by coercive or impartial means, and justice consists in norms that ought to be enforced impartially now if not forever, then that is a reason to say that, in Marx's vision, developed communism, in virtue of its fundamental principle, surpasses the horizon of justice (which is not necessarily to say that there is no justice in it).

105   *MEW*, 19, p. 21; *MECW*, 24, p. 87.

one means, but it has a devastating effect: the most complete publicity'.[106] A duty to ensure to the members of an organisation the greatest possible access to its workings is a duty that rests on the value of members' education in its processes, and on the value of their scrutiny. It is also a duty that (like the duty to ensure public access to court proceedings) gives no particular individual an unconditional advantage.[107]

If there are duties to the whole, then, contrary to Rawls, people can 'suffer from a greater liberty'.[108] To say that people cannot suffer from a greater liberty is to imply that there can be no reason not to treat liberty as a good that may be 'restricted only for the sake of liberty itself'.[109] It suggests that there is no reason not to ensure that, for any x it is possible for each individual to have the right to do, everyone ought to have a right to x, subject only to the proviso that the package of rights each individual enjoys securely is to be the best overall. If there are duties to the whole, however, it *is* possible for people to suffer from a greater liberty. People will suffer from a lack of community if secure liberty is the sole component of any package that is to be the best overall. If there are duties to the whole, liberty is limited by something other than liberty.

Suppose it were granted that it is possible for commodity form philosophy, unlike economic thought, to appeal to duties to the whole; that Marx appeals to duties to the whole; and that duties to the whole sustain a critique of contemporary liberal political philosophy. Some might *still* object that a *Marxist* project is *required* to acknowledge the impotence of normative appeals; that it is *bound* to study the forces developing within social reality, and not to propose ideals. The former formulation is suggested by Allen Wood's claim that Marx thought that all normative standards 'at odds with prevailing relations' were 'socially impotent'.[110] The latter captures Cohen's lament of Marx's '*obstetric* conception of political practice'.[111] An obstetric conception of political practice assumes that, on the occasion of dysfunctionality in a social form, the latter will have itself developed the means for its replacement, just as midwives 'deliver the form that develops *within* reality'.[112] Cohen infers that Marxism must present itself as 'the consciousness of a struggle within the world, rather

---

106   No author 1873, pp. 3–4; *MECW*, 23, pp. 458–9.
107   See also Marx's use of the term '*boni patres familias*' in *Capital* Volume III (*MEW*, 25, p. 784; *MECW*, 37, p. 763; Marx 1981, p. 911).
108   Rawls 1971, p. 143.
109   Rawls 1971, p. 244.
110   Wood 2004, p. 134.
111   Cohen 2001, p. 43.
112   Cohen 2001, p. 50.

than as a set of ideals proposed to the world'.[113] Thus, both Wood and Cohen
could accept Elster's gloss on Marx's remark in *The Civil War in France* that
'workers "have no ideals to realize"'.[114] For Elster, this remark suggests that, for
Marx, 'the class struggle is in no way moved by normative considerations'.[115]

Yet Marx's remark reads: 'they [the working-class – JF] have no ideals to realize, but to set free elements of the new society with which old collapsing bourgeois society itself is pregnant'.[116] This remark does *not* say that the working-
class has no ideals to realise. It says that the working-class can have *but one kind*
of ideal to realise. To use this remark as evidence that a Marxist project must
hold that workers have no ideals to realise, it would first be necessary to deny
that any principles tentatively exhibited in or suggested by the struggle that
workers must already have waged for bourgeois society to be faced with col-
lapse belong to the elements that workers may seek to set free. In other words,
it would first be necessary to deny that a Marxist project could here employ the
lesson that Marx reports having learnt from reading Hegel in 1837: look for 'the
idea in reality itself'.[117]

Capitalism may develop the means for its replacement in part because principles for organising a new society are exhibited in or suggested by struggles
prompted by its dysfunctionality. In that case, an obstetric conception of political practice can affirm normative principles. But if an obstetric conception
of political practice can affirm normative principles, principles that condemn
prevailing relations need not be impotent. Normative principles are impotent
if they are too demanding, or if they require but lack the backing of a form
of sanction. But normative principles exhibited in or suggested by organised
struggles need be neither.

Marx defines the goal of revolution, 'communist society', by 'the necessary
solidarity of the free development of all';[118] *and* Marx claims that 'solidarity' is
a 'fundamental principle of the International ... The revolution must display
solidarity'.[119] This combination of thoughts – solidarity is displayed in, and a
goal of, socialist revolution – is prima facie evidence for taking Marx's project
to combine the study of social reality with normative argument. It implies that
the obstetricism objection proves too little (obstetricism is compatible with

---

113   Cohen 2001, p. 102; see also p. 77.
114   Elster 1983, p. 289.
115   Ibid.
116   *MECW*, 22, p. 335.
117   *MEW*, 40, p. 8; *MECW*, 1, p. 18.
118   *MEW*, 3, p. 424; *MECW*, 5, p. 439.
119   *MECW*, 23, p. 256.

normative commitment), while the impotence objection proves too much (if organised struggles cannot adopt principles to any degree, there is no hope for a communist society). The ambition of combining the two types of argument need not compromise the Marxist pedigree of commodity form philosophy. All it must take care to do is limit the applicability of duties to the whole in capitalism so that such duties do not make it easier for a group to defeat a goal to which it is committed, having justified such limits on the grounds that that group may not complain.

5   The Commodity, Dialectical Contradiction and Real Abstraction

One use of the argumentative figure of dialectical contradiction essential to commodity form philosophy is to describe the commodity. Marx emphasises that the commodity is a dialectical contradiction in the First Edition of *Capital*, at the end of Chapter One:

> The commodity is an *immediate unity of use-value and exchange-value*, hence of two opposites. It is therefore an immediate *contradiction*. This contradiction must develop as soon as it is no longer observed analytically, as it has been up until now, at one time from the point of view of use-value, and at another from the point of view of exchange-value, but as a whole, actually related to other commodities. The *actual* relation of commodities to one another is their *exchange process*.[120]

As argued above, use-value and (exchange-)value are 'opposites' in respect of possession. Use-value *abstracts* from possession; it is conceived in abstraction both from the assertion of possession over it, and from any want to acquire possession. (Exchange-)value, on the other hand, *presupposes* possession in both respects. If A is to be able to offer (or offers) a commodity in exchange, A must be able to act (or acts) as if the only condition on another's receipt of it is whether A agrees to exchange it. A thereby asserts an exclusive claim to it. Moreover, A offers a commodity in exchange to acquire possession of a different commodity.

In virtue of generalised production for exchange, use-value and (exchange-)value also contain a characteristic of their opposite. Use-values produced as

---

120   *MEGA*, II, 5, p. 51; Marx 1967, p. 40; compare *MEW*, 23, p. 118; *MECW*, 35, p. 113; Marx 1976, p. 198.

commodities will tend to be consumed in forms that satisfy the want of a subject to know that a use-value is theirs, or that it would be worth a lot to them if they were to exchange it (that a house, stamps, paintings, etc., are a 'good investment'). (Exchange-)value, on the other hand, will have to assume a materiality suited to its realisation in the act of exchange. A commodity is a dialectical 'contradiction', because use-value is the opposite of (exchange-)value (in respect of possession); yet use-value takes on a character of exchange-value (a form that satisfies the want of a possessor) and exchange-value takes on a character of use-value (a materiality compatible with its realisation in exchange). As Lukács puts it: 'use-value and exchange-value are in dialectical interaction'.[121]

A further dialectical contradiction in commodity exchange is emphasised by Adorno:

> Dialectic is a self-movement in oppositions; it is unthinkable without the moment of reflection, that is, without the moment in which a thing becomes its own otherness by virtue of its consciousness of itself. Since it can only reflect itself in its otherness in consciousness, one cannot take the moment of subjectivity or reflection away from dialectic ... He [Marx – JF] traces everything back to the exchange process, or rather to the shape of abstraction lying in the exchange process itself; for in exchange, what is qualitatively distinct is reduced to a common denominator, to the equivalent form, as Marx calls it ... Through this implicit moment of reflection in the exchange process, the assumption of a dialectic makes good sense, which it immediately loses if it becomes a metaphysical principle hypostatised as an absolute.[122]

Suppose A wants to acquire some amount of commodity x. To that end, A cannot offer to part with that same type of commodity in return. If A were to part with x in return for x, A could only anticipate the result of the exchange to be an acquisition of x if A were to offer a lesser amount of x than A stood to receive. But if A were to offer a lesser for a greater amount of x, A's exchange partner, B, could not acquire whatever they want to acquire. A possessor of x cannot want to acquire in exchange a lesser amount of x than they already have. If B wanted to possess a lesser amount of x than they already had, B would just dispose of some amount of x. A commodity exchange, in which two possessors

---

121　　Lukács 1996, p. 48; Lukács 2000, p. 99.
122　　Adorno 1974, p. 215.

acquire whatever they want to acquire, is thus an exchange of some amount of two qualitatively different types of commodity, x and y.

In commodity exchange, a possessor treats the commodity they offer in exchange as a value, by treating it as just a means to acquire whatever they want to acquire. Their treating it as just a means to acquire whatever they want to acquire presupposes that they offer it in a context of generalised exchange, in which they *can* acquire whatever they want to acquire. But then, by relating to their possession in the context of generalised exchange as a means to acquire whatever they want to acquire, each possessor is led to regard their prospective acquisition as a means for its possessor to acquire whatever that possessor wants to acquire. For in the context of generalised exchange, the other possessor must be assumed to have chosen to engage in this particular exchange. They must be assumed to engage in this particular exchange because this is an exchange in which they acquire whatever they want to acquire. What they offer, they, too, offer in order to acquire whatever they want to acquire. So, they, too, treat their possession as a value. Insofar as each commodity exchanger regards both their own possession, and that of the other, as just a means for its respective possessor to acquire whatever they want to acquire, the attitude of each, in respect of both commodities' power of general exchangeability, is consonant with the thought: x and y are the same type of thing.[123]

In short: commodity exchange presupposes that the commodities exchanged are qualitatively different types of use-value; but it also ensures that, in virtue of their qualitative difference, the commodities exchanged are regarded by their exchangers as qualitatively homogeneous in respect of their power of general exchangeability.

More can be said, however, about what Adorno terms 'the shape of abstraction lying in the exchange process itself'.[124] As Adorno notes, 'abstraction' need not only denote the disregard of known sensible qualities, as with commodity exchangers' disregard of the known qualitative differences between their respective commodities in regarding them as values. Abstraction may also denote isolation from qualities that are yet to be known:

> [T]he concept of the abstract in Hegel sometimes means just the opposite
> of what it means in everyday language, namely, that which is isolated, i.e.
> that which is not yet so reflected in itself that, in virtue of this reflection

---

123   *MEW*, 23, p. 64; *MECW*, 35, p. 60; Marx 1976, p. 141.
124   Adorno 1974, p. 215.

in itself, in virtue of this unfolding of its inherent contradiction, it knows itself in its relation to the whole.[125]

Commodity exchange is also characterised by an abstraction in this second sense. Commodity exchangers treat one another in exchange as if the other is just the future possessor of what they part with. *A* treats *B* as if *B* were just the future possessor of what *A* parts with; and the same goes for *B*. For either to treat the other as anything more than that, conditions would have to be attached to the future use of what the other stood to receive. Yet that would undermine the acquisitive purpose of the exchange. The commodity parted with would no longer be a means to acquire whatever its possessor wanted to acquire, but only a means to acquire what could be acquired from someone willing to accept those conditions. In reflection on the result of their exchange, however, each commodity exchanger knows that it is not in fact the case that the other is just a possessor of what they have parted with. Each knows that the other has acquired a particular type of possession that can only be used in a further action or transaction, and hence that the other has a further end to pursue beyond the exchange that they conclude with them.

This second abstraction has the structure of what is here called a real abstraction.[126] An interaction exhibits a real abstraction if and because it *requires* at least one actor to treat or be treated by another as if *x* is the case; and yet, *by virtue of that very interaction*, it belongs to that actor's stock of experiences that *x* is not the case. In regard to this interactional conception of real abstraction, it would be correct to say, as Ritsert claims, that

> what is *real* about these processes of abstraction seems to be that they are performed by the actors themselves, in the course of their actual acts of exchange (consciously or unconsciously); they are not first construed from the perspective of an observer.[127]

As Ritsert says, an abstraction is real, if and because it is exhibited by the *action* of a participant in an interaction. But a participant's perspective is not only

---

125   Adorno 2010, p. 160.
126   The term 'real abstraction' originates with Georg Simmel (Simmel 2001, p. 32; Simmel 2004, p. 80; see also Sohn-Rethel 1971, p. 95; Sohn-Rethel 1989, p. 12; Sohn-Rethel 1978, p. 20). The interactional conception of real abstraction adopted here has little in common with those of Simmel or Sohn-Rethel, however. It attempts to take Adorno's aforecited remark on abstraction in the direction of the structure of dialectical contradiction outlined in ch. 2, sec. 2. On 'real abstraction', see Ritsert 1998; and Backhaus 2006.
127   Ritsert 1998, p. 335.

what makes a real abstraction real. It is also what makes it an abstraction. The action must abstract from something that a participant can become aware of, in virtue of the interaction to which it belongs. The concept of real abstraction is underspecified, therefore, in the statement: 'abstractions are real in that they are not merely mental generalisations, concepts, but are continually produced through social practices',[128] for this begs the question: *for whom* is a real abstraction an abstraction?

On this interactional conception of real abstraction, an absence of real abstractions in any system of interactions with a strong self-reinforcing dynamic is a condition for freedom. For otherwise, what actors can learn from their interactions may lead them to a judgement that remedial action is required that cannot be incorporated within that system. In *History and Class Consciousness*, Lukács suggests that the 'problem of dialectic' is 'solved' if a subject can 'move in a self-created world, whose conscious shape it is; whilst, at the same time, the validity of the world confronts it in its full objectivity'.[129] This statement implies that the capacity to respond to overcome real abstractions is a condition for freedom. If the system of capitalist production generates real abstractions, it falls short in this respect.

6   Antinomies of the Commodity Form

Even if there were no such thing as dialectical thinking, as Cohen suggests,[130] it would still not follow that Marxism has no valuable commitments that extend beyond what Hegel's *Encyclopaedia Logic* calls '[t]hinking as understanding [which] stops short at the fixed determinacy and its distinctness vis-à-vis other determinacies'.[131] Commodity form philosophy also makes use of the argumentative figure of antinomy.

The first author to insist on the connection between Marx's analysis of the commodity form and the argumentative figure of antinomy was Lukács. In *History and Class Consciousness*, Lukács claims that 'the thing-in-itself antinomies' of Kant's philosophy are but 'the greatest and most profound intellectual expression of those antinomies that underlie the being of bourgeois society [*dem Sein der bürgerlichen Gesellschaft*]'.[132] For Kant, antinomies define

---

128   Read 2003, p. 134.
129   Lukács 1977, p. 324; Lukács 1968, p. 142.
130   Cohen 2000, p. xvii, p. xxiv.
131   Hegel 1986c, § 80; Hegel 1991b, § 80.
132   Lukács 1977, pp. 330–1; Lukács 1968, pp. 147–8. The Lukács 1968 translation detracts from

human reason. Yet here Lukács insists that antinomies define the capitalist social world; and that its antinomies shine a critical perspective on Kant's philosophy. At issue, here, is merely the former claim.

In this book, 'antinomy' denotes an oscillation of thought or will between two incompatible assertions that leave no middle ground and appear to be valid, each of which rests on the same premise(s), at least one of which is false.[133] This conception of antinomy has two features: (a) two incompatible assertions that leave no middle ground; (b) the appearance of validity resting on the same premise(s), one or more of which is false. An antinomy is an antinomy of the commodity form if (c) the commodity form explains the acceptance of the premises. These features are now elaborated and defended.

(a)   *Two Incompatible Assertions That Leave No Middle Ground*
Two assertions are incompatible if they are contradictory opposites, or if they imply a contradictory opposition. A contradictory opposition describes the relation between the statements '*s* is *P*', and '*s* is not *P*'. The statements 'the rose is red' and 'the rose is not red' are contradictory opposites. The statements 'the rose is red' and 'the rose is entirely yellow' imply a contradictory opposition. For the latter statement, 'the rose is entirely yellow', implies 'the rose is not red', which is the contradictory opposite of 'the rose is red'. On the view taken here, an antinomy does not require an affirmation in the thesis, and its contradictory negation in the antithesis, as some Kant scholars have insisted.[134]

---

the provocation in Lukács's claim, by omitting to render '*dem Sein*'. On the translation of '*bürgerliche Gesellschaft*', see ch. 11.

133   In *Kant's* writings, an 'antinomy' can denote an oscillation of thought between: (1) a thesis and an antithesis that both seem true, although they are contradictory, and are both shown to be false (Kant 1999, A 426/B 454–A 443/B 471); or (2) a thesis and an antithesis that are both true, but apparently contradictory, and the contradiction is dissolved by distinguishing two distinct and non-contradictory points of view on the matter (Kant 1999, A 444/B 472–A 461/B 489; Kant 1987, 5: 338–9; Kant 1991, 6: 254–5, 417–18); or (3) a thesis and an antithesis that both seem false, although one must be true, and one is shown to be false only conditionally (Kant 1997, 5: 113–14). Commodity form philosophy identifies antinomies of type (1), which it explains by the commodity form, although thesis and antithesis need not be contradictory opposites. As argued below, thesis and antithesis must simply imply a logical contradiction and leave no middle ground.

134   For examples, see Wike 1982, pp. 2–3. As Victoria Wike notes, neither the fourth antinomy in Kant's *Critique of Pure Reason* (Wike 1982, p. 56) nor the antinomy of practical reason (Wike 1982, p. 17) have a thesis and antithesis that are contradictory opposites. However, the fourth antinomy is an antinomy of type (2), and the antinomy of practical reason is an antinomy of type (3). To relax the requirement for thesis and antithesis to be contradictory opposites for an antinomy of type (1), as here proposed, is a departure from Kant.

The requirement for two assertions to imply a contradictory opposition is shown up by a problem that arises for a conception of antinomy that lacks it. This problem is that, if no contradictory opposition is implied between thesis and antithesis, neither the false common premise, nor the thesis and antithesis, will have the appearance of validity that an antinomy also requires.

The problem is illustrated by Kojin Karatani's interpretation of *Capital*. According to Karatani, 'in the manner of Kant, Marx points out an antinomy'.[135] More specifically, *Capital* is said to identify an 'antinomy, which exposes the fact that both thesis and antithesis are nothing more than "optical delusions"'.[136] The evidence that Karatani presents for this claim is inadequate, however. Karatani claims that Marx identifies an antinomy of this type when 'he says, on the one hand, that surplus value (for industrial capital) cannot be attained in the process of production *in itself*, and, on the other hand, that it cannot be attained in the process of circulation *in itself*'.[137] The propositions Karatani reports here are not contradictory opposites; nor do they imply a contradictory opposition. So, as yet, there is no warrant to refer to them as a 'thesis' and an 'antithesis'.

The only way to take two propositions that do not imply a contradictory opposition to rest on a common false premise is to trace their assertion to the acceptance of a seemingly indubitable disjunctive premise, and to argue that that premise is false. In this case, the premise would have to be: surplus value must be attained *either* in production in itself *or* in circulation in itself. But *no* premise of the form 'either solely in x or solely in y', for any x and y which can be conceived as parts of a whole, can have an indubitable appearance. No premise can seem indubitable if it suggests possible options that it excludes; and any premise of this form suggests and excludes a third possibility that *combines x and y*. The disjunctive premise in this case cannot seem indubitable because its disjunction suggests and excludes the possibility that surplus value may be attained in the total process of production and circulation. More generally: as a premise will not seem indubitable if it is a disjunctive premise whose disjunctions are not contradictory opposites, any conception of an antinomy that does not require two assertions to imply a contradictory opposition will not satisfy (b) either.

---

135   Karatani 2002, p. 10.

136   Karatani 2002, p. 3.

137   Karatani 2002, p. 11; compare *MEW*, 23, p. 180; *MECW*, 35, p. 176; Marx 1976, p. 268. Arguably, what Marx takes his argument to show is that surplus value cannot arise in circulation, and yet must arise in circulation; but the correct interpretation is not at issue here.

While it is necessary for two assertions to imply a contradictory opposition, it is not sufficient. It is also necessary that they leave no middle ground. In other words, the notion of an '*antinomy* between two "poles"'[138] or extremes is in principle denied.

There can be no middle ground between two theses that are contradictory opposites. There is no middle ground between 'the world has a beginning' and 'the world has no beginning'. So, the requirement for no middle ground is satisfied by any antinomy whose thesis and antithesis are contradictory opposites. But to say that two assertions must leave no middle ground between them *is* to impose a further condition, if all that is required thus far is that thesis and antithesis must imply a contradictory opposition. A contradictory opposition is implied by the claims: 'utility ought to be maximised' and 'utility ought to be minimised'. If utility ought to be minimised, then utility ought not to be maximised. But there is some middle ground between these two extremes. It is possible to assert that a satisfactory level of utility (somewhere between maximum and minimum) ought to be sought. To require two incompatible assertions that leave no middle ground is a less strict view of the relation between the two theses of an antinomy than the view that requires them to be contradictory opposites. But even this less strict view excludes two claims that are opposite extremes from forming the thesis and antithesis of an antinomy.

On the present view, the thesis and antithesis of an antinomy could be provided by the claims: 'the pursuit of maximum utility ought not to be limited' and 'the pursuit of maximum utility ought to be limited'. But this is a case with which those who take the view that the thesis and antithesis of an antinomy must be contradictory opposites would be satisfied. To illustrate the difference between this view, and the view defended here, what is needed is an example of two incompatible assertions that leave no middle ground, but which are not contradictory opposites.

Marx offers an example in *Capital* when he refers to an 'antinomy' of 'right against right'.[139] No middle ground is left between two rights that are rights to states of affairs that are contradictory opposites. There is no middle ground between a right to the presence of something (a right to a limit on the working day) and a right to its absence (a right to no limit on the working day). But although these rights leave no middle ground, they are nonetheless not contradictory opposites. The contradictory opposite of one right is the absence of

---

138   Bidet 2008, p. 601.
139   *MEW*, 23, p. 249; *MECW*, 35, p. 243; Marx 1976, p. 344.

that right, not the presence of another antagonistic right. The thesis and anti-thesis of an antinomy need not be contradictory opposites, if they may consist in the assertion of rights to states of affairs that are contradictory opposites. As we shall see, this point is essential to the genius of *Capital's* antinomy pas-sage.

The requirement for two incompatible theses that leave no middle ground is less strict than the requirement for two theses that are contradictory opposites. From an interpretive perspective, the laxer view is not only unobjectionable but mandatory, just to affirm that what *Capital* identifies as an antinomy is indeed an antinomy. If Marx were of the stricter view, he would not describe this conflict of 'right against right' as an 'antinomy'. He would either seek to demonstrate an antinomy of 'right against no right', or else not invoke the argumentative figure of antinomy. The laxer view raises no problem from a substantive perspective, either. It is sufficient to ensure that an antinomy can betray a common false premise. Whether two theses are contradictory oppos-ites, or imply a contradictory opposition and leave no middle ground, either way, the awareness that a common premise licences them both must call that common premise into question.

The reason why two incompatible assertions may not leave any middle ground is that a lack of middle ground is a condition for an oscillation of thought or will between them. For there to be an oscillation of thought or will between two positions, it cannot appear to be the case that there is a third option different from them both. But for any two positions that leave some middle ground, a third option will appear available. No two positions that leave some middle ground can share a premise with an appearance of validity on which they exhaust the possible outcomes. The disjunctive premise 'either maximise x or minimise x' cannot seem indubitable, because it suggests and excludes the possibility of neither maximising nor minimising x. Like two assertions that do not imply a contradictory opposition, two assertions that leave some middle ground will not satisfy (b) either.

(b)   *The Appearance of Validity Resting on the Same Premise(s), at Least*
        One of Which Is False

Two incompatible assertions both have an appearance of validity if, on accept-ance of a seemingly indubitable premise or premises, an equally good proof can be offered for each. In each case, it must be possible to state the proof in the form of an argument that thematises and reasons from a premise in the proof of the other assertion. (Hence the argumentative figure of antinomy extends beyond what Hegel called '[t]hinking as understanding [which] stops short at the fixed determinacy and its distinctness vis-à-vis other determinacies').[140] It is not necessary, however, for the proofs to be convertible into the form of *modus tollens* proofs (if *p* then *q*; not-*q*; therefore not-*p*). To present both proofs in the form of *modus tollens* proofs, the thesis and the antithesis must be contradictory opposites. But, according to the argument for (a), an antinomy does not require a thesis and antithesis that are contradictory opposites. If an antinomy merely requires two incompatible theses that leave no middle ground, the proofs may not be convertible into the form of *modus tollens* proofs.

An equally good proof can be offered for two incompatible assertions if both proofs rest on the same premises. Yet, if two incompatible assertions can both be proven from the same premises, at least one of those premises must be false. If both assertions enjoy the appearance of validity, however, this common false premise cannot be a purely subjective error. It must be the result of an illusion, which remains even after a correct diagnosis.

The requirement for two incompatible assertions to enjoy an appearance of validity distinguishes an antinomy from a tension between values. There is a tension between the values x and y if x and y are equally desirable; some amount of each is indispensable; the more the one is realised, the less the other can be realised; and the maximum realisation of the one excludes any realisation of the other.[141] A tension between values will generate some cases where only one value, x or y, can be upheld, although either way, the result is equally desirable. But a tension between values stops short of an antinomy. If, in a given case of tension between values, the value of upholding x is worth +2 in respect of x but -2 in respect of excluding y; while the value of upholding y is worth +2 in respect of y but -2 in respect of excluding x; then the overall scores for both options is 0. But the fact that both options score equally does not mean that the arguments for each option reason to their conclusion from a premise in the other side's argument, or that any premise of either argument is false, or that any premise is accepted on account of an illusion.

Where there is a tension between values, some balance of both values is presumably to be affirmed. A tension between values therefore sets no radical learning process in train. By contrast, an antinomy is resolved by revealing a seemingly indubitable common premise to be false, so that both thesis and antithesis must be rejected. As a result, actors will be led to question thoughts or actions that rest on this premise, and/or to question the state of affairs that makes it seem indubitable. This has potentially radical consequences, if the common false premise is a widespread assumption that actors in a specific form

---

140   Hegel 1986c, § 80; Hegel 1991b, § 80.
141   This is how '*antinomy*' is conceived at Hidalgo 2014, p. 73; see, similarly, Martin 2011.

of society are led to make in a causally weighty context, and/or on account of
its fundamental features.

(c)   *The Commodity Form Explains the Acceptance of the Premises*
Kant's *Critique of Pure Reason* examines the theoretical antinomy of reason
in the section entitled 'Transcendental Dialectic'. The theoretical antinomy
of reason is a product of what Kant calls '*transcendental illusion* [Schein]'.[142]
According to Kant, transcendental illusion is that which leads us into the mistake of applying concepts to experience that do not apply to possible experience. The theoretical antinomy of reason arises because reason introduces the
thought of the unconditioned into the thought of the totality of the series of
conditions that make experience possible.[143] We either hold one object of possible experience to be unconditioned, or else we hold that the entire series of
objects of possible experience is unconditioned. The theoretical antinomy of
reason is exposed by demonstrating that both views share a 'groundless presupposition'.[144] The groundless presupposition is the assumption that the unconditioned can be given in experience at all.

Antinomies of the commodity form rest on illusion-generating social conditions. In *Capital* Volume I, Marx writes that commodity exchange generates
the 'objective semblance [*gegenständlichen Schein*]'[145] that products produced
for exchange have value by nature. The power of general exchangeability is a
power that products produced for exchange only have in virtue of the social
relations of generalised production for exchange. But they appear to possess
this power independently of these social relations: 'commodities' appear as one
of the 'natural forms of social life'.[146] As a product's power of general exchangeability is only realised in exchange, it can only be expressed in terms of what it
can acquire in exchange, another commodity. This form of expression suggests
that a product produced for exchange owes its power of general exchangeability to the same cause as that to which the other commodity, in which this power
is expressed, owes all its other properties. It suggests that the power of general
exchangeability is inherent to products as such. If generalised production for
exchange is an essential aspect of the capitalist form of wealth, then the belief
that products produced for exchange have value by nature is a characteristic
illusion of capitalism.

---

142   Kant 1999, A 295/B 352. Compare Marx's use of '*Schein*' in the next paragraph.
143   Kant 1999, A 416/B 444.
144   Kant 1999, A 485/B 513.
145   *MEW*, 23, p. 88, 97; *MECW*, 35, p. 85, 93; Marx 1976, p. 167, 176.
146   *MEW*, 23, pp. 89–90; *MECW*, 35, p. 86; Marx 1976, p. 168.

The illusion that products produced for exchange have value by nature generates a further, antinomy-producing illusion by virtue of the connection between value, possession and self-ownership.[147] To offer a product in exchange is a mode of possession. If, therefore, commodity exchange generates the illusion that products produced for exchange have value by nature, this must impact on how possession is viewed. To assume that products produced for exchange have value by nature is to assume that the possessing subject is a natural human subjectivity. As the will of a possessor is to act in regard to an object independently of anyone else's instruction or permission, the will of a possessor presupposes the will of a person, that is, a will to act in regard to one's parts and capacities independently of anyone else's instruction or permission. The subjectivity of personhood is articulated in law as the subjectivity of self-ownership. So, to assume that products produced for exchange have value by nature is to assume that there is a natural connection between law and self-ownership.

If the social origin of the possessing subject is not apparent, self-ownership must be thought of as a subjectivity of law that is without condition. The ambiguity in the thought of self-ownership as a subjectivity of law that is without condition can then generate antinomies. There is an ambiguity as to whether self-ownership is to be upheld as a subjectivity that is exercised in a given action, or as a subjectivity that is exercised in a series of actions. This helps to generate the rights-antinomy in capitalist production. There is also an ambiguity between self-ownership as the recipient of legal protection, and as the author of the law. This gives rise to an antinomy between natural rights and popular authorisation.

Three features of the use of the argumentative figure of antinomy by commodity form philosophy may be highlighted. First, as regards origin, both the thesis and antithesis of an antinomy of the commodity form share a common false premise concerning a type of subjectivity generated by the commodity form. Second, in regard to proof, the proof is to be intelligible from the point of view of actors' own stock of experiences. (All uses of the term 'antinomy' unaccompanied by a clear statement of a thesis and an antithesis, together with both proofs, are formally incomplete). Third, in terms of resolution, any resolution must be discoverable by a type of actor who asserts the thesis or antithesis of an antinomy of the commodity form. A resolution is found not by introducing a premise from a philosophical system, but solely from the resources provided by how actors are led to act as a result of their initial acceptance of the false premise of the antinomy.

---

147   For further elaboration of this connection, see ch. 7, sec. 3, and ch. 9, sec. 5.

CHAPTER 4

Action

Marx offers no explicit philosophy of action, and only a few asides on social relations. But something may be said about action to reconstruct Marx's concept of a social relation. It is possible to connect what Marx implies about action to one of Marx's asides on social relations by drawing on Alfred Schütz's *Phenomenology of the Social World* (1932) (*Der sinnhafte Aufbau der sozialen Welt*). This connection can then serve as a starting-point, in chapter 5, for reconstructing Marx's concept of a social relation.

In what is perhaps Marx's most interesting aside on social relations, from his *Economic Manuscripts of 1861–63*, Marx remarks: 'social relations only exist among human beings insofar as they think, and possess this capacity for abstraction from sensible [*sinnlich*] singularity and contingency'.[1] What *Capital* implies about action offers a way to defend this aside. For according to what *Capital* implies, action exercises a capacity for abstraction from sensible singularity and contingency. If action exercises the capacity for abstract thinking that human beings must possess and use for social relations to exist, a social relation can consist of actions.

Section 1 examines *Capital*'s description of human labour for what it implies about action in general. Section 2 introduces Schütz's distinction between an 'in-order-to motive' and a 'because motive'.[2] Section 3 argues that only in-order-to motives can orient behaviour, and section 4 notes their future perfect form. Finally, section 5 argues that it is in virtue of an in-order-to motive's future perfect form that action exhibits 'abstraction from sensible singularity and contingency'.[3]

1   *Capital*'s Description of Human Labour

Capital Volume I offers a description of human labour that, according to Marx, applies 'independently of every determinate social form'.[4] To describe human

---

1 *MEW*, 43, p. 226; *MECW*, 30, p. 232. *MECW* translates '*sinnlich*' as 'sensuous', which in some contexts would be apt, but '*sinnlich*' here means 'perceptible through the senses', in other words, sensible.

2 Schütz 2004, pp. 111–12, pp. 195–209; Schütz 1967, pp. 28–9, pp. 86–96.

3 *MEW*, 43, p. 226; *MECW*, 30, p. 232.

4 *MEW*, 23, p. 192; *MECW*, 35, p. 187; Marx 1976, p. 283.

© KONINKLIJKE BRILL NV, LEIDEN, 2019 | DOI:10.1163/9789004384804_005

labour independently of every determinate social form is to describe those transhistorical features of human labour that remain constant regardless of changes in social form (such as the replacement of pre-capitalism by capitalism, or capitalism by socialism). *Capital* states:

> Here we take labour in the form in which it is the sole preserve of human beings. A spider performs operations that resemble those of a weaver, and a bee puts many a human architect to shame with its construction of cells of wax. But what distinguishes from the outset the worst architect from the best bee is that the architect has built the cells in their mind [*die Zelle in seinem Kopf gebaut hat*] before they build them in wax. The end of the labour process bears a result that was already present ideally, in the worker's imagination, at the beginning. They do not simply transform nature; they realise their purpose in it – a purpose they know, determining, in law-like fashion, the mode of their activity, and to which they must subordinate their will.[5]

Statements that contrast facts about human beings with facts about animals provide one way for a theorist, such as Marx, whose writings largely concern historically specific types of society, to express and signal claims about transhistorical features of human life. An inter-species contrast indicates that the claim concerns human history in general. It marks the claim off from claims about specific periods of history only. But the contrastive statement need not be true in order for the part of the claim that concerns human beings to successfully identify a transhistorical feature of human life. If another species of animal were discovered to behave in such a way as to undermine Marx's contrast, the features in the contrast could not provide *differentia specifica* of human life.[6] The part of the contrastive statement that concerns human beings may still identify a transhistorical feature of human life, however. Nor is the existence or non-existence of a species of animal undermining any such contrast a reliable measure of the importance, to human life, of the transhistorical feature that the contrast identifies. At issue here is not whether Marx is right about animals, but whether what he says about human life, including what he says about human life through a (true or false) contrast with animals, identifies one or more transhistorical features of human life. In this respect, there are three points to note.

---

5   *MEW*, 23, p. 193; *MECW*, 35, p. 188; Marx 1976, pp. 283–4.
6   Leopold 2007, pp. 225–6.

One idea that Marx expresses here is that human labour is purposeful.[7] Humans do not simply effect a change in nature. They transform it in accordance with a 'purpose' or goal that they must regard as their own. They conceive themselves as bringing about the future state of affairs they realise.

A second point concerns the moment in time from which this goal is apparent. A producer anticipates the 'result' of their work 'at the beginning', prior to any given phase of their course of action. It is an antecedent goal. During any given phase in the course of an action, a producer can experience their action as fulfilling or missing its aim, by comparing its actual course with what they recall of their goal.

Third, a producer's antecedent goal has a future perfect form. *Capital* uses a perfective verb form, 'has built [*gebaut hat*]', in its example. The architect's course of action is oriented to realising an antecedently projected state of affairs in which they will have built a construction, as distinct from an antecedently projected state of affairs in which they are building it. Work is oriented to an antecedent vision of a future state of affairs in which an anticipated outcome is pictured as having already been achieved. Orientation to a goal requires the goal to be delimited, and delimitation is only provided by the thought of an end-state in which a course of action has already 'ideally' culminated.

The third point is lost to readers of English translations of *Capital*. It is only communicated by virtue of Marx's verb form, and both the first English translation of *Capital* by Samuel Moore and Edward Aveling as well as the later translation by Ben Fowkes replace Marx's perfective verb form with an imperfective verb form. The Aveling/Moore translation reads: 'the architect raises his structure in imagination before he erects it in reality'.[8] The Fowkes translation makes the same mistake with a different verb: 'the architect builds the cells in his mind before he constructs it in wax'.[9] The verb form 'builds', like 'raises',

---

7   A reader of Marx's *Grundrisse* in translation encounters the claim: 'the science which compels the inanimate limbs of the machinery, by their construction, to act purposefully, as an automaton, does not exist in the worker's consciousness but rather acts upon him' (Marx 1973a, p. 693). Use of the word 'purposefully' in this context (which also appears in the MECW translation at MECW, 29, p. 83) could be taken to suggest, contrary to what was just said, that a producer need not have a purpose, or that purposeful acts are not confined to living beings. The translation is incorrect, however. The word Marx uses is '*zweckgemäß*' (MEW, 42, p. 593), which means: in accordance with a purpose/in a manner fit for purpose. It does not mean 'purposefully' (which would be: '*zielgerichtet*'). To be sure, a producer need not understand the science they apply. But the same goes for a mobile phone user, and no one denies that a mobile phone user has a purpose. Translated aright, the claim is not evidence of an '"anthropological schema" ... completely shattered' (Read 2003, p. 119).

8   MECW, 35, p. 188.

9   Marx 1976, p. 284.

is imperfective,[10] whereas the verb form in the German editions of *Capital*, and in the French translation that Marx oversaw (*'a construit'*),[11] is perfective.

The English translations do not just differ from the German and French editions of *Capital*. If what Marx writes in German and French is true, what the English translations state in his name is false. Work cannot be oriented to the antecedent vision of an ongoing occurrence, because orientation requires delimitation, and the thought of an ongoing occurrence lacks delimitation. Schütz's philosophy of action illuminates the importance of this point.

2   In-Order-To Motives and Because Motives

In an influential work in the philosophy of action, G.E. Anscombe proposes that we 'defin[e] intentional action in terms of language – the special question "Why?" '[12] Intentional action, in Anscombe's view, is behaviour 'to which a certain sense of the question "Why?" is given application; the sense is of course that in which the answer, if positive, gives a reason for acting'.[13] Schütz's phenomenological approach to the philosophy of action reveals a problem with this view. The question 'why?' can be answered so as to give a reason for acting by reporting one of two different types of motive, an 'in-order-to motive' or a 'because motive', only one of which can orient behaviour.[14]

The in-order-to motive of an action is the future state of affairs that the actor expects their action to bring about. To discover an action's in-order-to motive, one asks: of all the various future events expected by the actor, which of them does the actor think their action will bring about? The in-order-to motive of, say, leaving the house, may be to go and see a friend.

The because motive of an action, by contrast, is the pre-existing state of affairs that prompts the action. The because motive of an action is discovered by asking: of all an actor's various experiences, which of them does the actor see as bringing about their action? The because motive of leaving the house to go and see a friend could be a feeling of loneliness.

H.L.A. Hart roughly restates Schütz's distinction between in-order-to motives and because motives when he distinguishes 'reason' in the sense of 'con-

---

10   'Builds/raises' could translate *'baut'*, but not *'gebaut hat'*.
11   *MEGA*, II, 7, p. 146.
12   Anscombe 1976, p. 86; compare p. 84.
13   Anscombe 1976, p. 9.
14   Schütz 2004, pp. 195–209; Schütz 1967, pp. 86–96.

sequence to which the action is a means (my reason for shutting the window was to keep out the cold)' from reason in the sense of 'some circumstance given which the action functions as a means to such a desired consequence (my reason for shutting the window was that I felt cold)'.[15] As Hart's two uses of the word 'reason' show, a why-question can be answered so as to give a reason for acting by reporting either an in-order-to motive or a because motive. Ask a person who is shutting a window 'why?' and one may receive either type of answer: in order to keep out the cold; or, because I feel cold.

Before using this fact to challenge Anscombe's approach, one may note that the distinction between in-order-to motives and because motives does not rest on use of the corresponding phrases ('in order to' or 'because') in answering a why-question. Indeed, the fact that a because phrase can be used to report both in-order-to motives and because motives is one reason that leads in-order-to motives and because motives to be confused with one another.

To simplify, let it be stipulated that any why-question that is answered so as to give a reason for acting may only be answered with phrases beginning 'in order to ...' or 'because ...'. With that stipulation in place, a because motive must be reported with a because phrase. A because phrase connects a given fact to a prior cause, while an in-order-to phrase connects a given fact to a future consequence. In the above case, the question 'why did you leave the house?' can be answered so as to report a because motive by using the phrase: because I was feeling lonely. It could not be answered so as to report a because motive by using the phrase: in order to feel lonely.

A parallel correspondence between motive and phrase does not hold for in-order-to motives, however. A why-question can be answered so as to report an in-order-to motive without using an in-order-to phrase. The question 'why did you leave the house?' can be answered so as to report an in-order-to motive by using either: in order to go and see a friend; or: because I am going to see a friend. In-order-to motives can be reported either with an in-order-to phrase or with a because phrase.

An actor's choice of phrase (in-order-to phrase or because phrase) in reporting their in-order-to motive will depend on their perspective when reporting this motive.[16] In reporting an in-order-to motive, an actor can have one of two things in view: the future state of affairs that the action is to bring about, or (since that future consequence is already ideally present in their plan) their plan to bring that future state of affairs about. Depending on which of these

---

15   Hart 1990, pp. 101–2; compare Anscombe 1976, p. 22.
16   Schütz 2004, p. 200; Schütz 1967, pp. 89–90.

two things the actor has in view, they will either choose an in-order-to phrase or a because phrase. Consider the factors that influence which of these two things an actor has in view.

There are two types of context in which an actor who responds to a why-question by reporting their in-order-to motive can have in view the future state of affairs their action is to bring about. An actor can have this future state of affairs in view if, at the time of their response, their action has yet to bring their in-order-to motive about. The future state of affairs that provides their in-order-to motive then lies in the future, and can be viewed as such in responding to the question. Second, an actor can have this future state of affairs in view after having completed their action, provided the question (or other accompanying circumstance) invites the actor to take some moment in time during the course of the action as their point of reference. Faced with the question 'why did you leave the house?' some circumstance may prompt the actor to picture themselves at the moment they left the house. With that point of reference, the actor can view the seeing of their friend, relative to the point in time at which they left the house, as lying in the future, even if they have already seen their friend.

In each of these two types of context, an actor may report their in-order-to motive with an in-order-to phrase. They are looking at their action from the perspective of the future state of affairs it is to bring about; an in-order-to phrase connects a given fact to a future consequence; therefore, they use an in-order-to phrase to report this motive. An actor who answers the question 'why did you leave the house?' by stating an in-order-to motive, and who has in mind the future state of affairs of seeing their friend, answers: in order to see a friend. Within the perspective of having in view the future state of affairs their action is to bring about, the actor cannot report that in-order-to motive with a because phrase. The answer: because I am going to see a friend, would connect the course of action of going to see a friend back to the formulation of the plan to go and see them.

Whether or not an actor finds themselves in either of these types of context, they are always *also* able to report their in-order-to motive from the perspective of looking back on their plan. Answering a question by reporting an in-order-to motive is only possible after an actor has at least formulated the plan to do something. So, if a question can be answered by reporting an in-order-to motive, there is always a plan to look back to. But if there is always a plan to look back to, an actor can always have that plan in view when they answer a why-question by reporting an in-order-to motive.

Suppose that an actor answers a why-question by reporting their in-order-to motive when having their plan in view. When an actor has their plan in view, they can (with the above stipulation: must) use a because phrase. Only a because phrase connects the given fact (the course of action) to a prior cause (the plan). In response to the question 'why did you leave the house?', they can answer: because I am going to see a friend. From within this perspective of having their plan in view, they cannot answer with an in-order-to phrase. An in-order-to phrase would connect the course of action to the future state of affairs to be brought about, not to the plan to bring it about.

In summary: the choice of an in-order-to phrase or a because phrase when reporting an in-order-to motive is determined by the actor's perspective when reporting their motive. Which perspective any given actor adopts will depend on the point of time at which they answer, the terms of the question, and their attitude.

From this analysis, it follows that any because phrase used to report an in-order-to motive can be converted into an in-order-to phrase. The conversion changes the perspective of the actor's report, but nothing more. The potential for conversion distinguishes because phrases that report in-order-to motives from those that report because motives. Because phrases that report because motives cannot be converted into in-order-to phrases, and state a motive, for a prior cause would then be presented as if it were an expected future consequence. Once the phrase: because I was feeling lonely, is converted into the in-order-to phrase: in order to feel lonely, it fails to state a motive of the actor who, because they are feeling lonely, leaves their house in order to see a friend.

The analysis thus far has brought out two points. Firstly, actions have two distinct types of motive, in-order-to motives and because motives, even if both types of motive can be reported with a because phrase. Secondly, the choice of phrase for reporting an in-order-to motive is determined by the actor's perspective when reporting this motive. As the choice of phrase for reporting an in-order-to motive is not a reflection of the reported action, but a reflection of the perspective an actor adopts in making their report; and as this reporting phrase may fail to lay bare something about the reported action (namely, whether the reported motive is its in-order-to motive or because motive), it impedes the purpose of an analysis of action to adopt as one's starting point an actor's response to a why-question. The impediment that this starting point represents will be compounded, moreover, if one of these two types of motive must be singled out from the other to examine a function that the one has but the other lacks. This is precisely the case, however, if only one of these two types of motive can orient action.

3   Orientation to an In-Order-To Motive

Having distinguished in-order-to motives from because motives, one question to ask is which type(s) of motive can orient action. Schütz raises this question in critical response to Max Weber's account of action in *Economy and Society*. Schütz accepts Weber's claim that action is '"meaningfully" oriented'.[17] Where Schütz sees a problem, however, is in Weber's claim that action can be oriented to some future *or pre-existing* meaningful state of affairs. This further claim is implied by Weber's statement that '[s]ocial action (including omissions and acquiescence) is oriented to the past, present or anticipated future behaviour of others'.[18]

The argument for holding that an in-order-to motive can orient action is straightforward. To say that action has an in-order-to motive is to say that it is guided by an anticipated future state of affairs that the actor seeks to realise, however patchy and dim. The anticipated future state of affairs may be patchy, as when I ask somebody a question or set out to write a text without knowing what words I will use. It may be dim, because I may be more attentive to other aspects of my surroundings, or other actions, at the same time. But if action has an in-order-to motive, there is *some* anticipated state of affairs that it seeks to realise. A course of action is oriented to an in-order-to motive, therefore, because an actor seeks to realise the future state of affairs (however patchy and dim) that they expect their action to bring about (and in so doing either realises it, or fails to realise it).

A because motive cannot orient action in exactly the same way, for a because motive is not something that an actor seeks to realise. But the question remains as to whether a because motive can orient action in some other respect. A because motive, like any motive, can only orient action if it is (or at some stage was) evident to the actor, however. Any argument to the effect that a because motive can orient action is therefore faced with the problem that there is an asymmetry in regard to how an actor relates to a because motive, as compared to how they relate to an in-order-to motive.

On the one hand, once a plan is formulated, an actor does not need to reflect on their because motive to retain their in-order-to motive. Once an actor has formulated the plan to go and see a friend, they do not need to be able to recollect that they are going to see them because they were feeling lonely to be able to continue to orient their action to the in-order-to motive of going to see

---

17   Weber 2005, p. 17, p. 18; Weber 1978, p. 25.
18   Weber 2005, p. 16; Weber 1978, p. 22.

them. On the other hand, an actor has no awareness of the because motive of an action independently of its in-order-to motive. To be linked back to a prior event in the past, action must be delimited. It is only possible to reflect on what caused a piece of action if it has already been singled out. But action can only be singled out if it is viewed as already completed, through an in-order-to motive. While attention to an in-order-to motive does not presuppose an awareness of a because motive, attention to a because motive does presuppose an awareness of an in-order-to motive.

This asymmetry has the following consequence. To become aware of the because motive of their action, an actor must perform a mental act of directing their attention to it by mentally taking a step back from what they are doing, as already defined by an in-order-to motive.[19] Prior to the mental shift by which an actor takes a step back from what they are already doing, and directs their attention to the because motive of their action, their because motive cannot orient their action, for it is not evident. So, if a because motive is to orient action, that can only be because an actor's reflection on the because motive of what they are doing, as already defined by an in-order-to motive, can orient their action.

The one possibility this suggests for how a because motive might orient action is for an actor to reflect on the because motive of their action, and alter their action mid-stride. To be sure, an actor can reflect on the because motive of their action, and alter their action mid-stride. But any modified action will be oriented to a new in-order-to motive, formulated in light of reflection on the because motive of the existing action. Suppose A has decided to go and see their friend, B. As A is leaving the house, A reflects that their because motive for going to see B is a feeling of loneliness. A's reflection on that because motive, in conjunction with A's awareness of their in-order-to motive, may prompt A to reconsider whether B is good company. If, in reconsidering their options, A decides to go and visit their neighbour, C, instead, A's behaviour is now oriented to the in-order-to motive to go and visit their neighbour. At no point was it oriented to their feeling of loneliness.

The finding that only in-order-to motives can orient action adds to the importance of distinguishing types of motive from types of reporting phrase. As argued above, there need be no correspondence between an in-order-to motive, and the phrase used to report it. An in-order-to motive can be reported with an in-order-to phrase or a because phrase. A conversion test is needed to separate because phrases that report in-order-to motives from those that report because motives. Accordingly, if attention is absorbed by the similar-

---

19   Schütz 2004, pp. 207–8; Schütz 1967, pp. 94–5.

ity of phrase, it is possible for because phrases reporting because motives to be assimilated to because phrases reporting in-order-to motives; and, as it is true that *some* because phrases (those that report in-order-to motives) can orient action, for the former to be mistaken for motives that orient action. 'Waving the flag because there is an accident ahead' is offered as an example of '[e]xplaining something in terms of what it is for';[20] but people do not wave flags for making accidents ahead. 'Suppose a person decides to eat a sandwich because she is hungry; her action, in this case, is purposeful in the direct sense';[21] but the direct purpose of people who eat sandwiches is not to be hungry. Phenomenological analysis is required to uncover the source of the confusion.

On this diagnosis, the fact that because motives are sometimes cited as if they orient actions (although they *cannot* orient actions) is explained by (i) an ambiguity in because phrases; and, in addition, (ii) the influence of philosophies of action that place undue emphasis on actors' responses to why-questions. But as (i) is sufficient to prompt the mistake and a feature of ordinary language, the confusion can be expected to arise in discussion of Marx's claims. Two cases are discussed in later chapters.[22]

4   The Form of an In-Order-To Motive

If action is behaviour oriented to an in-order-to motive, it is important, for an account of action, to pay special attention to the form of an in-order-to motive. Two points that Schütz makes in regard to the form of an in-order-to motive are brought together with his claim that action is '*antecedently projected* [vorher entworfen]'.[23]

First, an in-order-to motive is formed prior to the course of action. The antecedent character of an in-order-to motive accounts for the everyday fact that an actor experiences an action as realising or not realising its aim. They do so by comparing the course it has taken with what they recall of its in-order-to motive. For this experience to be possible during any given phase of a course of action, the in-order-to motive must be formulated prior to the course of action.

---

20   Stout 2005, p. 16.
21   Lovett 2010, p. 31.
22   See ch. 7, sec. 1; and ch. 12, sec. 5.
23   Schütz 2004, p. 157; Schütz 1967, p. 61. In Schütz 2004, '*vorher entworfen*' is a key term. Unfortunately, it is not rendered consistently in Schütz 1967. At Schütz 1967, p. 61, it is rendered as '*projected*'. In other words, '*vorher*' is not translated.

Second, an in-order-to motive has a future perfect form. An in-order-to motive is only sufficiently determinate to orient behaviour if it is delimited. An antecedent vision of a future state of affairs in which an actor will be x-ing (where x stands for an activity) does not delimit the future so that an actor can be guided by it to complete the action. A sufficiently delimited anticipation of the future is only provided by the anticipation of a future end-state;[24] that by a future point in time, the actor will have x-ed. As an in-order-to motive requires delimitation to orient action, and is only delimited if it takes a future perfect form, it must take a future perfect form.[25] (In-order-to motives, not objects of desire, must have a future perfect form. Listening to music is an action of mine if my behaviour is oriented to the antecedent projection of having listened to music, even if listening to music is what I desire. My desire to listen to music, a because motive, prompts the formulation of an in-order-to motive that has the form of my having listened to music, to which my behaviour is oriented).

5   Action and Abstraction

The antecedent *and* future perfect form of an in-order-to motive raises a further question, the answer to which connects *Capital*'s description of the antecedently projected form of human labour to Marx's aside, in his *Economic Manuscripts of 1861–63*, that social relations require the exercise of a 'capacity for abstraction from sensible singularity and contingency'.[26]

Considered separately, both the antecedent and the future perfect form of an in-order-to motive have their own ground. Its antecedency accounts for the fact that it is possible for an actor to experience a course of action as fulfilling or failing to fulfil its aim during any given phase of its course. Its future perfect form, on the other hand, provides the delimitation that orientation requires. Nevertheless, taken together, the antecedent *and* future perfect form of an in-order-to motive raises the following question. Under what condition is it possible for an actor to have an inkling of the future state of affairs that they expect their action to bring about as a state of affairs that they will have intentionally brought about, prior to embarking on the course of action to bring it about?

The answer to this question can only be: on the condition that this expected future state of affairs is similar in type to that brought about by an action

---

24   Schütz 2004, p. 156; Schütz 1967, p. 60.
25   Schütz 2004, p. 159; Schütz 1967, p. 61.
26   *MEW*, 43, p. 226; *MECW*, 30, p. 232.

with which the actor is already familiar. It is only possible for an actor to project a future state of affairs as one that they will have intentionally brought about prior to any given phase of a course of action to bring it about if they can recall a similar type of action from their 'stock of experiences [*Vorrat von Erfahrungen*]'.[27] An actor's stock of experiences includes not just the actions they recall themselves as having performed, intended or fantasised,[28] but also the actions that they can recall relevantly similar others as having performed.[29]

An actor's stock of experiences limits or conditions their action in several ways. It limits the imaginable future states of affairs that an actor can conceive themselves as being able to bring about, including those that they can conceive themselves as being able to bring about with others' cooperation. It also limits the means with which an actor can conceive themselves to bring about such future states of affairs. Further, it provides concepts with which to classify and evaluate the bringing about of future states of affairs, or the means used to bring them about. Finally, an actor's stock of experiences conditions the span of an action: 'the span of the projection itself depends on the intermediary aims that are unquestionably given, and so pre-experienced, at the moment of the projection'.[30] Particular means-ends connections become 'unquestionably given' through learning. The less an actor needs to attend to the means for a given step, the greater their ability to antecedently project a type of completed action that reaches beyond that step. To adapt an example from Donald Davidson: writing down the letter 'c' in the word 'action' is not a separate action to that of writing down the letter 'a',[31] unless each of these hand movements of writing down letters is the action of a child who is learning how to spell. People who have learnt how to spell do not antecedently project having written one letter, and then antecedently project having written down the next. They antecedently project having written a text, however patchy their projection of its content.

To antecedently project a given action, and thus to perform it at all, an actor must recall a similar type of action from their stock of experiences. To recall an action, an actor must single out a delimited phase of experience from the irreversible stream of their experience. Insofar as that delimited phase of experience is singled out as similar to an action to be performed in the different

27   Schütz 2004, p. 187; Schütz 1992, p. 80. In Schütz 2004, '*Vorrat von Erfahrungen/Erfahrungs-vorrat* [stock of experiences]' is a key term. It is rendered inconsistently in Schütz 1967. At Schütz 1967, p. 80, it is rendered first as 'supply of experience' and then as 'stock of knowledge'.
28   Schütz 2004, p. 186; Schütz 1967, p. 79.
29   On the interpretation of others' behaviour, see ch. 5, sec. 2.
30   Schütz 2004, p. 201; Schütz 1967, p. 91.
31   Davidson 2001, pp. 79–80.

context of here and now, it is recalled in an iterable form; that is, in the form: in situations like this, it is possible to do that. An antecedent projection of action is not only conditioned by *what* an actor can recall from their stock of experiences, therefore. It is also shaped by the iterable *form* of that recall. As Schütz puts it, '*the projection itself necessarily refers back* to similar actions *preceding* the projected action'.[32] More fully:

> Every act of projection, anticipating self-explication, 'interprets' the meaning being constituted in the projected action by relating it back (if rarely explicitly), in a synthesis of recognition, to previously executed actions of a 'similar kind', and identifying it with them.[33]

In antecedently projecting an action, an actor implicitly recalls similar actions from their stock of experiences, in iterable form, and identifies their present action as an action of the same type, in what Schütz calls a '*synthesis of recognition*'.[34] The antecedent projection thereby categorises the action as an action of a certain *type*.

We are now in a position to say how Schütz's account of action as antecedently projected behaviour, in the very respect in which it generalises *Capital*'s description of human labour, offers a way to defend Marx's remark that 'social relations only exist among human beings insofar as they think, and possess this capacity for abstraction from sensible singularity and contingency'.[35] If a social relation consists of action, then an actor in a social relation abstracts from sensible singularity, for, through the visor of seeking to realise their antecedent projection, they engage with the social world as a world that is coming to include a certain *type* of future state of affairs. They also abstract from contingency, for they regard the type of future state of affairs that they anticipate the social world as coming to include as the *necessary* outcome of their successful orientation to the antecedent projection of their action.

This use of Schütz's account of action to connect *Capital*'s description of human labour to Marx's aside on social relations also shows that to say that human labour has transhistorical features is not to presuppose an intentional subject outside history. One criticism levelled at *Capital*'s description of human labour is that it employs 'a fundamentally anthropological schema of the tran-

---

32   Schütz 2004, pp. 200–1; Schütz 1967, p. 90.
33   Schütz 2004, pp. 201–2; Schütz 1967, p. 90.
34   Schütz 2004, p. 184; Schütz 1967, p. 78.
35   *MEW*, 43, p. 226; *MECW*, 30, p. 232.

scendental conditions of any process of production'.[36] By positing invariant features of human life as conditions of any process of production, *Capital*'s description of human labour is said to share in the anthropology of classical political economy it is directed against, central to which is 'the implicit idea of a transcendental subject', a subject 'that acts on history insofar as he or she is posited outside history'.[37] *Capital*'s general description of human labour as a purposeful activity on an object using an instrument to produce a product does not presuppose a subject 'outside history', however, for this activity is described as a type of antecedently projected behaviour, which presupposes a stock of experiences acquired in life (and adds to it). If the concept of action as antecedently projected behaviour implicit in *Capital*'s description of human labour is transhistorically valid, then there is no intentional subject outside history.

Finally, a reply can be offered to the criticism, directed at *Capital*'s description of human labour, that Marx is constrained by a 'monological' model of action, on which 'purposeful or intentional activity is described with the help of a *prelinguistic* model' rather than being understood as 'linguistically mediated'.[38] If, as *Capital*'s description of human labour implies, work is a kind of antecedently projected behaviour, then it requires an actor to identify their present action with actions of a similar type that they recall from their stock of experiences. This stock of experiences includes the concepts that an actor has acquired, and that enable them to classify actions. As, on a conception of action as antecedently projected behaviour, action is projected as of a certain type; and, in this projection, an actor may in part be guided by the concepts they have acquired, which are linguistic; the intentional activities that actors perform are to be understood as subject to linguistic mediation, on the model of action that *Capital*'s description of human labour implies.

---

36   Read 2003, p. 115.
37   Read 2003, p. 16.
38   Benhabib 1986, pp. 134–5.

CHAPTER 5

Social Relations

'Social relation' is a key idea in Marx's work. Marx says as much on a number of occasions. His *Economic and Philosophic Manuscripts of 1844* praise Feuerbach for making 'the social relation "of human being to human being" the foundational principle of theory'.[1] *The German Ideology* complains of Max Stirner that he 'only knows "things" and "I's"; anything which does not fit these rubrics, all relations, he only knows as abstract concepts'.[2] In his *Economic Manuscripts of 1861–63*, Marx chides 'the standpoint of the economist, who only knows tangible things or ideas – relations do not exist for him'.[3] Yet on none of these occasions is Marx's praise or criticism accompanied by an elaboration of what (social) relations are. If a thesis connecting the capitalist economic structure with the state and classes is to be reconstructed from Marx's writings, it is up to the interpreter to fill in the gap.

Chapter 4 began this task by defending a conception of action as antecedently projected behaviour. From this conception of action, it was seen to follow that an actor categorises their action as action of a certain type, and views the existence of the state of affairs it is to bring about as the necessary outcome of their successful orientation to its antecedent projection. These consequences encourage a particular interpretation of Marx's aside in his *Economic Manuscripts of 1861–63* that 'social relations only exist among human beings insofar as they think, and possess this capacity for abstraction from sensible singularity and contingency'.[4] Social relations exhibit thinking, the capacity for abstraction, because they are comprised of action. The question of how to conceive of a social relation is resolved into the questions of the type(s) of action that comprise it, and their interconnection.

This chapter completes the task, by addressing these two questions. A social relation is principally comprised of a type of action called a standard action of social affecting. A standard action of social affecting by A is action in which A seeks to bring about action by B as a result of B identifying A as the author

---

1   *MEW*, 40, p. 570; *MECW*, 3, p. 328. Marx takes the phrase '"of human being to human being"' from Feuerbach's *The Essence of Christianity* (Feuerbach 1984, p. 444; Feuerbach 1989, p. 271; compare Feuerbach 1984, p. 274; Feuerbach 1989, p. 156).
2   *MEW*, 3, p. 346; *MECW*, 5, p. 362; see Stirner 1986; Stirner 1995.
3   *MEW*, 43, p. 142; *MECW*, 30, p. 150.
4   *MEW*, 43, p. 226; *MECW*, 30, p. 232.

© KONINKLIJKE BRILL NV, LEIDEN, 2019 | DOI:10.1163/9789004384804_006

of the action affecting *B*'s action. The actions of a social relation are interconnected such that each but the last standard action of social affecting affects a subsequent one. Thus conceived, a social relation is a relation of mutual affecting, or interaction.[5]

An interactional conception of a social relation as a relation of mutual affecting or interaction can be recommended on three counts. One is that it preserves two thoughts expressed in Marx's general remarks on social relations: an actor's awareness of a social relation they engage in is an aspect of that social relation (the *awareness condition* for a social relation); and, an actor in a social relation is aware of themselves as a being of a kind (the *species-awareness claim*). Second and more specifically, it suggests a plausible transhistorical conception of what Marx, in *Capital* and elsewhere, calls a 'social relation of production [*gesellschaftliches Produktionsverhältnis*]'.[6] A social relation of production, taken independently of its historically specific features, is an exercise of societal cooperation in the existence of use-value. Third, an interactional conception of capitalist relations of production permits them to be conceived of as distinct from both legal property relations, and norms. It can negotiate the problem known, since Cohen, as the problem of legality;[7] and a parallel problem of normativity.

Section 1 examines Marx's general remarks on social relations. It argues that these remarks hint at an interactional conception of a social relation. To outline a more precise conception of interaction, section 2 summarises Schütz's typology of social action. Section 3 then outlines a conception of interaction as a relation of mutual affecting. Section 4 argues that this interactional conception of a social relation can solve the problem of normativity. Section 5 then outlines an interactional conception of a social relation of production. Section 6 lists three objections that might be raised against it by appeal to Marx's *1859*

---

5 In this book, interaction always denotes a relation of mutual affecting.

6 *MEW*, 23, p. 93, p. 97; *MECW*, 35, p. 90, p. 93; Marx 1976, p. 172, p. 176; see also *MEW*, 6, p. 408; *MECW*, 9, p. 212; and *MEW*, 13, p. 22, p. 34; *MECW*, 29, p. 276, p. 289. It is worth noting that '*gesellschaftlich*' is related to '*Gesellschaft*', society; a more literal translation would be 'societal'. This suggests that a '*gesellschaftliches Produktionsverhältnis*' bears some connection to a whole; see sec. 5.

7 Cohen and Acton 1970, pp. 127–8; Cohen 1989, p. 95; Cohen 1978, p. 217. The problem of legality is raised in Acton 1962, pp. 154–5; Plamenatz 1956, pp. 22–8; and Plamenatz 1963, pp. 279–85. It is discussed, among others, by Cahan 1994–95, pp. 394–408; Chitty 1998, pp. 57–9, pp. 90–3; Collins 1982, pp. 77–85; Elster 1985, pp. 403–4; Hunt 1988, pp. 57–82; Lukes 1982a, pp. 211–22; Nozick 1974, p. 273; Rigby 1998, pp. 189–91; Sayer 1987, pp. 50–7; Taiwo 1996, pp. 45–54; and Wood 2004, pp. 82–7. See also Kelsen 1955, p. 93; Plekhanov 1956, p. 35, p. 173; and Rottleuthner 1975, pp. 231–2.

Preface. Sections 7–9 rebut these objections. Sections 7–8 address the objection from structure and the objection from consciousness. Finally, section 9 negotiates the problem of legality.

1   Marx's General Remarks on Social Relations

As suggested in chapter 4, a statement that contrasts human beings with animals offers a way for a theorist like Marx, whose writings largely concern historically specific types of society, to express and signal a claim about a transhistorical feature of human life. A contrastive claim about human beings and animals is a means for Marx to signal (to himself and/or to his readers) that he has broken off from analysing the features that only belong to a specific form of human society, such as capitalism. By reserving such contrastive statements for claims about transhistorical features of human life, Marx can intersperse claims about transhistorical features of human life in his analyses of capitalism, as part of an exploration of how capitalism shapes those transhistorical features, while reducing the danger of being read as if his whole text were operating at the same level of abstraction.

This point applies as much to Marx's general remarks on social relations as it does to *Capital*'s description of human labour. When Marx says that human beings relate in a way that animals do not, there is a good chance that he is attempting to advance a claim about a transhistorical feature of human life. Once again, it would not matter very much if what Marx says about animals were false. Marx's choice of device for separating transhistorical features of human life from historically specific features (a contrast with animals that supposedly lack the feature) may lead Marx to say something false about animals, if the feature that is to be identified as a transhistorical feature of human life is found in at least one species of animal. But the value of Marx's inter-species contrasts between humans and animals on the topic of social relations, as on any other topic of human life, rests on whether the part of the contrast that concerns human beings calls attention to an important transhistorical feature of human life. To get bogged down in the question of whether an existing (or hypothetical) species of animal could offer a counterexample to the contrast would be a smashing way to miss the point of Marx's claim.

Consider, in this light, the following marginal note from *The German Ideology*, written in a mixture of Marx's[8] and Engels's hand:

---

8 It has been claimed that this marginal note is one that 'Engels ... added' (Xiaoping 2010,

> Where a relation exists, it exists for me; the animal '*relates*' to nothing,
> does not '*relate*' at all. For the animal, its relation to others does not exist
> as a relation.[9]

In this marginal note, the word 'me' marks an attempt to adopt the perspective of a participant in a social relation, as distinct from the perspective of an
observer. To claim that a social relation 'exists for me' is to claim that an actor
is aware of a social relation they participate in. This claim is distinct from the
claim that a social relation exists for an observer. For all that is said here, a social
relation need not be observed by anyone else. Two people might engage in a
social relation in secret. They might be aware of their social relation even if no
one else was.

The statement 'where a relation exists, it exists for me', can be read in one
of two ways. On one reading, it asserts a constant conjunction between the
existence of a social relation, and a participant's awareness of it. On a constant conjunction reading, the awareness of a social relation on the part of its
participants is something that accompanies a social relation, without constituting an aspect of it. Alternatively, the statement can be read to explicate a
constitutive condition for a social relation. On a constitutive condition reading, the statement asserts that an actor's awareness of their social relation is a
constitutive condition for its existence.

One reason to favour the constitutive condition reading is that it supplies
a motivation for adding the second sentence. On the constitutive condition
reading, the second sentence can be added in an attempt to justify the first:
Marx offers the thought that an animal's doing to others 'does not exist as a
relation' for it as a reason to believe that an animal 'does not "*relate*" at all'. On
the constant conjunction reading, by contrast, the addition of the second sentence lacks motivation. There would be little point in adding a sentence to the
effect that an animal is not aware of a doing that (it has just been claimed) it

---

p. 493). However, *MEJ*, 2003, places m's around the scare-quoted word in its first sentence,
and also around the entire second sentence (p. 220); and 'm' is as an abbreviation for: 'identi-
fier for variations, marginal notes and independent passages of text in Marx's hand' (p. 155).
To be sure, 'Marx and Engels co-operated in composing the text [of *The German Ideology* –
JF]' (Uchida 2006, pp. 199–200). But the finding that a marginal note (which may be added
after composing the main text) is written in one author's hand might be thought to present
a bigger hurdle for the claim that it should also be regarded as a thought of the other author.
A two-sentence marginal note whose first sentence Marx alters by adding scare-quotes, and
whose second sentence is entirely in Marx's hand, is undeniably a thought of Marx's (whether
or not it is also a thought of Engels's).

9 *MEJ*, 2003, p. 16; *MEW*, 3, p. 30; *MECW*, 5, p. 44.

cannot do. The constitutive condition reading is better, because it suggests a reason to add the second sentence to the first.

Put aside whether what Marx says about animals is true or false, and consider it purely as an indicator of a claim about a transhistorical feature of human life. On a constitutive condition reading, this claim is: it is an aspect of a social relation between two human beings, A and B, that that relation exists for A and B. A's awareness of their social relation to B is a constitutive condition for A having a social relation to B; and the same goes for B.

The claim aligned to a constitutive condition reading of this marginal note is of a piece with Marx's aside in his *Economic Manuscripts of 1861–63* that 'social relations only exist among human beings insofar as they think, and possess this capacity for abstraction from sensible singularity and contingency'.[10] Both of these remarks assert that mental activity on the actor's part – their thinking or awareness – is constitutive of their social relation.

Although the point of these two remarks is very general, it compromises at least three views of a social relation offered in Marx scholarship. On one view (Cohen's), social relations are 'social relational properties';[11] in other words, rights, duties, powers or incapacities whose explication requires reference to the rights, duties, powers or incapacities of at least one other individual. A 'power to prevent others using means of production',[12] for example, is a social relational property, as it must be explicated by reference to others' incapacity to prevent that exclusion. On a second view (Elster's), social relations are instead 'internal relations';[13] that is, comparisons between two or more individuals' relational properties, each of whose description requires reference to a class of actors to which the other belongs. For example, A's greater popularity than B among voters is an internal relation, *if* A and B are themselves both voters. On a third view, a social relation is a kind of purely causal relation. Elster suggests this third view when he says that a social relation is characterised by 'mutual dependence', and he adds: 'the mutual dependence is causal'.[14] An example of a causal relation of mutual dependence, to expand a statement from E.O. Wright, would be: 'the rich are rich *because* the poor are poor',[15] and the poor are poor because the rich are rich.

---

10   *MEW*, 43, p. 226; *MECW*, 30, p. 232.
11   Cohen 1978, p. 90; see also p. 94.
12   Cohen 1978, p. 236.
13   Elster 1985, pp. 94–5.
14   Elster 1985, p. 93.
15   Wright 1985, p. 65.

Marx's two aforecited general remarks on social relations are not compatible with any of these views. None of them requires an actor to be aware of what each view identifies as the feature of a social relation for it to exist. Actors can have rights, duties, powers or incapacities that can only be explicated by reference to those of others without being aware that they have them.[16] Nor need actors be aware of their 'internal relations'.[17] A need not be aware of their greater popularity than B among voters to be more popular than B among voters. The view of a social relation as a kind of purely causal relation (of mutual dependence) falls at the same hurdle. An actor need not be aware of the property of theirs that stands in a causal relation to the property of another, or (if they are aware of the property) be aware that a causal relation links them to that other, or be aware of what that causal relation is, for the causal relation to pertain. In regard to the above example, someone who is rich or poor might not believe that they are rich or poor; and even if someone who is rich or poor does believe that they are rich or poor, they need not be aware that they are rich or poor on the account of others, or, in particular, on the account of others' poverty or wealth. Nor need they have any awareness of the cause of those others' poverty or wealth.

The idea that an actor's awareness of a social relation they engage in is an aspect of that social relation may be termed *the awareness condition* for a social relation. All of the above views fail to satisfy the awareness condition for a social relation. There is at least one way to satisfy this condition, however. The awareness condition for a social relation is satisfied if action is conceived of as antecedently projected behaviour, and a social relation is comprised of a type of action to another.

Action to another is action guided by an antecedent projection in which meaning is ascribed to another's behaviour. Thus, in action to another, an actor's sense of how their course of action is fairing is bound up with their interpretation of another's behaviour. Spying, for example, is an action to another, guided by an antecedent projection of having observed another's conduct without their knowledge. If A spies on B, A's sense of how A's course of action is fairing is bound up with A's view of whether A has seen everything that B has done.

If a social relation were comprised of at least one action to another by each actor, each actor would be aware of an aspect of another's behaviour, in virtue of their orientation to their antecedent projection. It requires something more

---

16   See Cohen 1978, p. 244.
17   Elster 1985, pp. 94–5.

than this, however, for an actor to be aware of their social relation. As the case of spying shows, an actor's awareness of some aspect of another's behaviour is not necessarily an awareness of any interconnection between their own action, and the action by another that they are aware of. Only a bad spy is spotted by, and so affects the behaviour of, their subject.

For an action to incorporate an awareness of an interconnection between it and action by another, its in-order-to motive must be of the type that seeks to get another to perform action. Such is the case if, say, A throws an object at B to get B to jump. A is then aware, by virtue of A's orientation to their antecedent projection, of an interconnection between A's action, and B's action. But nor is this sufficient for an actor to be aware of a social relation. What is required is a type of action with an in-order-to motive that, by orienting behaviour, provides an awareness of an interconnection between it, and action by another of the type that belongs to a social relation. Jumping out of the way of a projectile is not an action of the type that belongs to a social relation.

To provide an awareness of a social relation, the in-order-to motive of the action that each performs must be to get another to perform action to another. Each actor is then aware, by virtue of their orientation to their in-order-to motive, of an interconnection between their own action, and action by another of the type that belongs to a social relation. For example, when one actor asks another a question, and the other responds, each is aware of another as performing an anticipated action to another: responding to their question with an answer, and interpreting their answer. An action-based conception of a social relation satisfies the awareness condition, therefore, if it says that a social relation consists of actions that seek to get another to perform action.

A footnote in *Capital* Volume I implies that a social relation is comprised of action whose in-order-to motive is to get another to perform action:

> Since a human being is not born with a mirror, or as a Fichtean philosopher who says 'I am I', he first mirrors himself [*bespiegelt sich*] in another human being. The human being Peter first [*erst*] relates to himself as a human being through a relationship to the human being Paul, as his equal [*als seinesgleichen*]. Paul from head to toe, Paul in his Paul-like physicality, thereby counts for him as the form of appearance of the genus 'human being'.[18]

18   *MEW*, 23, p. 67; *MECW*, 35, p. 63; Marx 1976, p. 144. (1) '*Erst* (first)', an adverbial of time, is translated by *MECW* and Marx 1976 as 'only' (which would be: '*nur*' or '*allein*'). The error transforms a claim about origin into a claim about a necessary condition, to which Marx is not committed, and that is surely false. Capacities that first develop in social relations need

Marx here advances a claim about what 'first' gives a human being a sense of themselves as a being of a kind. Marx claims that a human being first gains a sense of themselves as a being of a kind in a social relation. A human being does not first gain a sense of themselves as a being of a kind in solitary self-reflection. Call the positive claim just expressed the *origination claim*. *Capital's* origination claim is not of direct concern here. But it is of indirect help, in virtue of how it fits together with what it presupposes about a social relation.

Capital's origination claim presupposes that *A* is implicitly aware, in their social relation to *B*, of *A* as a being of a kind. A human being can only 'first' gain a sense of themselves as a being of a kind in a social relation of whatever character if, in any social relation, they are aware of themselves as a being of a kind. Call the claim that an actor in a social relation is implicitly aware of themselves as a being of a kind the *species-awareness claim*. The species-awareness claim links up with the thought, common to both of Marx's aforecited general remarks, that an actor's awareness of a social relation they engage in is an aspect of that relation. Only if an actor's awareness of a social relation they engage in is an aspect of it can it be the case that, in a social relation they engage in, they are aware of themselves as a being of a kind.

Suppose that, in a social relation, there is something that the one actor, *A*, does, that another, *B*, also does. If what *A* does in a social relation with *B* is something that *B* also does in this relation, for *A* or *B* to be aware of their relation is for *A* or *B* to be aware of *A* and *B* as alike in that respect. An awareness of a similarity between two entities is a condition for thinking of them as belonging to the same kind. So if, in a social relation between *A* and *B*, *A* does something that *B* also does, an awareness on the part of *A* and *B* of their social relation is, implicitly, an awareness, on the part of *A* and *B*, that they belong to a kind defined by the capacity to perform that doing, a kind that includes both *A* and *B*.

Actors in a social relation are implicitly aware of themselves as beings of a kind, therefore, if each performs action that demands of the other that the

---

not only be exercised in them. (2) Marx 1976 renders '*bespiegelt sich* [mirrors himself]' ('*Spiegel*' is the German noun for 'mirror') as 'sees and recognises', and '*als seinesgleichen* [as his equal]' ('*seines*' is a genitive possessive pronoun and '*gleich*' means equal or alike) as 'in whom he recognises his likeness'. These renderings are inaccurate, and court confusion. Recognition (*Anerkennung*) is an important philosophical term for Fichte, but Marx does not use '*anerkennen*' here. The verb Marx uses, '*sich bespiegeln*', carries no normative connotation. If these errors are corrected, the footnote supports an argument against Plamenatz's claim that human beings only 'become self-conscious and conscious of other selves ... in the process of learning to see themselves in moral and customary (and therefore social) relations' (Plamenatz 1963, p. 284); see sec. 4 below.

other interpret it as an action. An action by *A* requires another, *B*, to interpret it as an action, if its success requires *B* to interpret it as an action. If *B* must interpret *A*'s action as an action for it to succeed, *A*'s antecedent projection includes *B*'s having interpreted *A*'s action as an action. By antecedently projecting an action whose success requires another to interpret it as an action, the actor ascribes a capacity for interpretation to this other. As, for their own part, the actor has interpreted their own action just by antecedently projecting it, it follows that, in any course of action by *A* in which *A* demands that another, *B*, interprets *A*'s action as an action, *A* is implicitly aware of both *A* and *B* as exercising a capacity for interpretation. *Capital*'s species-awareness claim is justified, then, if a social relation is comprised of action whose success is predicated on another interpreting it as action. Actors in a social relation are then implicitly aware of themselves as beings of a kind with the capacity for interpretation. For *Capital* to say that *A* views *B* as belonging to 'the genus "human being"' is to say that *A* views *B*'s body as the 'form of appearance' (Marx) or 'field of expression'[19] (Schütz) of something unobservable, *B*'s conscious experience.

Capital's origination claim, therefore, is that human beings are first aware of the fact that they belong to a kind with the capacity for interpretation in performing action whose success requires them to simultaneously exercise, and demand that another exercise, a capacity for interpretation. On this construal, *Capital*'s origination claim – hidden by the official translations – can be compared with George Herbert Mead's approach to the development of mutual self-awareness. For Mead, as William O'Meara puts it in his comparison of Marx, Husserl, Schütz and Mead, '[c]ontrolling one's gestures in terms of the expected responses of others establishes the individual with awareness of himself as a member of a group'.[20] Nonetheless, *Capital*'s origination claim need not be explored any further here. It suffices to have found a conception of a social relation that can both satisfy the awareness condition, and support the species-awareness claim: a conception on which a social relation is comprised of action to another whose success requires the other to interpret it as action.

---

19   Schütz 2004, pp. 104–5; Schütz 1967, pp. 22–3.
20   O'Meara 1986–87, p. 343.

2   Schütz's Typology of Social Action

This conception of a social relation can be refined by critically engaging with
Schütz's typology of social action. This typology helps to highlight the type of
action whose success is predicated on another's interpretation of it as action,
and which is able to enjoy a generalised existence.

Schütz's typology of social action is a modification and development of
Weber's account of social action in *Economy and Society*. In *Economy and Society*, Weber defines action as ' "social" ' when 'the intended meaning the actor(s)
gives to it is related to *others*' behaviour, and the course of the action is oriented
to this meaning'.[21]

We can begin with the first clause of Weber's definition. An actor who links
the meaning they give to their action to another's behaviour must attribute
meaning to that other's behaviour. How, then, does an actor give meaning to
another's behaviour? By imagining themselves in the other's place. *A* regards
B's behaviour as action, for instance, by implicitly imagining what *A* might have
antecedently projected if *A* were to find themselves doing what they take *B* to be
doing, drawing on anything they know about others in general and/or about *B*
in particular.[22] An antecedent projection is an interpretation of an action as of
a certain type. So, *A*'s interpretation of *B*'s behaviour as action in *A*'s antecedent
projection of social action categorises *B*'s action as action of a certain type, by
identifying it with similar doings that *A* recalls from *A*'s stock of experiences.

To attribute meaning to another's behaviour on the assumption that they
have the same temporal structure of consciousness as oneself is to adopt what
Schütz calls a *Fremdeinstellung*.[23] Schütz defines a *Fremdeinstellung* as 'a particular attitude of the ego to another's duration, founded on the general thesis
of the other as a conscious and experiencing being'.[24] *Fremdeinstellung* will
therefore be translated as 'attitude-to-the-other' and not, as in the official translation, as 'Other-orientation'.[25] The latter is a confusing choice, because Schütz
(following Weber) thinks of *action* as 'oriented [*orientiert*]'.[26] A *Fremdeinstellung* is not action, and it can be adopted to another without acting towards
them, such as in a feeling of love or hate.[27] (A feeling of love or hate is not

21   Weber 2005, p. 3; Weber 1978, p. 4.
22   Schütz 2004, pp. 241–2; Schütz 1967, p. 114.
23   Schütz 2004, p. 294; Schütz 1967, p. 146.
24   Schütz 2004, p. 294; Schütz 1967, p. 147.
25   'Other-orientation' would translate *'Fremdorientierung'*.
26   Schütz 2004, p. 292; Schütz 1967, p. 145; compare Weber 2005, p. 3; Weber 1978, p. 4.
27   Schütz 2004, p. 294; Schütz 1967, p. 147; compare the contrast of *'Fremdeinstellung* (atti-

an action, because it does not have the form of an antecedent projection). An attitude-to-the-other denotes the awareness of another conscious being as that awareness is tied up with an attribution of meaning to their behaviour.

Schütz's concepts of action and attitude-to-the-other suggest the following reformulation of Weber's definition: social action is behaviour oriented to an antecedent projection that includes an attitude-to-the-other to another. To take 'measures against future attacks',[28] which is one of Weber's examples, is a social action, because it is oriented to the antecedent projection of having taken measures against another's having launched attacks. To take the measures, another's future behaviour must be interpreted as 'attacks', in an attitude-to-the-other to them.

An action's because motive, on the other hand, has no bearing on whether it is social.[29] Action whose because motive is a feeling of attachment to another, as when someone lays flowers at a gravestone because they feel an attachment to the person whose name is engraved on the gravestone, is not, by virtue of its because motive, social action, although it may be social action in virtue of its in-order-to motive (if its in-order-to motive is to signal to others that that person is fondly remembered).

Four distinctions within social action reveal the type of action that defines an interaction. The first distinction to draw is between social action whose antecedent projection projects another's behaviour as having been affected by it, and social action whose antecedent projection does not project any such affect. Action of the former type has 'the in-order-to motive of bringing about certain conscious experiences in others, i.e. of *affecting* [*wirken*] others'.[30] Schütz calls this type of social action 'affecting-the-other [*Fremdwirken*]' or 'social affecting [*soziales Wirken*]'.[31] Asking someone a question, for example, is an action of social affecting. It is oriented to an antecedent projection in which the actor has asked a question and, as a consequence, another has answered. The addressee is antecedently projected as having answered because they were asked. The addressee's interpretation of the addressor's action as a question is antecedently projected by the addressor as the because motive of the addressee's response.[32]

---

tude-to-the-other)' to 'action' in the first passage cited in sec. 3 below to describe a 'relation of affecting'.

28   Weber 2005, p. 16; Weber 1978, p. 22.
29   Schütz 2004, p. 297; Schütz 1967, pp. 148–9. On because motives, see ch. 4, sec. 2.
30   Schütz 2000, p. 295; Schütz 1967, p. 147.
31   Schütz 2004, p. 296; Schütz 1967, p. 148.
32   Schütz 2004, p. 309; Schütz 1967, p. 159.

Social affecting is distinct from social action in which no affect on another is antecedently projected. In the latter case, another's meaningful behaviour is projected as a condition of the action, such as in the social action of pondering a creator's in-order-to motive in creating an artefact. Or consider spying: the other is antecedently projected as having behaved exactly as they would have behaved had they not been spied upon.

Schütz's concept of social affecting is too broad for present purposes, however, for two reasons. Firstly, it does not differentiate between actions by A that affect *action* by B (be the latter merely that B orients their behaviour to the antecedent projection of having interpreted A's action), and actions by A that affect B without affecting action by B (to get B to jump in fright). Action is a particular form of meaningful behaviour. It is distinct from meaningful behaviour not oriented to an antecedent projection, including meaningful behaviour in response to an external physical force or physiological cause (jumping in fright, suppressing pain, yawning) and 'position-taking acts'[33] such as feelings of love or hate. Thus, on Schütz's concept of social affecting, A's action of social affecting can affect B without affecting action by B. Relatedly, Schütz's concept of social affecting includes all action by A that leads B to interpret A's behaviour, whether or not B interprets A's behaviour as *action*. A may succeed in getting B to suppress a yawn by feigning a yawn in B's direction even if B does not interpret A's yawning in their direction as action.

From now on, the term 'social affecting' will be reserved for action by an actor, A, whose in-order-to motive is to affect *action* by another, B, in which B interprets A's action *as action* (whether or not B's action extends beyond an interpretation of A's action). The term 'affecting-the-other' will be reserved for Schütz's broader concept; that is, for action whose in-order-to motive is to affect another, whatever the form of that experience.

Finally, types of social affecting can be distinguished according to whether or not the other's affected action is antecedently projected as having been affected as a result of their having correctly identified *the actor* as the author of the affect (with a greater or lesser degree of anonymity). My action of asking a friend a question, for example, is oriented to an antecedent projection in which the friend has answered in virtue of having understood that *I* asked the question. Or suppose that a railway employee announces the evacuation of a railway station over the public address system. Their action is oriented to an antecedent projection in which those at the station have evacuated it in virtue of having understood that they have been requested to evacuate it by a railway employee

---

33   Schütz 2004, pp. 148–9; Schütz 1967, p. 54.

(rather than by some other sort of actor). Both of these cases can be contrasted with a second type of social affecting, where another's affected action is antecedently projected as a result of another's misidentification of, or uncertainty about, its author (at some greater or lesser degree of anonymity). As Schütz writes:

> ... not every act of *affecting-the-other* is oriented to the *other* having an *attitude-towards-the-other* to me. Affecting-the-other can even be oriented to the absence of such an attitude-to-the-other on the part of a partner, and hence to my remaining unobserved and unnoticed as the originator of the affect.[34]

An actor's in-order-to motive may be to confuse or mislead another, such as by throwing their voice, or by impersonating the voice of a railway employee. The first type of social affecting is thus the standard type. The second type of social affecting includes cases that are conceptually parasitic on it: an addressee is antecedently projected as having responded *as if* another had performed an action of social affecting of the first type (*as if* another person in the room had asked the friend the question without throwing their voice, or *as if* a railway employee had announced an evacuation).

Only standard actions of social affecting feature in the following conception of interaction, because its purpose is to prepare the ground for an analysis of two types of interaction that belongs to a form of society, and thus have a generalised existence. A form of society that was comprised of social affecting not of the standard type – in which, say, questions are only ever asked as if they had been asked by another – would be a very peculiar form of society. By contrast, a form of society comprised of interactions that consist of social affecting of the standard type is not, just by virtue of that, at all peculiar.

3   Interaction as a Relation of Mutual Affecting

There are two steps in going from the concept of a standard action of social affecting to the concept of interaction. First, Schütz's concept of a 'relation of affecting [*Wirkensbeziehung*]' is examined. Second, this concept is extended, to yield the concept of a relation of mutual affecting, or interaction.

---

34   Schütz 2004, p. 308; Schütz 1967, p. 159.

In the official translation of Schütz's *Phenomenology of the Social World*, the term '*Wirkensbeziehung*' is rendered as 'interaction'.[35] That is unfortunate, because the ordinary sense of interaction is that of two or more entities acting on one another, and a '*Wirkensbeziehung*', for Schütz, falls short of that. A '*Wirkensbeziehung*' only requires *one* actor to act to another:

> The relation of affecting [*Wirkensbeziehung*] does not, therefore, presuppose mutual affecting [*Wechselwirkung*], i.e. social affecting, or even action, posited by the partner in respect to me; it simply presupposes that the partner takes up an attitude-to-the-other [*Fremdeinstellung*] to me, the actor – takes note of me, has me in view, interprets the product posited by me as a sign of my conscious lived experiences, etc.[36]

> *Insofar as* affecting-the-other [*Fremdwirken*] is *oriented* to the other experiencing the effect of this affecting as produced *by me*, *a relation of affecting* [Wirkensbeziehung] *always exists*, since the partner's attentional conduct towards me entered into my projection of affecting-the-other, as the in-order-to motive.[37]

For Schütz, a 'relation of affecting' – my translation of '*Wirkensbeziehung*' – requires two things. It requires one actor, *A*, to perform a standard action of affecting-the-other to another, *B*. But (and in this respect the first of these passages corrects the second) it also requires that the other, *B*, adopt an attitude-to-the-other to *A*. The latter feature is independent of the first, although anticipated by it. There can be no guarantee that *B* will adopt an attitude-to-the-other to *A*. It is possible for *A* to ask *B* a question that goes entirely unnoticed by *B*, if it is drowned out by other noise. In this case, *A*'s action is so unsuccessful that it fails to establish a relation of affecting. Schütz's claim in the second passage is overstated, therefore. A standard action of affecting-the-other does not '*always*' establish a relation of affecting. It might go so disastrously wrong as to escape all notice by the other.

With three additions, a relation of affecting becomes what will be called a *relation of mutual affecting*, or interaction. First, each of at least two actors must perform at least one standard action of social affecting. Second, all these standard actions of social affecting must result in interpretation by another, in which

---

35   Compare Schütz 2004, pp. 308–9 and Schütz 1967, pp. 158–9. One German term for 'interaction' is '*Interaktion*'. But Schütz does not use '*Interaktion*' here.

36   Schütz 2004, p. 308; Schütz 1967, p. 158.

37   Schütz 2004, p. 309; Schütz 1967, p. 159.

they are interpreted as action. Third, all the standard actions of social affecting that belong to a single relation must be linked. Each (but the last) standard action of social affecting must affect (in virtue of being interpreted) another standard action of social affecting belonging to the relation. As a result of these three additions, each actor affects another (by performing a standard action of social affecting to them), and is affected by them (in an attitude-to-the-other to another's interpretation of their standard action of social affecting, and perhaps also – in two-person relations, always – by virtue of a standard action of social affecting by another to them).

As an illustration, take the simple case of a single question and answer between two people. In the case of a single question and answer, each actor performs one standard action of social affecting (asking a question in order to receive an answer, replying in order to give another an answer). Each standard action of social affecting leads the other to interpret it as action (the addressee interprets the addressor as having asked them a question, and the addressor interprets the addressee as having given them an answer). Finally, each but the last standard action of social affecting affects a subsequent one (the action of asking the question affected the action of answering it). A case of question and answer is thus a relation of mutual affecting, or interaction.

Two negative conditions may be stressed. First, not all actions by those who engage in a social relation are included in it. Suppose A advises B to go to bed earlier. What B does in following A's advice, going to bed earlier, does not belong to A and B's interaction. (Suppose, by contrast, that A commands B to go to bed earlier. If B's action is oriented to A having noted that B has carried out A's command, it is a standard action of social affecting by B to A, and so part of A and B's interaction). Further, no actor is part of a social relation unless they perform a standard action of social affecting. If A asks B to invite C to dinner, B invites C to dinner, and C replies to A and/or B, A, B and C interact. But if A hires B to shoot C, and B hides and shoots C, only A and B need interact.

On this conception of interaction, a given action can belong to more than one interaction, and a given interaction can encompass a number of distinct interactions. Suppose A asks B to get C to find out some information for A, B acknowledges A's request, B tells C to find out the information, and C acknowledges B. All those actions comprise one interaction between A, B and C. But A's request to B to get C to find out the information could be described, more simply, as a request by A to B. A's request to B and B's acknowledgement of A's request is itself an interaction, between A and B. Thus, A's request to B, like B's acknowledgement of A's request, belongs to at least two interactions of different spans: an interaction between A and B, and an interaction between A, B and C. The reason for this is that A's request to B affects both a standard action of social affecting by B to A, and a standard action of social affecting by B to C. Moreover, the interaction between A, B and C itself encompasses two interactions: one interaction between A and B (A's request to B, B's acknowledgement of A's request), and a second interaction between B and C (B telling C to find out the information, and C's acknowledgement of B).

The awareness condition – an actor's awareness of a social relation they engage in is an aspect of that social relation – must be qualified, therefore. An actor's awareness of a social relation arises from their orientation to the antecedently projected interconnection between their action and action by another. (In the case of the last standard action of social affecting belonging to the relation, the action by another is merely an action of interpretation). An awareness of that interconnection need not provide an awareness of *every* interaction of which the action, and hence the actor, is a part. In the example above, C's acknowledgement of B's request for C to find out information need not leave C aware of the part of the interaction between A, B and C that occurred between A and B. B need not communicate to C that B is collecting information on behalf of A. Hence, C need not be aware that A, B and C interact, even though their action is a part of it. This calls for a revision to the awareness condition, so that more complex, non-transparent social relations are not in principle in conflict with it.

The awareness condition may be revised to: an actor's awareness of (part of) a social relation they engage in is an aspect of that social relation. Any actor who performs a standard action of social affecting belonging to a relation of mutual affecting is aware of a connection between their action, and another's interpretation of it. If another were not to interpret it, it would not belong to a relation of mutual affecting. But if another does interpret it, then the actor, by virtue of their attitude-to-the-other to the other's interpretation of their action, is aware of an interconnection between their action, and that of another, and thus of themselves as affecting another and as affected by them. Each actor's awareness of (part of) the social relation is constitutive of that relation, for this awareness is an aspect of the orientation of their behaviour to their antecedent projection. An actor's awareness of (part of) a social relation they engage in need not stretch beyond a bit-part of it, however. It suffices that an actor is aware of a social relation that is encompassed by a social relation of a greater span to say that they are aware of part of the latter. In the above example, it suffices that C is aware of a social relation with B to say that C is aware of part of a social relation between A, B and C. This revision to the awareness condition is consistent with the species-awareness claim. Even if an actor is only aware of part of a social relation they engage in, they remain implicitly aware of themselves as a being of a kind with a capacity for interpretation.

4   The Problem of Normativity

An interactional conception of a social relation is a non-normative conception. It does not presuppose that actors who engage in social relations aim to
uphold norms. It is comprised of two types of action: standard actions of social
affecting, and actions of interpretation. An actor need not adopt an in-order-
to motive of upholding a norm to perform either of these types of action. This
point provides a basis for responding to John Plamanetz's critique of Marx on
the basis that social relations must be understood in normative terms.

Plamanetz offers two arguments for thinking that social relations must be
understood in normative terms. One is that social relations cannot but be
defined in normative terms. To ground his objection to 'Marx's doctrine' that
ideas are determined by social conditions, Plamenatz claims: '[s]ocial conditions consist, presumably, of social relations, and these relations are defined
in terms of conventional modes of behaviour'.[38] By 'conventional modes of
behaviour', Plamenatz has in mind something akin to what Weber calls a convention.[39] Plamenatz's objection to Marx's doctrine, then, is that, as social
conditions consists of social relations, and as social relations are defined by
conventions, it is not possible to say that social conditions determine ideas:
'[w]hat, then, can be meant by saying that men's social conditions determine
their ideas?'[40] To say that social conditions determine ideas is to say something
of the form '"A plus B determines B", which does not make sense'.[41]

Elsewhere, Plamenatz offers a wider version of this objection, by claiming
that the ideas by which social relations are defined include not just conventions, but also moral ideas:

> All properly social relations are moral and customary; they cannot be
> adequately defined unless we bring normative concepts into the defini-
> tions, unless we refer to rules of conduct which the persons who stand in
> those relations recognize and are required to conform to.[42]

We can call the problem of how to describe social relations so that they are
distinct from normative ideas (including moral and customary rules) the *problem of normativity*. So stated, the problem of normativity is a problem for those

---

38   Plamenatz 1970, p. 48; see, similarly, Plamenatz 1963, p. 283, p. 286; Collins 1982, pp. 78–9.
39   On Weber's view of a convention, see ch. 2, sec. 3.
40   Plamenatz 1970, p. 48.
41   Plamenatz 1963, p. 282.
42   Plamenatz 1963, pp. 283–4.

who wish to claim that social relations are (part of) what determine(s) normative ideas. Social relations can only be said to determine normative ideas if they are not already described in terms of them.

A second argument for why social relations must be understood in normative terms is implied by Plamenatz's remark that human beings 'become self-conscious and conscious of other selves ... in the process of learning to see themselves in moral and customary (and therefore social) relations'.[43] This remark suggests the following argument. Human beings become conscious of themselves and others in social relations. But it is only by recognising and conforming to rules of conduct that human beings can become conscious of themselves and others. Hence, social relations must 'involve'[44] rules of conduct. This argument is distinct from the first. The point as far as this second argument goes is that, irrespective whether or not it is possible to define social relations without reference to normative ideas, no such definition would be one on which it remained true to say that human beings become conscious of themselves and others in social relations.

The interactional conception of a social relation outlined above and the argument for how it preserves the species-awareness claim permit three responses to Plamenatz. One concerns the definition of a social relation. Implicit in Plamenatz's remarks is a conception of a social relation as any activity in which people recognise and conform to rules of conduct that concern how they are to behave vis-à-vis others. To adopt *this* conception of a social relation is to define a social relation in terms of the normative ideas that underpin these rules. Hence, to solve the problem of normativity, it is necessary to propose a different conception of a social relation, which avoids defining it by rules of conduct. An interactional conception of a social relation is one such conception.

Second, an interactional conception of a social relation allows particular social relations to be described so that their description avoids reference to normative ideas. If action is behaviour oriented to an in-order-to motive, then behaviour is only described as action when the description relates its course to an in-order-to motive. So, if a social relation is defined by standard actions of social affecting, and actions of interpretation, a description of a particular social relation is non-normative if the description of these actions' in-order-to motives avoids reference to normative ideas. In the case of A's action to B, no norms may be referred to, to describe the action by B that A aims to bring about,

---

43   Plamenatz 1963, p. 284.
44   Plamenatz 1963, p. 286.

or to describe *B*. An in-order-to motive is described with reference to a norm if it is characterised as the goal of having upheld a norm or of having avoided a sanction that a deviation from a norm is expected to receive. An in-order-to motive is described with reference to a convention if it is characterised as the goal of having strengthened others' beliefs that they can show their disapproval of deviant behaviour with assurance, or of having avoided another's approbation. As long as the descriptions of the actions of an interaction need not be descriptions of these sorts of in-order-to motive, the problem of normativity is open to an interactional solution.

The description of a simple interaction of question and answer in which a passer-by is asked the time and the answer received is '5.30pm' satisfies this condition. An interactional solution to the problem of normativity is therefore in principle possible. Cohen's claim that 'Plamenatz experiences difficulty when he confronts Marxian theoretical constructions because he is disposed to see in society only a collection of activities, not positions',[45] is a misdiagnosis, therefore. In supposing that the problem of normativity is insoluble, Plamanetz exemplifies the inability of sociological thought to conceive of an approach to the study of social activity that does not proceed on the basis of the concept of a social role.[46]

Finally, it is not necessary to describe social relations by reference to norms to have a description of them on which it is true to say that human beings become conscious of themselves and others in social relations. An interactional conception of a social relation preserves the species-awareness claim. In an interaction, each actor exercises, and demands another to exercise, a capacity for interpretation. Each does so whether or not their action is oriented to a norm or convention. The awareness of oneself as a being of a kind is one sort of awareness of oneself and others. So, whether or not a particular social relation is described by reference to norms, its description will be a description on which it is true to say that human beings become aware of themselves and others in social relations. If human beings become aware of themselves and others in social relations, then that is a reason to adopt a non-normative interactional conception of a social relation as a relation of mutual affecting.

---

45   Cohen 1988, 46.
46   See ch. 6, sec. 2.

5   An Interactional Conception of a Social Relation of Production

An interactional conception of a social relation refines Marx's general remarks on social relations, and can in principle negotiate the problem of normativity. But whether it also fits Marx's general remarks on social relations of production is a further question. The two sets of remarks might be inconsistent. At issue here and below is whether Marx's general remarks on social relations of production (as distinct from Marx's specific analyses of the social relations of production belonging to a specific form of society) are consistent with conceiving them as interactions; and whether an interactional conception of social relations of production can be defended against objections arising from the *1859 Preface*.

In his *Economic Manuscripts of 1861–63*, Marx refers to a '*relation of production*' as a 'social relation of individuals within production as a whole'.[47] To describe a relation of production as a kind of social relation implies that it links at least two actors. If one-person autarkic units of production coexisted side by side, there would be no social relations of production.

Because human production is not autarkic, *The German Ideology* can remark:

> The production of life, both of one's own in labour and that of another in procreation, already appears simultaneously as a twofold relation; on the one hand, as a natural relation, on the other, as a social relation – social to be understood in the sense of the cooperation [*Zusammenwirken*] of a number of individuals, whatever its conditions, mode and purpose.[48]

Changes in the social form of production (such as from capitalist production to socialist production) can only consist in changes to its 'conditions, mode and purpose'. To identify features of production that remain constant 'whatever' its conditions, mode and purpose is to identify features of production that endure irrespective of any changes of social form. One transhistorical feature of a social relation of production suggested by this remark is 'cooperation', which is a type of interaction. A further feature is that it also always has a 'natural relation'. It must give nature a form fit for human life. The in-order-to motives of actions of social relations of production must relate to something with or related to use-value.

---

47   *MEW*, 43, p. 140; *MECW*, 30, p. 148.
48   *MEJ*, 2003, pp. 14–15; *MEW*, 3, pp. 29–30; *MECW*, 5, p. 43.

An interactional conception of a social relation of production as cooperation in the existence of use-value is ambiguous, however, depending on whether 'cooperation' denotes cooperation in the production of a given type of product, or cooperation in the production of a total social product. The latter, societal cooperation, which *Capital* describes as 'the social relation of producers to total labour',[49] is meant here. As one interaction can encompass a number of distinct interactions, societal cooperation is conceivable as one all-encompassing interaction.

Relatedly, Marx argues in the *Grundrisse*:

> That the need of one can be satisfied by the product of another and vice versa; that one is able to produce the object for the need of another [*den Gegenstand dem Bedürfnis des andren zu produzieren*] ... shows that each, as a *human being*, outsteps their own particular need, etc., and that they relate to one another as human beings; that their common species-nature [*Gattungswesen*] is known by all. This does not happen elsewhere; elephants do not produce for tigers, or animals for other animals. E.g. a swarm of bees is essentially just one bee, and they all produce the same thing.[50]

By the fact of what they produce, no human being is precluded from identifying a type of product that they do not produce as suited for a certain type of use, or from developing a type of want that that other type of product can satisfy. Any human being with the relevant stock of experiences, which extends beyond that of a particular productive function, may do so. Hence, no productive function can exclude its performer from the potential usership of any type of product. Insofar as producers seek to make products that can be identified as

---

49   *MEW*, 23, p. 86; *MECW*, 35, p. 83; Marx 1976, p. 165.

50   *MEW*, 42, p. 168; *MECW*, 28, pp. 174–5; Marx 1973a, p. 243. (1) Marx 1973a translates the clause '*den Gegenstand dem Bedürfnis des andren zu produzieren*' as 'producing the object of the need of the other' (which would be: '*den Gegenstand des Bedürfnisses des anderen produzierend*'). The definite article '*dem*' is a *dative* indicating a beneficiary, however, a '*dativus commodi*' (Engel 1996, p. 193). It is not a *genitive* indicating a relationship of belonging (which would be: '*des*'). By eliminating the intentionality implied by Marx's phrase, the Marx 1973a rendering turns it into a redundant repetition of the sentence's first clause. (The *MECW* translation avoids this error). (2) Both *MECW* and Marx 1973a translate '*Gattungswesen*' as 'species-being', but 'species-nature' is better here, as Marx's concern is with the nature of the species to which a producer is aware of belonging. (Heinrich claims that, after 1845, this concept 'no longer surfaces in Marx's work' (Heinrich 2005, p. 20; Heinrich 2012, p. 22). Both the concept and – in this passage – the word, are there).

suited for certain types of use, and that can satisfy types of want, they do not anticipate anyone as excluded from the potential usership of what they produce. But if no one is anticipated as excluded from the potential usership of any product, there is no limit to the range of other productive activities that any given productive activity, and any producer performing it, can enable, by making a product that complements other products, as part of a total social product. Societal cooperation in the existence of use-value is conceivable, therefore, both from the point of view of its social component (one interaction of a certain type can encompass all interactions of that type), and from the point of view of its product component (each productive activity can enable every other).

The total social product is the total amount of all the types of product that are recognised in a society as products that can satisfy human wants. The test of whether a product is recognised in a society as a product that can satisfy a human want is whether, by virtue of the conditions of that society, the product is produced, and distributed to other people. To say that there is societal cooperation in the existence of use-value is to say that a producer produces a type of use-value in order to contribute to this total social product (whatever further purpose they may thereby realise, and whatever the conditions and mode of so doing are). As human beings have various needs that can only be satisfied by different types of object, any given productive activity can only be performed as a contribution to a total social product on the assumption that other productive activities producing complementary products are also performed by others. To cooperate in producing a total social product is thus to be aware (if only implicitly) of oneself and others as beings of a kind with the capacity to produce for anyone and have their needs satisfied by anyone. It is to be aware of this 'common species-nature'.

6   Some Objections

Cohen's interpretation of Marx raises or suggests three objections to an interactional conception of the social relations of production belonging to particular forms of society. Each objection relates to a sentence from Marx's *1859 Preface*:

> The totality of these relations of production constitutes the economic structure of society, the real basis from which a juridical and political superstructure arises, and to which determinate social forms of consciousness correspond ... It is not the consciousness of human beings that determines their being, but their social being that determines their con-

sciousness. At a certain stage of their development, the material productive powers of society enter into contradiction with the existing relations
of production, or, what is only a juridical expression for the same thing,
with the property relations in which they were previously put in motion.[51]

The objection related to the first sentence, the *objection from structure*, is that
social relations of production form a structure, and a structure cannot be comprised of interactions, because 'to represent the structure as itself a process is
to violate ... the concept of structure'.[52] The objection related to its second sentence, the *objection from consciousness*, is that a structure of social relations
of production is supposed to explain consciousness, and a structure of interactions cannot be distinguished from the consciousness it is supposed to explain:
'the economic structure, which is not an activity or set of activities, is central; and while moral and other ideas may enter the activity, the structure may
be so conceived that it is free of all such superstructural encumbrances'.[53] The
objection related to the third sentence, the *objection from legality*, is that the
structure of social relations of production is distinct from legal property relations, and a structure of interactions cannot be distinguished from the latter.
This is the implication of saying that Plamenatz held that 'relations of production ... are themselves legal in character'[54] because 'he is disposed to see
in society only a collection of activities'.[55]

7   The Objection from Structure

Take, first, the objection from structure. The response to the objection from
structure is that the features of a structure that Cohen identifies do not decide
between an effective control conception or an interactional conception of
social relations of production, or some third conception.

   One feature of a structure, Cohen says, is that it 'names no names'.[56] Its
description omits the identity of the individuals or means of production it
links. There is no change in a structure if one person dies and another takes
their position, or if two people swap positions. Thus, two different countries,

---

51   *MEW*, 13, pp. 8–9; *MECW*, 29, p. 263.
52   Cohen 1978, p. 86; see, similarly, Cohen and Acton 1970, p. 123; Wetherly 2005, p. 115.
53   Cohen 1988, p. 39.
54   Cohen 1988, p. 30.
55   Cohen 1988, p. 46.
56   Cohen 1978, p. 85.

Cohen says, could, in principle, have identical economic structures.[57] A second feature of a structure, Cohen says, is that it is comprised of positions. A 'position in the economic structure'[58] is defined by all of an individual's social relations of production. No single social relation of production constitutes a position, if no individual's total combination of social relations of production is exhausted by that one relation. One social relation of production merely 'contributes to defining'[59] an economic position. Drawing these features together, a structure, for Cohen, is comprised of anonymous positions.

Let it be granted that a structure is comprised of anonymous positions. (This view is rejected in chapter 6, but for now it is not challenged). It does not follow that to conceive a structure as comprised of interactions 'is to violate ... the concept of structure'.[60] In respect of the criterion of anonymity, interactions can be described by employing variables in place of expressions denoting particular individuals. Only the anonymised actions of an interaction need belong to a structure of interactions. The particular individuals who perform them need not. Second, in respect of the criterion of positionality, the notion of the total combination of an individual's social relations of production is neutral as between how a social relation of production is conceived.

If, as Cohen presumes, a structure of interactions is an inherently contradictory notion, a third unstated feature of a structure must have been silently assumed. But no such feature is likely to be both warranted as an interpretation of Marx, and decisive as between differing conceptions of social relations of production, for, contrary to what Cohen says, 'structure' is not a 'concept'[61] in Marx's writings. It is just one of several phrases – including 'skeleton',[62] 'organic system',[63] 'entire inner economic structure',[64] 'anatomy',[65] 'inner physiology'[66] and 'hidden foundation'[67] – indicating that, in Marx's view, a systematic study of social life cannot rest content with how isolated phenomena appear.[68] To suggest that an interactional conception of social relations of production viol-

---

57   Cohen 1978, p. 37.
58   Cohen 1978, p. 41, p. 73.
59   Cohen 1978, p. 41.
60   Cohen 1978, p. 86.
61   Ibid.
62   *MEW*, 42, p. 44; *MECW*, 28, p. 46; Marx 1973a, p. 110.
63   *MEW*, 42, p. 203; *MECW*, 28, p. 208; Marx 1973a, p. 278.
64   *MEGA*, II, 2, p. 68; *MECW*, 29, p. 481.
65   *MEW*, 13, p. 8; *MECW*, 29, p. 262.
66   *MEW*, 26. 2, p. 162; *MECW*, 31, p. 390.
67   *MEW*, 25, p. 799; *MECW*, 37, p. 778; Marx 1981, p. 927.
68   *MEW*, 32, p. 553; *MECW*, 43, p. 69.

ates Marx's concept of a skeleton would be absurd. It only seems less absurd to claim that an interactional conception of social relations of production violates Marx's concept of economic structure because 'structure' is a word that (unlike 'skeleton') has since taken on theoretical significance. The objection from structure reflects a misplaced desire to find profundity in a word where it is not to be found.

8   The Objection from Consciousness

The objection from consciousness is that a structure of interactions cannot be distinguished from the consciousness that the structure of society is supposed to explain. Cohen's use of the phrase 'moral and other ideas'[69] to describe the consciousness that the structure of society is supposed to explain permits two different versions of the objection, depending on whether 'other ideas' includes all other ideas, or simply all other normative ideas. Both versions may be rebutted.

The first version of the objection rests on an interpretation of the *1859 Preface*'s claim that 'social being ... determines ... consciousness'[70] which can be stated as follows:

(1)   the claim that social being determines consciousness is an explanatory claim

(2)   an *explanans* must be conceived free of its *explanandum*

(3)   social being includes all social relations

(4)   social being explains all consciousness

Interactions consist of actions, and actions exercise a capacity for abstraction, or thinking. So, if social being includes all social relations, as (3) asserts, to conceive of social relations as interactions is to include some thinking in social being. If social being includes some thinking, not all consciousness can be distinguished from social being. But according to (2), any consciousness conceived to belong to social being cannot be explained by social being. (4) cannot then be defended. Social being cannot explain all consciousness if it includes some consciousness. If, as (1) suggests, the claim that social being determines consciousness is an explanatory claim, an interactional conception of social relations of production limits the extent of that claim. A proponent of an interactional conception of social relations of production must either take issue

---

69   Cohen 1988, p. 39.
70   *MEW*, 13, p. 9; *MECW*, 29, p. 263.

with the above premises as an interpretation of the *1859 Preface*, or else accept that it artificially limits the extent of one of its claims.

To negotiate this first version of the objection, it is sufficient to replace premise (4) with: social being explains not all but only some consciousness; and to defend this replacement as an interpretation of the *1859 Preface*. If social being has only to explain some consciousness, it can include some thinking, and so consist of interactions, if the thinking that defines those interactions is distinct from the consciousness that social being explains.

The *1859 Preface*'s version of the claim that social being determines consciousness is just one part of an antithetical statement. It is immediately preceded by the denial that 'consciousness ... determines ... being'.[71] Accordingly, an interpretation of the *1859 Preface*'s version of the claim that social being determines consciousness must observe a constraint. The *antithetical constraint* is that social being and consciousness must be construed in such a way as to allow the possibility of believing (falsely, in Marx's view) that consciousness determines being. An interpretation of the *1859 Preface*'s claim that social being determines consciousness that presupposes an understanding of being and consciousness on which it is impossible to believe that consciousness determines being violates the antithetical constraint. It construes the *1859 Preface* as expending effort to deny something that no one could possibly believe, rather than (in Marx's view) a false belief. It would leave the *1859 Preface* engaged in empty rhetoric.

Premises (1)–(4) are not a valid interpretation of the *1859 Preface*, because they violate the antithetical constraint. They imply that social being excludes all consciousness, and no view of social being on which social being excludes all consciousness can satisfy the antithetical constraint. Consciousness can only determine being if it determines social being. To say that consciousness determines social being is to say that social being is *directed* by ideas whose institutionalisation is explained by the force of the better argument. For it even to be possible for social being to be directed by such ideas, social being would have to include something that was liable to be directed by ideas. It would have to include actions. But if social being includes actions, it includes some consciousness. To conceive social being as free from all consciousness is thus to violate the antithetical constraint. The antithetical constraint is observed by replacing (4) with the claim that social being explains not all but only some consciousness. The first version of the objection from consciousness is unfounded.

---

71   Ibid.

The second version of the objection, meanwhile, says that it is not possible to conceive of a structure of interactions that is distinct from all of the normative ideas that the structure of society is supposed to explain. This is a restatement of the problem of normativity posed by Plamenatz, which was addressed in section 4. An interactional conception of a social relation allows particular descriptions of social relations to avoid reference to normative ideas. No normative ideas need be cited to describe the in-order-to motives of actions that comprise particular social relations of production. The second version of the objection from consciousness may be raised against particular interactional accounts of social relations of production, but it cannot be raised against this conception itself.

9   The Problem of Legality

The final objection, the *objection from legality*, invokes the problem of legality. It says that an interactional conception of social relations of production cannot distinguish them from legal property relations.

The textual basis of the problem of legality, as noted above, is provided by the *1859 Preface*. It would be inconsistent to identify social relations of production, one of Marx's terms of art, with a type of relation they are said to explain, and hence must be distinct from. By claiming that social relations of production form an economic structure that explains a 'juridical ... superstructure' only then to suggest that the more familiar locution 'property relations' is a 'juridical expression for'[72] social relations of production, the *1859 Preface* leaves it unclear how these two types of relation are distinct. Any would-be conception of social relations of production must solve the *problem of legality*: how are social relations of production distinct from legal property relations? As Plamenatz asks: 'if they are not relations of property, what can they be?'[73]

Plamenatz's criticism of Marx is that the *1859 Preface*, in claiming that a structure of social relations of production explains legal phenomena, has said something 'which does not make sense'.[74] To defeat this criticism, it is necessary to argue that what the *1859 Preface* says is not 'necessarily false'.[75] It is not necessary to argue that what the *1859 Preface* says is true. It is not necessary to argue

---

72   *MEW*, 13, p. 8; *MECW*, 29, p. 263.
73   Plamenatz 1963, p. 280.
74   Plamenatz 1963, p. 282; compare p. 284.
75   Cohen 1983b, p. 212.

that social relations of production explain legal property relations, merely to solve the problem of legality. It is merely necessary to distinguish them. This point can be put another way. Suppose that the *1859 Preface* had not claimed that the structure of social relations of production explains legal phenomena. It would still generate a problem of legality. If, for argument's sake, the structure of social relations of production could only explain non-legal phenomena (art or religion, say), it would still be important to solve the problem of legality. Only then could it be denied that it is really legal property relations that explain those phenomena.

In fact, one may go further. A desire to solve the problem of legality does not presuppose *any* commitment to Marx's metaphor of basis and superstructure. There is only a superstructure if social relations of production explain something other than the (lack of) development of productive power. But even if social relations of production explained nothing except for the (lack of) development of productive power, and, consequently, there was no superstructure, one might still want to separate social relations of production from legal property relations, to distinguish their influence on the development of productive power from the influence of legal property relations on the development of productive power.

In other words, the problem of legality could be posed independently of its textual basis in the *1859 Preface*. It can be posed irrespective of how *Marx* conceives of property relations, in the *1859 Preface* or elsewhere; and regardless of whether Marx claims that social relations of production explain legal property relations. If Marx's term of art is to have any independent value, a common locution cannot be just as good. If 'x explains social relations of production' is just a more obscure way of saying 'x explains legal property relations', and if 'social relations of production explain x' is just a more obscure way of saying 'legal property relations explain x', there is no point in retaining Marx's term.

On an interactional conception, the basis for determining whether or not social relations of production are distinct from some other type of phenomenon is provided by the in-order-to motives of the actions that comprise them. If the description of these in-order-to motives does not refer to a type of phenomenon, social relations of production are distinct from it. Social relations of production are distinct from legal property relations if the in-order-to motives of the actions that comprise them can be described without reference to any legal phenomenon.

The in-order-to motive of a standard action of social affecting by A is to affect action by B. A description of A's action is distinct from x if neither B, nor the action by B that A aims to bring about, are described by reference to x. Here, the in-order-to motive of A's action must be described as that of getting B (who is described without reference to legal phenomena) to perform action that is described without reference to legal phenomena.

The in-order-to motive of an action is legal if its goal is to establish, uphold, alter or cancel a legal relation, or to avoid a legal sanction. An in-order-to motive of an action is *non-legal* if its goal is not to establish, uphold, alter or cancel a legal relation, or to avoid a legal sanction. If the actions of social relations of production are described by the latter, non-legal in-order-to motives, the problem of legality is solved. No interaction whose component actions are described in terms of non-legal in-order-to motives remains indistinct from legal property relations.

Potentially, three strategies are available, on an interactional conception of social relations of production, to solve the problem of legality. The straightforward strategy is to identify non-legal terms that Marx used to describe the in-order-to motives of the actions that comprise social relations of production. If Marx does not provide such non-legal terms, then a second, more indirect strategy is 'to formulate a non-legal interpretation of the legal terms in Marx's characterization of production relations'.[76] In Cohen's own version of the term replacement strategy, all rights-denoting terms that might otherwise be used to describe social relations of production are replaced with *de facto* power-denoting terms. But a different version of the term replacement strategy is also available to an interactional approach. It is possible, without varying an in-order-to motive's span, to replace a legal term that Marx uses to describe a social relation of production with a non-legal term. Finally, a third strategy might involve varying the span of an in-order-to motive. It might be possible to describe an in-order-to motive without reference to a type of phenomenon by extending or reducing an in-order-to motive's span, so as to avoid the need to refer to it. It is not necessary to dwell on the mechanics of the latter two strategies, however, for the straightforward strategy will be employed.

The interaction-recognition-antinomy thesis is a thesis about capitalism. To defend this thesis, what is required is a solution to the problem of legality as it pertains to a minimal description of the capitalist economic structure in terms of two generalised interactions: purchase and sale, and production with wage-labour for continuous money maximisation. Whether a non-legal description of the actions of these interactions provides a basis for deriving a juridical superstructure is a matter for later chapters. The task here is simply to provide an account of the capitalist economic structure on which it is not

---

76   Cohen 1978, p. 219.

necessarily false or confused to say that the juridical logic of freedom of choice is derived from a commodity form based conception of the capitalist economic structure.

The straightforward strategy adopted here uses the terms: possession, commodities, money, labour, agreement, offer, acceptance and instruction. Each of these terms can be described without reference to legal phenomena. If the social relations of production that belong to a minimal description of the capitalist economic structure are comprised of actions oriented to in-order-to motives described in these terms, they can be distinguished from all legal phenomena, including legal property relations.

A detailed analysis of possession, on which no terms denoting legal phenomena are required for its definition, is offered in chapter 7. The non-technical definition of possession offered in chapter 3 as control by someone who asserts an exclusive claim will do for now. For it is part of common sense, reflected in everyday expressions such as 'possession is nine-tenths of the law', to understand possession as something *de facto*. The point to focus on here is that the relevance of possession to the problem of legality is suggested by Marx himself. *Capital* uses possession in conjunction with legal terms in a way that suggests that property relations are a legal expression for interactions between possessors.

The relevant comment is found in the subsection entitled 'Purchase and Sale of Labour Power' within Chapter Four of the German edition of *Capital*, and which becomes, in the English translations, the main heading of Chapter Six, with the order of the terms 'Purchase' and 'Sale' arbitrarily reversed. Using 'he' to refer back to the 'possessor [*Besitzer*]' of 'labour power' who is also its 'free owner [*Eigentümer*]', Marx writes:

> He and the money possessor [*Geldbesitzer*] encounter one another in the market and enter into relation with one another as commodity possessors [*Warenbesitzer*] of equal birth, distinguished merely by the fact that the one is a purchaser, the other a seller, hence both are juridically equal persons [*Personen*].[77]

The Aveling/Moore and Fowkes translations of this sentence are misleading. Both obscure from the reader Marx's repeated use of the concept of possession, in connection with money and commodities. Both render '*Geldbesitzer* [money

---

77   *MEW*, 23, p. 182; *MECW*, 35, p. 178; Marx 1976, p. 271. On the distinction between possession and ownership, see ch. 7, sec. 3 and ch. 9, sec. 2.

possessor]' as 'owner of money';[78] while in the Aveling/Moore translation, '*Warenbesitzer* [commodity possessors]' is not rendered as a *nomen agenti* at all, and the Fowkes translation renders it as 'owners of commodities'.[79] Moreover, neither of these translations renders '*Personen* [persons]' with a *nomen agenti*. Each instead says that seller and purchaser are equal 'in the eyes of the law'.[80]

The only *nomen agenti* that appear in the Aveling/Moore and Fowkes translations of this sentence are defined in legal terms: 'owners', 'buyer' and 'seller'. As a consequence, both translations obliterate what ought to be straightforwardly recognisable as a double description of two human subjects as possessors and as persons (or as buyer/seller), the first a non-legal description and the second a legal description. The effect is to camouflage a resource for solving the problem of legality. If it is possible to refer to the subjects who enter into a relation of purchase and sale in legal language as persons (or as buyer and seller), but also in *de facto* terms as commodity possessor and money possessor, then capitalist relations of production can be distinguished from legal property relations by being described as interactions between commodity possessors and money possessors. 'Property relations' is merely a 'juridical expression for' capitalist relations of production because the latter are comprised of actions that seek to acquire or retain possession of commodities or money, or put someone else in the position of acquiring or retaining possession of commodities or money.

This solution to the problem of legality is not the indirect one that the official translations leave interpreters who rely on them to pursue, of formulating 'a non-legal interpretation of the legal terms in Marx's characterization of production relations'.[81] It is the straightforward strategy of building on the non-legal terms *Capital* uses to characterise such relations. Take, first, the relation of purchase and sale.

A contract of sale, according to Friedrich Carl von Savigny, Marx's teacher of jurisprudence, consists of two declarations of will whose content is in agreement.[82] A declaration of will is the signal of an intention to alter one's legal rights and/or duties. For a contract of sale, two declarations of will are in agreement if they indicate the same generic object of sale, and same value to be given in return. For example, *A* says to *B*, or does something that amounts to saying to *B*: I want to buy 1 coat for 100 euros. Likewise, *B* says to *A*, or does something that

---

78   'Owner of money' would be: '*Geldeigentümer*'.
79   'Owners of commodities' would be: '*Wareneigentümer*'.
80   'In the eyes of the law' would be: '*in den Augen des Gesetzes*'.
81   Cohen 1978, p. 219.
82   Savigny 1840, pp. 5–7, pp. 307–14.

amounts to saying to *A*: I want to sell 1 coat for 100 euros. If, as here, *A* and *B*'s declarations of will are in agreement, certain legal consequences follow; each incurs a legal obligation to transfer their respective item to the other.

To describe purchase and sale as a non-legal interaction between a commodity possessor and a money possessor, all the legal terms that might otherwise describe the in-order-to motives of its participants must be eliminated. There can be no reference to an in-order-to motive to alter legal rights and/or duties. One solution is offered by the concept of possession. To say that the possessor of an object agrees to let another possess it is to say that the first agrees both to cease to treat it as something that they may use without regard to anyone else's permission or instruction, and to bring about a state of affairs in which the other has control over it. Let A = a money possessor, and B = a commodity possessor. Substituting x and y for amounts of money and coats in the above example, purchase and sale begins when A signals their intention to let B possess x on condition that B lets A possess y, and B signals their intention to let A possess y on condition that A lets B possess x. A's offer is oriented to the antecedent projection of B having understood and accepted it. B's acceptance of the offer is a second standard action of social affecting, oriented to A having understood that their offer has been accepted. Each transfer, of money or commodities, is also a standard action of social affecting, oriented to an antecedent projection of the other possessor as having noted that part of their agreement has been performed.

One might worry that the term 'agreement' denotes a legally binding agreement. But *Capital* says that we may imagine that a 'relation of will' may be 'legally developed or not'.[83] We can abstract from the enforceability of an agreement by a court without prejudice to the fact that its upshot is to facilitate a money possessor becoming a commodity possessor, and a commodity possessor becoming a money possessor. After all, illegal (and hence non-enforceable) drug purchases are an instance of purchase and sale, on the above conception. It is possible, therefore, to provide an interactional solution to the problem of legality in respect of at least one social relation of production, namely purchase and sale. Generalised purchase and sale can belong to a capitalist economic structure, and be distinguished from legal property relations.

It might be objected that legal terms still feature in the phrase 'purchase and sale', which has been retained to designate a relation of the capitalist eco-

---

83   *MEW*, 23, p. 99; *MECW*, 35, p. 95; Marx 1976, p. 178. The full passage is translated in ch. 9, sec. 2.

nomic structure. But this objection is insubstantial. What matters is that the actions that comprise the social relation designated as 'purchase and sale' are non-legal. The phrase 'purchase and sale' is retained for simplicity.

The same terms also provide a means to describe the social relation of production with wage-labour for continuous money maximisation. This relation is comprised of the following actions: an offer of labour in return for money; acceptance of the offer; instruction of the labour to be performed; labour oriented to receiving money; and transfer of the money. All these actions can again be described as oriented to getting another to act so as to acquire or retain possession of commodities or money, and to others as possessors. Those that take place on the market may be described in the same terms used to describe the actions belonging to the relation of purchase and sale. In the production process, the money possessor's in-order-to motive is to instruct the one who confronted them in purchase and sale as the possessor of their labour power to produce a commodity that they will possess. The in-order-to motive of the latter is to get the money possessor to note that the labour they instructed has been performed by someone they agreed to give money to.

It might be objected that the action that is taken to comprise social relations of production would not exist in the absence of certain legal phenomena. For example, producers would not be able to act on the basis that they possess their labour power if it were not for the coercive enforcement of certain personal freedoms. The distinction required here is that between a necessary condition and a constitutive condition.[84] A necessary condition of x is a condition that (at least in our world) makes x possible; a constitutive condition of x is a condition for x to count as x. To say that a legal phenomenon makes a non-legal in-order-to motive possible is not to say that it constitutes it. The fact that social relations of production are comprised of actions that would not exist in the absence of certain legal phenomena may be a truth, but one that has not and need not be denied. To derive one phenomenon from another, it is not necessary to claim that the latter would be able to exist without the derived phenomenon.

This solution to the problem of legality also reveals how there can be an interactional solution to the problem of normativity. An interactional conception of a social relation can in principle solve the problem of normativity, it was

---

84   Cassam 2003, pp. 194–5. Cohen, too, relies on something like this necessary condition/constitutive condition distinction to defend his version of the term replacement strategy when he emphasises that 'my way of defining production relations does not stipulate how the powers they enfold are obtained and sustained' (Cohen and Acton 1970, p. 139; see, similarly, Cohen 1988, 35; Cohen 1989, p. 99).

argued above, because not all descriptions of the in-order-to motives of actions that belong to social relations need refer to a norm or convention. An interactional conception of social relations of production in terms of possession-oriented in-order-to motives does in fact solve the problem of normativity, because possession-oriented in-order-to motives are non-normative in-order-to motives. To describe actors as possessors is not to refer to a norm or convention; and to describe the above ways of getting another to act so as to acquire or retain possession of commodities or money, it is not necessary to refer to a norm or a convention. No reference to rights or duties, sanctions, disapproval or approbation is required.

One might worry that the term 'agreement' denotes something normative or conventional. But just as it is possible to abstract from the enforceability of an agreement, so it is possible to abstract from its normativity; that is, from participants' understanding that they *ought* to do what they agree to do. When it is said that money or commodities are transferred in order that another possessor takes note that a part of an agreement has been performed, 'agreement', here, simply denotes a meeting of the minds that creates an expectation on the part of another of likely future behaviour.

Consider Max Weber's remark in *Economy and Society* that, even if 'commerce' is 'lacking any normative regulation or coercive guarantee', exchangers can still count on 'the other's *own interest* in the continuation of a particular consensual act as such'.[85] Ordinarily, each will want to have the chance to continue to do deals with another, and/or with others who may learn of their dealings with that other. To that end, it is necessary to meet (or appear to meet) certain expectations of the other. When, to describe the capitalist economic structure, it is said that possessors transfer commodities or money to bring about the other's awareness that a part of their agreement has been performed, all that is meant is that possessors perform transfers to complete part of an arrangement that is commonly understood as a measure by which people decide whether it would be prudent to have future dealings with them. No norm or convention is thereby invoked.

The purpose of responding to the objection from structure, the objection from consciousness and the problem from legality is defensive. It is to show that the notion of a social structure and the need to distinguish the capitalist economic structure from normative ideas and legal phenomena do not preclude an interactional conception of capitalist relations of production. The positive interpretive argument for this conception is its consistency with Marx's

---

85   Weber 2005, p. 250; Weber 1978, p. 331.

aforecited general remarks. The positive substantive argument is its consistency with the awareness condition and the species-awareness claim, and the derivation of the juridical logic of freedom of choice in chapters 9 and 11.

CHAPTER 6

System and Bearer

The interaction-recognition-antinomy thesis characterises the capitalist economic structure in terms of two types of interaction: purchase and sale, and labour-exploitation. Chapters 7–8 present a separate analysis of each type of interaction. But first it may be asked how different types of interaction can combine to form a social structure.

A social structure can be conceived as a combination of generalised interactions. A system, more particularly, is a combination of generalised interactions whose tokens have an unintentionally constraining form imposed on them by the generalised existence of token interactions of their type. As a result, actors in a system are what *Capital* calls 'bearers [*Träger*]'.[1] That is, actors in each token interaction treat one another as if they did not have an end beyond it that they have.

The argument for conceiving the capitalist economic structure as a system in which actors are bearers challenges the sociological reception of Marx's writings. The fundamental concept of sociology, Ralf Dahrendorf argues, is the concept of a social role; that is, the 'expected modes of behavior' assigned to a position that are sustained by others' expected use of their positional powers.[2] To assimilate Marx's critique of political economy to the discipline of sociology is to treat it as a contribution to a theory of socio-economic roles. Dahrendorf,[3] the American sociologist Robert Merton[4] and others[5] take Marx's use of the term 'bearer' and other related phrases in *Capital* as expressions for the sociological concept of a role occupant. But that is unfounded. A bearer is not a role occupant.

---

1   *MEW*, 23, p. 16, p. 100; *MECW*, 35, p. 10, p. 95; Marx 1976, p. 92, p. 179. The *MECW* translation of *Capital* does not contain the term 'bearer' at all. At *MECW*, 35, p. 10, 'embodiments' is used (which would be: '*Verkörperungen*') and at p. 95, 'them'. Ben Brewster's glossary to *Reading Capital* suggests rendering '*Träger*' as 'support' (Althusser and Balibar 1975, p. 320). But '*Träger*', like 'bearer', is a *nomen agentis* (Engel 1996, p. 504). In English, the noun 'support', as in the phrase 'this beam is a support for the roof', is not a *nomen agentis*. 'Support' would not be a good translation of '*Träger*'.

2   Dahrendorf 1971, pp. 30–2; Dahrendorf 1973, pp. 16–17. Although a reference is supplied to a German edition of Dahrendorf's work, the translation (by Dahrendorf) is unaltered.

3   Dahrendorf 1971, p. 27; Dahrendorf 1973, p. 13.

4   Merton 1957, p. 462.

5   Iorio 2003, p. 76.

Section 1 defends a generalised interactions conception of the capitalist economic structure. Section 2 explains and problematises the sociological concept of a social role. Section 3 outlines the features of a system. Sections 4–5 argue that the capitalist economic structure can be conceived as a system. Finally, section 6 presents an abstraction-from-ends conception of an actor as a bearer, and distinguishes a bearer from a role occupant.

1   A Generalised Interactions Conception of Social Structure

In a famous passage from his *1859 Preface*, Marx claims that '[t]he totality of these relations of production' – the relations of production that correspond to a certain level of development of productive power – 'constitutes the economic structure of society'.[6] In chapter 5, this claim was discussed in the context of rebutting the objection from structure, which offered it as evidence against an interactional conception of social relations of production. In rebutting the objection from structure, two points were stressed. First of all, interactions can be described anonymously. Second, positions can consist of interactions. If a 'position in the economic structure'[7] is defined by a combination of all of an individual's social relations of production, that is no reason to believe that it is not defined by the combination of all of their relevant interactions. To rebut the objection from structure, it was not necessary to offer a positive account of the capitalist economic structure. It is now necessary to say something more positive.

If a social structure is formed from different types of social relation, the latter must be able to combine. One initial question, therefore, in conceiving of social structure, is: at what level are different types of social relation to be thought to combine? A conception of social structure on which the combination of different types of social relation is first conceived at the level of the positions occupied by individuals can be termed a *positional* conception of social structure. A conception of social structure on which their combination is first conceived at the societal level can be termed a *generalised relations* conception of social structure. On the latter conception, the question is: on the premise that each type of social relation is to be generalised, what types of social relation can combine? Different types of generalised social relation can combine if they would leave intact and/or reproduce enough of their conditions of existence to allow them to persist as generalised social relations.

---

6   *MEW*, 13, pp. 8–9; *MECW*, 29, p. 263.
7   Cohen 1978, p. 41, p. 73.

To see that the question of societal-level combination is distinct from that of individual-level combination, imagine two types of social relation, X and Y. The tokens of X and Y each involve two actors who have different functions vis-à-vis one another, designated as X1 and X2, Y1 and Y2. At the level of positions, there are then fifteen conceivable combinations of X1, X2, Y1 and Y2 (including none of them) that might exhaustively describe the position of any one individual in respect of X and Y. The questions of societal-level combination and individual-level combination are distinct, for the question of whether X and Y can combine if they are generalised is distinct from the question of which of the conceivable combinations of X1, X2, Y1 and Y2 it is possible for any one individual to hold.

A generalised relations conception of social structure treats the question of what positions individuals may have as subordinate to the question of what types of generalised social relations a society may have, and only counts the latter as a question of social structure.[8] There are no positions in a social structure, on a generalised relations conception. A positional conception of social structure, by contrast, pays no special attention to social relations with a generalised existence. Its primary concern is with positions, and its account of what positions can exist does not assume that only generalised social relations serve to define a position.

There is ample evidence that Marx favours and is committed to a *generalised interactions* conception of the capitalist economic structure; that is, a generalised relations conception on which social relations are interactions. The arguments for this conception are that: (i) it fits remarks related to the above claim from the *1859 Preface*; (ii) it unifies structural and capital-accumulation-related conceptions of capitalism; and (iii) it permits a societal account of an individual's position in a class formation.

(i) A generalised interactions conception of the capitalist economic structure is supported by two related remarks Marx penned shortly before composing the *1859 Preface*. One appears in the *Grundrisse*, while the other is taken from Marx's draft of *A Contribution to a Critique of Political Economy*, the so-called *Urtext*. They are best considered together:

---

8 Derek Sayer's response to *KMTH*, entitled *The Violence of Abstraction*, argues that *KMTH*'s effective control conception of economic structure ignores the richness of experience (Sayer 1987, pp. 51–7). The present critique, by contrast, is that its positional character eschews what *Capital* calls the 'power of abstraction' (*MEW*, 23, p. 12; *MECW*, 35, p. 8; Marx 1976, p. 90).

> If, in the mature bourgeois system, each economic relation presupposes [*voraussetzt*] the other in its bourgeois-economic form, and so everything posited is at the same time a presupposition [*Voraussetzung*], that is the case with every organic system.[9]

> within the bourgeois mode of production, simple circulation itself only exists as a precondition [*Voraussetzung*] of capital, and as presupposing [*voraussetzend*] capital.[10]

In German, a '*Voraussetzung*' may denote either a precondition, such as when it is said that the '*Voraussetzungen*' for admission to a degree are to have passed more elementary courses of study; or else it may denote that which is taken for granted (for something else to occur), as when the '*Voraussetzung*' of a question or argument is a premise accepted by the addressor. (A rough divider is whether or not the adjective 'tacit' can be added as a modifier). The first presented feature in the exposition of a complex whole may be a '*Voraussetzung*' in the former sense, and have '*Voraussetzungen*' in the latter sense. On the one hand, the exposition of this first feature may be an elementary precondition for the exposition of other features that follow it in the order of the exposition. On the other hand, the exposition of this feature will also take for granted the remaining features of the whole that is to be presented, if the first feature cannot exist in the form in which it is analysed, except in a whole characterised by those other features.

A generalised interactions conception of the capitalist economic structure allows the above remarks to offer three claims. One claim is that 'simple circulation', or generalised purchase and sale, is a precondition of 'capital', that is, generalised production with wage-labour for continuous money maximisation.[11] A second claim is that generalised purchase and sale cannot exist except

---

9   *MEW*, 42, p. 203; *MECW*, 28, p. 208; Marx 1973a, p. 278. *MECW* renders '*Voraussetzung*' as 'premiss', while Marx 1973a (correctly in my view) renders it as 'presupposition'. The clause 'and so everything posited is at the same time a *Voraussetzung*' is short for: 'and so everything posited in the description of the mature bourgeois system is at the same time a *Voraussetzung* of the description of each of its economic relations'. 'Premiss' is therefore incorrect. An expounded system of relations cannot function as a 'premiss', that is, be used to make further inferences about any of its relations, for an expounded system of relations already is the complete description of each of its relations.

10   *MEGA*, II, 2, p. 91; *MECW*, 29, p. 505. *MECW* renders '*Voraussetzung*' and '*voraussetzend*' as 'preposited' and 'prepositing'. But that is gobbledygook, not English.

11   The argument for why generalised production with wage-labour for continuous money maximisation may be characterised as capitalist labour-exploitation is given in ch. 8.

in a whole characterised by generalised production with wage-labour for continuous money maximisation. A third claim is that mature capitalism (that is, a capitalism whose production processes make money-maximising use of all the various kinds of productive power that capital accumulation can generate) is characterised by the combination of generalised purchase and sale, and generalised production with wage-labour for continuous money maximisation. A defence of these claims is offered below. The point to note here is that a positional conception of the capitalist economic structure must flounder in the face of the above remarks. A positional conception cannot explain why Marx should want to claim that the system of capitalist production consists of simple circulation and capital, as neither simple circulation nor capital are positions.

(ii) A generalised interactions conception of the capitalist economic structure preserves the unity of Marx's account of capitalism. Cohen inadvertently highlights the case for this claim by remarking: 'there are two equally standard but logically distinct Marxian definitions of capitalist society'.[12] According to Cohen, Marx offers both a '*structural* definition' of capitalist society in terms of the economic positions of capitalist and worker; and a '*modal* definition', which 'refers to the purpose of capitalist production ... to use exchange-value to produce more exchange-value' endlessly, and which 'serves the accumulation of capital'.[13]

The conclusion that there are two equally standard Marxian definitions of capitalist society is untidy. It is inevitable, however, as long as one adopts a positional conception of the capitalist economic structure, and yet retains a wish to define capitalism so as to preserve a connection with capital accumulation. Capital accumulates from T1 to T2 if all money-maximising firms taken together can purchase a greater proportion of the total social product at T2 than at T1. No positional conception of the capitalist economic structure can capture this macro-level dynamic, for no positional conception can capture any macro-level dynamic. A generalised interactions conception of the capitalist economic structure may be preferred for this reason. To define capitalism by the combination of generalised purchase and sale and generalised production with wage-labour for continuous money maximisation is to define it by a process of capital accumulation. A generalised interactions conception of social structure is a conception on which theorising capitalism in terms of its structure directs one to its macro-level dynamic of capital accumulation.

---

12   Cohen 1978, p. 181.
13   Ibid.

In fact, Roemer sketches a society that shows that the attempt to combine a positional conception of capitalist society with an interest in capital accumulation is faced with an even more acute problem. Cohen's 'structural definition' of capitalist society does not simply not direct one to its macro-level dynamic of capital accumulation. It is inconsistent with the study of this dynamic as definitive of capitalism.

Roemer begins: '[c]onsider a society which consists of many producers, which produces one good: corn'.[14] Each individual requires one bushel of corn per week to subsist. Two techniques for producing corn are available. Technique I uses no corn as input. After six days of labour, it yields one bushel of corn. Technique II uses one bushel of seed corn as input. The yield, after three days of labour, is two bushels net. Suppose there is only enough seed corn to employ half the population using technique II, and that it is all owned by a few people. The result, Roemer says, is that owners of seed corn will hire producers to use technique II for six days a week, at a rate of one bushel of corn. The producers' weekly reward is kept at one bushel of corn per week by the existence of a 'reserve army' of 'peasants'[15] who use technique I to produce on their own. The upshot, Roemer says, is that each owner of seed corn 'realises as many bushels of corn as *profit* as he employs workers'.[16]

In Roemer's sketch, owners of means of production (corn) are enabled, by differential private ownership of means of production, to hire individuals who perform surplus labour for their benefit. Owners of means of production must hire labour in order to maximise their net revenue. On either the effective control version or the optimising modal relational properties (OMRP) version of the positional conception of capitalist society, the judgement of Roemer's sketch (as indeed Roemer judges it) is that it is at least in part (ignoring the peasants) a capitalist society. The private owners of the corn who hire voluntary labour are 'capitalists';[17] while the producers who hire out their labour power may also be 'proletarians'.[18] On the effective control version, these producers are proletarians because each controls 'none' of the '*means of production he uses*'.[19] For there to be proletarians on the OMRP version, it would be necessary to suppose that their labour was better rewarded than that of the peasants.

---

14   Roemer 1982a, p. 9.
15   Roemer 1982a, p. 11.
16   Roemer 1982a, p. 10.
17   Roemer 1982a, p. 11.
18   Ibid.
19   Cohen 1978, p. 65.

If capitalist society is defined by capital accumulation, this judgement must be denied. *Capital* Volume I insists that a capitalist's end does not 'lie outside circulation', and that it is not 'the appropriation of use-value'.[20] A capitalist's end is 'the restless movement of accruing [*Gewinnen*]'[21] within circulation, where circulation denotes the totality of purchases and sales of products. Thus, each capitalist's aim is 'conquest of the world of social wealth'.[22] In *Capital's* view, each capitalist is driven by competition to acquire as great an amount of the value of the total social product as possible, and capital accumulation is the unintended macro-level result. The hirers in Roemer's sketch cannot be considered capitalists, on this capital-accumulation-related conception of a capitalist, if, however one plays around with hirers' preferences for product, hirers do not seek to accumulate as much value as possible.

In Roemer's sketch, product yields always allow each hirer, without selling any product, to begin a new round of production in which they hire others' labour to produce a surplus that, after satisfying the hirer's own needs, can be used to re-hire labour. In other words, a hirer is always able to reproduce themselves as a hirer of others' labour without selling any product, assuming a steady supply of labour. Thus, no hirer can be driven out of business by the selling power of any other hirer. A lack of competition between hirers means that, in order to assume that a hirer's end is not to obtain a finite amount of use-value (corn as food), but to produce the greatest possible surplus of corn to hire the largest possible number of producers again, and so on, endlessly, hirers must be stipulated to have an insatiable preference for possessing corn (or for the pride of hiring as many people as possible), or an overriding preference for possessing more corn than others (or for hiring more people than others). But even if a hirer continuously seeks to produce the greatest possible surplus of corn to satisfy such a preference, their end lies outside circulation. There is no circulation, or value. If a hirer's end has no relation to circulation, it is not the end of a capitalist. The result of each hirer pursuing their end is not capital accumulation. On a capital-accumulation-related conception of capitalist society, the society that Roemer sketches is not even a little bit capitalist. There are no capitalists in it at all.[23]

---

20   *MEW*, 23, p. 167; *MECW*, 35, pp. 163–4; Marx 1976, p. 254.

21   *MEW*, 23, p. 168; *MECW*, 35, p. 164; Marx 1976, p. 254. '*Gewinnen* (accruing)' is translated in *MECW* and Marx 1976 as 'profit-making' (which would be: '*Profitmachen*'). Marx only mentions profit later on, however (*MEW*, 23, p. 232; *MECW*, 35, p. 227; Marx 1976, p. 327). To render '*Gewinnen*' as 'profit-making' throws a reader off the track of *Capital's* order of exposition.

22   *MEW*, 23, p. 619; *MECW*, 35, p. 588; Marx 1976, p. 739.

23   In *Analytical Marxism: A Critique*, Marcus Roberts claims (following Ellen Meiksins Wood)

If a positional conception of the capitalist economic structure judges a society capitalist when it lacks any capital accumulation, it is not an option to believe that Cohen has identified 'two equally standard ... Marxian definitions of capitalist society'.[24] At least one of them must be rejected. A generalised interactions conception of the capitalist economic structure shows that it is possible to study capitalist production without giving up the label 'structural' *or* a focus on capital accumulation.

(iii) A generalised interactions conception of social structure subordinates the question of what types of position there are to that of what types of generalised interaction a society may have. Relatedly, whether a particular individual has a position in the class formation of a capitalist society will depend on whether capital accumulation is the predominant dynamic of production. A positional conception of social structure implies a more individualistic approach to class position. On a positional conception, to ascertain an individual's class position, the first and only thing to do is to determine all the social relations of production that they have. It is not necessary to consider the overall dynamic of production in the society to which they belong. Any two individuals with the same combination of social relations occupy the same position, regardless of any differences in the overall dynamics of production in the societies to which they belong.

The difference between these two approaches to class position is illustrated by the problem of modern slave labour. The problem of modern slave labour is: can there be uses of slave labour that are capitalist, or are all uses of slave labour non-capitalist?

In Marx's judgement (in the *Grundrisse*, the *Economic Manuscripts of 1861–63*, and *Capital*), the slaveholders in the *antebellum* South are 'capitalists'.[25] The slaveholding plantation owners are capitalists, on *Capital*'s definition, if they employ labour for ceaseless moneymaking in 'circulation';[26] in other words, if their aim is to employ labour to acquire an ever greater amount of the value of

---

that 'Roemer has, then, simply built the systematic imperative to accumulation inscribed within the capitalist mode of production into the preference structures of these allegedly *pre-social* individuals' (Roberts 1996, p. 174; compare Wood 1989, p. 49). Roemer has done no such thing. Roberts here fails to subject Analytical Marxism to critique. To offer a critique of analysis-NS in respect of the concept of capital, it is necessary to challenge the idea (not grant) that a 'systematic imperative to accumulation' can be built into hirers' preferences for product from their own production process.

24   Cohen 1978, p. 181.
25   *MEW*, 42, p. 420; *MECW*, 28, p. 436; Marx 1973a, p. 513.
26   *MEW*, 23, p. 168; *MECW*, 35, p. 164; Marx 1976, p. 254.

the total social product. The slaveholding plantation owners of the *antebellum* South are capitalists, therefore, because they compete with others on a 'world market'[27] to make as much money as possible, and to that end impose as much unpaid labour as possible on their workforce. What enables and unintentionally constrains them to act as capitalists is the 'bourgeois system'.[28] Although capital accumulation will be the predominant dynamic of production only if most labour is voluntarily recruited, it is still possible for some capitalists who operate where the dynamic of capital accumulation is predominant to employ slave labour, 'as anomalies'.[29] Some modern uses of slave labour are capitalist.

Consider, by contrast, the judgement dictated by a positional conception of the capitalist economic structure. On a positional conception, the position of slaveholders in the *antebellum* South is defined by their effective control over means of production and slaves, or else by the fact that, if they are to optimise their net revenue, they must use slaves to operate means of production. The class position of slaveholders in the *antebellum* South is of the same type as anyone with the same combination of powers or same optimising option, regardless of the predominant dynamic of production, and hence regardless of the historical epoch they live in. On a positional conception of the capitalist economic structure, slaveholders in the *antebellum* South are not capitalists any more than slaveholders in ancient Rome are capitalists. Although Cohen remarks of slaveholders in the *antebellum* South that 'Marx is prepared to consider them "capitalists"',[30] neither the effective control version nor the OMRP version of the positional conception of the capitalist economic structure supports Marx's judgement. If, as Jairus Banaji claims, 'a majority of Marxists are probably still reluctant to abandon the comforting idea that slavery precludes capitalism',[31] then one root cause of this reluctance is a positional conception of economic structure.

27   *MEW*, 26. 2, p. 299; *MECW*, 31, p. 516.
28   *MEW*, 42, p. 376; *MECW*, 28, p. 392; Marx 1973a, p. 464.
29   *MEW*, 42, p. 420; *MECW*, 28, p. 436; Marx 1973a, p. 513. See also *MEW*, 42, p. 376; *MECW*, 28, p. 392; Marx 1973a, p. 464; as well as *MEW*, 26. 2, p. 299; *MECW*, 31, p. 516; and *MEW*, 23, p. 350; *MECW*, 35, p. 244; Marx 1976, p. 345.
30   Cohen 1978, p. 185.
31   Banaji 2010, p. 144.

2   Sociological Thought and the Concept of Social Role

The aim in the previous section was to offer some positive reasons for holding that Marx's conception of the capitalist economic structure is a generalised interactions conception, rather than a positional conception. In fact, these two conceptions reflect the difference between commodity form philosophy, and economic thought. This difference provides the basis for a critique of sociological thought.

Capital begins with an analysis of the commodity as a general form of wealth. As a general form of wealth is a general feature by virtue of which a type of society is reproduced non-contingently, a commodity form based conception of the capitalist economic structure must be a generalised relations conception. Only a generalised relations conception of social structure is directly suited to theorise reproduction at the societal level. A commodity form based conception of the capitalist economic structure can define it by generalised purchase and sale and generalised production with wage-labour for continuous money maximisation, if the commodity form generates money, and generalised purchase and sale cannot exist except in a whole characterised by generalised production with wage-labour for continuous money maximisation. These arguments will be presented later on. What matters here is to show that only a positional conception of the capitalist economic structure is available to economic thought.

The basic concept of economic thought is the concept of an economic good.[32] The concept of an economic good presupposes a commanding subject who is economically rational; that is, who retains the good, conserves it, puts it to the most desired use first, and uses as little as is necessary to satisfy a given desire. Thus, the concept of an economic good presupposes a subject with a full preference order and full information, or else sufficiently exhaustive assumptions. An economic subject is only sufficiently informed, however, if they know all the relevant facts about their position, and that of any relevant others. So, an economic structure is only a structure by which to conceive of subjects as sufficiently informed to act economically if it includes their economic positions. In other words, a conception of an economic structure can only serve as a way to theorise the economically rational use of economic goods if it includes subjects' economic positions. Moreover, for economic thought, the question of whether certain types of generalised social relation can combine at the societal-level is a non-issue. An economic subject is sufficiently informed

---

32   See ch. 3, sec. 3.

if they are sufficiently informed about their own and any relevant others' positions. But whether those positions are defined by a type of generalised social relation or by a type of anomalous social relation is irrelevant. Hence, for economic thought, the structure of capitalist production must be positional. The difference between a generalised interactions conception and a positional conception of the structure of capitalist production reflects the difference between Marx's critique of political economy, and economic thought.

This difference also reveals the basis for a critique of sociological thought. In *Homo Sociologicus*, Ralf Dahrendorf offers 'the category of social role' as the answer to its search for 'an elementary category for the distinctly sociological analysis of the problems of social action'.[33] Dahrendorf writes:

> The term *social position* designates every place in a field of social relations ... Every position carries with it certain expected modes of behavior; every position a person occupies requires him to do certain things and exhibit certain characteristics; to every social position there belongs a *social role*.[34]

Again:

> People's regular behavior toward other people gains sociological meaning only insofar as it may be understood as behavior with respect to predetermined patterns that are assigned to the incumbent of a social position irrespective of his individual identity. It is these patterns, and not ... the behavior itself, that we have called social roles.[35]

On Dahrendorf's account, a 'social role' is distinct from a 'social position', because a social position is defined by (conventional or legal) rights and duties, which are not predictions, and which are open to interpretation. The rights and duties of a social position first generate the 'expected modes of behavior' that define a social role by being interpreted with a view to the expectations of others in different positions, who may wield powers of inducement or sanction. A 'social role' is also distinct from 'behavior itself'. It is explicated by statements about 'expected' behaviour that is merely probable, rather than by statements about actual behaviour. A definition of the social role of a doctor, for example, may include the expectation that he/she will serve anyone who is ill. If a doctor

---

33   Dahrendorf 1971, p. 5. Dahrendorf 1973, p. v, contains a later preface.
34   Dahrendorf 1971, pp. 30–2; Dahrendorf 1973, pp. 16–17.
35   Dahrendorf 1971, p. 63; Dahrendorf 1973, pp. 43–4.

were to refuse to treat someone who was ill, a patient or other health profession would be likely to complain, and likely lead to a sanction. But the social role of a doctor does not include a legal duty to serve anyone who is sick, or the fact of regularly serving anyone who is sick.

Social structure is often understood in terms of social roles. For Ralph Linton, '[t]he sum total of the ideal patterns which control the reciprocal behavior between individuals and between the individual and society constitute the social system'.[36] Similarly, the social anthropologist Alfred Radcliffe-Brown writes: 'in any relationship within a social structure a person knows that he is expected to behave according to these norms and is justified in expecting that others persons should do the same', whereby 'a person is a human being considered not as an organism but as occupying position in a social structure'.[37] Or as a more contemporary critical realist account puts it: 'the basic building blocks of society are *positions*, involving, depending upon, or constituted according to, social rules and associated tasks, obligations, and prerogatives' that are 'highly segmented'.[38] These statements articulate a common core idea, even if the language differs. For sociological thought, a social structure is comprised of different social roles, each of which is defined by the expected modes of behaviour that are sustained by relevant others' expected use of their positional powers.

The importance of the concept of social role to sociological thought is explained by the fact that this concept offers a way to respond to and correct economic thought. It offers a way to hold on to the idea that actors are economically rational to some extent while theorising the impact of social norms on action affecting the distribution of benefits and burdens in society. Economic thought, by virtue of the concept of an economic good, must adopt a positional conception of economic structure. It is only once agents' positions are specified sufficiently that economically rational behaviour can be theorised. What sociological thought *adds* is that, if we are to understand fully how agents in various positions typically act, we must also describe the normative expectations that they encounter; or as Plamenatz was seen to put it in chapter 5, we must also describe the 'rules of conduct which the persons who stand in those relations recognize and are required to conform to'.[39] The sociological correction of economic thought is that it is one-sided to focus on preference maximisation in respect of possessions when the existence of (unequal) power relations serves

36   Linton 1936, p. 105; compare Merton 1957, pp. 41–2.
37   Radcliffe-Brown 1952, pp. 9–10; see also p. 194, p. 198.
38   Lawson 1997, p. 165, p. 163.
39   Plamenatz 1963, pp. 283–4.

to ensure that actors may be enabled or constrained, formally or informally, by other role occupants, if they observe or depart from what is expected of them.

Insofar as the response of sociological thought to economic thought merely seeks to qualify it rather than to offer a critique, a commodity form based derivation of the concept of an economic good must be matched by a commodity form based critique of sociological thought for what it overlooks as soon as it treats the concept of social role as fundamental. Three points can be made in this regard. The common feature is that sociological thought cannot but ignore or misattribute to particular types of social role the causal power of generalised and non-differentiated behaviour that is characteristic of (a specific form of) society.[40]

Firstly, to treat the concept of social role as fundamental is to be blind to the fact that the generalised existence of a type of interaction may explain non-normative pressures even without further differentiation of those who take part in it. Actors may be constrained by having to bear in mind, instrumentally, what others will do in separate token interactions of a given type, even if all further differentiation is put aside. For example, the generalised existence of purchase and sale might (in part) explain why, say, people choose to study for a degree that they believe will provide them with a marketable skill, independently of any fact about differential pay or divisions of class. The effect in this case is the same as if the fact of everyone being a family member (which, as distinct from 'father', 'daughter', etc., does not designate a social role) were to create an interest with causal power that was not reducible to the interest that people have as types of family member.

Second, the generalised existence of a type of interaction may explain a normative expectation even without any further differentiation of those who take part in it. As we will suggest in chapter 9, a belief in the principle of self-ownership can be explained by appeal to generalised purchase and sale, and a social interest in security. Yet neither of these facts presupposes any further differentiation of those who engage in purchase and sale. It is misleading to attribute any explanatory power they have to role occupants, if a social role is an *exhaustive* description of the expectations that a position holder faces in a certain domain of action that includes *various* types of position.

Third, the generalised existence of a type of interaction may (in part) explain the existence of a social role. For a social role to exist, it must be the case that, at any given point in time, those who are expected to perform one (set of) functions in a certain domain of action are not expected to perform a different (set

---

40   The critique of Plamenatz in ch. 5, sec. 4, is summarised by removing the brackets.

of) functions belonging to that domain. If it is logically possible for a society to contain all the various functions that are actually expected of those with certain distinct social roles without containing these social roles, because all agents perform all the functions; and if the dynamic of this logically possible starting-point would tend, in time, to create these social roles; then their reproduction cannot be fully explained by sociological thought.

3   The Features of a System

A social structure qualifies as an 'organic system'[41] (hereafter: system) if its parts depend on one another not just for their existence, but for their nature. Not only does each type of generalised interaction in it have every other type of generalised interaction as a condition of its continued existence as a generalised interaction. The nature of each part rests on the whole. Consider the final part of the following remark from Carl Menger's *Investigations into the Methods of the Social Sciences*:

> The organism is distinguished from a mechanism on the one hand by the fact that, unlike the latter, it is not the product of human calculation, but the product of a natural process; on the other hand, by the fact that the individual part of the organism (each organ) is conditioned by the connection of the parts into a higher whole (the organism in its totality) and by the normal nature of the other parts (the other organs) not just in its normal *function*, but also in its normal *nature*. The latter is by no means the case with a mechanism.[42]

A minimal description of the capitalist economic structure in terms of two types of interaction is a description of it as a system if, in developed capitalism, the generalised existence of each type of interaction is a condition of the generalised existence of the other; and the tokens of each type of interaction owe their form to the generalised existence of token interaction of their type. If these two conditions are satisfied, no token interaction could have the form it has in the capitalist economic structure, as an isolated interaction. It is true to say, of such a structure, that the nature of each part (that is, each token interaction) depends on the whole.

---

41   *MEW*, 42, p. 203; *MECW*, 28, p. 208; Marx 1973a, p. 278.
42   Menger 1969, p. 144; Menger 1985, p. 132.

The generalised existence of token interactions of a given type may lend each token interaction a form in qualitatively different ways. The form that the generalised existence of a type of interaction imparts on each token interaction may be intended or unintended, depending on whether it is the intention of interaction partners that others engage in interactions of that type, or whether each merely bears in mind instrumentally that others will engage in separate interactions of that type. The generalised existence of capitalist relations of production imposes a form on each token interaction that is unintended. Each assumes that others will engage in separate token interactions of the same type, by means of which some number of human beings, including themselves, will reproduce their existence. But no one acts as if it were their intention that their interaction contribute to that process of social reproduction.

From now on, the term 'system' is reserved for a social structure in which the form imparted on each part is enabling and *unintentionally constraining*. In effect, unintentional constraint is treated as a third feature of a system. Whether or not the distinction between social structure and system drawn here maps current sociological usage, it fits a non-technical use of the term. The phrase 'the system', unlike 'the (social) structure', can characterise a stifling social arrangement. The capitalist economic structure is a system, on this more qualified conception, if simple circulation and capital are each defined by a type of interaction whose generalised existence imposes an enabling and unin-tentionally constraining form on each token interaction.

If the capitalist economic structure is a system, it is not an aggregated sum of social relations. Social relations form an aggregated sum if any number of tokens of any type of social relation can be added or subtracted with no change to the nature of the rest, and hence with no further change to the sum. By contrast, if one supposes, of a system, that all the tokens of one of its types of interaction did not exist, that would not leave the number of tokens of another type of interaction unaffected. It accords with saying that the capitalist eco-nomic structure is a system that, if one were to suppose that there were no token interactions of purchase and sale, there could be no token interactions of production with wage-labour for continuous money maximisation.

In *Karl Marx's Theory of History*, Cohen cites, no less than half a dozen times, a mistranslation of Marx's *1859 Preface* that says that a 'sum total' of relations of production constitutes the economic structure of society.[43] What the *1859 Preface* actually claims is that 'the totality [*Gesamtheit*] of these relations of

---

43   Cohen 1978, p. 28, p. 34, p. 87, p. 111, p. 216 and inside sleeve. Cohen cites a 1971 edition of
        the text, translated by Saro Ryazanskaya. The revised version of this translation for *MECW*
        (see *MECW*, 29, p. xxiv) says 'totality' (*MECW*, 29, p. 263).

production constitutes the economic structure of society'.[44] It thereby refines *Wage-labour and Capital*: 'the relations of production in their totality [*Gesamtheit*] constitute what are called social relations, society'.[45] A sum total of relations is a total to and from which token relations can be added and subtracted one at a time. If social relations of production constitute a sum total, an *OMRP* conception of the capitalist economic structure is a better interpretation of the *1859 Preface*.[46] Marx writes '*Gesamtheit* [totality]', however, not '*Summe*'.[47] What Cohen and others cite Marx as saying is, for Marx, false.

4   The Capitalist Structure as a System

One feature of a system is that each part depends on the others. The claim to be defended here is that, in developed capitalism, generalised purchase and sale and generalised production with wage-labour for continuous money maximisation are necessarily combined. In this claim, wage-labour is shorthand for: voluntarily recruited paid labour by a producer with private autonomy. (The phrase 'with private autonomy' excludes indentured labour that is voluntarily recruited). This shorthand is consistent with Marx's remark in *Results of the Immediate Process of Production* that insofar as 'wage-labour' is '*essential*' to the 'capitalist relation of production', that is, indispensable for developed capitalism, it has 'the form of salary', and is hired through 'a contract between equally entitled *commodity possessors* [Warenbesitzer] who confront one another as free and equal'.[48]

Take, first, the more straightforward question as to why generalised production with wage-labour for continuous money maximisation depends on generalised purchase and sale. A unit of production can only be oriented to continuous money maximisation if all potential inputs and outputs of production can be acquired in exchange, and their value can be identified or estimated using a single measure. A unit of production can only be oriented to a judgement that there is more money to be made by producing a certain number of

---

44   *MEW*, 13, p. 8; *MECW*, 29, p. 263.
45   *MEW*, 6, p. 408; *MECW*, 9, p. 212.
46   See ch. 2, sec. 1.
47   Compare Lukács's criticism of Heinrich Cunow's interpretation of the *1859 Preface*: 'the concept of the whole [*den Begriff des Ganzen (Gesamtheit, Totalität)*] is silently transformed into that of a "sum" ["*Summe*"]' (Lukács 1977, p. 185; Lukács 1968, p. 25; responding to Cunow 1921, p. 155).
48   *MEGA*, II, 4, pp. 128–9; Marx 1976, p. 1064; compare *MEW*, 25, p. 352; *MECW*, 37, pp. 337–8; Marx 1981, pp. 460–1.

a's with various amounts of *b*, *c* and *d* than by producing a certain number of *e*'s with various amounts of *f*, *g* and *h*, if there is a measure of value for *a*, *b*, *c*, *d*, *e*, *f*, *g* and *h*. Accordingly, for each prospective money-maximising investor to be able to ascertain the branch of production in which they can maximise their monetary wealth, there must be a measure of value for all the potential inputs and outputs of production. The judgements made with a single measure of value are only valid, however, if that measure also functions as the general means of exchange, and so if exchange, generally, is an exchange of commodities for money, or purchase and sale.

The reason why generalised purchase and sale depends on generalised production with wage-labour for continuous money maximisation is more complex: the subjectivity of a purchaser makes it relevant to distinguish degrees of generalised purchase and sale, based on the volume of purchases; and generalised production with wage-labour for continuous money maximisation is the most competitive form of production for circulation.

If all products circulate, all consumers are money possessors, who acquire whatever they want to acquire. As such, they cannot turn down the offer of the same commodity at a cheaper price. Purchasing a given type of commodity at a cheaper price is a means to acquire as much of whatever a money possessor wants to acquire as they can; and the comparison of possible purchases itself leads the wants of money possessors to expand. Thus, if purchase and sale is generalised, the volume of purchases is elastic, and may increase if commodities are produced more cheaply.

The most competitive units of commodity production are those that produce for continuous money maximisation. To be successful, units of production for circulation must be able to finance the re-purchase of all their inputs from their sale of outputs, and still keep their prices relatively low. The most sustainable way to do this is to invest in technological innovations. The means that a unit of production has at its disposal to invest in technological innovations are maximised by producing for money maximisation, and then reinvesting the maximum proportion in technological innovations whose use is likely to provide the opportunity to reinvest the most in technological innovations again, and so on, indefinitely. The most competitive units of commodity production are those that produce for continuous money maximisation, and adopt money-saving technologies and techniques unconditionally.

The same point may be expressed negatively. All non-money-maximising market production, where the adoption of money-saving technologies and techniques is conditional on some other aim, is not fully competitive. No such unit of production can reduce the price of its product as far as those units that adopt money-saving technologies and techniques unconditionally. If all consumers are money possessors, the inability of non-money-maximising units of production to match the price reductions of money-maximising units must leave the former vulnerable to being wiped out by the latter's undercutting strategies to enlarge market share. Non-money-maximising units of production for circulation are thus at most an anomalous source of niche products within a general trend of production for continuous money maximisation.

By encouraging production for continuous money maximisation, generalised purchase and sale encourages units of production to draw on the labour of multiple producers. The money-maximising option is to increase the number of producers whenever the resulting increase in the scale of production enables more money to be made. Insofar as cooperation in an enlarged division of labour brings efficiency savings, such moves impose a certain minimum size of workforce on competitors as well.

By encouraging money-maximising units of production to use the labour of multiple producers, generalised purchase and sale encourages units of production to recruit labour. Lending money as credit to groups of producers allows the latter to take investment and operational decisions themselves. That impedes production for continuous money maximisation, because the unconditional investment in and use of money-saving technologies and techniques requires their implementation, if necessary, at a workforce's own expense. It requires their implementation even when jobs are lost and/or deskilled (and hence cheapened) as a consequence. Capitalist cooperatives cannot be expected to organise labour within their control to their own members' detriment if all alternative employment is beyond their members' control. Groups of producers who act as their own capitalist will tend to be less competitive than capitalists who recruit others' labour, leaving them vulnerable to being wiped out or marginalised.

By encouraging money-maximising units of production to recruit others' labour, generalised purchase and sale encourages units of production to recruit voluntary labour. Generalised purchase and sale is not logically incompatible with generalised slave labour (as it is with serf labour, or labour rewarded in kind). But generalised production for continuous money maximisation is not feasible with generalised slave labour. Slave labour attaches costs and difficulties to technical change. It directly burdens slaveholders with costs of maintaining the slaves that new technologies and techniques displace, or of retraining and/or selling them. Further, slaves are increasingly less efficient producers, the more fragile or damageable the means of production. Slaves' frustrated will to be recognised as persons is expressed in the misuse of their tools. A slave, *Capital* remarks, 'creates for themselves the self-feeling of their distinction from them [from animals and other work implements – JF] by mistreating and wasting them *con amore*.[49] If a producer, whose will must be engaged, is treated as a thing, their frustrated will to be recognised as a person[50] can only be expressed in the misuse of the things that they are instructed to use. So, if purchase and sale encourages investment in technology, with the consequence that production for continuous money maximisation depends increasingly on its proper use, a type of labour with a relatively high propensity to misuse it is less and less optimal. Only voluntarily recruited labour allows money-maximising units of production to manage technical change over time.

Finally, by encouraging money-maximising units of production to recruit voluntary paid labour, generalised purchase and sale encourages units of production to recruit producers with private autonomy. Voluntarily recruited labour could still be indentured; that is, undertaken by someone bound to perform it. Its non-performance then permits punishment from the employer, as distinct from monetary claims for compensation. Indentured labour, such as the system of closed compounding imposed by South African mine-owners in the nineteenth and twentieth centuries, need not directly burden employers with the costs of maintaining, retraining and/or selling producers whose labour is displaced by more advanced technologies and techniques if it is renewed, say, a year at a time. Moreover, what Weber, following Adam Smith, emphasises as the irrational character of slave labour, the 'complete disappearance of the worker's own interest in optimal effort',[51] need not count against the economic rationality of indentured labour, if indentured labour is combined with variable pay scales, and/or the possibility of extending a period of bound service as punishment.

However, the *recognition*-based part of the argument for why generalised slave labour is incompatible with production for continuous money maximisation must also apply in the case of indentured labour. Like slaves, indentured

---

49   *MEW*, 23, pp. 210–11; *MECW*, 35, p. 207; Marx 1976, pp. 303–4.

50   Given that producers compare themselves to others, and that generalised purchase and sale is accompanied by the recognition of the personhood of commodity exchangers; see ch. 9.

51   Weber 2005, p. 94; Weber 1978, pp. 18–19; compare Smith 1979, pp. 488–9. Cohen claims that 'Weber-like arguments [for why slave labour is incompatible with developed capitalism – JF] turn on the supposed disutility to the capitalist of enslaved producers' (Cohen 1978, p. 192), the burden of maintaining or selling displaced slaves. The Marx-like argument, Cohen claims, is to focus on 'the consciousness and will of the producers themselves' (Cohen 1978, p. 192). Weber's aforecited remark undermines the accuracy of this contrast. The contrast it permits is that Weber's arguments all appeal to economic rationality, whether on the part of capitalists, *or* on the part of enslaved producers; while Marx's arguments need not be confined to economic rationality (as befits the project of commodity form philosophy).

labourers are treated as things. Their employer's contractual right to punish them for failing to do a job whose non-performance can be costed in monetary terms, together with the lack of a private sphere beyond the employer's policing, amounts to the judgement that they are nothing more than a thing. As long as a producer is made to feel that they are nothing more than a thing, their frustrated will to be recognised as a person can only be expressed in the misuse of the things that they are instructed to use, the cost of which increases as capitalism advances. Superintendence cannot pre-empt this misuse, for, besides the additional cost, indentured labour of superintendence would itself exhibit the same type of misuse.

This argument for why the capitalist economic structure exhibits the first feature of a system is in accord with Jairus Banaji's view that capitalism cannot be based on generalised slave labour or generalised indentured labour, although historical capitalism is characterised by some amount of each.[52] It employs a different defence of the former claim, however. Banaji offers a *mobility*-based argument. Banaji argues that capitalism is incompatible with generalised slave labour or generalised indentured labour on the grounds that 'the mobility of labour is essential to the mechanism of capital at *this* level'.[53] This mobility-based argument seems to conflate two different types of mobility, however. It is true, as Banaji says, that, historically, some capitalists have used various means in efforts to 'contain their [producers' – JF] mobility'.[54] It is also true that, if units of production generally could not get rid of producers they no longer need, or hire others they come to need, competition and capital accumulation would be impeded. But the type of mobility to be limited in the first case (the mobility$_1$ of labour on the initiative of producers) is not the type of mobility required in the second (the mobility$_2$ of labour on the initiative of capitalists). As the claim that capitalism precludes generalised immobility$_2$ does not imply that capitalism precludes generalised immobility$_1$, a mobility-based argument cannot show that capitalism is incompatible with generalised slave labour or generalised indentured labour. Indeed, Marx's claim, in the *Economic Manuscripts of 1861–63*, that 'capitalist production' occurs on the slave plantations in the *antebellum* South 'only formally'[55] invites the limits of the capitalist use of slave or indentured labour to be related back to features of the capitalist production process, such as technical change over time and recognition, rather than to conditions of the labour market.

---

52   Banaji 2010, pp. 142–3.
53   Banaji 2010, p. 142.
54   Banaji 2010, p. 150.
55   *MEW*, 26. 2, p. 299; *MECW*, 31, p. 516.

5   The Capitalist Structure as a System (Continued)

In a system, token interactions are enabled and unintentionally constrained by the generalised existence of token interactions of their type. To describe the capitalist economic structure as a two-relation system, therefore, it is also necessary to argue that simple circulation and capital impose a form on token interactions that is both enabling and unintentionally constraining.

Take, first, simple circulation. Marx writes in the *Grundrisse*:

> It lies in the nature of *circulation* that exchange appears as a process, as a fluid whole of purchases and sales ... [I]t results from conscious individuals' effect on one another, but it neither lies in their consciousness, nor is it subsumed under them as a whole. Their own collisions with one another produce an *alien* social power standing over them; their interaction [*Wechselwirkung*] exists as a process and force independent of them.[56]

In simple circulation, each exchange takes the form of an exchange of commodities for money, or purchase and sale. The form of exchange as an exchange of commodities for money both enables and unintentionally constrains actors in each token exchange. As Marx elaborates in *Capital* Volume I:

> It may indeed happen that A and B buy from each other, but that particular relationship is by no means conditioned by the universal relations of commodity circulation. We see here, on the one hand, how commodity exchange surpasses the individual and local limits of the immediate exchange of products, and develops the metabolic process of human labour; on the other hand, a whole circle of social connections to nature develops, uncontrollable by the acting persons. The weaver can only sell linen because the farmer has already sold wheat, the intemperate man can only sell bibles because the weaver sold linen, the distiller can only sell their *eau-de-vie* because the other has already sold the water of eternal life, etc.[57]

If A and B exchange products, B must want the product A has, and have the product A wants. If, by contrast, A and B exchange commodities for money, B

---

56   *MEW*, 42, pp. 126–7; *MECW*, 28, pp. 131–2; Marx 1973a, pp. 196–7. Compare Schütz's use of 'Wechselwirkung' in the passage cited in ch. 5, sec. 3.

57   *MEW*, 23, p. 126; *MECW*, 35, p. 122; Marx 1976, pp. 207–8.

must want the product *A* has, and have a product someone with money wants, but not necessarily *A*, or even anyone with *A*'s type of product, or even anyone in the same region as *A*. No one has to buy from anyone they sell to, or buy any type of product sold by those they sell to, or buy any type of product from the region of those they sell to. Each is enabled to sell the type of product anyone with money wants to acquire, and to acquire the type of product that anyone sells.

Each is also unintentionally constrained by the form of exchange as an exchange of commodities for money. *A*, who sells to *B*, may have an interest in *c* selling, if *B* only has the money to buy from *A* if *B* sells to *c*, who themselves must sell, to have money to buy from *B*. *A* then has an interest in *c* selling, *irrespective* of *what c* sells and *to whom c* sells, and despite the fact that *A* concludes no transaction with *c* and has no influence over *c*. As *B* may sell not only to one other person, *c*, but to any number of third parties; and every seller has concerns of the kind just attributed to *A*; circulation as a whole is an '*alien social power*' over each. Each actor can sell the type of product anyone wants to acquire, and acquire the type of product that anyone sells, but only if enough other money possessors, who acquire just whatever they want to acquire, have the fitting preferences.

Consider, second, capital. In the *Grundrisse* Marx claims:

> Conceptually, *competition* is nothing other than the inner *nature of capital*, its essential determination, appearing, and realised, as the mutual effect of many capitals on one another; its inner tendency as external necessity. (Capital exists, and can only exist, as many capitals, and its self-determination thus appears as the mutual effect of capitals on one another.)[58]

If production is for continuous money maximisation, then the volume of a firm's output rises as far as is profitable, in a context where every other firm requires inputs of a volume that allow it to raise its output as far as is profitable. But if the inputs for that greater volume of output are to be available in sufficient volume, then they, too, must be produced for an end that is open-ended in respect to volume, and so for continuous money maximisation. 'Capital ... can only exist, as many capitals', for the chain of dependence of one money-maximising unit of production on another extends as far as the outputs of one money-maximising unit are required as inputs for another.

---

58   *MEW*, 42, p. 327; *MECW*, 28, p. 341; Marx 1973a, p. 414.

Each unit of production is also, however, under an 'external necessity' or unintentional constraint to maximise its monetary returns, in order to reinvest and extract the maximum again, because competition attaches future disadvantages to non-accumulation. A reduction in accumulation decreases the sum available to expand production and/or purchase improved technologies. It thereby impedes undercutting strategies that use economies of scale and/or technological advantages to enlarge market-share. To postpone or dilute such changes in one's own firm gifts the opportunity to others, to the potential detriment of one's own firm's future moneymaking. Any money-maximising firm that is prompted to consider which technology or technique to adopt, and any revenue-oriented investor prompted to consider which branch to invest in, therefore has an incentive to pursue the money-maximising option, as determined by the opportunities presented in all branches of production.

6   Actors as Bearers

What remains to be argued is that actors in this system of capitalist production are bearers. Actors are bearers, it is argued here, if, in token interactions of a certain type, each treats the other as if the other lacked an end beyond their interaction that they have. The conception of a bearer as an actor who treats another and is treated by another as if they did not have an end beyond an interaction that they have is an *abstraction-from-ends* conception of a bearer.

Marx writes in his *Economic and Philosophic Manuscripts of 1844*:

> Animals are immediately one with their life activity. They do not distinguish themselves from it. They are *it*. Humans make their very life activity an object of will and consciousness. They have conscious life activity. It is not a determinateness with which they immediately coincide.[59]

A member of a species can be said to be 'immediately one' with an activity if the activity is not chosen with a view to the pursuit of further plans; and the experience of the activity provides no perspective on any further plans, in respect to whose promotion or frustration it is sensed to have a place. Activity is 'conscious life activity', by contrast, if it is chosen in light of further plans, and its experience is shaped by its fit with the further plans it brings into view, in light of an actor's stock of experiences. Human beings have conscious life activity

---

59   *MEW*, 40, p. 516; *MECW*, 3, p. 276.

in this sense. On an abstraction-from-ends conception of a bearer, the notion of conscious life activity is relevant for defining a bearer: to say that actors are bearers is to highlight a quality of conscious life activity on the part of the actors of a system.

Human beings have needs whose objects are not produced once and for all, but must be continually reproduced. Any given interaction in a system of production is therefore just one step in an actor's reproduction. It is one step in a series of steps for that actor, each of which is a part of the same system. Any given token interaction in it is a means, for its participants, to engage in a separate token interaction in it. In the system of capitalist production, actors sell one commodity in order to purchase another, or initiate production for money maximisation in order to initiate another round of production for money maximisation. The actions in a system are a kind of conscious life activity, therefore.

There is a peculiarity to this conscious life activity, however. In a system, actors do not interact with one another as if they intended separate token interactions of the same type. They merely bear them in mind, instrumentally. The only other token interactions of this type that they intend, beyond their present interaction, are their own future token interactions. Hence, no actor in a system intends for their interaction partner to engage in a further token interaction of that type. Thus, no actor in a system intends for their interaction partner to satisfy a further end in a separate token interaction. If a commodity/money possessor or a money-maximising firm could get what they acquire from a given interaction without parting with anything in return, and hence without parting with anything that could enable their interaction partner to engage in a further token interaction, they would. Thus, no actor in the system of capitalist production interacts with another as if they intended for that other to satisfy a further end in a separate token interaction of that system. The system of capitalist production turns actors into bearers, therefore, because it ensures that actors do not act towards one another as if they intended the other to satisfy a further end in a separate token interaction of that system; and because it ensures that each actor does in fact have such an end.

On the conception of real abstraction outlined in chapter 3, an interaction exhibits a real abstraction if it requires at least one actor to treat another as if x is the case; and yet, by virtue of that very interaction, it belongs to that actor's stock of experiences that x is not the case. Accordingly, one way for an interaction to exhibit a real abstraction is in respect to an end. An interaction exhibits a real abstraction in respect to an end if it requires one actor to treat another as if x is not an end of the other, or as if x may or may not be an end of the other; and yet, by virtue of that interaction, it belongs to that actor's stock of experiences that x is an end of the other, or that x must be an end of the other. An abstraction-from-ends-based conception of a bearer implies a potential for a real abstraction, for a bearer is not, by definition, aware of the fact from which their treatment of another abstracts.

Consider the following two comments from *Capital*. The first is taken from the Preface to the First Edition, and the second from Chapter Two:

> Persons feature here only insofar as they are personifications of economic categories, bearers [*Träger*] of definite class relations and interests. My standpoint, which grasps the development of the economic formation of society as a natural-historical process, is the last to make the individual responsible for relations whose creature they socially remain, however much they believe themselves above them.[60]

> In the course of the exposition, we will find, in general, that persons' economic character masks [*ökonomische Charaktermasken der Personen*] are merely the personifications of economic relations, as whose bearers they confront one another [*als deren Träger sie sich gegenübertreten*].[61]

On an abstraction-from-ends conception of a bearer, the fact that an actor is a bearer is a fact that concerns some one type of relation they engage in. It does not first become a fact about them as a participant in all the various relations of a given domain of action they engage in taken together. This is consistent with Marx's claim that actors are bearers throughout *Capital*'s exposition of economic categories. If the fact that an actor is a bearer were related only to all the various relations of a given domain of action they engage in taken together, actors would only emerge as bearers at the *end* of their mention in *Capital*'s exposition. Moreover, if actors are 'creature[s]' of relations that belong to a society's 'economic formation', for which 'the individual' is not 'responsible', that suggests that bearers are subject to an unintentional constraint irreducible to the powers wielded by particular responsible individuals. It implies that

---

60   *MEW*, 23, p. 16; *MECW*, 35, p. 10; Marx 1976, p. 92.

61   *MEW*, 23, p. 100; *MECW*, 35, p. 95; Marx 1976, p. 179. (1) The *MECW* and Marx 1976 translation of '*ökonomische Charaktermasken der Personen*' as 'characters that appear on the economic stage' is inaccurate. Marx does not refer to a stage (which would be: *'Bühne'*) or to what appears (*'erscheint'*). Unless '*Charaktermasken*' is rendered as 'character masks', Marx's statement cannot be used to assess Dahrendorf's identification of Marx's phrase '"character mask"' with the sociological concept of a 'social rol[e]' (Dahrendorf 1971, p. 27; Dahrendorf 1973, p. 13). (2) The Marx 1976 rendering of '*sich gegenübertreten*' as 'come into contact with one another' (which would be: '*in Kontakt miteinander kommen*') is misleadingly physical.

the unintentional constraint to which bearers are subject is not an interest in conforming to the expectations of a social role. On an abstraction-from-ends conception of a bearer, for *A* to 'confront' or encounter *B* as a bearer is for *A* to act towards *B* such that *B* counts, for *A*, as a bearer; that is, as someone without an end beyond the interaction that they have.

The system of capitalist production gives rise to a real abstraction in respect of an end if its actors treat one another merely as recipients of something they must part with in order to acquire something else for themselves; and yet, on reflection, they must know that the other has acquired something that they can only use in a separate interaction or action. Both purchase and sale, and production with wage-labour for continuous money maximisation, are interactions in which actors are not just bearers, but, in virtue of being bearers, can assume a critical stance towards the features from which they abstract.

In respect of commodity exchange, the *Grundrisse* remarks:

> The subjects in exchange are only for one another through the equivalents, as beings of equal worth [*Gleichgeltende*], and they prove themselves to be such through the change of objectivity in which the one is for the other. Since it is only thus that they are for one another in exchange, as beings of equal worth, as possessors [*Besitzer*] of equivalents and upholders of this equivalence, they are, as beings of equal worth, also indifferent to one another; their remaining individual differences do not concern them; they are indifferent towards all their remaining individual peculiarities.[62]

In commodity exchange, each actor regards themselves and treats the other as the current possessor of what they part with, and the future possessor of what they stand to receive. Each regards themselves as the possessor of what they offer for exchange, because each regards their will alone as making their agreement to exchange it valid. Each treats the other as the possessor of what they want to acquire from them, by directing their offer or acceptance of the other's offer only at that other. An offer, or its acceptance, aims at reaching agreement; and its initiator or acceptor could not hope to acquire a product

---

62   *MEW*, 42, pp. 167–8; *MECW*, 28, pp. 173–4; Marx 1973a, p. 242. There is no easy way to render 'Gleichgeltende (beings of equal worth)', particularly in a passage that already has a difficult sentence structure. But its three uses in this passage should be rendered consistently. Neither *MECW* nor Marx 1973a does so. In one instance, Marx 1973a renders 'Gleichgeltende' as 'equally worthy persons'. There is no mention of persons ('Personen') here, however. On possession, see ch. 7, sec. 3.

from another by means of agreement if they believed that a third party, besides the one to whom their offer or acceptance was directed, also had some say over its exchange. Finally, if each regards themselves as a possessor who concludes an agreement to exchange with another possessor, each must take both themselves and the other to possess what they receive from the other once the exchange is completed.

The action of taking possession is ends-indeterminate, however. It does not imply a will, or even the competence, to use the thing. Hence, to treat another as just a future possessor of commodities or money is to treat them in abstraction from any further end they may have with it. If each possessor parts with money or commodities in order to acquire commodities or money in return, they cannot attach conditions to the use of what they part with. As no conditions of future use can be attached to what a possessor parts with, and its recipient is only relevant as someone who, on condition of acquiring, supplies what the other wants to acquire, neither actor can act as if they ascribed an end to the other connected to what the other acquires from them, beyond acquisition. Each treats the other in abstraction from any further end, by treating the other simply as a possessor.

Indeed, each treats the other as a bearer. Each commodity exchanger treats the other as simply a possessor of what they acquire. Yet, as each thereby provides the other with a particular type of commodity or sum of money that can only be consumed or used in a further action, each must also suppose (to avoid regarding the other as without conscious life activity) that the other plans to exchange or consume what they acquire in a further action. In that each treats the other as a future possessor of commodities or money, neither acts towards the other as if the other has a further end to pursue. Yet each must know, in virtue of this interaction, that it is the other's end to exchange the money they acquire, or to consume or exchange the commodity they acquire.

For the same reason, actors are bearers of production with wage-labour for continuous money maximisation. Each treats the other as just a possessor of what the other acquires, money or commodities. To the end of money maximisation, a unit of production cannot attach conditions to the use or non-use of the money it pays the wage-labourer. Likewise, to the end of individual reproduction, a wage-labourer cannot attach conditions to the use or non-use of the commodities they agree to produce. Yet each necessarily has a further end beyond that interaction. Indeed, each must also suppose (if they are not to regard the other as without conscious life activity) that the other has a further end to pursue, given that the other's agreement would have no point unless it were a means to the end of using the commodities or money they acquire in a separate action or interaction.

So conceived, a bearer is distinct from a position holder or role occupant. Both Dahrendorf[63] and Merton[64] claim that Marx's use of the phrases '"character mask"' or '"personifications of economic categories"' or '"bearers"' can be replaced with the less metaphorical language of social roles. In defence of this sociological interpretation, it might be argued that the reason that individuals cannot be held 'responsible' for the relations to which *Capital* refers is that they are defined by general criteria, which abstract from changes of personnel. For Marx to say that actors jointly assume 'character masks' is then for Marx to say that *Capital* only considers actors as occupants of economic roles. That is the case that could be put for Merton's claim that 'Marx' is 'abstracting from other variables' and 'regarding men in their economic and class roles'.[65]

One truth in this sociological interpretation is that it is what Christoph Henning calls a '*de re*' interpretation.[66] A *de re* interpretation of Marx's conception of a bearer defines a bearer by something that an actor either actually does, or is actually expected to do. A *de re* interpretation contrasts with a purely methodological interpretation, on which a bearer is simply a deliberately one-sided description of an actor. The sociological interpretation is a *de re* interpretation, because social roles are defined by modes of behaviour expected *by other actors*. Certainly, Marx's aforecited remarks are only consistent with a *de re* interpretation. An actor cannot become a 'creature' of social relations just by virtue of an observer's reflection.

A sociological interpretation of Marx's conception of a bearer is not, however, the only or best *de re* interpretation, however. On the abstraction-from-ends conception of a bearer, a bearer is distinct from a position holder or role occupant on at least six counts. First, actors are bearers in virtue of what they actually do, rather than in virtue of anything they are expected to do. Second, the fact that an actor is a bearer is a fact that relates to some one type of generalised interaction they engage in. It is not a fact about them as a participant in all the various types of interaction they engage in within a given domain of action that necessarily includes various types of position. Third, actors are bearers only by virtue of their involvement in a system. (The concept of a position holder or role occupant does not presuppose the concept of a system). Fourth, the form of unintentional constraint to which bearers are subject would arise even in the absence of social norms. It does not (at least directly) take the form of a pressure to conform to normative expectations. Fifth, this constraint is an

---

63   Dahrendorf 1971, p. 27; Dahrendorf 1973, p. 13.
64   Merton 1957, p. 462.
65   Merton 1957, p. 462; see also Iorio 2003, p. 76.
66   Henning 2009, pp. 101–7.

upshot of the generalised interaction itself, rather than the sanctioning power of particular role occupants. Finally, bearers engage in a form of conscious life activity that is marked by an abstraction from actors' further ends.

CHAPTER 7

Purchase and Sale

The task in respect of purchase and sale is to explain the two functions of money appearing in the description of the capitalist economic structure as a system. It is to explain why a single measure of value serves as a general means of exchange. If the system of capitalist production is the most developed form of production to use money, an explanation of these two basic features of money in capitalism is also an argument for defining money by these two functions.

Commodity form philosophy is a project whose theses are all founded on an analysis of the commodity form, and which traces the effects, within individual disciplines, of its obscured significance. Insofar as the interaction-recognition-antinomy thesis belongs to the project of commodity form philosophy, its analysis of purchase and sale must observe these conditions. It must explain money by the commodity form, and diagnose the naturalisation of money in economic thought.

In the First Edition of *Capital* Volume I, Marx claims: '[t]he commodity is an *immediate unity of use-value and exchange-value*, hence of two opposites'.[1] Use-value and value are opposites in respect of possession.[2] If the subjectivity of possession is tied to the commodity form, a commodity form based explanation of money can appeal to the subjectivity of possession in the context of generalised production for exchange.

This possibility is cause to report one of the more comical features of the Anglophone reception of Marx's writings. In the first two chapters of *Capital* Volume I, Marx repeatedly uses the terms 'possessor [*Besitzer*]' and 'commodity possessor [*Warenbesitzer*]'.[3] Yet one would not know it from either the Aveling/Moore translation or the Fowkes translation of *Capital*. In these translations, '*Besitzer*' and '*Warenbesitzer*' are rendered as 'owner' and 'commodity owner/owner of a commodity' respectively.[4] The German terms for 'owner' and 'commodity owner/owner of a commodity' are '*Eigentümer*' and '*Wareneigentümer*'. Neither '*Eigentümer*' nor '*Wareneigentümer*' appears in *Capital*'s two opening chapters.

---

1   *MEGA*, II, 5, p. 51; Marx 1967, p. 40.
2   See ch. 3, sec. 1.
3   *MEW*, 23, pp. 78–9, pp. 99–103.
4   *MECW*, 35, pp. 74–5, pp. 94–9; Marx 1976, pp. 156–7, pp. 179–83.

© KONINKLIJKE BRILL NV, LEIDEN, 2019 | DOI:10.1163/9789004384804_008

A similar fate has befallen *A Contribution to the Critique of Political Economy*, which covers the same material as *Capital*'s two opening chapters. It uses the terms *'Besitzer'* and *'Warenbesitzer'* over 50 times.[5] Not one use of these terms is rendered as 'possessor' or 'commodity possessor' in the *MECW* translation.[6] It, too, uses the terms 'owner' or 'commodity owner/owner of a commodity'. Yet neither *'Eigentümer'* nor *'Wareneigentümer'* is used by Marx in this text.

Anglophone commentary on Marx has accepted and repeated these translations. The comical result is that, on the one hand, the term in current use in Anglophone commentary on Marx, 'commodity owner', is an equivalent for a term, *'Wareneigentümer'*, that there is no record of Marx ever having used, in any published or unpublished piece of writing; while on the other hand, virtually no mention or analysis is made of the term Marx repeatedly used, 'commodity possessor'.

The concept of possession was the object of a scholarly dispute between two of Marx's teachers of jurisprudence: Friedrich Carl von Savigny, and the Hegelian, Eduard Gans.[7] No diligent student of jurisprudence, let alone a thinker schooled in this dispute, can be assumed to use the terms possession and ownership interchangeably, as if they were synonyms. The difference between possession and legal ownership that matters for Marx interpretation is that possession is defined in phenomenological terms, whereas legal ownership is not. A possessor has a type of will that a legal owner, who enjoys an enforceable right, need not have. (As we will see in chapter 9, Marx also has a phenomenological concept of ownership. The different difference between possession and this phenomenological concept of ownership is that possession does not presuppose anything resembling recognition; but more on that later).

The relevance of possession to an explanation of money can be suggested by exposing two problems with Cohen's view of money. For Cohen, 'a sum of money is, *in effect*, a highly generalised form of such a ticket' that 'lays out a disjunction of conjunctions of courses of action that I may perform. That is,

---

5 *MEW*, 13, pp. 15–160.

6 *MECW*, 29, pp. 269–417. An older, lesser known translation, by Nahum Stone (Marx 1904), also uses 'owner' and 'commodity owner/owner of commodities' more often than not. On only one occasion does it render *'Warenbesitzer'* as 'possessors of commodities' (*MEW*, 13, p. 34; *MECW*, 29, p. 289; Marx 1904, p. 51).

7 Savigny's monograph on possession, *The Right of Possession (Das Recht des Besitzes)*, was first published in 1803 (Savigny 1803). In 1839, two years after the appearance of its sixth edition, Gans published a critique (Gans 1971, pp. 335–84). For a summary of the dispute, see Braun 1997, pp. 91–123. In what follows, the sixth (1837) German edition of Savigny's monograph is cited, because Marx read Savigny's monograph in late 1837 (see *MEW*, 40, p. 5; *MECW*, 1, p. 15). One important statement, indicated below, was only added in the sixth German edition.

I may do *A* and *B* and *C* and *D* OR *B* and *C* and *D* and *E* OR *E* and *F* and *G* and *A*, and so on'.[8] The qualifier '*in effect*' is added in acknowledgement of the fact that 'conditions other than possession of the required money are necessary' to 'supply the freedom' money-seekers seek.[9] For example, buyers have to be of age, and sellers may, but standardly do not, decline offers.[10] But assuming these other conditions are met, 'the whole point of money is to extinguish interference: that is its defining function'.[11] If I give money to travel on the train, the conductor's interference with my journey is extinguished, for his 'will' is 'to deny access except in return for money' and 'what the government in a money economy does is to enforce the asset-holder's will'.[12] For Cohen, what money renders commensurable, and its transfer facilitates, are uninterfered-with courses of action.

Cohen's view of money is flawed, even on its own premises. If the government in a money economy enforces 'the asset-holder's will', extinguishing interference is not the 'whole point' of money. An asset holder may will to exclude others from using their asset *whether or not* that use amounts to interference with any course of action they are free to perform with it. Money can therefore be used to purchase an asset with this in mind: *one* 'point' of purchasing land may be to acquire the power to keep trespassers off. Nor is it true that extinguishing interference with courses of action is money's 'defining function'. Money serves acquisition with or without any knowledge of what may be done with a purchasable item on the part of the purchaser. No deficiency in the sum of money used to acquire an item or in that acquisition itself would be exposed if, through ignorance or memory loss, a purchaser did not know what the item they purchased was for. Possession is relevant for an explanation of money precisely because it is exclusive and ends-indeterminate.

Section 1 examines the concept of exchange. Section 2 distinguishes a particular type of exchange, the independent exchange of products. Section 3 analyses possession, which the independent exchange of products presupposes. Finally, section 4 appeals to the subjectivity of possession to argue that generalised production for exchange cannot be thought without money.

---

8   Cohen 2011, p. 182.
9   Cohen 2011, p. 177.
10   Cohen 2011, p. 177, pp. 182–3.
11   Cohen 2011, p. 178.
12   Cohen 2011, p. 182, read with Cohen 2011, p. 176.

1   Exchange

One basic feature of exchange is conditionality.[13] In exchange, each actor only parts with something on condition that the other parts with something else in return. This is not the only basic feature of exchange, however. Otherwise, mutual aid to a third party would count as an exchange. Exchange is also acquisitional. Each actor who parts with something only on condition that the other does too is also the recipient of what the other parts with. Thirdly, exchange is voluntary. No party is denied the capacity to decline an exchange.

Standardly, the acquisitional conditional transfer is a result of an intended agreement. The agreement consists of an offer, described by Adam Smith as '[g]ive me that which I want, and you shall have this which you want',[14] and its acceptance. In the non-standard case, conceptually parasitic on the standard case, the acquisitional conditional transfer is merely viewed as if it rested on an intended agreement. One party may deny having had any intention to make or accept an offer, and still be bound by its terms, if, recklessly (or carelessly), they act in a way that another could honestly (and reasonably) understand as an offer or acceptance.[15] The law may then 'proceed as though [the actor] has signalled consent'.[16] Acquisitional conditional transfer as a result of an intended agreement remains the standard case, if neither party can be legally bound on account of a fact unrelated to what the other can understand as an offer or acceptance. Whether the agreement is real or fictional, no party is denied the capacity to decline an exchange.

An agreement to exchange is performed by the conditional transfer, which is also by agreement. It is not possible to perform part of an agreement to exchange by seizing something from the other, because it is not possible to seize something from another on condition that they seize something from oneself. Whilst a conjunction of events can occur in which *A* seizes from *B*, and *B* seizes something else from *A*, no seizure performs part of an agreement to exchange. In sum, exchange is an agreement between the acquisitional conditional terms of an offer and the acquisitional conditional terms of its acceptance, and a conditional transfer in accordance with that agreement.

Any exchange, so defined, is self-seeking. The argument runs as follows: if my in-order-to motive were just to give you something, I would not attach a condition to its receipt. As a condition is attached, your receipt of it is not, by

---

13   Chitty 2004, p. 534.
14   Smith 1979, p. 118.
15   Beyleveld and Brownsword 2007, pp. 190–5.
16   Beyleveld and Brownsword 2007, p. 194.

itself, of any evident independent value to me. Even if, in exchange, I must give you something, I do not act as though your receipt of it has any value for me, except as a means for me to get you to perform the condition I attach to your receipt of it. As the condition I attach is my receipt of some other thing from you in return, what I must be seeking is just to receive that other thing. As my end is just to receive a thing from you, my in-order-to motive is self-seeking.

This argument is not vulnerable to an objection from duty-based reciprocity. Imagine a society in which there is both a legal duty to give, and a legal duty to reciprocate any gift.[17] In principle, the same things transferred voluntarily by exchange could be transferred to and from the same people, by observing those duties. In principle, the physical appearance of behaviour in exchange, and the duty-based behaviour, could be identical. But the in-order-to motives would differ. The duty-based behaviour need not be oriented to a self-seeking in-order-to motive. An actor with a sense of their legal duty could attach an independent value to the other's receipt of a thing. They could believe that they ought to give the other what they give to the other, and conduct the transfer to the end of discharging that duty.

What prevents duty-based reciprocity from providing an objection to the argument for why exchange is self-seeking is that the concept of exchange, as an acquisitional conditional transfer standardly by intended agreement, does not include duty-based reciprocity. Reciprocity based on legal duties to give and reciprocate is not voluntary. Moreover, with duty-based reciprocity, no act of giving is founded on an acquisitional or a conditional agreement, even if a duty to reciprocate a gift with a gift to the giver ensures that no transfer is one-way. As duty-based reciprocity does not fall under the concept of exchange, the non-self-seeking character of acts that comprise duty-based reciprocity provides no basis for objecting to the claim that exchange is self-seeking.

It has nonetheless been claimed that voluntary reciprocity need not be self-seeking. 'Reciprocity' was a value championed by the manufacturer and early socialist Robert Owen as the basis for trade between cooperative associations.[18] More recently, Cohen affirms:

> Communal reciprocity is the antimarket principle according to which I serve you not because of what I can get in return by doing so but because you need or want my service, and you, for the same reason, serve me.[19]

---

17   Compare Mauss 1954, pp. 10–11.
18   Owen 1927, pp. 289–90.
19   Cohen 2009, p. 39, which modifies an earlier formulation at Cohen 2011, p. 217.

To assess this statement, we need to recall the distinction between in-order-to motives and because motives.[20] An in-order-to motive is a future state of affairs an actor expects their action to bring about. A because motive is a pre-existing state of affairs that prompts their action. Because phrases that report motives can be slippery: they can be used to report either in-order-to motives, or because motives.

The above statement of communal reciprocity is a victim of this slipperiness. For Cohen, a principle is only an 'antimarket principle' if its in-order-to motive is not self-seeking. 'The marketeer is willing to serve, but only in order to be served'.[21] Accordingly, 'communal reciprocity' is only an anti-market form of reciprocity if it is a form of two-way transfer whose in-order-to motives are not self-seeking. A non-self-centred because motive is not, however, evidence of a non-self-seeking in-order-to motive. If the because motive of my offer to serve you is that 'you need or want my service', my in-order-to motive may still be just to receive what I want from you in return. Hence, if Cohen's statement is to give a reason for supposing that 'communal reciprocity' really is an anti-market form of two-way transfer, the phrase 'because you need or want my service' (which is capable of being read as the report of a because motive, and, if read as such, is *irrelevant* to the pedigree of communal reciprocity as an anti-market principle) must be convertible into the phrase: in order to provide the service you need or want. The whole sentence must state a truth once it is rephrased as follows:

> Communal reciprocity is the antimarket principle according to which I serve you not in order to get something in return by doing so, but in order to provide the service you need or want; and you, for the same reason, serve me.

This statement is incoherent. If what I want to do is to serve you simply in order to provide you with the service you need or want, I will *not* attach a condition to my service, that you serve me. If I attach a condition, I place something in the way of achieving my goal of serving you. But *until* I attach such a condition, my service is no part of a voluntary two-way transfer in which you necessarily serve me too. Either the in-order-to motive of my service is just to serve you, in which case my service does not belong to a form of voluntary reciprocity; or our services are a form of voluntary reciprocity, in which case neither of us

20　　See ch. 4, sec. 2.
21　　Cohen 2011, p. 218.

seeks simply to serve the other. Once the two because phrases in Cohen's statement are converted into the less ambiguous form of in-order-to phrases, it is apparent that the statement offers no reason for thinking that there is a form of voluntary reciprocity that is not self-seeking.

To defend the claim that exchange is necessarily self-seeking, it is necessary to do more than just show that the above statement of communal reciprocity is incoherent, however. Even if the above statement is incoherent, the non-self-seeking character of communal reciprocity could be asserted in a different form. In a later passage from the same work, Cohen writes:

> My commitment to socialist community does not require me to be a sucker who serves you regardless of whether (if you are able to do so) you are going to serve me, but I nevertheless find value in both parts of the conjunction – I serve you *and* you serve me – and in that conjunction itself: I do not regard the first part – I serve you – as simply a means to my real end, which is that you serve me.[22]

The new argument for communal reciprocity Cohen suggests here is that exchangers may be motivated by the 'conjunction' of serving and being served. To hold that exchange is necessarily self-seeking, this final possibility, *communal reciprocity mark II*, must also be discounted as a possible non-self-seeking form of exchange.

The question here is whether communal reciprocity mark II implies, by virtue of the value that exchangers can put on the 'conjunction' of serving and being served, that their in-order-to motives in exchange are not self-seeking. Now, it follows from the fact that an exchanger values the 'conjunction' of serving and being served that they engage in exchange only if they want to be served. I cannot value the conjunction of serving and being served unless I value being served, and I cannot value being served unless I value a want that that service satisfies. If it is a condition of communal reciprocity mark II that an exchanger wants to be served, each exchanger's decision on the extent to which they engage in exchange will depend on their own wants.

If the extent to which people exchange depends on their own wants, each exchanger regulates the extent to which they exchange by deciding whether they want the wants they have, and that others' services may satisfy, to be satisfied, and how many of those wants they want to be satisfied. If A decides that they are content to leave some of these wants unsatisfied, A lessens the extent

---

22   Cohen 2009, p. 43.

to which *A* exchanges. If *A* decides that they will avail themselves of fewer services from others, *A* performs fewer services for others. At the most extreme end of the scale: if *B*, who may be a highly talented individual, decides that they will avail themselves of no services from others, the extent to which *B* exchanges is reduced to nil. Communal reciprocity mark II permits both full autarky, and cheap forms of suicide.

What these two extreme cases bring to the fore is that, if the extent to which actors exchange is a function of their decision to satisfy their own wants, each exchanger's in-order-to motive is self-seeking. If an actor exchanges only if and to the extent that that is what they prefer, any exchange they conduct is just a means to satisfy their preference order. Hence, communal reciprocity mark II is not a counterexample to the claim that exchange is necessarily self-seeking. (If actors instead have a moral duty to seek to make agreements to serve and be served, they could carry out an agreement in order to discharge a moral duty, rather than to serve themselves. But then each cannot be sure of providing another with a service they need or want).

What separates forms of reciprocity that need not be self-seeking from forms of reciprocity that are necessarily self-seeking is the presence or absence of a prior duty. If transfers occur on account of a prior duty, actors' in-order-to motives need not be self-seeking. Each actor can conduct their transfer in order to uphold their duty. If, by contrast, reciprocity is voluntary, both legally and morally, actors' in-order-to motives are necessarily self-seeking. As it is unattractive to rest a communal principle on legally or morally enforced reciprocity, and impossible to rest it on voluntary reciprocity, reciprocity is not a value suited to sustain criticism of self-seeking behaviour.

What the foregoing critique of communal reciprocity has revealed is that the self-seeking character of exchange is an implication of its voluntary acquisitional conditionality. Exchange is self-seeking, while reciprocity need not be, if it rests on a prior duty. Hence, not all inferences to be drawn from exchange can be drawn, once exchange is subsumed, as Cohen subsumes it, under the heading of reciprocity.[23]

One inference to draw from the self-seeking character of exchange relates to the fact that the object of self-seeking behaviour in exchange is the thing that the actor seeks to acquire, not the thing that they part with. Accordingly, if *A* exchanges with *B*, then *A* would hamper the pursuit of their own in-order-to motive if they were to attach conditions to the future use of what they part with (unless its use by *B* would impact negatively on further acquisition by *A* and *A*

---

23   Cohen 2009, p. 38.

is B's only potential supplier). If A were to attach any such conditions, A would have to find someone willing not only to part with what A wants, but also willing to accept those conditions. A would only have made it harder for themselves to achieve their self-seeking in-order-to motive. If, therefore, exchangers are clear about their in-order-to motive, and what its means are, they do not attach conditions to the future use of what they part with. *Capital* can remark that a commodity 'falls'[24] or drops out of the sphere of circulation into the sphere of consumption, because the distribution of products by means of exchange does not fix their particular use afterwards.

2 Independent Exchange of Products

Exchange, in virtue of its voluntary acquisitional conditionality, is necessarily self-seeking. But in capitalism, the exchange of products is also *independent*.

To say that the exchange of products is independent is just to say that products are exchanged as independent products. Products are exchanged as independent products if their exchange is not guided by a policy in respect of the total social product, in virtue of which they could be exchanged as shares of the total social product, instead of as independent products. If the total social product is in all phases of its distribution split between actors who have transactional rights vis-à-vis one another to exchange all products, it will not be possible for any exchange of product to be guided by a policy in respect of the total social product, because at no point will all products pass through the control of a single agency. Under this condition, exchange will have an independent character.

The independent character of an independent exchange of products is not an implication of voluntariness and conditionality in acquisition. It is possible to conceive of a hypothetical arrangement in which all transfers involving products are voluntary, conditional and acquisitional, but not independent.

Suppose a public agency controls the use of all productive facilities, and administers the distribution of means of individual consumption from a single fund. All withdrawals of means of individual consumption from the fund are regulated by a principle that specifies the respect in which like cases are to be treated alike. Assuming people do not desire to work, that is, work whether or not they are rewarded with means of individual consumption, no principle is feasible that does not make the withdrawal of at least some means of indi-

---

24   *MEW*, 23, p. 119, p. 129; *MECW*, 35, p. 114, p. 125; Marx 1976, p. 198, p. 211.

vidual consumption conditional on work. So imagine, further, that withdrawals from the fund are administered according to the principle that all means of individual consumption distributed to producers are to be distributed in proportion to work performed. Any given producer's withdrawal limit in respect of means of individual consumption will then be fixed in light of a projection of both the total size of the fund and the total amount of labour over a given period. But if any given producer's withdrawal limit cannot be specified without estimates of these totals, it cannot be specified without rendering all the components of or contributions to these totals commensurable as among themselves. If so, the *Grundrisse* says, a producer's withdrawal limit is 'not a definite particular product, but a certain share of communal production'.[25]

An independent exchange of products is not an implication of voluntariness and conditionality in acquisition, because it is possible to conceive of a version of this arrangement in which all labour contracts are voluntary. It is possible to imagine a version of the arrangement in which no individual has a duty to work, so that all labour contracts are voluntary on the side of individuals; and the public agency has no duty to employ any given individual, so that all labour contracts are also voluntary on the part of the public agency. (Voluntariness on the side of the public agency would be undesirable. But it is possible to conceive of undesirable arrangements). What matters here is that not even voluntariness on both sides would give the exchange an independent character. Each producer's withdrawal limit in respect of means of individual consumption would remain dependent on projections of both the total size of the fund, and the total amount of labour over a given period. The public agency would still have to render commensurable the components of or contributions to each total to determine any given producer's withdrawal limit.

As the independent character of the independent exchange of products is not an implication of voluntariness and conditionality in acquisition, the independent exchange of products is a particular type of exchange. Indeed, it is the particular type of exchange characteristic of capitalism. Exchange in capitalism cannot just be understood as self-seeking reciprocity.[26] Only if the exchange of products is independent are products exchanged as commodities. As the *Grundrisse* remarks in respect of the general kind of arrangement just imagined (not its specifically voluntary version):

---

25   *MEW*, 42, p. 104; *MECW*, 28, p. 108; Marx 1973a, p. 172.
26   As at Cohen 2009, pp. 39–41. For evidence that Cohen once knew better, compare what is said about 'marketeers' at Cohen 1978, pp. 119–20.

The individual's labour is posited from the outset as social labour. Hence whatever the particular material form of the product they create, or help to create, what they have bought with their labour is not a definite particular product, but a certain share of communal production. Thus, they also have no particular product to exchange. Their product is *not exchange-value*.[27]

The non-independent exchange of products is not a commodity exchange, because no value is expressed in it. If exchange is not an independent exchange, the expression of the commensurability of products as parts of the total social product does not occur in the form of the expression of their power of general exchangeability as independent products, that is, in the form of the expression of their value.

Relatedly, suppose, in the context of the general kind of arrangement just imagined, that the reward of labour by means of individual consumption is facilitated by what Marx's *Critique of the Gotha Programme* refers to as a 'certificate'[28] of labour. Labour is performed in return for a certificate of labour, and then a certificate of labour is redeemed for means of individual consumption. A certificate of labour that can be redeemed for means of individual consumption is a divisible, durable and transportable means of exchange usable by all. But it cannot render products commensurable by expressing a power of general exchangeability that they do not have. Hence, it is not a measure of value.

Suppose that all exchanges in a society are voluntary, acquisitional and conditional. That would still not entail that exchangers raise an unrestricted exclusive claim to any products they transfer. A public agency could be the sole agency permitted to alienate products, and it might be bound by a principle as to how to distribute all components of the fund of means of individual consumption. Nor need an independent product transfer dictate that actors raise an unrestricted exclusive claim to what they transfer. Even if the total social product is split between independent producers, so as to prevent transfers from being guided by a policy in respect of the total social product, all transfers might be a legal duty.[29] The *independent exchange* of products does, however, presuppose actors who raise an unrestricted exclusive claim to the products they transfer. To explicate the nature of the claim raised in exchange when exchange is an exchange of value, we must examine the concept of possession.

---

27   *MEW*, 42, p. 104; *MECW*, 28, p. 108; Marx 1973a, p. 172.
28   *MEW*, 19, p. 20; *MECW*, 24, p. 86.
29   See sec. 1.

3   Possession: Savigny and Marx

A community occupies land if, besides simply settling in it, its highest constituted power treats that land as a space to which that community has an
unrestricted exclusive claim. Samuel Pufendorf, in *Of the Law of Nature and
Nations*, identifies a first occupant as 'him who, before others, took bodily Possession of it, with Intention to keep it as his own [*animo, sibi habendi*]'.[30] In
specifying two conditions for first occupancy, Pufendorf implies that possession has two components, *corpore et animo*. Savigny's *The Right of Possession*
(*Das Recht des Besitzes*) explicates possession in these same terms.

Savigny's aim in *The Right of Possession* is to investigate the Roman law
concept of possession that provides a 'condition [*Bedingung*] of rights', as distinct from the concept of possession that is a 'consequence' of legal property.[31]
To say that possession is a condition of rights is just to say that possession is
a requirement for acquiring certain rights. It is not to say that possession is a
condition of property. Possession might be a condition of rights distinct from
property. Indeed, Savigny claims that possession can only establish a right of
property if it is acquired 'with *bona fides* and *justa causa*'.[32] Possession need not
be acquired with either *bona fides* or *justa causa* to ground a right of interdict,
however.[33] At issue here is not a list of all the rights that possession grounds,
but the concept of possession that Savigny elaborates as their common condition. In this respect, the concept of possession, as the right of interdict shows,
does not include *bona fides* or *justa causa*.

According to Savigny, possession has two components: 'in order to be a possessor, one must not merely have detention, but also want to have it'.[34] In
other words, possession consists of detention, and the will for detention, or, as
Savigny also says, '*animus domini*'.[35] As argued below, both detention and the

---

30   Pufendorf 1934, p. 388; Pufendorf 1729, p. 386.
31   Savigny 1837, p. 3; Savigny 1848, p. 3. Savigny 1848 translates '*Bedingung*' as 'foundation'
        (which would be: '*Grundlage*'), but that is unnecessarily vague.
32   Savigny 1837, p. 12; Savigny 1848, p. 9.
33   Savigny 1837, p. 91; Savigny 1848, p. 59.
34   Savigny 1837, p. 111; Savigny 1848, pp. 71–2. In a paper on Savigny and Marx, Jean Cahan
        writes: '[d]etention forms the larger part of *Besitz*, which amounts to detention plus two
        effects ... these are *usucapion* and *interdicte*' (Cahan 1994, p. 399). Unfortunately, this state-
        ment is inaccurate: possession [*Besitz*] requires detention and the will for detention; the
        effects of possession do not belong to its definition; and *usucapion* is not an effect of deten-
        tion or possession alone – *justa causa* and *bone fides* are also required (Savigny 1837, p. 91;
        Savigny 1848, p. 59).
35   Savigny 1837, pp. 113–14; Savigny 1848, pp. 72–3. Compare Hegel's Heidelberg lectures of
        1817/18 on natural right, paragraph §18: '[i]n order that a thing should become my posses-

will for detention (*animus domini*) exhibit exclusivity. Moreover, both deten-
tion and *animus domini* can be conceived in the absence of a legal system. On
Savigny's concept of possession, it is indeed possible, as Marx suggests in the
Grundrisse, that 'one can imagine an isolated savage possessing [*besitzend*]'.[36]

Marx's study of Savigny's *The Right of Possession* is documented in a letter
Marx wrote to his father, Heinrich Marx, in November 1837.[37] At one point,
Marx even uses a similar formulation. Savigny remarks in regard to '*occupancy*
of a thing*' that 'the acquisition of possession [*Besitz*] is the real ground of
property [*eigentliche Grund des Eigenthums*] itself'.[38] Marx's *Critique of Hegel's
Doctrine of the State* contains a similar formulation: '[t]he real ground of private
property [*eigentliche Grund des Privateigentums*], possession [*Besitz*], is a *fact*,
an *inexplicable fact*, not a *right*'.[39] To refer to possession not just as a fact, but as
an '*inexplicable*' fact, is to deny that it can be incorporated within an account
of the rational development of free will. To understand Marx's later use of the
concept of possession, it helps to examine Savigny's elaboration of detention
and *animus domini*.

Savigny defines 'detention' as 'the state in which not only one's own effect
on a thing is physically possible, but also every alien effect can be obstructed'.[40]
The first aspect of detention, the physical possibility to affect a thing, presupposes that a thing over which detention is held does not have an untamed life
of its own (for example, it is not a wild animal that is yet to be caught). Savigny
also adds the subjective test that 'the possibility of affecting a thing at will must
be capable of being thought as an *immediate present possibility* by he who wants
to acquire possession'.[41] An actor can think that they can affect a thing at will
if, for example, they can see that it is motionless and in their bodily presence.
But an actor would presumably not pass this subjective test if they were found
to have acted on the belief that the thing had an untamed life of its own (for
example, that it is a wild animal that is merely wounded), even if the thing did
not in fact have an untamed life of its own (it is in fact dead).

The criterion for the second aspect of detention, the capacity to obstruct
any uninvited effect by another, is the 'mere possibility of defence'.[42] It must

---

sion, my inner will is not sufficient; it is also necessary that I *take possession* of it' (Hegel
1983, p. 48; Hegel 2012, p. 66).

36   *MEW*, 42, p. 36; *MECW*, 28, p. 39; Marx 1973a, p. 102.
37   *MEW*, 40, p. 5; *MECW*, 1, p. 15.
38   Savigny 1837, p. 12; Savigny 1848, p. 9.
39   *MEW*, 1, p. 315; *MECW*, 3, p. 110.
40   Savigny 1837, p. 2; Savigny 1848, p. 2.
41   Savigny 1837, p. 268; Savigny 1848, p. 170.
42   Savigny 1837, p. 2; Savigny 1848, p. 2.

be possible for an actor to defend a thing from any uninvited effect by another, although it is not necessary for them to be able to succeed. An actor is able to defend an object from any uninvited effect by another if, for example, they have the object within their reach, or they have the set of keys to it.[43] Someone who is sailing on an open sea, by contrast, does not have detention of it,[44] because they cannot defend it from any uninvited effect on it by another. A sea is too vast and unbounded for anyone who is merely sailing on it to defend it from any uninvited effect by another.

Detention should not be confused with the capacity to use an object, or with its actual use. Neither is necessary or sufficient for detention. Although an actor is required to be able to affect an object at will, they are not required to have acquired any specific competence in regard to it, and hence to be able to affect it in a way that counts as a use. Moreover, whether or not an actor knows how to use an available object, or actually uses it, they only have detention of it if it is possible for them to defend it from any uninvited effect by another.

The second component of possession, the will for detention, or *animus domini*, is the will to affect a thing independently and to obstruct every alien effect on it. Savigny says:

> only he can count as a *possessor* who treats the thing whose detention he has as an *owner*, i.e. who wills [*will*] to dominate it factually just as an owner is empowered [*befugt*] to do by their right, and hence, more particularly, without willing to recognise [*anerkennen zu wollen*] another more entitled than himself.[45]

The clauses that follow 'i.e.' first appear in the sixth (1837) German edition of *The Right of Possession*.[46] It is quite possible that Savigny added these clauses to the sixth German edition to imply a criticism of Hegel and/or his followers. What matters at this point, however, is just their contribution to Savigny's concept of possession. (Their relevance for a dialectic of non-recognition and recognition is discussed in chapter 9).

---

43   Savigny 1837, p. 250; Savigny 1848, p. 158.

44   Savigny 1837, pp. 2–3; Savigny 1848, p. 2.

45   Savigny 1837, p. 113; Savigny 1848, p. 73. Savigny 1848 translates 'will', from the verb 'wollen (to want, to will)', as 'contemplate' (which could be: '*betrachtet*'), and omits to translate 'wollen'. These mistakes are unfortunate, because Savigny's aim is to elaborate a type of *animus* (*animus domini*), not a type of belief. Savigny 1848 also renders '*befugt* (to be empowered, to be entitled)' as 'accustomed' (which would be: '*gewöhnt*'). '*Befugt*' has a legal connotation that 'accustomed' lacks; and habit, here, is irrelevant.

46   Compare the first (Savigny 1803, p. 79) and fifth editions (Savigny 1827, p. 92).

First, for *A* to will to affect a thing 'without willing to recognise another more entitled' to affect it is for *A* to act as if they do not require anyone else's permission to affect the thing, and as if they are not affecting it on anyone else's instruction. If *B* acts as if they require another's permission or instruction to affect a thing (for example, by borrowing a book from a library), *B* has no will to affect it if that permission is not forthcoming, or if they are otherwise instructed. *B* does not will to dominate the thing just as an owner is empowered to do. Second, for *A* to will to defend a thing from any uninvited effect by another, without 'willing to recognise another more entitled' than *A*, *A* cannot act as if they require someone else's permission to defend it, or as if they are defending it on someone else's instruction. If *B* acts in this way by, say, looking after someone else's luggage, *B* does not will to dominate the thing just as an owner is empowered to do.

Note that the exclusivity that defines *animus domini* concerns an actor's rule over a thing, not the benefits of that rule. It is inaccurate to elaborate the will component of Savigny's concept of possession as 'an intention ... of being able to use it [an object – JF], with no limitation of time, exclusively for your own benefit (*animus domini*)'.[47] An intention to be the exclusive beneficiary of any use of a thing is neither necessary nor sufficient for possession. It is unnecessary, for possession, to intend to use a thing for one's own benefit, because *animus domini* can provide a state of mind in a paternalistic in-order-to motive. An intention to be the sole beneficiary of an effect on a thing is also insufficient for possession. To have possession of *x*, *A* must will to defend *x* from any uninvited effect by another, including any uninvited effect of the kind that *A* knows *A* is sure to be the sole beneficiary of. The point to hold on to here is that *animus domini*, like detention, is ends-indeterminate. Savigny's concept of possession does not say anything about the end for which possession is held.

A separate point: although Savigny has recourse to an analogy with legal ownership to define the will component of possession, *animus domini* is not a will to acquire a right of ownership. It is not a will to assume any legal consequence at all. The law may attach legal consequences to *animus domini*. But *animus domini* is not itself a will to bring about any legal consequences. For example, according to Savigny, the type of will required to acquire private property in a captured wild animal is *animus domini*.[48] As a recent legal commentary confirms, 'a particular will to acquire property is not presupposed'.[49] Possession is a fact, conceivable without a legal system, even if, with the existence

---

47   Posner 2000, pp. 543–4.
48   Savigny 1840, p. 6.
49   Gursky, Pfeifer and Wiegand 2004, § 958, 5.

of a legal system, it may be a fact with legal consequences.[50] As Marx suggests in the *Grundrisse*, 'one can imagine an isolated savage possessing [*besitzend*]. But then possession [*Besitz*] is not a legal relation'.[51]

Further, the will that is required to initiate possession, *animus domini*, is not a will that a legal private property owner must have. The legal private property owner of a thing is someone who is at liberty to use it as they please, and to whom others have a duty not to interfere. Accordingly, the legal private property owner of a thing is *permitted* to have *animus domini* in regard to it. But nothing stops them from seeking another's permission before they use it, or from following another's instruction to use it, or from tolerating another's uninvited effect on it. (They may be so disposed owing to a special relationship, or to an ethical attitude in respect of members of a particular group). The legal private property owner of a thing does not cease to be its owner by acting in such a way, although someone who acts in this way lacks the *animus domini* required for possession. A will not to recognise another in respect of a thing is constitutive of possession, but it is not constitutive of legal private property ownership.

Savigny adds in respect of the continuation of possession:

> Possession is *continued* by the continuation of the same conditions (*corpore et animo*) by which it was acquired; but it is natural that the immediate physical rule required at the start of possession is unnecessary for its continuation. What matters is rather the continuing *possibility* of *reproducing* that immediate relation at will.[52]

Possession only continues for as long as the one who takes possession is able to restore their detention of it (for example, return to where they kept it). Nor may a possessor cancel their *animus domini*, or become incapable of *animus domini*, without losing possession.

On Savigny's concept of possession as reproducible detention and *animus domini*, the independent exchange of products is a mode of possession. It is a mode of possession because, firstly, each exchanger can only perform their part of a voluntary acquisitional conditional transfer if they can reproduce their detention of what they agree to part with. Secondly and more importantly, however, in an independent exchange of products, both the offer and its accept-

---

50   Savigny 1837, p. 30; Savigny 1848, p. 20.
51   *MEW*, 42, p. 36; *MECW*, 28, p. 39; Marx 1973a, p. 102.
52   Savigny 1837, p. 270; Savigny 1848, p. 171.

ance are a mode of *animus domini*. Someone who offers or agrees to exchange an independent product acts as if their will alone makes its alienation valid.

Suppose *A* offers *x* to *B* in exchange for *y*. *A*'s offer amounts to a statement to *B* of the form: give me *y*, and I will give you *x*. As such, *A*'s offer to *B* asserts that, as far as *A* is concerned, the only condition to which *B*'s receipt of *x* is subject is whether or not *A* agrees. *A* is not after *B*'s permission to make their offer, or ready to be instructed by *B* in respect of *x*. *A*'s offer also provides a basis on which *A* could defend *x* from any uninvited effect from *B* in their own name. As the same goes for what *B*'s acceptance of *A*'s offer indicates of *B*'s will in respect of *y* vis-à-vis *A*, the independent exchange of products is a mode of possession on both sides. By contrast, neither a duty-based transfer of an independent product nor a voluntary but non-independent exchange is a mode of *animus domini* on both sides. In the former, the one to part with the product would have to regard themselves as requiring the permission of the authorities not to exchange. In the latter, the one to part with the means of consumption would have to regard themselves as under an instruction to exchange by those who enforce the principle of distribution that is to be applied.

4   Commodities and Money

If production for exchange is generalised, the exchange of products is independent, and a mode of possession. Hence, if the commodity form is a general form of wealth, possession is a general type of subjectivity. It is permissible, then, for a commodity form based explanation of money to appeal to the subjectivity of possession in the context of generalised production for exchange. Before reconstructing Marx's explanation of money, however, consider what can be said, from a commodity form perspective, about the explanation of the origin of money offered by economics.

For economic thought, founded on the concept of an economic good, it is a given that human beings seek to obtain goods to provide for their wants, including by means of exchange. Accordingly, Menger's explanation of money in *Principles of Economics* proceeds from the starting-point that 'every man, in regard to the goods they are to obtain from exchange, has just the use value in view'.[53]

The explanation takes the form of an illustration. Menger asks us to consider the plight of a 'weapon-smith' who has 'two suits of copper armour' and 'wishes

---

53   Menger 1968, p. 250; Menger 2007, p. 258; compare Smith 1979, p. 126.

to exchange them for copper, fuel, and food'.[54] The weapon-smith's problem is that few if any sellers of copper, fuel and food may want to exchange them for suits of copper armour. A solution to the problem lies in the fact that some goods are more 'marketable' than others, that is, will be accepted by more people, in a larger and more elastic quantity, with fewer spatial or temporal limits.[55] The weapon-smith can approach their goal, sparing themselves a 'significant loss of time', if they first exchange their copper armour for a good with 'greater marketability', and then exchange the latter for what they want to consume.[56] For Menger and others, money is the marketable good that first some, and then all, seek to acquire in exchange to get around the problem of non-complementary desires for use-values, so that it becomes the most marketable good.[57] The fundamental function of money, on this account, is its function as a general means of exchange.[58]

One point to note about this explanation is that it does not explain money simply by the existence of an unregulated economy in economic goods. The existence of an unregulated economy in economic goods only explains money in conjunction with an additional fact about human beings that is not implied by the concept of an unregulated economy in economic goods. An economy is unregulated if there are no prohibitions on exchange. An economist cannot explain money just by the existence of an unregulated economy in economic goods, however – that is, just by virtue of the coming into its own of the rationality bound up with the concept of an economic good – because it is conceivable for the total social product to consist entirely of one type of economic good, whose exchange is unregulated.

Recall, from chapter 6, the features of Roemer's sketch of a society that produces one good: corn.[59] A few owners of seed corn employ half the population at a subsistence wage, and reap a surplus of corn from each producer they hire; while the rest of the population produces for subsistence on their own. In this sketch, the total social product consists entirely of corn. It also has economic goods-character, because corn is only obtained by labour, and labour is undesirable.

As the total social product in this society consists of just one type of economic good, whose exchange is unregulated, its reproduction without money

54   Menger 1968, p. 252; Menger 2007, p. 259.
55   Menger 1968, pp. 233–49; Menger 2007, pp. 241–56.
56   Menger 1968, p. 252; Menger 2007, p. 259.
57   Menger 1968, pp. 253–4; Menger 2007, p. 260; see also Menger 1970, pp. 7–9; Mises 1924, pp. 2–7; Mises 1934, pp. 30–5.
58   Menger 1970, pp. 94–6; Mises 1924, p. 5; Mises 1934, p. 33.
59   Roemer 1982a, p. 11.

would prove that money cannot be explained simply by an unregulated economy in economic goods. The society Roemer sketches can indeed reproduce itself without anything an economist can regard as money. No exchange takes place in it apart from the exchange of corn for labour, and no economist can regard the corn that is exchanged for labour as money. It is not a good that any actor lacks, and which they must first acquire, in order then to make use of its greater marketability, in exchange, to acquire what they want to use. The hirers in Roemer's sketch already possess corn, first by stipulation, and subsequently as the direct result of a prior round of production; and the producers they hire, who acquire corn in return for labour, directly consume all their corn. Money cannot arise, because no one has any need to convert a good they have into a more marketable good in order, then, to go about using it in exchange to obtain what they want. Roemer's sketch proves that economists must appeal to an additional fact about human beings, extraneous to the rationality bound up with the concept of an economic good, to explain money. Money cannot be explained just by virtue of the coming into its own of the rationality bound up with the concept of an economic good.

The explanation of money in economic thought also rests on the following additional fact: human beings have a(n) (evolving) variety of wants. An economist must say: as human beings are a species with wants for a variety of different types of economic good, an unregulated human economy generates money. For if a species of being were to exist that only had wants for one type of economic good, that species could develop an unregulated economy without money. Yet the fact that human beings have a(n) (evolving) variety of wants is a transhistorical fact about human beings. It is true of human beings at all stages in their history. The economic explanation of money naturalises money, that is, traces it back to a transhistorical fact about human beings, because (i) its basic concept is that of an economic good, which has historically specific assumptions packed into it (possession) that are not acknowledged as such; and because (ii) only an extraneous transhistorical fact about human beings needs to be added to the rationality bound up with this concept, to explain money from an economic point of view.

Commodity form philosophy, by contrast, can offer an explanation of money that does not rely on empirical premises extraneous to its fundamental concept. The starting point of this explanation can be defended by showing up the derivative nature of Menger's starting-point. Menger's starting-point is that each exchanger 'has just the use value in view'.[60] By this, Menger seems to

---

60   Menger 1968, p. 250; Menger 2007, p. 258.

mean that every individual wants to acquire particular types of use-value, just as a weapon-smith wants to acquire copper, fuel and food. Yet, the particular types of use-value that any given individual wants to acquire will reflect broader life plans, formed in light of the society in which that individual lives. In the weapon-smith's case, the train of thought is: in this society, anyone may choose to work in any branch of production for exchange; I want to live by producing copper armour for exchange; therefore, I will acquire copper, fuel and food in return for the copper armour I produce. If we express the implication of the starting premise of this train of thought in a less artificially individualistic form, we can replace Menger's starting-point with the explicitly intrastructured starting-point: in a society defined by generalised production for exchange, each possessor seeks to acquire, in exchange, whatever product they want to acquire, in light of all other possessor's wanting to acquire whatever product they want to acquire. This brings us to Marx's remark in *Capital* Chapter Two:

> For each commodity possessor [*Warenbesitzer*], every alien commodity counts as a particular equivalent for their commodity, hence their commodity as a universal equivalent for all other commodities. But since all commodity possessors [*Warenbesitzer*] do the same, no commodity is a universal equivalent, and thus commodities also possess no general relative value-form in which they are equated as values, and their value magnitudes compared. Hence they do not confront one another as commodities at all, but only as products or use-values.[61]

Which particular type of product a possessor wants to acquire will depend on what all the various types of product they could acquire are worth. A possessor does not have a preference for acquiring one type of product over others independently of all information about what amounts of each type of product they would be acquiring. They do not have a preference to acquire commodity a over commodities b, c, etc. They have a preference to acquire z amount of commodity a over y amount of commodity b, x amount of commodity c, etc. A possessor may prefer to acquire a car than to acquire a television, but, given the possibility of re-sale, they cannot say that they prefer acquiring cars over acquiring televisions irrespective of what amounts of each they would be acquiring. So, to know what they want to acquire, a possessor must compare the worth of every type of product they could acquire. To do that, a possessor must know

---

61   *MEW*, 23, p. 101; *MECW*, 35, pp. 96–7; Marx 1976, p. 180.

what all the various types of product are worth in a single measure. So, to know what they want to acquire, a possessor must adopt a measure for comparing the worth of every type of product.

One type of product's exchangeability can only be expressed in another type of exchangeable product. Thus, only a particular type of exchangeable product can provide a measure of value.

A possessor's purpose in employing a measure of value is to ascertain what they want to acquire. To that end, there is no more direct measure of value than the type of product they possess, which they can immediately exchange. If a possessor adopted a type of exchangeable product they did not possess as a measure, they would have to measure the exchangeability of a type of product that they did possess in it, to know what they could acquire; and only after this conversion could they ascertain what they wanted to acquire. So, if D possesses w amount of d, D uses d as their measure of value by estimating, in d, all the amounts of all the types of product they could exchange it for.

No product can be acquired in exchange, however, without the agreement of *its* possessor, whose will is not subject to instruction, but is a will to acquire whatever *they* want to acquire. As the independent exchange of products is a mode of possession on both sides, both sides require a measure of value. Just as D estimates all the amounts of all the types of product for which they could exchange their possession, w amount of d, all the possessors of all those other types of product must also employ a measure of value in order to ascertain what it is that they want to acquire. Insofar as all the types of product that any given possessor could exchange their product for must be acquired from their current possessors, all of whom will to acquire whatever they want to acquire, and who can only determine this by employing a measure of value, any given measure of value that one possessor adopts must be consistent with every other possessor adopting a measure of value. Otherwise, it will not be able to inform action in a context in which all exchangers act as possessors.

No possessor has cause to consider all the amounts of all the types of product that something is worth just because another possessor possesses it. If a possessor is to acquire whatever they want to acquire, they must adopt, as their measure of value, something to which *they* relate as a possessor. So, the possessors of all the other types of product besides d do not all compare the amounts of all the types of product that their respective product is worth in amounts of d. Insofar as each possessor thinks like D, each possessor instead adopts a type of product that they possess as their measure of value, and so adopts a *different* measure of value.

It is not consistent, however, for possessors to adopt different measures of value. For then the thought that each possessor has, when employing their own particular measure of value, of the exchangers of the other types of commodity whose value is measured, is not a thought of them as employing their measure of value, and so not a thought of them as possessors. D's thought: 'w amount of d is worth z amount of a, or y amount of b, or x amount of c', is not a thought of A, B and C, the holders of a, b and c, as employing their measure of value.

What possessors must adopt if they are all, simultaneously and without contradiction, to compare the amounts of all the types of product that they could acquire, is a 'universal equivalent'.[62] A type of product is a universal equivalent if it is universally employed to express the power of general exchangeability of any type of product. A universal equivalent exists just by dint of the fact that the possessors of every type of product adopt it as a measure of value. The question, however, is how all possessors can adopt some one type of product as a measure of value, when generalised production for exchange presupposes that possessors do not all produce the same type of product, and so ensures that possessors cannot all settle on some one type of product as a measure of value on account of everyone possessing it in virtue of everyone having produced it.

A particular type of product can only be adopted by all possessors as a measure of value if it is something to which all can relate as a possessor. In the independent exchange of products, each regards themselves and treats the other as the current possessor of what they part with, and the future possessor of what they stand to receive. So, a particular type of product can become a universal equivalent if it is something to which all exchangers can relate either as the possession they part with or as the possession they stand to receive in their respective exchanges. A particular type of product can become a universal equivalent, then, if it is one or other of the two possessions that every possessor relates to in exchange. That is, a particular type of product can become a universal equivalent by serving as a 'universal means of exchange [*Tauschmittel*]'.[63] If one or other of the two possessions that each possessor relates to in exchange is a universal means of exchange, each possessor can adopt it simultaneously and without contradiction as a measure of value. For the thought that each then has, in so adopting it, is consistent with the thought of the exchangers of all the other types of commodity as acquiring just whatever they want to acquire,

---

62   *MEW*, 23, p. 101; *MECW*, 35, p. 96; Marx 1976, p. 180; and *MEW*, 13, p. 34; *MECW*, 29, p. 288.

63   *MEW*, 13, p. 34; *MECW*, 29, p. 288. *MECW* translates '*Tauschmittel* (means of exchange)' as 'medium of exchange' (which would be: '*Tauschmedium*'). That is confusing, for in the *Grundrisse*, Marx uses 'medium [*Medium*]' to refer to the function of money as a universal equivalent (*MEW*, 42, p. 74; *MECW*, 28, p. 77; Marx 1973a, p. 139). I am unaware of any use by Marx of the term '*Tauschmedium* (medium of exchange)'.

by virtue of what they exchange or seek to acquire in exchange. Its adoption as a measure of value can therefore inform action in a context in which every exchanger acts as a possessor. Although the logically first function of money is its function as a universal equivalent – a divisible, durable and transportable means of exchange used by all that lacks this function is *not* money – a type of product performs this function only by virtue of performing a second function, that of universal means of exchange.

Connecting both functions of money, *Capital* remarks:

> Commercial intercourse, in which commodity possessors [*Warenbesitzer*] exchange and compare their own articles with a variety of other articles, never takes place without the various commodity possessors' [*Warenbesitzer*] various commodities, within commercial intercourse, being exchanged for, and equated as values with, one further kind of commodity.[64]

The type of product that is both a universal equivalent and a universal means of exchange can be called the money commodity. The *first* type of product to serve as the money commodity will be a relatively marketable product. A product may be relatively marketable, Marx writes in *A Contribution to a Critique of Political Economy*, either on account of its being 'the most common use-value' in a given community, or on account of its acceptance in exchange by merchants who export it to 'other communities'.[65] But the function of money as a universal equivalent is *best* served by a product whose material is repeatedly divisible into indistinguishable exemplars.[66] Only then can it smoothly measure the value of every possible amount of every type of product. The type of money commodity best suited to serve the function of a universal means of exchange, meanwhile, is one whose material is durable and easily transportable.[67] Precious metals such as gold and silver combine the kinds of qualities well suited to perform both of these functions. Nonetheless, the divisibility and functional equivalence of quantities of a money commodity can be increased by coin;[68] and coin, insofar as its acceptance is guaranteed against effects of wear and tear, has an artificially enhanced durability.[69] The move from a money

---

64   *MEW*, 23, p. 103; *MECW*, 35, p. 99; Marx 1976, pp. 182–3.
65   *MEW*, 13, pp. 35–6; *MECW*, 29, pp. 290–1.
66   *MEW*, 13, p. 35; *MECW*, 29, p. 290.
67   Ibid.
68   *MEW*, 13, p. 87; *MECW*, 29, p. 342.
69   *MEW*, 23, p. 140; *MECW*, 35, p. 136; Marx 1976, p. 223.

commodity to coin can be explained as a deliberate intervention to remove the imperfections of a money commodity in respect of its functions as a universal equivalent and a universal means of exchange.

CHAPTER 8

Exploitation

What is now required, to support the interaction component of the thesis, is an argument for characterising production with wage-labour for continuous money maximisation as a kind of exploitation. If successful, it will show that exploitation is essential to capitalism.

Insofar as the interaction-recognition-antinomy thesis belongs to commodity form philosophy, the argument for characterising production with wage-labour for continuous money maximisation as capitalist labour-exploitation must rest on an analysis of the commodity form. Just as in the case of the explanation of money, it is not to introduce facts that are extraneous to the commodity form. It is to apply to a description of capitalism purely in terms that the commodity form presupposes.

As Backhaus puts it in *The Dialectic of the Value Form*, generalised production for exchange 'cannot be thought'[1] without money. A money commodity is what enables all exchangers to act as possessors, who acquire whatever they want to acquire. The conception of capitalist labour-exploitation presented below rests on the claim that not all possessors, however, can maximise their monetary wealth. Money maximisation, as a universal law of human nature, cannot be thought. Marx's distinction between use-value and value can explain why a maxim of money maximisation fails a system-level universalisability test.

Section 1 presents a case, against the quantitative Marxist view of exploitation, for conceiving exploitation in general terms. Section 2 cautions against defining exploitation in normative terms. Section 3 analyses the general conception of exploitation as instrumentalisation suggested by *The German Ideology*. Sections 4–8 elaborate its five conditions. In particular, section 5 outlines a system universalisability version of the harm condition, and distinguishes it from two other concepts: fallacy of composition (Elster), and collective unfreedom (Cohen). Section 9 formulates the system universalisability conception of exploitation in light of these elaborations. Section 10 then argues, on the basis of this conception, that production with wage-labour for continuous money maximisation is exploitative. Sections 11–13 argue that this conception facilitates a solution to three problems: the exploitation and need problem; the

---

1 Backhaus 2011, p. 32; compare p. 285.

agency problem; and the capitalism, rights and injustice problem. Section 14 concludes by listing the reasons to endorse a system universalisability conception of exploitation.

1   The Quantitative Marxist View of Exploitation

On the quantitative Marxist view of exploitation, the most popular view among advocates of Marx's value theory, there is no Marxist conception of exploitation in general. Rather, exploitation is regarded as a *sui generis* term for the appropriation of the product of unpaid labour. On the quantitative Marxist view of exploitation, production is the only context in which exploitation can occur, and capitalist exploitation concerns the difference between two quantities of value. Tony Smith, for example, writes:

> 'Exploitation' is defined in terms of the difference between the value that labor power creates, measured by socially necessary labor time, and the value of labor power, measured by the socially necessary labor time it takes to produce the commodities necessary for the production and reproduction of the commodity labor power.[2]

Similarly, Michael Heinrich states:

> The fact that the individual worker receives a lesser value from the capitalist than the value he produced through his labor is referred to by Marx as *'exploitation'* … Exploitation refers solely and exclusively to the fact that the producer only receives a portion of the newly produced value that he or she creates.[3]

These statements by Smith and Heinrich, which report a widespread view in the literature,[4] neatly state the quantitative Marxist view of exploitation.

On the quantitative Marxist view, exploitation in capitalism rests on four premises: a certain level of productive power; the commodification of the

---

2 Smith 1990, p. 114; whereby '[t]he category "labor power as commodity" defines a structure in which disparities of wealth lead one class to own/control considerable productive resources while another does not, with the latter class selling its labor power to the former' (Smith 1990, p. 112).

3 Heinrich 2005, pp. 93–4; Heinrich 2012, p. 96.

4 See also Arneson 1981, p. 203; Gordon 1991, p. 9, p. 50; Roemer 1988, p. 46.

human capacity to work; class division between those who sell their labour power and those who control productive resources; and a claim about the determination of value by socially necessary labour time. With a certain level of productive power, producers can produce the commodities that are required to reproduce their labour power in less than their total dispensable work time. Thus, on the quantitative Marxist view, if the exchange ratio of commodities, including labour power, is governed by their value, as determined by socially necessary labour time, capitalists who pay the full value of labour power, and put it to work, exploit wage-labourers by appropriating the product of what *Capital* calls 'surplus labour':

> We have seen that the worker, during one part of the labour process, merely produces the value of their labour power, i.e. the value of their necessary means of subsistence ... The second period of the labour process, in which the worker toils beyond the limits of necessary labour, costs them labour, is an expenditure of their labour power, but provides them no value. It constitutes surplus value ... I call this part of the working day 'surplus labour time', and the labour expended in it 'surplus labour'.[5]

Assuming the full value of labour power is paid (and nothing more than that), *Capital* continues,

> surplus value is in the same ratio to variable capital [money used by a capitalist to purchase labour power – JF] as surplus labour is to necessary labour ... The rate of surplus value is thus the exact expression of [*Ausdruck für*] the degree of exploitation [*Exploitationsgrad*] of labour power by capital, or of the worker by the capitalist.[6]

---

5 *MEW*, 23, pp. 230–1; *MECW*, 35, pp. 225–6; Marx 1976, pp. 324–5.

6 *MEW*, 23, pp. 231–2; *MECW*, 35, p. 227; Marx 1976, p. 326. '*Ausdruck für*' is translated as 'expression of' (not, as in *MECW* and Marx 1976, as 'expression for') because (1) '*Ausdruck für*' can denote a manifestation of something more fundamental or general; (2) if so, 'expression of' is the correct translation; (3) here, '*Ausdruck für*' denotes what (1) allows; (4) the corresponding phrase in the French edition of *Capital* is '*l'expression ... du*' (*MEGA*, II, 7, p. 179), which, for the same reason, may be translated as 'expression of'.

Some interpreters seem unaware of (1). Cohen claims that the 'natural interpretation' of 'Ausdruck dafür' as opposed to 'Ausdruck davon' is 'expression for' (Cohen and Acton 1970, p. 130). Yet '*Ausdruck für*' must sometimes be rendered as 'expression of'. When Marx writes in *Capital* that 'cooling is the technical expression for [*Ausdruck für*] the occasional escape from the drying room into fresh air' (*MEW*, 23, p. 314; *MECW*, 35, p. 301; Marx 1976, p. 410), '*Ausdruck für*' introduces an alternative term of description. Here, 'expression for' is correct and 'expression of' incorrect. But when, in *Outlines of a Critique of Political Economy*, Engels

Similarly, *Value, Price and Profit* (1865) contains the apposition: 'the real ratio between paid and unpaid labour, the real degree of the *exploitation* (you must allow me this French word) *of labour*'.[7]

It is easy to see how the above passages could give the impression that there is no Marxist conception of exploitation in general. The argument is as follows. A ratio is a proportional relationship between two quantities. As exploitation is a ratio that can only differ in degrees, both the benefit and the object of exploit-ation must always be of the same kind. If not only the benefit of exploitation, but also the thing exploited, are always of the same kind, exploitation is a *sui generis* term. As it is labour (power) that is exploited, production is the only context in which exploitation can occur.

There are four textual objections to the quantitative Marxist view of exploit-ation. The first narrowly concerns Marx's uses of the term 'exploitation'. The quantitative Marxist view goes beyond Marx's use of this term in the aforecited passages, while it is inconsistent with Marx's use of it in other passages.

On the one hand, the quantitative Marxist view of exploitation requires the above claims about the 'degree of exploitation of labour power', or the 'degree of *exploitation ... of labour*', to be understood as if they were claims about exploita-tion as such. That reading goes beyond the text. It is not, on that account, wrong. But it is undermotivated. Just because *Capital* refers to a 'degree of exploitation of labour power by capital' without first saying anything more general about exploitation, that is not to say that, for Marx, there can be no exploitation in capitalism that is not a 'degree of exploitation of labour power by capital'.

On the other hand, the quantitative Marxist view of exploitation is at vari-ance with the fact that Marx was not shy to suggest that capitalism engenders

---

writes that 'Malthusian theory is but the economic expression of [*Ausdruck für*] the religious dogma of the contradiction between spirit and nature and the resulting corruption of both' (*MEW*, 1, p. 520; *MECW*, 3, p. 439), Engels is claiming that an idea of one discourse (religion) is expressed in another (political economy). Here, 'expression of' is correct and 'expression for' incorrect. (*MECW* gets this one right.) Whether '*Ausdruck für*' is to be rendered as 'expression for' or as 'expression of' depends on the context.

In the above passage, Marx affirms *two* distinct ratios: a ratio between two quantities of value, and a ratio between two quantities of labour time. Hence, in Marx's conclusion that the rate of surplus value is the exact '*Ausdruck für*' the degree of exploitation, '*Ausdruck für*' must be translated as 'expression of'. To translate '*Ausdruck für*' here as 'expression for' creates the impression that there is only *one* ratio of interest to Marx (just as cooling is nothing other than the occasional escape from the drying room into fresh air). 'Expression for' thereby encourages talk about a 'rate of exploitation', a bogus phrase that illicitly con-joins terms from two different ratios, creating the false impression that there is only one (see below).

7   *MECW*, 20, p. 136.

other kinds of exploitation. The *Communist Manifesto* proclaims: 'the exploit-ation [*Exploitation*] of one nation by another will cease as the exploitation [*Exploitation*] of one individual by another ceases'.[8] *Capital* describes the rela-tion between landlord and tenant as 'secondary exploitation, accompanying the original exploitation that occurs immediately in the process of produc-tion itself'.[9] Marx's First Draft of *The Civil War in France* claims that the French 'middle-class' turned the 'immense machinery of government' into the object of 'a second exploitation of the people by assuring to their families all the rich places of the state household'.[10] As Marx's various uses of the term imply that neither the benefit nor the object of exploitation are always of the same kind, they presuppose a general conception of exploitation.

The second textual objection to the quantitative Marxist view of exploita-tion is that it begs the question: why, in the context of production, adopt 'this French word',[11] exploitation, at all? If Marx wanted a *sui generis* term to express a claim specific to production, is it not odd for him to adopt a term with a history of being applied, in French social criticism, beyond the context of pro-duction? Would not Marx have been better advised, when writing in German, to stick to the Germanic term '*Ausbeutung*', and to avoid the term '*Exploitation*', to emphasise that, for him, if not for French social critics, exploitation in pro-duction is *sui generis*?

The third textual objection is that Marx's project in *Capital* is not limited to, or primarily an exercise in, quantitative analysis. *Capital* is a study of 'the form of value'.[12] Just as it is one thing to ask what determines the magnitude of exchange-value, and another to ask what money is, so it is one thing to ascertain the 'degree' of capitalist labour-exploitation, and another to ask what capitalist labour-exploitation is. If *Capital* is the kind of work that studies what money is, that suggests it will also be concerned with what capitalist labour-exploitation is. But if one asks what capitalist labour-exploitation is, independently of its degree, one may answer with reference to a general conception of exploitation.

Finally, the quantitative Marxist view of exploitation does not even man-age to express Marx's quantitative claim faithfully, and expressing this claim faithfully adds urgency to the qualitative question of what it means to say that labour (power) is exploited. In the quotes cited above, both Smith and Hein-rich report that exploitation is a difference between two quantities of 'value'.

---

8   *MEW*, 4, p. 479; *MECW*, 6, p. 503.

9   *MEW*, 25, p. 623; *MECW*, 37, p. 604; Marx 1981, p. 745.

10   *MECW*, 22, p. 484.

11   *MECW*, 20, p. 136.

12   *MEW*, 23, p. 95; *MECW*, 35, p. 91; Marx 1976, p. 174.

In this they are not alone. Cohen states: 'the ratio of surplus value to variable capital is called the rate of exploitation'.[13] Wood remarks: 'Marx dubs the ratio of surplus value to variable capital the "rate of exploitation"'.[14] Norman Geras considers 'Marxian exploitation, the ratio between what the worker makes and what the capitalist takes'.[15] Fredric Jameson refers to the 'rate of exploitation of the variable capital (workers)'.[16] All these statements are false.

In the aforecited passage from *Capital*, the 'degree of exploitation' and the 'rate of surplus value' are distinguished. The former is a ratio between periods of socially necessary labour time, the latter a ratio between values. *Das Kapital never* refers to a 'rate of exploitation'. Occasional uses of this phrase in the English translations are all fabrications.[17] 'Rate of exploitation' is a bogus phrase that illicitly conjoins terms from two different ratios (rate from 'rate of surplus value' and exploitation from 'degree of exploitation'), creating the false impression that there is only one.

All of the above authors perform an economistic distortion. The monetary difference between what a producer can buy with their wage, and the value of the product they produce, is the basis of a complaint that can be formulated in terms of the economic goods that a producer is denied. By contrast, a complaint directed at the fact that the system of capitalist production maximises the ratio of surplus labour to necessary labour is beyond economic thought. It is not a matter of the economic goods that a producer does not possess. It is merely expressed in that form (in the absence of a redistributive tax scheme). In this context, it is instructive to recall Marx's remark in his *Economic and Philosophic Manuscripts of 1844*:

---

13   Cohen 1988, p. 211. See, also, Elster 1978a, p. 5; Elster 1985, p. 177, p. 187, p. 324; Schwartz 1995a, p. 277. In a subsequent work, Cohen says that exploitation, for Marxists, concerns labour time (Cohen 1995, pp. 145–7). In a still later work, Cohen reverts to saying that exploitation, for Marxists, concerns 'right to the product' (Cohen 2001, p. 108). Cohen never acknowledges a discrepancy.

14   Wood 2004, p. 250.

15   Geras 1992, p. 61; see, similarly, Geras 1985, p. 69.

16   Jameson 2011, p. 58.

17   See *MEW*, 23, p. 555; *MECW*, 35, p. 533; Marx 1976, p. 670; and *MEW*, 25, 401; *MECW*, 37, p. 385; Marx 1981, p. 511. Marx uses *'Rate der Exploitation'* in earlier unpublished manuscripts of 1861–63 (*MEW*, 26.2, p. 41; *MECW*, 31, p. 281; and *MEW*, 26.3, p. 66, p. 68, p. 294, p. 299; *MECW*, 32, p. 261, p. 263, p. 432, p. 438). But one reason for Marx later to stick with 'degree' of exploitation and 'rate' of surplus value is to avoid their confusion. (It is fair to refer to 'rate of exploitation' as a bogus phrase, for commentators who adopt it do not do so to refer to a phrase that Marx used in unpublished manuscripts of 1861–63. It is offered as a faithful report of Marx's position in *Capital*).

For to speak of *private property* is to believe one is dealing with a thing exterior to the human being. To speak of labour is to deal directly with the human being. This new formulation of the question already includes its solution.[18]

It is necessary to distinguish the degree of exploitation from the rate of surplus value to answer the questions: what is capitalist labour-exploitation? Why is the use of labour power for continuous money maximisation a kind of exploitation? If capitalist labour-exploitation is located in the dimension of labouring activity, rather than in the dimension of value, capitalist labour-exploitation may rest on a characterisation of the end pursued by hiring labour that produces what has value, on criteria applicable to the pursuit of other ends.

2 A Non-normative Concept of Exploitation

Exploitation is often defined in normative terms. Roemer once viewed exploitation as 'the distributional consequences of an unjust inequality in the distribution of productive assets and resources'.[19] For Cohen, 'a person is *exploited* when unfair advantage is taken of them'.[20] On this point at least, liberal theories of exploitation concur. Robert Goodin writes: 'built into the concept of exploiting a person is a notion of "unfairness"'.[21] Alan Wertheimer's book *Exploitation* discusses 'the morally relevant features of transactions and relationships in which it is claimed that one party is taking unfair advantage of another'.[22] Yet it is better to define exploitation non-normatively.

One reason not to define exploitation in normative terms is that, as Cohen says, it is a philosophical vice to regard other thinkers, with whom you disagree, as *obviously* wrong.[23] One form this vice can take is to define terms such that those with whom you disagree are obviously incoherent.[24] Exploitation always has an analytical component, from which, in any pejorative use, a speaker distances themselves.[25] If so, it is always possible for another speaker

---

18   *MEW*, 40, pp. 521–2; *MECW*, 3, p. 281.
19   Roemer 1986b, p. 281.
20   Cohen 2011, p. 5; compare Elster 1985, p. 167.
21   Goodin 1987, p. 167.
22   Wertheimer 1996, p. ix.
23   Cohen 2011, pp. 231–2.
24   Compare Cohen 1978, p. 217.
25   Consider Cohen's statement: 'some reduce their care [to things and people in their

to be of a different view, and not distance themselves from it. Only a non-normative definition of the term avoids making the speaker with that different view obviously incoherent. If free-riding were *defined* in normative terms, as a bad, someone who expressed a belief that free-riding is permissible would be regarded as obviously incoherent. Likewise, to define exploitation in normative terms is to understand an author, like Nietzsche, who 'assert[s] that exploitation is good or just', as 'contradicting only himself'.[26] The force of the assertion is lost. To define exploitation in non-normative terms is not, of course, to be committed to denying it normative significance, no more than free-riding lacks normative significance on account of a non-normative definition.

3   **Bazard, Marx and the Five Conditions for Exploitation**

Marx was aware of the history of 'this French word',[27] exploitation. *The German Ideology* hints at a general (and non-normative) conception of exploitation in appealing to the original French expression.

The expression 'exploitation of man by man [*exploitation de l'homme par l'homme*]' was coined in the *Doctrine de Saint-Simon. Exposition. 1829*,[28] authored mainly by Saint-Amand Bazard.[29] The *Exposition* appeared after Henri Saint-Simon's death, in what *The German Ideology* dubs 'the Bazard period' of Saint-Simonianism, its 'most significant theoretical development'.[30] *The German Ideology* adopts the French expression '*exploitation de l'homme par l'homme*' in the course of diagnosing the appeal of utilitarianism:

---

charge – JF] more than others do in the hope and expectation that they will thereby provide less care than others do, and thereby exploit and benefit from others' pains' (Cohen 2008, p. 308). People who reduce their care *need not* hope and expect, by reducing their care, to do something *unfair* to others. What they hope and expect is to *benefit*, irrespective of whether they *also* believe that what they do is unfair (and so hope and expect to do something unfair).

26   Wood 1995, p. 140; see also Wood 2004, pp. 242–5. Compare Geras's claim that 'the concept of an unequal exchange ... presupposes ... a notion of due entitlements and their being violated' (Geras 1992, pp. 52–3). In Geras's view, anyone who says: unequal exchange is not a wrong, is contradicting themselves. It is not inconsistent, however, to use the concept of unequal exchange analytically, and to believe that there is no moral entitlement to equal exchange.

27   *MECW*, 20, p. 136.

28   No author 1958, p. 63; see below for further uses of this phrase.

29   Cunliffe and Reeve 1996, p. 61.

30   *MEW*, 3, p. 493, p. 496; *MECW*, 5, p. 505, p. 508.

The real relations presupposed here are ... particular exercises of specific individual qualities. These relations are henceforth not to have their *characteristic* meaning; they are to express and represent a separate relation foisted upon them, the *relation of utility or utilisation*. Such *re-description* only ceases to be meaningless and arbitrary once those relations have validity for individuals not on their own account, not as self-activity, ...

Verbal masquerade is only significant if it is the unconscious or conscious expression of a real masquerade. In this case, the relation of utility has a very definite significance; namely, that I derive benefit for myself by my doing harm to another (*exploitation de l'homme par l'homme*).[31]

Marx's diagnosis of utilitarianism's appeal can be left to one side (although, as that diagnosis says that utilitarianism is a symptom of exploitation, it suggests that Marx's conception of exploitation is not underpinned by utilitarian concerns). The issue here is to consider what could have interested Marx in this French expression, and led him to render it as he did. Consider the following excerpts from the *Exposition*:

Let us turn, first, to the age in which the vanquished became the property of the victor, and the latter made of him an instrument of work or pleasure. In short, let us return to the institution of *slavery* ... [O]nly then did *exploitation* begin ...

In the beginning, exploitation encompasses the entire material, intellectual, and moral life of the man who is subject to it. The slave is placed outside humankind; he belongs to his master like the land he possesses, like his cattle and stock; the slave is *his thing* [*sa chose*] by the same title. The slave has no rights, not even the right to life: the master can dispose of his days, and mutilate him at will, to appropriate him for whatever functions he decides. The slave is not only condemned to misery and physical suffering, but also to intellectual and moral brutalisation: he has no name, no family, no property, no bonds of affection, and no recognised relation with man or the gods; for the slave has no gods, which only exist for the master. In short, *he cannot aspire to acquire any of the goods denied to him, or even to approach them*.[32]

---

31   *MEW*, 3, pp. 394–5; *MECW*, 5, pp. 409–10.
32   Bazard et al. 1830, pp. 85–6; No author 1958, p. 65. The published translation has 'property' for '*sa chose*' (which would be: '*propriété*') but 'his thing' is more literal.

The *Exposition* adds: '*the worker* is exploited *materially, intellectually* and *morally* as *the slave* was, only less intensely';[33] and concludes:

> it is evident that the constitution of property must be changed, since, by
> virtue of this constitution, some men are born with the privilege of liv-
> ing while doing nothing, that is, living at the expense of others, which but
> prolongs the exploitation of man by man [*exploitation de l'homme par*
> *l'homme*].[34]

As *The German Ideology* brackets the French expression '*exploitation de*
l'homme par l'homme' alongside its own phrase, let the following criteria be
adopted. The defining features of Marx's general conception of exploitation
must (i) appear in the phrase 'I derive benefit for myself by my doing harm to
another [*ich mir dadurch nütze, daß ich einem Andern Abbruch tue*]',[35] *and* (ii)
be connected, by the passages above, to this French expression.

On these criteria, exploitation requires one party to benefit. Marx refers to
'benefit', and the *Exposition* says the slave renders 'work or pleasure' to their
master.

Second, another party is harmed. '*Abbruch*' (literally: a breaking or tearing
off, or that which has been torn off) is non-committal as between a distributive
and an anthropological account of harm.[36] The *Exposition*, too, says the slave
is 'placed outside humankind', and brutalised.

Third, the beneficiary inflicts the harm. The beneficiary in Marx's first clause
('*mir*') is the subject causing the harm in the second ('*ich*'). Likewise, the *Expos-*
ition says the slave is the '*thing*' of the master who benefits.

Fourth, the benefit accrued is the consequence of the action causing harm
by the beneficiary. Syntactically, the conjunction '*daß*' subordinates the clause
it introduces to the preceding clause. The semantic effect here is that the event
in the subordinate clause (my doing harm to another) facilitates the event in
the former clause (my deriving a benefit). The *Exposition*, too, suggests that it
is in virtue of being '*his thing*' that the slave benefits the master.

---

33   Bazard et al. 1830, p. 105; No author 1958, p. 83.
34   Bazard et al. 1830, p. 108; No author 1958, p. 86.
35   *MECW* omits to render the second '*ich*', which is evidence in favour of the causal condition.
36   See sec. 5. Readers who cannot but take the English term 'harm' to denote 'loss of well-
      being' may cross out the following uses of 'harm', and replace them with 'disadvantage'. I
      have been unable to think of a better translation of '*Abbruch tue*' than 'doing harm', and
      so I have followed *MECW*.

Fifth, it is either intended or foreseen that the benefit will result from the action harming another. The adverbial *'dadurch'* suggests that the event described in the subordinate clause (my doing harm to another) is instrumental for the event described in the former clause (my deriving a benefit). The *Exposition*, similarly, says exploitation originates when one makes of the other 'an instrument'. (To say that action causing harm is an intended means for the benefit is not to say that harm is intended; to say that it is foreseen that action causing harm will result in the benefit is not to say that harm is foreseen).

The five conditions of *The German Ideology*'s general conception of exploitation as instrumentalisation can be stated as follows:

(1)   One party derives a benefit (the *benefit condition*)

(2)   Another party is harmed (the *harm condition*)

(3)   The harm is caused by the beneficiary (the *causal condition*)

(4)   The benefit is the consequence of action causing harm (the *consequence condition*)

(5)   The action causing harm is a means for the benefit (the *means-to-ends condition*)

Capital, too, describes capitalist labour-exploitation as a kind of instrumentalisation. It refers to 'unavoidable antagonism between the exploiter and the raw material [*Rohmaterial*] of their exploitation',[37] 'sheer brutal exploitation of the worker as material [*Arbeitermaterial*]',[38] and a 'mass of exploited human material [*Menschenmaterial*]'.[39] Echoing the *Exposition*'s phrase, *Capital* also refers to the capitalist's 'free exploitation of man by man [*freien Ausbeutung des Menschen durch den Menschen*]'.[40] An elaboration of these five conditions can therefore hope to cast light on Marx's later use of the term. The most controversial condition, the condition requiring the most elaboration, is the harm condition.

---

37   *MEW*, 23, p. 350; *MECW*, 35, p. 336; Marx 1976, p. 449.

38   *MEW*, 23, p. 495; *MECW*, 35, p. 474; Marx 1976, p. 601. The *MECW* and Marx 1976 translations of *'Arbeitermaterial'* as 'workpeople' and 'workers' respectively (which would be: *'Arbeiter'*) lose the connotation of instrumentalisation.

39   *MEW*, 23, p. 619; *MECW*, 35, p. 588; Marx 1976, p. 740. The *MECW* translation of *'Menschenmaterial'* as 'human beings' (which would be: *'Menschen'*) loses the connotation of instrumentalisation.

40   *MEW*, 23, p. 743; *MECW*, 35, p. 706; Marx 1976, p. 875.

4   The Benefit Condition

The benefit condition states: one party derives a benefit. The verb '*nützen* (to be of use or advantage to sby/sth, to benefit sby/sth)' has a beneficiary as its dative object. The benefit is thus distinct from any pleasure an actor might take in the action causing harm in the manner of the bully who just enjoys bullying. The benefit allows an actor to satisfy further wants, and is actually obtained, rather than merely striven for. To say that the benefit is enjoyed by 'myself' is to deny that it is enjoyed by all, or by the harmed party. It is an exclusive advantage, such as money, power, honour or leisure. The Germanic word '*Ausbeutung*' that Marx uses interchangeably with '*Exploitation*' is related to '*Beute*' ('loot'), an exclusive advantage.

The benefit condition distinguishes exploitation from behaviour towards others that produces no exclusive advantage (and hence from behaviour that satisfies the harm condition only). It implies that the exploitee is excluded from *a* benefit, in virtue of exploitation, rather than from all benefits altogether. Even a slave must be kept alive.

5   The Harm Condition

The harm condition states: another party is harmed. The harm condition is the most controversial condition, due to the need to elaborate the harm. Without an elaboration, it is unclear why those who are exploited are exploited.

Two types of elaboration of the harm condition can be distinguished: distributive elaborations and anthropological elaborations. Distributive elaborations require an exploitee to receive less than a given amount of something. Anthropological elaborations require the treatment of the exploitee to fall short on some other criterion, such as the valuing of a property of a whole. An anthropological elaboration can be defended by recalling the critique of the quantitative Marxist view of exploitation.

For as long as capitalist exploitation is located in the dimension of value, the fact that what labour produces has value at all is taken as given, as far as an analysis of capitalist exploitation is concerned. For if capitalist exploitation is located in this dimension, there will be a redistribution of value on which capitalist exploitation ceases. If, by contrast, capitalist exploitation is located in the dimension of labouring activity, it can rest on an assessment of the end pursued by hiring labour to produce commodities for money maximisation, which is served by maximising the ratio of surplus labour to necessary labour. *Capital* Volume III includes the apposition: 'exploitation, the appropriation of alien unpaid labour [*Exploitation, die Aneignung fremder unbezahlter Arbeit*]'.[41] Labour is 'alien' if the labourer's end is cut adrift from the end for which their labour is appropriated. This invites an anthropological elaboration of the harm condition that focuses on the end pursued by hiring labour for money maximisation.

The anthropological elaboration defended here is a system universalisability version of the harm condition. It says: another party features in a course of action whose maxim is reinforced by a system and cannot be thought as a universal law of human nature. In this section I shall: (i) suggest why it is plausible to take Marx to appeal to a universalisability test; (ii) explain what a maxim is and how a universal law of human nature can be contradictory in conception; (iii) explicate the harm; and (iv) respond to two difficulties.

(i) In his *Contribution to the Critique of Hegel's Philosophy of Right: Introduction*, Marx declares:

> The critique of religion culminates in the doctrine that *the human being is the supreme being for the human being*, and thus with the *categorical imperative to overthrow all relations* in which the human being is a debased, enslaved, abandoned, despicable being.[42]

This is a remarkable declaration, in two respects. Firstly, it is remarkable that Marx invokes a concept coined by Kant, the '*categorical imperative*', in an introduction to a critique of *Hegel*. Even if we know from a letter Marx wrote in 1837 that it was Hegel who first inspired Marx (against Kant) to 'seek the idea in reality itself',[43] this declaration and its appearance in a published critique of Hegel shows that Marx still thought it possible to draw critically on Kant's ethics in spite of that.[44]

Secondly, it is hard to imagine a '*categorical imperative*' that is more distant from Kant, both politically and philosophically. Politically, Kant could con-

---

41   *MEW*, 25, p. 399; *MECW*, 37, p. 383; Marx 1981, p. 509. The Marx 1981 translation, 'exploitation and appropriation of the unpaid labour of others' (which would be: '*Exploitation und Aneignung unbezahlter Arbeit anderer*'), loses Marx's appositional form, and (like *MECW*) renders '*fremder*' misleadingly as 'of others'. For analysis of '*fremd*', see ch. 10, sec. 3.

42   *MEW*, 1, p. 385; *MECW*, 3, p. 182.

43   *MEW*, 40, p. 8; *MECW*, 1, p. 18.

44   Within Marxism, Ernst Bloch (Bloch 1918, p. 406; Bloch 2000, p. 242) and Adorno (Adorno 1966, p. 356; Adorno 1973a, p. 365) invoke the concept of a categorical imperative; see, too, Lukács's ethical 'postulate' at Lukács 1977, p. 50; Lukács 1972, p. 8.

demn Marx's declaration. A call to '*overthrow*' defective relations seems to be a call for revolution, and Kant denied any right to revolution.[45] Philosophically, Kant would reject Marx's claim that a categorical imperative presupposes a 'critique of religion'. For Kant, religion, as the connection of the idea of freedom with immortality and god, provides the postulates of practical reason.[46] Further, Kant would deny that a categorical imperative is binding specifically on '*the human being*'. For Kant, a categorical imperative is binding on all rational beings. Finally, even after having put aside the revolutionary, anti-religious and anthropological air of Marx's declaration, Kant would *still* object to the thought that there could be a categorical imperative to replace all defective '*relations*'. Any categorical imperative that commands agents to adopt an end must, for Kant, have rational nature in an agent as its object. If its object is not the rational nature of an agent, but instead a state of affairs to be brought about, a categorical imperative to honour its value would entail that the rational nature of those agents it bound was merely of instrumental value. No rational agent could recognise such an imperative as categorical *and* regard their will as autonomous.

Marx's declaration represents a rejection of fundamental features of Kant's thought; yet Marx would only make such a declaration if he was attracted to something about it. I propose to take this as an invitation to elaborate a harm condition using an anthropological system-level version of the test of contradiction in conception (CC test) belonging to the formula of the categorical imperative known as the Formula of the Law of Nature (FLN). A system-level version of this test is able to justify what Marx, in *Value, Price and Profit*, describes as 'the *revolutionary* watchword, "*Abolition of the wages system!*"'[47] It also fits *The German Ideology*'s remark that 'the central relations of exploitation are determined independently of the will of individuals by production as a whole'.[48]

The suggestion[49] that Marx would endorse Hegel's criticism (in *Elements of the Philosophy of Right*) of Kant's moral philosophy as an '*empty formalism*'[50] is not fatal to this proposal, if there is a critical distance between an anthropological system-level universalisability test, and Kant's FLN.[51] The difference can be underscored by distinguishing four different conceptions of autonomy.

---

45   Kant 1996, 8: 299.
46   Kant 1987, 5: 474, Kant 1997, 5: 132.
47   *MECW*, 20, p. 149.
48   *MEW*, 3, p. 398; *MECW*, 5, p. 413.
49   Callinicos 2013, p. 274; Lukes 1982b, p. 196.
50   Hegel 1986b, § 135; Hegel 1991a, § 135.
51   I argue elsewhere (see Furner 2017a and Furner 2017b) that all of Kant's applications of

The general concept of autonomy is freedom in obeying a self-given law. Depending on whether an individual or a community is thought of as the autonomous entity, and whether or not autonomy is thought to rest on a capacity for normative action, four different conceptions of autonomy can be distinguished. An individual-level, non-normative autonomy consists in the exercise of the individual's capacity to regulate their action by rules that reflect their own personal values. This conception of autonomy informs Harry Frankfurt's account of a person, who can distance themselves from their first-order desires (as distinct from a 'wanton', who can impose no order on the direction in which their desires take them).[52] An individual-level, normative autonomy consists in the exercise of an individual's capacity to regulate their action by a universally binding moral law. This is Kant's conception of autonomy, and the one that Hegel criticises as an '*empty formalism*'.[53] By contrast, a community-level, non-normative autonomy holds that members of a community are free in obeying the laws that derive from their nature as self-interested agents. Rawls's account of the just society in terms of principles and policies that self-interested agents would agree to from behind a veil of ignorance is a version of this view.[54] Finally, a community-level, normative autonomy holds that members of a community are free in obeying laws derived from their nature as members of a community that can make ethical use of its organised power and knowledge. This conception of autonomy, which is in line with what Marx's *Theses on Feuerbach* refer to as 'human society, or social humanity',[55] may be called *self-legislative human community*. If an anthropological system-level universalisability test reflects a commitment to self-legislative human community, while Hegel's criticism of empty formalism is directed at an individual-level conception of autonomy, no claim to the effect that Marx would endorse Hegel's criticism need be fatal to the elaboration of the harm condition proposed here.

FLN in the *Groundwork* rely on a principle of natural teleology that we post-Darwinians cannot accept. As this interpretation of FLN is compatible with endorsing an anthropological system-level universalisability test that does not rely on this principle, one need not choose: *either* a critique of Kant's FLN, *or* a test of universalisability; one may have both. (Furner 2015 offered a shorter version of the argument below that took over Kant's CC test unmodified. At the time, I had not developed the interpretation of FLN defended in Furner 2017a and Furner 2017b, which differs from and criticises the dominant interpretations of FLN. I now regard the universalisability test attributed to Marx in Furner 2015 as differing from Kant's CC test; and I now emphasise that the test I defend is an anthropological, system-level test).

52   Frankfurt 1971.
53   Hegel 1986b, § 135; Hegel 1991a, § 135.
54   Rawls 1971.
55   *MEW*, 3, p. 7; *MECW*, 5, p. 5.

Marx's categorical imperative is in the spirit of self-legislative human community. Marx says in the same piece that the critique of religion enables the human being to 'revolve around himself and thereby around his true sun'.[56] However, '*the human being* is no abstract being encamped outside the world. The human being is *the world of the human being*, state, society'.[57] Human autonomy, for Marx, is an autonomy whose subject is the human community. In such a community, as *On the Jewish Question* puts it, the human being 'has cognised [*erkannt*] and organised his "forces propres" as *social* powers'.[58] A human community – not, as in Kant's ethics, the will of a rational being – is to be autonomous, for it is a human community that has the power to act universally; that is, create, abolish or modify types of generalised social relation. By formulating his categorical imperative, Marx is not making use of 'self-consciously Kantian vocabulary' to 'encourage us to think of the individual as having a value'.[59] Marx is using self-consciously *post*-Kantian vocabulary to encourage us to view a *human community* as having ultimate value.

A system universalisability version of the harm condition is in this spirit. If autonomy is conceived as self-legislative human community, any system that precludes human community by *dividing* society, as revealed by an anthropological system-level universalisability test, is contrary to autonomy.

(ii) A maxim is a subjective principle of action. It has the form: in conditions *x*, I will do *y*, in order to *z*.[60] Drinking coffee is a description of an action, but not a maxim. The maxim might be, for example: when I get up in the morning, I will do something to make myself alert.

Kant's FLN commands: '*so act as if the maxim of your action were to become by your will* A UNIVERSAL LAW OF NATURE'.[61] A law is universal if it holds for all the entities that satisfy its condition; it admits no exception. A maxim is a universal law, therefore, if its means and end are adopted by everyone who satisfies its condition. To take the alertness maxim: *everyone*, when they get up in the morning, will do something to make themselves alert. It is a widely-held view that the universality of a universal law of nature holds 'by causal neces-

---

56   *MEW*, 1, p. 379; *MECW*, 3, p. 176.
57   *MEW*, 1, p. 378; *MECW*, 3, p. 175.
58   *MEW*, 1, p. 370; *MECW*, 3, p. 168. *MECW* translates '*erkannt*' as 'recognised' (which would render: '*anerkannt*').
59   Leopold 2007, p. 155.
60   Allison 2011, p. 198; Herman 1993, p. 64; O'Neill 2013, p. 102; Pogge 1998, p. 189; Rawls 1989, p. 83.
61   Kant 2014, 4: 421.

sity'.[62] For example: everyone, when they get up in the morning, *cannot but* do something, to make themselves alert. To conceive of a maxim as a universal law of nature is to conceive of a hypothetical world in which (whatever other laws it has) a maxim is adopted by causal necessity by all those who satisfy its condition; for example, a hypothetical world in which, whatever other laws it has, everyone, when they get up in the morning, cannot but do something to make themselves alert.

Part of FLN is a test of contradiction in conception (CC test): FLN commands an agent to refrain from adopting a maxim if the thought of any hypothetical world in which that maxim is a universal law of nature contains a logical contradiction (p and not-p). There is a contradiction in the conception of any such world if we must suppose that at least one hypothetical agent who satisfies the conditions of the maxim's counterpart universal law of nature is unable to perform the action (cannot do y), or is unable to achieve their end by performing the action (cannot achieve z by doing y). FLN does not command an agent to refrain from adopting the alertness maxim, because there is no contradiction in the conception of a hypothetical world in which it is a universal law of nature. It is possible to imagine a hypothetical world in which everyone who gets up in the morning cannot but do something to make themselves alert. But it is widely believed that FLN does command an agent to refrain from adopting the following maxim of false promising: when I am in need of money, I will make a false promise, to obtain a loan.[63] Some believe that this is because the action of making a false promise would become impossible, while others believe that this is because the universalisation of the maxim would undercut the chance for an agent who makes a false promise to achieve their end of obtaining a loan.[64]

The anthropological system-level universalisability test proposed here differs from Kant's CC test. It says: a system that reinforces action on a maxim that cannot be thought as a universal law of human nature fails a system-level universalisability test. Three differences can be highlighted. First, the test is not a test of a maxim, which is a principle of individual action. It is a test of a system, albeit by reference to a maxim it reinforces. Hence, it is an ethical not a moral test.[65] It is not a test of a capacity that is exercised by an individual in their

---

62   Dietrichson 1964, p. 152; see also Allison 2011, p. 183; Herman 1993, p. 47; McNair 2000, p. 26;
      O'Neill 2013, p. 23; Rawls 2000, p. 168; Wood 1999, p. 80.
63   See Kant 2014, 4: 422.
64   For further discussion, see Furner 2017a.
65   See ch. 1, sec. 4.

own name, but a test of a property of society (the presence of a type of system). Second, the hypothetical world whose conception is to be non-contradictory is a hypothetical *human* world in which (whatever other laws it has) the system-reinforced maxim is a universal law of *human* nature. To imagine such a hypothetical world is to do no more and no less than incorporate into the thought of a hypothetical world two premises from *The German Ideology*: (a) human beings have vital needs that they must satisfy to live; and (b) human needs are open-ended.[66] Third, in conceiving of this hypothetical world, we suppose that its agents think of the adoption of the system-reinforced maxim as permissible. If we suppose that hypothetical agents (know that they) adopt a maxim by causal necessity, we must suppose that these agents do not think of its adoption as deserving censure.[67]

A system can fail the system-level universalisability test on two sorts of grounds. One sort of ground arises if a system-reinforced maxim presupposes others as addressees of '*normatively regulated action*'.[68] Universalising the maxim may then so change our understanding of what is permissible, and therefore so change actions proceeding from this normative understanding, that its pursuit is no longer possible, or could not succeed. There is, however, a second sort of ground on which a system may fail the system-level universalisability test, and in the present context, this is the ground to stress. A system-reinforced maxim may presuppose others in an *instrumental* capacity. Universalising the maxim may then preclude that service, rendering the maxim's pursuit impossible, or bound to fail. Take the *Exposition*'s phrase, cited above: 'the privilege of living while doing nothing'. This suggests the maxim: when I am in need of means of life, I will do no work, to receive my means of life. Any hypothetical world that contained the universal law of human nature: everyone, when in need of means of life, cannot but do no work, and cannot but thereby receive their means of life, is contradictory in conception. All being in need of means of life, and so all having done no work, nothing would be produced. No one acting on this maxim would achieve their end of receiving means of life. So, if a system reinforces the living-while-doing-nothing maxim, it fails the system-level universalisability test. A society with such a system is revealed as a divisive society, contrary to self-legislative human community.

---

66   *MEJ*, 2003, pp. 12–13; *MEW*, 3, p. 28; *MECW*, 5, p. 42.
67   For comparison with Kant, see Furner 2017a and Furner 2017b.
68   Habermas 1981, p. 127; Habermas 1986, p. 85.

A system will fail the system-level universalisability test if a maxim it reinforces implies a standard action of social affecting[69] to the maxim's performer (in the above example: another's work for them) that cannot go as planned, once the maxim is permissible and adopted by all who satisfy its conditions. Its thought as a universal law of human nature will give rise to an incompatibility between: (a) the type of actor another must treat the maxim's performer as for the latter to act successfully on their maxim (beneficiary of my work), and (b) how others must act, once the maxim is permissible and adopted by all who satisfy its conditions (do no work).

Accordingly, the system-level universalisability test is not a system-level version of a test for what Anthony Giddens calls 'contradictory consequences':

> Contradictory consequences ensue when every individual in an aggregate of individuals acts in a way which, while producing the intended effect if done in isolation, creates a perverse effect if done by everyone. If all the audience in a lecture hall get to their feet to obtain a better view of the speaker, no one will in fact do so.[70]

Thus defined, 'contradictory consequences' include both reciprocal blocking and what Jean-Paul Sartre called 'counter-finality',[71] that is, consequences that are even worse for everyone than reciprocal blocking. The system-level universalisability test is not a test for a system that reinforces action with 'contradictory consequences', for the laws of a hypothetical human world need not be in sync with the probabilistic laws that can be expected to hold in a given social situation; and 'contradictory consequences' may simply reflect the contingencies of a given situation. It is possible without contradiction to conceive of a hypothetical human world in which everyone whose view is impaired at a lecture cannot but stand up and get a better view, if the long-legged sit behind the short-legged. The reason why a system that somehow reinforced this standing-at-a-lecture maxim would not fail the system-level universalisability test is that my standing up at a lecture to get a better view does not require anyone else (here: any other audience member) to perform a standard action of social affecting to me.

Suppose Giddens's example describes an actual situation: everyone attending a lecture stands up to get a better view, the long-legged are not sat behind

---

69   Action to get another to perform action, as a result of their identifying its performer; see ch. 5, sec. 2.

70   Giddens 1984, p. 311; compare Elster 1978b, p. 110.

71   Sartre 1960, pp. 231–3; Sartre 2004, pp. 161–3; compare Elster 1985, p. 24.

the short-legged, and the result is a case of reciprocal blocking or 'counter-finality'. If so, that situation exhibits what Elster calls a 'fallacy of composition', that is, the fallacy that 'what is possible for any single individual must be possible for them all simultaneously'.[72] By implication, to describe a situation as exhibiting a fallacy of composition, it is not necessary to identify a maxim that cannot be conceived as a universal law of human nature. But nor does the pursuit of a maxim that cannot be conceived as a universal law of human nature imply that either the situation, or a belief of an actor in that situation, exhibits a fallacy of composition. For example: it need not be the case that everyone who satisfies the conditions of the false promising maxim *actually* adopts this maxim, nor need the agent who adopts it believe, or act as if they believed, that all could succeed if all were to adopt it. All that someone who makes a false promise to borrow money when in need believes, or acts as if they believed, is that *they* can get away with it. As the pursuit of a maxim that fails Kant's CC test is not a sufficient condition for applying the term 'fallacy of composition', Elster is mistaken to subsume this aspect of FLN under that term.[73]

The system-level universalisability test is also not a system-level version of the test that underpins Cohen's concept of '*collective unfreedom*'.[74] Cohen writes: 'a group suffers collective unfreedom with respect to a given type of action *A* if and only if performance of *A* by all members of the group is impossible'.[75] Both the system-level universalisability test and Cohen's concept of collective unfreedom rest on a counterfactual thought experiment. Both ask what would happen if all those in a certain situation act in a certain way, whether or not they do, in actual fact, all act in that way. Beyond this, however, the two concepts have little in common.

One difference is that the counterfactual thought experiment presupposed by the concept of collective unfreedom does not rest on any universal law of nature. The system-level universalisability test asks whether or not everyone can act successfully on a maxim if it is hypothetically assumed that everyone who satisfies a certain type of condition performs it whenever they satisfy that condition, and everyone knows that it is known by all to be permissible. By contrast, collective unfreedom may be avoided just by virtue of the fact that it is possible for all members of the group to perform action *A* one at a time (for example, all members of society at some time or other make a false promise to borrow money when in need).

---

72   Elster 1978b, p. 99.
73   See Elster 1978b, p. 100, p. 102, p. 163.
74   Cohen 1988, p. 264.
75   Cohen 1988, p. 268.

Further, when Cohen says that it is 'impossible' for all members of the group to perform action A, this is shorthand for: impossible in a given situation, with given resources and preferences. Thus, not every case of collective unfreedom to A will fail the system-level universalisability test even once this behaviour is converted into a universal law of human nature. Facts about existing resources and preferences cannot bear on whether any hypothetical world in which a maxim is a universal law of human nature is inconceivable.[76] To restate one example,[77] take the universal law of human nature: everyone, when they are a tourist at a hotel, will go on the hotel's coach trip, for fun. Now, a hotel may not be able to accommodate all its tourists on a coach trip if, for example, demand exceeds the number of coaches booked, or there are too few coaches available for hire. But facts about existing preferences or resources, although relevant to ascertain a situation-specific case of collective unfreedom, are irrelevant for a universalisability test that rests on the conception of a hypothetical world that is contradictory in conception in virtue of its including a universal law of human nature, *whatever* other laws it includes.

(iii) To say that a system fails the system-level universalisability test is not to pass normative judgement on that system. A normative condemnation presupposes a further belief in a type of community: no human community should include a system that encourages people to do what all cannot conceivably do. As the system-level universalisability test does not presuppose this belief, an elaboration of the harm condition for exploitation that rests on this test is non-normative. It does not state an argument for why exploitation is bad, and no terms it contains presuppose that any such argument has already been made. A system-level universalisability test can nonetheless elaborate a harm condition, if those who live in a system that reinforces such conduct can perceive themselves, in the words of Marx's *Theses on Feuerbach*, amidst a society split 'into two parts, one of which is superior to society';[78] and/or if they can perceive their dependence on nature with regret, as a condition that allows a part of society to act as if it were superior to society.

(iv) It is not necessary to address all the problems that Kant scholars raise in connection with Kant's FLN. This section considers just two problems among

---

76   Compare Furner 2017a, pp. 7–9.
77   Cohen 1988, pp. 270–1.
78   *MEW*, 3, p. 6; *MECW*, 5, p. 4.

them that are also faced by an anthropological system-level version of the CC test: the problem of *'false negatives'*,[79] and the problem of *'relevant descriptions'*.[80]

False negatives are examples of maxims that we regard as innocent, but which Kant's FLN purportedly prohibits. If there are false negatives, then it might be possible for some of them to be system-reinforced. If a system-level universalisability test disqualified systems for reinforcing innocent maxims, it would be questionable how the finding that production with wage-labour for continuous money maximisation is exploitative, on a system universalisability conception of exploitation, could sustain a normative condemnation.

One response to the problem of false negatives is to defuse some paradigm examples:

(A) 'I will buy clockwork trains but not sell them'[81] [the *clockwork train example*]

(B) when there is an after-Christmas sale, I will buy next year's Christmas presents, to save money[82] [the *Christmas present maxim*]

(C) ' "I will give a larger percentage of my income to charity than the average person does" '[83] [the *charity example*]

(D) ' "I will occasionally accompany others through a doorway, and on those occasions I will always go through the door last" '[84] [the *doorway example*]

As it stands, (A) is not a false negative, because (A) is not a maxim. Rather, (A) describes two consecutive actions. If (A) is to become a false negative, it must be further analysed and supplemented, just to acquire condition-means-end form:

(A1) when I have some disposable income, I will buy clockwork trains, to expand my collection

(A2) when I have bought a clockwork train, I will not sell it, to preserve my collection

There is, however, no contradiction in the thought of a hypothetical world that includes (A1), or (A2), or even (A1) and (A2), as universal laws of human nature.

---

79   Wood 1999, p. 105. It is not necessary to respond to the charge of false positives, that is, maxims which we regard as immoral, but which FLN purportedly does not prohibit, because the interaction-recognition-antinomy thesis does not say that a system-level universalisability test identifies all bads.

80   O'Neill 2013, p. 61.

81   O'Neill 2013, p. 163.

82   Herman 1993, p. 138.

83   Wood 2008, p. 72; see also Parfit 2011, p. 277.

84   Wood 1990, p. 157; see also Parfit 2011, p. 277.

A hypothetical world may include (A1) and (A2) as universal laws of human nature, because the universal counterparts of (A1) and (A2) permit all clockwork trains to be bought from those who *make* clockwork trains.

The claim that (B) is a false negative relies on an extraneous assumption about preferences: it assumes that Christmas presents form a significant proportion of annual sales. It is possible, however, to imagine a hypothetical world with a different annual sales pattern to ours, in which Christmas presents represent an insignificant proportion of annual sales. In such a world, firms may still have a reason to hold after-Christmas sales; for example, to clear stock for 1 January. Everyone who planned to give Christmas presents the following year could then buy presents in the after-Christmas sale following the previous Christmas, and save money. (B) is conceivable as a universal law of human nature, and therefore not a false negative.

(C) is not a false negative, because (C) is not a maxim. If (C) is to become a false negative, it must first acquire condition-means-end form. As (C) describes action that exceeds an average, (C) suggests a maxim whose condition is other people's performance of the same type of action, and whose end is to exceed the average:

(C1) When others give some of their income to charity, I will give a larger than average percentage of my income to charity, to outdo other people in my beneficence

(C1) is not a false negative, because (C1) is not innocent. It is not innocent to give money to charity for a reason other than to help the people who are to receive it. (If the agent's end was to help those to whom they give a charitable donation, giving more than the average person gives will not be a means to it; that different innocent maxim is conceivable as a universal law of nature).

(D) is similar to (C): (D) is not a false negative, because (D) is not a maxim. (D) suggests one or other of the following:

(D1) when others accompany me through a doorway, I will always go through the door last, to outdo others in courteousness

(D2) when others accompany me through a doorway, I will always go through the door last, to be courteous

(D1) is not a false negative, because, like (C1), it is not innocent. (D2) is not a false negative, because (D2) is not anyone's maxim: if my end is to be courteous, it is *not* my means always to go through the doorway last. Insisting on going through a doorway last if another person gestures to let me through is not a means for me to be courteous. Adopting an end commits an agent to avoid action that undermines its achievement; and steadfastly refusing others' offers to let one go first would undermine the end of being courteous. In either case, there is no false negative.

The problem of relevant descriptions is the problem of how to determine which of the many maxims that could describe an agent's conduct it is relevant to submit to a universalisability test. A system-level version of a universalisability test also faces this problem. But it solves the problem differently. Let us begin with Barbara Herman's solution to one aspect of the problem of relevant descriptions when applying Kant's FLN.[85]

Suppose (borrowing Herman's example) my car breaks down, and I take it to Joe's mechanics for repair. Consider two sincere reports I might give of my maxim:

(M1) When my car breaks down, I will take it to a mechanic, to get it repaired

(M2) When my car breaks down, I will take it to Joe's, to get it repaired

(M2) contains a more specific description of the means than (M1). We need a procedure that can be applied to determine which of (M1) or (M2) it is relevant to test.

First, we ask an agent what their in-order-to motive is (to get their car repaired), and what their because motive is (their car has broken down). This gives the end and the conditions of a possible maxim. Second, we ask what any rational being would do to achieve the reported in-order-to motive. This will give the most general possible description of the means of the maxim (take it to someone who can repair cars; a mechanic). Third, we determine whether the agent's powers, desires and beliefs would leave them willing to pursue options conceivably left open by this general description of their means, if the option they chose had not been available. We ask, for instance, if they would have taken their car to Dave's garage or Lucy's garage for repair, if Joe's garage had shut. If the answer to all these counterfactual questions is a yes, we accept the general description of the means. To the extent that the answers are no, we re-describe the means in more specific terms. Even if the agent is aware that Joe's is the only mechanic around, the counterfactual fact that they would have taken their car for repair at another mechanic if only that other mechanic (and not Joe's) had been around, establishes that taking the car to Joe's is not part of their maxim, but rather a choice they make in acting on a maxim whose means is to take the car to a mechanic.

Even if we accept this solution for determining the means of a maxim, there remains the problem of determining the end. Reliance on a sincere first-person report raises two worries. One is that the first-person report of an in-order-to motive may be more or less proximate. To continue with the above example, consider the following:

---

85   Herman 1990, pp. 114–20.

(M1) When my car breaks down, I will take it to a mechanic, to get it repaired
(M3) When my car breaks down, I will contact a tow away service, to take it to
     a mechanic
(M4) When my car breaks down, I will get it repaired, to be mobile

(M3) shortens while (M4) lengthens the span of the end in (M1). It is unsatisfactory just to go with the end that an actor happens to report, however, if the span of a reported in-order-to motive may simply reflect the context in which the report is given.[86]

A second worry is that, if an end is given by an agent's report, its description may not include all and only those facts that we would deem morally relevant. Derek Parfit offers the example: 'suppose that, being a whimsical kleptomaniac, I really *am* acting on the maxim of stealing from white-dress-wearing strawberry-eating women, whenever I can'.[87] The general point is that, if an agent truly is whimsical, their whimsy will be reflected in their maxim. It seems odd to allow an agent's whimsy to influence the assessment of their conduct.

A *system*-level universalisability test is not subject to either of these worries, however. A system-level universalisability test does not assess a maxim that is particular to an individual agent. It assesses a system-reinforced maxim. The end of the maxim whose universalisability is to be assessed is determined by the in-order-to motive that a system enables and unintentionally constrains. The generalised existence of tokens of that type of in-order-to motive must enable and unintentionally constrain tokens of that type. The end is determined by criteria that are not purely subjective. Once the end is determined, we can use a procedure for determining the means that borrows from the procedure just outlined. We can ask what any rational human being would do to achieve the end, *consistent* with the system in question. If we have selected the end of continuous money maximisation, because that is an end that the system of capitalist production enables and unintentionally constraints; we then ask what any rational human being would do to achieve it, consistent with the system of capitalist production. If, in this system, products are acquired by purchase and sale, then the means of the maxim may not disrupt purchase and sale (say, by seizing others' wealth). Whether the system of capitalist production fails the system-level universalisability test thus depends on the universalisability of the system-reinforced maxim: when my monetary wealth is at stake, I will put my possessions to economic use, to maximise my monetary wealth.

---

86   See ch. 4, sec. 2.
87   Parfit 2011, p. 297.

6   The Causal Condition

The causal condition states: the harm is caused by the beneficiary. The causal condition precludes harm-causing action from counting as exploitation if it is merely to the benefit of a third party. It makes exploitation self-serving.

The causal condition, as presently stated, is underdeveloped, however. Imagine that there are *several* beneficiaries – must each, or just one, cause harm? And is there any less exploitation if a beneficiary instructs a non-benefitting agent to perform the harm-causing action? In the above form, the causal condition cannot cope with these questions, which expose the limits of the first-person perspective of the phrase 'I derive benefit for myself by my doing harm to another'.[88] From a first-person perspective, the singular 'I' is required to avoid the implication that exploitation presupposes a plurality of beneficiaries. But this leaves the questions as to whether, when exploitation has a number of beneficiaries, each of them, or at least one of them, must cause harm; or whether exploitation might involve a non-benefitting agent of a beneficiary.

These questions suggest three types of scenario calling for judgement. In one, all the members of a group know that each member wants the same thing, and will share the spoils, and they decide that the harm-causing action is to be performed by whichever member is presented with the opportunity. In a second, a number of beneficiaries designate one of their number to perform the harm-causing action. In the third, a beneficiary instructs a non-benefitting agent to perform the harm-causing action. The principle to be applied across all three types of scenario is: so long as a beneficiary is the author of harm-causing action, there is no reason to deny that exploitation occurs on account of non-fulfilment of any causal condition. To judge all three types of scenario in conformity with this principle, the causal condition must be re-written as: harm is caused by a beneficiary, or someone instructed by a beneficiary.

A further modification can be made. The expectation that agents will carry out instructions to a certain effect is not so different from the expectation that an appointee will exercise their *discretion* to a certain effect. Marx remarks in his *Critique of Hegel's Doctrine of the State* that a bureaucracy's 'hierarchy' is its '*chief abuse*'.[89] One principle suggested by this remark is: if a hierarchy creates an expectation that the discretion of an appointee will be exercised to benefit an appointer (which an appointer takes insufficient measures to dispel), there is no reason to deny that exploitation occurs on account of non-

88   *MEW*, 3, p. 394; *MECW*, 5, p. 409.
89   *MEW*, 1, p. 249, p. 255; *MECW*, 3, p. 47, p. 52.

fulfilment of any causal condition if the author of the harm-causing action is not a beneficiary, provided that their appointer is a beneficiary. Modified in light of this principle, the causal condition reads: harm is caused by a beneficiary, or someone instructed or appointed by a beneficiary.

7   The Consequence Condition

The consequence condition states: the benefit is the consequence of action causing harm. The consequence condition has two functions.

One function of the consequence condition is that it requires the harm-causing action to be of a kind that yields a benefit. It excludes the case in which the connection between harm and benefit is merely that someone who is harmed happens also to be the source of a benefit. Call a harm-causing action that does not intrinsically yield a benefit 'abuse'. The consequence condition discounts cases where the abused just happen to benefit their abuser.

A second function of the consequence condition is to remove a deviant 'causal chain',[90] whereby the benefit is derived from an unplanned sequence of external events. Suppose that A's attempt to con B inadvertently leads B to seek C's advice, which B follows, yielding the benefit A sought. A obtains the benefit they sought, but inadvertently, because B follows C's advice. By discounting such cases, the consequence condition precludes exploitation by fluke (even when the harm-causing action is normally of the benefit-yielding variety).

8   The Means-to-Ends Condition

The means-to-ends condition states: the action causing harm is a means for the benefit. It also has two functions.

One function of the means-to-ends condition is to require that the benefit obtained must be intended or foreseen. It ensures that exploitation is not merely self-serving, but self-seeking.

Second, the means-to-ends condition removes a deviant causal chain, whereby the benefit is derived from an unplanned sequence of internal events. Consider Roderick Chisholm's story of a man who wants to enjoy a fortune, and believes he will inherit a fortune if he kills his uncle. And then

---

90   Davidson 2001, p. 72.

this belief and this desire agitate him so severely that he drives excessively fast, with the result that he accidentally runs over and kills a pedestrian who, unknown to the nephew, was none other than the uncle.[91]

Suppose that, prior to the drive, the man has resolved to kill his uncle, and is proceeding to the uncle's suspected whereabouts. The drive is then part of the man's plan to kill his uncle, and does serve as a means to bring about that result. But it does so inadvertently. The means-to-ends condition excludes flukes of this kind. It ensures that exploitation occurs by design.

9   The System Universalisability Conception of Exploitation

The five conditions for exploitation may now be restated as follows:
(1)   One party derives an exclusive benefit (the *benefit condition*)
(2)   Another party features in a course of action whose maxim is reinforced by a system and cannot be thought as a universal law of human nature (the *harm condition*)
(3)   The harm is caused by a beneficiary, or someone instructed or appointed by a beneficiary (the *causal condition*)
(4)   The benefit is the consequence of action causing harm (the *consequence condition*)
(5)   The action causing harm is a means for the benefit (the *means-to-ends condition*)
In short, the system universalisability conception of exploitation says that exploitation is self-seeking action that fails a system-level universalisability test.

The system universalisability conception is a *general* conception of exploitation, because it has any number of potential applications. Production (in capitalism) is not the only context in which exploitation can be said to occur. It is easy to see how a system of production that reinforces the use of slaves must be deemed exploitative, on this conception. Slaves must be owned, but slaves themselves cannot own anything. Thus, any system that reinforces the use of slave labour to acquire property is exploitative. If colonisation is analogous to slave ownership – in other words, if colonies must be colonised by a colonising nation but colonies themselves cannot colonise – it is possible to claim that a system of international relations that reinforces the pursuit of colonisation (as in the 'Scramble for Africa') is a system of 'the exploitation of one nation

---

91   Chisholm 1966, p. 30.

by another'.[92] A system that reinforces the charging of rent as a sole source of income will fail a system-level universalisability test for a similar reason as the *Exposition*'s idleness example. If everyone were to seek to obtain their means of life solely from renting out any shelter they own, then, all having done no work, no rent could be paid. If the system of production is already itself exploitative, such a relation between landlord and tenant counts as 'secondary exploitation'.[93]

A system that reinforces a maxim whose permissibility would remove the legitimacy its operations rely on will also fail a system-level universalisability test. Suppose that government administration only possesses the legitimacy it requires to function as such if it can be regarded as appointing people on the basis of an examination of their competence. Any system that reinforces a maxim to make government appointments on the basis that appointees hail from the class of their appointers (interpreted as an indication that they will exercise their discretion to the benefit of the class that the appointers belong to) will then fail a system-level universalisability test, and potentially constitute 'a second exploitation of the people'.[94]

Finally, any system that reinforces the pursuit of a maxim whose end is to outdo others will generate exploitation. This is the lesson of the non-innocent charity and doorway maxims discussed above. Suppose that there are a number of schools, some of which perform better than others, on certain widely desirable criteria. Suppose that the system of production is one that produces inequalities of wealth. Rich parents will then have the financial resources to relocate to the catchment areas of the better performing schools. To the extent that learning is dependent on access to cultural tools that rich parents can more easily afford, these schools will continue to perform better than the average, especially if parents are allowed to top-up school budgets from their private income. What may initially have been a random variation in schools' performance is now cemented by a social dynamic. If, as we begun by assuming, the system of production includes job hierarchies that produce inequalities of wealth; and if their experience of this system leads rich parents to aim to provide their children with an education that will prepare them for a high-ranking job in it; a system that reinforces the maxim: when I have a child, I will move into the catchment area of one of the better performing schools, to give my child a head start in life, will fail the system-level universalisability test, and count as a kind of exploitation.

92   *MEW*, 4, p. 479; *MECW*, 6, p. 503.
93   *MEW*, 25, p. 623; *MECW*, 37, p. 604; Marx 1981, p. 745.
94   *MECW*, 22, p. 484.

The system universalisability conception of exploitation is a plausible general conception of exploitation: it fits the kinds of phenomena beyond production that Marx identifies as exploitative; and it can be used to describe more contemporary phenomena.

10   Capitalist Labour-Exploitation

An actor who puts their possessions to economic use and thereby maximises their monetary wealth obtains several types of benefit. They obtain the power to re-invest that wealth; bargaining power vis-à-vis governments, in virtue of the power to re-invest; money for purchasing means of consumption; and the prestige of possessing money, which has advantages independent of its being spent.[95] The causal condition, consequence condition and means-to-ends condition for exploitation raise no special difficulties for characterising hired labour as labour that is exploited by its hirer; and production with wage-labour for continuous money maximisation was characterised as part of a system in chapter 6. All that remains to be shown, therefore, to characterise production with wage-labour for continuous money maximisation as capitalist labour-exploitation, is to describe its pursuit as the adoption of a money-maximising maxim that cannot be thought as a universal law of human nature.

In acting on a money-maximising maxim, it is necessary for agents to decide to hire wage-labour to produce. Without production, what some people gain must be taken from others. So, if money maximisation is to be a *universal* law of human nature, there must be production for money maximisation; and as argued in chapter 6, the money-maximising option in production is to hire wage-labour. To characterise production with wage-labour for continuous money maximisation as exploitative, what has to be shown is that a hypothetical human world that contains the money-maximising universal law of human nature

> everyone, when their monetary wealth is at stake, cannot but put their possessions to economic use, and cannot but thereby maximise their monetary wealth

is contradictory in conception. It is necessary to show that not all those who perform the function of wage-labour can maximise their monetary wealth by performing that function.

---

95   *MEW*, 40, p. 564; *MECW*, 3, p. 324.

It is worth stressing that a *system*-level universalisability test determines the identity of the agents who are thought to adopt a maxim by the criterion: the type of agent on whom a system imposes a constraint. Having determined the identity of one type of agent in this manner, the criterion 'types of agent presupposed by the constrained actions of the constrained agent' is used to identify the types of agent that must also belong to this hypothetical world. The system of capitalist production imposes money maximisation as a constraint on each capitalist firm. As money maximisation by firms presupposes wage-labourers, the system-level universalisability test is applied to the system of capitalist production by asking whether there could be a hypothetical human world in which all firms and all wage-labourers maximise their monetary wealth by virtue of these functions. We are examining behaviour at the level of the capitalist firm, and those it hires as wage-labourers.

As wage-labour is hired by money-maximisers, wage-labour must be assumed to be paid either by time worked, or in the form of piece-rates. To maximise their monetary wealth, each wage-labourer must maximise the time or output they hire themselves out for, perform the labour, and minimise their expenditures. Universal activities of these kinds are so far from enabling wage-labourers to maximise their monetary wealth, however, that the *Grundrisse* refers to them as 'the demand for *industriousness* and also for *saving*'[96] directed at them by capitalists. It remarks:

> if workers *generally* were to act on these demands, that is, as *workers* (what the individual worker does, or can do, in contrast to their genus, can only exist as an *exception*, not as a *rule*, because it does not lie in the nature of the relation itself), that is, as a *rule*, then (aside from the damage they would do to general consumption – the drop would be enormous – and hence to production as well, thus also to the number and volume of exchanges they could perform with capital, hence to themselves as workers) the worker would employ, absolutely, means that abolish their own end [*er absolut Mittel anwendete, die ihren eignen Zweck aufheben*], and which must directly degrade him to an Irishman, to a level of wage-labour at which the most brutal minimum of needs and means of subsistence appear as the sole object and end of his exchange with capital.[97]

---

96   *MEW*, 42, p. 210; *MECW*, 28, p. 214; Marx 1973a, p. 285.
97   *MEW*, 42, p. 211; *MECW*, 28, p. 215; Marx 1973a, p. 285. The Marx 1973a translation of the bracketed phrase, 'the worker would be employing means which absolutely contradict

This passage is valuable because its italics and syntax (the latter by bracketing irrelevant matters) confirm Marx's awareness of two distinctions that must be drawn in applying a universalisability test of contradiction in conception. First, to apply a universalisability test, one must imagine a hypothetical world in which some conduct is universalised. Accordingly, Marx asks what happens 'if' workers *generally* pursue the means of money maximisation available to them. The first pair of brackets indicates that it is irrelevant if some workers can maximise their monetary wealth as exceptions to a rule.

Second, to apply a universalisability test of contradiction in conception is to ask: if I try to conceive of a world in which everyone who satisfies a type of condition unfailingly performs a type of action and thereby unfailingly achieves a type of end, must I conceive of at least one agent who satisfies that condition as failing to perform that action or as failing to achieve that end by performing that action? To put money maximisation to this test is to ask: if I try to conceive of a world in which all wage-labourers as well as all capitalist firms cannot but maximise their monetary wealth, must I conceive of at least one wage-labourer as unable to perform the actions of working and saving, or as unable to maximise their monetary wealth by such actions? The second pair of brackets highlight that this question differs from the question of whether the unintended consequences of universalising money maximisation would increase its relative cost and difficulty. (Would the system contract, and capital hire fewer workers?)[98]

Marx implies that any such hypothetical world is contradictory in conception by stating that it would become every wage-labourer's 'sole ... end' to acquire means of subsistence to satisfy a minimum of needs. What would

---

their purpose', (which would translate: '*er Mittel anwendete, die ihren Zweck absolut widersprechen*') is inaccurate. '*Aufheben*' (here: to abolish, to cancel) is not '*widersprechen*' (to contradict). Moreover, '*eignen*' ('own') in 'their own end' (that is, the means' own end) is not translated; and 'absolutely' appears in the wrong place. To say that means 'contradict their purpose' is to convey a mistake in the choice of means to a (possible) end. Marx's claim is that the end is unachievable.

The passage does *not* describe a 'fallacy of composition', as Elster (1978b, p. 163; 1985, p. 26) and Lebowitz (2009, p. 6) claim. It conducts a counterfactual thought experiment, in which no worker need believe, or act as if they believed, that every worker would maximise their monetary wealth if all were to try. A worker must simply act as if they believed that *they* can maximise their monetary wealth if they try to do so (*however* other workers may fare). On fallacy of composition, see sec. 5.

98 The idea that Kant's CC test is a test of whether universalising a maxim would yield 'disastrous consequences' (Elster 1978b, p. 100) is a misinterpretation encouraged by John Stuart Mill (Mill 1962, p. 4, p. 49). For a critical discussion of the latter idea, see O'Neill 2013, pp. 77–92.

make wage-labourers' attempts at money maximisation unsuccessful is hirers' money-maximising response:

> If all or the majority are extra hard-working ..., they do not increase the value of their commodity, but merely its quantity, and thus the demands placed upon it as a use-value. If they all save, a general reduction of the wage will put them back on the right track; for the general saving would show the capitalist that their wage is generally too high, that they receive more than their equivalent for their commodity, for the capacity to dispose over their labour.[99]

Every *general* increase in work is evidence of the greater use-value of labour power. It shows that, over a given period, the average wage-labourer can work for longer or produce more output than was previously demanded. With any general increase, each money-maximising firm would be compelled by competition to impose that increased standard on their workforce as the norm, hiring fresh hands if its existing workers fail to maintain the pace. The value of labour power is not thereby increased, however. Second, every *general* saving by wage-labourers is evidence that labour power was purchased above its value. It reveals that, over a given period, labour power can on average be reproduced with fewer purchases than were affordable at the previous wage level. Money-maximising firms would take advantage of competition between those dependent on wage-labour to reduce wages to the level at which only the value of labour power was paid.

In combination, these responses leave wage-labourers expending maximum effort for minimal reward. Marx claims that this submission would make it 'impossible even to strive for wealth in general form, as money, stock-piled money',[100] by precluding the necessary self-control. But in any case, universal money maximisation is inconceivable. If all try, capitalists, but no wage-labourers, can succeed. For Marx, the distinction between use-value and value explains why.

To be sure, the system universalisability conception of capitalist labour-exploitation is based on a thin portion of text. To think of this as a decisive objection would be to raise an impossibly high bar, however. If a conception of capitalist exploitation can only be ascribed to Marx if it is fully elaborated in several explicit statements, *no* conception of capitalist exploitation can be

---

99   *MEW*, 42, p. 211; *MECW*, 28, p. 214; Marx 1973a, p. 285.
100   *MEW*, 42, p. 212; *MECW*, 28, p. 216; Marx 1973a, p. 287.

ascribed to Marx. The reconstructive response is to formulate a conception of capitalist exploitation in the spirit of Marx's project and texts. It would be a mistake to suppose that no criteria are left to assess such a reconstructive response. The question is whether a system universalisability conception of capitalist labour-exploitation can facilitate a solution to any of the problems that arise if Marx is read on his own terms. In this spirit, three problems will be discussed. While the exploitation and need problem is posed by Cohen, and the agency problem by Postone, the capitalism, rights and injustice problem is posed here for the first time.

11   The Exploitation and Need Problem

The *exploitation and need problem* is introduced by Cohen as follows:

> Particularly problematic, from the point of view of a socialist political philosopher, is the coming apart of the exploitation and need features [of the revolutionary agent of Marxism, which features, Cohen allows, used to converge somewhat on a single set of people – JF]. It forces a choice between the principle of a right to the product of one's labor embedded in the doctrine of exploitation and a principle of equality of benefits and burdens which negates the right to the product of one's labor and which is required to defend support for very needy people who are not producers and who are, *a fortiori*, not exploited. This is the central normative problem which Marxists did not have to face in the past.[101]

According to Cohen, it is a fact that there is now less overlap of the exploited and the needy than in the past. Although Cohen allows that any group of people who are *both* exploited and needy have 'a compelling interest' in replacing capitalism with socialism, now that this group is smaller, socialists face more pressure, Cohen says, 'to worry about the exact ideals and principles of socialism'.[102] It is now necessary, for practical reasons, to determine how a socialist political philosophy can consistently condemn exploitation *and* advocate support for the very needy, including very needy non-producers. Only with a solution

---

101   Cohen 2001, p. 108; compare Geras: 'Marx's story of unequal exchange or uncompensated labour effectively ignores any claims on the labour product that the non-producing needy might have' (Geras 1992, p. 59).

102   Cohen 2001, p. 108.

to this problem is it rational for a sufficient number of people to engage in a socialist revolution, Cohen implies.

The exploitation and need problem may be stated as follows: how can a socialist consistently combine a principled condemnation of exploitation with a principled defence of support for needy non-producers?

For the purpose of engaging, in the exploitation and need problem, even those who would deny the fact on which Cohen insists, two qualifying remarks may be made to clarify that the exploitation and need problem, as just stated, does not arise only for those who accept this fact. Firstly, it is not necessary to believe that there is greater social differentiation of the exploited and the needy in advanced capitalism than in earlier periods of capitalism to be exercised by the exploitation and need problem. If there has *always* been little convergence, the problem still arises as a practical and a theoretical problem. Secondly, the exploitation and need problem arises as a theoretical problem (even if not as a practical problem) even if one were to believe that at some future date at which society will become ripe for a transition to socialism, convergence between the needy and the exploited will be re-established. One may still want to know how a socialist can consistently condemn exploitation and defend support for needy non-producers. Even those who do not accept Cohen's factual claim, or deny the persistence of the fact it reports, can ponder the exploitation and need problem.

As the exploitation and need problem is a genuine problem, consider the form in which Cohen introduces it. Suppose, as Cohen says, that the socialist principle that condemns exploitation is 'the principle of a right to the product of one's labor', while the socialist principle that defends support for the needy is the principle of a right on the part of the needy to means of life. The exploitation and need problem must then be solved by means of an ordering principle. For without an ordering principle that establishes the priority of the one principle over the other, providing needy non-producers with means of life will violate producers' rights to the product of their labour; and distributing the product of labour to producers will violate needy non-producers' rights to means of life. An ordering principle that orders these two principles can either state that the anti-exploitation principle has priority, or that the need principle has priority. To endorse the former ordering principle is to be callous to the needy, while to endorse the latter is to be reconciled to compromise with capitalism, if workers are hired by needy capitalists.[103] In saying that the problem now faced by socialists 'forces a choice' between an anti-exploitation principle or a need principle,

---

103   Compare Cohen's infirm neighbour sketch, discussed in ch. 1, sec. 1.

Cohen reveals that he takes it to be unthinkable that a solution to the exploitation and need problem could be found without one or other of these ordering principles.

The system universalisability conception of capitalist labour-exploitation facilitates a solution to the exploitation and need problem without either of these ordering principles, and so without falling into the trap of believing that the exploitation and need problem (which is genuine) forces socialists to licence either callousness or compromise. It facilitates a *system universalisability principle of justice*, which says: exclusive advantages obtained by pursuing system-reinforced ends that cannot be universalised are unjust. This principle condemns capitalism, because money maximisation fails the system-level universalisability test. But as this principle does not rest on the premise that a producer has a right to the product of their labour, it is possible, without inconsistency, to use it to condemn capitalist exploitation, *and* to defend the provision of means of life for needy non-producers. What society sets about doing in enforcing the former principle against capitalist labour-exploitation is removing the system that enables and constrains the hire of wage-labour to produce for continuous money maximisation. Prohibiting capitalist labour-exploitation on this basis will create cases of conflict with a principle of providing means of life to needy non-producers only if it is possible for the latter to fall into a situation where the only way to provide them with means of life violates the system-level universalisability test. But it is implausible to suppose that, whatever policy of support for needy non-producers a socialist society adopts (whatever the means and end of such a policy may be), it will fail the system-level universalisability test.

The system universalisability principle of justice thus solves the exploitation and need problem. The problem appears acute only if one accepts the premise that an anti-exploitation principle must appeal to a producer's right to the product of their labour. Cohen's belief that a Marxist is committed to this premise[104] has led him to pose the exploitation and need problem in the form of a trap: callousness or compromise. The system universalisability conception of capitalist labour-exploitation allows the problem to be posed in a purer form, and to be solved, without licensing callousness or compromise.

---

104   Cohen 1988, pp. 226–9.

12   The Agency Problem

The *agency problem* is posed by Postone:

> Overcoming capitalism, then, must also be understood in terms of the
> abolition of proletarian labor and, hence, the proletariat. This, however,
> renders very problematic the question of the relation of working-class
> social and political actions to the possible abolition of capitalism; it
> implies that such actions, and what is usually referred to as working-class
> consciousness, remain within the bounds of the capitalist social forma-
> tion ... [C]apital rests ultimately on proletarian labor – hence, overcoming
> capital cannot be based on the self-assertion of the working-class. Even
> the 'radical' notion that the workers produce the surplus and, therefore,
> are its 'rightful' owners, for example, points to the abolition of the capit-
> alist class – but not to the overcoming of capital.[105]

According to Postone, the fundamental feature of capitalism is not a 'capitalist
class', but 'capital'. What is fundamental to capitalism, for Postone, is not the
differentiation of a propertyless group that produces from a property-owning
group that does not, but the dynamic of capital accumulation. Once capitalism
is analysed on this basis, however, Marx's belief in the revolutionary agency
of the working-class is said to be rendered 'very problematic'. According to
Postone, the ultimate goal of working-class social and political actions is the
abolition of classes, and this stops short of overcoming capitalism.

The agency problem may therefore be stated as follows: how can any group
within capitalism develop an interest that can lead it to seek to overcome capitalism? Or, as sceptics of Postone's conception of capitalism may prefer to
phrase it: how can a group within capitalism develop an interest that can lead
it to seek to overcome value production?

The solution presented here is formulated in the terms of the first statement of the problem. The reason for this is that the interaction-recognition-
antinomy thesis defines the system of capitalist production by two types of
generalised interaction: generalised purchase and sale, and generalised production with wage-labour for continuous money maximisation. These generalised interactions sustain the dynamic of capital accumulation that tends to
differentiate actors into classes without logically presupposing that this differentiation has already taken place. Even if, as Marx says in the *Grundrisse*, the

---

105   Postone 1993, pp. 370–1.

separation of the direct producers from the objective conditions of production is one of the 'historical conditions of capital',[106] it is not a logical condition. It is possible to conceive of a system of money-maximising production in which (at least initially) each individual performs wage-labour and co-owns a money-maximising unit of production (whether the same unit as that for which they work, as in a society of money-maximising producer cooperatives, or in a different unit). Such a system would facilitate a dynamic of capital accumulation, if competition led each unit of production to seek to accumulate as great a proportion of the value of the total social product as possible. Capital accumulation could still shape the techniques employed in production, the time devoted to labour, the kinds of product produced, and the occurrence of crises. The interaction-recognition-antinomy thesis offers no grounds for denying that such a system of capital accumulation is a form of capitalism, and so there is no cause, here, to substitute the first formulation of the problem with the second.

Although the agency problem is a genuine problem, it is possible to answer it by denying that working-class social and political actions must stop short of abolishing capital. In the above passage, Postone suggests two distinct reasons for holding that working-class agency cannot abolish capital: one related to self-assertion, and another related to the vindication of rights to product. Both may be challenged, although it is the second that relates the agency problem to exploitation.

Suppose it is accepted that overcoming capital involves overcoming 'proletarian labor'. If it is then argued that, as action by the working-class is a 'self-assertion of the working-class', working-class action cannot abolish 'proletarian labor', it follows that working-class action cannot abolish capital. This argument rests on an ambiguity, however. The actions of x will always exert x's capacities (= self-assertion$_1$). But only some of x's actions need aim to strengthen x (= self-assertion$_2$). While working-class actions are always acts of self-assertion$_1$, that is no reason to think that they are always acts of self-assertion$_2$. It is in general false that, if x is to be abolished, x cannot do the abolishing. The sense in which it is correct to say that actions of the working-class are self-assertions of the working-class is no reason to think that such actions cannot abolish an activity that its members perform, 'proletarian labor'. It is no reason to think that working-class agency cannot abolish capital.

Postone's second and more interesting suggestion is that the horizon of working-class action does not extend to the abolition of capital because it is

---

106   *MEW*, 42, p. 383; *MECW*, 28, p. 399; Marx 1973a, p. 471.

limited to vindicating workers' rights to what 'workers produce'. Even if the vindication of these rights precludes the existence of a separate group of non-producers who appropriate product and direct investment, it does not preclude capital accumulation under the management of producers themselves. To reject this second reason for denying that an interest of the working-class can lead it to seek to overcome capitalism, it is necessary to reject the claim that working-class social and political action is limited to the vindication of workers' rights to product.

What is surprising about this second suggestion is that Postone's endorsement of the idea that working-class agency is limited to vindicating workers' rights to product reflects a failure to question an assumption of traditional Marxism, the very tradition of thought that Postone purports to oppose. Traditional Marxism, according to Postone, is the critique of capitalism from the standpoint of labour as it is found in capitalism. Working-class actions that proceed from the standpoint of labour as it is found in capitalism are those that seek to prosecute the claims of workers that arise from a positive evaluation of the contribution that workers make in virtue of performing labour as it is found in capitalism. The traditional Marxist critique of capitalism rests on the premise that the working-class is the '"truly" productive'[107] class, and, as such, it alone has a right to product. It follows that, for traditional Marxism, there will be a redistribution of value from non-producers to producers on which capitalist exploitation ceases. Once all value is taken away from capitalists and returned to the producers,[108] that is the end of capitalist exploitation and of capitalism, for traditional Marxism. There is no outstanding claim for producers to prosecute. If the traditional Marxist account of working-class agency is sound, Postone is right to doubt that the agency problem can be solved by appeal to working-class agency. But it has yet to be shown that the traditional Marxist account of working-class agency is sound.

The case for saying that Postone's second suggestion reflects a failure to question the traditional Marxist account of working-class agency is that Postone remarks: 'the universality represented by the proletariat ultimately is that of value'.[109] This remark suggests that Postone is as confused as traditional Marxism is as to the dimension to which the most direct expression of working-class

---

107   Postone 1993, p. 64.

108   See, besides Cohen 2001, p. 108, Brown 2014, p. 373; Elster 1978a, p. 10; Honneth 2011, p. 420; Honneth 2014, p. 227; Pendlebury, Hudson and Moellendorf 2001, p. 210; Young 1978, p. 439.

109   Postone 1993, p. 368; compare p. 124.

resistance belongs. The most direct expression of working-class resistance to the system of capitalist production is not the assertion of a right to a greater share of value or product. To assert such a right already presupposes a willingness to submit to the discipline of value production. The most direct expression of working-class resistance to the system of capitalist production is resistance to the extension and/or intensification of the working day. It is directly expressed, that is, as resistance in what the system universalisability conception of exploitation acknowledges as the dimension of capitalist exploitation. If the most direct expression of working-class resistance concerns labour time, self-assertive working-class action need not be confined to the form of asserting a right to the product of value production. It need not be confined to the form of asserting a right whose vindication presupposes that 'proletarian labor' and capital continue to exist.

The system universalisability conception of capitalist labour-exploitation suggests that there may be a solution to the agency problem, by locating capitalist exploitation in the dimension of labouring activity, and defining it in terms of the systematic pursuit of money maximisation. There is no longer any reason to hold that working-class action is fixed on something short of the overcoming of capital on account of the centrality to it of resistance to capitalist exploitation. The overcoming of exploitation in capitalist production is not the overcoming of the unproductiveness of a class of non-producers, but the overcoming of value production itself. A positive solution to the agency problem can consist in an argument to the effect that participants in a working-class movement to limit the working day can conclude that workers have an interest in abolishing value production. An antinomy-based argument to this effect that relies on the system universalisability principle of justice is presented in chapter 12.

13   The Capitalism, Rights and Injustice Problem

The *capitalism, rights and injustice problem* is: how is it possible to hold that capitalism is unjust without appeal to rights?

The capitalism, rights and injustice problem arises on acceptance of two premises: (i) capitalism is unjust; (ii) capitalism is not to be condemned by appeal to rights. Before arguing that the system universalisability conception of capitalist labour-exploitation facilitates a solution to this problem, it is necessary to show why the problem arises. This will be done by arguing that socialists like Marx have reason to accept (i)–(ii). First, however, it is helpful to note some differences between what it is to solve the capitalism, rights and injustice problem, and the nature of the Anglophone debate on Marx and justice whose best known summary is an article by Norman Geras entitled 'The Controversy about Marx and Justice'.[110]

To solve the capitalism, rights and injustice problem, it is sufficient to condemn *one* injustice of capitalism without appeal to rights. It is not necessary to offer a comprehensive account of the (in)justice(s) of capitalism, according to Marx. This injustice need not be a *distributive* injustice, moreover. Distributive justice is concerned with the question of what benefits or burdens it is just for people to have equal amounts of.[111] To solve the capitalism, rights and injustice problem, however, it is sufficient to argue that capitalist labour-exploitation can be condemned as unjust without appeal to a right, although this injustice, because it is independent of any unequal distribution of labour (or product) within a society, is not a distributive injustice. If capitalist labour-exploitation is an injustice by virtue of the system-reinforced *end* it imposes on labour; if, that is, it is unjust because, in the words of the *Grundrisse*, it is '*theft of alien [fremder] labour time*';[112] then the capitalism, rights and injustice problem can be solved by showing that this charge of injustice does not rest on a right. Third, to offer a solution to the capitalism, rights and injustice problem based on Marx's writings, it is sufficient to show that Marx's writings contain the *resources* to solve it. Showing that Marx's writings contain the resources to respond to a problem is not the same thing as defending a view about what Marx had in mind.

These points are worth noting, for much of the Anglophone debate on Marx and justice takes the form of addressing the question of whether Marx (consistently) thought that capitalism was unjust on grounds of distributive justice. This is not the only question for debate on Marx and justice to address, and it is not the question directly addressed here. (After presenting a solution to the capitalism, rights and injustice problem, a critique of the Anglophone debate on Marx and justice will be offered). One upshot of these differences is a reduction in the textual burden of proof. To solve the capitalism, rights and injustice problem, it is not necessary to cite passages related to the (in)justice of phenomena other than capitalist labour-exploitation, or to multiply textual evidence for a given position, or to cite passages purely to defuse apparent inconsistencies. The important thing here is not how frequently or consistently Marx

---

110   Geras 1985. Geras also wrote a follow-up article, Geras 1992.

111   Cohen 2011, p. 3.

112   *MEW*, 42, p. 601; *MECW*, 29, p. 91; Marx 1973a, p. 705; compare the apposition in *Capital* Volume III cited in sec. 5, and the analysis of '*fremd*' in ch. 10, sec. 3.

expresses a view that solves the problem, but whether Marx's writings offer the resources to formulate a view that can solve it. With this in mind, we can turn to the task of motivating the problem's two premises.

The first premise of the capitalism, rights and injustice problem is: (i) capitalism is unjust. All this means is: capitalism stands condemned by a norm that ought to be enforced impartially, now if not forever. To say that a norm 'ought to be enforced' is to say that everyone it affects has a reason to accept it. The qualifier 'now' permits material or social circumstances, such as the level of productive power, to be taken into account in deciding what norms to enforce; while 'if not forever' indicates that the judgement is non-committal as regards whether or not the norm ought to be enforced in the best possible society. A norm is applied 'impartially' if it is applied without deference to the affected person's own assessment of the matter, by those in no special relationship with them. For example, the principle 'to each according to their needs!'[113] would not be applied impartially if its application deferred to each actor's self-assessment of their needs.

A commitment to (i) need not reflect a belief that 'justice is the first virtue of social institutions',[114] as Rawls says. Perhaps a norm ought to be enforced impartially now, although the best society is not one that includes impartially enforced norms (in a normatively fundamental role). It is consistent to believe that capitalism is unjust, and that the best society would realise other virtues only (or other virtues over justice). To motivate the capitalism, rights and injustice problem, it is not necessary to show that *Marx* held a view of justice as those norms that ought to be enforced impartially, now if not forever. Nonetheless, the Marxist pedigree of the ought-to-be-enforced-impartially view of justice is affirmed below.

Premise (i) also does not imply that capitalism is to be criticised on the basis of 'moral goods', that is, as contrary to or failing to promote 'valuing or doing something because conscience or the "moral law" tells us we "ought" to'.[115] Just norms may be observed for a variety of motives; may be valid and/or applicable in light of historical facts; and, rather than binding an individual's will, offer a mutual guarantee. Nor need action in accordance with just norms be prized for its instrumental value in promoting 'moral goods'. It can be prized for honouring the value of a property of a society. If Marx's rejection of morality – as in remarks of the kind: 'communists do not preach *morality* at all'[116] – is a rejec-

---

113   *MEW*, 19, p. 21; *MECW*, 24, p. 87.

114   Rawls 1971, p. 3.

115   Wood 2004, pp. 128–9.

116   *MEW*, 3, p. 229; *MECW*, 5, p. 247.

tion of 'moral goods', then the distinction between moral goods and nonmoral goods shows that this rejection is consistent with a belief in (i).[117]

One three-step argument for (i) as a claim that socialists like Marx have reason to accept is to say that anyone who regards a 'revolutionising'[118] agent as necessary to bring about a socialist society is committed to (i). First of all, it is reasonable to hold that a 'revolutionising' agent is necessary to bring about socialism, because socialism presupposes that wealth and power have been taken away from the enormously wealthy and the enormously powerful, and no enormously wealthy and powerful class gives up its wealth and power entirely voluntarily. No transition from capitalism to socialism will be possible without an agent at least raising the threat of physical force against the enormously wealthy and powerful. So, *if* socialists require a normative reason for replacing capitalism with socialism, this reason must licence a people's (threat of) physical force. In view of the reluctance of the enormously wealthy and powerful to give up their resources voluntarily, and adopting an ought-to-be-enforced-impartially conception of justice, we can say: *if* socialists require a normative reason for replacing capitalism with socialism, they require a principle of justice, on which capitalism, but not socialism, is unjust.

Second, all anti-capitalist revolutionaries require some principled reason for replacing capitalism. Those who attempt to bring about and/or who (tacitly) support a new order, to which the (previously) ruling class publicly voices its opposition, must be convinced of the validity of that new order, on grounds that they can give publicly and sincerely. Moreover, it is foreseeable that, to overcome the opposition of the enormously wealthy and powerful, those who bring about and/or support a new order will be required to make sacrifices, and to call on everyone willing to join them in doing so, to achieve their goal. But if that is so, given preferences alone cannot be expected to provide a sufficiently stable basis of revolutionary motivation. Some or other principled reason will have to provide a basis of revolutionary motivation.

---

117   Richard Miller portrays 'Marx as a critic of the moral point of view', where the latter consists of advocacy of any 'form of equality' as an end in itself, any norm offered as 'valid in all societies', or any claim to 'universality' (Miller 1984, p. 17). Miller's 'moral point of view' thus differs from Wood's 'moral goods'. Justice as here defined includes a claim to universality, and so is part of Miller's 'moral point of view'. But Miller neither acknowledges the possibility of duty-to-the-whole-based arguments about justice, nor discusses the passages in Marx relevant to advancing such an argument. Miller (like Wood) identifies 'the notion of justice' with 'rights-based morality' (Miller 1984, p. 79), and Miller (like Wood) does not discuss the *Grundrisse*'s counterfactual thought experiment, *Capital*'s account of recognition, or the rights-antinomy.

118   *MEJ*, 2003, p. 43; *MEW*, 3, p. 47, p. 271; *MECW*, 5, p. 60, p. 290.

The case for saying that anti-capitalist revolutionaries who are socialists like Marx require a principled reason for replacing capitalism that everyone affected has a reason to accept, and thus a principle of justice, relates to the fact that their goal, socialism, is a form of society in which everyone is treated equally in certain respects. In Marx's vision, emergent communism adopts the principle of an equal right to means of individual consumption proportional to productive contribution, while developed communism adopts the principle 'from each according to their abilities, to each according to their needs.'[119] No one denies that, in Marx's vision, emergent communism applies a type of 'equal standard';[120] while developed communism also adopts an equal standard (which is not a standard of equal right)[121] if an equal standard is a principle that applies to each in respect of attributes that any human being ordinarily has to some degree (such as abilities and needs).[122] If the goal of an anti-capitalist revolution is a form of society in which everyone is to be treated equally in certain respects, its agents must be able to give a public and sincere reason for replacing capitalism to anyone willing to help replace it that everyone affected has a reason to accept. For otherwise, the basis of revolutionary motivation does not prepare people for socialism. Anti-capitalists who aim to replace capitalism with an elitist culture or with a society based on principles that do not treat individuals as both distinct and equal are not committed to a principle of justice. But such anti-capitalists are not socialists like Marx.

To show that Marx is faced with the capitalism, rights and injustice problem, it is unnecessary to show that he would frame the problem in its terms. Hence, the above argument for (i) could afford to make no mention of Marx's view of justice. It may *also* be argued, however, that Marx has a view of justice that allows the problem to be framed in these terms. In other words, it may also be argued that Marx has an ought-to-be-enforced-impartially view of justice.

Two views of justice are standardly attributed to Marx. On the narrow view, justice consists of the 'juridical norms ... internal to each social order'.[123] On the broader view, justice consists of the 'proper ... distribution of advantages and disadvantages quite generally'.[124] The ought-to-be-enforced-impartially view of justice differs from the narrow view, for the norms that ought to be enforced

119   *MEW*, 19, pp. 20–1; *MECW*, 24, pp. 85–7.
120   Wood 2014, p. 258.
121   See ch. 3, sec. 4.
122   On this view, and contrary to Wood, the equal standard of developed communism is 'substantive'; it differs in kind from the 'equal standard' adopted in 'a caste system' that assigns to each 'what pertains to their caste position' (Wood 2014, p. 259).
123   Geras 1985, p. 71.
124   Ibid.

impartially (now if not forever) may be incompatible with an existing social order. It also differs from the broader view, on two counts. The broader view includes, as part of justice, any ethos operating within the bounds set by the norms that ought to be enforced impartially, and that contributes to the proper distribution of benefits and burdens.[125] The ought-to-be-enforced-impartially view of justice does not include any such ethos in its conception of justice. The broader view is also in one respect not broad: it is a view of *distributive* justice. The norms that ought to be enforced impartially (now if not forever) may include norms other than those that contribute to distributing a society's benefits and burdens.

Marx's vision of developed communism creates a problem for both the narrow view and the broad view that does not trouble the ought-to-be-enforced-impartially view. For Wood, who proposes the narrow view, Marx's view of justice is one on which 'the justice of an action, transaction or system of distribution consists in bearing a certain relation of adequacy, correspondence or functionality to the social mode of production within which it takes place'.[126] Yet Wood *also* says that Marx 'looks forward to a more distant future in which he hopes people will not have to think in terms of right or justice'.[127] The more distant future that Marx looks forward to includes a communist mode of production. No mode of production can exist without some activities being adequate to or functional for it, however. Nor can the adequacy or functionality of existing activities for an existing mode of production escape reflection. To look forward to the future to which, Wood says, Marx looks forward, Marx must have a view of justice different to the one that Wood attributes to him.[128] Geras, meanwhile, openly concedes that the broad view conflicts with what Marx says about developed communism, for Marx 'does not realize what he is doing'.[129] By contrast, the ought-to-be-enforced-impartially view of justice can be affirmed, while affirming that, on Marx's vision of it, developed communism surpasses the horizon of right (and the horizon of justice).[130]

The ought-to-be-enforced-impartially view of justice also captures the functions and drawbacks with justice that Marx identified. Impartially enforced norms offer a kind of guarantee and recognition. If they are clearly formu-

---

125 This is Cohen's view of justice; see Cohen 2008, p. 73, p. 116.
126 Wood 1984, p. 9; see, similarly, Wood 1979, pp. 269–70.
127 Wood 2014, p. 258.
128 For a complementary, antinomy-based argument not to attribute this narrow view of justice to Marx, see ch. 12, sec. 4.
129 Geras 1985, p. 71.
130 See ch. 3, sec. 4.

lated, have adequate sanctions, and are reliably enforced, impartially enforced norms are the kind of norms that self-interested actors can expect one another to conform to, as no one will wish to incur the sanction. Moreover, if impartially enforced norms are publicly declared, they are the kind of norms that can be recognised to have a content and standing that is independent of the judgement of the actor to whom they apply. These two functions distinguish impartially enforced norms from the norms of an ethos. But they also ensure that the conditions in which (a) progressive interests stand in need of a 'mutual guarantee'[131] are also the conditions in which (b) *'punishment, coercion,* contradict *human* conduct ... [L]aw must be one-sided, and *must abstract* from individuality'.[132] The ought-to-be-enforced-impartially view of justice accommodates both realist (a)-like statements as well as critical (b)-like statements. As the ought-to-be-enforced-impartially view of justice is in line with Marx's vision of developed communism, and accommodates both these sorts of statement, it is reasonable to suppose that Marx could have framed the above argument for why socialists like him are committed to premise (i) in its terms.

We can now turn to the second premise of the capitalism, rights and injustice problem: (ii) capitalism is not to be condemned by appeal to rights. Two arguments will be offered for why socialists like Marx have reason to accept (ii). The first is simply a broader form of the argument that exposed the limitation of the needs version of Cohen's product-based charge of capitalist exploitation.[133] The second is Marx's recognition-based critique of rights.

The needs version of Cohen's product-based charge of capitalist exploitation is limited by the fact that the principle of a right to product based on need cannot condemn capital accumulation if it is overseen by capitalists whose personal reward is limited to an amount of product calculated by need. The first part of the first argument for (ii) is that the same type of limitation will be exhibited by any socialist principle of right to product. If, say, the principle is that of a right to product 'proportional'[134] to productive contribution, the principle cannot condemn capital accumulation overseen by capitalists whose personal reward (like that of others) is proportional to their productive contribution. The form of reasoning is as follows:

I. Capitalism is a system of capital accumulation (in which purchase and sale and production with wage-labour for money maximisation are generalised)

---

131   *MEJ*, 2003, pp. 94–5; *MEW*, 3, p. 62; *MECW*, 5, p. 90; see also *MEW*, 7, p. 288; *MECW*, 10, p. 333.

132   *MEW*, 2, p. 190; *MECW*, 4, p. 179.

133   See ch. 1, sec. 1.

134   Husami 1978, p. 44; see, similarly, Elster 1983, pp. 292–3; Young 1978, p. 439.

II.   Whatever principle of right to product a socialist might advocate, it is logically possible for a tax scheme to regulate capital accumulation to yield that distribution

III. Therefore, no right to product that a socialist might advocate can condemn all capitalisms

IV.   Socialists condemn all capitalisms

V.   Therefore, socialists' condemnation of capitalism cannot appeal to a right to product

The form of reasoning is not that a socialist principle of right to product 'would not be rationally applicable to capitalism'.[135] Rather, it is that it would not *condemn* all possible capitalisms. The crucial step is step II, and what supports step II is that a principle of product distribution says nothing about the dynamic of production. If a tax scheme can be used to redistribute product, a principle of product distribution does not in principle exclude any particular production dynamic. Hence, it does not exclude capital accumulation.

The argument is incomplete, however, because capitalist labour-exploitation is not a matter of the distribution of value or product. It must be extended as follows:

VI.   Capitalist exploitation belongs to the dimension of labouring activity

VII. To condemn capitalist exploitation by appeal to a right, it is necessary to appeal to a producer's right not to perform surplus labour,[136] or to a producer's right to withhold surplus labour from a capitalist

VIII. A socialist cannot appeal to a right not to perform surplus labour, for then people whose impairments prevent them from producing cannot be guaranteed means of life, which is contrary to socialist values

IX.   A socialist cannot appeal to a producer's right to withhold surplus labour from a capitalist, for that *allows* each producer to choose to let a capitalist benefit, and if enough producers agree, some capitalist production can proceed

X.   Therefore, together with V, socialists' condemnation of capitalism cannot appeal to a right

The crucial steps are VIII and IX. But VIII is uncontroversial, and IX follows from IV.

A second argument for (ii) is Marx's recognition-based critique of rights. In its discussion of communist principles of distribution, *Critique of the Gotha Programme* suggests a problem in the form of right. This problem is that the

---

135   Wood 1972, p. 270; see, similarly, Wood 1979, p. 293.
136   Surplus labour is labour beyond necessary labour, that is, labour beyond the production of what is required to reproduce a given population of producers.

express standard of right does not reflect its actual content. 'Right', Marx says, 'can only consist in the application of an equal standard'.[137] To apply an equal standard of right is to treat rightsholders from a determinate point of view that 'sees nothing further in them, disregards everything else'.[138] Yet factors disregarded from a determinate point of view do not thereby cease to take effect. As a result, right is inherently short-sighted. Its standard may not express what it tacitly recognises.

Critique of the Gotha Programme offers one example: the right to product in proportion to productive contribution. This right applies an equal standard to all. The same output by any two different individuals gives each a right to the same amount of product. But this standard ensures that equal efforts are not equally rewarded. For unequally talented individuals must put in different amounts of effort to produce the same output. As the talented are able to put in less effort than the less talented to receive the same amount of product, this right 'tacitly recognises [*erkennt ... an*]' unequal talents as 'natural privileges'.[139] What right *tacitly* recognises differs from what it *expressly* recognises: this is Marx's recognition-based critique of rights.

Marx's recognition-based critique of rights revolves around the distinction between what is express and what is tacit, not around the distinction between universality and particularity. *Critique of the Gotha Programme* is often read as offering a critique of the universality of right. William Booth, for example, claims that its critique of right is that the 'universality' of right must 'pass over the irreducible particularity of the individual'.[140] This can be challenged, on two counts. First, Marx says that right disregards 'everything else'.[141] 'Everything else' is not reducible to: every other difference between individuals. Right remains subject to a recognition-based critique on the counterfactual assumption that all individuals are identical. The independent rightful actions of identical rights-endowed individuals could create a social dynamic that is not expressly recognised by right. Second, Marx does not here reject any 'system of general rules'.[142] A system of general rules leading to no divergence between what is expressly and what is tacitly recognised is not subject to a recognition-based critique.

---

137   *MEW*, 19, p. 21; *MECW*, 24, p. 86.
138   Ibid.
139   *MEW*, 19, p. 21; *MECW*, 24, p. 86. The next passage, from *On the Jewish Question*, uses the same verb; on 'recognition', see ch. 9, sec. 1.
140   Booth 1993, p. 257; see also Basso 2012, pp. 120–1; Lukes 1982b, pp. 199–200; Moore 1980, pp. 48–9.
141   *MEW*, 19, p. 21; *MECW*, 24, p. 86.
142   Moore 1980, pp. 48–9.

To say that recognition of *x* is but the recognition of *y* is to distinguish what is expressly recognised from what is tacitly recognised. Marx therefore also offers a recognition-based critique of individual human rights in *On the Jewish Question*:

> The liberty [*Freiheit*] of the egoistic human being and the recognition [*anerkennen*] of this liberty [as a human right – JF] is but the recognition of the *unbridled* movement of the intellectual and material elements which form the content of his life.[143]

To bestow rights on individuals is to presuppose that each individual, or at least some number of individuals, has a capacity that they would need to exercise, to make use of that right. Only then is there a practical point in awarding the right. Insofar as a legal order is based on right, the exercise of this capacity, in respect of what the right gives each a right to do, is subject only to the negative limits imposed by other individuals' rights and public order. The concatenation of every individual's rightful exercise of this capacity may, however, set in train a social dynamic. For example, one social dynamic set in train by the exercise of private property rights is capital accumulation. Another social dynamic set in train by the exercise of private property rights is the commercialisation of the press.[144] Whether or not such social dynamics are foreseen by a law-making body, they are not what a rights-based legal code expressly recognises. What it expressly recognises is the liberty. Yet all social dynamics set in train as a result of individuals' rightful exercise of their rights are public knowledge. So, if a social dynamic is set in train by individuals' rightful exercise of a right, any disparity between what the law expressly recognises and the social dynamic it tacitly recognises is public knowledge. But if it is public knowledge that such a disparity exists, laws are not, as Marx urges in *Debates on Freedom of the Press*, 'conscious reflections' of 'life'.[145] If laws are not conscious reflections of social life, then a member of society, in obeying them, is obeying something other than them. In that case, legal norms do not objectify freedom as self-legislative

---

143   *MEW*, 1, p. 369; *MECW*, 3, p. 167; Marx 1975a, p. 233; Marx 1994, p. 49. '*Freiheit*' is translated here and elsewhere as 'liberty' (not, as repeatedly in Marx 1975a and Marx 1994, as 'freedom') if it is Marx's term for 'la *liberté*', as the latter appears in the French constitution of 1793. German, unlike English, does not have two distinct words, 'freedom' and 'liberty'. (When writing in English on what the French constitution of 1848 guarantees, Marx uses 'liberty' (see *MECW*, 10, p. 568) where, when writing in German, he uses '*Freiheit*' (*MEW*, 8, p. 126; *MECW*, 11, p. 114)).

144   See *MEW*, 1, pp. 67–71; *MECW*, 1, pp. 171–5.

145   *MEW*, 1, p. 58; *MECW*, 3, p. 162.

human community. If socialists like Marx are committed to the value of self-legislative human community, they cannot condemn capitalism by appeal to rights.

Marx's recognition-based critique of rights is a critique of the form of right, rather than a critique of its content. That is, it is a critique of giving a fundamental role to outcome-independent constraints on conduct based on the notion of an individual's non-derivative value. This critique does not require that rights give expression to egoism,[146] or that rights lead individuals to see others as undesirable constraints on their action,[147] or that rights perpetuate inequalities.[148] Without doubt, rights are used in capitalism, by their holders, to pursue egoistic interests; in the context of their pursuit, individuals view others as undesirable constraints; and the result is inequality. But imagine a society with a rights-based legal code in which independent individuals use their rights for altruistic ends and thereby set in train a social dynamic that results in an egalitarian distribution. The social dynamic produced by the concatenation of everyone's rightful exercise of their rights may still lack express recognition in the law. If so, the law would not objectify freedom as self-legislative human community.

Leopold suggests three reasons for thinking that Marx and/or socialists confine (or should confine) criticisms of rights to their content as distinct from their form: (1) to suppose that human beings have a standing that inanimate objects do not, that 'people count in a way that filing cabinets do not',[149] is to be committed to rights; (2) to 'recognise that there are constraints on how we are permitted to treat' persons based on factors 'other than the goodness of outcomes'[150] is to be committed to rights; and (3) it is 'implausible' to think that a society could exist in which 'rights' are 'superfluous'.[151] These suggestions are not compelling, however. Firstly, to say that members of the human species have a value that transcends that of any type of inanimate object (or any other type of species) is not to imply that each individual also has a non-derivative value. Hence, it is not to be committed to rights. Secondly, to recognise constraints on how we ought to act towards other human beings that are independent of the goodness of outcomes is not to say that these constraints are owed on account of the value of a type of individual property. Hence, it is not

---

146   Schwartz 1995b, p. 163.
147   Leopold 2007, p. 160.
148   Ivison 2008, p. 183, pp. 185–6.
149   Leopold 2007, p. 150.
150   Leopold 2007, p. 152.
151   Leopold 2007, pp. 162–3.

to be committed to rights, as distinct from duties to the whole. Thirdly, to say that rights are never superfluous is not to say they must be normatively fundamental. To motivate a critique of the form of rights, it suffices to claim that a type of individual property is not the ultimate object of value, so that treating it as if it was, by adopting rights as fundamental, will require members of society, in obeying the law, to obey something other than it; and none of the above suggestions count against this claim.

The Communist Manifesto describes communism as an 'association, in which the free development of each is the condition for the free development of all'.[152] This suggests that freedom, for Marx, has a development component and an awareness component. Freedom consists in (a) the cultivation of one's abilities and the enjoyment of their exercise; and (b) the institutionalised awareness that this activity is in harmony with (rather than at the expense of) that of others. This is a wholly different sense of freedom to that in which 'a person's freedom is diminished when his private property is tampered with'.[153] It is a freedom in which, as *On the Jewish Question* puts it, the human being 'has cognised and organised his "forces propres" as *social* powers'.[154] If the principles of an association are to offer its members (b), they must accurately reflect harmonious social dynamics. If a legal code that prioritises rights is a legal code that cannot expressly recognise the social dynamics it sets in train, or that sets in train social dynamics in which actors' pursuit of ends is not harmonious, it cannot be the legal code of the association Marx envisioned. Formulated as a rejoinder to Hegel's *Philosophy of History*, Marx's recognition-based critique of rights is that, if 'world history is the progress in the consciousness of freedom',[155] a form of society characterised by a legal code that prioritises rights cannot be its end point. Socialists like Marx must be able to condemn capitalism without appeal to rights, to be able to insist on the freedom they value, the autonomy of 'social humanity'.[156]

In sum, socialists like Marx are faced with the capitalism, rights and injustice problem: how is it possible to hold that capitalism is unjust without appeal to rights?

The interaction-recognition-antinomy thesis says: by adopting a system universalisability principle of justice, according to which exclusive advantages

---

152   *MEW*, 4, p. 482; *MECW*, 6, p. 506; compare *MEW*, 23, p. 618; *MECW*, 35, p. 588; Marx 1976, p. 739, cited in ch. 3, sec. 1.
153   Cohen 2011, p. 155.
154   *MEW*, 1, p. 370; *MECW*, 3, p. 168.
155   Hegel 1986e, p. 32; Hegel 2001, p. 33.
156   *MEW*, 3, p. 7; *MECW*, 5, p. 5.

obtained by pursuing system-reinforced ends that cannot be universalised are unjust. A system universalisability principle is a principle of justice because it is enforceable (in the form of measures to remove the systems that enable and constrain non-universalisable ends), and if it can be recommended on the rational grounds that antinomies in the social world ought to be resolved.[157] It condemns capitalism, because money maximisation fails the system-level universalisability test. It is not a rights-creating norm, because it grounds prohibitive measures that give no individual an unconditional advantage.

To endorse the system universalisability principle of justice is not to be committed to rejecting rights. It is simply to be committed to a legal code in which rights are not prioritised, on the basis that what it is possible for all to have a right to do is an unsuitable basis for removing systematic incentives to do what it is inconceivable for all to achieve. If the libertarian conception of justice treats 'the nonviolation of rights as a side constraint upon action',[158] the interaction-recognition-antinomy thesis replies: a duty to the whole can be a 'side constraint' on a right. A duty to the whole can serve as a criterion for not awarding or for limiting a right. The normative charge accompanying the system universalisability conception of exploitation rests on the *same value*, self-legislative human community, informing Marx's recognition-based critique of rights. The basis for saying that capitalist labour-exploitation, and thus capitalism, is to be condemned as unjust, is also the basis for not condemning it by appeal to a right.[159]

Two different sorts of argument might be offered for denying that something like the system universalisability principle of justice is a principle of justice. One is to deny that any duty to the whole is a principle of justice on the grounds that no duty to the whole is enforceable. Hillel Steiner claims: '[o]ne of the properties standardly and distinctively attributed to correlative duties is that

---

157   See ch. 1, sec. 4; and ch. 12.

158   Nozick 1974, p. 30.

159   If this solution is plausible, why did Marx not articulate the grounds that underpin his use of the language of usurpation, theft and robbery to characterise capitalist production (see *MEW*, 42, p. 534, p. 601; *MECW*, 29, p. 22, p. 91; Marx 1973a, p. 634, p. 705; and *MEW*, 19, p. 339; *MECW*, 24, p. 535), which is naturally read as raising a charge of injustice? In the *Grundrisse*, Marx refers to its thought experiment as 'exoteric' (*MEW*, 42, p. 213; *MECW*, 28, p. 217; Marx 1973a, p. 287). It might belong to a 'critique of ... morality', as Marx promised in his *Economic and Philosophic Manuscripts of 1844* (*MEW*, 40, p. 467; *MECW*, 3, p. 231), but it does not belong to a critique of political economy. One answer, therefore, is that Marx chose to focus on the critique at hand, together with Marx's judgement that it was more important to write a critique of political economy.

they are *enforceable*'.[160] According to Steiner, duties for which there is no correlative right are not the kind of duties that can be enforced, because such duties are only discharged if they are discharged with an ethical motive. But that is false. A duty to the whole need not be discharged with an ethical motive: it may be underpinned by a value that can be promoted in a certain context without ethical motivation on the part of those it binds in that context. A duty on a government to keep the workings of its institutions open to the public is an enforceable duty that has no correlative right. No individual has an unconditional right to be admitted. It also has a value (or values), public access and public scrutiny, whose promotion does not depend on the ethical character of the motive of those who uphold it, who may be officials who seek to be paid. Likewise, self-legislative human community can be promoted by measures to remove the systems that enable and constrain non-universalisable ends, even if the motive of those who implement the measures is not specifically ethical.

A second type of argument is offered by Cohen. Cohen claims: 'it is an *insult to the status of persons* when certain acts are forbidden to them'.[161] A prohibition 'is an *insult to the status of persons*', Cohen says, if and because 'it seeks to make me unfree in a respect in which no one need be unfree'.[162] As the system universalisability principle of justice restricts liberty (that is, what one has no duty not to do) for the sake of something other than liberty, Cohen might deny the justice of the system universalisability principle of justice as follows:

(1)   Personhood is fundamental to justice
(2)   Restrictions on liberty insult personhood
(3)   Therefore, a principle that restricts liberty for the sake of something other than liberty is not a principle of justice
(4)   The universalisability principle restricts liberty for the sake of something other than liberty
(5)   Therefore, the system universalisability principle is not a principle of justice

(1) may be rejected. Prohibitions to uproot systems that reinforce ends whose universalisation cannot be thought without contradiction do not seek to stop anyone from doing what 'no one need be unfree' to do. Their prohibition does not 'make' it the case, but acknowledges it as the case, that members of a community cannot be free in that respect. Such prohibitions are the kind of prohibitions that Marx affirms in 1842 when he claims that the '[t]he lawgiver' does not '*make* the laws, he does not invent them; he merely formulates them, expressing

---

160   Steiner 2006, p. 89.
161   Cohen 2011, p. 191.
162   Cohen 2011, p. 192.

in conscious, positive laws the inner laws of relations of spirit [*geistiger Verhält-nisse*]'.[163] To be insulted by a prohibition licenced by the system universalisab-ility principle of justice, an actor must view themselves as outside 'relations of spirit'. They must view themselves as others' superior. They must demand respect for their end-setting capacities in disingenuous abstraction from the value of the community whose existence they presuppose when setting the end that is to be uprooted. Prohibitions on transactions designed to uproot systems that fail the system-level universalisability test cannot insult those who do not kid themselves that they are not equal members of a community. The liberty of persons is not fundamental to justice, but only to a particular conception of justice.

Marxists who believe that, if one avoids appeal to rights, one cannot appeal to justice; or that, if one rejects capitalism on grounds of justice, one must be appealing to rights, adopt an *economistic* version of Marxism. Econom-istic Marxism is a version of Marxism that loses sight of the implications of Marx's analysis of the commodity form, and instead adopts assumptions tied to the concept of an economic good. As argued in chapter 3, if the total social product is conceived as a total of economic goods, the only conceivable prin-ciples of justice in respect of product are principles with correlative rights. Economic thought, including economistic Marxism, cannot but identify justice with rights.

The entire Anglophone debate on Marx and justice is a symptom of econom-istic Marxism. Its three positions are articulated by Wood, Young and Cohen. According to Wood, Marx 'never' criticised capitalism on grounds of '*right*' or '*justice*'[164] but only on other values. According to Young, Marx did consist-ently think that capitalism is unjust because it violates the rights of workers, and any contradiction is merely apparent.[165] According to Cohen, 'Marx did not always realize that he thought capitalism was unjust'.[166] Cohen's claim –

---

163   *MEW*, 1, p. 149; *MECW*, 1, p. 308. *MECW* translates '*geistiger Verhältnisse*' as 'spiritual rela-tions'. But '*geistig*', for Marx, means 'related to/concerning the human spirit'; 'spiritual' relations has a religious connotation.

164   Wood 2004, p. 129; see, similarly, Allen 1981; Bensaïd 2002, pp. 133–4; Brenkert 1979; McCar-ney 1992; Miller 1984, pp. 78–9; Tucker 1969, p. 45; Tucker 1972, pp. 18–20. Extended to Engels (as in Tucker 1972, p. 19 and Wood 1979, pp. 277–8), the claim is in flat contradic-tion to Engels's reference in *The Development of Socialism from Utopia to Science* to '[t]he awakening insight [*Einsicht*] that the existing social institutions are irrational and unjust [*ungerecht*]' (*MEW*, 19, p. 210; *MECW*, 24, p. 306). (*MECW* translates '*Einsicht*' as 'perception', which would be: '*Wahrnehmung*'. '*Einsicht*' cannot be misleading as a perception can be).

165   Young 1978; see, similarly, Husami 1978; Kain 1988, pp. 156–70; Young 1981.

166   Cohen 1983a, p. 444; see, also, Cohen 2013, p. 12.

which, it is high time to acknowledge, echoes a century old Kantian critique of Marx[167] – has generated the largest chorus of approval. Steven Lukes, acknowledging Cohen, writes: 'Marx and Engels plainly believed that capitalism was unjust, but they did not believe that they believed this'.[168] Elster concurs: 'Marx may have thought that he had no theory of justice, but his actual analyses only make sense if we impute such a theory to him'.[169] According to Geras, 'Marx did think capitalism was unjust but he did not think he thought so'.[170] Ellen Meiksins Wood endorses Geras's 'persuasive argument that Marx himself did, if involuntarily, have a concept of justice'.[171] Kai Nielsen agrees that Cohen's is 'the right stance to take'.[172] Rodney Peffer accepts the conclusion that 'Marx seems to have explicitly held capitalist exploitation to be just while implicitly condemning it as unjust'.[173] Jeffrey Reiman endorses 'G. A. Cohen's wise and wily conclusion'.[174] Justin Schwartz concedes of Marx's views that '[w]e must throw out *something*, either his official views of justice or his use of terms like theft'.[175] David Leopold suggests a parallel claim to Cohen's: 'Marx did believe in moral rights although he did not think that he did so'.[176] John Rawls follows the fashion: 'Marx did condemn capitalism as unjust. On the other hand, he did not see himself as doing so'.[177] Alex Callinicos views Geras's case as a 'definitive solution'[178] to the Marx and justice debate, while Pablo Gilabert agrees with Geras that 'Marx did hold quite strong views about justice even though he was not fully aware that he did so'.[179]

Notwithstanding the difference in Wood's, Young's and Cohen's interpretive findings, *they all rest on the same false substantive premise.* They all survey

---

167   See Hermann Cohen's *Ethics of the Pure Will* (Cohen 1904, pp. 34–5, p. 296), and Leonard Nelson's lectures on Kant's *Critique of Practical Reason*. Nelson says: 'the theory of the natural necessity of this economic process [the dissolution of the capitalist form of economy – JF] is, in the MARXist's case, merely the belated attempt to provide an economic basis for the ethical idea that guides him, because he lacks the confidence to ground it as such scientifically' (Nelson 1917, p. 35).

168   Lukes 1982b, p. 197.

169   Elster 1983, p. 290.

170   Geras 1985, p. 70; repeated in Geras 1992, p. 65.

171   Wood 1989, p. 78.

172   Nielsen 1989, p. 119.

173   Peffer 1990, p. 339.

174   Reiman 1991, p. 148.

175   Schwartz 1995b, p. 164.

176   Leopold 2007, p. 156.

177   Rawls 2007, p. 336; compare the editorial note at Rawls 2007, p. x.

178   Callinicos 2012, p. 275.

179   Gilabert 2017, p. 563.

Marx's work on the premise that a duty of justice has a correlative right (call this the *correlativity premise*). Wood recommends that 'we use Mill's admirably clarifying and theoretically neutral definition of justice or right'[180] to decide whether or not exploitation is unjust, on which 'justice' requires 'a right in some person, correlative to the moral obligation'.[181] Accordingly, when interpreting Marx's texts, Wood treats the possibility of injustice in an economic transaction in which interest is paid to a lender as equivalent to the question of whether its payment is 'an injustice to the borrower'.[182] Likewise, for Wood, the judgement that an 'exchange between capitalist and worker' does no '"wrong or injustice (*Unrecht*) at all to the seller"' is equivalent to saying that it is 'a *just* transaction'.[183] Young, too, claims: 'if the extraction of surplus value is theft, workers must have some property right in surplus value'.[184] Cohen's comment that 'to steal is, in general, wrongly to take what rightly belongs to another',[185] signals Cohen's agreement with Young's claim. Wood, Young and Cohen all affirm the correlativity premise in the domain that they regard as central to the question of whether Marx thought capitalism unjust.

The correlativity premise is neither clarifying nor theoretically neutral, however. Although Wood cites Mill as an authority for the correlativity premise, not even all of Mill's own characteristic views are consistent with it. According to Mill, 'the peculiar evil of silencing the expression of an opinion' is that it is not 'simply a private injury' to one or more individuals, but an act of 'robbing the human race'.[186] Clearly, for Mill, justice in respect of freedom of expression is not exhausted by obligations that have correlative rights in some person. Nor

---

180   Wood 1995, p. 154; see, similarly, Arneson 1981, p. 216.

181   Mill 1962, p. 46.

182   Wood 1979, p. 270, interpreting *MEW*, 25, pp. 351–2; *MECW*, 37, pp. 337–8; Marx 1981, pp. 460–1. For some criticisms of Wood's interpretation of this passage, see Young 1978, pp. 435–8.

183   Wood 2004, p. 136, interpreting *MEW*, 23, p. 208; *MECW*, 35, p. 204; Marx 1976, p. 301; see, similarly, Tucker 1969, p. 44. There are two unsupported inferences in Wood's argument here. Wood's translation of '*Unrecht*' (wrong)' as 'wrong or injustice' (like its translation in Marx 1976 as 'injustice', which would be: '*Ungerechtigkeit*') portrays Marx as denying that the capitalist treats the seller of labour power unjustly. All that Marx denies is that the capitalist wrongs them. (To regard conduct as unjust, one need not blame someone as doing wrong). Second, to say that the capitalist does no wrong 'to the seller' is not to say that by this transaction they do no wrong. Neither the concept of a wrong nor the concept of an injustice presupposes the violation of an individual's right.

184   Young 1978, p. 439.

185   Cohen 1983a, p. 443; compare Cohen 1995, p. 146.

186   Mill 1962, p. 79. Cohen seems unwilling to entertain Mill's view as a view about justice. Cohen says: '[i]f freedom of speech is a dictate of justice, then a wrongly silenced would-be speaker has a *special* grievance when he is silenced' (Cohen 2008, p. 289).

does the literature on libertarianism make the mistake of assuming that a duty of justice has, by its very concept, a correlative right. '[L]ibertarians', as Peter Vallentyne notes, 'all hold that the only enforceable duties are interpersonal duties', where interpersonal duties are duties that are not 'impersonal duties'.[187] But this view, Vallentyne notes, is a 'controversial claim'.[188] It would be perverse to hold that those who do not define justice so as to make this libertarian premise true by definition fail to appreciate the 'neutral' character of the definition that would do so.

In the domain of property, the correlativity premise must be rejected. Theft or stealing is wrongful appropriation. But wrongful appropriation need not imply the violation of a right. If I steal the only copy of a book in the public domain, no one is at liberty to use it as they please. But I steal it nonetheless. Likewise, the theft of unallocated tickets to a public gallery need not violate a liberty. Would-be ticket-holders are not at liberty to enter, and the gallery may be duty-bound to admit the public.[189]

The correlativity premise is no more theoretically neutral than the concept of an economic good. It excludes all theories of justice that acknowledge enforceable duties to the whole. Marx's remark in the *Grundrisse* that 'the capitalist usurps the free time created by workers for society'[190] allows that Marx, too, rejected the correlativity premise in the domain to which the charge of capitalist labour-exploitation belongs, if 'society' is wronged. The Anglophone debate on Marx and justice has failed not only to identify the domain in which capitalist exploitation is located, but also to adopt a conception of justice suitable for assessing Marx's pronouncements.

Let us turn the tables on this debate. In 1981, Cohen claimed that 'the language of natural (or moral) rights is the language of justice, and whoever takes justice seriously must accept that there are natural rights'.[191] Later, however, in *Self-Ownership, Freedom and Equality*, Cohen allows justice to include enforceable duties that are not correlatives of rights. Having said of the case in which I have a non-contractual moral obligation to assist my mother if she falls ill that 'my having an obligation to her need not mean that my mother has any right against me',[192] Cohen says that a similar point can be made about the legal obligation of a state. If a state 'has a duty to tax' because 'the socialist constitu-

---

187   Vallentyne 2012, pp. 152–3; on 'impersonal duty', see ch. 3, sec. 4.
188   Vallentyne 2012, p. 153. Cohen acknowledges this at one point, too (Cohen 2008, p. 289).
189   Compare Jellinek 1919, p. 75.
190   *MEW*, 42, p. 534; *MECW*, 29, p. 22; Marx, 1973a, p. 634.
191   Cohen 1981a, p. 12.
192   Cohen 1995, p. 232.

tion requires the state to tax redistributively',[193] that does not mean that that duty is owed to some person with a right (to have the state set taxes).

Similarly, away from the context of Marx and exploitation, Wood says: '[i]n Kant's theory, the fact that nonrational beings have no rights does not entail that the general will of a state may not legislate restrictions on how they may be used or treated'.[194] Wood's point here is that, within a Kantian account of justice, there is room for duties that do not have correlative rights; for example, a duty not to hunt and kill members of an endangered animal species, which does not give animals (or non-hunters) rights. If Wood's point here is granted, namely, that there is a plausible account of justice on which not all duties of justice are correlative to rights, the entire Anglophone debate on Marx and justice is compromised.[195]

Cohen's and Wood's contributions to the Anglophone debate on Marx and justice are informed by a conception of justice that lacks the virtues claimed for it, and that *they themselves* do not always affirm. The only fitting response to the fashionable but superficial claim that this debate has cemented, therefore, that 'Marx did not always realize that he thought capitalism was unjust',[196] is that of a riposte: interpreters of Marx do not always realise that they think about justice like economists. Marxists who believe that Marx is confused about justice are themselves confused about justice.

---

193   Cohen 1995, p. 234.
194   Wood 1998, p. 192.
195   In a recent article discussing Marx's account of capitalist exploitation *and* Kant's account of how it is possible to 'do wrong without wronging any assignable person' (Wood 2017, p. 652), the *only* argument Wood offers to support his claim that Marx 'explicitly denies that capitalist exploitation is unjust' (Wood 2017, p. 641) is that 'implicit in the claim that capitalist exploitation is unjust' is the idea that 'the state is the mechanism for rectifying it' (Wood 2017, p. 655). Now, in Marx's view, 'the bourgeois state is merely the coercive mechanism through which the bourgeoisie imposes its class rule' (ibid.). So, if the affirmation of a principle of justice implied a commitment to its enforcement by (a modified version of) the bourgeois state, Marx could not, consistently with this view, affirm any anti-capitalist principle of justice. But affirmation of a principle of justice merely implies a commitment to its enforcement by a public power. Marx's praise for the 'communal constitution' (*MECW*, 22, p. 332) of the Paris Commune suggests that Marx believed that a revolutionary process may produce a new form of coercive public power that organises the previously disempowered and does not prioritise the protection of private property. If so, Marx can affirm a principle of justice without placing any faith in efforts to reform the bourgeois state. But then no implication of its enforcement prevents Marx from affirming an anti-capitalist principle that condemns capitalist exploitation as unjust. Wood's argument reads as an *ad hoc* defence of a thesis (Marx did not condemn capitalism as unjust) whose premise (the correlativity premise) Wood is no longer able to rely on.
196   Cohen 1983a, p. 444.

14   Summary

The system universalisability conception of exploitation is defended on the following grounds. What it identifies, in capitalism, as capitalist labour-exploitation, is
(1)   a systemic feature, not a merely individual trait
(2)   fundamental to the commodity form, not a contingent condition or consequence
(3)   activity of which a rate of surplus value can be an expression
(4)   suggestive of a solution to the agency problem
Further, the system universalisability conception of exploitation
(5)   identifies other kinds of exploitation (that Marx identified)
while its associated system universalisability principle of justice
(6)   rests on the value of self-legislative human community
(7)   offers a solution to the exploitation and need problem
(8)   offers a solution to the capitalism, rights and injustice problem
(9)   facilitates a critique of the Anglophone debate on Marx and justice from the perspective of commodity form philosophy.

CHAPTER 9

Recognition and Self-Ownership

In *The Gift*, Marcel Mauss reports that, in some early societies, a refusal to give or a refusal to accept a gift was thought to lead to illness or death, and could even be understood as a declaration of war.[1] Reciprocating a gift was viewed by clan members to confer authority and power on the donor.[2] In these various ways, gift-giving in early societies displayed a social significance irreducible to its effect in distributing goods.

From one angle, the system of capitalist production presents a marked contrast with such societies. Commodity exchange is conducted for the sole purpose of acquisition. Yet, even though (or rather just because) commodity exchangers' in-order-to motives are to acquire commodities or money, purchase and sale has an unintended social significance. It exhibits a kind of as-if mutual recognition that helps sustain, on the part of persons, a belief in the principle of self-ownership.

In chapter 8, it was argued that a society based on the system of capitalist production lacks self-legislative human community. However, that is not to say that this system yields no sense of community. Marx's *Economic and Philosophic Manuscripts of 1844* remark: 'under the semblance of the recognition [*Schein einer Anerkennung*] of the human being, national economy, whose principle is labour, is merely the consequential implementation of the denial of the human being'.[3] This chapter concerns the first part of Marx's remark. Notwithstanding Marx's judgement of production for money maximisation, what kind of recognition does purchase and sale exhibit, and what are its consequences?

Marx claims that commodity exchange exhibits a kind of recognition on two key occasions. Marx does not elaborate a conception of recognition to underpin this claim, however. Section 1 attempts to fill this gap, by outlining a pragmatic conception of recognition. Section 2 then draws attention to the peculiarity of Marx's conception of private property ownership in *Capital* Chapter Two: private property ownership is distinct, by virtue of recognition, both from commodity possession, and from law. Section 3 employs the pragmatic conception of recognition outlined in section 1 to defend this conception of private

---

1 Mauss 1954, p. 9, p. 11.
2 Mauss 1954, p. 10.
3 *MEW*, 40, pp. 530–1; *MECW*, 3, p. 291.

property ownership. It defends the idea that commodity exchange is characterised by the as-if mutual recognition of *animus domini*. Section 4 argues that such recognition implies the as-if mutual recognition of personhood. Finally, section 5 suggests that this as-if mutual recognition can lead actors to identify themselves as persons in virtue of commodity exchangers' social interest in security. If actors identify themselves as persons, then they will be led to affirm a principle of self-ownership.

1   A Pragmatic Conception of Recognition

In English there are three uses of the verb 'to recognise': (i) to identify someone or something already known or previously encountered (to recognise someone in a photo, for example); (ii) to cognise that something is so (to recognise the fact that x); and (iii) to appreciate someone or something as having a valued quality (for example, to recognise someone's achievements).[4] The German verbs for (i) are '*erkennen*' or '*wiedererkennen*', rather than '*anerkennen*'. The German '*anerkennen*' is only used for (ii)[5] or (iii).

A further distinction can be drawn within the evaluative use of '*anerkennen*'.[6] (iii) encompasses both the activity of acknowledging correctness (such as acknowledging the correctness of an opinion), as well as conduct that amounts to behaving appropriately to another. To interrupt a judge mid-flow by shouting 'yes, that's right!' would acknowledge the correctness of their opinion. But it would not be considered appropriate behaviour. To oversee a learning environment in which learners can make mistakes without being made fun of may be to treat them appropriately. But it need not acknowledge the correctness of their opinion. Unless explicitly indicated, the English word 'recognition' is reserved, from now on, for the evaluative-conduct-based use of '*anerkennen*'.

Arto Laitinen distinguishes two conceptions of recognition, a 'practical' and a 'symbolic' conception:

> The term 'recognition' can be taken to refer to the ethically adequate or
> inadequate *treatment* of persons, or to the treatment as interpreted to be

---

4   Compare Inwood 1992, p. 245. The final three meanings on Inwood's list are incorporated in
    (iii).
5   As when Marx remarks in the *Grundrisse* that a 'common interest' served in exchange is
    'recognised as a fact by both sides; but, as such, it is not the motive' (*MEW*, 42, p. 170; *MECW*,
    28, p. 176; Marx 1973a, p. 244).
6   See Kelsen 2008, p. 485.

an implicit delivery of a *message*: 'you are z and you ought to be treated accordingly' (for example, 'you are a person', 'you are a person with certain kinds of merit', 'you are a special person to me'). Let us call these the practical and symbolic conceptions of recognition.

The practical notion of recognition can be paraphrased as: 'A *treats* B in accordance with B's z-hood'. The symbolic notion can be paraphrased as: 'A reveals to B that A thinks that B is z and ought to be treated accordingly'. This 'revealing' can be implicit in the non-verbal treatment, there is no need to think dualistically that there are separate symbolic acts distinct from other behaviour. 'Reading' the message is a matter of interpreting how the recognizee is taken into account in the motives of the recognizer.[7]

I shall argue that neither the practical nor the symbolic conception of recognition is a satisfactory conception of the evaluative-conduct-based use of '*anerkennen*'.

The distinguishing feature of what Laitinen calls the 'practical' conception of recognition is that it suspends judgement about the recogniser's normative beliefs. Whether the recogniser believes that they ought to treat the other as they do ('ethically adequate'), or whether the recogniser has no such normative belief ('ethically inadequate') is immaterial, on the practical conception of recognition. All that matters is that the recogniser's conduct in regard to another is appropriate. The practical conception of recognition is distinct from the symbolic conception, for 'acting merely *as if* one has the attitudes is not the same as having the attitudes'.[8]

The problem with the practical conception of recognition is that, like the other senses of '*anerkennen*' listed above, recognition is a kind of judgement. To say that A recognises the fact that B has died is not to say that A merely acts if they believed that B has died. Similarly, to acknowledge the correctness of another's opinion is to do more than pay lip-service to its correctness. By the same token, if A recognises B, it must be possible for B to assume that A has normative beliefs as to how they ought to treat B in a given situation. B would revise their view that A had recognised them if B was to learn that A lacked mental capacity or that A simultaneously whispered something to C contrary to how A's behaviour otherwise appeared to B. The practical conception of recognition denies that any such revision of view would be required. This illustrates why it is not plausible.

---

7   Laitinen 2002, p. 465.
8   Laitinen 2011, p. 313.

The 'symbolic' conception of recognition avoids this objection. It requires conduct to be seen to involve a kind of judgement. It insists that a recognisee attributes normative beliefs to a recogniser in light of the latter's conduct. Three beliefs must be attributed by the recognisee to the recogniser. One belief is that personhood, or else a particular characteristic, or else a specific individual, is of value. A second belief is that the recognisee is a person, or has the particular characteristic, or is the specific individual, that is valued. The third belief is the belief that this fact ought to bear on the recogniser's actions in the given situation.

The objection to the symbolic conception of recognition is not *that* it requires the recognisee to attribute these three beliefs to the recogniser. Rather, the objection relates to the account of *how* a recognisee is led to attribute these beliefs to the recogniser.

On Laitinen's account of the symbolic conception of recognition, it is less than clear how the recognisee is to attribute these beliefs to the recogniser. Does the recognisee attribute these beliefs to the recogniser *in light of* behaviour that provides 'an implicit delivery of a *message*' about the recogniser's beliefs? Or is it rather the case, on the symbolic conception, that these beliefs are attributed to the recogniser in virtue of the recognisee's assumption that they *inform* the recogniser's behaviour, and so feature in its 'motives'? These are different elaborations.

'Expressive movements'[9] can provide an 'implicit delivery of a *message*'. If I see you blush, I may know that you believe you have been embarrassed. But expressive movements are not intentional. Blushing is not something done in order to achieve something else. Contrariwise, action that cannot be construed as an implicit delivery of a message may still lead a recognisee to attribute to a recogniser the normative beliefs that recognition is said to require. Let it be granted that action *without* any communicative intent can provide an 'implicit' delivery of a message about an actor's beliefs. For Laitinen (in a piece co-authored with Heikki Ikäheimo) distinguishes recognition 'in a broad sense' from recognition 'in a more limited sense', and argues that the former may be present 'even if *expressing* recognitive attitudes is not among the purposes of the action at all'.[10] Even granting this, action done with the specific intention that it *not* be communicated to another (for example, entries in a private diary) cannot be regarded even as an implicit delivery of a message to another. Yet a private diary can fall into the hands of someone who interprets the in-order-to

---

9   Schütz 2004, pp. 104–6, 245; Schütz 1967, pp. 22–3, 116.
10   Ikäheimo and Laitinen 2007, p. 44.

motive of an entry to be informed by normative beliefs about them. *A* may read an entry in *B*'s private diary which begins: 'I am writing this down to remind myself to treat *A* better'.

The cases of expressive movements or private diary entries are not brought forward as paradigm cases of recognition. Rather, they highlight the unacknowledged conceptual difference in the two elaborations that are offered for what is supposed to be one and the same symbolic conception of recognition. To hold that a recognisee attributes beliefs to a recogniser on account of behaviour by them that delivers a message about their beliefs is a different elaboration of how a recognisee attributes beliefs to a recogniser than an elaboration that appeals to an assumption on the part of the recognisee about the recogniser's 'motives'.

Only the *delivery-of-a-message elaboration* of the symbolic conception reflects Laitinen's true position, for two reasons. One reason is that Ikäheimo and Laitinen claim that 'actions … are not a necessary constituent of recognition at all'.[11] This directly rules out the *motive elaboration*. No normative beliefs can be taken to inform a recogniser's in-order-to motive unless they are taken to perform action. By contrast, as expressive movements show, some forms of behaviour can deliver a message about an actor's beliefs although they are not oriented to an in-order-to motive, and hence are not actions. If action is just a vehicle to deliver a message to the recognisee about the recogniser's normative beliefs, it is unnecessary if there are alternative ways to deliver that message (as indeed there may be).

The second reason why only the delivery-of-a-message elaboration reflects Laitinen's true position is that only it elaborates a conception of recognition that deserves to be called 'symbolic'. A conception of recognition is symbolic if it takes action that treats another appropriately to be just a symbol or test of what really constitutes recognition. For Laitinen, 'recognizing is a matter of having the *attitudes*', and '[a]ctions are a test of whether one genuinely has the attitudes'.[12] To hold that recognition is provided when an in-order-to motive is taken to be informed by certain normative beliefs is *not* to view action as just a symbol of what really constitutes recognition. The action is then constitutive of recognition. On the motive elaboration, to take the action out of recognition would be to deprive recognition of its medium.

From now on, the symbolic conception of recognition is identified with the delivery-of-a-message elaboration of how a recognisee attributes normative

---

11   Ibid.
12   Laitinen 2011, p. 313.

beliefs to the recogniser. The objection to this symbolic conception of recognition is that behaviour must do something other than deliver a message about its actor's beliefs, if it is to lead to recognition.

The argument for this objection proceeds from the premise that all interpretation in the social world is 'pragmatically conditioned',[13] in Schütz's phrase. In other words, the segment of another's behaviour that an actor singles out for interpretation depends on its relevance to the plans that this actor is pursuing; that is, on its relevance to their 'conscious life activity'.[14] One implication of this premise is that the extent to which A views others' behaviour as extending positive evaluation to A will depend on the standards A takes to apply to a given situation, as the latter is interpreted through the visor of A's plans. The crucial point is that the standards A applies are not simply standards concerning the beliefs that it is appropriate to communicate. They include other standards of appropriate conduct besides. If, for example, A has joined a queue, A will be less concerned with whether people communicate, expressly or implicitly, a belief in the rule of first come, first served, than in whether they observe it. If A views the situation as one in which it is appropriate for B to let A back in the queue once A has caught up with their runaway toddler, that action by B is an object of normative expectation in its own right, irrespective of whether the beliefs that A attributes to B suffice for recognition.

As the standards of appropriate conduct that A takes to apply to a given situation may include standards other than those about what message it is appropriate for others to communicate (implicitly or explicitly), what the symbolic conception of recognition counts as recognition, may not suffice for recognition. Depending on A's plans, it may be irrelevant to the fulfilment of the expectations arising from A's interpretation of the situation and the standards A thereby takes to apply, that A is aware that B is of a certain belief. The treatment that B's belief would warrant may still not be forthcoming from B. If the absence of conduct by B that B's belief would warrant foils A's plans on account of violating the standards A took to apply to the situation, A will not experience recognition from B.[15] If A is aware that B is of the belief that B ought to have done what they did not do, A's disappointment may be mitigated (although, if B's omission persists, there may come a point at which it will cease to be believable, for A, that B does in fact have that belief). But even so, A's awareness of B's belief, in combination with whatever was the vehicle for it, cannot suffice for

13   Schütz 2004, p. 201; Schütz 1967, p. 90.
14   *MEW*, 40, p. 516; *MECW*, 3, p. 276.
15   Compare Honneth 2003, pp. 221–2; Honneth 1995, p. 137.

recognition, if it is consistent with A's awareness that B has foiled their plans by not acting on it. The symbolic conception of recognition must be rejected, because, being an object of normative expectation in its own right, the function of action for recognition is more than just symbolic.

The pragmatic conception of recognition can avoid this objection. On the pragmatic conception of recognition, recognition requires a recognisee to take note of the recogniser's conduct, to interpret it as action that amounts to appropriate conduct, and to be able to view it as informed by normative beliefs about them.[16] The pragmatic conception of recognition, like the symbolic conception, does not suspend judgement about the recogniser's normative beliefs. It insists that the beliefs that the symbolic conception has the recognisee attribute to the recogniser are attributed. But it also rests on the premise that all interpretation in the social world is pragmatically conditioned. The recognisee must be able to experience the recogniser's conduct as extending positive evaluation to them, by virtue of the in-order-to motive they can ascribe to it, in light of their projects and stock of experiences (including their experiences of the recogniser, and/or of actors of a relevant type). The recognisee attributes beliefs to the recogniser by attributing them with an in-order-to motive that implies those beliefs, either by virtue of its goal, or its means.

The pragmatic conception of recognition differs not just from the practical and symbolic conceptions of recognition outlined by Laitinen, but also from Honneth's *expressive* conception of recognition. Honneth argues in *The Struggle for Recognition*:

> acts of recognition represent a distinctive phenomenon in the social world that is accordingly not to be understood as a by-product of an otherwise directed action [*andersgerichteten Handlung*], but rather must be grasped as the expression of an independent intention; whether we are talking of gestures, speech-acts or institutional procedures, expressions or measures are only cases of 'recognition' if their primary purpose is in some way positively directed to the existence of another person or group. This conceptual pre-commitment excludes, for example, counting as a form of 'recognition' the positive attitudes that unavoidably accompany the pursuit of a series of other interactional interests: if I have a strong desire to play chess regularly with a particular person, that probably

---

16   The recogniser's conduct need not consist of action *to the recognisee*; A may see B advance A's cause vis-à-vis C (whether or not B sees A).

expresses a special esteem for their intellectual abilities; but the primary purpose of my action's intention is directed at playing chess together.[17]

Honneth's conception of recognition here is neither practical nor symbolic. Contrary to the practical conception of recognition, Honneth does not abstract from a recogniser's normative beliefs. Contrary to the symbolic conception, action, for Honneth, is not merely a symbol of what really constitutes recognition. But further, and contrary to the pragmatic conception of recognition, Honneth requires recognition to provide an action's 'primary purpose'. For Honneth, only action whose primary purpose is to express a positive evaluation of another, counts as recognition. On the pragmatic conception of recognition, by contrast, it is immaterial whether a recognisee attributes normative beliefs to the recogniser in virtue of what they take to be the recogniser's goal, or in virtue of what they take to be the recogniser's choice of means to that goal. (It is also immaterial whether or not the action that leads a recognisee to attribute normative beliefs to the recogniser exhibits any communicative intent, towards the recognisee or to anyone else).

From the perspective of a pragmatic conception of recognition, two responses can be offered to Honneth's expressive conception. One is that Honneth misconstrues the force of his example. Suppose A plays chess regularly with B. B has licence to attribute to A the belief: 'it is worthwhile for me, A, to play chess with B'. By implication, B has licence to attribute to A the belief: 'B's intellectual abilities are such that it is worthwhile for me, A, to play chess with B'. But B does not have licence to attribute to A the belief: 'I ought to treat B in a way appropriate to B's intellectual abilities'. On *any* conception of recognition that requires normative beliefs to be attributed to the recogniser, B is not recognised by A. For those who share Honneth's judgement that B is not recognised by A, the example has no force in deciding between conceptions of recognition that require normative beliefs to be attributed to the recogniser.

The second response is that it is misguided to reject a pragmatic for an expressive conception of recognition on the basis that, because the pragmatic conception does not require recognition to be an action's primary purpose, it fails to capture the 'distinctive' character of recognition as a 'phenomenon of the social world'. It is false that a phenomenon is only distinctive of the social world if it provides an action's primary purpose. Expressive movements are a

---

17 Honneth 2003, p. 319; Honneth 2002, p. 506. The Honneth 2002 translation of '*anders-gerichteten Handlung*' as 'other-directed action' (which would be: '*anderer gerichtete Handlung*') is misleading. The adjective '*andersgerichtet-*' denotes a different aim, not an orientation to another human being. Only 'otherwise directed' fits with 'by-product'.

distinctive phenomenon of the social world, but they are never the primary purpose of an action. The social world certainly includes occasions on which a formally prescribed mode of procedure is specifically set aside for the purpose of ensuring that actors give special thought to the consequences they are incurring (for example, marriage vows). But as the social world cannot be reduced to the following of formal procedures, an expressive conception of recognition that requires recognition to be an action's primary purpose is artificially over-demanding.

A final point about the pragmatic conception of recognition is that some recognition may be mutual. No actor can value another's positive evaluation of themselves if, in the situation as they interpret it, the other is of lower value than themselves. Recognition can only come from someone the recognisee regards as at least their equal in the relevant respect. This carries a further implication, if A is to be recognised by someone, B, to whom A performs an action of social affecting. B must then feature in A's action as at least the equal of A. But if A demands recognition from B, B only features in A's action as A's equal if B features in A's action as someone who is entitled to demand the same recognition from A as A demands from B. Recognition can be mutual, therefore, if an action of social affecting by A to B that amounts to a demand for recognition from B aims to affect action by B that amounts to a demand by B for recognition from A that A must observe for A's initial action to succeed. For if it is a condition of the success of A's action that it leads to a demand by B for recognition from A that A is committed to honouring, A is committed to regarding B as someone who is entitled to demand recognition from A, and thus as their equal, and thus as someone who can recognise A; and A is also committed to recognising B. If A's action succeeds, A and B mutually recognise one another. As Hegel remarks in *Philosophy of Mind*, in mutual recognition, 'it is aware of its recognition in the free other, and is aware of this in so far as it recognizes the other and is aware that it is free'.[18]

What, then, is the effect of recognition? Honneth describes the effect of recognition as follows:

> only the person who knows that she is recognized by others can relate to herself rationally in a way that can, in the full sense of the word, be called 'free' ... [W]e can only actually direct [*verfügen*] our potential abilities if we can completely 'identify' ourselves with them ... In our recognitional attitudes, we respond appropriately to evaluative qualities that, by the

---

18   Hegel 1986d, § 436; Hegel 2007, § 436.

standards of our life-world, human subjects already possess but which they can actually direct [*aktuell verfügen können*] only once, in virtue of the experience of recognition, they can also identify themselves with them.[19]

Honneth makes two important claims: (i) recognition enables a recognisee to identify themselves with the qualities for which they are recognised; (ii) this identification permits a free self-relation that was not previously possible.

One elaboration of these claims, inspired by Frankfurt, to whom Honneth refers,[20] is to say that recognition enables a recognisee to take a certain attitude to their wants. Recognition allows a recognisee to want to be moved 'all the way to action'[21] that exercises the quality for which they are recognised. If an actor wants to be moved all the way to action, they can exercise 'freedom of the will'.[22] They can seek to bring the actions they actually pursue into line with what they want to be moved all the way to do.

Take, first, the claim that recognition allows a recognisee to identify themselves with a quality for which they are recognised. To be recognised is to take note of another's positive evaluation of oneself. It is natural for A to value qualities of A that are objects of esteem for others in the respect in which A holds them in esteem. But if A, too, values one of their qualities, it must make a difference to A if A fails to exercise it appropriately in what A interprets as an appropriate situation in which to exercise it.[23] A's attitude may exceed a sense of pleasure that A has a want to exercise a quality for which A is recognised (for example, A's sense of pleasure that A wants to tidy the house before visitors arrive). A's attitude may extend to wanting to be moved all the way to action that exercises that quality (A wants to be moved all the way to tidy the house before visitors arrive). In wanting to be moved all the way to this action, A can hope that there will be a value to what A will have done.

Suppose an actor is disposed, by the recognition they receive, to be moved all the way to exercise one of their qualities in the situations in which they deem

---

19   Honneth 2003, pp. 325–7; Honneth 2002, pp. 509–10. Honneth 2002 omits the second sentence. I can make no sense of its final sentence without replacing 'evaluative qualities' with 'abilities' (that are to be evaluated). The Honneth 2002 translation of '*aktuell verfügen können* (can actually direct)' as 'are actually available' (which might be: '*aktuell vorhanden sind*') is too vague; '*verfügen*' literally means 'to dispose over'.

20   Honneth 2003, p. 327; Honneth 2002, p. 510.

21   Frankfurt 1971, p. 8.

22   Frankfurt 1971, p. 15.

23   What A judges as an appropriate situation may depend, among other things, on their opinion of the reason why others positively evaluate that quality.

its exercise appropriate. They may then seek to bring the actions they actually perform into line with what they want to be moved all the way to do.

Two implications can be noted. First, an actor may withdraw from a want of theirs that is simply given. That is, they can give it no weight in their deliberation of what to do. If, for example, A wants, in conditions of visitors' impending arrival, to be moved all the way to tidy the house, and, in what A interprets as an instance of visitors' impending arrival, A wants to watch television, and A judges that it is impossible both to watch television and to tidy the house before their visitors arrive, A can withdraw from their want to watch television. As A believes it would lessen the value of what they will have done if A were not to tidy the house, A will not want their want to watch television to interfere. Second, an actor can prioritise between different actions they are moved all the way to do on grounds other than the intensity of their wants. Suppose A wants to be moved all the way to tidy the house before visitors arrive, *and* to watch the news at election time. If A judges that it would be impossible to watch election time news and to tidy the house before their visitors arrive, A may decide to watch the election time news, even if A's want to tidy the house is greater, provided A deems watching the election time news more important. A's judgement will depend on A's projects, stock of experiences, and interpretation and evaluation of the reasons for why their qualities are recognised.

In sum, ongoing recognition enables actors to develop dispositions to be moved all the way to exercise the qualities for which they are recognised. They need neither act purely on the relative strengths of their wants, nor randomly select one want to pursue over another. What kinds of qualities tend to be recognised, and so what kinds of action actors tend to be moved all the way to do, will vary from one form of society and context to another.

2   Possession, Private Property Ownership and Recognition

There are two key passages in which Marx says that commodity exchange exhibits a kind of recognition, one in *Capital* Chapter Two and the second in *Marginal Notes on Adolph Wagner's Lehrbuch der politischen Ökonomie* ('Notes on Wagner'). They are best studied together:

> Commodities cannot go to market and exchange themselves. We must therefore turn to their keepers, the commodity possessors [*Warenbesitzern*] ... In order to relate these things to one another as commodities, the commodity keepers must relate to one another as persons whose will resides in those things, such that it is only with the other's will, and thus

by means of an act of will common to both [*beiden gemeinsamen Willensakt*], that each appropriates the alien commodity, by alienating their own commodity. They must therefore mutually recognise [*anerkennen*] one another as private property owners [*Privateigentümer*]. This relation of right [*Rechtsverhältnis*], whose form is contract, whether legally developed or not, is a relation of will in which the economic relation is mirrored. The content of this relation of right or relation of will is given by the economic relation itself.[24]

For him [Wagner – JF], first there is law [*Recht*] and then there is commerce [*Verkehr*]; in reality, it's the other way around: first there is *commerce*, and then a *legal order* develops out of it. In the course of the analysis of commodity circulation I have shown that, in developed barter, the exchangers recognise [*anerkennen*] one another tacitly as equal persons and owners of the respective goods they are to exchange; they already *do* this while offering their goods to one another and reaching agreement on the deal. This *de facto* [*faktische*] relation, first arising through and in exchange itself, later receives *legal form* in contract, etc.; but this form creates neither its content – the exchange – nor the *relation of persons to one another existing* in it, but vice versa.[25]

---

24   *MEW*, 23, p. 99; *MECW*, 35, pp. 94–5; Marx 1976, p. 178. (1) '[B]*eiden gemeinsamen Willensakt*' is translated in *MECW* as 'act done by mutual consent' (which would be: '*Handlung im gegenseitigen Einvernehmen*') and in Marx 1976 as 'act to which both parties consent' (which would be: '*Akt dem beide Parteien zustimmen*'). Both of these translations lose the association with the 'relation of will to will' or 'common will' in Hegel's *Elements of the Philosophy of Right* (Hegel 1986b, § 71; Hegel 1991a, § 71). (2) Both, by translating '*Rechtsverhältnis*' as 'juridical relation', lose the association with what Hegel there called 'abstract right [*das abstrakte Recht*]' (Hegel 1986b, § 34; Hegel 1991a, § 34). (3) *MECW* says that each recognises 'the rights of private proprietors' (which would be: '*Rechte der Privateigentümer*'). But Marx does not mention 'rights' here. Marx is seeking to identify a kind of recognition that *explains* the capitalist legal order. This recognition *cannot* be a recognition of rights, for that would presuppose what was to be explained. (4) *MECW* translates '*Warenbesitzer*' as 'owners' (which would be: '*Eigentümer*'). The distinction between commodity possession (which does not require anything like recognition) and private property ownership (which does) is crucial to Marx's argument, however.

25   *MEW*, 19, p. 377; *MECW*, 24, pp. 553–4; Marx 1975b, p. 210. (1) The *MECW* and Marx 1975b translations of 'faktisch' as 'actual' or 'practical' respectively (which would be: '*wirklich*' or '*praktisch*') are unhelpful. The contrast is between what is *de facto* and what is *de jure* (compare the contrastive use of '*faktisch*' and '*rechtlich*' in Savigny 1837, p. 3; Savigny 1848, p. 3), not between what is actually done and what is potentially doable, or between practice and theory. (2) *MECW* renders '*anerkennen*' as 'acknowledge'. The reader is left unaware that Marx is using the same verb as in the aforecited passage from *Capital*. (3) Marx's

One common feature of these passages is that the connection they draw between commodity exchange and mutual recognition is not, in the first instance, a connection between commodity exchange and the mutual recognition of legal rights. Both passages say that there is a kind of mutual recognition in commodity exchange that does not, conceptually, presuppose law. Call this the *de facto recognition claim*. If these passages advance the *de facto* recognition claim, it would be incorrect to gloss them simply by saying: 'it is crucial that the owners of commodities should respect each other's property rights'.[26]

There are two pieces of evidence for interpreting the above passages as advancing the *de facto* recognition claim. One piece of evidence is Marx's insistence that commodity exchange exhibits a kind of mutual recognition irrespective of whether the agreement through which it occurs has a form that is 'legally developed'. Any kind of mutual recognition common to an agreement with a legally developed form and an agreement without a legally developed form cannot be the mutual recognition of anything legal, such as legal property rights bestowed by a constituted power. It must be the mutual recognition of something '*de facto*'.

The second piece of evidence is Marx's insistence that 'a *legal order* develops out of' the mutual recognition attached to commodity exchange, or that the latter 'creates' the '*legal form*' it receives. If commodity exchange is to exhibit a kind of mutual recognition that explains the legal order of capitalism, the mutual recognition it exhibits cannot be described in terms that presuppose any of the rights of that order, for that would be to presuppose what was to be explained.

The only terms in these passages that, taken in isolation, could sustain an objection to the *de facto* recognition claim, are 'private property owners/owners' and 'relation of right'. But they, too, can be accounted for, on the current interpretation.

The objection related to the term 'private property owners' is that the statement 'they must therefore mutually recognise one another as private property owners' implies that what commodity exchangers recognise is not non-legal.

---

comment beginning 'I have shown' refers back to *Capital* Chapter Two: '[f]or this alienation [i.e. an immediate exchange of products – JF] to be reciprocal, human beings must merely confront one another tacitly as private property owners of those alienable things, and thereby as independent persons' (*MEW*, 23, p. 102; *MECW*, 35, p. 98; Marx 1976, p. 182). An immediate exchange of products is 'developed' barter relative to barter of 'a chaotic mass of things as equivalent for another thing' (*MEW*, 23, p. 102; *MECW*, 35, p. 98; Marx 1976, p. 181).

26   Collins 1982, p. 108; compare point (3) two footnotes back.

The objection has three premises. The first is that, if the recogniser and recognisee of a kind of mutual recognition are defined by a legal status, that recognition cannot be non-legal. The second is that private property ownership is (for Marx) a legal status. As Emil Angehrn puts it, 'property is the legally legitimated, circumscribed form of possession secured by the state'.[27] The third is that *Capital* describes the recogniser and recognisee of the mutual recognition that accompanies commodity exchange as 'private property owners'. The conclusion is that the mutual recognition that *Capital* identifies as accompanying commodity exchange cannot be non-legal. (The same premises must lie behind the objection that the use of 'owners' in *Notes on Wagner* implies that recognition in commodity exchange is not *de facto*, but a recognition of legal property rights).

To rebut this objection, it is necessary to dispute the premise that private property ownership is a legal status, at least in the above passage. Now, Marx did at least *sometimes* use the term 'property' to denote something other than a legal status. *The German Ideology* claims that a thing 'only becomes a thing, actual property, in commerce [*Verkehr*], and independently of law [*Recht*]'.[28] The issue here, however, is whether 'private property owners' is used *in the above passage* from *Capital* to denote something other than a legal status. The argument for this is that *Capital* says that it is 'commodity possessors' or 'commodity keepers' who mutually recognise one another as 'private property owners'. As argued in chapter 7, possession is possible even in the absence of law. Its two conditions, detention and *animus domini*, can be described in non-legal terms. If possession is defined in non-legal terms, so can commodity possessors' actions. As the mutual recognition exhibited by commodity exchange consists of action by commodity possessors, it, too, can be grasped in non-legal terms. If actions of mutual recognition by commodity possessors turn commodity possession into private property ownership, 'private property owners' can denote a *de facto* status. Insofar as *Notes on Wagner* is an explication of what Marx says in *Capital*, its use of 'owners' can also denote a *de facto* status.[29]

Capital's non-standard use of 'private property owners' has a clear motivation. Marx needs a new term, distinct from commodity possession, if he is to identify a kind of *de facto* mutual recognition in commodity exchange. For it

---

27 Angehrn 1989, p. 96; see, similarly, Lohmann 1991, p. 93.

28 *MEJ*, 2003, p. 97; *MEW*, 3, p. 63; *MECW*, 5, p. 91. Note the similarity between this claim, and the second clause in the first sentence of the passage from *Notes on Wagner*, which uses the same pair of terms: '*Recht*' and '*Verkehr*'.

29 Henceforth, all uses of the term 'private property' without the adjective 'legal' should be understood to invoke Marx's non-standard conception of private property ownership.

would be wrong to claim that commodity exchangers mutually recognise one another as commodity possessors. The will of a commodity possessor is *animus domini*. To have *animus domini* is to have no regard to anyone else's permission or instruction in respect of a thing. To have no regard to another's permission or instruction in respect of a thing, it is both not necessary to recognise another as having a claim over some other thing, and impossible to recognise another's claim to the thing over which *animus domini* is asserted. As Savigny says:

> only he can count as a *possessor* who treats the thing whose detention he has as an *owner*, i.e. who wills to dominate it factually just as an owner is empowered to do by their right, and hence, more particularly, without willing to recognise [*anerkennen zu wollen*] another more entitled than himself.[30]

The will of a commodity possessor is not a will to recognise another. Nor does the will of a commodity possessor, *animus domini*, presuppose the effects of a prior recognition. An actor with no experience of recognition can have a want for a thing. As an actor can be led by a want for a thing to recognise no one else's permission or instruction in respect of it, *animus domini* does not presuppose any prior recognition. To describe the will of a commodity possessor as it is modified by mutual recognition necessitates a different term. The term Marx chooses, in *Capital*, is 'private property owners'. Using the term 'private property owners' in a non-legal sense (as advertised by the phrase 'legally developed or not') suggests a connection between *de facto* mutual recognition in commodity exchange, and the bestowal of legal property rights by a constituted power.

The final phrase to be squared with the *de facto* recognition claim is 'relation of right [*Rechtsverhältnis*]'. To characterise a kind of mutual recognition or relation of will as a 'relation of right' could again be taken to imply that it is the recognition of a legal status. What needs to be shown is that the substance of *Capital*'s argument remains unaffected if its first use of this term is replaced by 'relation of will', and its second use is eliminated.

The context of *Capital*'s use of the term 'relation of right' is a claim by Hegel in Part One of *Elements of the Philosophy of Right*, entitled 'Abstract Right [*das abstrakte Recht*]'. In § 71, Hegel claims that private property owners' 'relation of will to will is the distinctive and true ground in which freedom [the freedom of

---

30   Savigny 1837, p. 113; Savigny 1848, p. 73. On the translation of this passage, see ch. 7, sec. 3.

abstract right – JF] has *existence*'.[31] *Capital* refers to an agreement between commodity possessors as a 'relation of right' to signal a critique of Hegel's account of abstract right. The substance of this critique is that the 'relation of right or relation of will' characteristic of abstract right has a content 'given' by an economic relation. The substance of this critique would remain unaltered if *Capital's* two uses of 'relation of right' were replaced or eliminated. But without the term 'relation of right', readers of *Capital* (so Marx could think) might be less inclined to identify its implicit critique of Hegel's account of abstract right. Its use is understandable, but incidental. In *Notes on Wagner*, which was not written for publication, 'relation of right' does not appear.

Capital's implicit critique of Hegel's account of abstract right may be put as follows. Hegel seeks to offer a philosophy of recognition. He seeks to defend private property ownership by appeal to the freedom established by recognition in exchange. But generalised private property ownership presupposes commodity possession; and the will of a commodity possessor is *animus domini*, which is a will not to recognise another. By incorporating a defence of private property ownership in a philosophy of recognition, Hegel founds his philosophy of recognition on a will not to recognise another. As Hegel's philosophy of recognition is founded on non-recognition, Hegel does not offer a true philosophy of recognition. The term 'relation of right' does not need to be retained to advance this critique.

In sum: *all* the phrases in the above passages from *Capital* and *Notes on Wagner* can be accounted for if these passages are read as identifying a kind of mutual recognition that does not presuppose law; that is, as advancing the *de facto* recognition claim. By contrast, the majority of phrases in the above passages *cannot* be accounted for, if law is instead assumed to inform the recognition referred to. The common thought in these two passages is that a private property owner is a commodity possessor whose *animus domini* is recognised, and that this recognised will explains the legal order of capitalism.

Alas, no reader of the official translations of *Capital* is in a position to formulate this thought. The Aveling/Moore translation directly rules it out by the sentence: 'they must, therefore, mutually recognise in each other the rights of private proprietors'. If the object of mutual recognition were something legal, such as 'rights', then its object could not be *animus domini*, and it could not explain a legal order.

The Fowkes translation discourages this thought more indirectly, through its use of the bogus term 'commodity owner/owner of commodities'. (As the

---

31   Hegel 1986b, § 71; Hegel 1991a, § 71.

Aveling/Moore translation also contains this bogus term, it also discourages the thought indirectly). As noted in chapter 7, Marx repeatedly uses the terms 'possession' or '(commodity) possessor' in *Capital* Chapter One and Chapter Two. Marx *never* uses 'commodity owner/owner of commodities'. All appearances of the latter term in translations of *Capital* prior to the aforecited passage (and elsewhere) are bogus. The aforecited passage is the first paragraph in *Capital* to use 'owner' in connection with commodity exchange. But the fact that a reader of *Capital* in translation cannot know this has a certain effect.

Mutual recognition is not mentioned in connection with ownership until Chapter Two of *Capital*. By this time, however, a reader of *Capital* in translation has encountered '(commodity) owners/owners of commodities' in its opening chapter. So, it cannot strike a reader of *Capital* in translation that ownership is constituted by a kind of recognition: if ownership is constituted by a kind of recognition, Marx would have said so in introducing the concept in *Capital* Chapter One, or else not introduced it until the moment at which it was possible to say so. This reader must assume that recognition is incidental to ownership. But having made this assumption, there is no reason to suppose that Marx has a recognition-based reason to use 'private property owners' to denote something *de facto* in *Capital* Chapter Two. As recognition is incidental to ownership, it cannot determine the nature of private property ownership. Hence, there is no recognition-based reason to suppose that Marx departs from the standard view of 'private property owners' as a legal status in *Capital* Chapter Two. If Marx has no recognition-based reason to depart from this standard view, then the legal status of 'private property owners' must determine the character of the mutual recognition to which *Capital* refers. This must appear to be backed up by the fact that the Fowkes translation describes this mutual recognition as a 'juridical relation, whose form is the contract, whether as part of a developed legal system or not'.[32] From this description, a reader could infer that a 'juridical relation' is a legal relation, and that *Capital* is advancing a claim for which it is immaterial whether the legal system of which it is a part is developed or undeveloped.[33]

---

32   Marx 1976, p. 178.

33   Marx's phrase is: '*ob nun legal entwickelt oder nicht* (whether legally developed or not)' (*MEW*, 23, p. 99). In Marx 1976, this is translated as 'whether as part of a developed legal system or not' (which would be: '*ob nun Bestandteil eines entwickelten Rechtssystems oder nicht*'). *Capital* is advancing a claim for which it is immaterial whether the form of an act of will common to two individuals is thought to be in any way legally developed. It does not mention a 'legal system'.

A reader of *Capital* Volume I in translation who nonetheless picks up on the idea, visible from a translation of *Notes on Wagner*, that commodity exchangers recognise one another as owners irrespective of legal form, is left with a puzzle. The *puzzle of recognition and ownership* is:

(1) *Capital* ch. 1 refers to ownership without mention of recognition
(2) Therefore, recognition is not constitutive of its concept of ownership
(3) Therefore, there is no recognition-based reason for *Capital* to depart from the standard concept of ownership
(4) The standard concept of ownership is that of a legal status
(5) Therefore, *Capital*'s concept of ownership is that of a legal status
(6) Therefore, the recognition of 'private property owners' in commodity exchange is the recognition of a legal status

Yet:

(7) *Notes on Wagner* says exchangers are 'owners' irrespective of *'legal form'*
(8) Therefore, the recognition of owners in commodity exchange is not the recognition of a legal status
(9) But (6) and (8) are contradictory

The puzzle of recognition and ownership is solved by correcting the official translations of *Capital*. If these translations are corrected, it is apparent that (1) is false, and if (1) is false, (2) and (3) are false, as are (5), (6) and (9). The suggested contradiction between what Marx claims in *Capital*, and what Marx claims in *Notes on Wagner*, is unfounded. But it is perhaps as a result of the translation errors that produce the puzzle of recognition and ownership that the above passage from *Capital*, which Burkhard Tuschling could refer to as 'the most prominent remark of all'[34] in German language debate on Marx's account of law, is largely unremarked upon in Anglophone works on Marx's views of law and justice.[35]

According to Marx, a private property owner is a commodity possessor whose *animus domini* is recognised; and this recognised will explains the legal order of capitalism. To develop these thoughts, it is necessary to explicate the *de facto* mutual recognition exhibited in purchase and sale, and to link it to the legal order of capitalism.

---

34 Tuschling 1976, p. 12. For early receptions (1929–32) of this passage in German language debate on Marx's account of law by authors who were notable legal theorists in their own right, see Kelsen 1931, pp. 498–9; Paschukanis 2003, pp. 112–13, p. 162; Radbruch 1987, p. 553; Radbruch 1993b, p. 364. More recent analyses include Elbe 2008, p. 357, p. 362; Lohmann 1991, pp. 249–53; Maihofer 1992, p. 194; Reichelt 2008, p. 460; Stein 2012, pp. 30–1.

35 Buchanan 1982, Cohen, Nagel and Scanlon 1980, Cohen 1978, Cohen 1988, Cohen 1995, Geras 1985, Roberts 2017, Taiwo 1996, Wood 2004, Young 1978 and Young 1981 do not remark on the passage.

3   As-If Mutual Recognition in Purchase and Sale

The first task is to describe, in non-legal terms, a kind of mutual recognition in purchase and sale. If this argument is successful, it will show that the commodity form generates a dialectic of non-recognition and recognition; that is, that commodity possessors, precisely in virtue of being unwilling to recognise anyone else in respect of their own possession, nonetheless engage in a kind of mutual recognition.

A contract of sale, according to Savigny, consists of two declarations of will whose content is in agreement.[36] A declaration of will is the signal of an intention to alter one's legal rights and/or duties. Two declarations of will are in agreement if they indicate the same generic object of sale, and same value to be given in return. A non-legal account of these actions in terms of possession was offered in chapter 5. A signals their intention to let B possess x on condition that B lets A possess y, and B signals their intention to let A possess y on condition that A lets B possess x. What now needs to be shown is that a kind of mutual recognition can be identified in these actions.

Take the first action: A's offer to let B possess x on condition that B lets A possess y. As regards A's will in respect of x, A's offer is an assertion of *animus domini* by A over x. It exhibits A's will to dispose over x independently of B's permission or instruction. It asserts that, as far as A is concerned, the only condition to which B's possession of x is subject is whether or not A agrees; no one else has a say. The same goes for what B's counter-offer or acceptance of A's initial offer displays as regards B's will in respect of y. B thereby asserts *animus domini* over y.

Now consider what A's offer to B presupposes as regards B's will in respect of y. A's offer operates on the assumption that B has *animus domini* over y. A would not make an offer for y unless A wanted to acquire possession of y by agreement. As A's offer is directed only at B, A assumes that B is the only one who must accept it for an agreement to arise. A can suppose that only B need accept their offer, to acquire possession of y by agreement, if A supposes that B possesses y. For then A and B are agreed that no one but B has a say over the disposal of x. In directing an offer for y at B, A presupposes that B has *animus domini* over y.

Nor is that all. A's offer also abides by B's *animus domini* over y. By making an offer to B, or by accepting B's counter-offer, rather than coercing or deceiving B, A refrains from upsetting the *animus domini* that A presupposes B to have over y.

---

36   Savigny 1840, pp. 5–7, pp. 307–14.

In sum: *A*'s offer is both an assertion of *A*'s *animus domini* over *x*, and a non-disruption of *B*'s presupposed *animus domini* over *y*. Likewise, *B*'s counter-offer or acceptance of *A*'s offer is both an assertion of *B*'s *animus domini* over *y*, and a non-disruption of *A*'s presupposed *animus domini* over *x*. This assertion of *animus domini* and non-disruption of the other's presupposed *animus domini* by both commodity exchangers in reaching an agreement can be likened to mutual recognition.

It is apparent, on this analysis, why actions that can be likened to mutual recognition 'first'[37] arise when exchangers make offers and strike a deal, as *Notes on Wagner* says. The assertion of *animus domini* in exchange is detached from any pursuit of ends in relation to the use-value of the object over which *animus domini* is asserted. A thing cannot be offered for exchange in some respect and at the same time consumed in that respect. So, in exchange, each possessor's *animus domini* in respect of their own possession must appear to the other as unencumbered by any of the concrete ends for which that thing, as a use-value, might be used. In virtue of that lack of encumbrance, the will of each can and must appear to the other as of the same kind as their own, that is, as a will in the determination of *animus domini*, notwithstanding the differences in the use-value of what each offers. Each therefore features in the other's action as the same type of being the other asserts themselves to be. But it is only once trade begins that each features in the other's action as just the same type of being the other simultaneously asserts themselves to be. For prior to that point, the will of each in respect of their possession must appear to the other as bound up with its particular use-value.

The actions can only be likened to mutual recognition, however. For mutual recognition to be genuine, each commodity exchanger must be able to attribute to the other the judgement: 'you are a possessor, and your *animus domini* ought to be respected'. Each commodity exchanger must be able to construe the other's in-order-to motive as: acquisition of the other's possession, by means that respect the other's *animus domini*. But there is a difficulty in this. Each must assume that the other's in-order-to motive is self-seeking acquisition.[38] As the *Grundrisse* puts it, 'the other is also recognised and known as likewise realising their self-seeking interest'.[39] If each must assume that the other's in-order-to motive is self-seeking acquisition, each must assume that the other's choice of means to that end, acquisition by agreement, is based on nothing more than

37   *MEW*, 19, p. 377; *MECW*, 24, p. 553; Marx 1975b, p. 210.
38   See ch. 7, sec. 1.
39   *MEW*, 42, p. 170; *MECW*, 28, p. 176; Marx 1973a, p. 244; compare *MEW*, 23, p. 190; *MECW*, 35, p. 186; Marx 1976, p. 280.

self-interest, if, given their own stock of experiences, each can assume that the other is aware that their interest in acquisition is promoted by such means.

Here it is relevant to recall Weber's remark that, even if 'commerce' is 'lacking any normative regulation or coercive guarantee', the transacting parties can still count on 'the other's *own interest* in the continuation of a particular consensual act as such'.[40] Ordinarily, each will want to have the chance to continue to do deals with another, and/or with others who may learn of their dealings with that other. To that end, it is necessary for A to keep enough of their side of the bargain with B to ensure that the prospect of future dealings with A is regarded as an economically desirable prospect by those with whom A may need to have future dealings. Those with whom A may need to have future dealings will not regard future dealings with A as economically desirable, however, if they know that A is likely not to meet their expectations of what it is to keep to one's side of a bargain. They will not regard future dealings with A favourably if they know that A is likely to do what any bargainer would want another to avoid: engage in coercion or deception.

A, aware that they depend on future dealings with others, and aware that the prospect of future dealings with others is made more difficult if they are known not to meet transactional expectations that anyone may have of them, has an interest in meeting those expectations. Thus, each commodity exchanger, anticipating that the other is aware that it is in their interest to meet the transactional expectations that anyone may have, can anticipate that the other will meet those expectations. By implication, each can expect that the other will not disrupt their *animus domini*. Given generalised purchase and sale, it is unlikely that anyone known to disrupt *animus domini* would be regarded as someone with whom it was desirable to have future dealings. As each commodity exchanger can expect every other to be aware of that fact, each must assume that the other's non-disruption of their *animus domini* in commodity exchange is based on self-interest. But in that case, neither commodity exchanger can attribute normative beliefs to the other, either on account of their interpretation of the other's goal, or on account of their interpretation of its means. Hence, neither can experience the other as recognising them. No recognition can occur.

It therefore cannot be the case that

> the exchange relation is in itself, as a historically determinate type of social action, a relation of right because and insofar as the participants in

---

40   Weber 2005, p. 250; Weber 1978, p. 331.

this transaction recognise one another as free and equal persons, recognise the respective objects as parts of the other's sphere of will, and, thirdly and accordingly, perform this exchange as a common act of will.[41]

Rather, in making offers and reaching agreement, everything happens *as if* commodity possessors mutually recognise one another's *animus domini*. As Evgeny Pashukanis first put it, 'the commodity possessors conduct themselves as if they recognised each other as property owners'.[42]

There are two ambiguities in the concept of as-if recognition, however. One concerns the perspective from which an actor's behaviour is judged to be consonant with what genuine recognition would be. In Andrew Chitty's conception of as-if recognition as 'my behaving towards you exactly as if I cognitively recognised the thing as yours, but without necessarily having the corresponding thoughts',[43] it is the recogniser's perspective that is adopted. Recognition is merely as-if recognition if the *recogniser* knows that they do not have the beliefs that genuine recognition would require. On a pragmatic conception of recognition, by contrast, it is the *recognisee*'s perspective that determines whether behaviour counts as genuine recognition or not. To say that behaviour is merely consonant with what genuine recognition would be is to say that an as-if recognisee cannot assume that they enjoy more than an instrumental status in an as-if recogniser's in-order-to motive.

A second ambiguity in the concept of as-if recognition concerns the determinacy with which it is denied that normative beliefs inform the recogniser's conduct. For Chitty, as-if recognition is where an actor need not have the relevant normative beliefs. In contrast, Georg Lohmann's claim that commodity exchangers 'do not act out of moral duty, but only "in accordance with duty" in Kant's sense, insofar as their self-centred actions are contingently in accord with these moral norms'[44] suggests that behaviour counts as as-if recognition if it must be taken to lack normative motivation. On the pragmatic conception of recognition defended here, as-if recognition is conduct about which an as-if recognisee *must* conclude that they have an instrumental status in the as-if recogniser's end. What makes this behaviour as-if recognition is that, with a change in the as-if recognisee's stock of experiences about the

---

41   Maihofer 1992, p. 194.

42   Paschukanis 2003, p. 162; Pashukanis 2002, p. 162. The Pashukanis 2002 translation, which
       is from the German translation, renders '*Warenbesitzer*' as 'commodity owners'. It makes
       the same mistake as the MECW and Marx 1976 translations of *Capital*.

43   Chitty 1998, p. 82.

44   Lohmann 1991, pp. 275–6.

as-if recogniser (or actors of a relevant type), they *could* interpret their behaviour as genuine recognition.

The finding that purchase and sale merely exhibits as-if mutual recognition of *animus domini* is significant, as only genuine recognition allows actors to identify themselves with their qualities. If an actor cannot assume that a quality of theirs is an object of esteem for others in the respect in which they hold those others in esteem, others' conduct will not lead them to identify themselves with it. If purchase and sale merely exhibits as-if mutual recognition of *animus domini*, it will not ensure that actors develop an attitude of wanting to be moved all the way to act independently of anyone else's instruction or permission in regard to objects over which they have detention. If the as-if mutual recognition of *animus domini* in purchase and sale is to explain the legal order of capitalism by virtue of what it leads actors to be moved all the way to do, it can only do so in conjunction with some additional factor.

4   Marx's Concept of a Person

Before seeking this additional factor, it is important to note that *animus domini* is not the only object of recognition in purchase and sale that Marx identifies. In both of the aforecited passages from *Capital* and *Notes on Wagner*, Marx claims that commodity possessors recognise one another not merely as private property owners, but also as 'persons'. Similarly, later on in *Capital* Chapter Two, Marx says that exchangers must 'confront one another tacitly as private property owners of those alienable things, and thereby [*eben dadurch*] as independent persons [*Personen*]'.[45] This comment suggests that a commodity possessor's recognition as a private property owner already implies their recognition as a person. Accordingly, if Marx's use of 'private property owners' in *Capital* Chapter Two is *de facto*, then Marx's conception of a person, here, is also *de facto*. A person is an actor whose will in respect of their parts and capacities is recognised in the respect in which it is a condition for *animus domini*.

The type of will an actor must have in respect of their parts and capacities, to have *animus domini*, is an analogous, possessing will in respect of them. *Animus domini* is a will to act independently of another's instruction or permission in regard to a thing, including in the obstruction of any uninvited effect by

---

45   *MEW*, 23, p. 102; *MECW*, 35, p. 98; Marx 1976, p. 182. (1) The Marx 1976 translation of '*eben dadurch*' as 'precisely for that reason' (which would be: '*aus eben dem Grund*') is not literal. '*Dadurch*' means 'by means of that/in consequence of that'; '*eben*' is a particle emphasising simultaneity. (2) *MECW* translates '*Personen*' as 'individuals', but that would be: '*Individuen*'.

another. But it is only by willing to exercise one's parts and capacities that one can will to act in regard to a thing. So, to will to act independently of another's instruction or permission in regard to a thing, it is necessary to will to act independently of another's instruction or permission in regard to one's parts and capacities. One could not have *animus domini* over anything, if one were to treat the exercise of one's parts and capacities as subject to the instruction or permission of someone else.

A 'person', for Marx, is an actor whose will in respect of their parts and capacities, which has no regard to anyone else's permission or instruction, is recognised. The will of a person has the same exclusive character as the will of a private property owner. The difference lies in their object. The will of a person, unlike that of a private property owner, is not a will in respect of a part of the world beyond their own parts and capacities. If private property ownership is the post-recognition term corresponding to commodity possession as its pre-recognition term, 'person' is the post-recognition term corresponding to an actor's exclusive will in respect to their parts and capacities as its pre-recognition term.

Marx's concept of a person in these passages from *Capital* and *Notes on Wagner* is highly abstract. It is know-how-indeterminate, and ends-indeterminate. It is know-how-indeterminate for the same reason that the concept of *animus domini* does not presuppose the concept of use-value. Just as it is logically possible to take possession of mere stuff that cannot be used as a means to satisfy a want, it is logically possible for a person whose parts and capacities could not be used to accomplish anything to have an exclusive will in respect of their parts and capacities. Marx's conception of a person is also ends-indeterminate for the same reason that the concept of *animus domini* is ends-indeterminate. *Animus domini* is the will to rule over an object of the external world without regard to another's permission or instruction. It does not require an actor to want to put a thing to some particular use. Likewise, a person who is recognised as the exclusive decision-maker over their parts and capacities need not have any specific end in respect of their parts and capacities. In particular, it need not be a person's end to exercise their parts and capacities for their own benefit.

Accordingly, Marx's concept of a person is not an application of what Crawford Macpherson calls 'possessive individualism'. To exhibit possessive individualism is to behave 'with a view to [one's] own interest'.[46] Marx writes in *The Holy Family*:

---

46   Macpherson 1962, p. 263.

the members of bourgeois society are not *atoms*. The atom's *characteristic property* is to have *no* properties, and hence no relationship, conditioned by its *own natural necessity*, to other entities apart from itself ... The egoistic individual of bourgeois society, in their senseless imagination and lifeless abstraction, may inflate themselves into an *atom*.[47]

The know-how-indeterminate and ends-indeterminate concept of a person can be likened to the notion of an actor as an '*atom*', rather than to the notion of an 'egoistic individual', even if it is the pursuit of self-seeking motives in purchase and sale that leads actors to think of themselves as persons.

Lohmann has argued that, if a normative critique of capitalism is to be extracted from Marx's account of recognition in commodity exchange, the scope for recognition in commodity exchange must be counterposed to human beings' 'full intersubjective recognition as persons'.[48] The critical potential of Marx's account of recognition in commodity exchange rests, for Lohmann, on the idea that, in commodity exchange, personhood is recognised regardless of whether exchangers can avail themselves of the means that would allow their unconstrained development as persons.[49] On the current interpretation, by contrast, there is, for Marx, no aspect of personhood that remains to be recognised, as regards resource distribution, beyond what the recognition of private property ownership in commodity exchange delivers. If Marx had sought to appeal to the value of personhood to criticise the limited scope for recognition in commodity exchange, he would not have claimed, in *Notes on Wagner*, that commodity exchangers recognise one another as 'equal persons'.[50] Marx would have claimed that, while commodity exchangers recognise one another as persons, they do not recognise one another as equal persons. If Marx's account of recognition in commodity exchange is to support a normative critique of capitalism, it must do so in some other manner.

5   Security and Self-Ownership

We may now return to the task left hanging at the end of section 3, which is to find a factor in conjunction with which the as-if mutual recognition of *animus domini* in purchase and sale can explain the freedom of will of a per-

---

47   *MEW*, 2, pp. 127–8; *MECW*, 4, p. 120.
48   Lohmann 1991, p. 251.
49   Lohmann 1991, p. 250, p. 289.
50   *MEW*, 19, p. 377; *MECW*, 24, p. 553.

son. The argument presented here appeals to commodity exchangers' social interest in security. Together with as-if mutual recognition of *animus domini* in purchase and sale, a social interest in security leads commodity exchangers to advocate the principle that *animus domini* accompanying detention ought to be respected. Advocacy of this principle generates a type of genuine recognition promoting the freedom of will of a person. The freedom of will of a person can thus be explained by generalised purchase and sale, without contradicting the analysis of exchange (and independent exchange) in chapter 7 as necessarily self-seeking. This freedom of will can then also explain why commodity exchangers advocate a principle of self-ownership. The argument has six steps.

The first step is to connect the as-if mutual recognition of *animus domini* in purchase and sale to the concept of an exclusive will in respect of one's parts and capacities. As *animus domini* presupposes an exclusive will in respect of one's parts and capacities, purchase and sale, by exhibiting the as-if mutual recognition of *animus domini*, exhibits the as-if mutual recognition of personhood. Purchase and sale deposits the concept of an exclusive will in respect of one's parts and capacities in commodity exchangers' stock of experiences, as a concept they can apply, non-normatively, both to themselves and all others.

Second, generalised purchase and sale ensures that commodity exchangers have a social interest in security. Marx writes in *On the Jewish Question*:

> *Security* is the highest social concept [*höchste soziale Begriff*] of bourgeois society; it is the concept of *police*, i.e. that the entire society only exists to guarantee to each of its members the preservation of their person, their rights, and their property.[51]

A 'social concept' can be understood as a goal pursued by a power that acts in the name of society, whose promotion for all is a good for each. On this understanding, to say that security is a 'social concept of bourgeois society' is to say that a constituted power pursues the security of the members of bourgeois society as a goal; and the promotion of security for all is a good for each. Security is a social concept of bourgeois society if the satisfaction of any one member's

---

51 *MEW*, 1, p. 365; *MECW*, 3, p. 163. Mark Neocleous claims that 'Marx calls security "the supreme concept of bourgeois society"' (Neoclaus 2008, p. 30). Objections: (1) Neocleous's translation omits to render '*sozial*'; (2) the highest concept of society x (= the most x can achieve in some respect) need not be the supreme concept of society x (= the overriding principle in x). To say that security is bourgeois society's 'highest social concept' does not imply that it is its supreme concept. The first question posed by Marx's remark is: why is security a 'social' concept of bourgeois society at all? Only then can one ask: why is security its 'highest social concept'?

interest in security has general positive 'spillover effects'[52] on everyone's satis-faction of it. For if so, each member only tends to satisfy their interest in security under conditions that promote its satisfaction for all members.

The property and person of the members of bourgeois society are insecure if the *animus domini* asserted in purchase and sale is likely to be disrupted, and/or its members can reasonably fear that it is likely to be disrupted. It is likely to be disrupted if it is likely that another will seek to dispose over a commodity offered for exchange without its possessor's permission or instruction, by force, threat or deceit. The satisfaction of any one member's interest in security has general positive spillover effects if each stands to be disadvantaged by the char-acter traits that are promoted in perpetrators and/or victims by (the reasonable fear of) successful incidents of disruption. This claim rests on two premises.

The first premise is that, in a society characterised by generalised purchase and sale, money generates acquisitiveness. Money (a universal equivalent serv-ing as a general means of exchange) generates acquisitiveness, that is, a will to possess more means to acquire whatever one wants to acquire, because (i) there is no limit to what money can acquire; (ii) there is no limit to the amount of money one can acquire; and (iii) (whether or not money exists) people com-pare their judgement of how they are doing with others' judgement of how they are doing, and compare how they are doing with how others are doing. If money generates acquisitiveness, there is no reason to suppose that those who cause and gain from one incident of disruption to an exchanger's *animus domini* will stop there. The second premise is that the same amount of mon-etary wealth is no less worth gaining from one commodity exchanger by force, threat or deceit than from any other. On these premises, a rise in incidents of disruption to *animus domini* in purchase and sale is a disadvantage to each, on two counts. Firstly, as perpetrators are emboldened by their successes, *animus domini* in purchase and sale is now more likely to be disrupted. Secondly, a greater likelihood of disruption also creates a greater general level of reason-able fear of disruption. Security of *animus domini* accompanying detention is a social interest of commodity exchangers, that is, an interest that each com-modity exchanger only tends to satisfy under conditions that promote its sat-isfaction for all.

Third, commodity exchangers are led by their social interest in security to articulate the principle: *animus domini* accompanying detention ought to be respected. Self-interest presents no barrier to articulation of a practical principle, if the principle upholds a social interest. The principle that *animus*

---

52   Nozick 1974, p. 24.

domini accompanying detention ought to be respected upholds commodity exchangers' social interest in security. Hence, commodity exchangers' self-seeking in-order-to motives are no barrier to their articulation of this principle. Indeed, its articulation strengthens their security. It gives them added reason to hope for less future incidents of disruption to *animus domini* in purchase and sale. They can hope that such future incidents of disruption will not arise from those who conform to the principles they know others believe in, even if only because such conformity is in their self-interest.

Fourth, if commodity exchangers articulate this principle, its very articulation can provide the kind of genuine recognition lacking in purchase and sale. Firstly, each articulator of this principle must esteem every other articulator of it, if it is a principle they believe in. Secondly, what articulators of principles esteem are the qualities that the principles they articulate urge people to respect. Articulators of the principle '*animus domini* accompanying detention ought to be respected' esteem *animus domini* accompanying detention. As it is natural to value qualities that are objects of esteem for others in the respect in which one holds them in esteem, each of the articulators of this principle can, as a result of recognition, value *animus domini* accompanying detention. Each can develop a disposition to be moved all the way to act on their *animus domini* in respect of what they have detention over, and to genuinely respect others' *animus domini* in respect of what they have detention over.

Fifth, the relation of implication between *animus domini* and an exclusive will in respect of one's parts and capacities now assumes a new aspect. By articulating the principle that *animus domini* accompanying detention ought to be respected, commodity exchangers commit themselves to the principle that each exchanger's exclusive will in respect to their parts and capacities ought to be respected. So again, as a result of articulators recognising each other, each can value an exclusive will in respect of one's parts and capacities. Each can develop a disposition to be moved all the way to act as a person and to respect others as persons.

In this way, as-if mutual recognition in purchase and sale helps to lead commodity exchangers to enjoy the freedom of will of a private property owner and a person even without purchase and sale exhibiting genuine recognition. An actor exercises the freedom of will of a person by seeking to bring the actions they perform into line with what, as an exclusive decision-maker over their parts and capacities in a society of such decision-makers, they are moved all the way to do. For example, they may withdraw from a given want to follow another's instructions or to seek their permission in respect of their parts and capacities, or withdraw from a given want to instruct another's use of their parts and capacities without their agreement.

Finally, they may also be emboldened to articulate principles of legal private property ownership and self-ownership, as principles for guaranteeing this freedom of will. The principle of self-ownership, in John Locke's phrase, is that 'every Man has a *Property* in his own *Person*'.[53] It says that each individual, and only that individual, has enforceable rights over all their parts and capacities. Each is to have the enforceable right to do as they please with their parts and capacities provided others' rights in respect of their parts and capacities are not violated. No one is to be permitted to impose enforceable obligations on anyone else without their agreement. The principles of self-ownership and legal private property ownership provide the enforceable freedoms for satisfying actors with the freedom of will of persons, for they allow decisions taken by decision-makers with an exclusive will in respect of their parts and capacities to be given legal effect.

Indeed, there is both a negative and a positive reason for commodity exchangers to affirm the enforceable principles of private property ownership and self-ownership. The negative reason is that commodity exchangers are not immediately concerned with the motivation of the conduct that accords with the practical principles they articulate. As such, no barrier prevents them from believing that force may be used to uphold any practical principle they articulate. The positive reason is that a coercive guarantee would promote commodity exchangers' social interest in security, by preventing disruptions from those who do not will to conform to these principles; or by assuring those whose observance of them rests on an assurance that others will observe them, that others will face a coercive sanction if they do not observe them; or by allowing a settlement to be imposed in cases where people honestly and reasonably disagree about how these principles apply.

This explanation for the appeal of the principle of self-ownership is consistent with its rejection. If, as the principle of self-ownership holds, it is always wrong to impose enforceable obligations on anyone without their agreement, the rights of each individual over their parts and capacities are unconditional and conclusive. A principle that holds that rights are unconditional and conclusive presupposes a judgement about the value of their subject: that the subject of unconditional and conclusive rights is of value. In particular, it presupposes the judgement that the subject of self-ownership rights is of value because this subject is able to guide its conduct by any enforceable principle

---

53   Locke 1988, p. 287. Marx's *Economic Manuscripts of 1861–63* characterises Locke's view that 'natural right makes *personal labour* the limit of property' as the 'classical expression of the notions of right of bourgeois society as opposed to feudal society' (*MEW*, 26.1, p. 343; *MECW*, 34, p. 89; compare *MEW*, 23, p. 412; *MECW*, 35, p. 394; Marx 1976, p. 513).

that is of value; which is to say, by the principle of self-ownership. To affirm the principle of self-ownership is thus to be committed to the judgement that the subject of self-ownership rights has a capacity to limit its conduct by the principle of self-ownership. Indeed, it is to be committed to the judgement that the subject of self-ownership rights has this capacity in a pre-social situation.[54] For otherwise, the conditions of existence of those social phenomena that were taken to be conditions of this capacity would be taken to be conditions of there being subjects of self-ownership rights. In that case, measures to maintain these social phenomena would be of value to believers in this principle irrespective of individuals' choices to maintain them. Their value might have to be balanced against respect for self-ownership rights, and potentially override them. That would contravene the principle of self-ownership, however, which says that self-ownership rights are unconditional and conclusive.

The above explanation for the appeal of the principle of self-ownership did not grant that the subject of self-ownership rights has a capacity to limit its conduct by this principle in a pre-social situation, however. It said that actors learn to believe in and act on the principle of self-ownership in virtue of generalised purchase and sale. If, to affirm the principle of self-ownership, generalised purchase and sale must first be affirmed, as a social condition under which actors can learn to limit their conduct by this principle, and so possess the value that this principle presupposes the subjects of self-ownership rights possess, then self-ownership rights cannot be unconditional and conclusive. The maintenance of those social conditions is already taken to have a value that may need to be balanced against, and even override, self-ownership rights. This point casts doubt on Cohen's assertion that 'the thesis of self-ownership cannot be refuted'.[55] The thesis of self-ownership is refuted if its advocates are committed to the judgement that pre-social individuals have a capacity to limit their conduct by the principle of self-ownership when this capacity can only be acquired from a social learning process.

---

54 As Robert Nozick assumes: 'to the point, for deciding what goals one should try to achieve, would be to focus upon a nonstate situation in which people generally satisfy moral constraints and generally act as they ought … If one could show that the state … would arise by a process involving no morally impermissible steps … this … would justify the state' (Nozick 1974, p. 5; compare p. 17, p. 24).

55 Cohen 1995, p. 244.

CHAPTER 10

Recognition and Bureaucratic Domination

The concept of domination, as an asymmetrical power relation, admits of various different conceptions. The preceding accounts of exploitation and recognition impose negative and positive conditions on how domination is to be conceived. Negatively, they discourage a conception of domination on which the value of non-domination lies in an unsullied choice situation. Positively, they allow domination to be will-directed. These conditions are honoured by conceiving of domination as the command of an alien will. The interaction-recognition-antinomy thesis says that bureaucratic domination is an essential feature of capitalism.

Roemer once viewed domination as 'room for arbitrary exercise of power'[1] over another. Philip Pettit has since developed a systematic account of this view, as a contribution to republican political thought. For Pettit, one party dominates another 'to the extent that they have the capacity to interfere on an arbitrary basis in certain choices that the other is in a position to make'.[2] If, following Roemer and Pettit, domination is viewed as the capacity to arbitrarily constrain another's choices, then non-domination is a state of affairs in which individuals' choice situations are amended so that they are not sullied by this capacity.[3] Indeed, Pettit identifies freedom with such non-domination. Pettit takes, 'the goal of the state to be the promotion of freedom as non-domination';[4] the goal, not a goal. The interaction-recognition-antinomy thesis takes a different view of freedom and of non-domination.

To be sure, there are differences between viewing freedom in terms of an unsullied choice situation, and in terms of liberty (having no duty not to). Viewing freedom in terms of an unsullied choice situation does not presuppose that freedom is separable from the capacity to act, or that freedom is only reduced by actual interference. For Pettit, a choice situation consists of 'the range of options presented as available'.[5] An option is only available if a chooser is able to take it. An unsullied choice situation therefore presupposes capacities on the part of the chooser to pursue certain options. This distinguishes an unsul-

---

1 Roemer 1982b, p. 377.
2 Pettit 1997, p. 52 (numbering omitted).
3 See Pettit 1997, pp. 85–6; Pettit 2005, p. 102.
4 Pettit 1997, p. ix.
5 Pettit 1997, p. 53.

© KONINKLIJKE BRILL NV, LEIDEN, 2019 | DOI:10.1163/9789004384804_011

lied choice situation from liberty. I am at *liberty* to take a holiday in a faraway place just in case I am not prohibited from doing so, even if I am unable to go because I have no money. But taking a holiday in a faraway place is not one of my available options unless I am able to go. I must have enough money to go. Suppose that I know that the border guards at this faraway place have discretion to conduct humiliating strip searches on visitors. Their discretion sullies my situation in respect of my holiday choices *only if* I have enough money to go, for otherwise, it brings about no 'worsening'[6] of my choice situation; and *even if* their good mood leads them not to strip search me when I go.

Notwithstanding these differences, a policy of securing an equally unsullied choice situation for all individuals still provides a licence to exploit. It allows systems to reinforce ends that cannot be universalised (or that otherwise reproduce social antagonisms), provided that they proceed with others' agreement, and are enabled and constrained by impersonal dynamics, rather than by a need to kowtow to others' arbitrary exercise of power. Freedom is not to be identified with such non-domination, therefore. Rather, an account of domination is to be based on the same ultimate value as an account of exploitation. As the charge related to the system universalisability conception of exploitation rests on the autonomy of 'social humanity',[7] the interaction-recognition-antinomy must offer an account of domination that can support a charge related to the obstacles on individuals willing to engage in rewarding activities that are known to be in harmony with those of others.

In chapter 9, recognition was conceived pragmatically, as what a recognisee can experience as positive evaluation by another. The form of recognition encouraged by generalised purchase and sale is the recognition of *animus domini* and personhood. Although this founds recognition on non-recognition, it permits the assumption that actors in capitalism have a will. A thesis about domination in capitalism can extend this line of thought by conceiving domination as the kind of asymmetrical power relation that is directed to another's will, and precludes a will to engage in rewarding and evidently harmonious activity, and/or such activity itself; and by arguing that the bureaucratic command of an alien will is essential to capitalism.

To consider the place of domination in Marx's critique of capitalism is not, then, to be committed to recover Marx's thought for the tradition of Republican political thought. William Clare Roberts suggests that the 'explication of republican freedom as non-domination' provided, among others, by Pettit, 'tracks much more closely the range and types of Marx's concerns that does the more

---

6   Pettit 1997, p. 52.
7   *MEW*, 3, p. 7; *MECW*, 5, p. 5.

traditional attribution to Marx of a positive conception of freedom as collective self-realization'.[8] As Roberts's study is of Marx as the author of *Capital* Volume I, one reply to this suggestion is: if Roberts had not neglected Marx's accounts of recognition and of the rights-antinomy in *Capital* Volume I, he would have struggled to resolve the rights-antinomy without a principle reflecting the value of social humanity articulated in its vision of a 'higher form of society whose foundational principle is the full and free development of each'.[9] Even putting this aside, Roberts does not explain why a view of freedom typically advanced on premises that preclude the feasibility of *Capital*'s vision should be expected to illuminate its concerns. For one argument for the idea that the people ought to have powers to resist existing rules and author new ones, and so for freedom as non-domination, is that class conflicts or social inequalities are things that 'every political order necessarily abets'.[10] Incorporating a critique of the capitalist domination of labour in a thesis of commodity form philosophy committed to self-legislative human community is one way to challenge the idea that Marx's thought is susceptible to reconstruction within the Republican tradition.

The argument begins by identifying the three conditions of Marx's general conception of domination in the *Grundrisse*. Sections 2–4 elaborate each condition. Section 5 restates this conception as the command of an alien will. The analysis then shifts to the specific context of capitalist production. Section 6 offers an interpretation of what Marx refers to as the formal subsumption and the real subsumption of labour under capital. Sections 7–8 then argue that formal subsumption generates labour-domination, while real subsumption gives labour-domination a bureaucratic form. Section 9 presents an analysis of occupational identity, and offers a responsibility-related and an expertise-related reason for holding that the administrative personnel of a capitalist firm can assume that wage-labourers recognise their commands. Finally, section 10 summarises the respects in which bureaucratic domination is contrary to self-legislative human community.

---

8   Roberts 2017, p. 7.

9   *MEW*, 23, p. 618; *MECW*, 35, p. 588; Marx 1976, p. 739; see, similarly, *MEW*, 4, p. 482; *MECW*, 6, p. 506, cited in ch. 8, sec. 13.

10   Vatter 2005, p. 147; see, similarly, Hamilton 2014, p. 82. Vatter adds that, if the people desire freedom as non-domination (as an advocate of the value of freedom as non-domination may wish to claim), public office must be subject to 'the principle of political representation' (Vatter 2005, p. 149). This suggests a second reason why Marx's writings are not of the Republican tradition. On political representation, see ch. 11, sec. 5.

1 Marx's General Conception of Domination

Marx's most explicit general statement on domination is found in the *Grundrisse*:

> A relation of domination [*Herrschaftsverhältnis*] through appropriation cannot obtain over an animal, land, etc., although the animal serves. The appropriation of an alien *will* [*Aneignung fremden* Willens] is a presupposition of the relation of domination. That which lacks a will, an animal for example, can certainly serve, but that does not make the appropriator [*Eigner*] a *master* [Herren].[11]

Marx's general conception of domination can be stated in three conditions:
(1) One actor appropriates the will of another
(2) The other's will is alien to the appropriator
(3) The appropriation makes the appropriator a master
Each condition separates Marx's conception of domination from a conception of domination as the capacity to arbitrarily constrain another's choices. The capacity to arbitrarily constrain another's choices is neither necessary nor sufficient. Consider each condition in turn.

2 Domination and the Will

The first condition of the *Grundrisse*'s conception of domination says: one actor appropriates the will of another. It excludes any service on the part of a living organism that lacks a will from counting as an instance of domination.

Domination requires the dominated to have the specific attitude to their wants called a will. An actor's will is what they want, after consideration, to be moved all the way to do. For A to appropriate or direct B's will is for A to influence what B wants to be moved all the way to do, with the result that what B does contributes, as A anticipated, to the achievement of A's end. An animal

---

11   *MEW*, 42, p. 408; *MECW*, 28, p. 424; Marx 1973a, p. 500. (1) *MECW* and Marx 1973a translate '*Eigner*', which is related to the noun '*Aneignung* (appropriation)', as 'owner' (which would be: '*Eigentümer*'). 'Owner' is a post-recognition term (see ch. 9, sec. 2); 'appropriator' is not. Unlike ownership, appropriation can take place in a one-agent world. (2) *MECW* translates 'fremden *Willens*' as 'another's *will*' (which would be: 'anderen *Willens*'). 'Another's *will*' is ends-indeterminate; 'alien *will*' is not. For elaboration, see sec. 3. (3) For more uses of '*Herr*' and '*Herrschaft*', see secs 4, 6–7.

cannot be dominated, therefore, if an animal is not able to want, after consideration, to be moved all the way to action.

Frankfurt gives the name of 'a wanton'[12] to a being who is unconcerned with what they are moved all the way to do. A wanton simply does what they are most inclined to do, without caring what that might be. A wanton could not be dominated, therefore. A wanton's behaviour can be influenced by another, but not by means of domination. A wanton has no will for another to direct.

A wanton addict, for example, is an addict without a will. A wanton addict does not care that what they do is take a drug. Suppose someone tries to wean a wanton addict off the drug. They can offer them an object of greater pleasure instead, or try to entice them to an environment in which they have no inclination to take the drug. But, for the time being at least, they cannot reason with them. They cannot identify a goal, z, that the wanton addict wants to achieve, for which they would have to stop taking the drug; say to the wanton addict: 'if you really want to achieve z, you should stop taking this drug'; make available the means for the wanton addict to achieve z; and hope that they use their judgement not to take the drug. The only measures that can initially be used to wean a wanton addict off a drug are akin to the measures used to entice an animal.

The concept of a wanton reveals that the first condition of Marx's general conception of domination rests on an assumption. If a will-directed conception of domination is to identify a general phenomenon, it must generally be the case that actors have a will. If a will-directed conception of domination is to identify a general phenomenon of capitalism, actors in capitalism must generally have a will. Freedom of will is enabled by recognition. So, if a will-directed conception of domination is to identify a general phenomenon of capitalism, the system of capitalist production must generate a kind of recognition. A will-directed conception of domination can be used to theorise a general phenomenon of capitalism, therefore, because generalised purchase and sale is essential to capitalism; and generalised purchase and sale leads commodity exchangers to develop the freedom of will of persons. On Marx's own analysis of capitalism, Marx is entitled to use a will-directed conception of domination to theorise it.

The will-directed character of the *Grundrisse*'s conception of domination is one of three differences from the conception of domination advanced by Roemer and Pettit. According to the *Grundrisse*, not every arbitrary power to constrain the 'choices'[13] of another is a sign of domination. The arbitrary power

---

12   Frankfurt 1971, p. 11.
13   Pettit 1997, p. 52; Pettit 2005, p. 93.

to constrain another's choices does not suffice for domination, because it does not presuppose that the choice-constrained subject has a will. To say that *A* is able to exercise arbitrary power over *B*'s choice situation, it is not necessary to deny that *B* is a wanton. The capacity to arbitrarily seize a wanton addict's stash of drugs would alter their choice situation. But it is not an instance of domination.

3   Domination and Alien Will

The second condition of the *Grundrisse*'s general conception of domination says: the other's will is alien to the appropriator. From the appropriator's perspective, the other's will is alien or foreign. It features in their course of action as diverging from their own will, and thereby as potentially thwarting it. The will of the dominated does not feature in the course of action of the dominating party as identical with, or purely enabling for, the latter's will.[14]

To illustrate the possibility for the direction of another's will to be the direction of an identical will, consider the plight of an unwilling addict. If a wanton addict is an addict without a will, an unwilling addict, by contrast, suffers from weakness of will. An unwilling addict struggles against their want for a drug, but to no avail. They fail to bring what they do into line with their will. They are moved to act by a conflicting want. If someone concerned with the well-being of an unwilling addict seeks to get them to refrain from taking the drug, they can try to direct their will. But that direction is not domination. The director's will is for the addict to refrain, and the unwilling addict's will is to refrain. The directing actor cannot regard the unwilling addict's will as alien if they regard it as identical to their own. To illustrate the possibility for the direction of another's will to be the direction of a purely enabling will, imagine 'a jazz band each player in which seeks his own fulfilment as a musician'.[15] The wills of the jazz players are not identical. By playing together, each player seeks to hone their *own* skills. But one player may view the will of another as purely

---

14   Pashukanis writes: 'the logic of relations of domination and servitude can only be partly brought within the system of juridical concepts' (Pashukanis 2003, p. 95; Pashukanis 2002, p. 96), which is to say (for Pashukanis), within the system of concepts applicable to cases of conflict between private interests. Marx would rather say that authoritative direction is not always domination. But Marx and Pashukanis at least agree that scenarios where two wills are identical or purely mutually enabling are to be distinguished from scenarios where two wills diverge so as to constrain one another.

15   Cohen 1995, p. 122.

enabling. If one player directs the other's will, because the other is suffering from weakness of will, there is no domination.

The second condition of the *Grundrisse*'s general conception of domination is hidden, therefore, by the *MECW* translation of '*fremden* Willens' as 'another's *will*'. The adjectives '*fremd*' and '*ander*' are not interchangeable. A need not regard an attribute of another actor, B, as '*fremd*'; and an attribute A regards as '*fremd*' need not belong to another actor. To describe an individual attribute (a will, a power, an activity, and so on) as '*fremd*' is to presuppose a perspective from which it is regarded as foreign, just as a foreign language ('*Fremdsprache*') is not simply another language, and foreign soil ('*fremder Boden*') is not simply another country. Indeed, the perspective from which an individual attribute is regarded as foreign need not imply (as 'another' implies) a numerically distinct individual. André Brink's novel *On the Contrary* gives the following first person description of the plight of a prisoner in the dark hole of a castle:

> I cannot trust my own presence. When I clutch myself in the cold to cherish what meagre warmth a body fabricates, what I feel is alien. I have already taken my distance from it.[16]

Here, a prisoner describes their own body as alien; and the German translation of Brink's novel (fairly) renders the clause 'what I feel as alien' as '*halte ich etwas Fremdes in den Armen*'.[17]

The second condition of the *Grundrisse*'s general conception of domination is not satisfied by Erik Olin Wright's account of domination, which, like Weber's[18] and Pettit's,[19] is ends-indeterminate:

> To say that A dominates B is to say that A not only tells B what to do or in other ways directs B's activities, but also that A has the capacity to constrain B's attempts at transforming the relationship between A and B. To be a subordinate is not simply to be in a position in which one is given orders, but to be unable to transform the relationship of command-obedience.[20]

---

16   Brink 1993, p. 4.

17   Brink 1994, p. 12. For further uses of '*fremd*' in Marx's writings that are not interchangeable with 'other/another', see Mészáros 1970, pp. 222–6.

18   '*Domination* [Herrschaft] denotes the probability for a command with a specific content to be met with obedience by certain identifiable persons' (Weber 2005, p. 38; Weber 1978, p. 53).

19   For Pettit, interference in another person's choices remains interference 'even if it is for the person's overall good' (Pettit 2005, p. 93).

20   Wright 1982, p. 325.

Wright's account is subject to two doubts. One is that it subsumes cases of direction that merely seek to correct for another's weakness of will and cases of direction where actors' wills diverge so as to potentially thwart one another. On the evidence of this passage, there is, for Wright, no domination-relevant difference between directing a wage-labourer to produce in order to maximise profit, and directing an unwilling addict who cannot voluntarily withdraw from a rehabilitation programme. To apply ends-indeterminate terms to describe a form of society in which actors' ends are not identical or purely enabling is to leave unquestioned the nature of those ends.

Second, it is unclear why a subordinate's incapacity to transform their subordination (let alone the circumstance that the capacity to constrain such transformation is in the hands of the commander) is included in a conception of domination. One argument for including this incapacity would be to hold that, if a subordinate knew that they could transform their situation, they would not allow themselves to be dominated in the first place. But that is false, for it could be the case, as Rousseau claims, that

> Citizens let themselves be oppressed only so far as they are swept up by blind ambition, and, looking below more than above themselves, come to hold Domination [*domination*] dearer than independence, and consent to bear chains so that they might impose chains on others in turn. It is very difficult to reduce to obedience someone who does not seek to command [*commander*].[21]

Suppose A is in a position to offer B the option of dominating C, if B agrees to be dominated by A. If B prefers to dominate C and be dominated by A to doing neither, A could dominate B even though B may voluntarily terminate the arrangement with A in which B is dominated without any cost to themselves, other than the loss of an opportunity to dominate.

To be sure, domination is more stable if the dominated are unable to terminate it because of significant domination-independent costs, or if the dominating party is able to constrain their attempts to transform it. But it is one thing to elaborate a conception of domination, and another to explicate the conditions under which domination, as already defined, is more stable. Conditions that merely make domination more stable do not belong to a conception of domination. They are not necessary to ensure that the will of the dominated appears to the director as alien.

---

21   Rousseau 1944, p. 99; Rousseau 1997, p. 183.

4   Domination and Recognition

The third condition of the *Grundrisse*'s general conception of domination says: the appropriation makes the appropriator a master. The context in which to locate this condition is Hegel's account of the master-servant relation in the *Phenomenology of Spirit*. Where the master makes instrumental use of the servant, by putting them to work:

> This moment of recognition is present here such that the other consciousness sublates itself as being-for-itself, and it thereby itself does what the first does to it. This is equally the case for the other moment. What the second self-consciousness does is the first's own doing, for what the servant does is really the master's [*Herrn*] doing.[22]

Hegel here describes a kind of one-sided 'recognition' of the master by the servant. The servant does not just fear the master. The servant believes that instructions from their master ought to bear on their actions. The servant makes the master's instructions their will, by setting aside any contrary want (the first 'moment' of recognition) and acting on those instructions (the 'other moment' of recognition).

Accordingly, if, as the *Grundrisse* says, the direction that defines domination makes the director a master, then that is equivalent to saying that it meets with a kind of one-sided recognition. To count as domination, the direction of another's alien will must take a form by which the director *can* be recognised as a master; and that recognition must be forthcoming.

On a recognition-inclusive conception of domination, not every power to arbitrarily constrain the choices of another individual (with an alien will) is a sign of domination. A may be able to arbitrarily constrain B's choices only if A avoids being identified by B as the source of this constraint. A may be able to constrain B's choices by 'denying' B 'knowledge of the options available'.[23] To the end of exercising this power, it may be necessary for A to conceal not only the action by which A denies B knowledge of an available option, but also the fact that A had the opportunity to deny B knowledge of it. If so, A has the power to arbitrarily constrain the choices of another individual (with an alien will), but A cannot demand or receive recognition from that individual in virtue of holding or exercising this power.

---

22   Hegel 1986a, pp. 151–2; Hegel 2013, § 191.
23   Pettit 2005, p. 93.

One form of direction that intrinsically leads to a kind of one-sided recognition is the issue of a command. A command is a specific instruction to an identifiable group of persons, issued in the belief that it ought to be carried out obediently. Hobbes states: 'COMMAND is, where a man saith, *Doe this*, or *Doe not this*, without expecting other reason than the Will of him that sayes it'.[24] H.L.A. Hart highlights two features of this definition. One is that a command is 'peremptory'. The addressee is required to take the expression of the commander's will as a reason for acting 'in place of any deliberation or reasoning of his own'.[25] The addressee is not invited first to consider the merit of letting the commander decide what they are to do. Second, a command is 'content-independent'. Its addressee is required to take the expression of the commander's will as a reason for acting 'independently of the nature or character of the actions to be done'.[26] The addressee is not invited first to consider the merit of what they have been instructed to do. A command, then, is an instruction carrying the force of a peremptory, content-independent reason for acting. It is issued in the belief that its addressee is to do what is instructed of them because it has been commanded. The addressee is not taken to be owed any further explanation.

As a commander, by issuing a command, intends its addressee to make it their will, they presuppose that its addressee has a will. A kind of recognition is provided to a commander if (i) a commander can regard the addressee of their command as their equal in respect of possessing a will to engage voluntarily in the same domain of action as them; and (ii) a commander can interpret their addressee's response to be informed by the belief that they ought to do what they have been instructed to do in order to carry out a command of their commander.

In combination, three further implications of commanding add to the import of the recognition that obedience provides. One implication is that the issuer of a command must believe in its legitimacy. If *A* says to *B*: 'do *x*; but I am not sure you should', or *A* otherwise comports themselves to the effect of expressing that doubt, it cannot be clear to *B* that *A* has commanded them. *B* would have the same justification for making *A*'s doubt their will as they would to make *A*'s command to do *x* their will; if 'do *x*' carries peremptory, content-independent force, then so does the expression of the doubt that follows it. If *A* says to *B*: 'do *x*; but I am not sure you should', and *B* does *x*, *B* has not obeyed

---

24   Hobbes 1996, p. 176.
25   Hart 1990, p. 100.
26   Hart 1990, p. 101.

a command. If an instruction is to take effect as a command, it must be issued with conviction. A command can only be issued with conviction, however, if its issuer issues it in the belief that they are entitled to issue it. So, for a command to be issued with the conviction its effect requires, its issuer must believe in its legitimacy.

Second, commanding need not be arbitrary. Pettit writes: 'an act is perpetrated on an arbitrary basis, we can say, if it is subject just to the *arbitrium*, the decision or judgment, of the agent; the agent was in a position to choose it or not choose it, at their pleasure'.[27] On this definition of arbitrariness, decision-making is not arbitrary if the decision-maker is subject to others' scrutiny as to whether or not they followed a certain procedure, and/or if the decision-maker must respond to calls to justify the content of their decisions. If such a decision-maker were to make decisions just as they pleased, they could expect to incur disadvantages for doing so. Commanding need not be arbitrary, therefore, for a commander does not cease to command if their commands are subject to scrutiny in their procedure and/or to calls to justify their content (for example, by superiors in a command hierarchy).

Third, commanding effects exclusion. Commanding effects exclusion by virtue of the fact that the addressees of a command are required to obey it, and cannot be among its co-authors. For someone other than the commander to be the co-author of a command, that someone must appoint the commander, and be able to hold them to account. To the end of holding a commander to account, it must be possible to demand reasons from them for thinking that they have done their job. In that capacity, those who hold the commander to account must challenge any command from the commander. Faced with a commander who responds to an awkward question about the job they have done with a command to stop asking questions, those who hold them to account must restate the question. A readiness to challenge a commander's commands in the capacity of holding them to account must, however, jeopardise any obedience to the same outside of that capacity. Those with both the functions of obeying a commander's commands *and* of holding them to account must first, before obeying, consider for *themselves* (or ask a third party they delegate that decision to) whether the situation is one in which they are to obey or hold the commander to account. But if the addressee of an instruction must *first* consider such a question for themselves (or ask a third party they delegate that decision to) before they execute it, they have ceased to regard it as a command. An instruction would lack the force of a peremptory, content-independent reason

---

27   Pettit 1997, p. 55.

for acting if its issuer issued it in the belief that its execution was properly preceded by this consideration. Commanding effects exclusion, therefore, as the
addressees of commands cannot be their co-authors.

If commanding (i) rests on a commander's belief in the legitimacy of their
commands, (ii) need not be arbitrary, and (iii) effects exclusion, then that adds
to the import of the recognition that obedience provides. This recognition may
provide a commander with a sense that their decision-making has an objective value that does not extend to the addressees of their commands. By virtue
of recognition in the form of obedience, a commander is not simply moved
all the way to command, and to respect other commanders' commands. They
are moved all the way to act to express the fact that commanders are entitled
to command and their addressees are not entitled to hold them to account;
for example, by putting the addressees of commands in their place. In so acting, a commander can hope that there will be an objective value to what they
will have done. Relatedly, if several commanders command in a domain of
action, commanding can yield a sense of 'us' and 'them' among commanders vis-à-vis the commanded, due to each commander's sense of the objective
value common to each commander's commands, their common entitlement
to command, and their addressees' common lack of entitlement to hold them
to account.

The relation between command and recognition through obedience must
be qualified, however. Commanding is an exercise of 'de facto practical authority'[28] because a command is issued in the belief that it is a conclusive reason
for acting (whether or not it really is a conclusive reason for acting). As the
addressee of a command need not respond as this belief anticipates, however,
a command must be accompanied, if only implicitly, by a threat of sanction.
Hart continues:

> Of course the commander may not succeed in getting his hearer to accept
> the intended peremptory reason as such: the hearer may refuse or have no
> disposition at all to take the commander's will as a substitute for his own
> independent deliberation, and it is typical of commanding, therefore, to
> provide for this failure of the primary peremptory intention by adding fur-
> ther reasons for acting in the form of threats to do something unpleasant
> to the hearer in the event of disobedience.[29]

---

28   Murphy 2007, pp. 7–8.
29   Hart 1990, p. 101.

The threat of sanction is what Hart terms a 'secondary provision'[30] of commanding, for it aims to give the addressee a reason to act in the event that a command's peremptory, content-independent force (that is, the assertion of *de facto* practical authority) goes unrecognised. The designation of authority as primary and the threat of sanction as secondary is a phenomenological ordering from the commander's perspective. A commander cannot regard their authority as what they fall back on when their threats of sanction hold no fear. Rather, they regard their threats of sanction as what they fall back on when their practical authority holds no sway. This phenomenological ordering does not imply a corresponding claim in respect of the relative causal impact of authority and threats of sanction, however. It is possible for a commander to be convinced of the legitimacy of their commands and to continue to issue them in that belief although they are aware that the influence of their authority is outweighed by their threats, and/or by their capacity to threaten. Phenomenological priority (authority backed by threat of sanction) is distinct from, and not an indication of, relative causal weight.

Indeed, the fact that a commander's capacity to threaten to initiate a sanction does not remove their need to believe that their command is legitimate imposes a condition on any threat of sanction. A threat of sanction must not only warn an addressee of a disadvantage that a commander can cause to be brought about; that is, be a credible threat. To endure as a secondary provision of commanding, as distinct from constituting a bare threat, the form in which a sanction is threatened as well as its type and nature of execution must all be consistent with a belief in the legitimacy of the command it is to support. The threat and execution of a sanction are then further contexts in which commanders in a given domain of action can bond as a group that is marked off from those they command.

5   Marx's Conception of Domination Restated

The three conditions of Marx's general conception of domination in the *Grundrisse* may now be re-stated as follows:
(1)   One actor issues a command to another (the *command condition*)
(2)   The addressee's will is not identical with or purely enabling for the commander's will (the *alien will condition*)

---

30   Ibid.

(3)   The commander is recognised through the addressee's obedience (the *recognition condition*)

In short, domination is the command of an alien will. Types of domination can be distinguished by their domain of action, the source of belief in the legitimacy of a command, and the type of sanction. At issue, here, is domination in the context of the system of capitalist production.

6   Formal Subsumption and Real Subsumption

In purchase and sale, commodity exchangers act as if they mutually recognise one another as private property owners and persons. Neither treats the other as someone who has to follow anyone else's instructions, or get anyone else's permission, to exchange. By implication, neither acts as though they thought of themselves as entitled to command the other to alienate their commodity. No domination takes place, therefore, by virtue of a single token interaction of purchase and sale. *Capital* says that 'commodity exchange includes, in and of itself, no other relations of dependence [*Abhängigkeitsverhältnisse*] than those that arise from its own nature',[31] that is, debt and compensation for breach of contract. But to say that commodity exchange can include relations of dependence is not to say that it can include *relations of domination* (*Herrschaftsverhältnisse*). A credible threat to take someone to court over non-payment or non-performance is not just for that reason a secondary provision of commanding.

If circulation consists in the totality of purchases and sales, no domination takes place in circulation, either. The circulation of commodities ensures that market actors can only achieve their ends by falling into line with unpredictable movements in prices that result from 'nothing but the caprices of their customers and competitors'.[32] But this sort of dependency cannot lead domination to take place in circulation. It does not subject anyone to the commands of an alien will, or lead to their recognition. It does not subject anyone to a will at all. Movements in prices do not have a will of their own. The *Grundrisse* describes circulation as an '*alien* social power',[33] rather than as a power of an alien will. Just as a system that aggregates *x* is not itself *x*, so a 'system for aggregating *arbitria*'[34] is *not itself* an arbitrary will. If *A*'s dependency on movements

---

31   *MEW*, 23, pp. 181–2; *MECW*, 35, p. 178; Marx 1976, pp. 270–1.
32   Roberts 2017, p. 57.
33   *MEW*, 42, p. 127; *MECW*, 28, p. 132; Marx 1973a, p. 197; see ch. 6, sec. 5.
34   Roberts 2017, p. 93.

in prices is a dependency on a 'system for aggregating *arbitria*', it is not dependency on a will. If domination is 'nothing more than a metaphor' if it 'loses all reference to an arbitrary, incontestable will',[35] then the notion that there is impersonal domination in circulation is 'nothing more than a metaphor'. The premises of those who locate domination in circulation can be used to deny that it is located there.

If the system of capitalist production is to generate domination, that can only be on account of its production process. Elster, however, advances a claim that suggests an objection to this view. Elster claims:

> The exercise of power occurs when the contract is signed, by the capitalist taking advantage of the lack of property of the worker. The enforcement of the contract is not then a further exercise of power.[36]

Elster claims that, as the capitalist exercises power over the worker when the labour contract is signed, and as the capitalist production process is merely an enforcement of this contract, to count the capitalist production process as a further instance of the capitalist's exercise of power is illicit double-counting. Now, from the fact that an enforcement of a contract is not a further contract, it does not follow that enforcing it involves no further exercise of power. But even if it did follow, and even if it were true (which it is not)[37] that the capitalist production process merely enforces a labour contract, it would not be illicit double-counting to count the actions in this production process as domination, because no domination – no command of an alien will – takes place in the purchase and sale of labour power.

Further, if a wage-labourer is dominated in the capitalist production process, that need not be on account of any imperfection in their labour contract. Roemer has claimed that 'domination' in the capitalist production process is 'a substitute for a perfect contract'.[38] An imperfect contract, Roemer says, is a contract that fails to 'specify precisely the terms' of what is bought and sold, so as to avoid 'disagreements in the terms'.[39] Accordingly, an imperfect contract may allow one contracting party (= A) to arbitrarily constrain the other (= B), *if* A is less dependent on B than B is on A. Imperfections in the contract's terms will then give A the capacity to get B to do what only an interpretation of

---

35   Roberts 2017, p. 92.

36   Elster 1985, p. 200; compare p. 327.

37   See sec. 7 below.

38   Roemer 1982b, p. 377.

39   Roemer 1982b, pp. 376–7.

the contract favourable to *A* would require *B* to do. If, due to competition with the unemployed, a wage-labourer is more dependent on a capitalist firm than the latter is on them, an imperfection in a labour contract will give a capitalist firm the capacity to get the wage-labourer to do what only an interpretation of the labour contract favourable to the capitalist firm would require them to do. But the capacity to arbitrarily constrain another's choices is neither necessary nor sufficient for domination. Even if a labour contract were perfect, including its specification of who was to instruct whom, domination in the capitalist production process would still occur. The explanation for domination in the capitalist production process lies elsewhere.

The cause of domination in the capitalist production process is capital itself, that is, generalised production with wage-labour for continuous money maximisation. In other words, the cause of domination in the capitalist production process is what Marx refers to as the formal subsumption and the real subsumption of labour under capital (to some degree). To subsume one thing under another is to treat the former as a particular instance of the latter. To say that labour is subsumed under capital is to say that it is subject to just those conditions that arise from capital. The formal subsumption of labour under capital (hereafter: formal subsumption) is the subjection of labour to just those conditions of purchase and sale that arise from capital, while the real subsumption of labour under capital (hereafter: real subsumption) is the subjection of labour to just those conditions of the technical production process that arise from capital. This section merely attempts to explicate the notions of formal and real subsumption.

Marx's *Results of the Immediate Process of Production* describes formal subsumption in terms of two features:

> The essential features of *formal subsumption* are (1) the purely monetary relation between the one who appropriates surplus labour, and the one who provides it ... (2) ... the worker's *objective conditions of labour* (means of production) and *subjective conditions of labour* (means of life) confront them as *capital*, as monopolised by the purchaser of their labour capacity.[40]

Regarding point (1), there is a 'purely monetary relation' between a producer and the appropriator of their labour if their relation is a result of the producer's sale of their labour power for a determinate period, and the concrete

---

40   *MEGA*, II, 4.1, pp. 96–7; *MECW*, 34, p. 430; Marx 1976, pp. 1025–6.

type of labour power hired is determined purely by monetary considerations. As argued in chapter 6, the optimal money-maximising arrangement for capital is to hire wage-labour. The concrete type of labour power that is hired is determined purely by monetary considerations, because the system of capitalist production allows money-maximisers to hire any number of wage-labourers for all types of labour. Money-maximisers need not remain in a less profitable branch of production just because they have technical skills specific to that branch, for they can hire a workforce large enough for them not to have to perform a productive function. If money-maximisers are able to switch to more profitable branches of production irrespective of their technical skills, then the concrete type of labour power they hire will be determined solely by monetary considerations.

Point (2) encompasses two additional aspects of formal subsumption: all means of production are monopolised by capital; and all means of subsistence are produced by capital. Each aspect arises from the facts that (a) any alienable resource, including all alienable inputs used in the production of means of production or means of individual consumption, can be bought by money-maximisers; and (b) capitalist firms can out-compete non-capitalist hirers of wage-labour who produce for the market.[41]

What real subsumption entails is indicated by and under the subheading: 'Real Subsumption of Labour Under Capital, or the Specifically Capitalist Mode of Production'.[42] Under this subheading, Marx discusses the 'social productive power of labour' created by 'cooperation, the division of labour in the workplace, the application of machinery'.[43] The social productive power created by cooperation is the power of two or more individuals doing the same thing together to produce, in less overall labour time and/or with fewer costs, what the same number of uncoordinated individuals can achieve. The phrase 'doing the same thing together' is here intended to include performing the same action together, and/or using the same conditions of production (for example, the same building). The social productive power created by a division of labour in the workplace is the power of two or more individuals assigned with different sets of tasks to produce, in less overall time and/or with fewer costs, what the same number of individuals periodically rotated between those sets of tasks could achieve. The social productive power created by the use of machinery is the power of one or more machine operators to produce, in less overall labour

---

41   See ch. 6, sec. 4.
42   *MEGA*, II, 4.1, p. 95; *MECW*, 34, p. 428; Marx 1976, p. 1023.
43   *MEGA*, II, 4.1, pp. 95–6; *MECW*, 34, p. 428; Marx 1976, p. 1024.

time and/or with fewer costs, what the optimal number of individuals could achieve by using hand-held tools in place of a machine incorporating their functions.

To outdo or match its competitors, a capitalist firm will employ *any and only* those social productive powers that promise to raise the productive power of *its* workforce to make a product *it* can own, and/or reduce the costs that *it* bears, *provided* it can expect to recoup *its* outlay. The unintended consequence of competition between capitalist firms is the general adoption of social productive powers, *within these limits*.

A further aspect of real subsumption arises from social productive powers, however: the utilisation of social productive powers' scope for what Lukács calls 'rational calculation'.[44] The use of social productive powers within the above limits increases a capitalist firm's scope to calculate what use of power will yield what volume of output, by reducing the effect of wage-labourers' individual idiosyncrasies. In regard to cooperation, the social productive power of two or more wage-labourers producing the same thing together is more likely to approximate to the average productive power of that number of individuals, than the productive power of a single individual acting alone is likely to approximate to the average productive power of one individual. In regard to a division of labour in the workplace, it is easier to ascertain the time it ought to take to accomplish x, y and z, and to identify any cause of failure, if x, y and z are assigned to different wage-labourers than if three wage-labourers do some of each of x, y and z. In regard to the application of machinery, automated rhythms can be used to steady the pace of work in advance.

The scope for calculation attached to the adoption of social productive powers is independently significant, because the money-maximising use of productive power is not necessarily the use that yields the greatest volume of output. 'Use-value', *Capital* says, 'is never to be regarded as the capitalist's immediate end'.[45] If the greatest volume of output that given productive powers could yield is unmarketable at a given price, it may be more advantageous to lower output, rather than to incur storage or disposal costs, or to reduce the price. A production process run for continuous money maximisation will therefore be organised to make use of social productive powers' scope for calculation. The ideal situation for a capitalist firm is to have each of the following:

---

44   Lukács 1977, p. 262; Lukács 1968, p. 88.
45   *MEW*, 23, p. 168; *MECW*, 35, p. 164; Marx 1976, p. 254.

(i)   the (social) productive power to produce as much of a given type of product that it can expect to sell in the foreseeable future at the price that will yield the highest return (a capitalist firm's ideal *level of productive power*);

(ii)   the capacity to control its use of power to yield the intended output with minimal wear and tear to its power (a capitalist firm's ideal *capacity for efficiency*);

(iii) the capacity to calculate what use of power will yield what output (a capitalist firm's *capacity for calculation*).

Due to the upkeep and depreciation costs of dormant productive powers (and any lost opportunity to hire them out), a capitalist firm will not aim to acquire or keep hold of a vast excess of productive power for long. In effect, therefore, a capitalist firm will tend to organise its production process to accord with its calculation of what it can achieve near to full capacity, with the expected degree of efficiency.

For the purpose of the above analysis, formal subsumption and real subsumption were distinguished. In reality, however, they are intertwined. Formal subsumption and real subsumption do not correspond to discrete historical periods of capitalism, let alone admit of definition in historical terms. One without the other is no more than a hypothetical; and each promotes the other.

Consider, first, why neither may be defined in historical terms. One positive piece of evidence for this claim is that the above quotes do not mention historical periods. In particular, neither of the two features of formal subsumption Marx notes is defined in historical terms. Yet Marx does seem to imply that formal subsumption and real subsumption are to be understood in historical terms elsewhere. Just prior to the quote from *Results of the Immediate Process of Production* cited above that notes the two features of formal subsumption, Marx says that '*formal subsumption of labour under capital*' is so called because 'it is only *formally* distinguished from earlier modes of production'.[46] It is easy see how one might be led to conclude from remarks such as this that formal subsumption is to be defined as the form of a capitalist production process that is technologically unchanged from a pre-capitalist period.[47]

But here is the objection. To say that the production process at T_2 (capitalism) is technologically unchanged from an earlier production process at T_1 (pre-capitalism) is to say nothing about the technological character of the production process at T_1. For all the lack of technological change from T_1 to T_2

---

46   *MEGA*, II, 4.1, p. 96; *MECW*, 34, p. 430; Marx 1976, p. 1025.

47   The view of Read 2003, p. 10, pp. 105–10; and Heinrich 2005, p. 117; Heinrich 2012, p. 118.

implies, the production process at T_1 may have used social productive powers (cooperation, for example). Yet the use of social productive powers is what, for Marx, defines *real* subsumption. If formal subsumption is defined as the form of a capitalist production process that is technologically unchanged from a pre-capitalist period, any social productive powers thought of as belonging to the technological production process of that earlier period are counted twice, both as an aspect of formal subsumption, and as an aspect of real subsumption. As formal subsumption and real subsumption are not meant to overlap, and a historical definition of formal subsumption would fail ensure a lack of overlap, formal subsumption is not to be defined in historical terms. But in that case, neither is real subsumption.

We can now ask why neither formal subsumption nor real subsumption without the other is more than a hypothetical. To imagine formal subsumption without any degree of real subsumption, one must suppose that, when the money-maximising option is to hire several wage-labourers, this is consistent with having each of them produce a product under wholly separate conditions (not even under the same roof). Any phase of any one employee's tasks must be supposed to be technically independent of any phase of every other employee's tasks. Formal subsumption without any degree of real subsumption is no more than a hypothetical, therefore, for it is hard to imagine a scenario where the money saved (in accountancy costs) by using a single budget for several separate production processes cannot be increased by technical cooperation. Real subsumption without any degree of formal subsumption is also no more than a hypothetical, for producers subject to personal (non-monetary) relations of dependence cannot be expected to use expensive machinery with the minimum of wear and tear and damage.[48]

Moreover, formal subsumption and real subsumption also promote one another. Formal subsumption promotes real subsumption, because purely monetary relations between hirers and hired and a total monopolisation of resources by the former, such that the latter are entirely dependent on work for capital, make for the type of producer most responsive to a hirer's monetary incentives. Their labour is the most amenable to calculation. Real subsumption also promotes formal subsumption, for as the *Grundrisse* remarks, it is only with the 'greatest development of production based on capital' that the '*general conditions of production*, such as roads, canals, etc.' can be organised by 'capital' rather than by 'government'.[49] Capital must have developed, in part by means

---

48   See ch. 6, sec. 4.
49   *MEW*, 42, p. 437; *MECW*, 28, p. 455; Marx 1973a, pp. 530–1.

of real subsumption, to afford the investment that would enable it to monopolise all branches of production, and so remove the related job opportunities from government auspices.

7   Domination and Formal Subsumption

To show that formal subsumption is a cause of capitalist labour-domination is to show that formal subsumption (to some degree) gives rise to a relation that satisfies the three conditions for domination outlined above. This section focuses on the first two conditions: the command condition and the alien will condition. Discussion of the recognition condition is postponed to section 9.

The command condition for domination says: one actor issues a command to another. The idea that the command condition is satisfied by virtue of formal subsumption is suggested by a remark in *Capital* where Marx recapitulates his argument up to that point:

> the commanding power [*Kommando*] of capital over labour originally appeared to be merely a formal consequence of the fact that the worker labours for the capitalist, rather than for himself, and hence labours under the capitalist.[50]

In considering why labour that is formally subsumed (to some degree) satisfies the command condition, two issues can be distinguished: why it is possible for a capitalist firm to command its wage-labourers; and why it is necessary. To show that it is possible for a capitalist firm to command its wage-labourers involves showing that it is possible for the capitalist to believe in the legitimacy of instructions issued to the wage-labourer, and to reinforce such instructions with the credible threat of a sanction.

First of all, one actor can only command another by relating to the other's will. The case of the wage-labourer presents no difficulty on this score. The

---

50   *MEW*, 23, p. 350; *MECW*, 35, p. 335; Marx 1976, p. 448. Both *MECW* and Marx 1976 translate *'Kommando'* (of capital) as 'subjection' (of labour) (which would be: *'Unterwerfung'*). The 'subjection' of labour can occur in various forms, not all of which need rely on commands. *'Kommando'* is more specific: its exercise is essentially the issuing of commands. Read suggests that Marx's use of military terms (of which *'Kommando'* is one) may be viewed as 'figures standing in the place of a concept that is absent' (Read 2003, p. 85). A command-based conception of domination would have been suggested to Marx by Rousseau and Hegel (see sec. 3–4), however. The interest of Marx's thoughts on domination, understood as the command of an alien will, does not depend on 'a concept that is absent'.

wage-labourer has a will by virtue of their recognition as a person. Moreover, their labour power is not like a pair of prosthetics or false teeth that may be taken away from them while they sleep, put to use, and then returned. Whoever uses a wage-labourer's labour power must engage the wage-labourer's will.

Call the doctrine that an individual is bound by an obligation if it results from an exercise of their right to bind themselves the doctrine of individual responsibility. A commander can believe in individual responsibility as a source of legitimacy for their instructions if they can believe that each has a right to perform a certain type of action and to choose whether or not to follow instructions in how they perform it; and if they can believe that others have in fact chosen to perform such action under their instruction, and that they have in fact chosen to instruct them. If a commander has these four beliefs, they may view their instructions as a form of respect for their addressees, as beings who, like them, may assume the consequences they choose to assume. They may view an attempt to disrupt them from instructing, or an attempt not to comply with their instructions, as a form of disrespect. A capitalist has acted as if they have the first two of these beliefs (beliefs of right) by seeking a wage-labourer's agreement, and only that wage-labourer's agreement, before instructing them. They have the remaining two beliefs of fact, if they believe that the instructions they issue remain within the agreed remit.

The sanction available to a capitalist is to terminate a wage-labourer's contract. A wage-labourer who fails to carry out a capitalist's instructions within the remit of their contract is in breach of contract. To let them go is consistent with a belief in individual responsibility as a source of legitimacy of the capitalist's commands, if that sanction is only employed when a wage-labourer breaks conditions of employment they agreed to be bound by. If contracts are enforceable, the threat is credible provided there is what *Capital* calls 'a relative overpopulation'[51] of wage-labourers. In reference to a relative overpopulation of wage-labourers, *Capital* remarks: 'the silent compulsion of economic circumstances [*Verhältnisse*] seals the domination [*Herrschaft*] of the capitalist over the worker'.[52] In other words: a wage-labourer's anticipation of the

---

51   *MEW*, 23, p. 765; *MECW*, 35, p. 726; 1976, p. 899.
52   *MEW*, 23, p. 765; *MECW*, 35, p. 726; Marx 1976, p. 899. (1) *MECW* translates 'Herrschaft' (of the capitalist) as 'subjection' (of the wage-labourer) (which would be: 'Unterwerfung'). (2) *MECW* and Marx 1976 translate 'Verhältnisse' as 'relations'. The plural of 'das Verhältnis (relation)', 'die Verhältnisse', can denote relations, but it may instead (as in this sentence) denote circumstances. The finale of the first act of Brecht's *Three Penny Opera*, for example, is (fairly) translated as 'On the Uncertainty of Human Circumstances [*Verhältnisse*]' (Brecht 1967, p. 430; Brecht 1960, p. 129). In that finale, 'Human Circumstances' refers to the lack of a right to nourishment, an inability to live in peace, and a lack

undesirable uncertainty attached to being in the position of having to compete
with the unemployed to find work in order to live gives force to the capitalist's
threat to let them go. A capacity to execute this credible threat 'seals' capitalist labour-domination by prompting compliance where a capitalist's authority
yields no obedience.

True, breaches of contract may not be automatically detectable. Nor may
it be possible for responsibility to be automatically pinned on particular individuals. But a capitalist firm is able to monitor labour, both to pre-empt shirking
and to pin shirking on particular individuals; and to adopt disciplinary procedures. It is able to take the steps that it must take to ensure that its threat to let
a particular wage-labourer go is credible.

The necessity for a capitalist firm to command its wage-labourers is three-
fold. Firstly, it is unconvincing to object that commanding is possible but not
necessary because a wage-labourer could read through their contract, which
they cannot be commanded to accept, and honour it without instruction. No
agreement can regulate every eventuality in advance.

Moreover, the capitalist production process cannot conceivably consist in
just the enforcement of a labour contract. If production is with wage-labour
and for continuous money maximisation, both the purchase of labour power,
and production, are intermediary steps in the firm's pursuit of continuous
money maximisation. A labour contract only limits the actions of a capitalist
firm by limiting the arrangements in production by which continuous money
maximisation can be pursued. It only limits the firm by limiting its means. As a
labour contract only limits its means, the capitalist production process is never
merely the execution of a labour contract.

Imagine that all contractual terms admit just one interpretation, all violations have adequate sanctions, and all sanctions are instantly enforceable (even
against a firm). An unquestionably lawful option is then the firm's money-
maximising option. But to say that an unquestionably lawful option is the
money-maximising option is not to say that the firm has only one unquestionably lawful option. To grant that all contractual terms admit just one interpretation is not to say that they permit only one course of action. (Even if there
is only one way to interpret the prohibition 'do not walk on the grass', there
are many ways to observe it). Which unquestionably lawful option is the firm's

of humanity – all phenomena that it is unnatural to describe in English as 'relations'.
Likewise, the phenomena that Marx's use of the term 'Verhältnisse' refers to, having to
look for work and a context of unemployment, are circumstances, not relations. The
'canonical' phrase 'dull/silent compulsion of economic relations' is questionable, therefore.

money-maximising option cannot be determined by the labour contract, for it is only determined once labour contracts are interpreted, and factored into projections of every relevant actor's likely behaviour over the period for which the firm is seeking to ascertain its money-maximising option. The interpretation of labour contracts, together with trends among competitors and buyers with whom the firm has no special relationship, are the data for estimating that likely future behaviour. Likely future behaviour is what a firm takes into account when making its decisions, because all its decisions revolve around what investments to make and which conditions of work to implement in order to continue to accumulate as much capital as possible. As a capitalist firm regards a labour contract as just one of the data for estimating the likely future behaviour to which its production process is adjusted, no labour contract can remove the ongoing need to issue instructions to wage-labourers.

Finally, there is the compulsion imposed by competition. Assuming that commands are well-directed, then, in combination with the threat of sanction and the monitoring that gives this threat credibility, their effect, Marx writes in *Results of the Immediate Process of Production*, is greater 'continuity and intensity of labour, and greater economy in the application of the conditions of labour'.[53] But if that is so, because commands adjust the production process to the firm's money-maximising option without using up any more of the wage-labourer's time than they require to understand what they have been commanded to do; then each capitalist firm must command wage-labour, just to match the productivity of its competitors, whose own level of productivity already includes this effect.

We can now turn to the alien will condition. The commands of the capitalist firm satisfy the alien will condition if the wage-labourer's will is not identical with or purely enabling for the capitalist's will, which is for the firm to maximise its monetary wealth. The wage-labourer's will is not identical with or purely enabling for this will, because the firm's pursuit of continuous money maximisation generates a displacement-based antagonism. A displacement-based antagonism arises from the fact that the unconditional investment in and use of money-saving technologies and techniques requires their implementation, where necessary, at a workforce's own expense, and thus even when jobs are lost and/or deskilled (leading to a fall in wages) as a consequence. To the extent that the capitalist firm is aware of this possibility, and that it may meet with resistance on the part of its wage-labourers, it must regard any wage-labourer's will as an alien will. If wage-labourers recognise the commands of their firm, there

---

53   *MEGA*, II, 4.1, p. 97; *MECW*, 34, p. 431; Marx 1976, p. 1026.

can be no reason to deny that domination occurs on account of non-fulfilment of the alien will condition.

Already by this point, we can agree and yet disagree with Postone's claim:

> In Marx's analysis, social domination in capitalism does not, on its most fundamental level, consist in the domination of people by other people, but in the domination of people by abstract social structures that people themselves constitute ... Within the framework of Marx's analysis, the form of social domination that characterizes capitalism is not ultimately a function of private property, of the ownership by the capitalists of the surplus product and the means of production; rather, it is grounded in the value form of wealth itself, a form of social wealth that confronts living labor (the workers) as a structurally alien and dominant power ... A central hallmark of capitalism, then, is that people do not really control their own productive activity or what they produce but ultimately are dominated by the results of that activity. This form of domination is expressed as an opposition between individuals and society, which is constituted as an abstract structure.[54]

In this passage, Postone broaches two questions. One is the question of the cause of domination in capitalism: what it is 'ultimately a function of' or 'grounded in'. Here Postone considers two possibilities. Either domination in capitalism is explained by class division (a division between owners of means of production and product, and non-owners), or it is explained by the value form of wealth. Postone suggests that domination in capitalism is explained by the value form of wealth. A second question is what domination in capitalism 'consists in' or by what it is 'constituted'. Either domination in capitalism consists in domination by other people, or it consists in domination by an abstract social structure. Postone takes the latter view. It is possible, however, to agree that what Postone refers to as the value form of wealth is the cause of capitalist labour-domination (because its cause is formal and real subsumption), but to take a different view of what capitalist labour-domination consists in.

It is unclear what is supposed to justify Postone's contrast between 'domination of people by other people' and 'domination of people by abstract social structures'. If what distinguishes 'domination of people by other people' from 'domination of people by abstract social structures' is intentional activity on the part of a dominating actor, the notion of 'domination of people by abstract

---

54   Postone 1993, p. 30.

social structures' should be rejected; rejected, indeed, on the basis of Marx's *Grundrisse*, the text from which Postone claims inspiration.[55] If, on the other hand, domination by 'social structures' consists in an intrastructured intentional activity of domination, and 'abstract' domination is domination in the pursuit of abstract wealth; then the distinction can be upheld. Capitalism, as a system of production that reinforces the pursuit of money maximisation, gives rise to 'domination of people by abstract social structures' in this sense; that is, to the intrastructured (because competitively imposed) command of an alien will in the pursuit of money maximisation. On this latter elaboration, however, capitalist domination is conceived differently to Postone, for whom domination has nothing specifically to do with commanding.

On a command-based elaboration, too, the main cause of capitalist labour-domination is formal and real subsumption, not class division. It is possible to conceive of a system of money-maximising production in which (at least initially) each performs wage-labour in a different money-maximising unit of production to one they co-own; and in which shares cannot be exchanged for money, and dividends can only be converted into shares. If so, formal and real subsumption is logically possible without initial class division. But if formal and real subsumption is logically possible without initial class division, and is sufficient to give rise to capitalist labour-domination, then the value form of wealth must be regarded as the primary cause of capitalist labour-domination. (By contrast, if all that is stipulated about a society is that it is initially divided into private owners of means of production and product and free non-owners, it need not possess the productive power required for capitalist production. Class division without formal and real subsumption is not sufficient to give rise to capitalist labour-domination).

8   Domination and Real Subsumption

We have already seen, in connection with formal subsumption, that it is both possible and necessary for a capitalist firm to command wage-labour. Part of this argument consisted in showing that a capitalist can believe in the legitimacy of the commands issued to a wage-labourer on account of a belief in the doctrine of individual responsibility. To this we can now add that real subsumption generates a belief that the commands of a capitalist firm possess a second type of legitimacy.

---

55   Postone 1993, p. xi; compare sec. 1 above.

Capital Volume I implicitly distinguishes the aspect of command that is tied to the capitalist use of social productive powers from the aspect of command that results from formal subsumption in its remark:

> With the cooperation of numerous wage-labourers, the commanding power [*Kommando*] of capital develops into a requirement for carrying out the labour process itself, a real condition of production. The capitalist's command [*Befehl*] in the field of production now becomes as indispensable as the general's command on the field of battle.[56]

Before providing a positive account of how real subsumption accentuates capitalist labour-domination, however, it is important to reject one line of thought that relates to a mistranslation of a neighbouring passage in *Capital* Volume I:

> All immediately social or communal labour on a large scale requires, in varying degrees, a directing organ [*Direktion*] that harmonises individual activities, and assumes the general functions arising from the workings of the entire productive organism, as distinct from the movements of its independent parts.[57]

To say that 'all' large-scale social processes of work, whether in a capitalist firm or not, require a 'directing organ', is to say that they all require the administrative tasks of planning and execution to be assumed by certain identifiable people. All large-scale social processes of work generate a need to decide between various views of how to realise one and the same goal, and to reconcile each actor to that decision. Second, all large-scale social processes of work depend on continuity. To that end, the requisite means must be supplied without delay, in sufficient quantity, to the correct people; and tasks must be distinguished and assigned so that they can be performed no later than the moment at which their non-performance interrupts others.

Sadly, in both the Aveling/Moore and the Fowkes translations of *Capital* Volume I, '*Direktion*' is rendered as 'directing authority'. That is inaccurate, because *Capital* does not refer to '*Autorität* (authority)' here.[58] It is misleading, as a '*Direktion*' is an administrative unit, and an administrative unit need not

---

56   *MEW*, 23, p. 350; *MECW*, 35, p. 335; Marx 1976, p. 448. *MECW* and Marx 1976 translate '*Kommando*' as 'sway' or 'command' respectively. '*Kommando*' is a synonym for '*Befehlsgewalt* (commanding power)', not '*Befehl* (command)'.

57   *MEW*, 23, p. 350; *MECW*, 35, pp. 335–6; Marx 1976, p. 448.

58   The phrase used in the French edition of *Capital* is '*une direction*' (*MEGA*, II, 7, p. 283).

exercise *de facto* practical authority. In other words, it need not issue instructions with peremptory content-independent force in the belief that it is legitimate for it to do so. If Marx had wanted to imply that *de facto* practical authority is required for any large-scale social process of work, nothing would have been easier than for Marx to have written '*Kommando*' where in fact he wrote '*Direktion*'.

A reader of *Capital* in translation may infer that Marx believes that, in virtue of the twin administrative tasks of planning and execution, all large-scale social processes of work require the exercise of *de facto* practical authority. One interpreter to defend this conclusion is Ali Rattansi. Rattansi repeatedly cites the Aveling/Moore translation of this passage as 'crucial' proof that Marx came to regard 'authoritative regulation' as an aspect of any large-scale work process.[59] Similarly, David Harvey's companion to *Capital* says: 'any cooperative endeavor requires some directing authority'.[60] Nothing could be further from the truth.

In and of themselves, administrative planning and execution lack all three qualities of domination: a command, an alien will, and the recognition of a command. Neither administrative planning nor execution requires a command or its recognition. The exercise of administrative skill is conceivable without the exercise of *de facto* practical authority. It is conceivable for administrative policy and administrative appointments to be subject to the approval of a forum, constituted on the initiative of those whose activities are to be administered, in which their rationale is scrutinised. Any instructions issued by people who assume administrative tasks are then issued with the implicit acknowledgement that it may be proper for their addressees to question them. They may be owed a further explanation, if that would bear on how the forum is to scrutinise the rationale of the instruction or the rationale of having them assume administrative tasks. As instructions issued with this acknowledgement lack peremptory, content-independent force, they are not commands. They do not effect exclusion. Their execution is not the recognition of a command. Nor need administrative planning and execution imply the direction of an alien will. Administration need not serve an end from whose perspective the wills of those whose activities are administered appear as foreign.

The official translations of *Capital* prevent readers from concluding that, if it were not for certain features of capitalism, social productive powers could

59   Rattansi 1982, p. 138, pp. 165–6, p. 193.
60   Harvey 2010, p. 174.

(Marx allows) be used without the use of commanding power. They preclude those who want a Marxist analysis of capitalism to focus on its distinctive features from employing a command-based conception of domination to analyse capitalism. What those who are duped by the ideology in the official translations of *Capital* must fail to grasp is this. Marx's claim is that real subsumption modifies the character of domination in the capitalist production process due to the conjunction of a large-scale social process of work, and the separation of those who own the firm from those who perform the activities that are administered (and not because of the fact of a large-scale social process of work alone).

Commands presuppose a belief in the legitimacy of issuing instructions with peremptory, content-independence force. The legitimacy of commands issued to a wage-labourer by a capitalist firm can rest on a belief in individual responsibility, and a belief that the facts accord with it. By the same token, if a capitalist concludes separate contracts with several wage-labourers to work with and on the same means of production, then, provided those contracts provide for a social process of work, a belief in individual responsibility will allow a capitalist to issue commands in respect of wage-labourers' interactions with these means. Indeed, if a capitalist can believe, on grounds of individual responsibility, that they are entitled to command wage-labourers they hire in a social process of work, they can also believe, on the same grounds, that those they hire to command others they hire are entitled to issue commands to the latter, provided that suitable provision is made in wage-labourers' contracts. The same applies to these administrative personnel themselves. A capitalist can believe, on grounds of individual responsibility, and subject once again to the same contractual provision, that the administrative personnel they hire to command other administrative personnel they hire are entitled to command the latter.

This arrangement has a specific consequence. If administrative personnel are all hired by a capitalist who decides who works with, under or over whom, administrative personnel will be bound not to deliberate with subordinates, or explain the rationale of their decisions to subordinates, if they are so instructed by someone authorised by the capitalist to issue that instruction to them. Its purpose may be to keep a firm's special knowledge or strategy from competitors; or to confine controversy or disagreement among members of a workforce, whose will is alien. With this instruction, they are bound to secrecy. Occasions may arise in which subordinates come to administrative personnel with a problem related to a matter on which administrative personnel are bound to secrecy. On such occasions, administrative personnel have no option but to exercise *de facto* practical authority. To solve the problem, they must issue instructions; but as they are bound to secrecy, they cannot explain these instructions. Even if it were not the most time efficient option, their response would have to take the form: do this, because I say so. The exercise of *de facto* practical authority by administrative personnel is thus an inherent feature of the administration of a large-scale social process of work in an entity (like a capitalist firm) whose legal owners are separate from those who perform the activities that are administered. Marx's claim in *Critique of Hegel's Doctrine of the State* that the '*authority*' of administrative personnel is based in a 'hierarchy' of '*secrecy*'[61] applies to capitalist firms as well.

To be sure, administrative personnel (= A) can believe in individual responsibility as a basis for the legitimacy of their commands, just as the capitalist (= c) can. A need only suppose that those they command contract with c to be instructed by A, just as A contracts with c to instruct them. But a belief in a second type of basis for the legitimacy of these commands may also arise. As no plan can regulate every eventuality in advance, administrative personnel will need to respond to unforeseen problems of an administrative nature. But as the problems they must respond to are administrative in nature; and as administrative personnel are employed on account of their administrative ability; any command by administrative personnel can be accompanied by a belief in administrative expertise as a basis of its legitimacy.

This belief takes the form: it is legitimate for me to issue you with an instruction carrying peremptory content-independent force because *I have* administrative skill (or else because the person whose instruction I relay has administrative skill). The form of the belief is not: it is legitimate for me to issue you with an instruction carrying peremptory content-independent force because *it* is *informed by* administrative skill. As the latter belief is a judgement about the instruction, it is not the kind of belief that can underpin a belief that an instruction has content-independent force. The former belief is backed up by a suitable credible threat of sanction if the power of dismissal is delegated to administrative personnel, and/or if they have the discretionary power to vary a wage-labourer's exposure to capture by company records, and that surveillance is regarded as tiresome and/or humiliating.

Capital makes three further points about the occasions for domination in a capitalist firm:

> The capitalist's direction is not just a particular function arising from and inherent to the nature of the social process of work; it is also a function

---

61   *MEW*, 1, p. 249; *MECW*, 3, p. 47.

of the exploitation of a social process of work, and thus conditioned by the unavoidable antagonism between the exploiter and the raw material of their exploitation. Likewise, the imperative to control the proper use of the means of production, which confront the wage-labourer as alien property, grows with their advance. Further, the cooperation of wage-labourers is a mere effect of the capital that simultaneously deploys them ... The connection of their labours therefore confronts them intellectually as the capitalist's plan, and practically as the capitalist's authority [*Autorität*], as the power of an alien will [*fremden Willens*] subjecting their doings to its purpose.[62]

The first point Marx makes here is that occasions for domination are increased by the fact that a firm's pursuit of continuous money maximisation may antagonise its producers, who do not share this end. A capitalist firm may wet the ambitions of its workforce by encouraging them to increase their own monetary wealth by acting to maximise the firm's. But that must wet their ambitions for higher positions. *The Communist Manifesto* refers, like *Capital*, to 'surveillance from a full hierarchy of lieutenants and officers'.[63] If the loyalty of those who monitor labour must be purchased by status and reward, the apparatus for imposing domination is also a career path, and thus an object of potential conflict in its own right, potentially calling for more domination.

Second, real subsumption permits calculation, and calculation is entwined with domination. In the above passage, Marx says that, as investment in technology increases, capital accumulation increasingly depends on its 'proper use', that is, on capitalist efficiency. The damage of technology that is a relatively greater part of outlay is more crucial for a capitalist firm to avoid. But capitalist efficiency rests on capitalist calculation. To get wage-labourers to put a given technology to its intended use with minimum wear and tear presupposes a target for what counts as a proficient use. Thus, if the damage of technology is increasingly crucial to avoid, it is increasingly crucial to devise firm predictions as to what counts as a proficient use. That gives capitalist labour-domination an extended licence. Commands are required not just to uphold capitalist effi-

---

62   *MEW*, 23, pp. 350–1; *MECW*, 35, pp. 336–7; Marx 1976, pp. 449–50. (1) *MECW* and Marx 1976 render '*Macht eines fremden Willens*' as 'the powerful will of another' (which would be: '*der mächtiger Wille eines anderen*') or 'the powerful will of a being outside them'. These renderings lose Marx's stress on a will whose end, from the worker's perspective, appears as 'alien [*fremd*]'; see sec. 1.

63   *MEW*, 4, p. 469; *MECW*, 6, p. 491; compare *MEW*, 23, p. 351; *MECW*, 35, p. 337; Marx 1976, p. 450.

ciency, but to ensure a firm's efforts at calculation; in other words, to ensure that its employees keep, and are captured by, company records.

Third, real subsumption ensures that it is the social process of work that provides the focus of a firm's commands. Just as a firm's concern is with the money its total output represents, and only with the use-value of that output because nothing without use-value can be of any monetary value; so its interest in any wage-labourer's set of tasks is as a contribution to the monetary value of its total product, and to minimising the costs of total wear and tear to all its means of production. What a capitalist firm seeks from any given wage-labourer, therefore, is that they perform their tasks without delaying or coun-teracting the tasks assigned to its other employees, in circumstances where the division and length of tasks is oriented to continuous money maximisation. The effect of that orientation on a workforce is that each member is encour-aged to see in the tasks of every other member a potential prompt for their own domination, which must again give rise to further conflicts to be managed.

As real subsumption includes a division of labour in the workplace, it in-cludes an administrative division of labour. Some administrative personnel draw up the 'plan' that others execute 'practically'. But if a capitalist firm imple-ments an administrative division of labour, by hiring separate planners and executors, planners and executors must then relate to each other. A remark from Marx's *Critique of Hegel's Doctrine of the State* implies that the internal relations of a bureaucracy, that is, a professional administration in which a belief in administrative expertise underpins a belief in the legitimacy of its commands, will be characterised by a degree of collusion:

> The top echelons entrust the lower orders with knowing the details, whilst the lower orders trust the top echelons with knowing general matters, and in this way they mutually deceive themselves.[64]

R.D. Laing and Aaron Esterson have argued that if, to live out a phantasy of myself, I treat another not as they are, but as a figure in my phantasy system, 'collusion' arises if it is the case for each that 'the other person's phantasy of what one is, coincides with one's own phantasy of what one is'.[65] As Martin Howarth-Williams elaborates:

---

64   *MEW*, 1, p. 249; *MECW*, 3, pp. 46–7. The translation of this sentence in Furner 2011, p. 209
     contains inaccuracies (without affecting the argument advanced therein).
65   Laing and Esterson 1958, p. 120.

> The particular function of collusion seems to be the mutual confirmation of the player's phantasy positions by each other. Thus, suppose p phantasises that he is an intellectual and o that he (o) is a 'he-man', whereas in fact they are neither. Collusion would occur if p tacitly agreed to confirm o as a he-man in return for o confirming him, p, as an intellectual. This elaborate phantasy system is not, of course, made explicit by the players.[66]

In the case of a capitalist firm, planners are in the default position of having a duty not to disclose the rationale behind their plans. A firm's special knowledge, competitive strategy or internal work atmosphere might otherwise be compromised. Yet planners may not be able to extract from executors a relevant account of executors' actions without being prepared to risk some disclosure of the rationale behind the plans that executors are supposed to implement. To the extent that that risk is to be avoided, planners 'entrust' executors with a plan's execution. Yet, insofar as planners entrust executors with a plan's execution, they will be unable to ascertain the extent to which the plans they drew up were applied, and thus were apt to be applied. All they can then do is verify, from company records, whether or not executors' captured behaviour is in order and has yielded the projected results. Planners thus need to believe in the image of good executors (which they cannot confirm) to believe in themselves as good planners (which they cannot confirm). Executors, on the other hand, are in the default position of having to exercise *de facto* practical authority over wage-labourers. In doing so, they may have to relay instructions from superiors in the administrative hierarchy and so 'trust' in planners' administrative expertise. Yet executors cannot properly implement a plan, as distinct from achieve its targets, if they are not privy to the rationale behind it. So, executors, too, need to believe in the image of good planners (which they cannot confirm) to believe in themselves as good executors (which they cannot confirm).

9   The Recognition Condition and Occupational Identity

The argument thus far has focused on the link between formal and real subsumption on the one hand, and the command condition and alien will condition for domination on the other. We now turn, finally, to the recognition condition for domination, which says: the commander is recognised through

---

66   Howarth-Williams 1977, p. 20.

the addressee's obedience. The question is whether the administrative personnel of a capitalist firm can experience the response of wage-labourers to their
commands as one of recognition.

Capital offers the suggestive remark:

> It is not enough for the conditions of labour to amass at one pole, as
> capital, while human beings with nothing to sell but their labour power
> gather at the other. Nor is it enough to compel them to sell themselves vol-
> untarily. As capitalist production advances, a working-class develops that,
> by education, tradition and custom, recognises [*anerkennt*] the require-
> ments of that mode of production as self-evident laws of nature.[67]

Marx here insists that the lack of alternative options of the propertyless to
selling their labour power is no guarantee of the survival of capitalist production. The survival of capitalist production requires 'education, training and custom' of the kind that leads wage-labourers to 'recognis[e]' its 'requirements'. As
these requirements include the execution of commands, Marx implies that we
can infer from the survival of capitalist production that the recognition condition for domination is satisfied. In other words, the administrative personnel of
capitalist firms who issue its commands can believe that the in-order-to motive
of their addressees is: working for a wage in order to live, by obeying the firm's
commands.

To account for this recognition, Marx refers obliquely to 'education, tradition
and custom'. Whatever 'education, tradition and custom' includes, it includes
the cultural effects of formal and real subsumption. The following analysis is
confined to this effect. It may also be born in mind that the question here
is simply whether it is possible for the administrative personnel who issue
the commands of a capitalist firm to believe that their commands are recognised. The recognition condition is satisfied even if its relative causal weight in
explaining why commands are observed is modest in comparison to the threat
of being let go or the prospect of career advancement.

---

67 *MEW*, 23, p. 765; *MECW*, 35, p. 726; Marx 1976, p. 899. Both *MECW* and Marx 1976 translate
    '*anerkennt*' as 'looks upon' (which would be: '*betrachtet*'). On these translations, it is as if
    Marx's concern here is with workers' opinions. To say that an actor 'looks upon' a require-
    ment as self-evident is to say that they are of the opinion that it is self-evident. But Marx is
    concerned here with the conditions of capitalist production. What capitalist production
    presupposes is a kind of behaviour. To use the verb '*anerkennen*' in this context is to make a
    claim about the normative beliefs that can be taken to inform wage-labourers' in-order-to
    motives.

One contributing factor, related to formal subsumption, is the attribution of a belief in individual responsibility. By signing a contract all by themselves and only for themselves, a wage-labourer can be understood to assert a right to work and to be instructed in that work. The administrative personnel of a capitalist firm who issue its commands can also reason from the fact that, as *Results of the Immediate Process of Production* puts it, each wage-labourer is 'responsible to himself for the manner in which he spends his wages'.[68] If a commander can assume that a wage-labourer believes that a means of consumption they purchase ought to be delivered to them, then, by the same token, a commander may assume that a wage-labourer's in-order-to motive in observing their commands can be informed by a normative belief that they ought to do as instructed in order to carry out a command of someone they agreed to be instructed by.

A second contributing factor relates to real subsumption. As we have seen, a further basis for administrative personnel to believe in the legitimacy of the commands they issue is a belief in their administrative expertise. The recognition condition for domination can also be satisfied, therefore, if it is possible for administrative personnel to believe that a wage-labourer does as they instruct in order to carry out a command of an administrative expert.

This possibility rests on an additional premise: that a wage-labourer who is the addressee of a command identifies themselves with their productive activity. If A obeys B's commands on account of a belief in B's administrative expertise, A can feel assured that their work is in safe administrative hands. But A must identify themselves with their activity for this assurance to be of value to them. In fact, for this assurance to be of value to them, A must identify themselves with their activity so as to identify no ability of their own to assess the administrative tasks it generates. Otherwise, it is unclear why A's interest in an assurance that their activity is in safe administrative hands should not lead A to challenge B's *de facto* practical authority.

The German Ideology insists that productive activities do more than just yield output. They also mould individual identity:

> [A] mode of production is not merely to be observed as the reproduction of individuals' physical existence. It is also a definite type of activity by these individuals, a determinate way of expressing their life, their distinctive *mode of life*. The manner in which individuals express their life makes them what they are.[69]

---

68   *MEGA*, II, 4.1, p. 103; *MECW*, 34, p. 437; Marx 1976, p. 1033.
69   *MEJ*, 2003, p. 107; *MEW*, 3, p. 21; *MECW*, 5, p. 31.

One form of identity generated by the system of capitalist production is occupational identity. *The German Ideology* remarks that an occupational title like that of 'painter' is a 'name already capturing well the parochial character [*Borniertheit*] of their occupational development and dependence on the division of labour'.[70] If receipt of means of individual consumption is conditional on performing work, and if all offers of work are offers to perform activities for firms that operate in particular branches of production, then each wage-labourer tends to face pressures to continue to remain in a particular occupation. Each is led by that occupational confinement to assert an occupational identity (painter, baker, train-driver, tailor, doctor, and so on), because each cannot simply quit their current occupation and maintain their standard of living; because each is recognised as making a productive contribution to social wealth only through a paid occupation; and because each is led to cultivate indifference to general affairs beyond their occupation by continual exposure to contexts in which a single sectional interest is articulated, and by the difficulty of switching occupations.

For *A* to assume an occupational identity is for *A* to want to be moved all the way to action by the value bestowed on *A* as a practitioner of an occupation on which value is bestowed. Suppose *A*'s occupation is driving. Insofar as *A* assumes the occupational identity of a driver, *A* will want to be moved all the way to action by the value bestowed on *A* as a driver. If an interest is what an actor, in light of their will, can believe they have a reason to do or to favour, then *A*'s occupational identity gives *A* an interest to do or to favour what *A* judges necessary to express or preserve the value bestowed on *A* as a driver.

The assumption of an occupational identity is not to be confused with an actor's identification of themselves with a normatively regulated activity. For *B* to identify themselves with a normatively regulated activity is for *B* to want to be moved all the way to action by the norms of that activity. For *B* to identify themselves with driving is for *B* to want to be moved all the way to uphold the norms of driving. *B*'s will is to drive well, by the standard of those norms. *B*'s will to perform an activity well is, however, a different kind of will to *A*'s will to express or preserve the value bestowed on *A* as a practitioner of a valued occupation. The will to drive well is distinct from the will to express or preserve the value bestowed on oneself as a driver.

---

70   *MEW*, 3, pp. 378–9; *MECW*, 5, p. 394. Feuerbach uses '*borniert*' to denote 'indifference towards everything that is not immediately connected to well-being of the self' (Feuerbach 1984, p. 210; Feuerbach 1989, p. 114). That is a good way to understand Marx's current claim, if 'self' is replaced with 'occupational self'.

To be moved all the way to action by the norms of an activity, an actor need not assume an occupational identity. Indeed, an occupational identity can even incline an actor to violate the norms of the corresponding activity. Suppose that there are traffic regulations such as speed limits for good driving. If *B* identifies themselves with the activity of driving, then *B* will want to be moved all the way to observe these traffic regulations, to drive well. *B* can want to be moved all the way to observe them even if *B* does not think of themselves as a driver. Perhaps *B* only thinks of themselves as someone who drives to work. It is possible, moreover, to imagine that someone whose occupation leads them to adopt the identity of driver believes that, as they are such a great driver, by the criterion, say, of how much money they make from driving compared to what other drivers make, or of how many more kilometres than other drivers they have driven, they need not observe the traffic regulations that other drivers ought to observe. They need not regard it as necessary to abide by a speed limit to preserve their value as a driver when they can measure their value as a driver by an independent criterion; a criterion that compares them as a driver to other drivers, rather than their driving to norms of driving. An occupational identity is so far from being equivalent to the identity provided by a normatively regulated activity that it is conceivable for it to lead an actor to violate that activity's norms.

This difference can also be illustrated in the terms of Marx's famous Eleventh Thesis of the *Theses on Feuerbach*: 'philosophers have only *interpreted* the world in various ways; the point is to *change* it'.[71] Marx is not claiming that *philosophies* only interpret the world in various ways, and the point is to change it. If that had been Marx's claim, it would have represented a rejection of his earlier view, in *Letters from the Deutsch-Französische Jahrbücher*, that 'philosophical consciousness itself has been drawn into the torment of the struggle not merely externally, but intrinsically'.[72] Rather, the Eleventh Thesis says that *philosophers* only interpret the world. The occupational identity of philosopher will not move philosophers to change the world, even if it is anti-philosophical not to. Cohen gets things exactly wrong when he provides the Eleventh Thesis with the gloss: 'commitment as a philosopher will compel him to become a political activist'.[73] It is not the value bestowed on an actor as a philosopher that may lead them to a revolutionary commitment. Rather, one thing that, for Marx, may produce this commitment is the value an actor puts on philosophising well. If,

71   *MEW*, 3, p. 7; *MECW*, 5, p. 5.

72   *MEW*, 1, p. 344; *MECW*, 3, p. 142.

73   Cohen 2001, p. 97.

as Marx believed, the capitalist world order is one that generates illusions, antinomies, collusion, secrecy and lies, all of which impede a search for truth, then
someone who values philosophy, understood as a search for truth, has a reason
to change the world, even if a philosopher does not.

Just as commodity form philosophy utilises the concept of use-value, which
is distinct from the concept of a good, so it distinguishes normatively regulated
activity from occupational identity. The concept of use-value abstracts from all
forms of distribution. It is distinct from the concept of a good, because a good
presupposes the thought of a subject with the will of a possessor. Likewise,
the knowledge of what it is to perform an activity well and the sense of self
that is enjoyed by performing it well abstracts from its distribution as a paid
occupation, and from the associated occupational confinement and occupational identity. Marx's *Economic and Philosophic Manuscripts of 1844* urge that
'all physical and intellectual senses' are to be freed from 'the sense of having'.[74]
This is a plea not just for a critique of goods and a discipline of thought in which
use-value only exists in the form of (economic) goods, but also for a critique of
occupational identity and any inquiry in which occupational identity is treated
as a natural form that a sense of self related to productive activity is to take.

Occupational identity is neither a sufficient nor a necessary condition for
meaningful work. An occupational identity is not sufficient for meaningful
work, for even mechanically repetitive jobs that are resented as a form of
drudgery may form the basis of an occupational identity. The assumption of an
occupational identity is not necessary for meaningful work, either. An actor can
take a sense of accomplishment from their work if they can affirm its intrinsic
value for a life worth living, and occupational identities are not necessary to
affirm a life plan that includes productive activities as ends in themselves. A
world is possible in which an actor takes a sense of accomplishment from having spent part of their life writing a book, for no other end than that of expand-
ing human knowledge, without either writing as a paid occupation, or thinking
of themselves as a writer.

However, for actors in a system of production that imposes occupational
confinement, and who therefore assume occupational identities, it must seem
that their own value rests on their continued performance of the corresponding
activity, and that the world depends on them for it. It is impossible for someone,
within the occupational identity they assume, to conclude that they have the
ability to help meet a need that goes beyond it. Nor, insofar as they regard others
within the occupational identities they assume, can they conclude that others

---

74   *MEW*, 40, p. 540; *MECW*, 3, p. 300.

have the ability to help meet needs that go beyond those occupations. Paint-ers – as distinct from 'human beings who amongst other things, also paint'[75] – cannot conclude that they are able to help meet the need for coats or for driv-ing; and a painter cannot believe that tailors or drivers (as distinct from human beings who make coats or drive) are able to help meet the need for painting. As a painter cannot conclude that they, as a painter, have the ability to meet needs besides the need for painting, or that tailors or drivers can help meet the need for painting, a painter must suppose that their own value rests on their con-tinuing to paint, and that the world depends on painters like them to meet its need for painting. The same goes for every actor who assumes an occupational identity.

Occupational identities therefore sustain two jointly acting reasons for a capitalist firm's administrative personnel to assume that wage-labourers do as they instruct in order to carry out a command of an administrative expert. The occupational identities that administrative personnel can attribute to wage-labourers in non-administrative jobs do not allow administrative personnel to assume that wage-labourers identify any ability in themselves to perform administrative tasks. But wage-labourers attributed with non-administrative occupational identities can be thought to welcome *administrators'* expertise for managing the only productive contribution that their occupational iden-tities allow them to believe they can make. Indeed, administrators may believe that wage-labourers who assume occupational identities obey their commands on the grounds of their administrative expertise even if they cannot believe that wage-labourers obey them on the grounds of individual responsibility. An actor succeeds in terms of their occupational identity if they meet their tar-gets. To achieve this success, they need not believe that their targets represent no more than the amount of work they agreed to perform. If administrators who view wage-labourers in terms of their occupational identities can assume that the latter have a reason to strive to meet a target even if it exceeds what they agreed to do, they may suppose that wage-labourers obey their commands even when they cannot believe that a belief in individual responsibility gives wage-labourers a reason to do so.

Further, occupational identities not only reinforce wage-labourers' obedi-ence. They also reinforce compliance. They allow the sanction of terminating a labour contract to derive its force not just from the undesirable uncertainty of having to compete with the unemployed for work in order to live, but also from the undesirable state of having no recognised identity, in virtue of being

---

75   *MEW*, 3, p. 379; *MECW*, 5, p. 394.

deprived of the employment that gave them one. *The German Ideology's* claim that everyone is 'a hunter, fisherman or shepherd, or a critical critic, and so they must remain if they do not wish to lose their means of life'[76] is irreducible to the claim that everyone must continue to hunt, fish, breed stock or philosophise if they do not wish to lose their means of subsistence.

10   Summary

The foregoing account of capitalist labour-domination reflects a commitment to the value of self-legislative human community. From this perspective, capitalist-labour domination is concerning, because:

(1)   A system that relies on commanding effects social division. As the addressees of commands cannot be their co-authors, the recognition of commands encourages commanders to express the fact that while they are entitled to command, their addressees may not hold them to account. This yields a sense of 'us' and 'them'.

(2)   When the commanding that a system relies on has individual responsibility as a source of belief in its legitimacy, commanding will also (a) encourage each individual to care exclusively for their own powers, or for achieving the targets imposed on them, whether as a result of recognition, threat of sanctions, or incentives; (b) bind commanders not to disclose the position in a command chain that an instruction, which they may not be permitted to explain, originates from.

(3)   When the commanding that a system relies on has administrative expertise as a source of belief in its legitimacy, it will also thereby be prone to: (a) a degree of collusion among the personnel at different administrative levels; (b) a degree of disinterest towards matters beyond a given occupational identity; and (c) a degree of violation of the norms of normatively regulated activities.

These concerns are occluded by the official translations; and they lie beyond the vision of Marxist accounts of domination that focus on 'room for arbitrary exercise of power'[77] or dependency on a 'system for aggregating *arbitria*'.[78] They could remain live concerns even if contracts were perfect, and even if the conduct of owners and managers of firms was subject to effective third party scrutiny based on an evaluative judgement that compared needs for products.

---

76   *MEJ*, 2003, p. 20; *MEW*, 3, p. 33; *MECW*, 5, p. 47.
77   Roemer 1982b, p. 377.
78   Roberts 2017, p. 93.

CHAPTER 11

Antinomy and State Form

A philosophical analysis of the state of capitalist society differs from a comparative analysis of the states of historical capitalism. 'State of capitalist society' is the term used here for the most developed type of state that is compatible with the system of capitalist production, and its culture of recognition.[1] The state of capitalist society is a rights-based and popular-sovereignty-based state with a parliamentary-bureaucratic government. It cannot avoid an antinomy of natural rights and popular authorisation.

On the Jewish Question declares its concern with the state of capitalist society in its claim that *'political* emancipation' is 'not the final form of human emancipation in general', but 'the final form of human emancipation *within* the existing world order'.[2] In other words, the existing world order is said to be able to do no more than provide a limited type of freedom, called political freedom. A limit in 'the existing world order' is not merely a limit common to all instances of a given type of phenomenon that exists in the world at a certain point in time. It is a limit that is characteristic of a type of phenomenon that is essential to a world historical epoch. No matter how developed instances of this type become, they (and therefore the epoch) exhibit the limit. The difference between a philosophical analysis of the state of capitalist society and a comparative analysis of the states of historical capitalism is apparent when one considers that not a single state in the world at the time Marx wrote *On the Jewish Question* (1843) had yet to test the limit of political emancipation. It would have been clear to Marx that his was a philosophical claim.

Critique of the Gotha Programme advances a related sort of claim: '[r]ight can never be higher than the economic formation of society, and the development of culture this conditions'.[3] The degree to which a society can exhibit principles of right is said to rest on material, social and cultural factors other than those principles themselves. Should a society's 'economic formation' and 'culture' be limited, its principles of right will be limited. This claim can be linked to that of *On the Jewish Question* on the uncontroversial assumption that, for Marx, the system of capitalist production is a limited form of social wealth. For then

---

1 'Law of capitalist society' is used analogously.
2 *MEW*, 1, p. 356; *MECW*, 3, p. 155.
3 *MEW*, 19, p. 21; *MECW*, 24, p. 87; compare Marx 1972, p. 329.

the *Critique of the Gotha Programme*'s claim in respect of capitalism is that its principles of right are limited because its system of production and culture of recognition is limited; and *On the Jewish Question* insists that one limit of right in the capitalist world order is that it can do no more than provide political freedom. What needs to be explained, on this interpretation, is how the system of capitalist production, along with its culture of recognition, generates political representation; and why the freedom provided by a representative form of government is inherently limited.

An explanation of the state of capitalist society by its economic formation and culture presupposes a term, such as '*bürgerliche Gesellschaft*', translated either as 'civil society' or 'bourgeois society',[4] by which this economic formation can be singled out. In the first text in which Marx uses the term '*bürgerliche Gesellschaft*', his *Critique of Hegel's Doctrine of the State* of 1843, Marx claims:

> The constitution is nothing but an accommodation between the political and the unpolitical state; hence it is necessarily, in itself, a treaty [*Traktat*] between essentially heterogeneous powers.[5]

In *Elements of the Philosophy of Right*, Hegel uses '*Traktat*' to denote an agreement between independent states with 'particular *wills*'.[6] By referring to the constitutional relation between powers of the *same* state as a 'treaty', Marx suggests that no power of this state can root out the other, although each asserts its particular interests vis-à-vis the other. Marx thereby implies that the state of capitalist society cannot realise freedom as self-legislative human community. In writing for the *Kölnische Zeitung* the previous year, Marx suggests that the state in which the individual 'obeys, in the laws of the state, only the laws of

---

4   *The German Ideology* distinguishes (i) '*bürgerliche Gesellschaft*' as a 'social organisation' common to 'all epochs' with states and nations; and (ii) '*bürgerliche Gesellschaft* as such' that 'first develops with the bourgeoisie' (*MEJ*, 2003, p. 93; *MEW*, 3, p. 36; *MECW*, 5, p. 89). Uses of the first kind are translated as 'civil society', and uses of the second kind as 'bourgeois society', with the exception that, if Marx uses the term to report or comment on Hegel's view, it is also translated as 'civil society'. Even if, for Hegel, '*bürgerliche Gesellschaft*' marks a distinctively modern period, it includes institutions, such as the corporations, that purportedly mediate between market self-interest and the universal interest of the state. A term suggestive of a particular class is therefore inappropriate.

5   *MEW*, 1, p. 260; *MECW*, 3, p. 57; Marx 1975a, p. 120. In Marx 1975a, '*Traktat*' is rendered as 'synthesis' (which would be: '*Synthese*'); the last clause reads: 'it [the constitution – JF] is itself a synthesis of essentially heterogeneous powers'. There is no suggestion here of a 'synthesis', however, that is, a unity in which conflict is resolved; quite the opposite.

6   Hegel 1986b, § 336; Hegel 1991a, § 336.

nature of his own reason, human reason' is a 'great organism'.[7] A type of state can be likened to an 'organism' only if it possesses what Kant, in *Critique of Judgment*, terms 'organisation'; that is, only if 'each member in such a whole should indeed be not merely a means, but also a purpose'.[8] If a type of state can only realise freedom as self-legislative human community if its powers relate to one another harmoniously instead of asserting particular interests vis-à-vis one another; and if the constitutional relation between the powers of the state of capitalist society is that of a 'treaty'; then the state of capitalist society is not able to realise freedom as self-legislative human community. A type of state that can do no more than provide political freedom is limited on account of that fact, if political representation is but part of a constitutional arrangement in which the various powers of state assert particular interests vis-à-vis one another, precluding freedom as self-legislative human community.

Marx's claim in *Critique of Hegel's Doctrine of the State* may be defended as follows. To accommodate popular sovereignty and freedom of choice, the law-making power of the state of capitalist society must have the form of a representative assembly. As a representative assembly requires law-implementation to be left to a state bureaucracy, and representative discussion and bureaucratic authority are opposed both in spirit and in practice, the state of capitalist society is not a real unity. One backdrop to this conflict is an antinomy of natural rights and popular authorisation.

Section 1 derives the juridical logic of freedom of choice by outlining a guarantee related reason and a recognition related reason for commodity exchangers to call for legal norms of private property ownership and self-ownership. Section 2 recasts these legal norms in terms of absolute innate rights, and examines Marx's claim that absolute innate rights must appear as natural rights. Natural rights are not, however, the only apparent supra-legal source of justification on which the state of capitalist society can rely. Section 3 argues that the system of capitalist production precludes monarchical sovereignty; and, if only for the sake of equal liberty, necessitates an appeal to, and institutionalisation of, popular sovereignty. Section 4 summarises the resulting antinomy: it necessarily appears to be the case both that government action is only justified if and because it remains within the limits of natural rights, *and* that government action is only justified if and because it is authorised by a decision of the people for equal liberty. Section 5 presents a representative assembly as the form of law-making power that accommodates freedom of choice, and

---

7   *MEW*, 1, p. 104; *MECW*, 3, p. 202.
8   Kant 1987, 5: 375.

popular sovereignty. Section 6 argues that its representative form requires law-implementation to take a separate bureaucratic form, with which it must collide.

1   A Derivation of the Juridical Logic of Freedom of Choice

Capital and *Notes on Wagner* suggest an explanation of the law of capitalist society that begins from commodity exchange.[9] In commodity exchange, buyer and seller act as if they mutually recognise one another as private property owners, and, by implication, as persons. Through such as-if mutual recognition, generalised purchase and sale deposits the concepts of *animus domini* accompanying detention and an exclusive will in respect of one's parts and capacities in commodity exchangers' stock of experiences. Commodity exchangers are led to apply these concepts, by their social interest in security. A commodity exchanger's interest in the security of *animus domini* accompanying detention is a social interest, because no significant subgroup of individuals can withhold from others the general positive spillover effects of the satisfaction of their interest in its security. Commodity exchangers' self-interest is thus no barrier to their articulation of the principle that *animus domini* accompanying detention ought to be respected. But if such a principle is articulated, the ensuing recognition allows commodity exchangers to develop the freedom of will to use their possessions, parts and capacities without regard to anyone else's permission or instruction, and to respect such uses by others. That can embolden them in calling for the enforcement of legal norms of private property ownership and self-ownership.

Commodity exchangers have two reasons to call for legal norms of private property ownership and self-ownership. One reason relates to the guarantee function of law. Laws offer a 'mutual guarantee'[10] or 'mutual insurance'[11] for the interests they protect. If legal norms are clearly formulated, have adequate sanctions, and are reliably enforced, each can act on the expectation that, since no one will wish to incur the sanction, no one will obstruct them if their actions are permitted by these norms. The guarantee is 'mutual' if it removes the risks for one actor to perform a certain type of action only by removing the risks for all, by means of a general norm.

---

9   See ch. 9, sec. 2.
10   *MEJ*, 2003, pp. 94–5; *MEW*, 3, p. 62; *MECW*, 5, p. 90.
11   *MEW*, 7, p. 288; *MECW*, 10, p. 333.

The second reason relates to the recognition function of law. Marx writes in *Debates on Freedom of the Press* (1842) that 'laws' are 'positive, clear, general norms in which freedom has obtained an impersonal, theoretical existence independent of individual caprice'.[12] To be sure, Marx rejects this view of the relation between law and freedom in *The Holy Family* (1844), due in part to a reassessment of the impact of coercion on freedom: *'punishment, coercion,* contradict *human* conduct'.[13] Relatedly, Marx's vision of developed communism in *Critique of the Gotha Programme* is one in which 'society' will ultimately 'write on its flag: from each according to their ability, to each according to their needs!'[14] A 'flag', or public declaration, can serve a recognition function, but not a guarantee function. This reassessment does not negate the point at issue, however, which is that Marx identifies a public recognition function of law. Marx's re-assessment simply shows that he came to believe that coercively guaranteed law is not the *only* form that can serve this recognition function. Whether a publicly declared principle is guaranteed by coercive force or not, if it is publicly declared, it is proclaimed as having a standing above any individually held view to the contrary.

To put this into relief, imagine a society in which liberty is coercively guaranteed but in which each person is told what they are at liberty to do by being given a set of tickets detailing what their liberties are.[15] We may suppose that the tickets inform the holder of three further things: that every other person is at liberty to do the same things as them; that the tickets received by every other person also inform their holder that everyone else's tickets give them the same liberties; and that no one is to speak publicly of this. The coercion used to uphold these liberties could serve a guarantee function, if the liberties are clearly formulated, have adequate sanctions, and are reliably enforced. But as their enforcement is not an enforcement of publicly declared liberties, it would not serve a recognition function.

Accordingly, a second reason for commodity exchangers to call for legal norms of private property ownership and self-ownership is that they can will for it to be publicly declared that these norms ought to be upheld, to express their will that they ought to regulate how everyone behaves. The public declaration of these legal norms flags that they have a standing above any individually held belief to the contrary. Enforceable and publicly declared (and publicly

---

12   *MEW*, 1, p. 58; *MECW*, 1, p. 162.
13   *MEW*, 2, p. 190; *MECW*, 4, p. 179.
14   *MEW*, 19, p. 21; *MECW*, 24, p. 87.
15   See Cohen 2011, p. 181.

declared as enforceable) general norms are the means to guarantee and recognise principles that articulate persons' social interests.

Commodity exchangers have a social interest in the security of *animus domini* accompanying detention, and, by implication, of an exclusive will in respect of one's parts and capacities. This is not their only social interest in security, however. In the words of *Debates on Freedom of the Press*, commodity exchangers also have a social interest in a 'positive, clear',[16] which is to say, *determinate*, formulation of legal norms (as distinct from a vague public declaration, backed by coercive force). Commodity exchangers have a social interest of security in the determinate formulation of legal norms of private property ownership and self-ownership, because a norm can only serve as a 'common measure',[17] in Locke's phrase, if it obtains a determinate formulation.

As we saw in chapter 7, for a measure of value to exist, all commodity possessors must regard one and the same type of commodity as a measure. Likewise, it is unsatisfactory for a commodity exchanger to view their own conception of the legal norm of private property ownership as applying to all. Each commodity exchanger has a social interest in a situation where everyone knows that everyone knows that everyone knows ... that a legal norm of private property ownership entails such and such. The extent to which ignorance or uncertainty over what it covers can contribute to the prevalence of the character traits that have disadvantages for all is then minimised. So, each commodity exchanger has a social interest in a determinate formulation of the legal norms that guarantee and recognise private property ownership and self-ownership. But if so, each commodity exchanger may articulate the determinate formulation of these norms as a principle. They can recognise attempts to give these norms a determinate formulation.

To articulate the principle that *animus domini* accompanying detention ought to be respected as a determinate, enforceable and publicly declared norm generates a new logic. A legal private property owner is someone who enjoys *freedom of choice* in respect of their private property; and a self-owner is someone who enjoys *freedom of choice* in respect of their parts and capacities. As Savigny writes in Volume Three of *System of the Modern Roman Law*:

> In the sphere of law we do not engage with the speculative difficulties of the concept of freedom; what concerns us is simply freedom in appearance, that is, the ability to make a choice from several conceivable decisions.[18]

---

16   *MEW*, 1, p. 58; *MECW*, 1, p. 162.
17   Locke 1988, p. 351.
18   Savigny 1840, p. 102.

Or as Marx remarks, in *Comments on the Latest Prussian Censorship Instruction*:

> For the law, I do not exist, am no object for it, apart from in *my act*. That is the only thing to which the law is to hold me; for it is the only thing for which I demand a right of existence.[19]

The juridical logic of freedom of choice may be put into relief by recalling Frankfurt's analysis of addiction.[20] Neither a wanton addict, nor an unwilling addict, enjoys freedom of will. Neither is able to bring the actions they pursue into line with what they want to be moved all the way to do. But the law may safeguard the freedom of choice of both types of addict, provided the drug to which each is addicted is legal. If the drug is legal, no one is entitled to interfere with its consumption simply on the grounds that its consumer is addicted. If, say, either type of addict turns violent as a result of taking the legal drug, the law may permit their arrest. But the ground of their arrest is not that they have indulged an addiction to a legal drug. The ground of their arrest is the violent act they have performed. As the grounds on which an addict lacks freedom of will are not by themselves grounds for others to interfere with their legal drug-taking, freedom of choice does not imply freedom of will;[21] and the discipline of jurisprudence, Savigny insists, is not directly concerned with freedom of will. That someone has indulged an addiction is irrelevant both to whether they are to be held responsible for their choice of act, and to whether another is infringing their freedom of choice. What unwilling addicts 'demand a right of existence' for, that is, *demand* to have effects that are not cancelled, as distinct from what they merely *will* to take effect, are their chosen acts of drug-taking. It is only chosen acts that may prompt a sanctioning use of force.

The legal norms of private property ownership and self-ownership cannot guarantee a person's freedom of will in regard to their possessions, parts and capacities directly. Legal norms can only guarantee that will *indirectly*, by guaranteeing freedom of choice. Although a specific type of will, the will of a private property owner and a person, explains the existence of legal norms of private property ownership and self-ownership, what the latter secure is freedom of choice, which has its own logic.

An explanation is a derivation if the logic it explains is revealed as a logic that is bound to register its cause as just one of the phenomena that is subject to it.

---

19   *MEW*, 1, p. 14; *MECW*, 1, p. 120.

20   See ch. 10, sec. 2.

21   See Frankfurt 1971, p. 14.

The explanation offered for the juridical logic of freedom of choice is a derivation. Its cause is the freedom of will generated by the commodity form; and yet freedom of choice is safeguarded even for those who do not enjoy this freedom of will. Even if an addict ceases to have the will of a private property owner – if, say, they would not regard it as interference if someone sold their stuff behind their back, and gave them their drug of choice in return – they enjoy the same legal protection. They are legally entitled to complain about the invasion. Or suppose that an actor acts out of a sense of a nonvoluntarily assumed moral duty. The fact that they have not acted as a person will not stop a legal system based on norms of private property ownership and self-ownership from holding them individually responsible for their choice. Suppose an environmental activist violates a legal norm of private property ownership for the sake of an ecological principle, from which they take care not to exempt themselves, and that they regard as a nonvoluntarily assumed duty on all rational inhabitants of the world. They are not permitted to petition anyone who also regards the action they performed as entailed by this duty to serve any share of imprisonment they receive as punishment.

The German Ideology claims:

> This same jurists' illusion [of property as the freedom to choose what to do with an object – JF] explains the fact that for them, and for any code, it is entirely contingent that individuals enter into relations with one another, e.g. contracts; and [*und*] that, for any code [*ihm*], these relations are valid [*gelten*] as relations that one [can] enter into or not at will, and as relations whose content [rests] entirely on the individual volition of the contracting parties.[22]

---

22   *MEJ*, 2003, pp. 97–8; *MEW*, 3, p. 64; *MECW*, 5, pp. 91–2. (1) The *MECW* translation of '*gelten*' as 'consider' in its version of Marx's penultimate clause ('they consider that these relations [can] be entered into or not at will') is inaccurate. 'Consider' could translate '*betrachten* (to regard, look upon)' but not '*gelten*'. The difference is that, if relations have '*Geltung* (validity)', one can ask after the 'ground' ('*Grund*') of that '*Geltung*' (hence the compound noun: '*Geltungsgrund*'). To say that the relations regulated by a legal code are *valid* as relations that one can enter into or not at will is to say that freedom of choice is the *ground* of their legal effect. By contrast, to say that jurists *consider* the relations regulated by a legal code to be relations that one can enter into or not at will would be to say that jurists view their formation *to reflect nothing but* the parties' choices. The *MECW* translation thereby turns the clauses following the semi-colon into redundant repetitions of the clauses preceding it. No wonder, then, that *MECW* omits to translate the conjunction '*und*' after the semi-colon, for it signals that Marx is not repeating the same thought. The *MECW* translation misleads Donna Kline into saying of these clauses: 'it would appear, then, that Marx intended to attribute ... a view that the act of will involved in entering contracts was an arbitrary

The German Ideology's claim in the part of this sentence following the semi-colon is that the law of capitalist society codifies freedom of choice as the ground on which agreements are to be given legal effect. Agreements are to be given legal effect to respect the choices people make. To this end, it is not necessary for judges (a) to take a view of the facts on which any interaction given legal effect as a binding agreement is viewed to reflect nothing but the parties' preferences. Freedom of choice can serve as the ground on which an agreement is given legal effect even when it is known to be a fact that one or more of the parties had no other easy, costless or satisfactory option, and so agreed to something they would have preferred not to have agreed to.

For freedom of choice to provide the ground on which agreements are to be given legal effect, it is also not necessary for judges (b) to take a view of the facts on which both parties are viewed to have intended to enter into the agreement. Freedom of choice can serve as the ground on which an agreement is given legal effect even if it is known that one party did not intend for their behaviour to be taken as an offer or acceptance, provided they were negligent or reckless and the other is found to have honestly and/or reasonably taken it as such.[23]

Indeed, *The German Ideology*'s claim is that freedom of choice is the ground on which agreements are to be given legal effect at the level of a legal 'code' *as a whole*. This claim is consistent with believing that the law of capitalist society (c) includes some norms that, if they were applied as part of a differ-ent code of a different type of society, need not give legal effect to freedom of choice. Consider, for example, the law of unjust enrichment, which rectifies the outcomes of mistaken payments. Suppose *A* mistakenly pays *B*. A law against unjust enrichment says that *B*, the recipient of the mistaken payment, is under an obligation to pay *A* back. The reason why *B* must pay *A* back is neither a contract nor a wrong.[24] *B* may be required to pay *A* back even though *B* did nothing to bring about *A*'s mistake. So, *B*'s obligation to reimburse *A* need not be incurred by virtue of anything that could be construed as a choice on *B*'s part vis-à-vis *A*. But still, in capitalism, a law against unjust enrichment may serve to

---

one free of any external constraint' (Kline 1987, pp. 73–4). (2) *MECW* errs in rendering '*ihm*', a dative *singular* pronoun, as 'they' (which would be: '*ihnen*'). Thus, *MECW* errs in suppos-ing that the illusions in the clauses following '*ihm*' are illusion of 'jurists', rather than of 'any code'. Illusions of jurists can be illusions about matters of fact common to particular cases. Illusions of a legal 'code' are unrelated to such matters of fact; this supports point (1). (3) For why Marx can call jurists' view of property as the freedom to choose what to do with an object an 'illusion', see the discussion of Marx's recognition-based critique of rights in ch. 8, sec. 13.

23   Beyleveld and Brownsword 2007, pp. 190–5.
24   Birks 2005, p. 8.

return *A* and *B* back to a position in which freedom of choice is to be given legal effect, because this law is part of a legal code whose other norms give effect to freedom of choice. In socialism, by contrast, a law against unjust enrichment would instead serve to return *A* and *B* back to the position they would have been in had *B* not received something from *A* to which they were not entitled. It would neither give legal effect to a choice nor return *A* and *B* to a position in which freedom of choice is to be given legal effect above all. As the example of a law against unjust enrichment shows, the claim that the law of capitalist society adopts freedom of choice as the ground on which agreements are to be given legal effect must be advanced at the level of a legal code as a whole.

The law of capitalist society does not just secure personhood only indirectly, then, by guaranteeing freedom of choice. It guarantees any individual's freedom of choice only indirectly, by (a) guaranteeing everyone's freedom of choice, (b) using typical interpretive schemes to judge individual acts, and (c) bringing to bear an entire legal code.

A further aspect of commodity exchangers' security interest in respect of the legal norms of private property ownership and self-ownership is an interest in bringing closure to disputes over their implications, and the consequences for punishment. It is a form of insecurity to know that a norm's application to a given case can always be altered, or that any punishment can always be resumed. It would be to live with a constant fear of future disruption. It is a security interest to know when an interpretation is final, that is, cannot be disputed or annulled; and to know when a punishment has been served, that is, cannot be augmented. A single determinate procedure is required in each case.

Commodity exchangers' security interests in a single determinate procedure for the interpretation of legal norms and in a single determinate procedure for the punishment of violations are social interests. It is unsatisfactory for a commodity exchanger simply to suppose that on their own conception of the procedure for interpretation or punishment, the latter has run its course. Unless everyone can be sure that everyone can be of the same mind in regard to whether the procedure has run its course, no one can be sure that it has run its course. A security interest in closure over these disputes can only be satisfied, therefore, by publicly determining that a procedure for interpretation and punishment is to be used. Everyone can then tell whether or not interpretation and punishment in a given case has run its course. As a single measure for interpretation and punishment can only be obtained for one if it is obtained for all, a security interest in a single determinate procedure for interpretation and punishment is a social interest. As commodity exchangers' self-interest is no barrier to their affirming a principle whose object is a social interest, commodity exchangers can recognise attempts to establish a single determinate procedure for interpretation and punishment.

Part of what it is to know if and when an interpretation or punishment is final is to be able to identify the individuals who are to interpret and punish. But in addition to that, it is an aspect of the recognition function of the law of capitalist society that those who interpret legal norms, and punish norm violations, should be independent of all parties to the dispute. That is, they should be non-identical with them and in no special relationship with them. The recognition related reason for commodity exchangers to call for legal norms of private property ownership and self-ownership is to flag that these norms have a standing above any individually held view to the contrary. To enjoy that standing, their interpretation and the punishment of violations must be seen to be more than just the judgement that certain particular individuals' private property ownership or self-ownership is to be upheld. It must be seen as giving effect to a general principle. In order for interpretation and punishment to enjoy the standing of the implementation of a general principle, both must be assigned to those with no particular interest at stake, beyond the social interest in security that any commodity exchanger has. To say that the responsibilities for interpretation and punishment are to be assigned to an independent instance is to say that they are to be assigned to a court. The recognition based reason for commodity exchangers to call for legal norms of private property ownership and self-ownership is therefore also a reason for them to call for their interpretation and the punishment of violations to be assigned to a court.

Marx writes in the *Grundrisse*:

> every form of production generates its own legal relations, form of government, etc. The crudity and lack of conception lies in relating contingently, bringing into a merely reflective connection, what organically belongs together. All that occurs to bourgeois economists is that production is better with the modern police than e.g. with self-help [*Faustrecht*]. They forget that self-help is also a right, and that the right of might [*Recht des Stärkeren*] lives on in another form even in their '*Rechtsstaat*'.[25]

---

25   *MEW*, 42, p. 23; *MECW*, 28, p. 26; Marx 1973a, p. 88; Marx 1996, p. 133. (1) '*Faustrecht*' is the right of those who are wronged to redress the wrong by their own force, without involving a court (Osman 2007, p. 89; see, also, Welcker 2001, p. 83). To render '*Faustrecht*' as 'the principle of might makes right' (Marx 1973a) (which would be: '*das Prinzip "Macht macht Recht"*') or 'club-law' (*MECW*) (which could translate: '*das Recht des Stärkeren*') or 'law of the jungle' (Marx 1996) (which would be: '*das Gesetz des Dschungels*') is misleading, for (i) the wronged need not be the mighty; (ii) rule by the mighty does not contrast with

Marx's rebuke is directed at John Stuart Mill. In *Principles of Political Economy*, Mill suggests that the 'protection of industry' provided by 'the soldier, the policeman, and the judge' is arranged by government on account of efficiency. Such services are 'of better quality at a much smaller cost' if they are financed from taxes than if producers obtain them directly by 'engaging armed men' themselves.[26]

In Marx's rebuke, the qualifying phrase 'all that occurs' implies that, even if one were to assume, for argument's sake, that it was no more expensive for producers to hire qualified armed men themselves than for a government to arrange their employ, the crucial question can *still* be posed: why does the law of capitalist society include a 'modern police', and not 'self-help', that is, a right on the part of those who are wronged to re-dress the wrong by their own force, without involving a court? The interaction-recognition-antinomy thesis says: generalised purchase and sale leads actors to conceive themselves as private property owners and persons, who can only guarantee their social interest in security and give the norms of private property ownership and self-ownership the standing they believe they ought to have through determinate, coercively enforced and publicly declared general norms with independent procedures for interpretation and punishment.

This explanation avoids the *Grundrisse's* charge of being 'merely reflective', for it does not simply cite an economic function, but appeals to actors' self-conceptions. It also implies, like the *Grundrisse's* scare-quotes, a critique of the concept of a *Rechtsstaat*. A *Rechtsstaat* is a state whose sole task is to uphold right, and hence is organised in accordance with right. As Carl Welcker, a German liberal, remarks in *Die letzten Gründe von Recht, Staat und Strafe* (*The Ultimate Grounds of Law, State and Punishment*) (1813): '[r]ight must necessarily be prior to the *Rechtsstaat*, for the latter can only ground its rightful existence upon it'.[27]

'modern police', as Marx's use of *'Faustrecht'* is intended to do. (2) *'Das Recht des Stärkeren'* is the capacity to use a right to compel others, through fear, to serve one's desires (Welcker 2001, pp. 15–17). To confuse *'Faustrecht'* and *'das Recht des Stärkeren'* muddies the nature of Marx's complaint against Mill. (3) The Marx 1973a translation of *'"Rechtsstaat"'* as *'"constitutional republics"'* is incorrect. Boldt observes: *'"bürgerlicher Rechtsstaat"* ... For this specific form of modern state, whether it appeared as a monarchy or as a republic was a sideissue' (Boldt 1967, p. 100; compare Schmitt 2003, p. 201; Schmitt 2008, p. 236). A better Anglicism is 'constitutional state' (as in *MECW*). I follow Franz Neumann's practice (Neumann 1986, p. 179), and retain *'Rechtsstaat'*.

26   Mill 1965, Bk. I, ch. II, 5.

27   Welcker 2001, pp. 80–1; compare Kant 1991, 6: 312–13.

One line of critique of the concept of a *Rechtsstaat* is to argue that the centrality of right as a principle of social organisation arises from generalised purchase and sale. For then, if a state is to be a *Rechtsstaat*, it must uphold generalised purchase and sale, as the condition under which actors, as private property owners and persons, can believe in the fundamental status of the right that a *Rechtsstaat* is organised to uphold. But if so, its task cannot just be to uphold right. If it does not uphold generalised purchase and sale, there are no persons to demand right as the fundamental principle of social organisation. To secure its existence, it must uphold generalised purchase and sale, even if necessary at the expense of right. Yet a state that upholds generalised purchase and sale even at the expense of right is not a *Rechtsstaat*. The demand for a *Rechtsstaat* is the kind of demand that, in the words of a phrase Marx uses elsewhere in the *Grundrisse*, 'can only be satisfied under conditions in which it can no longer be raised'.[28]

2   Individual Human Rights

The character of a legal code in which freedom of choice is the ground for giving agreements legal effect can be illuminated by considering Marx's account of human rights in *On the Jewish Question*, in light of a classification of legal norms.

On one classification of legal norms, which uses two criteria, there are four types of legal norm. First, a legal norm may impose a duty and no right (no unconditional advantage), or award a right. Second, that duty or right may require non-interference from all others, or a particular action from another specific agent.

Some legal norms that regulate public office impose duties on officials without creating a right on the part of those they serve. A legal norm may impose a duty on an official not to exclude, arbitrarily, those who qualify for an advantage. An official may have a duty not to exclude, arbitrarily, any willing individual, who satisfies the relevant criteria, from accessing a public facility (a park, gallery, etc.). No right is thereby awarded, because the advantage is subject to capacity, and the conditions for maintaining the facility.[29] Alternatively, a legal norm may impose a duty on an official to require a particular

---

28   *MEW*, 42, p. 105; *MECW*, 28, p. 109; Marx 1973a, p. 172.
29   In Jellinek's terms, legal norms of this kind create a 'reflex right' or conditional advantage for others, not a 'subjective right' (Jellinek 1919, pp. 67–81).

action from an individual, or group of individuals, who fulfil the relevant criteria. An official may be under a duty, in defined circumstances, to conscript able-bodied adults of a given age. While the first type of duty-creating legal norm leads no particular action to be imposed on anyone but the duty-bound official, the second type of duty-creating legal norm does, in some circumstances, lead a particular action to be imposed on ordinary citizens, regardless of choice.

Alternatively, legal norms may award rights. A rightsholder's advantage is only cancelled or waived on a given occasion if they (are taken to) agree. Rights-awarding legal norms can also be classified according to whether they require non-interference from all others: *absolute* rights; or a particular action from another specific agent: *relative* rights. An example of the former is a right of private property. If A has a right of private property over x, then the advantages in respect to x that A enjoys cannot be taken from A without A's (real or fictional) agreement. From a phenomenological point of view, what makes this right an absolute right is that, if it is violated, then, in the absence of other modifying relations, the thought of its violation is separable from the thought of a special relation to another agent. It may be B, or C, or D, or ... who violates it. An example of a relative right, besides those that arise from the exercise of the right to contract, is a right to legal representation before a court, or a right to government benefits. Again, these advantages can only be waived by the rightsholder. But if the right is relative, the thought of its non-performance cannot be separated from the thought of a special relation. It is always some specific agent, B, who does not perform.

The thrust of self-ownership and private property ownership is that, if, without my agreement, another can enforce that I do something, or enforce that I part with fruits of what I do or property I own, they wrongfully infringe on my freedom of choice. Self-ownership, like private property ownership, is guaranteed by legal norms of the form that award absolute rights, including the right to contract. As awarding such rights only on the condition that a person performs some act would itself violate self-ownership, the absolute rights that guarantee self-ownership are also innate, rather than acquired. Indeed, self-ownership and private property ownership do not leave the other three types of legal norm in the above classification any obvious role, except as means to support absolute innate rights, or as outcomes of their exercise.

One upshot of this classification of legal norms, together with the distinction between innate and acquired rights, is that, if *Capital* and *Notes on Wagner* suggest a plausible explanation of the law of capitalist society, then its critique is a critique of a legal code that prioritises innate absolute rights. A critique of a legal code that prioritises innate absolute rights need not imply a critique of all possible legal codes. But it need not simply be a critique of 'the values and interests which are protected and promoted by particular rights'.[30] Not every critique of rights that is not a critique of their form[31] need focus on the values or interests they protect or promote, because a critique of the content of rights may include a critique of an illusory status that they enjoy. Nor need a critique of the content of rights (be it of the values and interests they promote, or of an illusory status) be confined to a critique of their content in a particular jurisdiction. It may be intrinsic to that type of right.

On Leopold's reading of *On the Jewish Question*, the latter offers a critique of the individualistic 'content' that 'two particular categories of rights' have in jurisdictions dominated by an egoistic civil society, but no critique of a content intrinsic to any right or category of rights, and no critique of the form of rights, or of a category of right.[32] By implication, *On the Jewish Question*, on Leopold's reading, offers no critique of a legal code that prioritises absolute innate rights, beyond a critique of the individualistic content such rights may be used to pursue in jurisdictions dominated by an egoistic civil society. Leopold is right that *On the Jewish Question* merely discusses individual human rights and political human rights, and such rights do not exhaust all rights. Neither category of rights includes all relative rights, such as rights to government benefits. Nor do individual human rights include acquired individual rights, such as the rights that a professional acquires in virtue of meeting professional standards or obligations. But besides overlooking the passage in which *On the Jewish Question* offers a recognition-based critique of the form of individual human rights similar to that of Marx's *Critique of the Gotha Programme*,[33] Leopold goes too far in saying of Marx's attitude to each individual human right ('liberty, property, equality, and security') that 'Marx does not reject the value of the relevant good as such';[34] and Leopold also does not remark on *On the Jewish Question*'s illusion-based critique of the type of legal code that prioritises innate absolute rights.[35]

By way of introducing his analysis of individual human rights in *On the Jewish Question*, Marx says that he will examine 'human rights' in the 'authentic form'[36] they enjoy in North America and France. To take an interest in

---

30   Leopold 2007, p. 157.

31   On the form of right, see ch. 8, sec. 13.

32   Leopold 2007, pp. 156–7, pp. 160–1.

33   See ch. 8, sec. 13.

34   Leopold 2007, p. 160.

35   Kouvélakis 2005 draws attention to the illusion-based critique.

36   *MEW*, 1, p. 362; *MECW*, 3, p. 160.

the constitutions of these two places as constitutions in which human rights obtain their 'authentic form' is not to take an interest in two merely contingent arrangements of human rights. If Marx cites a definition of a human right from these constitutions, this definition is not (according to *On the Jewish Question*) to be taken as a particular conception of this human right, the value of which one might reject while continuing to affirm the value of the human right itself. Any defect in the authentic form of something is a defect in its essence. That Marx singles out France's 'most radical constitution, the constitution of 1793'[37] is in line with the thought that Marx is out to examine the limits of individual human rights in their authentic form.

Marx's analysis of individual human rights begins with his citing, from the French constitution of 1793, the list: "'l'*égalité*, la *liberté*, la *sûreté*, la *propriété*"'.[38] The first item from this list that Marx discusses is '*la liberté*'. After quoting further statements from the French constitution of 1793, Marx concludes: '[l]iberty [*Freiheit*] is thus the right to do anything that does not harm another'.[39] The implicit standard of harm is harm to another's right. One individual harms another if they violate the right of any other individual. If people are to be at liberty to do 'anything' provided that no one else is harmed, then liberty is only to be constrained for the sake of liberty. According to *On the Jewish Question*, the fundamental idea of individual human rights is that liberty may only be constrained for the sake of liberty.

The rationale for counting events that violate rights as harm, but not counting other events as harm, is that the avoidance of the former has special importance. But the only value that justifies assigning special importance to the former's avoidance is the value of freedom of choice. The absence of rights violations cannot guarantee freedom of will. A nation of law-abiding citizens may be a nation of drug addicts, or a nation whose culture is one in which members of certain social groups are systematically not recognised as competent or as properly engaged or seen within certain domains of action (as long as this informal culture stops short of what counts as illegal discrimination). An absence of rights violations also cannot guarantee that rights will be used to advance some particular end. The prioritisation of the individual human right of liberty in a legal code is therefore a prioritisation within it of the value of freedom of choice.

If the individual human right of liberty is to be awarded, it must regulate individuals' relation to their parts and capacities, by characterising the indi-

---

37   *MEW*, 1, p. 364; *MECW*, 3, p. 162.
38   Ibid.
39   Ibid. On the translation of '*Freiheit*' as 'liberty' (here and below), see ch. 8, sec. 13.

vidual's relation to their own parts and capacities. An individual's parts and capacities are the means by which they give effect to their choices. So, *if* the individual human right of liberty is to be awarded, then, in the absence of further legal norms, each individual is to be awarded rights of self-ownership.

The individual human right of '[*é*]*galité*', Marx writes, 'is nothing other than the equality of the *liberté* described above'.[40] The principle of *equal* liberty is the principle that, for any *x* it is possible for each individual to have the innate absolute right to do, everyone ought to have the innate absolute right to do *x*, subject only to the proviso that the overall package of innate absolute rights enjoyed by each individual is to be the best overall. The principle of equal liberty therefore already incorporates the individual human right of '*la propriété*', in the form of private property: 'the practical utilisation of the human right of liberty is the human right of *private property*'.[41] 'La *sûreté*', as we have seen, incorporates the modern police, and the courts.[42] The core principle of material (non-procedural) individual human rights is the principle of equal liberty.

Besides the right to private property, *On the Jewish Question* mentions several other material individual human rights. These include: the right to practice a religion[43] (the freedom to choose to practice a religion, or none); the right to publish views and opinions[44] (the freedom to choose what, if anything, to communicate publicly); the right to 'assemble [*sich zu versammeln*]'[45] (the freedom to choose whether or not to gather together); the right of private correspondence[46] (the freedom to choose with whom if anyone to correspond); and the right to practice a trade[47] (the freedom to choose what employment, if any, to seek). This list of material rights may presumably be extended, however, by any right that can assume the form of an equal liberty, and contribute to an overall package of innate absolute rights.

Even allowing for this type of extension, it is apparent that Marx's conception of 'human rights' in *On the Jewish Question* is narrow, when compared to the Universal Declaration of Human Rights (1948). Articles 25 to 27 of the Uni-

---

40   *MEW*, 1, p. 365; *MECW*, 3, p. 163.

41   *MEW*, 1, p. 364; *MECW*, 3, p. 163.

42   See sec. 1.

43   *MEW*, 1, p. 362; *MECW*, 3, p. 161.

44   *MEW*, 1, p. 363, p. 367; *MECW*, 3, p. 161, p. 165.

45   *MEW*, 1, p. 363; *MECW*, 3, p. 161. *MECW* translates '*sich zu versammeln*' as 'to hold meetings'. The latter would fall under a right to associate. Although *On the Jewish Question* does not refer to an '*Assoziationsrecht*', it could be added to a list of rights extended as indicated.

46   *MEW*, 1, p. 367; *MECW*, 3, p. 165.

47   *MEW*, 1, p. 369; *MECW*, 3, p. 167.

versal Declaration of Human Rights include, as human rights, the right to the satisfaction of vital needs, to healthcare, education, and culture.[48] Such rights, which are not political rights, amount to claims vis-à-vis a government, or other international public body, for certain forms of positive assistance. They therefore do not take the form of equal liberties. The positive assistance they require from a public body qualifies as 'harm', on the standard of harm implicit in the concept of liberty. To place a public body under a duty to provide specific groups of individuals with certain forms of positive assistance is to leave it *no* choice but to provide that assistance.

One reason to continue to separate individual human rights from the kind of rights that appear in Articles 25 to 27 of the Universal Declaration of Human Rights is that generalised purchase and sale only leads commodity exchangers to affirm the former. Whether or not any social, economic and cultural relative rights vis-à-vis a public body can be explained as the result of class struggle, or by other phenomena generated by the commodity form, their explanation is distinct from that of innate absolute rights. Moreover, if relative rights vis-à-vis a public body for forms of positive assistance are recognised in circumstances where innate absolute rights appear as natural rights, and one of the latter, private property rights, must be taxed to fund them, then they 'cannot claim the same legal status'[49] as innate absolute rights.

On the Jewish Question's illusion-based line of critique of individual human rights is that individual human rights appear to possess a supra-legal legitimacy that they do not have: *'droits de l'homme* appear as *droits naturels'*.[50] To claim that innate absolute rights appear as natural rights is to claim that they appear to be grounded in the nature of human beings. To make this claim is to advance an illusion-based critique, if the appearance is no accident, but false. *On the Jewish Question* explains this appearance as follows:

> The *droits de l'homme* appear as *droits naturels*, because *self-conscious activity* is concentrated in [*konzentriert sich auf*] the *political act*. The egoistic human being is the *passive*, merely *found* result of the dissolved society, an object of *immediate certainty*, hence a *natural* object. *Political revolution* dissolves civil life into its components without *revolutionising* these components themselves and subjecting them to critique. It relates to bourgeois society, the world of needs, labour, private interests

48   Boersema 2011, pp. 386–7.
49   Kouvélakis 2005, p. 716.
50   *MEW*, 1, p. 369; *MECW*, 3, p. 167.

and private law, as to the *foundation of its existence*, as a *precondition* that has no further grounding, hence as its *natural basis*.[51]

'[P]*olitical revolution*' is the process whereby the right to hold and vote for representative office comes to be awarded in abstraction from religious, economic, sexual, tribal and other differences, leaving the nationality and maturity of those who live in a state's territory as the only prerequisites. To treat the nationality and maturity of those who live in a state's territory as the only prerequisites for the right to hold and vote for representative office is to treat all adults of the same nationality as equals, as far as these political rights are concerned. Insofar as representatives are elected by everyone who satisfies certain basic prerequisites, representatives must exhibit a commitment to a set of objectives that they can present as reasonable for everyone to accept. Political activity is '*self-conscious*' activity in the sense that it is would-be common-good-promoting activity.

'[D]*roits de l'homme*' can only 'appear as *droits naturels*' if social life is regulated by '*droits de l'homme*'. Everyone is permitted to pursue whatever projects they choose, with whomever they choose, just as long as they do not harm the rights of others. As this principle leaves everyone having to fend for themselves in order to meet their needs, however, it leads to the pursuit of egoistic interests. Representatives' relation to social life is thus a relation of would-be common-good-promoting activity to a domain of particular-interest-pursuing activity. Representatives view the latter domain as the '*foundation*' of their activity insofar as they view it both as falling outside of their own domain, which is that of would-be common-good-promoting activity, and as the domain from which they are to extract a common good.

If social life is a domain of particular-interest-pursuing activity, however, it will include attempts to influence representatives to uphold particular interests, rather than the common good. Representatives' activity can only be would-be common-good-promoting activity, therefore, if it *abstracts* from or

---

51   *MEW*, 1, p. 369; *MECW*, 3, p. 167; Marx 1975a, p. 233; Marx 1994, p. 49. To say that wealth is concentrated in a few families (in German: '*der Reichtum konzentriert sich auf wenige Familien*') is to say that wealth is a monopoly of, is only possessed by, a few families. To say that '*self-conscious activity* is concentrated in the *political act*' is to say that self-conscious activity is a monopoly of, is only exhibited by, acts of the political domain. The phrase 'concentrated on' in the *MECW* translation 'conscious activity is concentrated on the political act' (which could translate: '*die bewußte Tätigkeit fokussiert sich auf den politischen Akt*'), like the phrase 'concentrated (up)on' in Marx 1975a and Marx 1994, leaves the false impression that political action is instead the object of activity that is 'conscious' (whether or not this 'conscious' activity is itself of the political domain).

disregards any purely particular interests of social life when devising law: 'the *political* human being is merely the abstracted, artificial human being'.[52] By contrast, lawful particular-interest-pursuing activity in social life does not abstract from or disregard some other known interest. It is not formed by inoculating itself from a type of interest other than itself. Unlike representatives' activity, therefore, it appears basic to human beings. But then the rights that enable its pursuit must appear to be grounded in human nature. Hence, '*droits de l'homme* appear as *droits naturels*'.

If this is Marx's argument, it is not convincing. One activity can appear more basic than another without appearing to be transhistorical; while the pursuit of particular interests could be enabled by rights besides absolute innate rights, leaving no special reason why it should be '*droits de l'homme*' that appear as natural.

Capital Volume I suggests a better argument to this conclusion, however, based on the connection between value, possession and self-ownership. The first part of this argument was outlined at the end of chapter 3. As the exchangeability of one type of commodity can only be expressed in another, the form in which a commodity's power of general exchangeability is expressed cannot make it apparent that it only has this power in virtue of social relations of generalised production for exchange. Rather, it appears to have this power of general exchangeability by nature, by the same cause that gives the other commodity, in which this power is expressed, all its other properties. But if commodities appear to have value by nature, then the subjectivity through which their value is realised, and any presupposition of this subjectivity, must appear as natural. As argued in chapters 7 and 9, commodity exchange, in which value is realised, is a mode of possession on both sides; and possession presupposes an analogous, exclusive will in respect of one's own parts and capacities. So, if commodities appear to have value by nature, possession, and an exclusive will in respect of one's parts and capacities, appear as natural human subjectivities. If these subjectivities are guaranteed and recognised in law by absolute innate rights of private property ownership and self-ownership, then these absolute innate rights appear as natural rights.

If this argument holds, it provides an alternative basis for affirming Marx's claim in *On the Jewish Question* that rights-discourse in capitalism is inherently skewed. For if innate absolute rights appear as natural rights, they appear to constitute external constraints on the exercise of political human rights. That is, they appear to be justified independently of any procedure by which they

---

52   *MEW*, 1, p. 370; *MECW*, 3, p. 167.

are posited. '[T]he *citoyen* is declared the servant of the egoistic *homme*',[53]
for representatives' activity appears to be justified only if it confines itself to
upholding supposedly natural absolute innate rights, which, by leaving everyone fending for themselves to meet their needs, cement the pursuit of egoistic
interests.

3   The System of Capitalist Production and Popular Sovereignty

On the analysis thus far, absolute innate rights occupy pride of place in the law
of capitalist society. Yet the call for equal liberty also connects the state of capitalist society to popular sovereignty. This connection must now be examined.

One approach is suggested by a remark in Marx's *Critique of Hegel's Doctrine
of the State*: 'sovereignty of the monarch, or sovereignty of the people, that is
the question'.[54] If monarchical sovereignty or popular sovereignty are the only
two options, then, if the state of capitalist society is connected to popular sovereignty, it ought to be possible to establish this connection by arguing that, were
the system of capitalist production to coexist with monarchical sovereignty, it
would lead to a call for equal liberty based on an appeal to popular sovereignty,
and to the institutionalisation of that call.

To begin, we can examine the claims advanced on behalf of monarchical
sovereignty by one of its defenders, Julius Friedrich Stahl, author of *Die Philosophie des Rechts nach geschichtlichen Ansicht* (1830–37) (*Philosophy of Law in
Historical Perspective*). This work formed the basis of Stahl's intellectual reputa-
tion when, in 1840, the then crown prince of Prussia, Friedrich Wilhelm (soon
to become King Friedrich Wilhelm IV), intervened in Stahl's move to the University of Berlin,[55] a position from which Stahl could combat the influence of
Hegelianism.

In this work, Stahl argues that equal liberty in private matters can only be
guaranteed in a monarchy, not a republic.[56] Equal liberty in private matters is
said to be owed to all persons on account of their likeness to God;[57] and only a
state whose authority is acknowledged to derive from God is said to be able to
cultivate the obedience that the existence of a state, and thus the guarantee of

---

53   *MEW*, 1, p. 366; *MECW*, 3, p. 164.
54   *MEW*, 1, p. 230; *MECW*, 3, p. 28.
55   Lens 1910, p. 551.
56   Stahl 1837, p. 308.
57   Stahl 1833, p. 130; Stahl 1837, pp. 38–9, p. 240.

equal liberty in private matters, requires.[58] According to Stahl, equal liberty in private matters is not the state's ultimate end, and so the true state is never simply a mutual insurance or guarantee. The state's ultimate end is to realise its Christian purpose. (A guarantee or insurance, by contrast, removes risks from action whose performance is conceivable without it). But a monarchy is nonetheless the only type of state that can provide this guarantee, according to Stahl.

As a sovereign monarch can bestow supra-legal legitimacy on equal liberty in private matters, and as monarchical sovereignty is compatible with an independent judiciary to decide civil cases,[59] the system of capitalist production can be connected to popular sovereignty only if monarchical sovereignty and popular sovereignty have differing implications for law-making or law-execution. A sovereign monarch is incompatible with the system of capitalist production if the implications of monarchical sovereignty for law-making and/or law-execution compromise its guarantee of equal liberty in private matters.

State power is characterised by monarchical sovereignty if its authority expressly derives from God, and the head of the state is a monarch with 'personal power'.[60] A monarch has personal power if the constitution gives the hereditary monarch a power to rule that cannot be compelled by any other organ of state, whether an assembly, a minister, or a court. The monarch, in their capacity as law-maker, may be required to seek the approval of an (estates-based) assembly, and the latter may be able to dispute the actions of ministers who exercise the monarch's executive power.[61] But there is no capacity in which the monarch themselves can be held responsible.[62] A sovereign monarch is both the law-maker, and the head of the executive;[63] and no judicial finding on the illegality of a minister's conduct sets a precedent for the interpretation of the constitution.[64] There is then, as Marx puts it in his speech at the trial of the Rhenish District Committee of Democrats in 1849, 'no law, no custom, no organic institution, which imposes upon it the limitations of a constitutional executive power'.[65] A sovereign monarch could only be reduced to the role of a constitutional executive power if they were made subordinate to a separate law-making power; and the latter would presuppose a source of authority

---

58   Stahl 1837, p. 280.
59   Stahl 1837, p. 50.
60   Stahl 1837, p. 254.
61   Stahl 1837, p. 146, pp. 153–4.
62   Stahl 1837, p. 74.
63   Stahl 1837, pp. 43–4.
64   Stahl 1837, p. 176.
65   *MEW*, 6, p. 248; *MECW*, 8, p. 331.

distinct from and higher than the monarch. As no sovereign monarch could recognise any such power, monarchical sovereignty would cease with its recognition. In the event of its recognition there could at most be 'a republic with a monarchical appearance'.[66]

The argument for saying that monarchical sovereignty is incompatible with the system of capitalist production is that equal liberty in private matters cannot be guaranteed by an assembly that has influence, but no share of state power. The argument rests on the premise that the system of capitalist production is unlike a cultural relic that can be preserved by ensuring that everything stays the same. A cultural relic whose preservation were assured if everything around it stayed the same, and whose surroundings could only be altered following a change in the law, could be guaranteed by an agency with a mere veto power. The need to obtain the agency's approval for any change to the law would allow it to veto any threat to the relic's conditions of existence, and thus guarantee its preservation.[67] But the system of capitalist production is not like a cultural relic. As the *Communist Manifesto* claims, '[t]he bourgeoisie cannot exist without constantly revolutionising the instruments of production, hence the relations of production, and thus all social relations'.[68]

It is for this very reason that the *Communist Manifesto* proceeds to claim: '[a]ll status [*Ständische*] and standing evaporates, and all that is holy is desecrated'.[69] A system of production for continuous money maximisation involves constant technical change, in both the means of production, and the means of communication. But no assembly that lacks the power to compel a monarch to act can ensure that each aspect of equal liberty relevant for capital accumulation will be guaranteed as and when the technical possibility of its use arises. No sovereign monarch can be counted on to do so by themselves, moreover, when they are bound, by conscience, to view individual interests as subordinate to the majesty of the realm of the state, and its religious purpose.

The system of capitalist production can only be guaranteed, therefore, by means of a law-making power with independence from a monarch. The exist-

---

66 Stahl 1837, p. 134.
67 An estates-based assembly does not even have a veto power if a monarch may dissolve it as and when they no longer trust it; see Stahl 1837, p. 206.
68 *MEW*, 4, p. 465; *MECW*, 6, p. 487.
69 Ibid.; compare *MEW*, 3, p. 182; *MECW*, 5, pp. 200–1. The German phrase is '*Alles Ständische und Stehende verdampft*'. The *MECW* translation, 'all that is solid melts into air' (literally: '*Alles Feste zerrinnt in die Luft*'), has a poetic quality, but it is not accurate. It omits the nominalised adjective '*Ständische*'; '*ständisch*' literally means 'of estates'. The poetic quality of the translation comes at the cost of losing the implication that the abolition of estates is an effect of the revolutionising nature of capitalist production.

ence of such a power is indefensible in terms of monarchical sovereignty, however. Hence, the system of capitalist production is incompatible with monarchical sovereignty.

Moreover, as no sovereign monarch can recognise a law-making power that is independent of it, the establishment of such a law-making power, for the sake of securing the equal liberty that the system of capitalist production requires, can only be achieved in opposition to a sovereign monarch. This opposition sets in train a certain dynamic. In *The Bourgeoisie and the Counterrevolution*, Marx writes:

> The bourgeoisie had to vindicate its share of political power to itself, already for the sake of its material interests. Only the bourgeoisie itself could give its commercial and industrial needs statutory validity ... To achieve its end, it had to be able freely to debate its own interests and views, and the actions of the government. It called that 'the *right* [Recht] *of freedom of the press'*. It had to be able to *associate* unhindered. That it called 'the *right* [Recht] *of freedom of association*' ... To oppose the court, it had to court the people.
>
> Perhaps it really took itself to constitute an opposition *for* the people.
>
> The rights and liberties it sought *for itself* could naturally only be demanded from the government under the slogan of *popular rights* and *popular liberties*.[70]

The bourgeoisie's desire for a law-making power independent of a monarch and willing to guarantee equal liberty in commercial and industrial matters always has some historical occasion. It is bound up with its desire for a guarantee of some aspect of equal liberty, related to the issues of the day. Agreement on such issues can only arise among private competitors, however, through some degree of negotiation in public, by which each can be seen by others to commit to a common position. So, as a condition of any common agitation for a new law-making power, the bourgeoisie must negotiate some common ground in public on the issues of the day.

Some public exchange of ideas is allowed even from the perspective of the private law of a monarchy. Insubordination only occurs if public statements raise demands in respect to the form or function of public office, or encourage others to raise such demands. While a monarchy might permit the publication of demands directed by one private individual to another, to raise demands in

---

70   *MEW*, 6, pp. 104–5; *MECW*, 8, pp. 158–9. In both cases, *MECW* omits to translate *'Recht'*.

respect to the form or function of public office is a different prospect. Any such demand presupposes that state power is properly subject to public contestation by an agent lacking any formally constituted power. Just as a sovereign monarch cannot recognise an independent law-making power, no sovereign monarch can permit such demands. Their toleration would be the toleration of 'a second sovereignty'.[71] A bourgeoisie that publicly articulates a desire for a law-making power independent of a monarch must articulate this desire as a demand, to exert pressure on a sovereign monarch otherwise unwilling to recognise any such law-making power. Yet any use of the press by an agent without formal power to raise demands in respect to the form or function of public office, as distinct from other tones of commentary on public affairs, or demands by one private person to another, must be defended not only on a basis other than the law of the existing monarchy, but on a basis other than the law of any possible state claiming direct authority from an otherworldly source.

To defend a use of the press to raise demands in respect to the form or function of public office is to defend the press as a means that, among other things, may be used to exert pressure on public office. Any such defence implies that the state has no licence to censor the press beforehand,[72] and thereby deny it this effect. Any such defence therefore re-doubles the challenge to monarchical sovereignty. A challenge is posed to monarchical sovereignty both by the principle demanded (a law-making power independent of a monarch, to guarantee aspects of equal liberty related to the issues of the day), and by the claim to have the right to raise such a demand.

A similar double challenge to monarchical sovereignty is posed by any association that does not simply pursue merely private affairs, but seeks to promote the idea of a new law-making power. An 'association', as distinct from a corporation, is a form of organisation whose 'formation, activity and dissolution fundamentally lies at the disposal of its members'.[73] To found an association to promote monarchical sovereignty would be a performative contradiction. Any such association would have to be viewed by a sovereign monarch as a second sovereignty, and so as undercutting its declared aim. Any association that promotes the idea of a new law-making power independent of the monarch therefore challenges monarchical sovereignty both by virtue of the idea it promotes, and by claiming the right to (encourage others to) raise the demand.

One feature common to the two rights that Marx mentions in the foregoing passage – the right of press freedom and the right of association – is that a right

71   Stahl 1837 p. 223.
72   The topic of *MEW*, 1, pp. 3–25; *MECW*, 1, pp. 109–31.
73   Müller 1963, p. 15.

whose restricted use can be justified irrespective of the choice between monarchical sovereignty and popular sovereignty – may, if exercised to the end of exerting pressure on or opposing a sovereign monarch, be exercised in a way that can only be justified on the basis of popular sovereignty. To use the press or an association to raise a demand in respect to the form or function of public office is to issue a demand to institute a particular principle. But regardless of the particular principle demanded, the right of an informal agency to raise such a demand presupposes popular sovereignty. It rests on the premise that the authority of state power derives from the people. If, in seeking to establish a new law-making power, the bourgeoisie must publicly defend the right of press freedom and the right of freedom of association it asserts in demanding this law-making power, it can only establish a new law-making power consistently with this defence by resting its case for it on popular sovereignty.

Any informal agency that raises a demand for a law-making power independent of a monarch is compelled, by its invocation of popular sovereignty, to address issues that, in the conjuncture, must be addressed, to successfully lay claim to speak on behalf of the people. No informal agency can have full control of what these issues are, however. Anyone in a monarchy who holds no office may take themselves to belong to the people; and no group can control whether or not other groups will use the press and/or associations to assert their own, potentially conflicting demands in the name of the people. The bourgeoisie may unite other groups behind it if it can articulate a social interest it shares with other groups, requiring the removal of a common foe,[74] such as the principle that birth should not determine life chances. But it may not wish to prolong a political revolution if the uncontrollable effect of its appeal to the people, on which its political leadership rests, stands to destabilise the status quo to an extent from which its own particular interests may not recover.

Yet, whatever the extent of political revolution, the institutionalisation of a law-making power independent of a monarch is the victory of one supralegal source of authority of constituted power over another, of the people over God. In that victory, there is no continuity of power. The most fundamental level of constituted power is the constitution-making power; that is, the power that draws up the constitution. As Marx puts it in his *Critique of Hegel's Doctrine of the State*: 'the constitution has also not made itself of its own accord ... A law-making power [*eine gesetzgebende Gewalt*] must exist, or have existed, *prior* to the constitution and *outside* the constitution'.[75] But there can be no continuity between a sovereign monarch, and the constitution-making power

74   See *MEW*, 1, p. 388; *MECW*, 3, p. 185.
75   *MEW*, 1, p. 257; *MECW*, 3, pp. 54–5; Marx1970b, p. 55. The phrase '(*eine/die*) *gesetzgebende*

that establishes a constitution whose law-making power is to be independent of a monarch. No sovereign monarch is entitled, as a sovereign monarch, to transfer its power to any such power, for they would thereby abandon their duty, in terms of the old constitution, to uphold the old constitution. Any such constitution-making power, no less than a politically confrontational use of the press or of an association, must derive its authority from the people.

Concluding his trial speech of 1849, Marx says of the relation between a sovereign people and the constitution-making power:

> The National Assembly has no rights for itself, the people has simply transferred to it the assertion of its own rights. If it does not execute its mandate, the mandate is extinguished. The people itself, in its own person, then enters the stage, and acts on its own supreme power [*Machtvollkommenheit*].[76]

To appreciate what Marx says here, let us recap the argument so far. The system of capitalist production must lead to conflict with a sovereign monarch, because a sovereign monarch cannot guarantee equal liberty even in private matters. By using the press and associations to publicly tie certain issues of the day to a demand for a law-making power independent of a monarch, the bourgeoisie commits itself to popular sovereignty. This compels it to seek to unite any other self-assertive group behind it. Insofar as the bourgeoisie obtains popular backing for its demands, it creates the conditions for convoking a power tasked with drawing up a new constitution. It is only if such demands are popular that a constitution-making power can be convoked and meet unobstructed. As these demands must already be publicly raised and recognised for the constitution-making power to meet and be recognised, they constitute its 'mandate'. If the constitution-making power cannot exist without a popular mandate, it is not the constitution-making power that is sovereign, but

---

Gewalt' is translated here and below as '(a/the) law-making power', rather than, as in MECW and Marx 197b, 'legislative authority' or 'legislature' (the latter would be: '*die Legislative*'). First, 'law-making power' is a more literal translation. A '*Gewalt*' is not an 'authority' (an '*Autorität*'), but a 'power' (in German, 'the separation of powers' is '*die Trennung der Gewalten*'). Second, a constitution-making power is a kind of law-making power, not a kind of 'legislature'. A 'legislature' presupposes a contrast with an executive, and a constitution-making power must first establish that separation. It makes no sense to say: '[a] legislature must exist or have existed before and outside of the constitution' (Marx 1970b).

76   MEW, 6, p. 256; MECW, 8, p. 339. MECW renders '*Machtvollkommenheit*' as 'authority' (which would be: '*Autorität*'). 'Supreme power' is power whose possession does not presuppose an act by another agency conferring it, and that transcends any other power.

the people. By provoking the formation of a constitution-making power with a mandate from the people, the system of capitalist production entails the institutionalisation of popular sovereignty.

4   The Antinomy of Natural Rights and Popular Authorisation

In combination, the foregoing arguments point to an antinomy in the justification for government action,[77] an antinomy of natural rights and popular authorisation. On the one hand, *if* some rights appear to be natural rights, it must seem that the standard by which government action is justified is the extent to which it guarantees these rights. This standard is independent of any popular decision, because independent of any act or procedure by which such a decision could be taken. On the other hand, *if* state power is authorised by a decision of the people for equal liberty, then government action is justified if it falls within the terms of this authorisation. The proofs take the form of latching on to a premise in the argument for the other assertion (the premise that each individual has an exclusive claim to their parts and capacities) and reasoning to an incompatible positive position for how government action is justified in relation to it:

Thesis: government action is only justified if and because it guarantees natural rights.

Proof: suppose that government action is only justified if and because it is authorised by a decision of the people for equal liberty. If adherence to the terms of this popular authorisation is to justify government action, the people must be entitled to authorise the government to uphold equal liberty. It would be contrary to equal liberty to suppose that the people are so entitled, however, unless they have the permission of everyone whose liberty they are to authorise the government to uphold. Every individual taken together can give the people the permission it requires if each has an exclusive claim to their parts and capacities. But if, prior and therefore independently of constituted power, each individual has an exclusive claim to their parts and capacities, the task

---

77   'Government' here denotes all constituted power under a given constitution. It is broader than 'government of the day', but narrower than 'state'. 'State' is used to denote all constituted power (including a constitution-making power) together with its effects on public life (such as public opinion). Marx's *Critique of the Gotha Programme* distinguishes 'state' and 'government' (*MEW*, 19, p. 29; *MECW*, 24, p. 96) without saying how they are distinct.

of government is to guarantee innate absolute rights as natural rights. Hence, government action is only justified if and because it guarantees natural rights.

Antithesis: government action is only justified if and because it is authorised by a decision of the people for equal liberty.

Proof: suppose that government action is only justified if and because it guarantees natural rights. If the guarantee of natural rights is to justify its action, that can only be because each individual has an exclusive claim to their parts and capacities. But if so, a government can only justly come into being if it comes into being without violating these claims. To justly come into being, it must be authorised by all of the individuals within the territory it is to govern. Only all of the individuals taken together as a people have all of the permissions that it must acquire. But if the government justly comes into being by the people authorising it, its action is justified if and because it falls within the terms of the authorisation it receives: to uphold equal liberty. Hence, government action is only justified if and because it is authorised by a decision of the people for equal liberty.

The thesis asserts that government action is only justified by the conditions of its intervention. It asserts that the government is bound to act to protect actions that are sound and to repair actions that are defective, where the criterion for soundness and defectiveness is whether or not they give effect to the choices of the holders of natural rights. The antithesis, by contrast, asserts that government action is only justified by its observance of a means-ends relation. It asserts that the government is bound to adopt the means to bring about the end-state that it is authorised by the people to maintain; namely, equal liberty.

It is possible to imagine a government that seeks to utilise both types of justification for its actions. In *The Eighteenth Brumaire of Louis Bonaparte* ('*The Eighteenth Brumaire*'), Marx examines the case of a government that guarantees the right of private property, inheritance and freedom of religion, while curtailing political uses of liberty as a means to providing the former guarantee.[78] But the two justifications are not compatible. Giving legal effect to the choices of rightsholders need not serve to bring about the equal liberty that the state is authorised to bring about; and the means necessary for ensuring that equal liberty is upheld may not give legal effect to the choices of rightsholders.

---

78   *MEW*, 8, p. 154; *MECW*, 11, p. 143.

By way of illustration, consider the case of conscription. If the thesis of the antinomy is adopted as the standard, conscription cannot be justified. Conscription violates the innate absolute right to one's parts and capacities. It is false that 'full compensation for that violation nullifies it', for the right 'entails … a liberty and power to do what is necessary to prevent such incursions [on what one owns – JF]'.[79] By the standard of the thesis, a prospective conscript is entitled to flee from any agency that tried to detain them for conscription purposes, and to lay a cease-and-desist order against it. If, by contrast, the antithesis of the antinomy is taken as the standard, conscription may be justified. A popular authorisation to uphold equal liberty permits a government to adopt the means to minimise the violation of the equal liberty it is authorised to uphold. In some contexts, these means may include the conscription of some of those who authorised it, to positively assist in preventing or redressing violations of the liberty of others who authorised it. Conscription illustrates that the thesis and antithesis can sustain incompatible judgements.

Or consider the declaration of a *'state of siege'*.[80] Marx's comment in *The Eighteenth Brumaire* that the declaration of a state of siege is 'regulated' by the French constitution of 1848 'as an organic institution',[81] together with his claim (in *Revolution in Vienna*) that it is a 'universal means' that 'like revolution, has toured around the world',[82] suggests that Marx considered the legal institution of a state of siege to serve a specific purpose in the law of capitalist society. The declaration of a state of siege allows certain liberties to be suspended, including personal liberty, freedom of the press and association; subordinates civil administration to military command; and permits offences to be tried by court martial.[83] Liberties are merely suspended, however, their exercise temporarily postponed, as the state of siege is to recreate the conditions for restoring their centrality. The declaration of a state of siege is not justified by the standard of the thesis, but it may be justified by that of the antithesis.

If a justification may be said to be asserted even when it is merely implied by conduct whose purpose is practical, the antinomy of natural rights and popular authorisation may inform Marx's remark in *On the Jewish Question* that:

---

79   Steiner 2006, pp. 100–1.
80   *MEW*, 8, p. 130; *MECW*, 11, p. 118; see also *MEW*, 6, pp. 493–9; *MECW*, 9, pp. 440–7.
81   *MEW*, 8, p. 148; *MECW*, 11, p. 137.
82   *MEW*, 5, p. 417; *MECW*, 7, p. 457.
83   Boldt 1967, p. 14; compare *MEW*, 8, p. 130; *MECW*, 11, p. 118.

> The human right of liberty [*Freiheit*] ceases to be a right as soon as it enters into conflict with *political* life, whereas in theory political life is only the guarantee of human rights, of the rights of the individual human being.[84]

To uphold equal liberty, a government must preserve its own existence. Conflicts between the needs of '*political* life', and the guarantee of individual human rights, are thus one form of expression of the antinomy of natural rights and popular authorisation. To take two of the rights mentioned in *On the Jewish Question*: the antinomy may be expressed in incompatible judgements about, say, the justification for the secret services to read private correspondence, or for the police to profile suspects on the basis of likely religious beliefs.

The antinomy of natural rights and popular authorisation may also find expression in constitutional limitations imposed on rights. Marx claims in *The Eighteenth Brumaire* that 'every paragraph' of the French constitution of 1848 'contains its own antithesis', for:

> Each of these liberties [*Freiheiten*] is proclaimed as the *unconditional* right of the French citizen, but always with the proviso that it is unlimited insofar as it is not restricted by the '*equal rights of others* and the *public safety*', or by 'laws' which are to mediate this harmony of individual liberties with one another, and with the public safety.[85]

In *Legalität und Pluralismus* (*Legality and Pluralism*), Ulrich Preuß formulates the general point at issue. Preuß suggests that the law of capitalist society can be expected to contain a 'substance term' that informs the interpretation of all the rights-related articles of a constitution, and 'whose realisation the behaviour of subjects is to serve'.[86] In other words, a 'substance term' is a term that encapsulates the mandate to uphold equal liberty that the government receives from the people, and that can be cited to limit rights, allowing a government to depart from the task of giving legal effect to them. A 'sub-

---

84   *MEW*, 1, p. 367; *MECW*, 3, p. 165; compare Paschukanis 2003, p. 80; Pashukanis 2002, p. 82. In *Political Power and Social Classes*, Poulantzas writes of an 'internal contradiction' in which 'the private individual's freedom suddenly appears to vanish before the authority of the state which embodies the general will' (Poulantzas 1982, p. 237; Poulantzas 1978, p. 219). Poulantzas neither says what an 'internal contradiction' is, nor offers a clear account of its genesis, however.

85   *MEW*, 8, p. 126; *MECW*, 11, p. 114; translated in accordance with *MECW*, 10, p. 568.

86   Preuß 1973, pp. 23–4.

stance term' provides a government with a legal licence to adopt the means it deems necessary to bring about the conditions for a future in which equal liberty is upheld. If, as in the case of the French constitution of 1848, this licence is filled out by ordinary laws, the guarantee function of the law of capitalist society will not match the constitution's recognition function. The extent to which the constitution encapsulates the thesis of the antinomy will be out of sync with the extent to which a government acts on its antithesis. As Marx puts it in *The Eighteenth Brumaire*: 'the constitutional existence of liberty [*Freiheit*] remains unbroken, inviolate, however much its *ordinary* existence is destroyed'.[87]

5 Parliamentary Representation

According to the argument thus far, the system of capitalist production gives actors reason to adopt a legal code that prioritises freedom of choice, and to institutionalise their appeal to popular sovereignty. The form of the law-making power must therefore incorporate both values: freedom of choice, and popular sovereignty.

Marx remarks in *Critique of Hegel's Doctrine of the State*: 'civil society would renounce itself, if all were the law-maker'.[88] To uphold freedom of choice, responsibility for law-making must be assumed voluntarily. But universal voluntary participation, where every individual is allowed to decide for themselves whether or not to assume any law-making responsibility, is excluded. Even if universal voluntary participation were possible from a technical point of view, it is ruled out on principle. *If* the law-making power is to be a popular power, no individual of bourgeois society may share in its responsibilities just by virtue of their own choice when this choice cannot be dissociated from the pursuit of a particular interest.

The law-making power *must* be a popular power, for it concretises the constitution. The constitution-making power is itself a popular law-making power. It executes its popular mandate by drawing up a constitution, which consists of principles. But the constitution it devises must be extended not merely formally, by constitutional amendment, but informally, by ordinary laws. Marx's remark in *Critique of Hegel's Doctrine of the State* that '[t]he constitution is, by definition, unalterable, although it does actually alter; only, this alteration

---

87   *MEW*, 8, p. 127; *MECW*, 11, p. 115.
88   *MEW*, 1, p. 325; *MECW*, 3, p. 119.

is unconscious, it does not have the form of an alteration',[89] can be related to Ernst-Wolfgang Böckenförde's distinction between interpretation and concretisation:

> Interpretation is the discovery of the content and meaning of something already given, which may thereby become more complete and internally differentiated, and so also richer in content; concretisation is the (creative) elaboration of what is only fixed in direction or principle, but otherwise remains open, and first requires defining determination to become an executable norm.[90]

If a constitution includes principles, where principles, as a condition of their application, require further determination, a constitution requires 'concretisation' by ordinary laws to fully apply. If so, those ordinary laws, even if they do not formally belong to the constitution, are an integral part of it. To regard a document drawn up with the aim of regulating social life, which includes principles that cannot be applied without further determination, as complete in itself, is an illusion. It is an illusion to suppose that a constitution does not alter when the ordinary laws that concretise it are altered.

If the law-making power is to promulgate laws that concretise the constitution, it must be exercised in the same spirit as the constitution-making power whose product it is to concretise. Its laws, and thus the law-making power, must be mandated by the people, if the people are not to alienate their will in respect of how the principles of their constitution are to be concretised; which is to say, in respect of the aim for which the constitution was drawn up in the first place. Popular sovereignty therefore requires a law-making power that concretises a constitution to be authorised by the people.

As bourgeois society rests on freedom of choice, and its law-making power must be a popular power, the members of this law-making power cannot be identical with the individuals of bourgeois society, but must be chosen by them. But that is not all. The members of the law-making power must be chosen by a popular means. If *A* chooses *B* to carry out a function for *A*, *A* need not authorise *B*. A member of the Christian church may *choose* their confessor, but that does not mean that they *authorise* them.[91] If the non-performer of a function can choose another person to perform it for them without authorising this other

---

89   *MEW*, 1, p. 258; *MECW*, 3, p. 56.
90   Böckenförde 1991, p. 186.
91   Stahl 1837, p. 187.

person, to say that members of the law-making power are chosen by the individuals of bourgeois society is not yet to say that the law-making power has a popular character. The means by which its members are chosen must be of the type that can display their popular mandate.

The only selection procedure to respect freedom of choice is selection by vote (as distinct from selection by birth, lottery, expert appointment or acclamation). Indeed, selection by vote only fully expresses the value of freedom of choice if anyone can stand, and the principle of one individual, one vote, is combined with universal suffrage.[92] Selection of the law-making power by a general vote also has popular significance, however. According to Marx's *Critique of Hegel's Doctrine of the State*, its '*election* is the *immediate, direct*, not *imaginary* [bloß vorstellend], *but existent* relation of civil society to the political state'.[93] As candidates for election publicly declare a commitment to a set of law-making objectives, an election result is a verdict directly from the people on how the constitutional mandate to uphold equal liberty is to be concretised.

The combination of popular sovereignty with freedom of choice also explains why the elected law-making power is an *independent assembly*. Marx writes in *Debates on Freedom of the Press*:

> It is a senseless contradiction that the function of the state that exhibits, more than any other, the *self-activity* of the individual provinces, is even removed from their *formal* participation, *joint knowledge*; the senseless contradiction that my self-activity is to be another's act of which I am unaware.[94]

Popular sovereignty requires the elected law-making power to be responsible. Popular law-makers, unlike a sovereign monarch, must be bound by the law they make. If law-makers were above the law they make, they would not be of the people. The people, through them, would not make the law. Law-making would not be a people's 'self-activity'. Further, this elected and responsible law-making power must be a publicly deliberating plurality, or 'assembly'.[95] If law-making was delegated to a single person, that person could announce their

92   *MEW*, 1, p. 326; *MECW*, 3, p. 121.
93   Ibid. In *MECW*, 'bloß vorstellend' is translated as 'merely representative' (which would be: '*nur repräsentativ*'). '*Vorstellen* (to conceive of, to envision)' is not to be confused with '*repräsentieren* (to represent)'. That which is '*bloß vorgestellt*' is that which exists merely in thought. Representation, by contrast, is a political term. 'Civil society' cannot have any kind of 'representative' relation to 'the political state', although it can be represented.
94   *MEW*, 1, p. 44; *MECW*, 1, p. 148.
95   *MEW*, 1, p. 329; *MECW*, 3, p. 123.

decision. But, lacking political equals, they could not publicly discuss it beforehand. Only through a plurality of law-makers, who discuss in view of the public, can the people enjoy '*formal* participation'. Only the form of an assembly allows everyone to know that the reasoning that precedes a decision is conducted in the name of the people.

The value of freedom of choice explains the *independent* character of this assembly. The specific characteristic of independent public deliberation is that it guarantees deliberators' freedom of choice. Marx comments in *Critique of Hegel's Doctrine of the State* that the members of an independent assembly 'are formally commissioned [*formell kommittiert*], but as soon as they are *actual* [wirklich], they are *no* longer *commissaries* [Kommittierte]'.[96] Candidates for popular elections must be identifiable and cannot voluntarily substitute themselves. That is what it means to say that they are 'formally commissioned'. No candidate, if elected, can withdraw and select their replacement, or from time to time confer their voting rights on certain matters to others, for that would imply that the people had alienated their will. However, when the members of an *independent* law-making assembly are '*actual*', that is, discuss and vote, they do not act on a formal mandate or instruction. A formal mandate or instruction would not only abolish members' freedom of choice, by taking away their freedom to choose whether or not, and for what position, to speak and vote. It would abolish citizens' freedom of choice too. For if members of the law-making assembly were to be given a formal instruction or mandate, at least some number of citizens would be required to issue them; but freedom of choice includes the freedom not to express any opinion on public affairs at all.

As the form of law-making power that incorporates popular sovereignty and freedom of choice is an elected, responsible, independent assembly, modern politics is defined by a dialectical contradiction: the mandate that must be given by the people to the constitution-making power, namely, to ratify a constitution that upholds equal liberty, can only be fulfilled through its opposite, independence from mandate. The system of capitalist production brings it about that bourgeois society must mandate a law-making power to establish the independence of a law-making power from mandate. As Marx claims

---

96   Ibid. The *MECW* translation, 'formally they are commissioned, but once they are *actually* commissioned they are *no* longer *mandatories*', is nonsense. '*Wirklich* (actual)' – which contrasts with 'potential' – is not '*actually* commissioned' (which would be: 'wirklich *kommittiert*'); Marx does not say that representatives are '*actually* commissioned' (Marx says they are 'formally' commissioned); and it is contradictory to say of those 'actually commissioned' that they are '*no* longer *mandatories*'.

in his *Critique of Hegel's Doctrine of the State*: '[t]he separation of the political state from civil society appears [*erscheint*] as the separation of the deputies from their mandators'.[97] A law-making power has 'mandators' if it is created by a constitution-making power in execution of a mandate it has received from the people. Any law-making power of capitalist society must also uphold freedom of choice, however. To that end, it must be independent, and so exclude mandate. Mandate must appear as its opposite, as 'separation' or independence from mandate.

Marx remarks in *Capital* that 'all science [*Wissenschaft*] would be superfluous, if the form of appearance [*Erscheinungsform*] and the essence of a thing were immediately to coincide'.[98] One way to interpret this remark is to say that derivation is central to commodity form philosophy. Capitalism is characterised by multiple logics, each of which has a commodity-form-related cause. Just as the freedom of will generated by the commodity form explains the juridical logic of freedom of choice; the system of capitalist production generates a popular mandate that explains the logic of political representation. Just as the juridical logic of freedom of choice must register a rightsholder with the will of a person as simply one of the phenomena subject to it; the logic of political representation must register the people as mandators of equal liberty as just one of the phenomena subject to it. To defend this claim, it is first necessary to clarify what is meant by political representation.

The German Ideology claims: '[r]epresentation [*Repräsentation*] is an entirely specific product of modern bourgeois society'.[99] Representation is a specific product of modern bourgeois society if modern bourgeois society explains the existence of a law-making power with a certain form, and representation is conceived of as an act of a law-making power with this form. A conception of representation as an act of an elected, responsible, independent law-making assembly, albeit as an act conceptually distinct from law-making

---

97   Ibid. Compare '*erscheint*' here with '*Erscheinungsform*' in the next citation.

98   *MEW*, 25, p. 825; *MECW*, 37, p. 804; Marx 1981, p. 956; compare *MEW*, 23, p. 73, p. 559, p. 562, p. 564, p. 594; *MECW*, 35, p. 69, p. 537, p. 540, p. 542, p. 568; Marx 1976, p. 150, p. 677, p. 680, p. 682, p. 714. On '*Wissenschaft*', see ch. 3.

99   Bahne, p. 100; *MECW*, 5, p. 200. (The passage of text from which this quotation is taken is not reproduced in the *MEW*). *MECW* translates '*Repräsentation*' as 'representative system', which would be: '*Repräsentativsystem*'. The representative system is the system in which the people are represented in an elected assembly. '*Repräsentation*' is a more general concept. The claim that 'the representative system is a very specific product of modern bourgeois society' (*MECW*) is trivial. No one, including Stahl, would dispute it. *The German Ideology*'s claim that *representation* is a specific product of modern bourgeois society is a controversial claim: monarchists (such as Stahl) must dispute it.

itself, is in line with Marx's remark in *Critique of Hegel's Doctrine of the State* distinguishing 'the law-making power, as the actual *law-making* function, and as the *representative, abstract-political* function'.[100] Political representation is the making present of a people before a public audience by an elected, responsible, independent law-making assembly that claims a monopoly on representation.

One defining feature of political representation, on this conception, is that a people, and not some other entity, must be represented. The law-making power, Marx says, is 'representative of the people'.[101] To put this into relief, consider Stahl's account of political representation.

For Stahl, a sovereign monarch is the 'representative of the state'.[102] The monarch is the representative of the state, because the state authorises their power. A monarch owes their personal power to their office, which they assume in accordance with the constitution.[103] A monarch does not represent the people, because a monarch does not owe their personal power to the people. The people is instead 'the obedient part in the state'.[104] Indeed, as, for Stahl, the essence of the state is personality, the monarch is the only representative of the state. The essence of the state is personality, according to Stahl, because there is to be an isomorphism between God's superiority over the Torah, and the role of personality in supplying dignity to the laws that enable the state's creative intervention.[105] As the state is essentially personality, it can only be represented by the highest person in the state, the monarch.

If, by contrast, state power is authorised by the people, any representatives must represent the people, and be responsible. Further, the people, as a plurality, must be represented in a plural form, rather than in a personal form. Only an assembly allows it to be known, through its public deliberation, that its decisions are made in the name of the people. As Marx remarks in *The Eighteenth Brumaire*: '[t]he National Assembly exhibits, through its individual representatives, the manifold sides of national spirit'.[106]

A law-making assembly makes a people present if its law-making is regarded as a common-good-promoting activity in a society otherwise characterised by the pursuit of particular interests. A representative law-making assembly

---

100   *MEW*, 1, p. 325; *MECW*, 3, p. 120.
101   *MEW*, 1, p. 260; *MECW*, 3, p. 57.
102   Stahl 1837, p. 77.
103   Stahl 1837, pp. 78–81, pp. 88–9.
104   Stahl 1837, p. 246.
105   Stahl 1833, p. 203.
106   *MEW*, 8, p. 128; *MECW*, 11, p. 117.

is thus an *independent* assembly. The condition under which the law-making assembly can be representative is the condition under which, to be representative, it must be independent.

Further: if the people must be represented by an independent law-making assembly, then representation requires a public audience. Representation must be asserted by the representative, and believed in by the author. But the fact that representation must be believed in by the author has a further implication, if the representative is independent of their author. It must occur before them. Only if acts of representation occur before the represented can they effect the belief in representation that representation requires.

Consider, by way of contrast, representation in the sphere of private law. In the sphere of private law, one actor (the agent) may act on another's behalf (the principal). An agent is not independent of their principal, however. The agent is under an obligation to report back to their principle, and follow additional instructions. A principal can be assured of their representation by the fact that their agent is under these obligations. As political representatives are independent from formal mandate or instruction, their author can only be assured of their representation if they are included in the audience before whom representation occurs. As political representation must occur before an audience that includes its author, and must represent its author, it follows, as Marx writes in *Debates on Freedom of the Press*, that '[r]epresentation removed from the consciousness of those who commission it [*Kommittenten*] is no representation'.[107] No non-public act is representative, for no non-public act can include the people as its audience. Without the people's inclusion in the audience of representation, the people cannot believe they are represented. Although a public sphere may be conceivable without representation, representation is inconceivable apart from a public sphere.

Marx claims in *The Eighteenth Brumaire*: 'it is impossible to create a moral power by paragraphs of law'.[108] Going by this claim, an independent law-making assembly is not a representative assembly simply by dint of the fact that a constitution declares its members to be representatives of the people. Representation must be asserted and accepted. The main formal channel by which the people can accept representatives' claims to represent them is through their

---

107   *MEW*, 1, p. 44; *MECW*, 1, p. 148. The *MECW* translation of '*Kommittenten*' as 'those whom it represents' (which would be: '*Repräsentierten*') is too nebulous. It is not on every account of how political representatives relate to those they represent that those they represent are '*Kommittenten*'. The latter suggests that political representatives are authorised and mandated by those they represent.

108   *MEW*, 8, p. 128; *MECW*, 11, p. 116.

election. Members of an independent law-making assembly must publicly discuss and vote on laws. Insofar as they do this as members of the people, they cannot deny the people the right to publicly discuss and vote. For by such a denial, they would elevate themselves above the people. As these rights are exercised by the people in an election, it is in the form of their own election that representatives must have their claim to represent the people accepted.

The people accepts a responsible independent law-making assembly as its representative by casting votes for its election, provided its votes are cast for those who accept the existing constitution, and provided that it does not heed any other would-be law-maker. According to Marx's *Critique of Hegel's Doctrine of the State*, an independent law-making assembly's claim to represent the people is a claim to a 'monopoly'[109] on its political representation. A representative assembly is an independent assembly, and an assembly only asserts its independence by formally refusing all mandates or instructions, such as any other law-making power would have to issue to it. If a representative assembly that recognised another law-making power alongside itself would thereby confess that it was not free from mandate and instruction, and hence not representative, any claim to represent the people is a claim to a monopoly on its political representation.

This conception of political representation as the making present of a people before a public audience by an elected, responsible, independent law-making assembly that claims a monopoly on representation offers a way to interpret the *'representative, abstract-political* function'[110] of the law-making power. In the sphere of private law, not only can an agent represent their principal without the latter as an audience. The agent's acts of receiving instructions from and reporting back to their principal may also be entirely distinct from the acts of representing this principal vis-à-vis a third party, that is, asserting the principal's interests vis-à-vis a third party to win the latter's agreement. By contrast, in political representation, the people has three roles. Firstly, representatives represent the people. Secondly, the people are the public audience before whom representation occurs. Thirdly, the people are to be won over by representation. Acts of political representation effect the belief in representation that representation requires by winning over the people who are thereby represented. The function of representation is to offer (to the end of arguing for or against a set of electoral objectives, a law, a minister, etc.) an image of the people to the people that the people accept.

---

109   *MEW*, 1, p. 268; *MECW*, 3, p. 65.
110   *MEW*, 1, p. 325; *MECW*, 3, p. 120.

In section 1, the juridical logic of freedom of choice was derived from the commodity form. Although a legal code that prioritises freedom of choice can be explained by the commodity form, freedom of choice can be given legal effect even for those who do not possess the will of a person. It can be given legal effect for those who lack freedom of will (addicts), and for those with freedom of will who do not act as persons (such as those who act from a non-voluntarily assumed duty). So, from the perspective of this legal code, its cause appears as just one phenomenon subject to its logic. The same goes for the logic of political representation. The commodity form explains the logic of political representation by the popular mandate generated by the system of capitalist production, which must be fulfilled by a representative law-making power. But its cause, too, appears as just one phenomenon subject to its logic. The logic of political representation must register the people as mandators of equal liberty as just one of the many possible representations of the people. For political representatives can also represent the people as a people that is not sovereign, that is, as a people that is not entitled to mandate a constitution-making power; or as a people that is entitled to mandate a new constitution-making power. From the perspective of political representation, its cause is just one possible image of the people that can be offered to the people for the people to accept.

Indeed, a representative assembly may represent the people as inherently bound to an existing constitution, however that constitution is thought to come about, and have its claim accepted on any occasion on which it is formally required to have that claim accepted. Elections are the main formal occasion on which a representative assembly permits the people to accept or reject its claim to represent it, and elections are verdicts on how to concretise an existing constitution. A representative assembly can therefore represent the people as bound to the existing constitution, and have its claim accepted on any occasion on which it takes itself to be required to have this claim accepted.

6   The Separation of Powers

Marx's *Critique of Hegel's Doctrine of the State* attempts to explain the separation of powers by saying of the 'lie' that 'the *people* is the *interest of the state*':

> This lie ... has established itself as the *law-making* power precisely because the law-making power has the universal as its content, is more a

matter of knowledge than will, is the *metaphysical* state *power*; while the same lie, as the power of government, etc., would either have to dissolve at once, or be transformed into a truth.[111]

The premise of the explanation is that a representative assembly is a '*lie*'. A representative assembly is a '*lie*' if its members' claim to represent the people rests on something they know to be false. What is it about representatives' claim to represent the people that they know is false?

Marx's recognition-based critique of rights in *On the Jewish Question* and *Critique of the Gotha Programme* suggests an answer.[112] Marx's recognition-based critique of rights concerns the disparity between the liberties that rights-creating norms expressly recognise and the social dynamics they tacitly recognise. A constitution that includes a right of property does not expressly recognise the capital accumulation to which it gives rise, just as a constitution that includes a right of freedom of expression or a right to form a political party does not expressly recognise the commercialisation of the press or the hierarchisation of electoral political parties. A significant, publicly known disparity between what the law expressly recognises and what it tacitly recognises nonetheless ensures that, in obeying the law, members of society know that they are obeying something other than the law: the furtherance of whatever dynamics form as a result of the concatenation of rightsholders' independent exercise of their rights.

As far as a representative assembly is concerned, the main formal occasion on which representatives must have their claim to represent the people accepted is at elections. A representative assembly counts an election as a verdict on how the constitution is to be concretised just as long as the people exercise their freedom of choice by voting, in conditions of legality, for candidates who declare a commitment to a set of constitutional law-making objectives. That is to say, a representative assembly deems the successful candidates to be representatives of the people just in case their election can be viewed as the culmination of a legal process.

But as just argued, rights-creating norms tacitly recognise dynamics that they do not expressly recognise. So, by adopting the legality of the election process as the test of whether its result is to be recognised, a representative assembly allows dynamics not expressly recognised by law, but which merely form as a result of it, to influence the objectives that candidates declare a com-

---

111   *MEW*, 1, p. 268; *MECW*, 3, p. 65.
112   See ch. 8, sec. 13.

mitment to and/or the reasons that votes are cast for them, at no cost to its recognition of the result. In other words, it regards the successful candidates as representatives of the people notwithstanding the fact that the dynamics that influence whether or not they triumph are not expressly recognised in the name of the people. To hold that, simply by virtue of being returned at a legally binding election, candidates have had their claim to represent the people accepted, is a lie, if their success depends on whether their declared commitments or appeal are in line with opinions that flourish by virtue of dynamics that are known not to be expressly recognised in the name of the people. But that is just what representatives hold, and is a lie, if a representative assembly treats the legality of the election process as the test of whether its result is to be recognised, and the law is founded on innate absolute rights.

The fact that political representation is a lie helps to explain the separation of powers because, if political representation is a lie, some implementation of the law will have to be conducted out of the public glare. Law-implementation must be conducted in private if (the anticipation of) prior public debate and announcement of a decision would increase the degree of public controversy to an unmanageable level. The number of full-blown public controversies must be limited, if the law is to perform its guarantee and recognition functions. When, however, the law is to be implemented in contexts that affect particular interests buoyed by dynamics that the law does not expressly recognise, its public implementation (starting with holding all meetings of ministers in public) would increase public controversy to an unmanageable level. If the law-making power is a representative assembly, some law-implementation must be conducted out of the public glare.

If law-implementation must be conducted in private, it cannot be conducted by a representative assembly. If an assembly had two functions to perform, one of which had to be conducted in private, it would first have to decide which function the deliberation of a given issue belonged to. That decision could not itself be taken in public, for its aim would be to determine whether or not an issue was to be aired in public at all. So, if an assembly had two functions, one of which had to be conducted in private, its entire activity would first have to be cleared by an initial round of private deliberation. But if an assembly with responsibility for law-making had first to meet in private, to determine whether or not it was to meet in public, it could not retain its representative character. The people could not know that its discussion was conducted in their name.

As the form of law-making power in the state of capitalist society is a representative assembly, which must deliberate before a public audience; and as law-implementation must be conducted in private; the law-making power and the executive power must be separated. The government administration in the charge of this executive power then assumes a bureaucratic form. Marx writes in *Critique of Hegel's Doctrine of the State*:

> The universal spirit of bureaucracy is *secrecy*, mystery; preserved on the inside by hierarchy, and from the outside as a closed corporation. Public state spirit, even state conviction, thus appear to bureaucracy as a *betrayal* of its mystery. *Authority* is therefore the principle of its knowledge, and reverence to authority its *conviction*.[113]

The successful implementation of the laws passed by a representative assembly rests on an administration's capacity for '*secrecy*', that is, its capacity to control the disclosure of information to the public. Other things being equal, this capacity will vary with an administration's capacity to control the disclosure of information internally. The latter requires access to information to be made conditional on objective criteria that can be enforced; that is, to be attached to offices with defined areas of competence.

A government administration must also be accountable, however, where to be accountable is to be liable to scrutiny, and to be subject to calls to justify decisions. If the aim of law-making is to regulate social life, by means of implementation, any executive power in charge of government administration must be responsible to the legislature, if the people is not to have alienated its will. As an executive power can only exercise this responsibility if it is in charge of a government administration that is accountable, government administration must be accountable. Accountability is only meaningful, however, if it can reveal information that is not already known, or not known with sufficient certainty. As a government administration must limit its internal disclosure of information *and* be accountable, it must be organised hierarchically. In an administrative hierarchy, the accountability of offices is asymmetrical: office a is not accountable to b, but b is accountable to a; b is not accountable to c, but c is accountable to b; and so on.

To describe government administration as a 'closed' corporation, meanwhile, is to say that it controls its own appointments. If access to information depends on the office one holds, the disclosure of information is only controlled by controlling appointments via the same hierarchy that imposes accountability. Government administrators must then be appointed. As the implementation of laws passed by a representative assembly requires a single

---

113   *MEW*, 1, p. 249; *MECW*, 3, p. 47; compare *MEW*, 8, p. 196; *MECW*, 11, p. 185.

hierarchy both to impose accountability and to control appointments, government administration has the form of a 'bureaucracy', where a belief in administrative expertise underpins a belief in the legitimacy of the commands issued by one office-holder to a subordinate office-holder.

The fact that the law-making power takes the form of a representative assembly, and a separate executive power is in charge of a bureaucratic government administration, produces an inherent conflict between them, however:

> From this discordant [*zwiespältig*] nature of the law-making power, as the actual *law-making* function, and as the *representative, abstract-political* function, a peculiarity arises ... A question only arouses special attention once it becomes *political* ... Why this appearance? Because the law-making power is at the same time the representation of the political existence of civil society; because the political essence of a question in general exists in its relation to the various powers of the political state; and because the law-making power represents political consciousness, and this can prove itself to be *political* only in conflict with the power of government.[114]

Not only is the executive power in charge of a state bureaucracy opposed in spirit to a representative law-making assembly, as bureaucratic authority to independent public discussion; or, as Marx puts it in *The Eighteenth Brumaire*, as '*power without words*' to '*the power of words*'.[115] They are opposed in practice, as each is led by its own spirit into conflict with the other. A representative law-making assembly not only requires a separate executive to take charge of a government bureacracy. It must also hold it to account. Its exercise of the capacity to hold members of the executive to account is one aspect of the assertion of its representative character. A representative assembly must be able to discuss any issue of principle that it identifies as impacting on its concretisation of the constitution, including in the executive's actions. Only by this means can it assert its 'monopoly'[116] on representation – even if the antinomy of natural rights and popular authorisation introduces indeterminacy into what actions it will scrutinise, and what justifications it will accept. If a representative assembly were

---

114   *MEW*, 1, pp. 325–6; *MECW*, 3, p. 120; compare *MEW*, 8, p. 167; *MECW*, 11, p. 155. *MECW* translates '*zwiespältig*' as 'twofold' (which would be: '*zweifach*'). 'Twofold' is a neutral term. A thing of twofold nature (such as a twofold objective) need not be internally riven. But that is the connotation of '*zwiespältig*'.

115   *MEW*, 8, p. 196; *MECW*, 11, p. 185.

116   *MEW*, 1, p. 268; *MECW*, 3, p. 65.

to concede its inability to deliberate on any issue, it would abdicate its representative character; while a state bureaucracy retains its capacity to act by disclosing as little information to it as possible. Paradoxically, the representative function that is supposed to integrate the people within the state leads its separated powers into conflict. The state of capitalist society is not the 'organism'[117] that it would have to be, to realise freedom as self-legislative human community.

117   *MEW*, 1, p. 104; *MECW*, 3, p. 202.

CHAPTER 12

The Rights-Antinomy and Class Struggle

What now remains to be shown is that classes are connected to the system of capitalist production and the state of capitalist society by a further antinomy. Insofar as the interaction-recognition-antinomy thesis belongs to commodity form philosophy, this second antinomy must also be traceable to the commodity form.

The famous chapter of *Capital* Volume I entitled 'The Working Day'[1] expounds the antinomy in question. The system of capitalist production is said to sustain the assertion of a right to an unlimited working day, and the assertion of a right to a limited working day, both with equal justification. This 'antinomy' of 'right against right, both equally licenced by the law of commodity exchange'[2] will be referred to as *the rights-antinomy*, and the passage in which it appears *Capital's antinomy passage*.

The rights-antinomy serves two functions. On the one hand, it connects the system of capitalist production to classes. Engendered by the system of capitalist production, the rights-antinomy is the first form of the antagonistic interdependency that defines the capitalist and working-classes. On the other hand, it connects classes to the state of capitalist society. Workers' practical response to the rights-antinomy opens up a standpoint from which not only the rights-antinomy but also the antinomy of natural rights and popular authorisation can be resolved.

The rights-antinomy is central, therefore, to the interaction-recognition-antinomy thesis, and this chapter offers a long overdue analysis of it. Notwithstanding the vast literature on *Capital*, the antinomy it describes has yet to receive proper analysis. Only one author in the history of philosophy could claim to provide a concept with which to grasp its significance. The reasons for its neglect are multiple.

One set of reasons stem from the official translations, discussed below.[3] Put simply, the official translations make it harder than it should be to identify

---

1   *MEW*, 23, p. 245; *MECW*, 35, p. 239; Marx 1976, p. 340.
2   *MEW*, 23, p. 249; *MECW*, 35, p. 243; Marx 1976, p. 344. Marx first remarks on an 'antinomy' in capitalist production's 'general relation itself' in the *Economic Manuscripts of 1861–63* (*MEW*, 43, p. 172; *MECW*, 30, p. 184).
3   See sec. 4.

an antinomy. Even commentators with no theoretical pre-commitments that would prevent them from grasping the rights-antinomy are left flailing about in the dark.

Second, some Marxist projects do not permit the rights-antinomy to assume any importance. One project of this kind is Analytical Marxism. Analytical Marxists have eschewed all argumentative figures that exceed 'thinking as understanding'.[4] As such, they cannot attend to any antinomy. A second project of this kind is Althusserian Marxism. According to Louis Althusser, 'one could and should ... approach ideologies *in terms of Ideological State Apparatuses*'.[5] To follow this cue is to be condemned to neglect the root of the rights-antinomy. The premises of its thesis and antithesis are supplied by the system of capitalist production, and its culture of recognition. Neither of the latter belongs to a so-called 'Ideological State Apparatus'. If the premises underpinning the rights-antinomy do not arise from an 'Ideological State Apparatus', then Althusserian Marxism, too, must remain silent about it. Symptomatically, half a dozen studies influenced by the projects of Analytical Marxism or Althusserian Marxism that get as far as citing *Capital*'s antinomy passage offer no analysis of it.[6] Others do not get this far. In a study subtitled 'The Political Theory of *Capital*', William Clare Roberts claims: 'the length of the working day is the crucial point of contestation'.[7] Although the rights-antinomy characterises this 'crucial point of contestation' and is relevant politically, Roberts does not mention it.

Nor, thirdly, has the label 'Hegelian Marxism' (under which interpretations of Marx from outside Analytical Marxism and Althusserian Marxism have sometimes proceeded) encouraged attention to the rights-antinomy. The label 'Hegelian Marxism' emphasises the author whom Marx, in *Capital*, identifies as the source of his interest in dialectical contradiction.[8] Yet it does so at the price of de-emphasising any other insights that Marx's analysis of the commodity form incorporates, and for which Hegel could not have been the source of Marx's interest. As the term 'antinomy' may be associated with Kant, the label 'Hegelian Marxism' need not encourage attention to how Marx's analysis of the

---

4 Hegel 1986c, § 80; Hegel 1991b, § 80.
5 Althusser 1994, p. 499; Althusser 2006, p. 138; see Althusser 1995; Althusser 2014, and Althusser 1970; Althusser 1971.
6 Bidet 2007, p. 80, Callinicos 2014, p. 304, Elster 1985, p. 186, Peffer 1990, p. 335, Read 2003, p. 96 and Wetherly 1992, p. 185 all cite parts of *Capital*'s antinomy passage, yet offer no analysis of the antinomy.
7 Roberts 2017, p. 139.
8 *MEW*, 23, p. 623; *MECW*, 35, p. 592; Marx 1976, p. 744.

commodity form makes use of the argumentative figure of antinomy. For their part, authors in the tradition of Kantian socialism have not analysed the rights-antinomy.[9] Kantian socialists have focused on defending the claim that Kant's *ethics* (and in particular the Formula of Humanity or the Formula of the Realm of Ends) can provide a justification for socialism.

Finally, the Anglophone debate on Marx and justice is not in a position to emphasise the rights-antinomy. As shown in chapter 8, Anglophone debate on Marx and justice has not proceeded either from a clear and correct understanding of the domain in which capitalist exploitation is located, or from a suitable conception of justice. If capitalist exploitation is located in the domain of value, it is natural to organise an assessment of *Capital*'s pronouncements on the justice or injustice of capitalism around a contrast between the exchange of equivalents in circulation, and the one-way appropriation of value in production.[10] As *Capital*'s antinomy passage has no obvious place in this contrast – the antinomy it identifies concerns the working day – it is often ignored in this debate. Moreover, both to identify the premises of the rights-antinomy, and to resolve it, it is necessary to reject the correlativity premise that Wood, Young and Cohen have all affirmed.

It has therefore come to pass that only one author in the history of philosophy has offered a concept with which to grasp the significance of *Capital*'s antinomy passage, in a work that both reconstructs Marx's critique of capitalism and mounts a critique of Kant's theoretical philosophy: Lukács, in *History and Class Consciousness*.[11] As Lukács perceives, *Capital*'s antinomy passage identifies 'the problem of labour time' as the moment where a worker's 'consciousness as the consciousness of the commodity arises'.[12] Only the antithesis of the rights-antinomy exhibits '*the self-consciousness of the commodity*'.[13] If one way to understand Lukács's concept of an 'identical subject-object of the social process of development'[14] is as an agent that need only reflect on its response

---

9   Van der Linden 1988, p. 262; Staudinger 1907; Vorländer 1911. There is no discussion of *Capital*'s antinomy passage in Negt 2010, or the *Kantian Review* Special Issue on Kant and Marx (2017), either.

10 As in Geras 1985, Young 1978 and others.

11 As Sonja Buckel notes, neither the critical theorists Otto Kirchheimer and Franz Neumann, nor Pashukanis, establish a systematic connection between class struggle, and the commodity form (Buckel 2007, p. 115). One explanation is their neglect of *Capital*'s antinomy passage.

12 Lukács 1977, p. 363; Lukács 1968, p. 178.

13 Lukács 1977, p. 352; Lukács 1968, p. 168.

14 Lukács 1977, p. 394; Lukács 1968, p. 206; see also Lukács 1977, p. 331; Lukács 1968, p. 149.

to its conditions to identify principles that could be used to found a superior form of society, then *Capital*'s antinomy passage can be read as beginning an argument for the working-class as an 'identical subject-object'.

Sections 1–2 present an antagonistic interdependency account of the capitalist and the working-classes. Section 3 then examines Lukács's concept of 'the self-consciousness of the commodity'.[15] With its aid, section 4 reconstructs *Capital*'s antinomy passage. Sections 5–9 chart the significance of this rights-antinomy for class struggle. Section 5 rebuts the claim that capitalist class interests are such as to render it of little import. Section 6 elaborates the concept of possible practical awareness, on which a standpoint rests, and suggests that interest privilege can arise from a learning process defined by antinomy, recognition and real abstraction. Sections 7–8 then argue that working-class organisation and movements can initiate such a learning process. Finally, section 9 argues that it is possible for this learning process to facilitate a resolution to the rights-antinomy, and to the antinomy of natural rights and popular authorisation.

1   An Antagonistic Interdependency Conception of Classes

In *Reading Capital*, Althusser remarks of Marx's *Capital*: 'the reader will know how Volume Three ends. A title: *Classes*. Forty lines, then silence'.[16] Whether the absence of a systematic account of classes is just evidence of *Capital*'s unfinished state, or, as Althusser more strongly claims, one of Marx's 'omissions'[17] (implying that the material Marx published ought to have contained a systematic account of classes), can be left to one side. Either way, the fact remains that the absence of a systematic account of classes from *Capital* means that Marx's most explicit statement on the conditions for classes is found not in *Capital* but in *The Eighteenth Brumaire*, in the course of its analysis of the French peasantry:

> Insofar as millions of families live under economic conditions of existence that separate their mode of life, their interests and their culture from those of the other classes, and place them in hostile confrontation [*feindlich gegenüberstellen*], they form a class. Insofar as a merely local connection links these small-holding peasants, and the sameness of

---

15   Lukács 1977, p. 352; Lukács 1968, p. 168.
16   Althusser and Balibar 1969, p. 71; Althusser and Balibar 1975, p. 193.
17   Ibid.

their interests generates no commonality, national association or political organisation among them, they do not form a class.[18]

As noted in both English language and German language literature, this passage suggests two distinct concepts of classes.[19] Its first sentence delineates one concept of classes, while both sentences taken together delineate a second, more demanding concept of classes. In the standard terminology, the first concept is termed 'class in itself', while the more demanding concept is termed 'class for itself'.[20] Prepositions are not especially clarifying means to mark theoretical distinctions, however. It is more informative to say that the less demanding concept of classes posits antagonism at the micro-level only, while the more demanding concept of classes also includes the conditions for antagonism at the macro-level.

In the first sentence of the passage, classes are defined by separation and opposition. That move admits various interpretations. It is ambiguous between a definition of classes in terms of the tendency of certain conditions to generate separation and opposition, and a definition of classes as separate and opposed. Are classes identical with or formed from this tendency?

The latter reading is to be favoured. In its comparison of Europe and North America, *The Eighteenth Brumaire* asks if, when 'classes already exist', they have 'become fixed', or 'instead continually alter and transfer their component parts in a constant flux'.[21] In other words, *The Eighteenth Brumaire* raises the question of the degree of class mobility. The question of class mobility can only be raised if the tendency of certain conditions to separate and oppose individuals in class terms has born fruit. A separation and opposition must already exist before one can compare the ease or likelihood for individuals in different societies to move from one class to another in spite of that separation and opposition. By implication, members of classes are separate and opposed to one another; they do not simply live under conditions that tend to produce that separation and opposition. Classes have memberships that do not overlap. (That is not to say that everyone in a class society belongs to a class).

A second ambiguity concerns the nature of class opposition. Is it merely causal, or is it characterised by interdependency? On a causal interpretation, classes have memberships that do not overlap, whose members' interests can

---

18   *MEW*, 8, p. 198; *MECW*, 11, p. 187. The significance of '*feindlich*', an adverb related to the noun '*Feind* (enemy, adversary)', is discussed below.

19   Brunkhorst 2007, p. 237; Cohen 1978, p. 75.

20   Brunkhorst 2007, p. 237; Cohen 1978, p. 76.

21   *MEW*, 8, pp. 122–3; *MECW*, 11, p. 111.

be satisfied to different degrees, and whose satisfaction is inversely related to the satisfaction of the interests of members of another class. On an interdependency interpretation, classes are groups with non-overlapping memberships, whose members' ends presuppose standard actions of social affecting[22] to themselves by members of another class, and whose degree of achievement is inversely related. A 'group', in this definition, is a number of individuals who all have a certain property, and who all perform social action[23] related to that property to at least one other member of the group. A number of individuals form a reading group, for example, if they all read a text, and exchange opinions on it.[24] In expressing their opinion on the text to the group/a member of the group, an individual performs a social action related to the property of having read the text. By inviting others to consider their opinion of the text, they assume that others, like them, have read it.[25]

Note, firstly, what the causal interpretation and the interdependency interpretation of the opposition requirement for classes have in common. Both make what Marx's *1859 Preface* refers to as 'antagonism growing up out of individuals' social conditions of life'[26] a defining feature of classes. As, for both of these interpretations, antagonism is a defining feature of classes, there is no such thing, on either interpretation, as class in the singular.

Both interpretations differ in this respect from a modal definition of class.[27] To define class modally, by what a given distribution of resources ensures a type of actor *must* do, is to define classes independently of one another, rather than by antagonism. Even if a description of what one type of actor must do refers to facts about others, if it avoids reference to facts about what others must do, it avoids reference to any other modally defined class position. Paul Wetherly, for example, describes 'the ownership position of proletarians' as: 'proletarians ... lacking ownership of means of production, apparently have no choice but to sell their labour power to a capitalist who does own means of production'.[28] There is no reference, in this description of the proletarian's modally defined class position, to what a capitalist must do. Hence, the proletarian's class position is defined independently of the capitalist's class position. On a

---

22   Action to get another to perform action, as a result of their identifying its performer; see ch. 5, sec. 2.

23   Action that includes an attitude-to-the-other to another; see ch. 5, sec. 2.

24   A reading group is a voluntary group. A group is involuntary if the property that all members have is involuntarily acquired (for example, ethnicity).

25   The class of people who have read a text is not, just as such, a group.

26   *MEW*, 13, p. 9; *MECW*, 29, p. 264.

27   Advocated at Cohen 1978, p. 72; Elster 1985, p. 174; Roemer 1982a, p. 14, 77.

28   Wetherly 2005, p. 112.

modal definition of class, it is possible to conceive of a world in which there are proletarians but no capitalists, or a world in which there are capitalists but no proletarians. A modal definition of class is straightforwardly incompatible with the first sentence of the above passage from *The Eighteenth Brumaire*, therefore. If 'hostile confrontation'[29] or antagonism defines classes, then one class is not even conceivable without another.

Both the causal and the interdependency interpretation also differ from what Cohen calls a 'structural definition of class'.[30] A 'structural definition of class', Cohen writes, is a definition of class 'purely in terms of production relations', where 'production relations', for Cohen, denote types of effective control over productive resources.[31] Types of effective control over productive resources place conditions on production. They may[32] give rise to antagonism. But they are not an antagonism. Their description as types of effective control is not even a description of a tendency of economic conditions to generate antagonism. The 'structural definition of class', like the modal definition, is straightforwardly incompatible with the first sentence of the above passage from *The Eighteenth Brumaire*.

Where the causal interpretation and the interdependency interpretation of the opposition requirement for classes differ is over interdependency. The causal interpretation does not imply interdependency. The causal interpretation construes opposition in terms of inversely related interests only. Inversely related interests can be interests in counterposed distributions of x, where the distribution of x does not require recipients with inversely related interests in its distribution to act to one another. Suppose a parent has a fixed amount of disposable income to split between two children. On a causal construal, the two children may have separate and opposed interests in the distribution of their parent's disposable income, even if they are raised in different households, do not act to one another, or even know of the other's existence. But if so, the children are not interdependent. The concept of causally opposed interests does not presuppose interdependence between those with opposed interests.

There are two reasons to favour an interdependency interpretation of the opposition requirement for classes. One reason is that an interdependency interpretation is a better fit with Marx's general remarks on social relations.

---

29   *MEW*, 8, p. 198; *MECW*, 11, p. 187.
30   Cohen 1978, p. 75.
31   Cohen 1978, p. 75, p. 63.
32   But not necessarily: an autarchic individual on a desert island would have a type of effective control over productive resources that could not give rise to social antagonism.

Social relations require standard actions of social affecting.[33] On the interdependency interpretation of the opposition requirement for classes, classes exist in virtue of social relations between members of different classes. The same cannot be said on the causal interpretation.

The second reason is that the interdependency interpretation is a better fit with the above passage from *The Eighteenth Brumaire*, which describes the relation between classes as 'hostile [*feindlich*]'. A relation cannot be 'hostile' unless it is an object of awareness. One may have an illness without being aware of it. But one cannot have an enemy (*Feind*) without being aware of them. The concept of an enemy presupposes the possibility of struggle, fought by the respective sides. There is only a possibility of struggle, however, if its possibility can be felt by the respective sides. By implication, an attributive reference to an enemy-like (*feind-lich*) or hostile stance assumes an awareness of the possibility of struggle on the part of those to whom it is attributed. It presupposes an awareness of opposition on their part. By its use of this adverbial, which also features in the next passage cited, *The Eighteenth Brumaire* implies that actors' awareness of opposition is constitutive of classes.

It is one of the myths of Marx interpretation, then, that the difference between the two concepts of classes Marx outlines in *The Eighteenth Brumaire* is a difference between a consciousness-free and a consciousness-inclusive concept of classes.[34] The phrase 'hostile confrontation' appears in the first sentence of the aforecited passage. Thus, elements of consciousness define both its concepts of classes. It is unwarranted to suppose that, if Marx had a concept of classes besides that of classes in struggle, then he must have had a consciousness-free concept of classes. The difference between the two concepts of classes in *The Eighteenth Brumaire* is that the less demanding concept of classes posits antagonism at the micro-level only. The more demanding concept of classes also includes the conditions for antagonism at the macro-level. Both concepts, however, are consciousness-inclusive concepts of classes.

Whereas the interdependency interpretation of the opposition requirement for classes is sensitive to the implications of the adverbial '*feindlich*', the causal interpretation is not. On the interdependency interpretation, the end of each member of a class presupposes a standard action of social affecting to that member by one or more members of another class. If so, class members can become aware, however dimly, of a class opposition, whenever they reflect on their end, if the ends of class members are opposed; that is, if the degree to

---

33   See ch. 5.
34   See Cohen 1978, p. 76. It is revealing that Cohen merely refers to *The Eighteenth Brumaire* without reproducing the aforecited passage.

which each achieves their end depends on opposed uses of the same determinant. For then by reflecting on their own end, they are at least implicitly reflecting on action by a member of another class belonging to the pursuit of an opposed end. Nothing about the causal interpretation of the opposition requirement, by contrast, ensures that class members can become aware of class opposition. As the case of the two children raised in different households illustrates, inversely related interests do not guarantee the possibility of an awareness of the other, let alone the possibility of an awareness of opposed interests.

On an antagonistic interdependency conception of classes, the (perhaps only implicit) awareness of opposition that helps to define the capitalist and working-classes arises in virtue of production. It cannot arise in virtue of distribution. From the perspective of distribution, Marx remarks in his *Economic Manuscripts of 1861–63*, it appears that:

> The different revenues flow from entirely different sources, one from land, another from capital, another from labour. They thus stand in no hostile [*feindlich*] connection, because in no inner connection at all ... Insofar as an opposition [*Gegensatz*] arises between them, it only springs from competition as to which of the agents is to appropriate more of the product, more of the value they jointly created; and if it occasionally leads to a scrap, what then finally emerges as the end result of this competition between land, capital and labour is that, by quarreling with one another over the division, they have, through their rivalry, so increased the value of the product that each receives a larger piece,[35]

The value of the total social product can increase, if more socially necessary labour is performed within a given duration of time than was previously performed in the same duration of time. If more socially necessary labour is performed, the value that capital and labour each receive as profit and wages could both increase. But if profits and wages may rise (or fall) together, *and* the 'sources' or ultimate determinants of each amount *appear* to be 'entirely different' or independent, no opposition between capitalists and workers need be apparent from the perspective of distribution. As *The Eighteenth Brumaire* requires an opposition to be apparent to class members for classes to exist; and as, on Marx's own analysis, the distribution of value as profit and wages

---

35   *MEW*, 26.3, p. 493; *MECW*, 32, pp. 502–3. In *MECW*, '*Gegensatz*' is rendered as 'contradiction' (which would be: '*Widerspruch*').

need not reveal an opposition; Marx must look to a sphere logically prior to the distribution of value, to hold that capitalist and working-classes exist. In other words, Marx must locate the awareness of opposition that is constitutive of these classes, and thus these classes themselves, in production.

An awareness of opposition can be located in production, by identifying two ends that require opposed uses of labour power, where each end presupposes a standard action of social affecting by someone pursuing the other end. Two such ends are: production with wage-labour for continuous money maximisation; and minimisation of labour, at a given wage. Every reduction of labour performed, at a given wage, impedes production for continuous money maximisation; and if production is for continuous money maximisation, more labour in the present would not be a means to less labour for the same wage in the future. Generalised production for continuous money maximisation creates incentives for those who invest in and control production to use advances in productive power not to decrease the future labour time of their workforce, but instead to impose higher standards of what quantity of output is to be produced within a given period.[36]

Some of Marx's statements corroborate the thought that an awareness of opposition of this kind can be located in capitalist production. *Capital* contrasts the capitalist's 'sole driving motive [*Motiv*]' of 'an increasing appropriation of abstract wealth'[37] to the worker's need for free 'time'.[38] It also suggests that there is an awareness of opposition. In reference to capitalist production, *Capital* comments: 'in this atmosphere, the formation of surplus value by surplus labour is no secret'.[39] A capitalist firm controls its wage-labourers' time to ensure that their output per time unit worked meets or exceeds the industry standard (that is, the standard for an industry when it is run for continuous money maximisation); and to ensure that all its wage-labourers' contracted time, or more time than that, is spent working. To this optimising end, a capitalist firm monitors and keeps records in light of a plan to overcome potential reticence on wage-labourers' part. Monitoring is necessary, as there are few circumstances in which an overlooker cannot '"fear that a skilfully concealed and only too comprehensible laziness may make him [a labourer – JF] hold back half his strength"' or '"fear that the hope of *remaining employed longer*

---

36   See Postone 1993, pp. 286–91.

37   *MEW*, 23, pp. 167–8; *MECW*, 35, pp. 163–4; Marx 1976, p. 254. *MECW* and Marx 1976 translate '*Motiv*' as 'force' (which would be: '*Kraft*' or '*Zwang*'). An elemental movement can have force. A '*Motiv*' is an attribute of action performed for a reason.

38   *MEW*, 23, p. 246; *MECW*, 35, p. 241; Marx 1976, p. 341.

39   *MEW*, 23, p. 257; *MECW*, 35, p. 250; Marx 1976, p. 352.

on the same task may stay his hands and blunt his tools".[40] The experience of labour time discipline also leads to an awareness of opposition on the part of a wage-labourer, moreover, for it is shaped by the imposition of upwardly revised targets in the event of advances in productive power, and by monitoring that anticipates their potential reticence.

Capitalists are a group insofar as each seeks to supply or outdo other capitalists; and workers are a group insofar as each seeks to minimise their labour at a given wage in a context of a social process of work by snatching free time with, or at the expense of, co-workers. On an antagonistic interdependency conception, capitalists and workers are classes because both are groups; because their non-overlapping memberships seek to use labour power to the opposed ends of continuous money maximisation, and the minimisation of labour at a given wage; and because they are thereby aware of their antagonism. An antagonistic interdependency conception of classes, although consciousness-inclusive, does not reduce classes to class struggle, therefore. Class struggle presupposes an opposition between distinct organisations, each of which is recognised by class members to act in their name. The awareness of opposition that is constitutive of capitalist and working-classes does not presuppose such organisations.

From a logical point of view, the system of capitalist production does not presuppose capitalist and working-classes. Rather, the existence of capitalist and working-classes presupposes the system of capitalist production. There are two reasons for this. One is that classes can only exist if certain activities to some extent fall to separate groups: upward and downward class mobility is possible, but at any given point in time, (some of) those who adopt the end defining one class do not adopt the end defining another. For capitalist and working-classes to exist, non-wage-labourers must pursue continuous money maximisation by hiring non-capitalists as wage-labourers. As the same ends are conceivable without separate groups, however, the system of capitalist production does not logically presuppose classes. Second, the system of capitalist production does not presuppose an awareness of opposition. It is conceivable for a worker to identify with the capitalist firm that hires them, that is, to affirm the value of labouring for its benefit, and to affirm the steps they take to that end for no contrary value. Even if all workers identified with their firm, the system of capitalist production could still exist. But capitalist and working-classes would not exist. If workers could be pre-programmed to identify with their firm, then, in that science fiction scenario, there would be no capitalist

---

40   *MEW*, 26.1, p. 324; *MECW*, 31, p. 244. Marx is quoting Linguet's *Théorie des loix civiles*.

and working-classes, even if the activities of capital and wage-labour were performed by separate groups.

Two implications may be noted. First, the relation between exploitation
and classes is the reverse of that suggested by Analytical Marxists. For Elster,
'exploitation tends to obtain between actors of different classes, as defined
by some independent criterion'.[41] The same belief informs Roemer's 'Class-
Exploitation Correspondence Principle': exploitation corresponds to class, as
already defined.[42] Likewise, Erik Olin Wright claims that 'the typical institu-
tional form of capitalist class relations is capitalists having full ownership rights
in the means of production and workers none', leading to 'exploitation based
on property relations in means of production'.[43] On the present account, all
these claims are rejected. There can be *no such thing* as a 'Class-Exploitation
Correspondence Principle' in the case of capitalism, because capitalist labour-
exploitation, which is a characterisation of generalised production with wage-
labour for continuous money maximisation, is logically prior to classes. The
benefit condition for capitalist labour-exploitation requires socially necessary
labour to be appropriated by a party from which the exploitee is excluded.
But this is logically consistent with an initially classless scheme in which each
capitalist firm is run by the exploitees of another firm, and hence with the
non-existence of a class who exploit, without being exploited. Only the competitive dynamic of capital accumulation over time (in other words, the system
of capitalist production) explains why that hypothetical scenario is unsustainable.[44]

Second, phrases like 'class relation between capital and labour'[45] are to be
avoided. 'Capital' and 'labour' do not imply either a differentiation of groups, or
an awareness of opposition.[46] As 'capital' and 'labour' do not presuppose a differentiation of groups, 'capital' cannot be attributed with *any* of the properties

---

41   Elster 1985, p. 323.

42   Roemer 1986a, pp. 89–90.

43   Wright 1985, pp. 82–3; see, similarly, Wright 2005, pp. 4–30.

44   Compare the anti-capitalist argument against luck egalitarian justice in ch. 1, sec. 1.

45   Harvey 2006, p. 24.

46   When Marx first refers to class struggle in *Capital* Volume I, he uses the phrase 'a struggle
      between the collective capitalist [*Gesamtkapitalisten*], i.e. the class of capitalists, and
      the collective labourer [*Gesamtarbeiter*], or working-class' (*MEW*, 23, p. 249; *MECW*, 35,
      p. 243; Marx 1976, p. 344.) Unfortunately, *MECW* and Marx 1976 both render '*Gesamtkapit-
      alisten*' as 'collective capital' and '*Gesamtarbeiter*' as 'collective labour' (which would be:
      '*Gesamtkapital*' and '*Gesamtarbeit*'). They thereby imply, misleadingly, that, for Marx, all
      capitals taken together and all labours taken together are alternative expressions for the
      capitalist class and the working-class.

that individuals, as members of groups, possess. Marx says in *Capital* that a 'capitalist' is 'personified capital, capital endowed with will and consciousness'.[47] That strongly suggests that 'capital' as such has neither will nor consciousness. If capital has neither will nor consciousness, then capital is not a term in a 'class relation', for a 'class relation' presupposes a will and consciousness on two sides. Likewise, capital as such cannot have interests, if an interest is something that an actor can believe they have a reason to do or to favour. Only capitalists, either individually or collectively (through an association), can have interests.

2   Class Antagonism at the Macro-Level

We can now return to the second sentence of the aforecited passage from *The Eighteenth Brumaire*:

> Insofar as a merely local connection links these small-holding peasants, and the sameness of their interests generates no commonality [*Gemeinsamkeit*], national association or political organisation among them, they do not form a class.[48]

Marx here identifies four criteria that, together with antagonistic interdependency at the level of individual ends, yield a more demanding concept of classes. The ends of members of a class must be advanced by means of (1) cooperation with other class members beyond a given locality; and (2) generate a 'commonality', that is, a class-specific social interest. Further, (3) some class members must have formed an organisation capable of pursuing this class-specific social interest. Finally, (4) the class-specific social interest it pursues must inform, or sustain a stance vis-à-vis, a representative body.

The key condition of the four is the requirement for a commonality, that is, a class-specific social interest. '*Gemeinsamkeit*' is an abstract noun built from the adjective '*gemeinsam*', which means 'belonging to several people or things'. If, for example, A, B and C share a mutual friend, D, D is the '*gemeinsamer Freund*' of A, B and C. Having D as a mutual friend is a '*Gemeinsamkeit*' of A, B and C.

---

47   *MEW*, 23, p. 168; *MECW*, 35, pp. 163–4; Marx 1976, p. 254; compare *MEW*, 23, p. 619; *MECW*, 35, p. 588; Marx 1976, p. 739.

48   *MEW*, 8, p. 198; *MECW*, 11, p. 187; Marx 1973b, p. 239; Marx 1996, p. 117. Both *MECW* and Marx 1996 translate '*Gemeinsamkeit*' as 'community' (which would be: '*Gemeinschaft*') while Marx 1973b translates it as 'feeling of community' (which would be: '*Gemeinschaftsgefühl*'). For why these inaccuracies are misleading, see the main text.

This example shows that the translation of *'Gemeinsamkeit'* as 'community' is too demanding. A *'Gemeinsamkeit'* is insufficient for groupness, and thus insufficient for community, understood as an organised group. *A*, *B* and *C* need not be a group or community in virtue of *D*, their mutual friend: the actions of *A*, *B* and *C* to one another might be uninformed by the fact that *D* is a mutual friend, if they were unaware of that fact.

A class-specific social interest is an interest common to all individuals of a class such that either (i) no one member satisfies it without all other members satisfying it; or (ii) each member only tends to satisfy it in conditions that promote its satisfaction by all members. A class-specific social interest is thus a type of 'commonality', albeit one that does not suffice for groupness or community: it is possible for a number of individuals to have a social interest but not to act on it, and so not to be a group or community by virtue of it. However, if, as just argued, *'Gemeinsamkeit'* should not be translated as 'community', the objection to saying that the type of *'Gemeinsamkeit'* Marx had in mind could not have been a class-specific social interest falls away. It is not necessary to show that the existence of a class-specific social interest amounts to the existence of a community to defend the claim that a class-specific social interest is the type of *'Gemeinsamkeit'* that Marx had in mind.

On this reading, class for itself requires members of a class in itself to share a social interest whose satisfaction is inversely related to the satisfaction of a social interest of another class. An inversely related class-specific social interest is analytically distinct from antagonistic interdependency at the micro-level. To illustrate the distinction, imagine that there are a number of individuals who each need one and only one unit of a certain type of product that is sold only by suppliers who have no need for it. Each individual obtains it from a supplier only by paying for it. But imagine, further, that instead of the product having a general price, its price in an individual transaction is determined by a roll of dice, performed after buyer and seller agree to transact. In this scenario, the product's consumers and suppliers have separate and opposed interests. Each consumer wants the roll of dice governing the price of their transaction to be as low as possible, while their supplier wants it to be as high as possible. But without a general price, there can be neither a consumer-specific social interest in the general reduction of the product's price, nor a supplier-specific social interest in its general increase. '[T]he sameness of their interests generates no commonality'. What this imaginary scenario puts into relief is that a class-specific social interest is an interest in a *general* state of affairs that favours all class members.

Inversely related class-specific social interests can be identified in the case of the capitalist and working-classes. With a given technology, wage and workforce, capitalist firms can increase their returns by extending the length and/or increasing the intensity of the working day. So, assuming that wage-labourers can change employers in the pursuit of minimising labour at a given wage, capitalists have a class-specific social interest in the highest possible *average* length and intensity of the working day across all firms in a given space and time. As Marx writes in *Capital* Volume III:

> every individual capitalist, like the entirety of all capitalists in each particular sphere of production, is involved in the exploitation of the entire working-class by total capital, and in the degree of that exploitation – not just out of general class sympathy, but directly economically – because, other things being equal (including the value of the total constant capital advanced), the average rate of profit depends on the degree of exploitation [*Exploitationsgrad*] of total labour by total capital.[49]

Capitalists have a class-specific social interest in the highest possible average length and intensity of the working day in a given space and time, because, other things being equal, each capitalist's ability to increase their profits is determined by the average length and intensity of the working day. Wage-labourers, on the other hand, have a class-specific social interest in a reduction of the average length and intensity of the working day, relative to a given wage. Any reduction in that average reduces the labour that their capitalist employer, or another hiring firm, will expect to impose on someone they hire.

A class-specific social interest is related to (1), cooperation with other class members beyond a given locality, if it must be promoted by general norms, and the latter can only be enforced, demanded or preserved by the actions of class members on a supra-local scale. A class-specific social interest is related to the third and fourth additional conditions for class at the macro-level, if the general norms that uphold class-specific social interests are to be guaranteed and recognised by a representative government, which a separate class organisation may need to influence.

In respect of the capitalist class as a class for itself, *The German Ideology* remarks:

---

49   *MEW*, 25, p. 207; *MECW*, 37, pp. 195–6; Marx 1981, pp. 298–9. '[D]egree of exploitation [*Exploitationsgrad*]' is the same term as used in *Capital* Volume I. It should be translated uniformly. Here, *MECW* translates it as 'intensity' of exploitation (as if it were: '*Exploitationsintensität*') and Marx 1981 as 'level' of exploitation (which might be: '*Exploitationsstufe*').

> The bourgeoisie is already compelled, because it is a *class* and no longer
> an *estate*, to organise itself no longer locally, but nationally, and to give its
> average interest a general form.[50]

The characteristic of an estate, Stahl writes, is that 'every estate, even a private
estate, is nonetheless something public'.[51] Occupations have a public character
as estates if everyone has a fixed place in state life by virtue of their occupation,
whose assumption may be subject to hereditary conditions. A society divided
into estates can only be thought of as unified, then, on account of an otherworldly unifying power, in whose name the state rules. '[T]he common interests
of the estate are expressed in the particular locality',[52] Stahl writes, because the
ultimate end of such a state, obedience and order, rests on continuity, and continuity is ensured by the official oversight of particular occupations in fixed
locations.

By contrast, capital, *The German Ideology* says, is 'indifferent to whether it
is put in this thing or that'.[53] Just as money as capital must be transferrable
from one branch of production to another in pursuit of the greatest returns, it
must be moveable from one location to another on that basis. Capitalists' class-
specific social interest in the highest possible average length and intensity of
the working day is not guaranteed by subjecting investments to particular conditions designed to secure the fixed employment of a local population, the local
quality or local circulation of a product, or other local interests. It is guaranteed
by general norms of equal liberty enforced on any given area as just one area of
territory among others. As Marx notes in *Capital*, if 'one law holds in Yorkshire,
another in Lancashire', then, from capital's point of view, that is 'a condition of
things altogether abnormal and anarchical'.[54] The organisational requirements
for the capitalist class to be a class for itself are satisfied, therefore, with their
establishment of a representative government that upholds equal liberty uniformly across its territory.

Capital's explanation for the existence of organisations that advocate workers' class-specific social interest vis-à-vis (and even against) a representative
government relates to its discovery of an antinomy. In over 150 years since
Das Kapital's first publication in 1867, Lukács's *History and Class Consciousness*
remains the only work to propose a concept that aids its understanding.

---

50   *MEJ*, 2003, p. 94; *MEW*, 3, p. 62; *MECW*, 5, p. 90.
51   Stahl 1833, pp. 310–11.
52   Stahl 1833, p. 294.
53   *MEJ*, 2003, p. 53; *MEW*, 3, p. 52; *MECW*, 5, p. 66.
54   *MEW*, 23, p. 309; *MECW*, 35, p. 296; Marx 1976, p. 405.

3   The Self-Consciousness of the Commodity

What Lukács terms '*the self-consciousness of the commodity*'[55] is a wage-labourer's practical awareness of their labour power as a value *and* a use-value. Like any other commodity exchanger, a wage-labourer must refrain from consuming or otherwise diminishing the use-value of the commodity they wish to exchange (labour power). Yet a wage-labourer, unlike any seller of a commodity produced for exchange, relates to their commodity as a use-value even at its point of sale. It is only because a wage-labourer relates to their labour power as a use-value even at its point of sale that there is a rights-antinomy.

For a possessor to treat a product as a value is for them to treat it as a means to acquire whatever they want to acquire. To the end of treating it as just a means to acquire whatever they want to acquire, a possessor can attach no conditions to its use by a potential purchaser. Otherwise, it is no longer a means to acquire whatever its possessor wants to acquire, but a means to acquire what can be acquired from someone willing to accept those conditions. So, if and to the extent that a wage-labourer attaches conditions to the use of the labour power they exchange, besides the receipt of a wage, they cannot be said to treat their labour power, at the point of sale, as just a value.

A wage-labourer relates indirectly to the use-value of their labour power, at its point of sale, by attaching conditions to its use that seek to preserve it for hire for future periods in time, following the period of its current hire. To be able to hire out their labour power for a future period in time, a wage-labourer must preserve its use-value, for otherwise, no one would buy it. So, if, at the point of a given sale, a wage-labourer attaches conditions to the use of their labour power designed to preserve it for hire for future periods of time, then, even at the point of sale, they relate to their labour power indirectly as a use-value.

It is necessary for a wage-labourer to preserve their labour power for hire for future periods of time, following the period of its current hire. Generalised production with wage-labour for continuous money maximisation cannot relieve everyone who was already dependent on the sale of their labour power to live,

---

55   Lukács 1977, p. 352; Lukács 1968, p. 168. Postone chides Lukács's *History and Class Consciousness* for failing to break with traditional Marxism (Postone 1993, pp. 72–4, pp. 275–6). Yet this work identifies the problem of labour time as a problem in its own right, and links it to working-class consciousness (Lukács 1977, p. 363; Lukács 1968, p. 178). Its concept of the self-consciousness of the commodity conceptualises working-class struggles as irreducible to struggles over value, which is how traditional Marxism, with its distributive view of exploitation, must conceive them. In respect of how to think about working-class politics, it is Postone's *Time, Labor, and Social Domination* that fails to challenge the assumptions of traditional Marxism (see ch. 8, sec. 12).

from having, in the future, to sell their labour power to live. By virtue of wage-labour, wage-labourers cannot all acquire the means with which to live without selling their labour power. For if only cooperative labour is viable in terms of productivity, then, as Marx argues in the *Grundrisse*, for any wage-labourer to live without selling their labour power, their money (and/or credit) 'would have to become capital, i.e. purchase labour', in which case, 'the opposition that is to be cancelled at one point is created at another point'.[56] At the end of each period of hire, the same general compulsion on wage-labourers to hire out their labour power reasserts itself, for as long as wage-labourers continue to sell their labour power.

Assuming that a wage-labourer does not regard themselves as an exception to the rule that wage-labourers must continue to perform wage-labour to continue to live,[57] and assuming that they are not indifferent to whether or not they continue to live, they must seek to attach conditions to the sale of their labour power to preserve it for hire for future periods. They must seek to negotiate conditions of sale that allow them to adopt a future perfect perspective on themselves as someone who, after any given period of sale apart from the very last one, will have preserved labour power that can be sold to a capitalist.

To put this point into relief, imagine, by contrast, a stuntman who is to be hired to perform a dangerous stunt. The stunt is so dangerous that it is certain to leave physical or psychological scars so deep that its performer could not be expected to continue their career as a stuntman. In lieu of that fact, the stuntman is offered a fee that would allow them to enjoy, for the rest of their life, the standard of living that stuntmen are accustomed to, without having to perform any more stunts. There are just so many people who want to see the stunt that there is still a great deal of money to be made by hiring them. Let it also be stipulated that the stuntman has no other skill. Their penchant for stunts has rendered them otherwise unemployable. Now, the stuntman who agrees to perform the dangerous stunt may be said to sell their labour power. But from a phenomenological perspective, their relation to their labour power, at the point of sale, is unlike that of a wage-labourer. At the point of sale, there is no future point in time from whose perspective the stuntman can picture themselves as having preserved their labour power for sale, although nor does the stuntman regard themselves at any point as a slave.

---

56   *MEW*, 42, p. 213; *MECW*, 28, p. 218; Marx 1973b, p. 288.

57   A practical awareness of the exceptional, and a will to avoid basing plans on an exceptional outcome, implies no pursuit of a class-specific social interest. It falls within class in itself.

The case of the stuntman reveals, contrastively, the type of condition that a wage-labourer must seek to attach to the conditions of sale of their labour power, in respect of its use. They must seek to attach conditions to ensure that, however their labour power is used, its use will leave them in a position to hire out the quality and quantity of labour power that a capitalist firm requires a wage-labourer to exercise, for the rest of their working life. The length of the latter can be defined as the future period for which wage-labourers generally could hire out their labour power in the quality and quantity that capitalist firms require, for a wage they could live off, if their labour power was not prematurely damaged or destroyed. A wage-labourer cannot will for their labour power to be sold for a use that is likely to deprive them of it for any period in that future, and so deprive them of their means of existence for any period in that future. Their will is then a will to preserve possession of their labour power's use-value for capital; or, as Lukács says, 'the self-consciousness of the commodity'.[58]

By virtue of the will to attach this type of condition to its sale, a wage-labourer's relation to their labour power at the point of sale is a more complex relation than a relation to it as just a value, that is, as that with which to acquire a wage to purchase means of existence. It is a relation to their labour power as a *commodity*. This relation is also distinct from and does not imply the claim that a wage-labourer relates to their labour power as a *good*. To say that a wage-labourer relates to their labour power as a good would be to say that they relate to it as that over which their will is the necessary and sufficient condition of its satisfying a want of theirs. However, a wage-labourer does *not* relate to their labour power as a good: they cannot force anyone to purchase it; and their labour power is of little direct use to themselves if they lack the means to make a product with it that would relieve them of the compulsion to sell it. As a wage-labourer does not relate to their labour power as a good, there is no 'self-consciousness of the good', and hence *no economic theory of class struggle*.

One need giving content to the type of condition that a wage-labourer must seek to attach to the conditions of sale of their labour power is the need for rest. Labour power consists of skills that, *Capital* says, 'exist in the physical form, in the living personality of a human being'.[59] As these skills are developments of general human capacities, which require periods of rest to be restored, a wage-labourer must rest periodically, to restore their labour power. Uses of labour

---

58   Lukács 1977, p. 352; Lukács 1968, p. 168.
59   *MEW*, 23, p. 181; *MECW*, 35, p. 177; Marx 1976, p. 270.

power that disrupt or postpone this rest may damage or destroy labour power to an extent that jeopardises its future use-value for capital. A wage-labourer must seek to attach conditions to the sale of their labour power in respect of its use that exclude such effects; unless the reward is so great that they need not work again (in which case, like the stuntman, they cease to be a wage-labourer), or the reward is great enough that they need not work until they have fully recovered.

Even the latter possibility is generally unrealistic, however. The effects of work-induced exhaustion, injury or illness that overly delay a wage-labourer's return to full fitness could only be compensated for by a sharp increase in hourly earnings.[60] A capitalist will not pay that sharp increase if it is cheaper for them to hire another instead; and if labour power sells at its value, it is always cheaper. Given competition among wage-labourers for jobs, therefore, a wage-labourer must always seek to attach conditions to the use of their labour power that exclude disruptions or postponements of rest that may damage or destroy it – even leaving aside the fact that an individual can put a certain value on not enduring a condition of (temporary) powerlessness. In short, a wage-labourer must seek to attach conditions to the use of their labour power that guard against *excessive labour*, non-normatively defined as an amount of labour in the short or medium term that, through exhaustion, injury or illness, would reduce significantly the total time (years and months) for which they could sell their labour power in the quality and quantity that capitalist firms would require if they were to not to impose excessive labour, for a living wage.[61]

Other needs, besides the need for rest, may give content to the type of condition that a wage-labourer must seek to attach to the use of their labour power. They include the need to avoid premature death, reflected in a will to attach conditions that guard against dangerous work; the need to avoid obsolescent labour power, reflected in a will to attach conditions of sale that render labour power suitable for future capitalist employment; and so on. In all these cases, the will in which the need is reflected differs in kind to the will to sell labour power for a wage that suffices to purchase the means of a wage-labourer's reproduction. It is a will in respect to the use of labour power, rather than to its value. A wage-labourer's will to sell labour power only for a wage above the threshold

---

60   Compare *MEW*, 23, p. 549; *MECW*, 35, p. 527; Marx 1976, p. 664.

61   Suppose producers who perform surplus labour throughout their life become unable to do so week-in week-out at 70. An amount of labour that exhausts them by 50 is excessive. But if they can perform various amounts of surplus labour until about 70, the greatest amount determines the non-excessive quantity of labour that capitalist firms would require if they were not to impose excessive labour.

required for purchasing means of their reproduction is, of course, one aspect of '*the self-consciousness of the commodity*',[62] but only one aspect.

The difference is important for grasping the rights-antinomy, for the following reason. In *Capital*, Marx claims, prior to its antinomy passage, that it is a 'law of commodity exchange' that 'equivalent' is 'exchanged for equivalent'.[63] Any antinomy rooted in the commodity form must be consistent with the operation of this law. In other words, it must be taken as a given both in the proof of the thesis and in the proof of the antithesis that labour power is purchased for the sum of money required to purchase the means of its reproduction.[64] The presence or absence of an appeal to the value of labour power cannot be what distinguishes one proof from the other, therefore.[65] Rather, one proof can only differ from the other in *how* it appeals to the value of labour power. Both proofs can appeal to the value of labour power, and yet support opposed claims, if each proof views its value in relation to different time periods: as equal to the value of the means required to reproduce labour power over its period of hire, or as equal to the value of the means required to reproduce it over a period proportional to the extent to which the labour performed uses it up. The worker will appeal to the latter period, because only the latter period anticipates the *future* use of *their* labour power by a capitalist firm. In other words, only the proof voiced by the worker will exhibit '*the self-consciousness of the commodity*'.

4   *Capital*'s Antinomy Passage: a Reconstruction

Reasoning first from the perspective of the capitalist and then from the perspective of the worker, *Capital* Volume I identifies the following rights-antinomy:

> The capitalist has purchased labour power at its daily value. Its use-value throughout a working day belongs to him ... But what is a working day?

---

62   Lukács 1977, p. 352; Lukács 1968, p. 168.

63   *MEW*, 23, p. 209; *MECW*, 35, p. 205; Marx 1976, p. 301; compare *MEW*, 23, p. 173; *MECW*, 35, p. 169; Marx 1976, p. 261.

64   *MEW*, 23, pp. 184–5; *MECW*, 35, pp. 180–1; Marx 1976, pp. 274–5.

65   Contrary to the claim: 'the capitalist only appeals to the juridical form of the exchange' (Wildt 1997, p. 233). The first sentence of *Capital*'s antinomy passage reproduced in section 4, read with the first paragraph's penultimate sentence, has the capitalist also appeal to a premise about value.

It is certainly shorter than a natural day. But by how much? The capitalist has his own view of this *ultima Thule* ... The time the labourer works is the time in which the capitalist consumes the labour power he purchased from him. If the labourer consumes his disposable time for himself, he steals [*bestiehlt*] it from the capitalist.

The capitalist thus appeals to the law of commodity exchange. Like every other buyer, he seeks to extract the greatest possible utility from the use-value of his commodity. But all of a sudden a labourer's voice pipes up ...

The use of my daily labour power therefore belongs to you. But by means of its sale price for the day, I must be able to reproduce it daily, and hence be able to sell it anew. Leaving aside natural deterioration with age, etc., I must be able to work with the same normal amount of strength, health and freshness tomorrow, as I do today ... Like a sensible, thrifty innkeeper, I shall be economical with my singular fortune, labour power, and abstain from wildly squandering it. Each day I will realise, set in motion, put to work, only so much of it as its normal duration and healthy development can bear ... The use of my labour power, and the deprivation [*Beraubung*] of it, are entirely different things ... I demand the normal working day, because, like any other seller, I demand the value of my commodity.

... [T]he nature of commodity exchange itself provides no limit to the working day, hence no limit to surplus labour. The capitalist asserts his right as a purchaser when he tries to make the working day as long as possible, and, if possible, to turn one working day into two. On the other hand, the specific nature of the commodity sold includes a limit on its consumption by the purchaser, and the labourer asserts his right as a seller when he wills to limit [*beschränken will*] the working day to a certain normal magnitude. An antinomy therefore arises, of right against right, both equally licenced by the law of commodity exchange. Between equal rights, force decides. Hence, in the history of capitalist production, the regulation of the working day presents itself as a struggle over the limits of the working day – a struggle between the collective capitalist, i.e. the class of capitalists, and the collective labourer, or working-class.[66]

---

66   *MEW*, 23, pp. 247–9; *MECW*, 35, pp. 241–3; Marx 1976, pp. 341–4; compare *MEW*, 43, p. 172; *MECW*, 30, p. 184. (1) *MECW* and Marx 1976 render '*bestiehlt*' as 'robs' (which would be: '*raubt*'); relatedly, *MECW* renders '*Beraubung*' as 'spoliation' while Marx 1976 renders it as 'despoiling' (both of which would translate: '*Plünderung*'). Marx does not portray the capitalist or the worker as asserting that the other violates their right with *violent* means. Insofar

On the conception of antinomy defended in chapter 3, an antinomy is an oscillation of thought or will between two incompatible assertions that leave no middle ground and appear to be valid, but each of which rests on the same premises, at least one of which is false. Here, the oscillation is between the assertion of a right to an unlimited working day, and the assertion of a right to a limited working day. It cannot be the case that there ought to be a right to an unlimited working day (the thesis), and that there ought to be a right to a limited working day (the antithesis). Yet *Capital* says that the system of capitalist production sustains both assertions. (A right is asserted even if its assertion must be inferred from conduct whose primary purpose is not to assert a right; compare the two when-clauses in the final paragraph).

There are two reasons for saying that the rights-antinomy is an antinomy of the type in which both assertions turn out to be false. One reason is that *Capital* leaves us in no doubt that the thesis and the antithesis both seem true to someone; while it cannot be disputed that they are in fact contradictory. If a thesis and an antithesis both seem equally justified, although they are in fact contradictory, then an oscillation of thought or will can occur between them if the arguments for each rest on the same premises, at least one of which is false. Second, both the thesis and the antithesis are asserted by a type of actor in a form of production of which *Capital* is a critique. Earlier on in *Capital*, Marx argues that commodity exchange, in which both of these types of actor engage, generates an illusion.[67] *Capital* itself provides grounds, prior to its antinomy passage, for believing that both assertions can rest on a common false premise. The form of the antinomy *Capital* identifies nonetheless involves a departure from Kant if its thesis and antithesis are not contradictory opposites, but assert rights to states of affairs that are contradictory opposites. I return to this below.

The rights-antinomy is an antinomy between assertions of rights by actors in a system of production. It is a separate matter whether a *legal system* contains an antinomy. There are several problems with saying that *Capital* has unearthed an 'antinomy of the bourgeois legal system',[68] or 'insofar as there are two equally compelling legal arguments, it will be *force* that chooses between them'.[69] In *Capital's* presentation, the actors who assert the rights that form the antinomy do not have any legal competence to legislate or adjudicate; they

---

as the *MECW* and Marx 1976 translations of '*bestiehlt*' as 'robs' and '*Beraubung*' as 'spoliation' or 'despoiling' imply the use of violent means, they mislead. (2) On '*beschränken*', see below. (3) On '*ultima Thule*', see Romm 1992, pp. 121–71.

67   See ch. 3, sec. 6, (c).
68   Tuschling 1976, p. 26.
69   Knox 2016, p. 318.

assert rights implicitly vis-à-vis one another, rather than explicitly before a competent legal instance; and neither is said to appeal to a positive legal provision. An antinomy between legal arguments could not, in any case, allow Marx to say: '[b]etween equal rights, force decides'. If no legal arguments can settle a matter, it is still possible that moral arguments can.

Before reconstructing the proofs, it is instructive, first, (i) to attend to some errors of translation and interpretation that relate to the concept of an antinomy; and, second, (ii) to reject three interpretations of the antithesis of the rights-antinomy in German language scholarship. An alternative interpretation of the rights-antinomy is then proposed (iii), and, finally, some implications drawn out (iv).

(i) First of all, readers of *Capital* in translation are misled by the Aveling/Moore and Fowkes rendering of '*beschränken* (to limit, to restrict)' as 'to reduce'.[70] Both translations state: 'the worker maintains his right as a seller when he wishes to reduce the working day'. Read in conjunction with the previous sentence, in which Marx says that the capitalist tries to make the working day 'as long as possible', the phrase 'wishes to reduce' spoils the antinomy.

If one side seeks to make something's length as long as possible, and the other side seeks to reduce its length, there is a conflict between the two sides. Yet the two sides might still find some middle ground. Imagine that the broadcaster of a marathon sought to make its length as long as possible, while an Association of Marathon Runners sought to reduce its length. The two sides could still find middle ground by leaving its length unaltered.

No two endeavours that leave some middle ground can share a premise with an appearance of validity on which they exhaust the possible outcomes. Hence, there is no premise that could lead to an oscillation of thought or will between them. Without an oscillation of thought or will between two incompatible positions, there is no antinomy. The Aveling/Moore and Fowkes translations 'reduce' *Capital*'s antinomy passage to empty bluster. The two positions they describe do not form an antinomy. The assertion of the right to make x as long as possible and the assertion of the right to reduce x cannot form an antinomy. What Aristotle said of Anaxagoras, Marx could say of his official translators: 'that an intermediate exists between two contradictories, makes everything false'.[71]

---

70   *MECW*, 35, p. 243; Marx 1976, p. 344. The verb '*beschränken*' is related to the noun '*Schranke* (limit, restriction)'. 'To reduce' would be '*reduzieren*'.
71   Aristotle 1924, 1012a26–7; Aristotle 1966, 1012a26–7.

Consider again, for the purpose of contrast, the case of a dispute over the proper length of a marathon. A judgement that kept the marathon's length unaltered *might* be acknowledged by both sides to balance their respective rights. Alternatively, the two sides could settle on a compromise that left the marathon's length unaltered. By contrast, there can be no balancing of a right to an unlimited working day and a right to a limited working day, if the arguments for both rights rest on common premises that leave the assertions of these rights as the only two possible positions. There can also be no possibility of compromise, if there is no middle ground between the presence and the absence of a limit.

In Anglophone commentary, two types of mistake predominate, each of which goes wrong in exactly the same respect as the official translations. One type of mistake is to misconstrue the issue in such a quantified way that no antinomy can possibly arise. Harry Cleaver refers to *Capital*'s analysis of 'the struggle over the length of the working day'.[72] David Harvey claims: 'the only issue concerns how much use-value ... the laborer is going to give up to the capitalist'.[73] Fredric Jameson writes of 'that quantity that comes into play in the struggle to shorten the working day'.[74] In *Capital*, Marx *never* refers to a struggle to shorten the working day, for good reason. A dispute over a 'length' or a 'quantity' or over 'how much' always admits of compromise. It is in principle impossible for conflicting claims over quantities to form an antinomy. An antinomy can inform a struggle over the presence or absence of legal limits on the working day precisely because the latter is not simply a struggle over quantities.

A second type of mistake is to fail to describe a thesis and antithesis between which there is no middle ground. Consider three recent examples:

> capitalists are entitled to make workers work as long as humanly possible. Similarly, workers are entitled to make the working day as short as reasonably possible. From this Marx concludes that: '[t]here is here therefore an antinomy'.[75]

> [t]he worker wants as much as possible for her labour power, while the capitalist wants to buy it cheaply and extract the most value from it. As Marx writes, 'Between equal rights, force decides'[76]

---

72   Cleaver 1979, p. 79.
73   Harvey 2010, p. 137.
74   Jameson 2011, p. 111.
75   Cannon 2015, p. 176.
76   Read 2016, pp. 280–1.

the capitalist with his attempts to prolong the working day, as well as workers with their attempt to shorten it ... there is therefore 'an antinomy' ...[77]

An entitlement to make others work 'as long as humanly possible' and an entitlement to work for 'as short as reasonably possible' cannot provide the thesis and antithesis of an antinomy, for they leave some middle ground. A length need neither be as short as reasonably possible nor as long as humanly possible. There is also middle ground between acting on a want to sell labour power for 'as much as possible' and acting on a want to buy it 'cheaply' and extracting the most value from it: purchase it for an amount less than the maximum, but not cheaply either. Finally, no antinomy can arise between attempts to 'prolong' and to 'shorten' the working day, for that suggests the option of keeping the working day at its current length.

Besides the issue of translation (Heinrich is, after all, German), one possible diagnosis of these errors is as follows. A rights-antinomy in 'the being of bourgeois society',[78] as Lukács puts it, must be socially explained *and* described. It is necessary to offer 'explanatory reasons' for why each actor asserts a right (reasons that explain why someone acts as they do) and 'justifying reasons' for each actor to assert that right (reasons that that actor can give for why what they assert is just).[79] These twin tasks have been confused. Maximising behaviour features in Marx's explanation for why the capitalist makes the rights claim they make. Insofar as the difference between describing the justification of a claim that belongs to an antinomy and explaining it is confused, maximising language may enter the proof and description of the thesis or antithesis. Using maximising language to describe counterposed positions will leave some middle ground between them, and encourage a view of the issue on which it is purely quantitative. There is then no antinomy.

This confusion is not the only barrier to understanding *Capital*'s antinomy passage, however. Everyone knows that Marx was on the side of the workers and against the capitalists. It is a layman's temptation, therefore, to read Marx as affirming any argument that *Capital* has a worker voice against a capitalist. In *Capital*, a worker asserts one of the rights in the rights-antinomy. It is a

---

77   Heinrich 2005, p. 101; Heinrich 2012, p. 103.

78   Lukács 1977, p. 331; Lukács 1968, p. 148. On the translation of this phrase, see ch. 3, sec. 6.

79   Rawls 2000, p. 166. In *Capital*'s antinomy passage, the capitalist's justifying reason is described at the start and end of the first of the paragraphs translated above, and the explanatory reason in the second paragraph. The worker's justifying reason is described in the bulk of the third paragraph, and the explanatory reason in its final sentence.

layman's temptation, therefore, to identify Marx's position with the argument for the right to a limited working day that *Capital* has the worker voice. Any sympathy for Marx must then get in the way of reflection on what *Capital* says. To reflect on an antinomy is to reflect on the problematic status of two claims. If Marx's own view is equated with the argument that *Capital* has the worker voice, any antinomy in which the worker's claim is implicated can only problematise 'Marx's' own view. Victims of this layman's temptation who are sympathetic to Marx must withdraw from examining the features of the rights-antinomy that make it an antinomy.

It is this layman's temptation, however, that vitiates German language discussion of *Capital's* antinomy passage. In what is the most influential interpretation of *Capital's* antinomy passage in German language scholarship,[80] Andreas Wildt claims: '[e]ven if Marx often asserted the contrary, at this point in *Capital* he, too, actually advocates a theory of just wages'.[81] Heinrich, similarly, equates 'Marx's argumentation' with 'the claim of the worker'.[82] Wildt and Heinrich treat the position that *Capital* has the worker voice as if what it commits the worker to is something Marx is committed to. If Marx wanted to affirm the position that *Capital* has the worker voice, or even merely an implicit presupposition of this position in respect of 'just wages', Marx would not present it as part of an antinomy! To treat what the worker is committed to as something Marx is committed to is to view the conflict as one where two claims seem true, although they are contradictory, and one is shown to be false. But both thesis and antithesis are shown to be false, for they both rest on the same premises.

(ii) As German language scholarship succumbs to this layman's temptation, it has focused on the worker's argument (the proof of the antithesis). Between them, Wildt and Heinrich offer three interpretations of this argument, here labelled the *total value* interpretation, the *basic right* interpretation and the *maximum advantage* interpretation. All three interpretations fail to reconstruct the worker's argument for a right to a limited working day.

Wildt offers the following account of the worker's argument:

---

80   Wildt's account of *Capital's* antinomy passage (in Wildt 1986, pp. 161–6; see also Wildt 1997, pp. 233–4) is endorsed by Honneth 2003, p. 238; Honneth 1995, p. 197; Lohmann 1991, p. 79, p. 283; and Nutzinger 1984, pp. 128–30. More critical are Heinrich 2006, p. 374 and Maihofer 1992, p. 70.
81   Wildt 1986, p. 165; compare p. 166; and Nutzinger 1984, p. 129.
82   Heinrich 2006, p. 374.

The worker then argues, however, with a more extensive concept of the value of labour power, namely, with the concept of a 'total value' of his 'substance of labour' ... This substance of labour, which relates to the entire life of the worker, determines the 'total value' of his labour power. A boundless extension of the working day would be a 'deprivation' or theft of the substance of labour, thereby of value, and so 'contrary to the law of commodity exchange'.[83]

There are two suggestions in Wildt's account. One is a total value interpretation. In elaborating this interpretation, Wildt remarks:

The worker deploys his concept of the 'total value' of the substance of labour of a complete working life to establish that, with the extension of the working day and the corresponding curtailment of a working life – constant wage evidently presupposed – the capitalist only pays the worker a fraction of the daily value of his labour power. The issue of the length of the working day is thereby treated as a wage issue.[84]

On the total value interpretation, the worker's argument seems to run as follows:
(1)   If someone totally consumes a commodity, they must pay its total value
(2)   Excessive labour destroys labour power prematurely
(3)   Therefore, the capitalist who imposes excessive labour and pays its daily value still has something to pay
(4)   As the capitalist does not make this additional payment, the worker has a right to a limited working day

Only part of this argument is coherent. While (3) follows from (1) and (2), (4), which is needed to complete the argument, is incoherent. From the fact that a capitalist who imposes excessive labour and pays its daily value still has something to pay that they do not pay, it does not follow that a worker has a right to a limited working day. It follows that the capitalist still has something to pay. The only right this argument gets close to supporting is the worker's right to an additional payment. But that right is not a right in the correct dimension, of labouring activity.

Wildt suggests a second interpretation, however: '[t]he plausibility of the position that Marx's worker voices is not, in the nature of the matter, depend-

---

83   Wildt 1986, pp. 162–3.
84   Wildt 1986, p. 165.

ent on any 'law of value'. It can also be grounded directly on a basic right to an uncurtailed life and working life'.[85] On this basic right interpretation, the worker's argument would have to run as follows:

(1)   Everyone has a basic right to an uncurtailed life, and, as one aspect of this, a basic right to an uncurtailed working life
(2)   Excessive labour would deprive the worker of an uncurtailed working life
(3)   Therefore, the worker has a right to a limited working day

The basic right argument is coherent, and does not depend on a premise about value. But the basic right argument is not only not an argument that *Capital* has the worker voice. It is an argument that *Capital* cannot have the worker voice. A basic right to an uncurtailed life gives everyone a right to an uncurtailed life, including those who cannot work. It gives people who are unable to work rights vis-à-vis the government for means with which to enjoy an uncurtailed life. To this end, a government must be entitled to finance its provision of these means by imposing taxes on the fruits of commodity exchange. Hence, actors who affirm this right must have rejected the principle of self-ownership. However, there is no reason at this stage in *Capital* for Marx to suppose that workers reject the principle of self-ownership, if, as argued in chapter 9, a belief in this principle is encouraged by generalised purchase and sale. Before *Capital* could have a worker voice appeal to this basic right, it would have to show that the worker can be led to reject the principle of self-ownership. The rights-antinomy may contribute to this, but only if its premises do not already presuppose that the principle of self-ownership has been rejected.

Let us now turn to Heinrich's maximum advantage interpretation, which is offered in response to Wildt's account:

> The point of Marx's argumentation consists, however, in the fact that it makes do without this normative foundation [a normative argument for a 'just wage' – JF]: the worker's claim that his labour power will not be so heavily used up by its daily use that it leads to a shortening of its 'typical life span' can be grounded solely on the fact that the worker relates to his labour power as a commodity. The normality that he claims is its normal physical life span, i.e. he (like the capitalist) wills to extract the maximum advantage from this commodity.[86]

---

85   Wildt 1986, p. 164; compare Wildt 1997, p. 234.
86   Heinrich 2006, pp. 374–5; compare the interpretation of Wolfgang Müller and Christel Neusüss: 'the excessive extension of the working day beyond its normal measure prevents the normal regeneration of his labour power, and so results in the *premature* depletion of the worker's only asset. Hence, for the worker, the labour time that extends beyond the

On the maximum advantage interpretation, the worker's argument to the conclusion that there is a right to a limited working day seems to run as follows:

(1) Everyone ought to have a right to seek to extract the maximum advantage from their commodity (subject to its purchase at value)[87]

(2) For the worker to extract the maximum advantage from their commodity, labour power, the working day must be limited

(3) Therefore, the worker has a right to a limited working day

The problem with the maximum advantage reading is that (3) does not follow from (1) and (2). If A has a right to seek to negotiate their preferred terms in a transaction with B, B respects A's right by not deceiving or coercing A during their negotiations. B is not bound to conclude an agreement with A on (some of) A's preferred terms. Thus, the right in (1) does not make (2) normatively relevant. Nor (as part of an attempt to give (2) normative relevance) can (1) be revised to: everyone has a right to what would result from extracting the maximum advantage from their commodity (subject to its purchase at value). That is not something that anyone could think everyone had a right to. (1) does not make (2) normatively relevant, and if (1) is revised to make (2) relevant, (1) is not a possible premise.

At bottom, the maximum advantage interpretation confuses explanatory reasons and justifying reasons. *Capital* does indeed report that every 'buyer' seeks 'to extract the greatest possible utility from the use-value of his commodity'.[88] Yet this report offers an explanatory reason for the capitalist's claim. Utility maximisation explains why the capitalist (the 'buyer' of labour power) asserts a right to an unlimited working day. But from the fact that utility maximisation is an explanatory reason, it does not follow that it is a justifying reason. As an individual's utility maximisation is of no concern to anyone but that individual, it cannot help to justify a rights claim. A capitalist cannot *justify* their right to an unlimited working day by arguing that only an unlimited working day allows them to extract the greatest possible utility from the labour power they purchase.[89] Even if we grant that the *explanatory* reason

---

normal working day is theft' (Müller and Neusüss 1971, p. 48). If a 'premature' depletion' of labour power is its depletion prior to the maximum possible period of use, then this interpretation is also a maximum advantage interpretation.

87   The bracketed phrase is added to maintain consistency with Marx's claim that both rights of the antinomy are 'licenced by the law of commodity exchange' (*MEW*, 23, p. 249; *MECW*, 35, p. 243; Marx 1976, p. 344).

88   *MEW*, 23, p. 247; *MECW*, 35, pp. 241–2; Marx 1976, p. 342.

89   Maihofer (1992, p. 70) and Wildt (1986, p. 162) also appear to report the explanatory reason for the capitalist's claim as if it was (part of) a justifying reason.

for the worker's rights claim is that a *seller* of labour power wishes to draw the maximum advantage from its sale to capitalists, by insisting on conditions of use that preserve it for the maximum possible period of future use by capitalists (as distinct, say, from a period of future use sufficient to raise children to a working age), we have not yet offered a *justification* for the antithesis.

The total value interpretation cannot justify a right in the correct dimension; the basic right interpretation rests on a premise foreign to the nature of commodity exchange; and the maximum advantage interpretation is missing a possible premise about rights. If there is to be an antinomy of 'right against right, both equally licenced by the law of commodity exchange',[90] both arguments, the proof for the thesis no less than the proof for the antithesis, must rest on a possible, commodity exchange related premise about rights that has an implication beyond the dimension of value, as well as a premise about value. If both the thesis and the antithesis rest on these premises, that may help to explain, in a manner conducive to a solution to the agency problem,[91] why the first form of expression of class antagonism on the part of the worker is to assert a right in the dimension of labouring activity (a right to a limited working day), as distinct from a right in the dimension of value.

Let us draw together the criticisms advanced thus far. In *Capital*, Marx reproaches the political economists Adam Smith and David Ricardo for treating 'the value-form as something of complete indifference'.[92] *Capital* says, in respect of labour and the form of value, that political economy 'has never even asked the question as to why this content assumes that form'.[93] A similar sort of criticism can be levelled at the entire reception of Marx's *Capital* over the last 150 years, with the sole exception of Lukács's *History and Class Consciousness*. Interpreters of *Capital* have never even asked the question as to why class in itself must be expressed in the form of a rights-antinomy. This is partly because class in itself has not been adequately understood. The modal, structural and causal conceptions of class discussed above do not identify an antagonism that it is possible to articulate in the form of a rights-antinomy. Yet it is also because the projects of Analytical Marxism and Althusserian Marxism, the assignment of exploitation to the dimension of value, mistranslations, a failure to treat justifying reasons as distinct from explanatory reasons, a layman's

---

90   *MEW*, 23, p. 249; *MECW*, 35, p. 243; Marx 1976, p. 344.
91   See ch. 8, sec. 12, and the final three sentences of the proof of the antithesis reconstructed below.
92   *MEW*, 23, p. 95; *MECW*, 35, p. 91; Marx 1976, p. 174.
93   Ibid.

temptation, and the difficulty of assimilating *Capital*'s heterodox[94] concept of an antinomy, have all prevented considered analysis of this rights-antinomy, or made it tougher. Even those who cite and interpret *Capital*'s antinomy passage appear unexercised by the question of how its thesis can be justified by the same premises as its antithesis; in other words, unexercised by its form as an antinomy.

(iii) The interaction-recognition-antinomy thesis approaches *Capital*'s antinomy passage on the following basis:

(A) Labour power is an object of two opposed ends on the part of the capitalist and the worker, each of which presupposes social affecting by the other

(B) In pursuing these ends, capitalist and worker implicitly assert, respectively, a right to an unlimited working day, and a right to a limited working day

(C) These rights form an antinomy: they conflict, leave no middle ground and appear valid, yet rest on the same premise(s), one or more of which is false

(D) These premises include a premise about value as well as a premise about the recognition of rights

(E) Marx is not committed to either the thesis or the antithesis

(F) The opposed ends of (A) are expressed in the rights described in (B) and (C) because, in virtue of commodity exchange, capitalist and worker each conceive themselves to have a claim vis-à-vis the other to the labour or labour power they stand to lose on the other's account.

In clarification of (C): *Capital* characterises the antinomy as an antinomy of 'right against right',[95] and not as an antinomy of right against no right. An antinomy of right against right is not an antinomy in which the antithesis is the contradictory negation of the thesis. Rather, both sides are positive assertions. The proofs are to take the form of latching on to a premise of the other side's argument, and reasoning to an incompatible positive position.

The interpretation of *Capital*'s antinomy passage defended here incorporates separate premises about value and the recognition of self-ownership. Hence, it will be termed the *value and recognition of self-ownership interpretation*. On this interpretation, the arguments for the thesis and the antithesis of the rights-antinomy share two premises:

---

94   While the antinomy is of the type where both thesis and antithesis are shown to be false, they are not contradictory opposites; see ch. 3, sec. 6.

95   *MEW*, 23, p. 249; *MECW*, 35, p. 243; Marx 1976, p. 344.

(1)   commodities may only be purchased for a price proportional to value

(2)   commodity exchangers are to recognise one another as self-owners

What needs to be shown is that the system of capitalist production allows these premises to be taken as given by both the capitalist and the worker; and that, once they are taken as given, they can support conclusive arguments for both the thesis and the antithesis of the rights-antinomy.

Premise (1) restates, in imperative form, Marx's claim, prior to *Capital*'s antinomy passage, that it is a 'law of commodity exchange' that 'equivalent' is 'exchanged for equivalent'.[96]

The rights-antinomy depends on premise (1), because an antinomy can only arise if at least one of its premises can be taken in different ways. An antinomy in respect of a limit to the working day can only arise if one of its premises is indeterminate, for the types of actor who raise its thesis and antithesis, in respect of the time period relative to which labour power is to be paid. Ask both a capitalist and a worker, and you will not have a single determinate answer as to whether the value of labour power is to be calculated by its value for the period of hire, or by its value for a period proportional to the extent to which the labour performed uses up the worker's labour power. As the value of labour power is indeterminate in this respect, and (1) introduces the concept of the value of labour power by stating that commodities, and thus labour power, may only be purchased for a price proportional to value, (1) introduces an indeterminacy that the rights-antinomy requires.

Premise (1) is not sufficient to engender the rights-antinomy, however. The rights-antinomy is an antinomy of 'right against right',[97] and (1) cannot ground any rights claim. If, as (1) says, it is only permissible to purchase commodities for a price proportional to value, then no one has a right to purchase a commodity for less than that. If someone fails to pay a commodity's full price, they act impermissibly. But to say that action is impermissible is not to say that anyone's right is violated. Duties do not, by definition, have correlative rights. To say that another acts impermissibly by failing to pay a commodity's full price is not yet to say that anyone else's right to its full price is violated. As both the thesis and antithesis are assertions of rights, at least one further premise must be identified to produce the rights-antinomy.

To illustrate the insufficiency of premise (1), consider the antithesis: there is a right to a limited working day. From (1), it follows that labour power may not be purchased for a price less than proportional to its value. If excessive labour

---

96   *MEW*, 23, p. 209; *MECW*, 35, p. 205; Marx 1976, p. 301; compare *MEW*, 23, p. 173; *MECW*, 35, p. 169; Marx 1976, p. 261.

97   *MEW*, 23, p. 249; *MECW*, 35, p. 243; Marx 1976, p. 344.

is effectively a purchase of labour power for a price less than proportional to its value, then, given (1), a purchaser of labour power acts impermissibly by imposing excessive labour. They have no right to impose it. But that conclusion is not the assertion of a right. In a recent account of the antithesis of the rights-antinomy, Guido Starosta argues that if 'the excessive prolongation of the working day actually involves the payment of labour power below its value', then 'the realisation of the full value of labour power' may give a worker 'reaso[n] for his refusal to let the capitalist impose her/his will on the determination of the length of the working day'.[98] That may be all well and good. But a 'refusal' of another's right to *p* is not the assertion of a right to not-*p*. So, this reasoning cannot be the reasoning that justifies the antithesis of the right-antinomy. As *Capital* makes plain, the worker's conclusion is not of the form: '*you* may not ...'. It is of the form: '*I* demand ...'.

Premise (2) states, in imperative form, the result of the argument offered in chapter 9 (and supported by quotes from *Capital* that appear prior to its antinomy passage) that generalised purchase and sale leads commodity exchangers to articulate a belief in self-ownership. If commodity exchangers articulate a belief in self-ownership, they must believe that they ought to recognise one another as self-owners in commodity exchange. Accordingly, to the extent that generalised purchase and sale provides the context of belief for both capitalist and wage-labourer, both can believe that they must recognise one another as self-owners in commodity exchange. If both the capitalist and the wage-labourer have this belief, each can assert a *right* against the other, by asserting, respectively, that it is a condition for their (*and* consistent with the other's) recognition as a self-owner that the working day should be unlimited or limited.

Maybe premise (2) is not the only conceivable premise to allow the purchaser and the seller of labour power to assert rights to an unlimited or limited working day vis-à-vis the other. But what we require is a premise that supports these rights claims *and* can be taken as given if commodity exchange is generalised. (2) satisifes both conditions, as we shall see.

The only way to deny that (2) is a premise of the rights-antinomy is to argue that it is superfluous, on account of the availability of an alternative further premise that also satisfies these conditions. So, consider the following alternative premises:

---

98   Starosta 2016, pp. 207–8. As the rights-antinomy rests on a further premise, besides (1), the worker's resistance is not 'only a concrete manifestation of the broader question about the realisation of the full value of labour power' (Starosta 2016, p. 208); it does not carry 'no content other than' this (Starosta 2016, p. 214).

(3)   there are to be no relations of personal dependence
(4)   labour power may only be purchased for a limited period
(5)   people have a right to what is created by their labour

Premise (3) restates, in imperative form, Marx's claim, prior to *Capital's* anti-nomy passage, that 'commodity exchange includes, in and of itself, no other relations of dependence than those that arise from its own nature'.[99] But (3) is not a plausible alternative premise of the rights-antinomy. The absence of rela-tions of personal dependence is a necessary but not a sufficient condition for the worker to assert a right of their own. An absence of relations of personal dependence is consistent with the non-existence of rights in general. There are no relations of personal dependence in 'Nowheresville', where all duties are owed to a sovereign.[100] But there are no rights in Nowheresville either. As the antinomy is only a rights-antinomy if both capitalist and worker can each assert a right of their own, and (3) does not suffice for this, (3) is not a possible alternative to (2).

Premise (4) restates, in imperative form, *Capital's* claim, prior to its anti-nomy passage, that 'the continuation of this relation' – that is, the purchase of labour power from the person whose power it is – presupposes that labour power is always purchased 'only for a limited period'.[101] (4) does not create a right, however. If labour power may only be purchased for a limited period, then the capitalist would act impermissibly if they were to attempt to pur-chase it without allowing the worker the option of terminating the agreement. But to say that action is impermissible is not to say that anyone's right is viol-ated.

Even if it were supposed that premise (4) *did* create a right, namely, a right of each side to terminate a labour contract, it would not be the kind of right that the rights-antinomy requires. It is not sufficient (in conjunction with (1) and (3)) to engender the rights-antinomy. A wage-labourer who has the right not to lease their labour power to a particular firm in the future does not just by vir-tue of that have a right to attach any conditions to its *use* of their labour power. As the right to a limited working day is a right that concerns the use of labour power by a firm, the right that (3) would establish would not be sufficient to justify the antithesis. To put the point a different way: the right to terminate a contract does not presuppose that, after the contract is terminated, the produ-cer has any labour power to supply.

---

99   *MEW*, 23, pp. 181–2; *MECW*, 35, p. 178; Marx 1976, pp. 270–1.
100   See Feinberg 1970, p. 247.
101   *MEW*, 23, p. 182; *MECW*, 35, p. 178; Marx 1976, p. 271.

Premise (5), the labour principle of property, is sometimes regarded as a belief that commodity exchange encourages.[102] It is not, however, a premise of the rights-antinomy. The rights-antinomy rests on the worker's assertion of a right to their labour power. The deprivation that the worker holds the capitalist responsible for is a deprivation of their labour power. (5) cannot support this rights claim, as (5) says nothing about property in what is not created by labour, labour power is not created by the labour of the person whose power it is, and no one could think that it was. Upbringing, culture and formal schooling obviously also play their part.

There is no alternative to premise (2), the premise that commodity exchangers are to recognise one another as self-owners, that capitalist production (on *Capital*'s account of it) allows to be taken as given, and that can justify the worker's assertion of a right to a limited working day. (2) is a necessary premise of the rights-antinomy.

A comparison with premise (5), the labour principle of property, is instructive for another reason. The aspects of self-ownership crucial to the rights-antinomy are the exclusive rights to use and to alienate one's parts and capacities, rather than the exclusive right to enjoy the fruits of their use. The self-ownership rights whose recognition gives rise to the rights-antinomy are just those self-ownership rights analogous to *jus utendi* and *jus disponendi* within private property ownership, rather than the self-ownership right analogous to *jus fruendi*.[103] The rights-antinomy concerns the use of hired labour power during the working day, not the ultimate claims on its product. The antinomy would remain even if it was supposed that the government had a right to force the capitalist to pay part of their profits in tax that was not justified by the principle of self-ownership.

We can now reconstruct the proofs. Depending on whether the payment of value and the recognition of self-ownership are taken to apply, in the sale of labour power, to that sale *as a single sale*, or to that sale *as just one sale in the entire future series of the wage-labourer's sales* of their labour power,[104] there arises one of the following two claims:

Thesis: there is a right to an unlimited working day.

---

102   See Lohmann 1991, pp. 48–51; Cohen 2011, p. 126.

103   The distinction is from Pound 1939, p. 997.

104   The contrast is between a sale viewed as an isolated sale and a sale viewed as part of a series of sales of the same item. It is not a contrast between 'the perspective of circulation' and 'the point of view of production' (Tomba 2013, pp. 128–30).

Proof: suppose the wage-labourer has a right, against any hirer of their labour power, to a limited working day. They have that right, because they have exclusive property in their parts and capacities. But as a self-owner, they must also have the right to sell or not to sell the use of their labour power for the remaining hours in that day. They must have the right to sell the use of their labour power for any stretch of time within a given time frame. So, for whatever daily stretch of time the wage-labourer sells the use of their labour power, they can have no objection to the hirer's use of it in that time if its value for this time frame is paid. If this value is paid, then when the wage-labourer unilaterally slackens or breaks off from the use of their labour power, during the time they sell it for, however long that may be, they steal what the hirer has acquired by right from them.

Antithesis: there is a right to a limited working day.

Proof: suppose it is the capitalist's right to use the labour power they hire for whatever stretch of time in the day is agreed, provided its daily value is paid. For them to have acquired that right, its seller must have had the right to sell the use of their labour power to them for any stretch of time. The seller has that right, because they have exclusive property in their parts and capacities. But if so, their sale of the use of their labour power for one stretch of time cannot abrogate their right to sell its use for a later stretch of time. The seller of the use of a commodity for a definite period is entitled to receive it back, at the end of that period, in the same state as before, natural wear and tear excepted. If what was sold yesterday was the use of labour power for a day, the seller is entitled to receive back the same labour power at the end of that day. If, by excessive labour, the capitalist deprives the wage-labourer of their labour power for any period beyond the period of hire, then, unless they pay its value for that future period as well, they steal the wage-labourer's property in their labour power. As a self-owner, the capitalist does not offer to pay for something they have yet to hire. Still, the wage-labourer can and must assert a right against them to a limit on the work in the period for which they are hired, to directly put a stop to the theft of their property.

(iv) Five features of this interpretation may be noted.

First, the value and recognition of self-ownership interpretation of *Capital*'s antinomy passage allows the rights-antinomy to take on a broader significance. The reason for this is that it allows both proofs to rest on the same premises, while allowing the proof of the antithesis a specific character. While both proofs rest on the same premises, only the proof of the antithesis exhibits *'the self-consciousness of the commodity'*.[105] Only the proof of the antithesis appeals to a wage-labourer's relation to their labour power as a future use-value for capital, as well as to their relation to it as a value. If it can be shown that, by virtue of workers' position in and practical response to the rights-antinomy, participants in a working-class movement can arrive at a privileged standpoint, then *'the self-consciousness of the commodity'*, by characterising the proof of the antithesis, may help to explain this standpoint.[106]

Second, the point of departure for *Capital's* account of struggle between the capitalist and the worker is a *struggle for recognition*. This point is worth underscoring, for two reasons. Firstly, it implies a critique of existing interpretations of *Capital's* account of this struggle. Its point of departure is not, as Postone claims, a struggle to 'gain some control over the conditions of sale'[107] of labour power. Nor is it, as Harvey supposes, a struggle over 'control over time'.[108] Conditions of sale and labour time in a firm are not the sort of things that can *possibly* be brought under *one* party's 'control'. *Capital* says that conditions of sale and labour time in a firm are objects of a 'relation of will';[109] and no actor can control another's will. Nor is *Capital's* account of the struggle between capitalist and worker reducible, as Honneth says (having endorsed Wildt's account of *Capital's* antinomy passage), to a struggle for material resources.[110] As the premises of the rights-antinomy and the proof of its antithesis dictate, the point of departure for *Capital's* account of struggle between capitalist and worker is a struggle in the dimension of labouring activity, and for recognition. For as long as a worker performs excessive labour, they experience a lack of recognition as a self-owner. This is significant, because the need for recognition cannot be extirpated. The criterion that the value and recognition of self-ownership interpretation imposes on a reconstruction of Marx's account of class struggle is that it must identify a moment of recognition *in every subsequent phase* in the working-class's journey from a class in itself to a class for itself.

Third, the value and recognition of self-ownership interpretation clarifies that the rights-antinomy expresses class in itself, not class for itself. *Capital* attributes the rights claims that form the rights-antinomy to the individual capitalist and individual worker. Indeed, their opposed ends must be expressed in the assertion of these antinomic rights, for they are led, by commodity

105   Lukács 1977, p. 352; Lukács 1968, p. 168.
106   See secs. 7–9.
107   Postone 1993, p. 275.
108   Harvey 2010, p. 139.
109   *MEW*, 23, p. 99, pp. 350–1; *MECW*, 35, p. 95, pp. 336–7; Marx 1976, p. 178, pp. 449–50.
110   Honneth 2003, pp. 235–9; Honneth 1995, pp. 148–50.

exchange, to conceive of themselves as exclusive claimants to the labour or labour power they stand to lose on the other's account. But it does not follow from this that class for itself is also expressed in (antinomic) rights. It is mistaken to say that 'the class struggle manifests itself as a conflict of "right against right"'.[111] The struggle for and against limits on the working day only takes the form of a class struggle as the *result* of the rights-antinomy; and the demand of workers in this *class* struggle is not for a right. It is for a legal limit *on* rights. *Capital* says:

> For 'protection' from the serpent of their sorrows, labourers must ... as a class, compel a state law, an irresistible social shackle, which prevents them, by voluntary contract with capital, from selling themselves, and their kin, into death and slavery. In place of the grandiose catalogue of 'inalienable human rights' comes the modest Magna Charta of a legally limited working day.[112]

If a legal norm is an 'irresistable social shackle' that limits the right of contract, it is a rights-restricting norm, not a rights-creating norm. If a working-class movement that struggles for a limited working day has a rights-restricting norm as its objective, its objective is not a right. If its objective is not a right, class struggle over excessive labour cannot take the form of a struggle of right against right. Only antagonism at the micro-level takes the form of the assertion of two antinomic rights.

Fourth, the value and recognition of self-ownership interpretation is instructive in respect of Marx's conception of justice. One aspect of this is that it shows that the author of *Capital* is not a meta-ethical relativist in respect of justice. A meta-ethical relativist is someone who believes that 'there are no objectively sound procedures for justifying one moral code or one set of moral judgments'.[113] To claim that the author of *Capital* is a meta-ethical relativist in respect of justice is to claim that, judged by *Capital*, there is, in Marx's view, no objective standard for evaluating claims about justice. Robert Tucker suggests that Marx is a meta-ethical relativist in respect of justice by offering *Capital's* antinomy passage as evidence that, on the issue of 'the length of the working day ... according to Marx, there is simply no determining what is right and just'.[114]

---

111 Blackledge 2012, p. 49.
112 *MEW*, 23, p. 320; *MECW*, 35, pp. 306–7; Marx 1976, p. 416.
113 Nielsen 1989, p. 7.
114 Tucker 1969, pp. 44–5.

Now, the rights-antinomy cannot support Tucker's claim, because its antithesis is not the contradictory negation of its thesis, and Marx does not endorse either. For all *Capital*'s antinomy passage proves, Marx's view of the justice of limiting the working day may be any one of the views that remain after the thesis and antithesis are rejected. These views include the view: an unlimited working day is unjust, but not on grounds of right. Nor, more generally, can the rights-antinomy support the idea that the author of *Capital* is a meta-ethical relativist in respect of justice.[115] It is conclusive proof against this idea. A thinker who identifies an antinomy of the type described above within a topic of belief can only believe that there is no standard for evaluating claims on that topic at the cost of renouncing reason itself. To take a meta-ethical relativist position in respect of justice while identifying a rights-antinomy, it would be necessary to deny that there was any basis for saying that a set of beliefs about justice that does not include a claim that belongs to an antinomy is in one way better than a set of beliefs about justice that does include such a claim. That denial exhibits an indifference to reason itself. It is profoundly implausible, then, to regard the author of *Capital* as a meta-ethical relativist in respect of justice.

Relatedly, *Capital*'s antinomy passage offers a further reason to reject Wood's view that, according to Marx, the justice of an action 'consists in bearing a certain relation of adequacy, correspondence or functionality to the social mode of production within which it takes place'.[116] For a thinker to affirm this conception of justice in respect of what they take to be an antinomy-generating 'mode of production' would be for them to affirm the logical contradiction between the thesis and antithesis of the antinomy it generates. If the rights-antinomy arises from the nature of commodity exchange, then it cannot be denied that action on the thesis, and action on the antithesis, are both adequate to capitalist production. Someone with this conception of justice would have to say that both actions were just, and would thereby make a logical contradiction part of their own thought. Their identification of a rights-antinomy would lead not just to a questioning of the state of affairs that generated it, but to the exposure of the logical inconsistency of their own thinking. No wonder, then, that in all his accounts of Marx and justice over the last 40 to 50 years, Wood has remained silent about *Capital*'s antinomy passage. *Capital*'s antinomy passage

---

115   Besides Tucker, see Callinicos 2013, p. 274; and Harvey 2010, pp. 137–8.
116   Wood 1984, p. 9; see, also, Wood 1979, pp. 269–70. Harry van der Linden suggests that *Capital*'s antinomy passage supports Wood's attribution of this narrow view of justice to Marx (Van der Linden 1984, p. 128), but without offering a reason why, or a reconstruction of the antinomy.

and a commitment to reason require the author of *Capital* to reject the conception of justice that Tucker and Wood attribute to Marx.

It is symptomatic of the implausibility of Tucker's view (which Wood develops) that Marx regards 'the only applicable norms of justice – those operative in the existing mode of production and exchange' that Tucker follows up this view by remarking of the rights-antinomy: 'according to Marx, there is simply no determining what is right and just'.[117] This remark is inadequate to *Capital*'s antinomy passage, because it is unnecessary to identify an antinomy between two views on an issue to say that there is 'no determining' it. One non-antinomic reason that there may be 'no determining' an issue with certain principles is if the latter are insufficiently concrete, as when Hegel replies to Fichte that there is no determining, by principles of right, what the correct passport regulations should be.[118] Hegel does not thereby grant that principles of right generate an antinomy in respect of passport regulations. For an antinomy to pertain, it must be the case that there is no determining an issue because certain principles have *contradictory* implications (rather than insufficient implications) in respect of it. To identify a rights-antinomy is to say that the same premises equally justify two rights between which there is a logical contradiction. That no one who offers a mode-of-production-relative account of Marx's view of justice has got any further in the interpretation of *Capital*'s antinomy passage than Tucker's inadequate 'no determining' remark is symptomatic of the fact that *Capital*'s antinomy passage is a nail in its coffin. A thinker who identifies an entity as rights-antinomy-generating would make a logical contradiction *part of their own thought* by affirming a view of justice on which the only applicable norms for judging the justice of the actions that belong to it were its own.

Finally, the value and recognition of self-ownership interpretation reveals two aspects to *Capital*'s oft-cited but only partially understood remark: '[b]etween equal rights, force decides'.[119] One aspect is causal and the other is normative. The more straightforward causal aspect of Marx's remark is: force (of numbers) will decide. No government committed to upholding commodity exchange need intervene on its own initiative in favour of one side and against the other if both sides can claim to be in the right on the basis of commodity exchange. The nature of a government's intervention will be determined by the tide of public pressure, in which class struggle plays a role.

---

117   Tucker 1969, p. 45.
118   Hegel 1986b, p. 25; Hegel 1991a, p. 21.
119   *MEW*, 23, p. 249; *MECW*, 35, p. 243; Marx 1976, p. 344.

There is, however, a normative aspect to Marx's remark, for which it must be kept in mind that the 'equal rights' of which Marx is speaking belong to an antinomy of the type described above. If two sides genuinely have equal rights, then either side may be entitled to feel aggrieved if force is used against it, in favour of the other side. But if two sides assert rights that form an antinomy, there is nothing compelling about the argument of either side. The further aspect of Marx's remark is thus: there can be no complaint from either side of a rights-antinomy if force decides. Between antinomic rights, there can be no complaint from right by either side if a normatively irrelevant factor, such as force, or tossing a coin, decides the matter. A contrast with Marx's assessment of the American Civil War provides one way to clarify and insist on this second aspect of *Capital*'s remark.

On Marx's assessment, the American Civil War was not a struggle between two sides equally in the right. On Marx's assessment, slavery was fundamental to the American Civil War;[120] and slavery in the American South must appear 'unjust'[121] even from the perspective of those whose beliefs chime with the system of capitalist production. On the premise that there are to be no relations of personal dependence, the American Civil War was a struggle of right and wrong. Yet, just because, from this perspective, the North was in the right and the South was in the wrong, the North did not cease to require force to beat the South. The judgement here is: between right and wrong, force may be used to prosecute the cause of those in the right. By contrast, the judgement in the case of two sides equally in the right, between which there is no rights-antinomy, is: between equal rights, *either* side may feel aggrieved if force is used to prosecute the other side's cause. Finally, the judgement in the case of antinomic equal rights is: between equal rights, *neither* side may feel aggrieved if force is used to prosecute the other side's cause.

This insistence on the twofold nature of Marx's remark is not, however, to grant that neither side can have any grounds to complain about an injustice if the other side wins. Commodity form philosophy, by virtue of the concept of use-value, avoids and diagnoses the misidentification of justice with rights. It permits duty-to-the-whole-based arguments for exerting public pressure on a government to curtail equal liberty. Marx describes the North's victory in the American Civil War not as a victory for force, but as a victory for 'reason',[122] notwithstanding the fact that the North required force to beat the South. Likewise, if an enforced limit on the working day can be justified on non-rights-based

---

120   *MEW*, 15, p. 419; *MECW*, 19, p. 115.

121   *MEW*, 25, p. 352; *MECW*, 37, p. 338; Marx 1981, p. 461.

122   *MEW*, 15, p. 552; *MECW*, 19, p. 249.

grounds, that enforced limit, too, is a victory for reason, even if an initial appeal to an antinomic right was required for that victory. Insofar as the other side appeals to an antinomic right, they cannot complain.

Insofar as *Capital*'s tone is one that condemns the suffering experienced by those whose lives are mangled by excessive labour,[123] *Marx* implicitly adopts a non-rights-based perspective from which a limit on the working day ought to be enforced. But if, as Marx put it in 1843, 'the rational is actual' in virtue of 'the *contradiction* of *irrational reality*',[124] that tone is not enough. Marx needs to show that a type of *actor* is able to adopt a non-rights-based perspective from which a limit on the working day ought to be enforced. On the above reconstruction of *Capital*'s antinomy passage, both the purchaser and the seller of labour power affirm the principle of self-ownership, which prohibits all non-rights-based normative arguments about norms that ought to be enforced. So, if a type of actor is to adopt a non-rights-based perspective from which they can believe that a limit on the working day ought to be enforced, it must be shown that this perspective can become available to them by virtue of their practical response to the rights-antinomy.

5   The Rights-Antinomy and the Capitalist Class Interest Claim

Before considering workers' practical response to the rights-antinomy, two claims are denied. First, it is denied, as Wildt and others claim, that legal limits on the working day that forestall excessive labour 'correspond to capital's objective interests';[125] or rather, since capital cannot have interests any more than it can be white,[126] it is denied that such limits are in capitalists' class interest. Unless this claim is denied, legal limits on the working day that forestall excessive labour could not be an object of genuine antagonism between the capitalist and working-classes. Such limits are an object of genuine antagonism not just between individuals, but also at the macro-level, between classes as a whole. Second, it is denied that, *even if* such legal limits *were* in the interest of the capitalist class, it would follow that the rights-antinomy was not

---

123   See, for example, *MEW*, 23, pp. 269–71, pp. 285–6, p. 320; *MECW*, 35, pp. 261–3, pp. 275–6, pp. 306–7; Marx 1976, pp. 364–6, p. 381, p. 416.

124   *MEW*, 1, p. 266; *MECW*, 3, p. 63. On the translation of this phrase, see ch. 1, appendix.

125   Wildt 1986, p. 164; Harvey 2006, p. 30; Harvey 2010, p. 155, p. 157; Müller and Neusüss 1971, p. 49; Taiwo 1996, p. 87.

126   'White monopoly capital' is a term in current use in South Africa by some African nationalists.

enduring. Wildt advances this second claim when he adds: '[o]n Marx's historical presentation, the antinomy of the working day is therefore not enduring'.[127]

Call the claim that legal limits on the working day that forestall excessive labour are in capitalists' class interest the *capitalist class interest claim*. The capitalist class interest claim is a premise in some arguments for the view that Marx offers a functional explanation of the passage of the Factory Acts.[128] But the nature of Marx's explanation of the passage of the Factory Acts is not at issue here. To deny that Marx endorsed the capitalist class interest claim, it is neither sufficient nor necessary to reject functional-explanation-based interpretations of Marx's account of the passage of the Factory Acts. The capitalist class interest claim could serve as a premise in an intentional explanation of their passage; and not every conceivable functional explanation of their passage need appeal to a dispositional fact with benefits for the capitalist class.

Three preliminary points may be made about the capitalist class interest claim. One is that it is a claim about the interest of all money-maximising firms over an extended time and space (in circumstances of class division). Proponents of the capitalist class interest claim need not deny that there is an antagonism between the interest of an individual wage-labourer, and a firm's interest in imposing excessive labour on them in its pursuit of continuous money maximisation. They need only deny that there is genuine class antagonism over legal limits that forestall excessive labour at the macro-level.

Second, proponents of the capitalist class interest claim defend a possible position. It is conceivable for the imposition of excessive labour by individual firms to have a negative effect on capitalists' class interest. Assuming a constant wage, all capitalist firms over an extended time and space have a class-specific social interest in the highest possible average length and intensity of the working day over that time and space. Anything whose nature is such that it decreases this average, or increases the wage while keeping the length and intensity of the working day constant, is contrary to the capitalist class interest, even if it is in the capitalist class's short-term interest, or in the long-term interest of a few capitalists. If, as a result of individual firms' actions in imposing excessive labour, labour power cannot be put to work for as long and as intense a period (over an extended time and space) than if those firms desisted from imposing excessive labour, the latter act against capitalists' class interest by imposing excessive labour.

---

127   Wildt 1986, p. 164.
128   Elster 1985, pp. 186–91; Wetherly 1992, p. 181.

Accordingly, the imposition of excessive labour by individual firms can conceivably have detrimental consequences for capitalists' class interest in one or
more of three ways: by (i) decreasing the average endurance of labour power
to an extent that lowers the average length and intensity of work that can be
sustained; or by (ii) eroding the supply of labour such that the average wage
increases, if capitalists' appropriation of the additional labour fails to recoup
the cost; or by (iii) creating more 'expenses'[129] to maintain labour power than
otherwise (such as health-related expenses), if capitalists' appropriation of the
additional labour fails to recoup the part of the cost of those expenses born by
capitalists. (i)–(iii) are all distinct from a concern with wage-labourers' health
in and of itself. If excessive labour leads to unhealthy but functioning wage-
labourers, that raises no immediate problem, as far as the capitalist class is
concerned.

To deny the capitalist class interest claim, it is not necessary to dispute these
points. One may begin, rather, by noting some of its proponents' ambiguous
formulations. Elster claims: 'the capitalists have an interest in the survival and
reproduction of the workers'.[130] Wetherly writes: 'the system requires reproduction of labour power, which in turn requires that the hours of labour be
kept within the physical bounds of labour power'.[131] Both formulations occlude
the difference between the claim that capitalists require wage-labour, and the
claim that capitalists must re-hire the current population of producers. If,
between them all, capitalists in a given space *had* to re-hire the current population of producers in that space at a living wage for the *maximum* possible
period for which the latter could perform non-excessive capitalist wage-labour,
excessive labour would quite possibly[132] be detrimental to capitalists' class
interest. If excessive labour was imposed, total labour per producer would
probably not be optimal. But capitalists need not re-hire the current population of producers, let alone re-hire them for this maximum period. Hence, the
capitalist class interest claim cannot be true in the abstract. It is only possibly

---

129   *MEW*, 43, p. 173; *MECW*, 30, p. 185.
130   Elster 1985, p. 377; compare p. 193.
131   Wetherly 1992, p. 195. Wetherly could drop this claim from his interpretation of Marx's
       account of the passage of the Factory Acts by regarding their passage as an instance where
       'in the interests of maintaining political order ... office-holders may make concessions to
       working-class demands even where these go against capitalist class interests' (Wetherly
       2005, p. 179).
132   Not necessarily, for even then, capitalists in an extended time and space might have a brief
       window of opportunity to make huge gains vis-à-vis other nations' capitalists by imposing
       excessive labour.

true in particular contexts, in light of facts that make a capitalist class in a given space dependent on the long-term performance of its current population of producers.

It is also Marx's view that, in the abstract, the capitalist class interest claim is false. In *Capital*, Marx is adamant that, so long as other wage-labourers, from however far afield, and from whatever generation, remain to be hired, '[c]apital does not inquire into labour-power's length of life'.[133] The existence of successive generations of wage-labourers who live artificially short working lives due to excessive labour may be a mark of the degree to which capitalists' class interest in the highest possible average length and intensity of the working day is being met, provided capitalists avoid enough of any of the extra expenses; and there are enough bodies for the scrap-heap. In the *Economic Manuscripts of 1861–63*, Marx insists that the capitalist class interest claim is also false for a particular period of history:

> the history of modern industry has shown that a continuous overpopulation is possible, even though it is a stream formed of human generations who are quickly ruined, swiftly succeed one another, and are picked unripe, so to speak.[134]

> If the average age of the generations of workers declines, there is an ever-superfluous and constantly increasing mass of short-lived generations on the market, and that is all that capitalist production requires.[135]

Three factors intrinsic to capital (and thus common to all particular contexts in which the capitalist class interest claim could be advanced) distinguish the reproduction of labour power from the reproduction of the current population of producers for its maximum possible period. First, capital 'produces the transformation of women and children into wage-labourers'.[136] Money-maximisers are indifferent to whom they hire, just as long as the labour of one is as good a means of moneymaking as the next. So, if there is a latent surplus population in domestic households, it matters less, for the capitalist class, if current pro-

---

133   *MEW*, 23, p. 281; *MECW*, 35, p. 271; Marx 1976, p. 376. Compare Marx's use of 'at the very least' in *Capital*'s claim: '[t]he labour power withdrawn from the market by wear and tear, and death, must at the very least be continually replaced by an equal number of fresh labour powers' (*MEW*, 23, p. 186; *MECW*, 35, p. 182; Marx 1976, p. 275).

134   *MEW*, 43, p. 173; *MECW*, 30, p. 185.

135   *MEW*, 43, p. 297; *MECW*, 30, p. 302.

136   Ibid.

ducers are prematurely exhausted. Second, 'capital also produces an absolute increase of the number of people, above all of the working-class'.[137] Capital, by generating advances in productive power, reduces the cost of means of individual reproduction, and thus the cost of raising children to a working age. It enables a more rapid replenishment of the human pool from which capitalists can draw to replace current producers. So again, it will matter less, for the capitalist class, if some proportion of them is prematurely exhausted.

Third, capital extends the catchment area of the human pool available to each firm, by generating advances in transport and communication that ease prospective wage-labourers' migration. Unless the globalised human pool of potential producers that capitalists in a given nation can draw from has dried up, it is in that national capitalist class's interest to extend its use of this human pool, ahead of restricting the labour of its current population of producers. Any unilateral move within a given territory to restrict working hours gifts an advantage to the capitalist classes of other countries, who, by imposing excessive labour (perhaps using the same globalised human pool of potential producers spurned by the first), can accumulate quicker, and undercut them. As *Capital* puts it: '"*Après moi le déluge!*" is the watchword of every capitalist, and of every capitalist nation'.[138] Elster and Wetherly ignore the final clause of this phrase.

The pretext for an interpretive stance so at odds with the above passages from *Capital* and Marx's *Economic Manuscripts of 1861–63* is a reading of a passage in *Capital* that discusses the reasons for the restriction of factory labour in England:

> Aside from the daily more threatening growth of the workers' movement, the restriction of factory labour was dictated by the same necessity with which guano was spread over the English fields. The same blind thirst for robbery which, in the former case, exhausted the soil, in the latter case, seized the life-force of the nation at its root. Periodic epidemics speak as clearly on this point as the diminishing military standard of height in Germany and France.[139]

Marx here explains the restriction of factory labour in England by a second factor alongside that of placating a workers' movement with concessions. Elster

---

137   Ibid.

138   *MEW*, 23, p. 285; *MECW*, 35, p. 275; Marx 1976, p. 381; see, also, the reference to 'Ireland' and 'Africa' at *MEW*, 23, pp. 281–2; *MECW*, 35, p. 272; Marx 1976, pp. 377–8.

139   *MEW*, 23, p. 253; *MECW*, 35, p. 247; Marx 1976, p. 348.

claims that this second factor is the advancement of the 'collective capitalist interest'.[140] Others, too, hold that the life-force of the nation is to be restored to satisfy capitalists' need for labour.[141] If the restriction of factory labour in England at this time was explained by Marx even partly to satisfy a 'collective capitalist interest' in increasing the supply or endurance of labour, that would count as evidence for Marx's commitment to the capitalist class interest claim, in one particular context. The reading goes arbitrarily beyond the text, however. There is no mention here of a 'collective capitalist interest' as an *in-order-to* motive for restricting factory labour. The passage implies, rather, that capitalists' 'blind thirst' for labour was a *because* motive for this restriction.[142]

The second in-order-to motive for restricting factory labour is elaborated in the final sentence, which refers to 'periodic epidemics'. In the *Economic Manuscripts of 1861–63*, Marx claims that 'as a result of the excesses, pests broke out whose devastation was equally threatening to capitalists and workers'.[143] Recurrent bouts of disease have general negative spillover effects in any type of society, if their effects cannot be localised. The second reason that Marx offers for the restriction of factory labour in England, therefore, was to pre-empt circumstances conducive to recurrent bouts of disease. This second factor is independent of any desire to advance capitalists' class interest. If pests kill people of all classes, and unrestricted factory labour leads (in this one instance or quite generally) pests to spread, one reason to restrict factory labour (in this one instance or quite generally) is to root out a cause of people dying, *whether or not* pests leave enough of those that they do not kill able to sustain the length and intensity of labour that they would maintain in their absence. As *Capital*'s suggestion that an interest in public safety contributed to the restriction of factory labour in England does not imply that Marx endorsed the capitalist class interest claim even in this one particular context, and proponents of this claim present no other genuine[144] evidence for believing that Marx endorsed it, there is no evidence that Marx endorsed the capitalist class interest claim.

---

140   Elster 1985, p. 188.
141   Cohen 1978, p. 295; Harvey 2010, p. 141, pp. 145; Wetherly 1992, pp. 192–5.
142   On in-order-to motives and because motives, see ch. 4, sec. 2.
143   *MEW*, 43, p. 206; *MECW*, 30, p. 216.
144   Cohen cites a remark in *Capital* Volume I: '"the interest of capital itself points in the direction of a normal working day"' (Cohen 1978, p. 295, citing *MEW*, 23, p. 281; *MECW*, 35, p. 272; Marx 1976, p. 377; also cited to this effect in Starosta 2016, pp. 212–13; and Roberts 2017, p. 131). But the translation is inaccurate: 'to point' would be '*hinweisen*', but Marx's verb is '*scheinen*', 'to seem'. The remark is better rendered: '[t]hus capital seems [*scheint*] directed by its own interest to a normal working-day'. Owing to the contrast between '*Schein*

But suppose, for the sake of argument, that the capitalist class interest claim is in fact true in all particular contexts in which excessive labour is imposed. Would it follow that 'the antinomy of the working day is therefore not enduring'?[145] No. The capitalist class interest claim is a macro-level claim. The rights-antinomy is a form of antagonistic interdependency at the micro-level. As there is an enduring difference between an individual capitalist's interest and capitalists' class interest, the truth of the capitalist class interest claim cannot establish that the rights-antinomy is not enduring. If the capitalist class interest claim is true in a particular context, an association of the capitalist class can argue for legal limits on the working day to forestall excessive labour on the basis of enlightened class interest; and, being enlightened, it would not seek to repeal such limits once passed. But the achievement of a legally limited working day on this basis would not cause the premises that engender the rights-antinomy to cease to be believable. Even if, due to legal limits forestalling excessive labour, no conduct in production implicitly asserts the rights of the rights-antinomy, the proofs can still be articulated, either by capitalists who resent these limits, or in reply to them.

The rights-antinomy could still be of practical import in production, moreover, for two reasons. If a capitalist firm uses the means at its disposal to evade any profit-reducing effects of a limit on its own operations, then it may succeed in imposing excessive labour in spite of the law (if the law lacks adequate sanctions, and/or is not enforced reliably or timely). Moreover, as competition encourages capitalist firms to invest in more profitable technologies and techniques, including by intensifying the labour performed within a given time period, a legal limit need not permanently prevent excessive labour even on the assumption that capitalist firms act within the law. New technologies and techniques may so intensify labour that observance of a legal limit dating from T_1, whose observance at T_1 prevented excessive labour at T_1, nonetheless allows capitalist firms using technologies and techniques discovered since T_1 to impose excessive labour at T_2. *Capital* suggests:

(appearance)' and '*Wirklichkeit* (reality)' (compare the first Marx quote in ch. 9), '*scheinen*' is often used to cast doubt on an assertion. Cohen leaves his readers with an impression contrary to Marx's point: as a workforce of wage-labourers is not exclusively owned like a machine whose replacement must be funded by the owner who exhausts it, it need not be the case that the capitalist who suspends excessive labour in their firm thereby reduces their costs. It merely seems to be the case that a capitalist has an interest in suspending excessive labour in their firm.

145   Wildt 1986, p. 164.

the tendency of capital, as soon as it is cut off by the law, once and for all, from an extension of the working day, is to feast on [*sich gütlich zu tun*] a systematic increase in the degree of intensity of labour, and to twist every improvement in machinery into a means for a greater sapping of labour power; which must soon spell another new turning point, where a further reduction of working hours becomes unavoidable.[146]

A distinction can be drawn between the conditions of the rights-antinomy, and the conditions for the rights-antinomy to be of practical import in production. If purchase and sale and production with wage-labour for continuous money maximisation are essential to capitalism, and sustain a belief in the principle of self-ownership, the rights-antinomy is an essential ideological feature of capitalism. But the rights-antinomy can only be of practical import in production on the further condition that the amount of labour actually performed is excessive. Whether or not it is excessive rests on empirical facts related to different dynamics: (i) the technologies and techniques used, (ii) the length and intensity of the working day, and (iii) the time and energy required to satisfy needs that are recognised as needs (such as commuting, raising a family or entertainment), whose satisfaction then ought not to depend on a worker sacrificing the rest they require to reproduce their labour power for the maximum possible period. While (i) relates to the development of productive power, (ii) is influenced by class struggle, and (iii) is affected by what *Capital* describes as the historical 'customs and lifestyle demands the class of free labourers has cultivated'.[147] Even if excessive labour is an always reinstateable possibility under capitalism, it need not be a current reality, due to the class struggle it and the rights-antinomy occasion. So, the rights-antinomy need not always be of practical import in production.

6   Interest Privilege and Possible Practical Awareness

A standpoint is defined by interest privilege and capacity privilege. A type of actor has interest privilege if, by virtue of their pursuit of their initial in-order-

---

146   *MEW*, 23, p. 440; *MECW*, 35, p. 420; Marx 1976, p. 542. '[*S*]*ich gütlich zu tun*', here translated as 'to feast on', is not 'to compensate' (*MECW*; Marx 1976) (which would be: '(*sich*) *entschädigen*'). It might be in capitalists' interest to increase the intensity of labour even if the working day is not limited, and hence even if they have nothing to 'compensate' in respect of its length.

147   *MEW*, 23, p. 185; *MECW*, 35, p. 181; Marx 1976, p. 275.

to motive, they can come to will a principle that there is an impartial reason to apply; while at least one other type of actor in the same society cannot. A type of actor has capacity privilege if, by virtue of their pursuit of their initial in-order-to motive, actors of their type can develop the capacity to bring about a form of society in which a principle that there is an impartial reason to apply is applied, without entering into coalition with one specific other type of actor. The latter type of actor must also be incapable of bringing about this form of society without entering into a coalition that includes the first.

An actor is a bearer of an interaction only if the in-order-to motive they pursue in it is enabled and unintentionally constrained by the generalised existence of that type of interaction. Any in-order-to motive (such as working in return for a wage in order to live) is an intellectual construct reflecting the interests of its constructor. But bearers are thought of as pursuing in-order-to motives in types of interaction with a generalised existence and self-reinforcing dynamic. To study the possible practical awareness of an actor insofar as they are the bearer of one or more types of interaction is to investigate the possible practical awareness of a type of actor non-incidental to a form of society with such a dynamic.

As the bearer of one or more types of interaction, an actor is ascribed with a minimal initial stock of experiences, and a minimal initial set of capacities and external resources. Their initial stock of experiences consists simply of their awareness of the type of end-state they are to bring about, by pursuing their in-order-to motive, as a possible end-state for them to bring about; and their awareness of the means by which they bring it about as possible means for them to bring it about. Their initial set of capacities and external resources consist simply of the capacities and external resources necessary for them to bring about the type of end-state they are to bring about by pursuing their in-order-to motive.

In the pursuit of their in-order-to motive, an actor interprets the actions of those they relate to, and may acquire new beliefs and interests. Any practically relevant belief or interest that an actor can acquire in pursuit of their in-order-to motive and in the light of their stock of experiences belongs to their possible practical awareness. Belief b belongs to the possible practical awareness of actor A, the bearer of relation r, if b is a belief that A can hold in light of A's pursuit of their in-order-to motive in r and A's stock of experiences; or, more derivatively, if b is a belief that A can hold in light of A's in-order-to motive in r, A's stock of experiences, and any further action A performs on account of the beliefs A can hold.

An interest is what an actor, in light of their will, can believe they have a reason to do or to favour. An actor's will is initially defined by their in-order-to motive as a bearer of one or more types of interaction. Their interests depend on their initial in-order-to motive, stock of experiences, capacities and resources; and any beliefs, will, capacities and resources they can acquire from that starting-point. There can be no guarantee that an actor can acquire the capacities and external resources they require to successfully act on the beliefs and will they can acquire. In other words, it is conceivable for an actor to have interests they cannot satisfy. But an actor's interests are defined from that actor's perspective, not from an observer's perspective.

The steps that an actor takes in pursuit of their in-order-to motive may include an experience of recognition. An actor can then want to be moved all the way to exercise the qualities for which they are recognised. That may create new interests. They may be more prepared than before to adopt the means for something they want to achieve, despite the fact that their adoption is undesirable in some other respect.

The beliefs and will that an actor can acquire need not be confined, moreover, to the discovery of means that better serve the achievement of their in-order-to motive as a bearer of one or more types of interaction, or to greater determination in the pursuit of that in-order-to motive, or to renewed belief in it. The horizon of an actor's possible practical awareness may exceed the horizon of their initial in-order-to motive. An actor's possible practical awareness records a potential to acquire *new* in-order-to motives. By virtue of A's possible practical awareness, A may be able to evaluate action that forms no part of the interaction(s) of which they are the bearer as having a value that is independent of, or more important than, the value A places on their in-order-to motive as a bearer of such interaction(s). A may prioritise action to which their in-order-to motive as a bearer has led them, over action that defines them as a bearer.

To ascertain that an actor's possible practical awareness includes all the beliefs and interests they would have to act on, to achieve a certain goal, is not to predict that they will act to achieve it (or to say that they will succeed if they do). It may be that, in the normal course of things, many actors will simply continue to pursue their initial in-order-to motive as a bearer of one or more types of interaction. But in respect of an actor's possible practical awareness, '[i]t is not a matter of what this or that proletarian, or even the whole proletariat, for the time being *regards* as its aim',[148] as Marx puts it in *The Holy Family*. It is a matter of objective possibility. There is no inconsistency in affirming a standpoint while believing that, in the normal course of things, few will approach

---

148   *MEW*, 2, p. 38; *MECW*, 4, p. 37.

its horizon, or that there will be few occasions on which its horizon will be approached; no more than a Rawlsian need admit to a problem in their theory of justice just by virtue of believing that, in the normal course of things, few will adopt the original position.

To generate a standpoint, a type of actor must be able to undergo a distinctive learning process, in which they acquire all the beliefs and interests they would have to act on, to apply a principle to a domain of action that should be applied to that domain. If the system of capitalist production engenders a rights-antinomy, therefore, in which two types of actor assert antinomic rights, it is possible to consider whether a standpoint can arise from the distinctive learning process set in train by one type of actor's position in and practical response to the rights-antinomy.[149] The rights-antinomy also provides a measure of interest privilege: a type of actor has interest privilege if, by virtue of their position in the rights-antinomy, they can acquire the beliefs and interests they would have to act on, to will a principle that resolves the rights-antinomy. If, moreover, the system of capitalist production contains real abstractions, it is possible to ask whether these real abstractions compound the distinctiveness of this learning process. For if a type of interaction is characterised by a real abstraction, and one type of actor, unlike their counterpart, has an interest in acting on the knowledge that that real abstraction reveals, then that actor will have a distinctive learning process.

7   The Rights-Antinomy, Recognition and Union Organisation

The rights-antinomy is the first form in which the antagonistic interdependency of class in itself is expressed. Unregulated production with wage-labour for continuous money maximisation must lead to excessive labour; and the first response of a wage-labourer who (like the capitalist) adopts the self-conception of a self-owner sustained by generalised purchase and sale, is to implicitly assert a right to a limited working day, by unilaterally snatching free time.

---

149   Werner Bonefeld may be right that 'the standpoint of labour does not reveal an ontologically privileged position' (Bonefeld 2014, p. 3). As the interaction-recognition-antinomy thesis is not a thesis of traditional Marxism, this claim is not in dispute. A traditional Marxist argument for a 'privileged position' (where traditional Marxism is a critique of capitalism from 'the standpoint of labour') is not the only type of (Marxist) argument for a standpoint, and it is not the type of argument advanced here.

The all-important question, the question that Lukács poses, is: 'how far it lies in the nature of the interests of a given class to go beyond this immediacy'.[150] In other words: to what extent is the rights-antinomy a productive antinomy? The above denial of the capitalist class interest claim in the abstract suggests that, if either party to the rights-antinomy is to undergo a macro-level learning process creating an interest in a *principle* that can be recommended on the impartial ground that antinomies in the social world ought to be resolved, it will be the wage-labourer. Perhaps this learning process can bear out *The German Ideology*'s claim that

> proletarians only approach this unity [revolutionary unity – JF] through a long process of development; a process of development in which the appeal to their right also plays a role. This appeal to their right is simply a means to make them into a 'they'.[151]

This passage does not say that appeals to right are 'without effect'.[152] On the contrary: it asserts that workers' appeals to rights can serve to promote revolutionary unity. Nonetheless, it displays an instrumental attitude to workers' appeals to rights. The premises of this instrumental attitude are: (i) workers' appeals to rights can make the working-class a ' "they" ', that is, organise them and give rise to a spirit of recognition among them; (ii) there is more to value in this result than in the appeals to rights that initially give rise to it.

The rights-antinomy identified in *Capital* suggests a qualified defence of (i)–(ii). If two rights form an antinomy, a critical distance from them is a rational requirement, to avoid the 'sceptical hopelessness' or 'dogmatic stubbornness'[153] that an antinomy can produce. It is permissible for this critical distance to translate into an instrumental attitude to the right asserted in the antithesis if workers, by virtue of their position in and practical response to the rights-antinomy, can unite in a spirit that suggests a principle with which they can resolve it.

In *Capital*'s presentation of the rights-antinomy, the proof of the thesis is assigned to a capitalist, while the proof of the antithesis is voiced by a worker. That pairing is a result of their initial in-order-to motives. A capitalist's pursuit of continuous money maximisation leaves them indifferent to who supplies the labour. They must construe the payment of value and the recogni-

---

150   Lukács 1977, p. 227; Lukács 1968, p. 54.

151   *MEW*, 3, p. 305; *MECW*, 5, p. 323.

152   Wildt 1997, p. 217.

153   Kant 1999, A 407/B 434.

tion of self-ownership, in any given purchase of labour power, to apply to that sale as a single sale. They cannot entertain any concern the worker raises in respect of future periods, for which they have yet to hire them. By contrast, a wage-labourer's in-order-to motive of working in return for a wage in order to live gives them an interest in continuing to be able to sell their labour power for the duration of their working life. A wage leaves them dependent on the sale of their labour power for future periods. It is in their interest to construe the payment of value and the recognition of their self-ownership, in any given purchase of labour power, to apply to that sale as a sale in an ongoing series of sales of their labour power. To that end, the worker must assert a right to a limited working day that puts a stop to the theft of their property.

For as long as a wage-labourer performs excessive labour, a capitalist believes that self-ownership is recognised, while a wage-labourer experiences a lack of recognition as a self-owner. To demand their recognition as a self-owner, the worker must assert a right to a limited working day. But as their appeal to a right to a limited working day is met by a capitalist's appeal to their right to an unlimited working day, and each of these appeals is licenced by the nature of commodity exchange, neither the capitalist nor the government volunteers to recognise the worker's right. A worker can only obtain recognition as a self-owner if they are prepared to struggle for it.

Between a capitalist and a worker, 'the silent compulsion of economic circumstances seals the domination of the capitalist over the worker'.[154] If anyone may hire anyone, workers must compete with each other for jobs that not all are guaranteed to get, but on which, if labour power is purchased at value, each immediately depends. This leaves an individual worker with insufficient bargaining power, in the form of credible warnings and/or promises about the future, to negotiate a limited working day, when a capitalist has the power to fire and hire. Paradoxically, a worker cannot obtain recognition as a self-owner by themselves.

If a capitalist firm has greater bargaining power than an individual worker, and it is the capitalist firm that initiates production, its bargaining advantage can only be eroded as an unintended consequence of its exercise of this initiative. Indeed, one way to maximise monetary returns is to increase the scale of production, which increases the number of wage-labourers hired. Insofar as cooperation in an enlarged division of labour brings efficiency savings, such

---

154   *MEW*, 23, p. 765; *MECW*, 35, p. 726; Marx 1976, p. 899. On the translation of this claim, see ch. 10, sec. 7.

moves tend to impose a certain minimum size of workforce on competitors as well. Each capitalist firm in a given branch then employs a number of wage-labourers, and is as interested in increasing the degree of exploitation of the one as it is of the other. That circumstance reduces the capitalist's bargaining advantage, if the bargaining power of an entire workforce to withdraw all its labour at once is a greater threat to the firm's continuous money maximisation, the larger the workforce. As Marx's *Instructions for the Delegates of the Provisional General Council* remark: '[t]he only social power of the workmen is their number'.[155] To the extent that a workforce has power in number, a limited working day in the firm is a workforce-specific social interest. In the face of an individual worker's lack of bargaining power, each member of a workforce can only satisfy their interest in a limited working day by obtaining a limit for all workers across the firm.

But Marx's *Instructions* add: '[t]he force of numbers, however, is broken by disunion'.[156] Even a single workforce is divided by competition for jobs, and by advancement in the hierarchy of command. If a workforce is to overcome those divisions and to act jointly to limit its working day, that can only be because there are factors relativising those sources of division. Two real abstractions may have this effect. One is that a capitalist firm treats all the wage-labourers it hires as if they had no determinate end, beyond receipt of a wage, by attaching no conditions to its use. Yet it must know that wage-labourers have a further end to pursue, individual reproduction. For wage-labourers to become aware of that real abstraction is for them to become aware of their firm's common indifference to their reproduction. Second, a capitalist firm must correct any behaviour or delay within its workforce that hampers its total output, calculated in light of likely future behaviour. It must exercise its commanding power to that end, as if its workforce intended that calculated target, although it must know that the contract to which each wage-labourer agrees is merely an input for this calculation. For wage-labourers to become aware of that real abstraction is for them to become aware of their firm's common indifference to their will.

The members of a workforce pursue a workforce-specific social interest in a limited working day in the firm by engaging in collective bargaining. Collective bargaining is based on an agreement between the members of a workforce. The latter agree with one another 'to cease contracting with a third party – the employer – until his offer meets certain conditions'.[157] The agreement facilit-

---

155   *MECW*, 20, p. 191; compare *MEW*, 23, p. 350; *MECW*, 35, p. 336; Marx 1976, p. 449.
156   *MECW*, 20, p. 191.
157   Cohen 1978, p. 242.

ates the raising of a threat to collectively withdraw labour power 'from some capitalist(s) without offering it to any other'.[158]

To bargain collectively, the members of a workforce must agree to refrain from selling their labour power to their employer until a particular condition is met for all. If each member of the workforce can believe in the greater bargaining power of a larger number, then, whether or not any member believes that there is a duty on each member to redress the workforce disadvantage of excessive labour, each has an interest to act in accordance with what a belief in that duty would require.

Marx remarks in *Notes on Wagner* that commodity exchangers 'already *do* this' – act as if they recognise one another – 'while offering their goods to one another and reaching agreement on the deal'.[159] By the same token, in seeking to agree to bargain collectively for a limited working day in the firm, the members of a workforce begin to recognise one another as entitled to, and as prepared to bargain collectively for, a limited working day. They are genuinely recognised by one another as entitled to a limited working day, for each can believe of every other member that every other member, like them, regards the objective of their agreement, a limited working day, as something to which every member is entitled. Each can believe this of every other, as each knows that every other could make the same argument they made in asserting the antithesis of the rights-antinomy. They are genuinely recognised by one another as prepared to bargain collectively, because each also knows that every other regards this preparedness, signalled in the act of agreeing to bargain collectively, as a preparedness to consciously seek a valued objective.

If, by seeking to agree to bargain collectively, the members of a workforce recognise one another in these respects, then each is recognised as having an equal basis to complain if their objective is foiled on account of any member's violation of the agreement to bargain collectively. It is not only one particular individual within the group, to the exclusion of others, who may complain. The duty to recognise the preparedness to bargain collectively is a duty to the whole. To undermine this preparedness would be to undermine a valued property of the workforce.

Each member also has a reason to articulate a belief in a duty to recognise the preparedness to bargain collectively. Its articulation reinforces how each has acted in agreeing to bargain collectively. Each can believe that violations of the agreement are less likely to occur if a belief in this duty is articulated.

---

158 Cohen 1978, p. 241.
159 *MEW*, 19, p. 377; *MECW*, 24, pp. 553–4.

Those who conform to the principles they know others believe will be encouraged to conform to it.

Indeed, it is possible for members of a workforce to regard disunion created by those among them who have yet to agree to bargain collectively as a wrong. What makes this possible is an *author-recognition tension* in a voluntary agreement whose objective is to bring about a type of equality among those who conclude it.

Through a voluntary agreement whose objective is to bring about such an equality, a difference can arise between: (a) the original beliefs its authors have concerning what entitles them to conclude the agreement, why its objective ought to be realised, and what binds each to pursue it; and (b) what each recognises the others as, as soon as agreement is sought. (b) may supply an alternative reason for each to believe that they are entitled to make the agreement, or that its objective ought to be realised, or that each is bound to pursue it. A tension exists if, in any of these respects, the alternative reason is incompatible with the original belief.

In the case of workplace collective bargaining for a limited working day in the firm, a difference arises between the answer to: 'what does a member of the workforce believe entitles them to agree to bargain collectively for a limited working day, why is the objective to be realised, and what binds each to pursue it' (answer: self-ownership and a voluntary agreement); and the answer to: 'what do members of the workforce begin to recognise one another as, as soon as they seek to agree to bargain collectively for a limited working day' (answer: as equally entitled to, and prepared to bargain collectively for, a limited working day).

What this mutual recognition adds is members' positive evaluation of one another's preparedness to bargain collectively. If a preparedness to bargain collectively for a limited working day in the firm is valued, a belief may arise that it is of sufficient value that those who display it are owed assistance from others who have a capacity to assist, and who would be relieved of the same disadvantage were the objective achieved. The idea that this assistance was owed could only be resisted on the basis that all duties must be assumed voluntarily, or that the objective could be achieved by other means. But the former belief is discredited in the eyes of workforce collective bargainers by the fact that it echoes the capitalist's argument for the thesis of the rights-antinomy, which they are committed to oppose; and the latter belief is also discredited, in light of the imbalance of bargaining power at the individual level.

In the case of workforce collective bargaining for a limited working day in the firm, the author-recognition tension is productive of a new belief. It allows members of a workforce to believe that members of a workforce ought to assist any critical mass of co-workers who decide to bargain collectively for a limited working day. Insofar as this assistance must take the form of agreeing to bargain collectively, the author-recognition tension is productive of a belief that there is a duty on each member to redress the workforce disadvantage of excessive labour by bargaining collectively.

A duty to redress a group disadvantage is distinct from solidarity. Solidarity is also a kind of duty to the whole. But solidarity is a duty to the whole, reciprocated by the whole to each. If x = a disadvantage, and y = action to redress that disadvantage, the concept of solidarity is: if *any* member of a group acquires x, each member has a duty to y, if they can assist.[160] A duty to redress a group disadvantage, by contrast, has the form: if *every* member of a group acquires x, each member has a duty to y, if they can assist, and if a critical mass of other members is prepared to redress x. A belief in a duty to redress a group disadvantage can generate a belief in a duty of solidarity, however, through the possibility for anyone who discharges it to be singled out for punishment.

A workforce's attempt to limit its working day cannot succeed, however. The prospective gain for any firm in abandoning any voluntary limit on working hours would increase, at the expense of firms maintaining a limit, with every increase in the number of firms maintaining it. Collective bargaining by a workforce for a limited working day must reveal a firm's resistance to a limited working day, on account of the competitive handicap it would bring for that firm.

According to the aforementioned *Instructions for the Delegates of the Provisional General Council*:

> Trades' Unions originally sprang up from the *spontaneous* attempts of workmen at removing or at least checking that competition [competition among workers – JF], in order to conquer such terms of contract as might raise them at least above the condition of mere slaves.[161]

'Slaves' have no right to a limited working day. So, although wage-labourers are free agents, their condition may still have something in common with slaves: excessive labour. One reason to say that workers form unions to raise themselves 'above the condition of mere slaves' is if workers form unions to resist excessive labour.

---

160   On solidarity, see ch. 3, sec. 4.
161   *MECW*, 20, p. 191.

If excessive labour is to lead workers to form a union, un-unionised workers must be able to believe that all the workers of their trade are more likely to obtain a limited working day in their branch of production, than all the members of their workforce are to limit the working day of their employer. They can believe this, if workplace collective bargaining has failed, and branch-level collective bargaining has yet to be attempted. The strength of that belief must also outweigh the costs and difficulties of maintaining a union, however. So to some extent, the workers who are led to form a union must believe that it is important for the workers of their trade to obtain a limited working day in their branch of production.

One reason for workers to believe this is their occupational identity. Occupational identities arise from occupational confinement, such as the system of capitalist production induces.[162] Occupational identities move actors to action by the value they bestow on themselves, as practitioners of an occupation on which value is bestowed. In the context of a struggle against the firms of a particular branch of production, an occupational identity can provide a source of worth separate from and opposed to the identity of any firm whose excessive labour is to be limited. By prematurely ruining the labour power of workers in a given trade, excessive labour ruins the power to perform such work that those who embrace its occupational identity can identify and value.

From the perspective of an occupational identity, fellow workers of a trade, employed in other firms, are entitled to nothing less than the members of one's own workforce. A shared occupational identity allows workers who believe in a duty on all members of their workforce to redress the workforce disadvantage of excessive labour (if they can assist, and a critical mass of co-workers are prepared to redress it) to believe that there is a duty on all workers of their trade to redress the general disadvantage of excessive labour in their trade (if they can assist, and a critical mass of workers in the trade are prepared to redress it). But if the members of various workforces of a given trade can believe in a duty on all workers in that trade to redress the disadvantage of excessive labour in their trade, they can value a union that acts in the name of all the workers of their trade, as a means to coordinate their efforts to limit the working day in their trade, even, perhaps, to the extent of putting up with the costs and difficulties of maintaining the union.

Attempts by individual unions to limit the working day in their branch of production face a problem, however. Just as an unlimited working day in a small minority of firms gives them an individual advantage vis-à-vis their com-

---

162   See ch. 10, sec. 9.

petitors, so an unlimited working day in a small minority of branches would allow firms in those branches to reap a higher than average profit. Again, therefore, capitalist competition will unravel any voluntary agreement between an individual union and trade representatives to limit the working day in a single branch of production.

The formation of trade unions can nonetheless lead to new beliefs, not only from an evaluation of their failures, but also on account of the capacities that their formation first creates. The formation of individual trade unions makes it possible to form 'a point of union' in a *National Association of United Trades*.[163] That prospect allows union members to believe that it is more likely that a legal limit on the working day could be obtained for all if an association of unions were formed, than that their union will secure its members' sectional interest in a limited working day in their branch of production. They can believe that, were a general legal limit on working hours to be declared, and violations reliably and timely enforced and adequately sanctioned, each firm could rest assured that no route to continuous money maximisation required it to violate that limit.

In his *Economic Manuscripts of 1861–63*, Marx reports: 'the struggle had first to assume the form of a class struggle, and thereby provoke the intervention of state power, before the daily total labour time received certain limits'.[164] A 'struggle' over excessive labour whose first form is provided by individuals' antinomic rights claims only assumes 'the form of a class struggle', that is, the form of a struggle between classes, each of which is a class for itself, on certain conditions. Workers' objective in this struggle must be to advance their class-specific social interest in a general legal norm limiting working hours. The pursuit of this objective must enjoy, formally and/or in spirit, the backing of an organisation that all workers can recognise to act in the name of their class. No struggle is a *class* struggle unless workers can recognise it as a struggle of their class; for which it must enjoy, formally and/or in spirit, the backing of an organisation that all workers can recognise to act in their name. Finally, this struggle must be waged vis-à-vis a representative government that is recognised by capitalists as guaranteeing their class interest (by guaranteeing the status quo).

Workers can recognise an association of unions as an organisation of their class by virtue of the mutual recognition that begins with its foundation. Already by forming an association of unions to bring about a general legal limit on the working day, each associated union recognises every other as

---

163   Marx 1970a, p. 226; *MECW*, 6, p. 210.
164   *MEW*, 43, p. 173; *MECW*, 30, p. 184.

entitled to a limited working day, and as prepared to support the association. Associated unions genuinely mutually recognise one another as entitled to a limited working day, for each knows that every other associated union could make the same type of argument it made for preserving its members' power to perform their type of work. Associated unions genuinely mutually recognise one another as prepared to support the association, because each knows that every other regards this preparedness, signalled in the act of agreeing to join the association, as a preparedness to consciously seek a valued objective.

Indeed, each associated union has a reason to articulate a belief in a duty on all associated unions to redress the working-class disadvantage of excessive labour. The articulation of that duty reinforces how each has acted in negotiating the formation of the association. Each can believe that a violation of the association is less likely to occur if a belief in that duty is articulated.

The effects of mutual recognition in the formation of an association of unions extend to ordinary union members. If a worker of a given trade is able to identify themselves with their union by virtue of their occupational identity, then a worker of a trade whose union is accepted into an association of unions can identify themselves with an association that their union joins as an equal. From this newly acquired perspective, the workers of one trade of the association are owed nothing less than those of any other trade. A belief in a duty on all workers of a trade to redress excessive labour in their trade (if they can, and a critical mass of other workers in that trade are prepared to do so) can become a belief in a duty on all workers of various trades to redress the working-class disadvantage of excessive labour (if they can, and a critical mass of other workers are prepared to do so).

Moreover, associated unions are committed to allowing any further union to join the association, and so to partake in offering and receiving support. Each knows that any worker can assert the antithesis of the rights-antinomy, and that any trade union can make the same type of argument the associated unions made for preserving its members' power to perform their type of work. Hence, each knows that there is no reason not to recognise any union as an associated union, if it is prepared to support the association. If the association is seen to welcome, on these terms, any union as an associated union, it can be recognised as an organisation of the working-class. It can speak in the name of the working-class on account of a belief that even those workers who have not joined it, can and ought to join it, to redress a working-class disadvantage. By maintaining an openness based on a criterion created by the mutual recognition in its formation, an association of unions enables the working-class to become a class for itself.

The formal terms of an association of unions need not, however, settle the scope of a duty to redress working-class disadvantages. Any voluntary agreement whose objective is a type of equality among those who conclude it may give rise to a *formal-spirit tension* as well as an author-recognition tension.

A formal-spirit tension is a tension between the formal terms of an agreement (the terms that have in fact been agreed upon), and the terms that *ought* to be agreed by those who recognise one another as its authors recognise one another. A formal term is in the spirit of an agreement if it can be viewed as a term that ought to be agreed by those who recognise one another as entitled to, and prepared to bring about, what all authors of the agreement are owed. If a formal term can be assessed in this way, then so can any merely hypothetical term. One may ask of any term, formally approved or not, whether it falls within this spirit. A tension arises between the formal terms of an agreement, and its spirit, if the spirit of an agreement licences terms that have not been formally agreed, or if it cannot licence terms that have been formally agreed.

If unions agree to form an association of unions, a formal-spirit tension takes the form of a tension between the answers to the questions: 'what are the formally agreed terms of the association of unions?'; and 'what terms ought (now) to be agreed by unions that recognise one another as prepared to support an association of unions in the pursuit of what all its members are owed?' A tension between the formal terms and the spirit of an association of unions could arise if, say, its spirit licenced the association to use means that its formal terms prohibit (illegal means, for example); or if the formal terms narrowly focus on one objective (ending excessive labour), but ignore others (ending dangerous labour or unequal pay).

Accordingly, even if a struggle is only a class struggle if it enjoys the backing of an organisation that can be recognised as a class organisation, such backing need not be formal. Any class-specific social interest counts as an objective of a class struggle if it is articulated and accepted as an objective of struggle by those who recognise one another as prepared to support an association of unions in the pursuit of what all its members are owed. It is not necessary to offer a criterion for judging when an objective qualifies as an objective of a class struggle to insist that the conditions for working-class struggle do not allow its scope to be formally limited in advance.

8   Working-Class Movements

The conditions for working-class struggle just outlined are also conditions of
what Marx calls a working-class movement. Marx writes in a letter to Friedrich
Bolte:

> every movement in which the working-class, as a *class*, confronts the rul-
> ing classes, and seeks to compel them by pressure from without, is a polit-
> ical movement. E.g. the attempt to enforce a restriction of labour time
> [*Beschränkung der Arbeitszeit*] upon individual capitalists, in a single fact-
> ory or even in a single trade, through strikes etc., is a purely economic
> movement; by contrast, the movement to compel an eight hour etc. *law*
> is a *political* movement. And in this way, from all the isolated economic
> movements of workers, a *political* movement springs up, i.e. a movement
> of the *class*, to implement its interests in a general form, in a form with
> general, socially binding force.[165]

A 'movement' is a number of actions interlinked in the beliefs of the participants in the latest action. At least some of its participants must be able to
recollect previous actions as attempts to achieve the same goal, and to conceive
of future actions to that goal. That is relatively straightforward if the objective is
a change in the law. A statute law ties legal consequences to general antecedent
conditions, without temporal limitation. A participant in a movement whose
objective is a change in the law recollects previous actions or projects future
actions as attempts to achieve the same goal by recollecting or projecting such
actions as attempts to bring about the same type of legal (dis)advantage for the
same type of actor. A movement is a working-class movement, therefore, if the
participants in its latest action can regard that action, and actions they recollect and project as having the same goal, as enjoying (formally or in spirit) the
backing of an association of unions, and as aiming at a change in the law that
would redress a working-class disadvantage.

A working-class movement becomes a '*political* movement', however, only
if it exerts 'pressure from without' on a 'ruling' class. A class is a 'ruling' class

---

165   *MEW*, 33, pp. 332–3; *MECW*, 44, p. 258. (1) *MECW* renders '*Beschränkung der Arbeitszeit*' as
'shorter working day' (which would be: '*kürzerer Arbeitstag*'), repeating the error of *MECW*
and Marx 1976 noted in sec. 4. (2) The phrase 'pressure from without' is written in English, as it is in Marx's remark elsewhere that: '[b]y pressure from without, the English
understand large extra-parliamentary popular demonstrations' (*MEW*, 15, p. 454; *MECW*,
19, p. 153).

if it can count on constituted power being exercised to observe its members' instructions and/or to accede to its members' bargaining power, and not (or only exceptionally) to observe the instructions or to accede to the bargaining power of an opposed class. The capitalist class is a ruling class, therefore, notwithstanding the formal independence of representative government, if it can count on the latter heeding the instructions its members issue through employer associations or ownership of the press, and/or if it can count on its members' power of investment to ensure that the government will anticipate and tailor its policies to its members' interests, to achieve its own goals.[166]

To 'compel' a representative government by 'pressure from without' is to challenge the power of the capitalist class as a ruling class by demanding that the government take a particular step it would otherwise be reluctant to take on account of the power of the capitalist class. To hand in a petition is to acknowledge that its recipient is to have the final say. To apply pressure from without is to act as if one believes that it is justified to *instruct* a representative government to take a particular step. The twin features that a working-class movement must display to count, for Marx, as a political movement, mirror the double nature of the challenge posed by use of the press and associations to oppose monarchical sovereignty.[167] A working-class movement is political not just by virtue of what it seeks, but how it seeks it.

A movement has no formal power to instruct a representative government, of course. Elections are the only context in which representative institutions lead representatives to regard their claim to represent the people to be challengeable. The participants in a movement can only regard it as entitled to instruct a representative government by regarding it as entitled to sanction the government's non-observance of its demand. For that, it must reserve to itself the right to commit acts of civil disobedience in the event of the government's non-observance of its demand. A working-class movement applies pressure from without, then, if its participants invoke the backing of an association of unions to raise a credible warning about how its power may be used to inconvenience government if no concession is made to the movement's demands.

A working-class movement must resort to pressure from without, to the extent that it must create a counterweight to ruling class power. The existence of a ruling class will tend to render ineffective forms of mass action, such as mass petitioning that stop short of pressure from without, when their objective is to redress a working-class disadvantage. An extra-parliamentary class move-

---

166 Here I draw on Wetherly 2005, pp. 88–92.
167 See ch. 11, sec. 3.

ment can succeed in prompting reforms, Marx here implies, because a representative government may be swayed by capitalists' concessionary response to its pressure.

9 A Resolution of Both Antinomies

Can participation in a working-class movement to limit the working day suggest a principle with which to resolve the rights-antinomy? A type of actor can resolve an antinomy if they can conceive of and will a principle with which to resolve it. A participant in a working-class movement to limit the working day can will a principle, if participation in this movement provides them with a positive reason to will it. To resolve an antinomy, it is necessary to reject a common premise of both of the proofs while better satisfying any need expressed in but separable from a rejected premise.

For a working-class movement to exist, its participants must be able to believe that it is backed (formally and/or in spirit) by an organisation that is recognised as a class organisation. They can therefore formulate the concept of a duty to redress a working-class disadvantage. They formulate this concept by abstracting from the content of the movement, and focusing on the form of a class organisation's commitment to it. They then have the concept: if every member of the working-class acquires a disadvantage, each member of the working-class has a duty to redress it (if they can, and a critical mass of workers is prepared to redress it).

The concept of a duty to redress a working-class disadvantage is a stepping stone to a principle with which to resolve the rights-antinomy. If a duty to redress a working-class disadvantage requires each worker to redress a disadvantage acquired by every worker, it presupposes that that duty can conceivably be discharged by all workers. Only if all those bound by a duty can conceivably discharge it, can each be subject to it. There can be no duty on all to do what all cannot conceivably do. The concept of a duty to redress a working-class disadvantage suggests a test of universalisability, if only as a limit on what the duty to redress a working-class disadvantage may entail. The concept of a duty to redress a working-class disadvantage is a stepping stone to a resolution of the rights-antinomy, because the latter can be resolved with the aid of a universalisability principle.

On the recognition and self-ownership interpretation of the rights-antinomy, both the proof of a right to an unlimited working day and the proof of a right to a limited working day rest on two premises: (1) commodities may only be purchased for a price proportional to value; (2) commodity exchangers are to recognise one another as self-owners. A universalisability principle can be used to resolve the rights-antinomy if it can be used to reject one or other of these premises.

Consider how a universalisability principle can be used to reject premise (2). (2) can be rejected by rejecting the idea that each person has exclusive property in their parts and capacities, and is therefore to be recognised as such. A universalisability principle can be used to reject (2), because it entails that no one may do what everyone cannot conceivably achieve, even if such action would not interfere with anyone's self-ownership. No one is to be recognised as a self-owner, for that would be to recognise a licence to do what everyone cannot conceivably achieve. All rights claims based on an appeal to the recognition of self-ownership must then be rejected. As both rights of the rights-antinomy rest on an appeal to the recognition of self-ownership in commodity exchange, both must then be rejected.

A universalisability principle also undermines premise (1). A universalisability principle can be used to reject (1) by rejecting the system of which (1) is but a part, if the conditions under which (1) can apply are the conditions of a system that reinforces the pursuit of a maxim that cannot be universalised. For it to be a law that commodities are purchased at prices proportional to value, labour power must be a commodity, and be purchased for a wage that purchases the means of reproducing labour power. These are the conditions of the system of capitalist production. If labour power generally is purchased for this wage, a competitive dynamic will lead wage-labour to be put to work for continuous money maximisation. But not all firms and all wage-labourers can simultaneously maximise their monetary wealth by performing the functions of capital and wage-labour.[168] If (1) is but a component of a system that reinforces the pursuit of continuous money maximisation, which cannot be universalised, (1) can be rejected on the same basis as (2).

A participant in a working-class movement to limit the working day can will the principle that a system-reinforced end that cannot be universalised is prohibited. First of all, this principle is consistent with participation in a working-class movement. It is not contrary to this principle to discharge a duty to redress a working-class disadvantage by participating in a movement. Yet something more needs to be said, for it is not consistent with all of the premises of the antithesis of the rights-antinomy, that there is a right to a limited working day. Assertion of this right allowed workers to recognise one another as equally entitled to a limited working day in the first place. If a participant in a working-

---

168   See ch. 8, sec. 10.

class movement to limit the working day is to be able to will a principle that requires them to reject the premises of the proof of this right, it must serve to fill the void left by abandoning the rights claim it undermines. It must supply an independent justification for the movement's objective. The justification supplied by a system universalisability principle is: a limit on the working day in capitalist firms is a restriction of money maximisation, and hence a restriction of the pursuit of what no one is permitted to do. It is consistent with a commitment to a movement to limit the working day to will this principle, for it offers a participant a non-rights-based reason to value their participation in it.

A participant in a working-class movement to limit the working day also has a more positive reason to will the principle that a system-reinforced end that cannot be universalised is prohibited. For it is relevant for them to resolve the rights-antinomy. If the thesis and antithesis of the rights-antinomy rest on the same premises, anyone who articulates one of its proofs cannot entirely escape the intellectual force of the other. A doubt about either argument must remain, if these rights form an antinomy. In the worker's case, this doubt could affect the resoluteness with which they prosecute their interest in a limited working day by participating in a movement to limit it. As the principle that a system-reinforced end that cannot be universalised is prohibited offers a non-antinomic reason to participate in a working-class movement to limit the working day, a participant in this movement has a positive reason to adopt it, to have a principle with which they can value their participation in it without the doubt induced by appeal to a right that is part of an antinomy.

This is not the end of the matter, however. As the system universalisability principle condemns the system of capitalist production, it is necessary to show that a participant in a working-class movement has a reason to condemn the system of capitalist production, to show that they have a positive reason to adopt it; and to show that the need for recognition that is separable from premise (2) can be better satisfied, if not only (2) is rejected, but the system of capitalist production is abolished. It is necessary, in other words, to show that 'the *revolutionary* watchword, "*Abolition of the wages system!*"'[169] voices an interest of a participant in a working-class movement to limit the working day. The latter has an interest in the abolition of the system of capitalist production if they can believe that its abolition would remove the cause of the type of effect that this movement seeks to cancel. For it is wearisome, as

169   *MECW*, 20, p. 149.

Marx writes in *Value, Price and Profit*, to be 'fighting with effects, but not with the causes of those effects'.[170]

Consider, first, what the failure of workplace and trade-specific struggles to limit the working day that precede this working-class movement reveals. It reveals that capitalist firms are compelled to impose excessive labour by the competitive handicap they would suffer if they did not impose it. If the compulsion to impose excessive labour is known to result from competition, it is known to be a tendency inherent to all capitalist firms, in the absence of legal limits preventing it. So, from these failures, a participant in the working-class movement to limit the working day can believe that all capitalist firms are indifferent to whom they hire, as long as one individual's labour is as good a means for their money maximisation as the next's.

In light of this, they can conclude that capitalist firms, both individually and collectively, will always oppose restrictions on labour contracts or taxes on their returns that seek to guarantee the reproduction of the current population of producers for no further reason than that they are producers; which is to say, *whether or not* the conditions of the labour market leave capitalist firms dependent on re-hiring them. By implication, they can believe that any movement to guarantee their reproduction just as such will encounter capitalist firms' opposition. As long as the system of capitalist production remains, movements to guarantee current producers' reproduction for no further reason than that they are producers will have to struggle against it. Yet the movement to limit the working day to forestall excessive labour is but one such type of movement. It is but one such type of movement that an association of unions may support, in the pursuit of what all its members are owed. So, even if excessive labour is suspended by the success of a movement to limit the working day, any other measure to reproduce the current population of producers for no further reason than that they are producers that would place a restriction on labour contracts or a tax on firms will have to be fought for. Only if the system of capitalist production is itself abolished can the cause of such struggles be removed. A participant in a working-class movement to limit the working day has a positive reason to adopt a principle that condemns the system of capitalist production, for its application would abolish the cause of the type of effect that it is foreseeable that working-class movements like the one to limit the working day may always have to combat.

The application of the system universalisability principle would also satisfy the need for recognition that is expressed in the form of premise (2). (2) gives

---

170   *MECW*, 20, p. 148.

expression to the need for recognition in a form, self-ownership, that sustains an antinomy. While commodity exchangers cannot recognise one another in some other form, it is possible to satisfy the need for recognition in a form of production that lacks commodity exchange. Commodity exchange is an independent exchange: products exchange as separate products. As the exchange of commodities is not guided by a policy in respect of the total social product, there can be no recognition, in commodity exchange, of actors as members of society as a whole. In commodity exchange, *recognition is founded on non-recognition*; that is, on commodity possession.[171] The application of a system universalisability principle in the context of other principles of self-legislative human community could better satisfy the need for recognition, then, if such principles enable the recognition, in production, of actors as members of society. They do this if they inform a form of society in which actors engage in rewarding and evidently harmonious activity. For then actors are recognised as its members, in virtue of knowing that structures are in place that encourage them to contribute to a total product through rewarding and evidently harmonious activity. For in knowing this, each can assume that others, like them, put a value on productive activities being harmonious, and so each can assume that they have more than just an instrumental status in valued others' ends.

While a participant in a working-class movement to limit the working day to forestall excessive labour can will a principle with which to resolve the rights-antinomy even if it condemns capitalism, a capitalist cannot. It is impossible to will two incompatible states of affairs. As a capitalist pursues continuous money maximisation, a capitalist cannot will anything that prohibits its pursuit. If the system universalisability principle is the only principle with which to resolve the rights-antinomy, then the capitalist is not able to resolve it. If so, a participant in a working-class movement has interest privilege over a capitalist, for only the former could will a principle that there is an impartial reason to apply, the latter being that of resolving an antinomy in 'the world's own principles'.[172]

Imagine, for the sake of argument, that a different defensible principle, other than the system universalisability principle, could resolve the rights-antinomy. The mere availability of such a principle would not compromise the existence of a 'standpoint of the proletariat'.[173] To reject the claim of interest privilege, it would be necessary to argue that a *capitalist* is able to conceive of and will such a principle. This is denied.

---

171   See ch. 9, sec. 2.
172   *MEW*, 1, p. 345; *MECW*, 3, p. 144.
173   Lukács 1977, p. 331; Lukács 1968, p. 149.

As argued in denying the capitalist class interest claim, the fact of excessive labour is not, in and of itself, contrary to the interest of the capitalist class. As excessive labour may accord with the capitalist class interest, a capitalist cannot be led by their class interest to develop an interest in a principle that, if applied, would root out the cause of excessive labour. Class interest does not give a capitalist a principled reason to reject any premises of the rights-antinomy. Depending on the conditions of the labour market, the risks for public health or the levels of unrest that may be provoked, it may be advantageous for a capitalist class in a *particular time and place* to refrain from imposing excessive labour. But as it is only ever advantageous for a capitalist class to do so under certain contingent conditions, and not as a matter of principle, a capitalist cannot will to reject a premise of the rights-antinomy by virtue of willing a principle. Hence, a capitalist cannot resolve the rights-antinomy.

The rights-antinomy is not the only antinomy of the commodity form. The commodity form also generates an antinomy of natural rights and popular authorisation.[174] It seems to be the case both that government action is only justified if and because it guarantees natural rights, *and* that government action is only justified if and because it is authorised by a decision of the people for equal liberty. It is a further question whether a participant in a working-class movement to limit the working day can resolve this antinomy.

Before asking whether a participant in a working-class movement to limit the working day can affirm a principle with which to resolve the antinomy of natural rights and popular authorisation, a question of relevance arises. It is directly relevant for them to resolve the rights-antinomy. A resolution of the rights-antinomy removes a doubt that could only lessen their resoluteness in the pursuit of this movement's stated objective. By contrast, the relevance of a resolution of the antinomy of natural rights and popular authorisation may seem open to question. It is not this movement's express objective to remove a type of justification for government action.

Yet it is still relevant for a participant in this movement to resolve the antinomy of natural rights and popular authorisation. A working-class movement to limit the working day is likely to confront conduct licenced by its thesis, and conduct licenced by its antithesis. It is likely to confront government inaction justified by non-interference in the natural right of contract, and police measures to curtail a movement whose objective is to restrict equal liberty, even, perhaps, at the cost of its participants' rights. To the extent that a working-class movement confronts actions that draw on each of these justifications, a res-

---

174   See ch. 11, sec. 4.

olution of the antinomy of natural rights and popular authorisation can only embolden its participants. As a resolution of the antinomy of natural rights and popular authorisation is relevant for a participant in a working-class movement to limit the working day, we can turn to the question of whether they possess the concept and the will to resolve it.

To resolve an antinomy, it is necessary to reject one or more of its premises. In the case of the antinomy of natural rights and popular authorisation, both proofs rest on the premises: each individual has an exclusive claim to their parts and capacities; and government action is justified in relation to this. So, the antinomy of natural rights and popular authorisation rests on a premise similar to premise (2) of the rights-antinomy; both posit self-ownership. The system universalisability principle used to reject (2) can also, therefore, be used to reject a premise of the antinomy of natural rights and popular authorisation. If the same principle can be used to reject premises of both antinomies, the argument for why a participant in the working-class movement to limit the working day has the concept and will to resolve the rights-antinomy is also an argument to the effect that they can reject a premise of the antinomy of natural rights and popular authorisation.

An antinomy is only resolved, however, by showing that any need separable from it can be better satisfied after the rejected premise is rejected. If a need for constituted power under a constitution remains even after both antinomies of the commodity form are avoided, it is necessary to show that, if the premise of self-ownership is rejected, government action can be justified in some other way. Even if constituted power is to operate under the kind of 'communal constitution'[175] Marx praised in *The Civil War in France*, it requires some sort of justification.

A participant in a working-class movement to limit the working day is committed to popular sovereignty, in virtue of the fact that this informal movement applies pressure from without vis-à-vis a representative form of government to achieve its end. So, the justification of government action to be given after both antinomies of the commodity form are avoided must be consistent not only with a resolution of the rights-antinomy, but also with popular sovereignty. The resolution of the rights-antinomy rests on a duty to the whole, the system universalisability principle. So, to resolve the antinomy of natural rights and popular authorisation, it must be possible to justify a government that upholds a duty to the whole as normatively more fundamental than rights as a more radical realisation of popular sovereignty. Just as a need for recognition can

---

175   *MECW*, 22, p. 332.

be said to be better satisfied if recognition is freed from non-recognition; so a need for a popular constituted power can be said to be better satisfied if it is freed from something opposed to popular sovereignty. A government is no longer based on something opposed to popular sovereignty if it ceases to presuppose an executive power in charge of a government administration whose spirit is bureaucratic authority. For if the aim of law-making is to regulate social life, to have laws implemented in a spirit opposed to the spirit in which they are proclaimed is for the people to have alienated its will in respect of their implementation. A government that upholds a duty to the whole as normatively more fundamental than rights can free popular sovereignty from what is opposed to it, by enforcing duties to the whole that make all its powers public powers.

All that remains is to relate the possibility of resolving both antinomies to the thesis of political awareness from without. In *What is to be Done?*, Lenin advances the thesis that workers can acquire class political awareness only from without their movements to improve their terms of employment.[176] The thesis admits of two versions, however. The strong version says that both (a) the sociological understanding required for the comprehensive context-dependent judgement of bads, and (b) the capacity to identify and order bad principles from a revolutionary socialist point of view, can only be acquired by workers from without the movements to improve their terms of employment. The weak version merely says that (a) can only be acquired by workers from without such movements.

The interaction-recognition-antinomy thesis rejects the strong version of the thesis of political awareness from without. Workers' position in and practical response to the rights-antinomy allow a participant in a working-class movement to limit the working day to resolve both antinomies, from the revolutionary socialist point of view of the system universalisability principle, which rests on the value of 'social humanity'.[177] Not all of the conditions for class political awareness must be acquired from without the movements to improve workers' terms of employment.

To be sure, the limited goals of movements to improve workers' terms of employment do not require participants to reflect on all the conditions of life they would need to grasp to take an informed public stance on every issue. That being said, the thesis of political awareness from without is of limited value. The tricky part is to explain, by appeal to antinomy, real abstraction and recog-

---

176   Lenin 2006, pp. 745–6; see ch. 1, sec. 4.
177   *MEW*, 3, p. 7; *MECW*, 5, p. 5.

nition, why its strong version is false. As a first step, 'the problem of labour time'[178] must be singled out from other terms of employment, such as wages. The thesis of political awareness from without is as much an unclear statement of a problem as a thesis.

---

178   Lukács 1977, p. 363; Lukács 1968, p. 178.

Conclusion

The interaction-recognition-antinomy thesis connects capitalist production, the state and classes through a conception of interaction, recognition and antinomy. Rather than recapitulate the overall argument of the thesis, the significance of three specific points may be brought out, concerning the nature and injustice of exploitation; the derivation of the state; and the transition from class in itself to class for itself. The first suggests a novel explanation for Analytical Marxism's 'total disappearance'.[1]

1 Exploitation and Injustice

Production with wage-labour for continuous money maximisation was characterised as exploitative by adopting a system universalisability conception of exploitation. As this conception of exploitation rests on a system-level universalisability test, it raises the challenge of explaining why some maxims cannot be thought as universal laws of human nature. An interactional account of a social relation suggests an answer. A maxim may require another to perform a standard action of social affecting to the one who adopts it. The conception of a hypothetical world that includes a maxim's counterpart universal law of human nature will contain a logical contradiction if this standard action of social affecting is incompatible with how others must act once the maxim is known to be permissible, and adopted by all who satisfy its conditions.

To characterise capital as exploitative, there must be a logical contradiction in the conception of a hypothetical world that includes the universal law of human nature: everyone, when their monetary wealth is at stake, cannot but put their possessions to economic use, and cannot but thereby maximise their monetary wealth. The issue is whether all capitalist firms and all those who perform the function of wage-labour can maximise their monetary wealth, just by virtue of these functions. Wage-labourers cannot succeed, owing to capitalist firms' money-maximising response. Marx's value theory is relevant for a conception of capitalist labour-exploitation, for its distinction between use-value and value explains why this is so.

The system universalisability conception of exploitation facilitates a system universalisability principle of justice, which says: exclusive advantages

---

1 Evans 2007, p. xvi; see also Bertram 2010, p. 33.

obtained by pursuing system-reinforced ends that cannot be universalised are unjust. A system universalisability principle is a principle of justice if it is enforceable, and if it can be recommended on the basis that antinomies in the social world ought to be resolved. A system universalisability principle of justice condemns capitalism as unjust, because money maximisation fails the system-level universalisability test.

This principle of justice shows up the mistake in Cohen's argument that advocates of Marx's value theory can only believe that it can serve as a premise in an argument for the injustice of capitalist exploitation by embracing the different (and, according to Marx's value theory, false) view that 'labour and labour alone creates value'.[2] On the system universalisability conception of exploitation, the argument for saying that capitalist production is exploitative is elaborated by distinguishing use-value and value. It does not require a premise about the *creation* of value, such as the premise that producers create value (which, according to Marx's value theory, is false, since the socially necessary labour time that determines value 'is that required now, not that required when [the commodity] was produced').[3] Cohen's argument, supposedly a 'demolition'[4] of the relevance of Marx's value theory for a charge of exploitation against capitalism, is a symptom of Cohen's own false belief that exploitation rests on the premise that labour creates something. For Cohen, 'what matters, ideologically, is what creates that thing',[5] the product. Rather than confronting value-based charges of capitalist exploitation on their own terms, Cohen ungraciously saddled them all with a version of this belief. Cohen assumed that advocates of Marx's value theory could only concoct a charge of capitalist exploitation by illegitimately transferring this creation claim into the dimension of value, which is the object of this theory.[6] But a charge of capitalist exploitation need not rest on any creation claim. It may rest on a claim about the non-universalisability of a system-reinforced end. By supporting this claim, Marx's value theory supports a charge of exploitation against capitalism.

The value underpinning the system universalisability principle of justice is the autonomy of 'social humanity',[7] or self-legislative human community. The general concept of freedom as autonomy is freedom in obeying a self-given law.

---

2   Cohen 1988, p. 213. The sole piece of evidence Cohen presents for ascribing this premise to Marx is a miscitation of a mistranslation. Compare Cohen 1988, p. 222 with *MEW*, 23, p. 53; *MECW*, 35, p. 48; Marx 1976, p. 129.
3   Cohen 1988, p. 217.
4   Cohen 2013, p. 153.
5   Cohen 1995, p. 174.
6   To be sure, *some* Marxists use the language of creation; see ch. 8, sec. 1.
7   *MEW*, 3, p. 7; *MECW*, 5, p. 5.

Human autonomy can be conceived at the level of a human community, for it is the human community that has the power to act universally. If autonomy is conceived at the level of a human community, it consists in acting in accordance with public principles that accurately reflect the harmonious dynamics of generalised relations. The system of capitalist production is contrary to self-legislative human community, because it is systematically divisive.

One reason for believing that the system universalisability principle of justice can belong to a reconstruction of Marx's thought is that it reconciles two far less controversial commitments. No one could reasonably doubt that Marx advocated the revolutionary overthrow of capitalism in favour of a classless society initially based on enforceable principles that treat everyone equally in the relevant respect; or that he valued freedom. The system universalisability principle of justice, unlike many other principles, can reconcile the implications of these views. This is what the capitalism, rights and injustice problem aimed to test. Those who seek to overthrow a wealthy and powerful class must be prepared to (threaten to) use force against them, and to call on all their supporters to make sacrifices, for the sake of their objective. But for socialists like Marx, this entails a commitment to a principle of justice; for otherwise, the revolution is not a preparation for socialism. Further, for Marx, freedom requires an institutionalised awareness that individuals' rewarding activities are harmonious. This awareness presupposes public principles that accurately reflect harmonious social dynamics. As a legal code whose basic principle is a principle of right would tacitly recognise (disharmonious) social dynamics that are not publicly proclaimed, a free association cannot rest on such a legal code. Marx's commitments to socialist revolution and freedom in association can only be reconciled, therefore, by a principle of justice that avoids appeal to right. The system universalisability principle of justice answers to this need. Indeed, the interaction-recognition-antinomy thesis shows that Marx's writings suggest an argumentative strategy for affirming this principle that those who reject the idea that Marx affirms any principle of justice have not anticipated. For this argumentative strategy is consistent with believing that Marx does not condemn capitalism by appeal to eternal truths, moral goods, rights, or post-capitalist standards of distribution; that a principle of justice must be recommended on impartial grounds; and that the best society, for Marx, is beyond right and beyond justice.

It has been repeatedly noted that questions of justice are irreducible to questions of rights. The enforcement of a duty need not give anyone a right, understood as an unconditional advantage. An analysis of the concept of use-value and how it differs from the concept of an economic good allowed questions of justice to be posed as irreducible to questions of rights. The value of self-legislative human community explains the importance of principles of justice that are not principles of rights. If a value underpins a principle of justice, the latter must be enforced in a form that respects this value. If freedom of choice is the value underpinning a principle of justice, this principle must be enforced in a form that allows individual preferences to be respected: namely, in the form of rights. But if the value that underpins a principle of justice is self-legislative human community, this principle need not be enforced in the form of rights. As the system universalisability principle of justice is underpinned by the value of self-legislative human community, it is not enforced in the form of rights.

The account of the injustice of capitalism defended here is therefore distinct from all three existing positions within the Anglophone debate on Marx and justice, although it asks a different question. The question addressed in the Anglophone debate on Marx and justice is: did Marx think that capitalism is unjust? Three positions are defended: Marx was consistent in never condemning capitalism on grounds of justice or right; Marx consistently condemned capitalism as unjust by appeal to right; Marx condemned capitalism as unjust by appeal to right but did not always realise that he did so. The arguments for these positions all rest on two false premises. They rest on the false substantive premise that all duties have correlative rights; and on the false interpretive premise that capitalist exploitation belongs to the dimension of value. Marxists who believe that Marx is confused about justice are themselves confused about justice.

Accordingly, it is possible to hold a fourth position, namely: Marx condemned the use of labour in capitalism as unjust, but did not condemn capitalism by appeal to right, and simply by virtue of this, Marx is not inconsistent. The interaction-recognition-antinomy thesis is compatible with taking this fourth position. But it is not addressed to the same question. A reconstruction extends an author's claims in a direction consistent with the text, to bring out an underlying thesis. It is distinct from an interpretation of what an author had in mind. The system universalisability principle of justice belongs to a reconstruction, because it justifies the *Grundrisse*'s description of labour for the capitalist as a usurpation of 'free time' that wrongs 'society'[8] by developing the thought behind its counterfactual thought experiment. As Marx never put these thoughts together, however, or connected them to *Capital*'s account of recognition and the rights-antinomy, the system universalisability principle of justice is not offered as an interpretation. Rather, what the interaction-

---

8   *MEW*, 42, p. 534; *MECW*, 29, p. 22; Marx, 1973a, p. 634.

recognition-antinomy thesis says is that an assessment of the justice of capital-ism that is of value to Marx's project and suggested by Marx's texts is: the use of labour in capitalism is unjust, not by the standard of a rights-creating principle, but by a system universalisability principle of justice. Two points in favour of this claim are that the interaction-recognition-antinomy thesis is able to offer a critique of capitalist labour-domination, and the state of capitalist society, from the perspective of the same value that underpins this principle, self-legislative human community; and that it is able to show that a participant in a working-class movement can will this principle, to resolve the rights-antinomy that *Capital* describes.

What may be added here is a note to defuse a kind of scepticism towards the system universalisability principle of justice. A sceptic might hold that this principle imports an idea from Kant that is foreign to Marx. One response to this scepticism was given above: the system universalisability principle of justice can belong to a reconstruction of Marx's texts, because, without depart-ing from Marx's value theory, it reconciles Marx's commitments to socialist revolution and freedom. One additional reason to regard this extension of Marx's texts as fruitful is that it can solve the exploitation and need problem. But a further response can be suggested.

It is one thing to engage explicitly with a thinker and another to accept their premises. The argument for the system universalisability principle of justice engaged with Kant. Nonetheless, it rejects two features of Kant's thought that some contributions to the Anglophone debate on Marx and justice cannot claim to reject, even if they do not engage with Kant. Kant divides the doc-trine of right and the doctrine of virtue on the basis that duties belonging to the former are grounded without appeal to ends.[9] Further, the universalisabil-ity test that belongs to Kant's ethics is an individual-level test, not a system-level test. The system universalisability principle of justice departs from Kant on both scores. It is a system-level test that presupposes that a principle of justice can evaluate ends.

By contrast, some contributions to the Anglophone debate on Marx and justice cannot claim to depart from Kant on these scores. Insofar as some con-tributions conclude that Marx condemns capitalism on grounds of distributive justice, Marx is not taken to raise a charge of injustice against capitalism based on an evaluation of ends. The charge Marx is taken to raise can be raised while holding that principles of justice abstract from ends. Moreover, insofar as authors like Cohen and Roemer evaluate candidate principles of exploita-

---

9   Kant 1991, 6: 230, 239.

tion by their implications for *two*-person societies,[10] and no two-person society can contain a *system* of relations, some contributions suppose that the Marxist charge of exploitation that is to be levelled against capitalism is not aimed at a system. The charge of exploitation these contributions defend is consistent with the anti-Marxist view that, contrary to what Marx says in the Preface to the First Edition of *Capital*, principles of justice may make 'the individual responsible for relations whose creature they socially remain'.[11] On both of these scores, the system universalisability principle of justice is both less Kantian and closer to Marx than some contemporary thinking about justice among Marx scholars that does not engage explicitly with Kant.

If, as the *Grundrisse* claims, there is '*theft of alien [fremder] labour time*',[12] it must be possible for a principle of justice to evaluate ends. If, as *The German Ideology* says, 'the central relations of exploitation are determined independently of the will of individuals by production as a whole',[13] it must be possible to define capitalist labour-exploitation at the level of a system. The further response to the sceptic of the system universalisability principle of justice who believes that it has too much of a Kantian whiff about it, therefore, is this: *you* cannot oppose the inclusion of the system universalisability principle of justice within a Marxist thesis on the grounds that it is too Kantian for a Marxist thesis only to return to a position that is tacitly even more Kantian. But how is that not the effect of opposing the inclusion of this principle in a Marxist thesis, if the consequence of opposing its inclusion is to return to a conception of justice (whether positively taken up or negatively dismissed) that both abstracts from ends and focuses on individuals?

2   The Disappearance of Analytical Marxism

If a system universalisability principle of justice can belong to a Marxist thesis, it is possible to shatter the self-told narrative around the disappearance of Analytical Marxism. Analytical Marxism has long ceased to be a live movement, of course. But it is one thing for Analytical Marxism to cease as a live movement, and another for its influence on how Marx is read or viewed to die out. One reason to undermine the self-told narrative around Analytical Marxism's disap-

---

10   Cohen 1995, pp. 94–5, p. 205; Roemer 1986b, pp. 272–3.
11   *MEW*, 23, p. 16; *MECW*, 35, p. 10; Marx 1976, p. 92; compare Cohen's emphasis on individual 'responsibility' at Cohen 2011, p. 19.
12   *MEW*, 42, p. 601; *MECW*, 29, p. 91; Marx 1973a, p. 705.
13   *MEW*, 3, p. 398; *MECW*, 5, p. 413.

pearance is to embolden other Marxist projects. Cohen's account of Analytical Marxism's disappearance is that Analytical Marxism's Marxism led to its undoing. By contrast, the interaction-recognition-antinomy thesis suggests that the analytical constraints of Analytical Marxism led to its undoing.

Consider, first, how Cohen could view his intellectual trajectory, from *Karl Marx's Theory of History* (1978) to *Self-Ownership, Freedom and Equality* (1995).[14] In the former, history is presented as the development of productive power, and the rise and fall of forms of society as they enable and constrain that development.[15] This theory of history, Cohen comes to concede, ignores some of the trends that make it harder for the final form of society it predicts, socialism, to come about. It overstates the level of material wealth that socialism can promise;[16] and it exaggerates the growth of the agent that is to bring socialism about, the working-class, and the coincidence of its characteristics.[17] As Marx's theory of history is in part wrong about the facts, the coming of socialism requires a task that Marx did not sufficiently anticipate. People will have to be more convinced of socialism's normative superiority to capitalism in the context of scarcity than Marx had thought, by more finely grained arguments than Marx provides. On Cohen's account, then, the disappearance of Analytical Marxism is explained by the fact that Analytical Marxists acknowledged an intellectual task that Marxism was not equipped to tackle. For in Cohen's view, 'scientific socialism offers no ideals or values to the proletariat'.[18]

The interaction-recognition-antinomy thesis allows and requires this explanation of Analytical Marxism's disappearance to be rejected. The fact that it is true that socialism will only come about if at least some people are convinced of its ethical superiority in a context of scarcity, and hence that an intellectual project in its defence will need to come up with some such argument to be politically relevant, is not a reason to downgrade the Marxist character of its intellectual defence. It is possible to argue for socialism's normative superiority from a Marxist perspective by appeal to the value of self-legislative human community. This value informs a system universalisability principle of justice that condemns the system of capitalist production as unjust. This value and principle can be defended by reconstructing Marx's texts. Arguably, they cannot be defended without reconstructing Marx's texts.

---

14   For further remarks, see Furner forthcoming (2019).
15   Cohen 1978, p. x, p. 148.
16   Cohen 1995, pp. 6–7; Cohen 2001, p. 115.
17   Cohen 1995, pp. 154–5.
18   Cohen 2001, p. 64.

If the system universalisability principle of justice can belong to a Marxist thesis, it is false that an interest in normative questions left Analytical Marxists acknowledging an intellectual task that Marxism was not equipped to tackle. Analytical Marxism's disappearance cannot then be explained by the fact that it took on a task that Marxism was not equipped to tackle. A different explanation must be sought: Analytical Marxism disappeared because it could only look to Marx's texts for answers to its normative questions from within its own analytical constraints.

The reason why Analytical Marxism disappeared is found in Cohen's *Self-Ownership, Freedom and Equality* (*SFE*), which largely expands articles dating from the mid-1980s to the early 1990s.[19] Cohen's aim in *SFE* was to 'diminish the appeal'[20] of the libertarian principle of self-ownership. The idea of socialism was on the defensive, and libertarianism was a thorn in the side of arguments against the retrenchment of the welfare state.[21]

In seeking to diminish the appeal of the principle of self-ownership, *SFE* judged Marx unhelpful at best, and complicit at worst. According to *SFE*, Marx's critique of capitalism and vision of communism either avoid normative arguments about justice,[22] or tacitly rely on the principle of self-ownership.[23] To oppose self-ownership, it concluded, 'in the spirit of Marxism, it is necessary to embrace the anti-self-ownership tenet' in the doctrines of distributive justice proposed by 'Ronald Dworkin and John Rawls', that people's 'talents' are 'resources over the fruits of whose exercise the community as a whole may legitimately dispose'.[24]

To support this reading of Marx's attitude to self-ownership, Cohen misquoted a text, and utilised a shoddy translation.[25] This philological tangle might

---

19   Cohen 1995, p. x.

20   Cohen 1995, p. 230.

21   Cohen 1995, p. 151.

22   Cohen 1995, p. 6, p. 126, p. 139.

23   Cohen 1995, pp. 134–5, p. 145, p. 197.

24   Cohen 1995, pp. 118–19.

25   (1) To support the claim that Marx's critique of capitalist exploitation tacitly relies on a principle of self-ownership, Cohen repeatedly misquotes a translation of the *Grundrisse* that correctly renders '*fremd*' as 'alien' (see ch. 10, sec. 3) as if it had instead used the ends-indeterminate words 'another' or 'another person' (compare Cohen 1995, p. 145, p. 150, p. 197, Cohen 1983a, p. 443 and Cohen 1990, p. 365 with *MEW*, 42, p. 601; *MECW*, 29, p. 91; Marx 1973a, p. 705). (2) To ram home *SFE*'s claim that Marx thought that equality would be delivered by material abundance (Cohen 1995, pp. 6–7; see also Cohen 2001, p. 115), making it unnecessary for him to reject the principle of self-ownership, *SFE* uses the words 'abundance/abundantly' over 50 times. They are attributed to Marx at Cohen 1995, p. 126, on the basis of the mistranslation documented in the appendix to ch. 1.

be unremarkable, if it were not a symptom of the fact that the analytical constraints of Analytical Marxism are obstacles on using Marx's texts to diminish the appeal of self-ownership. As the interaction-recognition-antinomy thesis shows, Marx's texts can be read to suggest that as-if mutual recognition in purchase and sale explains (and so problematises) the belief in a principle of self-ownership; that the principle of self-ownership maximises equal liberty and therefore licences an exploitative system that reinforces the pursuit of ends that cannot be universalised; and that it serves as a premise in antinomies. The analytical constraints of Analytical Marxism preclude the uptake of these arguments, however.

Mutual recognition, where each actor is both recogniser and recognisee, and is only the one because they are the other, has a structure beyond the purview of analysis-NS. The latter eschews any *explanans* in which actors are conditioned by others in the same respect in which they condition those others. Tellingly, Analytical Marxists do not examine *Capital*'s account of mutual recognition in commodity exchange that was once said to be 'the most prominent remark of all'[26] in German language debate on Marx's view of law. Analysis-NS also precludes any universalisability test that tests if everyone can successfully adopt a maxim if it is hypothetically assumed that any one performance of it is but an instance of everyone in the same conditions performing it by causal necessity. Tellingly, Elster misconstrues Kant's CC test as a test for a fallacy of composition, which *is* consistent with analysis-NS. The argumentative figure of antinomy, which exceeds 'thinking as understanding',[27] also appears to lie beyond analysis-BS. Tellingly, even those Analytical Marxist commentaries that get as far as citing a part of *Capital*'s antinomy passage offer no account of the rights-antinomy it describes.[28]

If, therefore, SFE regarded Marx's texts as unhelpful for constructing arguments with which to diminish the appeal of self-ownership, that had little to do with Marx's texts. But that did not stop SFE from having a fateful consequence for Marx's texts. It had set a practical political problem that any socialist had to answer, but any Analytical Marxist must struggle to answer, from an Analytical Marxist reading of Marx's texts. SFE thus provided sufficient cause for any Analytical Marxist to move away from Marx's texts. It had to spell the end of Analytical Marxism, notwithstanding the fact that an anti-self-ownership Marxist who is not an Analytical Marxist can get further with the *Grundrisse*

---

26   Tuschling 1976, p. 12.
27   Hegel 1986c, § 80; Hegel 1991b, § 80.
28   See Elster 1985, p. 186; Peffer 1990, p. 335; Wetherly 1992, p. 185.

and *Capital* than an anti-self-ownership socialist can get with Dworkin's or Rawls's doctrines of distributive justice.

3   The State of Capitalist Society

Capital and *Notes on Wagner* suggest a distinctive, commodity form based approach to the state of capitalist society. Other than Pashukanis, however, few have attempted to develop these suggestions. The interaction-recognition antinomy thesis develops them by relating them to Marx's writings from the 1840s. As-if mutual recognition of private property ownership and personhood in purchase and sale can be linked to a social interest in security, to explain the freedom of will that encourages commodity exchangers to demand equal liberty. This demand is related to popular sovereignty, by imagining how the system of capitalist production would lead actors to respond to a sovereign monarch. Developing Marx's remarks in this way led to the formulation of an antinomy in the justification of government action, and to a derivation of the juridical logic of freedom of choice and the political logic of representation.

The first step was to outline a pragmatic conception of recognition, on which recognition consists of action that a recognisee can experience as another's positive evaluation of them. Whether an actor can experience another's action as extending positive evaluation to them will depend on the in-order-to motive they can ascribe to the other, in light of their own stock of experiences and projects. This pragmatic conception of recognition was used to give contour to Pashukanis's notion of as-if recognition.

The challenge that then arose can be represented as one of reconciling three premises: only genuine recognition enables freedom of will; purchase and sale does not provide genuine recognition; actors in capitalism possess freedom of will in virtue of purchase and sale. Given the latter premise, and the absence of genuine recognition in purchase and sale, there is a temptation to water down the conception of recognition. The result of giving in to that temptation is illustrated by Honneth's account of recognition in *Freedom's Right*. In attempting to defend a reformed capitalism from the perspective of a social theory of recognition, *Freedom's Right* adopts a watered-down conception of recognition, on which it suffices, for recognition, to experience another as pursing plans that enable one's own.[29] This is some way off the earlier, expressive

---

29   See ch. 1, sec. 2.

conception of recognition that Honneth defended in *Struggle for Recognition*, and which was examined in chapter 9.

The challenge, then, is to offer a recognition-based account of the fact that actors in capitalism exhibit the freedom of will of persons in virtue of purchase and sale, while retaining a robust conception of recognition and entertaining no illusions about commodity exchangers' motivations. The strategy pursued was to identify a social interest in security leading commodity exchangers to articulate the principle that *animus domini* accompanying detention ought to be respected, and to argue that, by virtue of that articulation, commodity exchangers can recognise one another as persons. If, as a consequence, commodity exchangers are moved to use their parts, capacities and possessions without regard to another's permission or instruction, then that explains their belief in a principle of self-ownership, in a form that undercuts this belief.

Each commodity exchanger, as a person and private property owner, has a guarantee related reason and a recognition related reason to call for absolute innate rights, as the basis of government. Further, capital accumulation cannot be guaranteed by a sovereign monarch. Any confrontation between the two must lead to the raising of a demand for equal liberty in the name of the people. Two incompatible supra-legal justifications for government action then arise: natural rights, and the popular decision for equal liberty. It appears that government action is justified only if it guarantees natural rights, and that government action is justified only if it adopts the means to (including the means for preserving itself as the condition to) uphold equal liberty. This antinomy implies that a law-making assembly's representation of the people is only limited one way or the other if and insofar as a constitutional court recognises a relation of priority in favour of norms that guarantee rights or norms that acknowledge a government's authorisation, a decision that is not itself determined one way or the other by a constitution. Even then, if a representative assembly holds the executive to account for its actions in what is understood to be a new situation, the antinomy introduces indeterminacy into what actions it will scrutinise, and what justifications it will hear and accept.

A derivation is a type of causal explanation that shows that an *explanandum* must register its *explanans* as just one of the phenomena subject to its logic. Commodity form philosophy permits derivations in which the commodity form, or something explained by the commodity form, provides the starting point. The juridical logic of freedom of choice is derived from personhood, because the legal code guaranteeing freedom of choice that persons demand guarantees freedom of choice even for those who do not have the will of a person. Political representation is the making present of a people before a public audience by an elected, responsible, independent law-making assembly that claims a monopoly on representation. It is explained by the popular mandate for equal liberty given to the constitution-making power that must be brought into being if a system of capitalist production encounters monarchical sovereignty. The logic of political representation is a derived logic, for by this logic, the image of the people as mandators of equal liberty is just one possible representation of the people.

The interaction-recognition-antinomy thesis offers a variant of state derivation theory, therefore, because its explanation for the antinomy of natural rights and popular authorisation relies on a derivation of the juridical logic of freedom of choice; and because it also derives the political logic of representation. The antinomy of natural rights and popular authorisation, the derivation of these logics, and the above concept of political representation offer elements for a commodity form based approach to the state of capitalist society that remains true to Marx's critique of political economy, through its employment of the argumentative figure of dialectical contradiction. What is specific and fundamental to modern politics, the logic of political representation, is understood as the form of appearance of its opposite, popular mandate. Bourgeois society must mandate a law-making power to establish the independence of a law-making power from mandate.

4   Revolutionary Awareness

The second antinomy identified by the interaction-recognition-antinomy thesis is the rights-antinomy. The rights-antinomy provides the first form in which the micro-level antagonism between capitalist and worker is expressed. Grasping this point is instructive in three respects.

Firstly, it can serve as a guide for the theorisation of classes. Respect for the fact that the rights-antinomy is the first form in which micro-level antagonism between capitalist and worker is expressed can serve as a criterion for assessing conceptions of these classes. The main aim of a Marxist theorisation of classes is to explain how groups related to each other in virtue of a form of production come to engage in class struggle. If the assertions of the rights belonging to the rights-antinomy are the first form of expression of the micro-level antagonism between capitalist and worker, and prompt wider macro-level struggle, any Marxist conception of classes must be based on features that are expressed in and result from this rights-antinomy. In other words, a Marxist conception of class in itself must define the capitalist and working-classes by the interdependent pursuit of antagonistic ends that, if combined with beliefs explained by the relations that these ends have in common, yield the claims forming the rights-antinomy. As modal and all consciousness-free conceptions of class in itself fail in this regard, they are all inadequate. Only an antagonistic interdependency conception of class in itself is adequate to the rights-antinomy. (A developed account of class in itself would, among other things, connect the antagonistic interdependency between capitalist and wage-labourer to capitalist labour-domination, to differentiate middling strata between them. This was not attempted. The interaction-recognition-antinomy thesis is merely a starting point for a more developed account of classes from the perspective of commodity form philosophy).

Secondly, an analysis of the rights-antinomy offers a way to understand what kind of awareness revolutionary awareness is. On the value and recognition of self-ownership interpretation, one of the premises of the rights-antinomy is: commodity exchangers are to recognise one another as self-owners. Now, the practical response set in train by the rights-antinomy is a learning process by which a participant in a working-class movement can come to possess the concept and the will to reject this premise, and resolve the rights-antinomy. So, to say that a belief provides a premise of the rights-antinomy is not to say that those who voice its claims are destined to maintain it. But even if it is the case that a participant in a working-class movement can resolve the rights-antinomy by means of rejecting this premise, that is not to say that everything about it is rejected. A need for recognition cannot be extirpated. Even if a participant in a working-class movement can come to reject the recognition of self-ownership, they cannot extirpate their need for recognition. They can only alter the form in which this need is asserted. One implication of the value and recognition of self-ownership interpretation of the rights-antinomy, therefore, is that *Capital*'s account of the antagonism between capitalist and worker is an account of an antagonism that, from the outset, is reflected in a struggle for recognition. As the need for recognition cannot be extirpated, even if the course of working-class struggle leads to a rejection of the recognition of self-ownership, it is permanently a struggle for recognition.

If working-class struggle is permanently a struggle for recognition, a need for recognition must be reflected in every phase of its development, up to and including its final objective. If working-class struggle is to adopt the abolition of value production as an objective, then that can only be because its abolition can be regarded by a participant in a working-class movement as answering to a need for recognition. As commodity exchange is an independent exchange, there can be no recognition, in commodity exchange, of actors as members of society; recognition is instead founded on non-recognition. The application of a system universalisability principle along with other principles of self-legislative human community could better satisfy a need for recognition, therefore, by freeing recognition from non-recognition, in virtue of freeing production from the independent exchange of products. The need for recognition as a member of a human community could then be satisfied by virtue of the institutionalised awareness that the principles that structures encourage people to observe are principles that harmonise rewarding activities. Accordingly, revolutionary awareness is the awareness that an existing form of society is unable to become a free association, and of the steps necessary to achieve it. Or, put the other way around, Marxism, by theorising such an association as the outcome of the abolition of value production through class struggle, is (in Lukács's phrase) 'the theory of proletarian class struggle'.[30]

Finally, an analysis of the rights-antinomy provides a starting-point for explaining how revolutionary awareness is possible. To ground the possibility for a type of actor to assume a critical stance towards the essential features of capitalism is a necessary task for any critical theory of capitalism that aims to locate a potential in its object to raise itself into a higher form. An antinomy-based account of how a participant in a working-class movement to limit the working day can believe that value production ought to be abolished provides a solution to the agency problem that entails a modification of the idea that 'to assert strong claims of necessity ... and ... to ground revolutionary politics ... [S]tands or falls with his [Marx's] use of dialectical logic'.[31] The grounding of revolutionary politics can at most stand or fall with the use of argumentative figures that exceed what Hegel termed 'thinking as understanding'.[32] The latter include, besides dialectical contradiction, the argumentative figure of antinomy. If not even the tradition of Hegelian Marxism has subjected *Capital*'s antinomy passage to detailed analysis, perhaps this unmodified idea helps to explain why.

It is possible for a participant in a working-class movement to limit the working day to will to abolish value production just by virtue of that participation, because this participant can affirm a system universalisability principle of justice that prohibits the pursuit of continuous money maximisation. The working-class response to excessive labour represented by this movement has the form of a duty to redress a working-class disadvantage. Implicit in this belief is the concept of a prohibition on action that cannot be universalised. A participant in a working-class movement to limit the working day can affirm this prohibition, for, by resolving the rights-antinomy, it removes a doubt that

---

30   Lukács 1977, p. 558; Lukács 1970, p. 52.
31   Smith 1990, p. x.
32   Hegel 1986c, § 80; Hegel 1991b, § 80.

must plague their resoluteness; and, by condemning the system of capitalist production, it condemns the cause of the effects against which working-class movements of its type must otherwise struggle. Not all features of class political awareness need be acquired only from without.

Bibliography

Works by Marx

[No author] 1873, *L'alliance de la democratie socialiste et l'association internationale des travailleurs. Rapport et documents publies par ordre du congres international de la haye*, London: A. Darson.

Bahne, Siegfried 1962, '"Die deutsche Ideologie" von Marx und Engels. Einige Textergänzungen', *International Review of Social History*, 7: 93–104.

Marx, Karl 1970a [1847], 'Misère de la Philosophie', in *Marx-Engels Gesamtausgabe. Erste Abteilung. Band 6. Werke und Schriften von Mai 1846 bis März 1848*, edited by V. Adoratskij, Glashütten im Taunus: Detlev Auvermann.

Marx, Karl 1972, *The Ethnological Notebooks of Karl Marx: Studies of Morgan, Phear, Maine, Lubbock*, edited by Lawrence Krader, Assen: Van Gorcum.

Marx, Karl 1982, 'Über Friedrich Lists Buch "Das nationale System der politischen Ökonomie"', in Friedrich List, *Das Nationale System der politischen Ökonomie*, Berlin: Akademie-Verlag.

Marx, Karl and Friedrich Engels 1956–90, *Werke*, Berlin: Dietz Verlag.

Marx, Karl and Friedrich Engels 1975–, *Marx-Engels-Gesamtausgabe (MEGA)*, herausgegeben von der Internationalen Marx-Engels-Stiftung, Berlin: Akademie Verlag.

Marx, Karl, Friedrich Engels and Joseph Weydemeyer 2004, *Marx-Engels-Jahrbuch 2003. Die deutsche Ideologie. Artikel, Druckvorlagen, Entwürfe, Reinschriftenfragmente und Notizen zu I. Feuerbach und II. Sankt Bruno*, edited by Inge Taubert and Hans Pelger, Berlin: Akademie Verlag.

Translations of Marx's Works

Marx, Karl 1904 [1859], *A Contribution to the Critique of Political Economy*, translated by Nahum Isaak Stone, Chicago: Charles H. Kerr.

Marx, Karl 1967 [1867], 'The Commodity', in *Value: Studies by Marx*, edited and translated by Albert Dragstedt, London: New Park Publications.

Marx, Karl 1970b [1927], *Critique of Hegel's 'Philosophy of Right'*, edited by Joseph O'Malley, translated by Annette Jolin and Joseph O'Malley, Cambridge: Cambridge University Press.

Marx, Karl 1973a [1939], *Grundrisse: Foundations of the Critique of Political Economy (Rough Draft)*, translated by Martin Nicolaus, Harmondsworth: Penguin Books.

Marx, Karl 1973b, *Surveys from Exile. Political Writings. Volume 2*, edited by David Fernbach, translated by Ben Fowkes and Paul Jackson, Harmondsworth: Penguin Books.

Marx, Karl 1974, *The First International and After. Political Writings. Volume 3*, edited by David Fernbach, translated by Joris de Bres, David Fernbach, Paul Jackson, Rosemary Sheed, and Geoffrey Nowell-Smith, Harmondsworth: Penguin Books.

Marx, Karl 1975a, *Early Writings*, translated by Rodney Livingstone and Gregor Benton, Harmondsworth: Penguin Books.

Marx, Karl 1975b, 'Notes (1879–80) on Adolph Wagner', in *Karl Marx. Texts on Method*, edited and translated by Terrell Carver, Oxford: Basil Blackwell.

Marx, Karl 1976 [1867], *Capital. A Critique of Political Economy. Volume 1*, translated by Ben Fowkes, Harmondsworth: Penguin Books.

Marx, Karl 1981 [1894], *Capital: A Critique of Political Economy. Volume 3*, translated by David Fernbach, Harmondsworth: Penguin Books.

Marx, Karl 1994, *Early Political Writings*, edited and translated by Joseph O'Malley, Cambridge: Cambridge University Press.

Marx, Karl 1996, *Later Political Writings*, edited and translated by Terrell Carver, Cambridge: Cambridge University Press.

Marx, Karl and Friedrich Engels 1975–2005, *Collected Works*, London: Lawrence and Wishart.

Other Works

[No author] 1958, *The Doctrine of Saint-Simon: An Exposition; First Year, 1828–1829*, translated by Georg G. Iggers, Boston: Beacon Press.

Acton, Harry B. 1962, *The Illusion of the Epoch: Marxism-Leninism as a Philosophical Creed*, London: Cohen and West.

Adler, Max 1925, *Kant und der Marxismus*, Berlin: E. Laubische Verlagsbuchhandlung.

Adorno, Theodor W. 1966, *Negative Dialektik*, Frankfurt am Main: Suhrkamp.

Adorno, Theodor W. 1973a [1966], *Negative Dialectics*, translated by E.B. Ashton, London: Routledge.

Adorno, Theodor W. 1973b, *Philosophische Terminologie. Band 1*, Frankfurt am Main: Suhrkamp.

Adorno, Theodor W. 1974, *Philosophische Terminologie. Band 2*, Frankfurt am Main: Suhrkamp.

Adorno, Theodor W. 2010, *Einführung in die Dialektik*, Frankfurt am Main: Suhrkamp.

Allen, Derek P.H. 1981, 'Marx and Engels on the Distributive Justice of Capitalism', *Canadian Journal of Philosophy. Supplementary Volume*, 7: 221–50.

Althusser, Louis 1970, 'Idéologie et appareils idéologiques d'État (Notes pour une recherché)', *La Pensée*, 151: 3–38.

Althusser, Louis 1971 [1970], 'Ideology and Ideological State Apparatuses (Notes Towards an Investigation)', in *Lenin and Philosophy and Other Essays*, translated by Ben Brewster, London: Verso.

Althusser, Louis 1994, *Écrits philosophiques et politiques. Tome I. Textes réunis et présentés par François Matheron*, Paris: Stock/IMEC.

Althusser, Louis 1995, *Sur la reproduction*, Paris: Presses Universitaires de France.

Althusser, Louis 2006, *Philosophy of the Encounter: Later Writings, 1978–87*, translated by G.M. Goshgarian, London: Verso.

Althusser, Louis 2014 [1995], *On the Reproduction of Capitalism. Ideology and Ideological State Apparatuses*, translated by G.M. Goshgarian, London: Verso.

Althusser, Louis and Étienne Balibar 1969, *Lire le Capital II*, Paris: François Maspero.

Althusser, Louis and Étienne Balibar 1975 [1969], *Reading Capital*, translated by Ben Brewster, London: New Left Books.

Anderson, Elizabeth 2012, 'Feminist Epistemology and Philosophy of Science', in *The Stanford Encyclopedia of Philosophy (Fall 2012 Edition)*, edited by Edward N. Zalta, available at https://plato.stanford.edu/archives/fall2012/entries/feminism -epistemology/.

Angehrn, Emil 1989, 'Besitz und Eigentum', *Zeitschrift für philosophische Forschung*, 43: 94–110.

Anscombe, Gertrude E.M. 1976, *Intention*, Oxford: Basil Blackwell.

Aristotle 1924 [350 B.C.E.], *Metaphysics. Volume I*, Oxford: Clarendon Press.

Aristotle 1966 [350 B.C.E.], *Metaphysics*, translated by Hippocrates G. Apostle, Bloomington: Indiana University Press.

Arneson, Richard J. 1981, 'What's Wrong with Exploitation', *Ethics*, 91, 2: 202–27.

Arthur, Christopher J. 1997, 'Against the Logical-Historical Method', in *New Investigations of Marx's Method*, edited by Fred Moseley and Martha Campbell, Atlantic Highlands, NJ: Humanities Press.

Arthur, Christopher J. 2002, *The New Dialectic and Marx's* Capital, Leiden: Brill.

Backhaus, Hans-Georg 1999, 'Über den Doppelsinn der Begriffe "Politische Ökonomie" und "Kritik" bei Marx und in der Frankfurter Schule', in *Wolfgang Harich zum Gedächtnis. Band II*, edited by Stefan Dornuf and Reinhard Pitsch, München: Müller und Nerding.

Backhaus, Hans-Georg 2006, 'Die Kritische Theorie als Forschungsprogramm: "Systematische enzyklopädische Analyse der Tauschabstraktion"', in *Für einen realen Humanismus: Festschrift zum 75. Geburtstag von Alfred Schmidt*, edited by Michael Jeske and Wolfgang Jordan, Frankfurt am Main: Peter Lang.

Backhaus, Hans-Georg 2011 [1997], *Dialektik der Wertform*, Freiburg: ça-ira.

Banaji, Jairus 2010, *Theory as History: Essays on Modes of Production and Exploitation*, Leiden: Brill.

Basso, Luca 2012, *Marx and Singularity: From the Early Writings to the* Grundrisse, Brill: Leiden.

Bazard, Hippolyte Carnot, Prosper Enfantin, Olinde Rodrigues, Henri Fournel, Charles Duveyrier and Gustave d'Eichthal [1830], *Doctrine de Saint-Simon*, Milton Keynes: BiblioBazaar.

Becker, August 1844, *Was wollen die Kommunisten?*, Lausanne: S. Irmel.

Beecher, Jonathan and Richard Bienvenu (eds) 1971, *The Utopian Vision of Charles Four-ier: Selected Texts on Work, Love, and Passionate Attraction*, translated by Jonathan Beecher and Richard Bienvenu, Columbia, MO: University of Missouri Press.

Benhabib, Seyla 1986, *Critique, Norm and Utopia: A Study of the Foundations of Critical Theory*, New York: Columbia University Press.

Bensaïd, Daniel 2002 [1995], *Marx for Our Times: Adventures and Misadventures of a Critique*, translated by Gregory Elliott, London: Verso.

Bertram, Christopher 2008, 'Analytical Marxism', in *Critical Companion to Contempor-ary Marxism*, edited by Jacques Bidet and Stathis Kouvélakis, Leiden: Brill.

Bertram, Christopher 2010, 'Analytical Marxism', in *Encyclopaedia of Political Theory. Volume One*, edited by Mark Bevir, London: Sage.

Beyleveld, Deryck and Roger Brownsword 2007, *Consent in the Law*, Portland: Hart.

Bhaskar, Roy 2008 [1993], *Dialectic: The Pulse of Freedom*, London: Routledge.

Bidet, Jacques 2007 [2000], *Exploring Marx's* Capital: *Philosophical, Economic and Polit-ical Dimensions*, translated by David Fernbach, Leiden: Brill.

Bidet, Jacques 2008, 'Bourdieu and Historical Materialism', in *Critical Companion to Contemporary Marxism*, edited by Jacques Bidet and Stathis Kouvélakis, translated by Gregory Elliott, Leiden: Brill.

Birks, Peter 2005, *Unjust Enrichment*, Oxford: Oxford University Press.

Blackledge, Paul 2012, *Marxism and Ethics: Freedom, Desire, and Revolution*, Albany, NY: SUNY Press.

Blanc, Louis 1851, *Plus de Girondins*, Paris: Charles Joubert.

Bloch, Ernst 1918, *Geist der Utopie*, München und Leipzig: Dunckler und Humblot.

Bloch, Ernst 2000 [1918], *The Spirit of Utopia*, translated by Anthony A. Nassar, Stanford: Stanford University Press.

Böckenförde, Ernst-Wolfgang 1991, *Staat, Verfassung, Demokratie*, Frankfurt am Main: Suhrkamp.

Boersema, David 2011, *Philosophy of Human Rights*, Boulder, CO: Westview Press.

Boldt, Hans 1967, *Rechtsstaat und Ausnahmezustand*, Berlin: Duncker und Humblot.

Bonefeld, Werner 2014, *Critical Theory and the Critique of Political Economy: On Subver-sion and Negative Reason*, New York: Bloomsbury.

Booth, William James 1993, 'The Limits of Autonomy: Karl Marx's Kant Critique', in *Kant and Political Philosophy: The Contemporary Legacy*, edited by Ronald Beiner and Wil-liam James Booth, New Haven, CT: Yale University Press.

Braun, Johann 1997, 'Der Besitzrechtsstreit zwischen Friedrich Carl von Savigny und Eduard Gans', in *Judentum, Jurisprudenz und Philosophie. Bilder aus dem Leben des Eduard Gans (1797–1839)*, edited by Johann Braun, Baden Baden: Nomos Verlags-gesellschaft.

Brecht, Bertolt 1960 [1928], 'The Threepenny Opera', in *Plays. Volume 1*, translated by Desmond I. Vesey and Eric Bentley, London: Methuen.

Brecht, Bertolt 1967 [1928], 'Die Dreigroschenoper', in *Gesammelte Werke. Band 2*, Frankfurt am Main: Suhrkamp.

Brenkert, George G. 1979, 'Freedom and Private Property in Marx', *Philosophy and Public Affairs*, 8, 2: 122–47.

Brink, André 1993, *On the Contrary*, London: Secker and Warburg.

Brink, André 1994 [1993], *Im Gegenteil*, translated by Hans Hermann, Berlin: Volk und Welt.

Brink, Bert van der and David Owen (eds) 2007, *Recognition and Power: Axel Honneth and the Tradition of Critical Theory*, Cambridge: Cambridge University Press.

Brown, Alexander 2014, 'Marx on Exploitation: A Kantian Perspective', *Rethinking Marxism*, 26, 3: 260–81.

Brunkhorst, Hauke 2002, *Solidarität. Von der Bürgerfreundschaft zur globalen Rechtsgenossenschaft*, Frankfurt am Main: Suhrkamp.

Brunkhorst, Hauke 2005 [2002], *Solidarity: From Civil Friendship to a Global Legal Community*, translated by Jeffrey Flynn, Cambridge, MA: MIT Press.

Brunkhorst, Hauke 2007, 'Kommentar', in Karl Marx, *Der achtzehnte Brumaire des Louis Bonaparte*, Frankfurt am Main: Suhrkamp.

Buchanan, Allen E. 1979, 'Exploitation, Alienation, and Injustice', *Canadian Journal of Philosophy*, 9, 1: 121–39.

Buchanan, Allen E. 1982, *Marx and Justice: The Radical Critique of Liberalism*, Totowa: Rowman and Littlefield.

Buckel, Sonja 2007, *Subjektivierung und Kohäsion. Zur Rekonstruktion einer materialistischen Theorie des Rechts*, Weilerswist: Velbrück Wissenschaft.

Cahan, Jean Axelrad 1994–95, 'The Concept of Property in Marx's Theory of History: A Defense of the Autonomy of the Socioeconomic Base', *Science and Society*, 58, 4: 392–414.

Callinicos, Alex 1987, *Making History: Agency, Structure and Change in Social Theory*, Cambridge: Polity.

Callinicos, Alex 2001, 'Having Your Cake and Eating It', *Historical Materialism*, 9: 169–95.

Callinicos, Alex 2013, 'Marxism and Contemporary Political Thought', in *The Routledge Companion to Social and Political Philosophy*, edited by Gerald F. Gaus and Fred D'Agostino, Oxon: Routledge.

Callinicos, Alex 2014, *Deciphering* Capital: *Marx's Capital and its Destiny*, London: Bookmarks.

Cannon, Bob 2015, 'Marx, Modernity and Human Rights', in *Constructing Marxist Ethics: Critique, Normativity, Praxis*, edited by Michael J. Thompson, Leiden: Brill.

Carchedi, Guglielmo 2011, *Behind the Crisis: Marx's Dialectics of Value and Knowledge*, Leiden: Brill.

Carver, Terrell and Paul Thomas (eds) 1995, *Rational Choice Marxism*, Basingstoke: Macmillan.

Cassam, Quassim 2003, 'Can Transcendental Epistemology be Naturalized?', *Philosophy*, 78: 181–203.

Chisholm, Roderick M. 1966, 'Freedom and Action', in *Freedom and Determinism*, edited by Keith Lehrer, New York: Random House.

Chitty, Andrew 1998, 'Recognition and Social Relations of Production', *Historical Materialism*, 2: 57–98.

Chitty, Andrew 2004 [1993], 'The Early Marx on Needs', in *Karl Marx's Social and Political Thought: Critical Assessments. Second Series. Volume 8*, edited by Bob Jessop and Russell Wheatley, London: Routledge.

Cleaver, Harry 1979, *Reading* Capital *Politically*, Brighton: Harvester Press.

Cohen, G.A. 1978, *Karl Marx's Theory of History: A Defence*, Oxford: Oxford University Press.

Cohen, G.A. 1981a, 'Freedom, Justice and Capitalism', *New Left Review*, I/126: 3–16.

Cohen, G.A. 1981b, 'Functional Explanation: Reply to Elster', *Political Studies*, 28, 1: 129–35.

Cohen, G.A. 1983a, 'Karl Marx. By Allen W. Wood', *Mind*, 92, 367: 440–5.

Cohen, G.A. 1983b, 'Reply to Four Critics', *Analyse und Kritik*, 5: 195–222.

Cohen, G.A. 1986, 'Walt on Historical Materialism and Functional Explanation', *Ethics*, 97, 1: 219–32.

Cohen, G.A. 1988, *History, Labour, Freedom*, Oxford: Clarendon Press.

Cohen, G.A. 1989, 'Base and Superstructure: A Reply to Hugh Collins', *Oxford Journal of Legal Studies*, 9, 1: 95–100.

Cohen, G.A. 1990, 'Marxism and Contemporary Political Philosophy, or: Why Nozick Exercises Some Marxists More than He Does any Egalitarian Liberals', *Canadian Journal of Philosophy*, Supplementary Volume, 16: 363–87.

Cohen, G.A. 1995, *Self-Ownership, Freedom and Equality*, Cambridge: Cambridge University Press.

Cohen, G.A. 1998, 'Once More into the Breach of Self-Ownership: Reply to Narveson and Brenkert', *The Journal of Ethics*, 2: 57–96.

Cohen, G.A. 2000 [1978], *Karl Marx's Theory of History. 2000 Edition*, Oxford: Oxford University Press.

Cohen, G.A. 2001, *If You're an Egalitarian, How Come You're So Rich?*, Cambridge, MA: Harvard University Press.

Cohen, G.A. 2008, *Rescuing Justice and Equality*, Cambridge, MA: Harvard University Press.

Cohen, G.A. 2009, *Why Not Socialism?*, Princeton: Princeton University Press.

Cohen, G.A. 2011, *On the Currency of Egalitarian Justice*. Princeton: Princeton University Press.

Cohen, G.A. 2013, *Finding Oneself in the Other*, Princeton: Princeton University Press.

Cohen, Gerald A. and Harry B. Acton 1970, 'On Some Criticisms of Historical Materialism', *Proceedings of the Aristotelian Society*, Supplementary Volume, 44: 121–56.

Cohen, Hermann 1904, *Ethik des reinen Willens*, Berlin: Bruno Cassirer.

Cohen, Marshall, Thomas Nagel and Thomas Scanlon (eds) 1980, *Marx, Justice and History*, Princeton: Princeton University Press.

Collins, Hugh 1984, *Marxism and Law*, Oxford: Oxford University Press.

Cunliffe, John and Andrew Reeve 1996, 'Exploitation: The Original Saint Simonian Account', *Capital and Class*, 20, 2: 61–80.

Cunow, Heinrich 1921, *Die Marxsche Geschichts-, Gesellschafts- und Staatstheorie. Grundzüge der Marxschen Soziologie. Band II*, Berlin: Vorwärts.

Dahrendorf, Ralf 1971 [1965], *Homo Sociologicus. Ein Versuch zur Geschichte, Bedeutung und Kritik der Kategorie der sozialen Rollen*, Opladen: Westdeuscher Verlag.

Dahrendorf, Ralf 1973 [1965], *Homo Sociologicus*, translated by Ralf Dahrendorf, London: Routledge and Kegan Paul.

Davidson, Donald 2001 [1980], *Essays on Actions and Events*, 2nd edition, Oxford: Oxford University Press.

Descartes, René 1988 [1637], 'Discourse on the Method', in *Selected Philosophical Writings*, edited by John Cottingham, translated by John Cottingham, Robert Stoothoff and Dugald Murdoch, Cambridge: Cambridge University Press.

Descartes, René 1990 [1637], *Discours de la méthode. Französisch-deutsch*, übersetzt und herausgegeben von Lüder Gäbe, Hamburg: Felix Meiner.

Dimoulis, Dimitri and Jannis Milios 1999, 'Werttheorie, Ideologie und Fetischismus', *Beiträge zur Marx-Engels-Forschung. Neue Folge*, edited by Richard Sperl and Rolf Hecker, Berlin: Argument.

Elbe, Ingo 2008, *Marx im Westen. Die neue Marx-Lektüre in der Bundesrepublik seit 1965*, Berlin: Akademie Verlag.

Elder-Vass, Dave 2010, *The Causal Power of Social Structures: Emergence, Structure and Agency*, Cambridge: Cambridge University Press.

Elster, Jon 1978a, 'Exploring Exploitation', *Journal of Peace Research*, 15, 1: 3–17.

Elster, Jon 1978b, *Logic and Society: Contradictions and Possible Worlds*, Chichester: John Wiley and Sons.

Elster, Jon 1983, 'Exploitation, Freedom and Justice', *Nomos*, 26: 277–304.

Elster, Jon 1985, *Making Sense of Marx*, Cambridge: Cambridge University Press.

Engel, Ulrich 1996 [1988], *Deutsche Grammatik. 3., korrigierte Auflage*, Heidelberg: Julius Groos Verlag.

Evans, Mark 2007, *Self-Realization: Politics and the Good Life in Modern Times*, New York: Nova Science.

Feinberg, Joel 1970, 'The Nature and Value of Rights', *Journal of Value Inquiry*, 4, 4: 243–60.

Feuerbach, Ludwig 1984 [1841], *Gesammelte Werke. Band 5: Das Wesen des Christentums*, Berlin: Akademie Verlag.

Feuerbach, Ludwig 1989 [1841], *The Essence of Christianity*, translated by George Eliot, New York: Prometheus.

Fine, Robert 2009, 'An Unfinished Project: Marx's Critique of Hegel's *Philosophy of Right*', in *Karl Marx and Contemporary Philosophy*, edited by Andrew Chitty and Martin McIvor, Basingstoke: Palgrave Macmillan.

Flatow, Sibylle von and Freerk Huisken 1973, 'Zum Problem der Ableitung des bürgerlichen Staats', *Probleme des Klassenkampfs*, 7: 83–154.

Fourier, Charles 2015 [1829], *Le nouveau monde industriel et sociétaire – Tome I: 1*, Createspace Independent Publishing.

Frankfurt, Harry G. 1971, 'Freedom of the Will and the Concept of a Person', *Journal of Philosophy*, 68, 1: 5–20.

Freire, Paolo 2000 [1968], *Pedagogy of the Oppressed*, 30th anniversary edition, translated by Myra Bergman Ramos, New York: Bloomsbury.

Furner, James 2004, 'Marx's Critique of Samuel Bailey', *Historical Materialism*, 12, 2: 89–110.

Furner, James 2011, 'Marx's Sketch of Communist Society in *The German Ideology* and the Problems of Occupational Identity and Occupational Confinement', *Philosophy and Social Criticism*, 37, 2: 189–215.

Furner, James 2015, 'Marx with Kant on Exploitation', *Contemporary Political Theory*, 14, 1: 23–44.

Furner, James 2017a, 'Kant's Contradiction in Conception Test: A Causal-Teleological Version of the Logical Contradiction Interpretation', *Theoria*, 152, 64, 3: 1–23.

Furner, James 2017b, 'Kant's Contradiction in the Will Test: An Extravagant Imperfect Nature Interpretation', *The Philosophical Forum*, 48, 3: 307–23.

Furner, James forthcoming (2019), 'G.A. Cohen', in *Routledge Handbook of Marxism and Post-Marxism*, edited by Alex Callinicos, Stathis Kouvelakis and Lucia Pradella, London: Routledge.

Gans, Eduard 1971 [1839], 'Über die Grundlage des Besitzes – Eine Duplik', in *Philosophische Schriften*, Glashütten im Taunus: Detlev Auvermann.

Geraets, Theodore F. and Henry S. Harris 1991, 'Introduction: Translating Hegel's Logic', in Georg Wilhelm Friedrich Hegel, *The Encyclopaedia Logic. Part 1 of the Encyclopaedia of Philosophical Sciences with the Zusätze*, translated by Theodore F. Geraets, Henry S. Harris and Wal A. Suchting, Indianapolis: Hackett.

Geras, Norman 1985, 'The Controversy about Marx and Justice', *New Left Review*, I/150: 47–85.

Geras, Norman 1992, 'Bringing Marx to Justice: an Addendum and Rejoinder', *New Left Review*, I/195: 37–69.

Gerstenberger, Heide 1975, 'Klassenantagonismus, Konkurrenz und Staatsfunktion', in

Gesellschaft. Beiträge zur Marxschen Theorie 3, edited by Hans-Georg Backhaus, Hans-Dieter Bahr et al., Frankfurt am Main: Suhrkamp.

Giddens, Anthony 1984, *The Constitution of Society*, Cambridge: Polity.

Gilabert, Pablo 2017, 'Kantian Dignity and Marxian Socialism', *Kantian Review*, 22, 4: 553–77.

Goethe, Johann Wolfgang von 1833, *Werke. Neun und Vierzigster Band*, Stuttgard: J.G. Cotta.

Goethe, Johann Wolfgang von 1998 [1833], *Maxims and Reflections*, translated by Elisabeth Stopp, London: Penguin Books.

Goodin, Robert 1987, 'Exploiting a Situation and Exploitation a Person', in *Modern Theories of Exploitation*, edited by Andrew Reeve, London: Sage.

Gordon, David 1991, *Resurrecting Marx: The Analytical Marxists on Freedom, Exploitation and Justice*, New Brunswick: Transaction.

Gould, Carol C. 1978, *Marx's Social Ontology*, Cambridge, MA: MIT Press.

Green, Michael 1983, 'Marx, Utility, and Right', *Political Theory*, 11, 3: 433–46.

Günther, Klaus 1989, 'A Normative Conception of Coherence for a Discursive Theory of Legal Justification', *Ratio Juris*, 2, 2: 155–66.

Gursky, Karl-Heinz, Axel Pfeifer and Wolfgang Wiegand 2004, *J. von Staudingers Kommentar zum Bürgerlichen Gesetzbuch, Drittes Buch, Sachenrecht, §§ 925–984*. Berlin: Sellier – de Gruyter.

Habermas, Jürgen 1981, *Theorie des kommunikativen Handelns. Band 1. Handlungsrationalität und gesellschaftliche Rationalisierung*, Suhrkamp: Frankfurt am Main.

Habermas, Jürgen 1986 [1981], *The Theory of Communicative Action, Volume 1*, translated by Thomas McCarthy, Cambridge: Polity.

Hamilton, Lawrence 2014, *Freedom is Power: Liberty Through Political Representation*, Cambridge: Cambridge University Press.

Harré, Rom and Edward H. Madden 1975, *Causal Powers: A Theory of Natural Necessity*, Oxford: Basil Blackwell.

Hart, Herbert Lionel Adolphus 1990, 'Commands and Authoritative Legal Reasons', in *Authority*, edited by Joseph Raz, New York: New York University Press.

Harvey, David 2006, *The Limits to Capital*, London: Verso.

Harvey, David 2010, *A Companion to Marx's* Capital, London: Verso.

Hegel, Georg Wilhelm Friedrich 1969–71, *Werke in zwanzig Bänden*, Frankfurt am Main: Suhrkamp.

Hegel, Georg Wilhelm Friedrich 1983, *Die Philosophie des Rechts. Die Mitschriften Wannenmann (Heidelberg 1817/18) und Homeyer (Berlin 1818/19)*, Stuttgart: Klett-Cotta.

Hegel, Georg Wilhelm Friedrich 1986a [1807], *Werke 3: Phänomenologie des Geistes*, Frankfurt am Main: Suhrkamp.

Hegel, Georg Wilhelm Friedrich 1986b [1821], *Werke 7: Grundlinien der Philosophie des Rechts*, Frankfurt am Main: Suhrkamp.

Hegel, Georg Wilhelm Friedrich 1986c [1830], *Werke 8: Enzyklopädie der philosophischen Wissenschaften im Grundrisse 1830. Erster Teil. Die Wissenschaft der Logik*, Frankfurt am Main: Suhrkamp.

Hegel, Georg Wilhelm Friedrich 1986d [1830], *Werke 10: Enzyklopädie der philosophischen Wissenschaften im Grundrisse 1830. Dritter Teil. Die Philosophie des Geistes. Mit den mündlichen Zusätzen*, Frankfurt am Main: Suhrkamp.

Hegel, Georg Wilhelm Friedrich 1986e [1837], *Werke 12: Vorlesungen über die Philosophie der Geschichte*, Frankfurt am Main: Suhrkamp.

Hegel, Georg Wilhelm Friedrich 1991a [1821], *Elements of the Philosophy of Right*, edited by Allen W. Wood, translated by H.B. Nisbet, Cambridge: Cambridge University Press.

Hegel, Georg Wilhelm Friedrich 1991b [1817], *The Encyclopaedia Logic. Part I of the Encyclopaedia of Philosophical Sciences with the Zusätze*, translated by Theodore F. Geraets, Henry S. Harris and Wal A. Suchting, Indianapolis: Hackett.

Hegel, Georg Wilhelm Friedrich 2001 [1837], *The Philosophy of History*, translated by J. Sibree, Kitchener: Batoche.

Hegel, Georg Wilhelm Friedrich 2007 [1830], *Hegel's Philosophy of Mind*, translated by William Wallace and A.V. Miller, revised by Michael J. Inwood, Oxford: Clarendon Press.

Hegel, Georg Wilhelm Friedrich 2012 [1983], *Lectures on Natural Right and Political Science: The First Philosophy of Right*, edited by J. Michael Stewart, translated by Peter C. Hodgson, Oxford: Oxford University Press.

Hegel, Georg Wilhelm Friedrich 2013 [1807], *The Phenomenology of Spirit*, translated by Terry Pinkard, available at: https://www.marxists.org/reference/archive/hegel/works/ph/pinkard-translation-of-phenomenology.pdf.

Heinrich, Michael 2012 [2004], *An Introduction to the Three Volumes of Karl Marx's Capital*, translated by Alexander Locascio, New York: Monthly Review Press.

Heinrich, Michael 2005 [2004], *Kritik der politischen Ökonomie. Ein Einführung*, Stuttgart: Schmetterling.

Heinrich, Michael 2006 [1999], *Die Wissenschaft von Wert. Die Marxsche Kritik der politischen Ökonomie zwischen wissenschaftlicher Revolution und klassischer Tradition. Überarbeitete und erweiterte Neuauflage*, Münster: Westfälisches Dampfboot.

Heller, Agnes 1976, *The Theory of Need in Marx*, New York: St. Martin's Press.

Henning, Christoph 2010, 'Charaktermaske und Individualität bei Marx', *Marx-Engels-Jahrbuch*, 2009: 100–22.

Herman, Barbara 1990, *Morality as Rationality: A Study of Kant's Ethics*, New York: Garland.

Herman, Barbara 1993, *The Practice of Moral Judgment*, Cambridge, MA: Harvard University Press.

Hidalgo, Oliver 2014, *Die Antinomien der Demokratie*, Frankfurt: Campus Verlag.

Hobbes, Thomas 1996 [1651], *Leviathan*, Cambridge: Cambridge University Press.

Hollis, Martin 1994, *The Philosophy of Social Science*, Cambridge: Cambridge University Press.

Holloway, John and Sol Picciotto (eds) 1978, *State and Capital: A Marxist Debate*, Austin: University of Texas Press.

Holmstrom, Nancy 1977, 'Exploitation', *Canadian Journal of Philosophy*, 7, 2: 353–69.

Honneth, Axel 1995 [1992], *The Struggle for Recognition: The Moral Grammar of Social Conflicts*, translated by Joel Anderson, Cambridge: Polity Press.

Honneth, Axel 2002, 'Grounding Recognition: A Rejoinder to Critical Questions', *Inquiry*, 45: 499–520.

Honneth, Axel 2003 [1992], *Kampf um Anerkennung: Zur moralischen Grammatik sozialer Konflikte*, Frankfurt am Main: Suhrkamp.

Honneth, Axel 2011, *Das Recht der Freiheit. Grundriß einer demokratischen Sittlichkeit*, Frankfurt am Main: Suhrkamp.

Honneth, Axel 2014 [2011], *Freedom's Right. The Social Foundations of Democratic Life*, translated by Joseph Ganahl, Cambridge: Polity.

Houlgate, Stephen 2006, *The Opening of Hegel's* Logic, West Lafayette: Purdue University Press.

Howarth-Williams, Martin 1977, *R.D. Laing: His Work and its Relevance for Sociology*, London: Routledge.

Hunt, Alun 1988, 'On Legal Relations and Economic Relations', in *Law and Economics*, edited by Robert N. Moles, Stuttgart: Franz Steiner Verlag.

Husami, Ziyad I. 1978, 'Marx on Distributive Justice', *Philosophy and Public Affairs*, 8, 1: 27–64.

Husserl, Edmund 1929, *Formale und transcendentale Logik. Versuch einer Kritik der logischen Vernunft*, translated by Dorion Cairns, Halle: Max Niemeyer.

Husserl, Edmund 1969 [1929], *Formal and Transcendental Logic*, The Hague: Martinus Nijhoff.

Ikäheimo, Heikki and Arto Laitinen 2007, 'Analyzing Recognition: Identification, Acknowledgment, and Recognitive Attitudes towards Persons', in *Recognition and Power: Axel Honneth and the Tradition of Critical Theory*, edited by Bert van der Brink and David Owen, Cambridge: Cambridge University Press.

Inwood, Michael 1992, *A Hegel Dictionary*, Oxford: Blackwell.

Iorio, Marco 2003, *Karl Marx – Geschichte, Gesellschaft, Politik*, Berlin: Walter de Gruyter.

Ivison, Duncan 2008, *Rights*, Stocksfield: Acumen.

Jameson, Fredric 2011, *Representing Capital: A Commentary on Volume One*, London: Verso.

Jellinek, Georg 1919, *System der subjektiven öffentlichen Rechte*, Tübingen: J.C.B. Mohr.

Jütten, Timo 2015, 'Is the Market a Sphere of Social Freedom?', *Critical Horizons*, 16, 2: 187–203.

Kain, Philip J. 1988, *Marx and Ethics*, Oxford: Clarendon Press.

Kant, Immanuel 1902–, *Kants gesammelte Schriften*, Berlin: de Gruyter.

Kant, Immanuel 1987 [1790], *Critique of Judgment*, translated by Werner S. Pluhar, Indianapolis: Hackett.

Kant, Immanuel 1991 [1797], *The Metaphysics of Morals*, translated by Mary Gregor, Cambridge: Cambridge University Press.

Kant, Immanuel 1996 [1793], 'On the Common Saying: "That May Be Correct In Theory, But It Is Of No Use In Practice"', in *Practical Philosophy*, edited and translated by Mary J. Gregor, Cambridge: Cambridge University Press.

Kant, Immanuel 1997 [1788], *Critique of Practical Reason*, translated by Mary Gregor, Cambridge: Cambridge University Press.

Kant, Immanuel 1999 [1781], *Critique of Pure Reason*, edited and translated by Paul Guyer and Allen W. Wood, Cambridge: Cambridge University Press.

Kant, Immanuel 2014 [1785], *Groundwork of the Metaphysics of Morals: A German-English Edition*, edited and translated by Mary Gregor and Jens Timmermann, Cambridge: Cambridge University Press.

Karatani, Kojin 2002 [2001], *Transcritique: On Kant and Marx*, translated by Sabu Kohso, Cambridge, MA: MIT Press.

Kelsen, Hans 1931, 'Allgemeine Rechtslehre im Lichte materialistischer Geschichtsausfasung', *Archiv für Sozialwisssenschaft und Sozialpolitik*, 66, 3: 449–521.

Kelsen, Hans 1955, *The Communist Theory of Law*, London: Stevens and Sons.

Kelsen, Hans 2008, *Werke Band 2. Veröffentlichte Schriften 1911. Zweiter Halbband*, Tübingen: Mohr Siebeck.

Keynes, John Maynard 1939, *The General Theory of Employment, Interest and Money*, London: Macmillan.

Kline, Donna 1987, *Dominion and Wealth*, Dordrecht: D. Reidel.

Knoll, Heiko and Hans-Jürgen Ritsert 2004, *Das Prinzip der Dialektik. Studien über strikte Antinomie und Kritische Theorie*, Münster: Westfälisches Dampfboot.

Knox, Robert 2016, 'Marxist Approaches to International Law', in *The Oxford Handbook of the Theory of International Law*, edited by Anne Orford and Florian Hoffman, Oxford: Oxford University Press.

Kouvélakis, Stathis 2005, 'The Marxian Critique of Citizenship: For a Rereading of *On the Jewish Question*', *The South Atlantic Quarterly*, 104, 4: 707–21.

Kuhlen, Lothar 1975, '"Ableitung" und "Verdoppelung" in der neueren marxistischen Diskussion über den Staat', in *Probleme der marxistischen Rechtstheorie*, edited by Hubert Rottleuthner, Frankfurt am Main: Suhrkamp.

Kymlicka, Will 1989, *Liberalism, Community and Culture*, Oxford: Clarendon Press.

Laing, Ronald D. and Aaron Esterson 1958, 'The Collusive Function of Pairing in Analytic Groups', *British Journal of Medical Psychology*, 31: 117–23.

Laitinen, Arto 2002, 'Interpersonal Recognition: A Response to Value or a Precondition of Personhood?', *Inquiry*, 45: 463–78.

Laitinen, Arto 2011, 'Recognition, Acknowledgment, and Acceptance', in *Recognition and Social Ontology*, edited by Heikki Ikäheimo and Arto Laitinen, Leiden: Brill.

Lawson, Tony 1997, *Economics and Reality*, London: Routledge.

Lebowitz, Michael A. 2009, *Following Marx: Method, Critique and Crisis*, Leiden: Brill.

Lenin, Vladimir 2006 [1902], 'What is to be Done? Burning Questions of Our Movement', in Lars Lih, *Lenin Rediscovered*: What is to be Done? *in Context*, Leiden: Brill.

Lens, Max 1910, *Geschichte der Königlichen Friedrich-Wilhelms-Universität zu Berlin, Vierter Band: Urkunden, Akten und Briefe*, Halle: Buchhandlung des Waisenhauses.

Leopold, David 2007, *The Young Karl Marx: German Philosophy, Modern Politics, and Human Flourishing*, Cambridge: Cambridge University Press.

Leopold, David 2008, 'Dialectical Approaches', in *Political Theory: Methods and Approaches*, edited by David Leopold and Marc Stears, Oxford: Oxford University Press.

Lih, Lars T. 2006, *Lenin Rediscovered*: What is to be Done? *in Context*, Leiden: Brill.

Linden, Harry van der 1984, 'Marx and Morality: An Impossibly Synthesis?', *Theory and Society*, 13, 1: 119–35.

Linden, Harry van der 1988, *Kantian Ethics and Socialism*, Indianapolis: Hackett.

Linton, Ralph 1936, *The Study of Man: An Introduction*, New York: Appleton-Century-Crofts.

Locke, John 1988 [1690], *Two Treatises of Government*, edited by Peter Laslett, Cambridge: Cambridge University Press.

Lohmann, Georg 1991, *Indifferenz und Gesellschaft. Eine kritische Auseinandersetzung mit Marx*, Frankfurt am Main: Suhrkamp.

Lovett, Frank 2010, *A General Theory of Domination and Justice*, Oxford: Oxford University Press.

Lukács, Georg 1968 [1923], *History and Class Consciousness*, translated by Rodney Livingstone, London: Merlin Press.

Lukács, Georg 1970 [1924], *Lenin: A Study on the Unity of his Thought*, translated by Nicholas Jacobs, London: Verso.

Lukács, Georg 1972, *Political Writings 1919–1929*, edited by Rodney Livingstone, translated by Michael McColgan, London: New Left Books.

Lukács, Georg 1977 [1968], *Werke Band 2. Frühschriften II. Geschichte und Klassenbewußtsein*, Darmstandt und Neuwied: Luchterhand.

Lukács, Georg 1996, *Chvostismus und Dialektik*, Budapest: Áron Verlag.

Lukács, Georg 2000 [1996], *A Defence of* History and Class Consciousness: *Tailism and the Dialectic*, translated by Esther Leslie, London: Verso.

Lukes, Steven 1982a, 'Can the Base be Distinguished from the Superstructure?', *Analyse und Kritik*, 4: 211–22.

Lukes, Steven 1982b, 'Marxism, Morality and Justice', *Royal Institute of Philosophy Lecture Series*, 14: 177–205.

Macpherson, Crawford Brough 1962, *The Political Theory of Possessive Individualism*, Oxford: Clarendon Press.

Maihofer, Andrea 1992, *Das Recht bei Marx*, Frankfurt am Main: Nomos.

Maker, William 1994, *Philosophy Without Foundations: Rethinking Hegel*, Albany, NY: SUNY Press.

Martin, Wayne 2011, 'Antinomies of Autonomy: German Idealism and English Mental Health Law', *International Yearbook of German Idealism*, 9: 191–213.

Mauss, Marcel 1954 [1925], *The Gift: Forms and Functions of Exchange in Archaic Societies*, translated by Ian Cunnison, London: Cohen and West.

Mayer, Tom 1994, *Analytical Marxism*, Thousand Oaks, CA: Sage.

McCarney, Joseph 1992, 'Marx and Justice Again', *New Left Review*, I/195: 29–36.

McCarney, Joseph 2009, 'The Entire Mystery: Marx's Understanding of Hegel', in *Karl Marx and Contemporary Philosophy*, edited by Andrew Chitty and Martin McIvor, Basingstoke: Palgrave Macmillan.

McNair, Ted 2000, 'Universal Necessity and Contradictions in Conception', *Kant-Studien*, 91, 1: 25–41.

Meek, Ronald L. 1956, *Studies in the Labor Theory of Value*, New York: Monthly Review Press.

Menger, Carl 1968, *Gesammelte Werke Band I. Grundsätze der Volkswirtschaftslehre (1871)*, Tübingen: J.C.B. Mohr.

Menger, Carl 1969 [1883], *Untersuchungen über die Methode der Socialwissenschaften und der politischen Ökonomie*, Tübingen: J.C.B. Mohr.

Menger, Carl 1970 [1892], 'Geld', in *Carl Menger Gesammelte Werke. Band IV. Schriften über Geld und Währungspolitik*, edited by Friedrich A. Hayek, Tübingen: J.C.B. Mohr.

Menger, Carl 1985 [1883], *Investigations into the Method of the Social Sciences with Special Reference to Economics*, edited by Louis Schneider, translated by Francis J. Nock, New York: New York University Press.

Menger, Carl 2007 [1871], *Principles of Economics*, translated by James Dingwall and Bert F. Hoselitz, Auburn: Ludwig von Mises Institute.

Merton, Robert King 1957, *Social Theory and Social Structure*, Glencoe: The Free Press.

Mészáros, István 1970, *Marx's Theory of Alienation*, London: Merlin.

Mill, John Stuart 1962 [1910], *Utilitarianism, Liberty, Representative Government*, London: Dent.

Mill, John Stuart 1965 [1848], *Principles of Political Economy Books I–II*, Toronto: University of Toronto Press.

Miller, Richard W. 1984, *Analyzing Marx: Morality, Power and History*, Princeton: Princeton University Press.

Mises, Ludwig H.E. von 1924 [1912], *Theorie des Geldes und der Umlaufsmittel*, Berlin: Duncker und Humblot.

Mises, Ludwig H.E. von 1934 [1912], *The Theory of Money and Credit*, translated by H.E. Batson, London: Jonathan Cape.

Moore, George E. 1919–20, 'External and Internal Relations', *Proceedings of the Aristotelian Society*, New Series, 20: 40–62.

Moore, Stanley 1980, *Marx on the Choice between Socialism and Communism*, Cambridge, MA: Harvard University Press.

Müller, Friedrich 1963, *Korporation und Assoziation. Eine Problemgeschichte der Vereinigungsfreiheit im deutschen Vormärz*, Dissertation der Albert-Ludwig-Universitaet zu Freiberg im Breisgau.

Müller, Wolfgang and Christel Neusüss 1971, 'Die Sozialstaatsillusion und der Widerspruch von Lohnarbeit und Kapital', *Probleme des Klassenkampfs*, 1, 1: 7–70.

Murphy, Mark C. 2007, *Philosophy of Law*, Malden, MA: Blackwell.

Murray, Patrick 1988, *Marx's Theory of Scientific Knowledge*, Atlantic Highlands, NJ: Humanities Press.

Murray, Patrick 2006, 'In Defence of the "Third Thing Argument": A Reply to James Furner's "Marx's Critique of Samuel Bailey"', *Historical Materialism*, 14, 2: 149–68.

Murray, Patrick 2016, *The Mismeasure of Wealth: Essays on Marx and Social Form*, Leiden: Brill.

Negt, Oskar 2010, *Kant und Marx*, Göttingen: Steidl.

Nelson, Leonard 1917, *Vorlesungen über die Grundlagen der Ethik. Erster Band. Kritik der praktischen Vernunft*, Leipzig: Veit und Comp.

Neocleous, Mark 2008, *Critique of Security*, Edinburgh: Edinburgh University Press.

Neumann, Franz L. 1986 [1936], *The Rule of Law: Political Theory and the Legal System in Modern Society*, Leamington Spa: Berg.

Nielsen, Kai 1989, *Marxism and the Moral Point of View: Morality, Ideology, and Historical Materialism*, Boulder, CO: Westview Press.

Nozick, Robert 1974, *Anarchy, State, and Utopia*, New York: Basic Books.

Nutzinger, Hans G. 1984, 'Gerechtigkeit bei Marx und Mill. Zur Schwierigkeit "positiver" und "normativer" Fundierungen der Politischen Ökonomie', in *Ökonomie und Gesellschaft, Jahrbuch 2: Wohlfahrt und Gerechtigkeit*, edited by Peter de Gijsel, Thomas Schmid-Schönbein and Johannes Schneider, Frankfurt am Main: Campus.

Ollman, Bertell 1993, *Dialectical Investigations*, London: Routledge.

O'Meara, William M. 1986–87, 'The Social Nature of Self and Morality for Husserl, Schutz, Marx, and Mead', *Philosophy Research Archives*, 12: 329–55.

O'Neill, Onora 2013 [1975], *Acting on Principle: An Essay on Kantian Ethics*, 2nd edition, Cambridge: Cambridge University Press.

Osman, Nabil 2007, *Kleines Lexikon untergegangener Wörter*, München: C.H. Beck.

Owen, Robert 1927 [1849], *A New View of Society and Other Writings*, London: J.M. Dent and Sons.

Parfit, Derek 2011, *On What Matters. Volume One*, Oxford: Oxford University Press.

Paschukanis, Eugen 2003 [1924], *Allgemeine Rechtslehre und Marxismus. Versuch einer Kritik der juristischen Grundbegriffe*, translated by Edith Hajós, Freiburg: ça ira-Verlag.

Pashukanis, Evgeny Bronislavovich 2002 [1924], *The General Theory of Law and Marxism*, translated by Barbara Einhorn, New Brunswick: Transaction.

Peffer, Rodney G. 1990, *Marxism, Morality, and Social Justice*, Princeton: Princeton University Press.

Pendlebury, Michael, Peter Hudson and Darrel Moellendorf 2001, 'Capitalist Exploitation, Self-Ownership, and Equality', *The Philosophical Forum*, 32, 3: 207–20.

Pettit, Philip 1997, *Republicanism: A Theory of Freedom and Government*, Oxford: Clarendon Press.

Pettit, Philip 2003, 'Groups with Minds of Their Own', in *Socializing Metaphysics: The Nature of Social Reality*, edited by Frederick F. Schmitt, Lanham, MD: Rowman and Littlefield.

Pettit, Philip 2005, 'The Domination Complaint', in *Nomos XLVI: Political Exclusion and Domination*, edited by Melissa S. Williams and Stephen Macedo, New York: New York University Press.

Plamenatz, John 1956, *German Marxism and Russian Communism*, London: Green and Co.

Plamenatz, John 1963, *Man and Society: Political and Social Theory: Bentham through Marx. Volume 2*, Gateshead: Northumberland Press.

Plamenatz, John 1970, *Ideology*, London: Pall Mall Press.

Plekhanov, Georgi V. 1956 [1895], *The Development of the Monist View of History*, translated by Andrew Rothstein and A. Fineberg, Moscow: Progress.

Popper, Karl R. 1940, 'What is Dialectic?', *Mind*, 49: 403–26.

Popper, Karl R. 1950, *The Open Society and Its Enemies*, Princeton: Princeton University Press.

Posner, Richard A. 2000, 'Savigny, Holmes and the Law and Economics of Possession', *Virginia Law Review*, 86, 3: 535–67.

Postone, Moishe 1993, *Time, Labor, and Social Domination: A Reinterpretation of Marx's Social Theory*, Cambridge: Cambridge University Press.

Poulantzas, Nicos 1978 [1968], *Political Power and Social Classes*, translated by Timothy O'Hagan, London: Verso.

Poulantzas, Nicos 1982 [1968], *Pouvoir politique et classes sociales de l'état capitaliste*, Paris: François Maspero.

Pound, Roscoe 1939, 'The Law of Property and Recent Juristic Thought', *American Bar Association Journal*, 25: 993–9.

Preuß, Ulrich K. 1973, *Legalität und Pluralismus*, Frankfurt am Main: Suhrkamp.

Pufendorf, Samuel 1729 [1672], *Of the Law of Nature and Nations. Eight Books*, translated by George Carew, London: J. Walthor.

Pufendorf, Samuel 1934 [1672], *De Jure Naturae et Gentium. Libri Octo*, Oxford: Clarendon Press.

Radbruch, Gustav 1987 [1930], 'Paschukanis, E.: Allgemeine Rechtslehre und Marxismus', in *Gesamtausgabe. Band 1. Rechtsphilosophie I*, Heidelberg: C.F. Müller.

Radbruch, Gustav 1993a [1929], 'Klassenrecht und Rechtsidee', in *Gesamtausgabe. Band 2. Rechtsphilosophie II*, Heidelberg: C.F. Müller.

Radbruch, Gustav 1993b [1914], 'Rechtsphilosophie, 3. Auflage 1932', in *Gesamtausgabe. Band 2. Rechtsphilosophie II*, Heidelberg: C.F. Müller.

Radcliffe-Brown, Alfred R. 1952, *Structure and Function in Primitive Society: Essays and Addresses*, Glencoe: The Free Press.

Rattansi, Ali 1982, *Marx and the Division of Labour*, London: Macmillan.

Rawls, John 1971, *A Theory of Justice*, Cambridge, MA: Harvard University Press.

Rawls, John 2000, *Lectures on the History of Moral Philosophy*, Cambridge, MA: Harvard University Press.

Rawls, John 2007, *Lectures on the History of Political Philosophy*, Cambridge, MA: Harvard University Press.

Read, Jason 2003, *The Micro-Politics of Capital: Marx and the Prehistory of the Present*, Albany, NY: SUNY Press.

Read, Jason 2016, *The Politics of Transindividuality*, Leiden: Brill.

Reichelt, Helmut 2001 [1973], *Zur logischen Struktur des Kapitalbegriffs bei Karl Marx*, Freiburg: ça-ira.

Reichelt, Helmut 2008, *Neue Marx-Lektüre. Zur Kritik sozialwissenschaftlicher Logik*, Hamburg: VSA Verlag.

Reiman, Jeffrey E. 1987, 'Exploitation, Force, and the Moral Assessment of Capitalism: Thoughts on Roemer and Cohen', *Philosophy and Public Affairs*, 16, 1: 3–41.

Reiman, Jeffrey E. 1991, 'Moral Philosophy: The Critique of Capitalism and the Problem of Ideology', in *The Cambridge Companion to Marx*, edited by Terrell Carver, Cambridge: Cambridge University Press.

Ricardo, David 1821 [1817], *Principles of Political Economy*, London: John Murray.

Rigby, Steve H. 1998, *Marxism* and *History: A Critical Introduction*, Manchester: Manchester University Press.

Ritsert, Jürgen 1997, *Kleines Lehrbuch der Dialektik*, Darmstadt: Primus.

Ritsert, Jürgen 1998, 'Realabstraktion. Ein zu recht abgewertetes Thema der kritischen Theorie?', in *Kein Staat zu machen – zur Kritik der Sozialwissenschaften*, edited by Christoph Görg, Münster: Westfälisches Dampfboot.

Roberts, Marcus 1996, *Analytical Marxism: A Critique*, London: Verso.

Roberts, William Clare 2017, *Marx's Inferno: The Political Theory of* Capital, Princeton: Princeton University Press.

Roemer, John E. 1981, *Analytical Foundations of Marxian Economic Theory*, Cambridge: Cambridge University Press.

Roemer, John E. 1982a, *A General Theory of Exploitation and Class*, Cambridge, MA: Harvard University Press.

Roemer, John E. 1982b, 'Reply', *Politics and Society*, 11, 3: 375–94.

Roemer, John E. 1986a, 'New Directions in the Marxian Theory of Exploitation and Class', in *Analytical Marxism*, edited by John E. Roemer, Cambridge: Cambridge University Press.

Roemer, John E. 1986b, 'Should Marxists be Interested in Exploitation', in *Analytical Marxism*, edited by John E. Roemer, Cambridge: Cambridge University Press.

Roemer, John E. 1988, *Free to Lose: An Introduction to Marxist Economic Philosophy*, Cambridge, MA: Harvard University Press.

Roemer, John E. 1994, *Egalitarian Perspectives: Essays in Philosophical Economics*, Cambridge: Cambridge University Press.

Romm, James S. 1992, *The Edges of the Earth in Ancient Thought: Geography, Exploration, and Fiction*, Princeton: Princeton University Press.

Rosenthal, John 1998, *The Myth of Dialectics: Reinterpreting the Marx-Hegel Relation*, Basingstoke: Macmillan.

Rottleuthner, Hubert 1975, 'Marxistische und analytische Rechtstheorie', in *Probleme der marxistischen Rechtstheorie*, edited by Hubert Rottleuthner, Frankfurt am Main: Suhrkamp.

Rousseau, Jean-Jacques 1944 [1754], *Discours sur l'origine et les fondements de l'inégalité parmi les hommes*, Cambridge: Cambridge University Press.

Rousseau, Jean-Jacques 1997 [1754], *The Discourses and Other Early Political Writings*, edited and translated by Victor Gourevitch, Cambridge: Cambridge University Press.

Rubin, Isaak Illich 1973 [1928], *Essays on Marx's Theory of Value*, Montréal: Black Rose Books.

Rubin, Isaak Illich 2012 [1926–28], 'Studien zur Geldtheorie von Marx', in *Beiträge zur Marx-Engels-Forschung Neue Folge. Sonderband 4. Isaak Il'jič Rubin Marxforscher – Ökonom – Verbannter (1886–1937)*, edited by Rolf Hecker, Richard Sperl and Carl-Erich Vollgraf, Hamburg: Argument.

Sartre, Jean-Paul 1960, *Critique de la raison dialectique (précéde de Questions de méthode). Tome 1. Théorie des ensembles pratiques*, Paris: Gallimard.

Sartre, Jean-Paul 2004 [1960], *Critique of Dialectical Reason. Volume 1. Theory of Practical Ensembles*, edited by Jonathan Rée, translated by Alan Sheridan-Smith, London: Verso.

Savigny, Friedrich Carl von 1803, *Das Recht des Besitzes. Eine civilistische Abhandlung*, Giessen: Georg Friedrich Heyer.

Savigny, Friedrich Carl von 1827 [1803], *Das Recht des Besitzes. Eine civilistische Abhandlung. Fünfte, vermehrte und verbesserte Auflage*, Giessen: Georg Friedrich Heyer.

Savigny, Friedrich Carl von 1837 [1803], *Das Recht des Besitzes. Eine civilistische Abhand-lung. Sechste, vermehrte und verbesserte Auflage*, Giessen: Georg Friedrich Heyer.

Savigny, Friedrich Carl von 1840, *System des heutigen Römischen Rechts. Dritter Band*, Berlin: Veit und Comp.

Savigny, Friedrich Carl von 1848 [1803], *Treatise on Possession; or the Jus Possessionis of the Civil Law*, translated by Sir Erskine Perry, London: S. Sweet.

Sayer, Derek 1987, *The Violence of Abstraction: The Analytical Foundations of Historical Materialism*, Oxford: Basil Blackwell.

Schmitt, Carl 2003 [1928], *Verfassungslehre*, Berlin: Duncker und Humblot.

Schmitt, Carl 2008 [1928], *Constitutional Theory*, edited and translated by Jeffrey Seitzer, Durham, NC: Duke University Press.

Schütz, Alfred 1967 [1932], *The Phenomenology of the Social World*, translated by George Walsh and Frederick Lehnert, Evanston, IL: Northwestern University Press.

Schütz, Alfred 2004 [1932], *Der sinnhafte Aufbau der sozialen Welt*, Konstanz: UVK.

Schwartz, Justin 1995a, 'In Defence of Exploitation', *Economics and Philosophy*, 11: 275–307.

Schwartz, Justin 1995b, 'What's Wrong with Exploitation?', *Noûs*, 29, 2: 158–88.

Sensat, Julius 1984, 'Exploitation', *Nous*, 18, 1: 21–38.

Shandro, Alan 1995, '"Consciousness from Without": Marxism, Lenin and the Prolet-ariat', *Science and Society*, 59, 3: 268–97.

Shandro, Alan 2014, *Lenin and the Logic of Hegemony: Political Practice and Theory in the Class Struggle*, Leiden: Brill.

Simmel, Georg 2001 [1900], *Philosophie des Geldes*, Köln: Parkland.

Simmel, Georg 2004 [1900], *Philosophy of Money*, edited by David Frisby, translated by Tom Bottomore, London: Routledge.

Smith, Adam 1979 [1776], *The Wealth of Nations. Books I–III*, London: Penguin Books.

Smith, Tony 1990, *The Logic of Marx's* Capital: *Replies to Hegelian Criticisms*, Albany, NY: SUNY Press.

Sohn-Rethel, Alfred 1971, *Warenform und Denkform*, Frankfurt: Europäische Verlagsan-stalt.

Sohn-Rethel, Alfred 1978 [1970], *Intellectual and Manual Labour: A Critique of Epistem-ology*, translated by Martin Sohn-Rethel, London: Macmillan.

Sohn-Rethel, Alfred 1989 [1970], *Geistige und körperliche Arbeit. Zur Epistemologie der abendländischen Geschichte*, Weinheim: VCH Verlagsgesellschaft.

Stahl, Julius Friedrich 1833, *Die Philosophie des Rechts nach geschichtlichen Ansicht. Zweyter Band. Christliche Rechts- und Staatslehre. Erste Abteilung*, Heidelberg: J.C.B. Mohr.

Stahl, Julius Friedrich 1837, *Die Philosophie des Rechts nach geschichtlichen Ansicht. Zweyter Band. Christliche Rechts- und Staatslehre. Zweite Abteilung*, Heidelberg: J.C.B. Mohr.

Stalin, Joseph 1977 [1938], *Dialectical and Historical Materialism*, New York: International Publishers.

Starosta, Guido 2016, *Marx's Capital, Method and Revolutionary Subjectivity*, Brill: Leiden.

Staudinger, Franz 1907, *Wirtschaftliche Grundlagen der Moral*, Darmstadt: Eduard Roether.

Stein, Kilian 2012, *Die juristische Weltanschauung. Das rechtstheoretische Potenzial der Marxschen 'Kritik'*, Hamburg: VSA Verlag.

Stein, Lorenz von 1852, *System der Staatswissenschaft*. Erster Band, Tübingen: J.G. Cotta'schen Verlag.

Steiner, Hillel 2006, 'Self-Ownership and Conscription', in *The Egalitarian Conscience: Essays in Honour of G.A. Cohen*, edited by Christine Sypnowich, Oxford: Oxford University Press.

Stirner, Max 1986 [1845], *Der Einzige und sein Eigentum*, Berlin: Verlag der Mackay-Gesellschaft.

Stirner, Max 1995 [1845], *The Ego and its Own*, edited by David Leopold, translated by Steven T. Byington, Cambridge: Cambridge University Press.

Stout, Rowland 2005, *Action*, Chesham: Acumen.

Suchting, Wal 1982, ' "Productive Forces" and "Relations of Production" in Marx', *Analyse und Kritik*, 4, 2: 159–81.

Taiwo, Olufemi 1996, *Legal Naturalism: A Marxist Theory of Law*, Ithaca, NY: Cornell University Press.

Tomba, Massimiliano 2013, *Marx's Temporalities*, translated by Peter D. Thomas and Sara R. Farris, Leiden: Brill.

Torrance, John 1995, *Karl Marx's Theory of Ideas*, Cambridge: Cambridge University Press.

Tucker, Robert C. 1969, *The Marxian Revolutionary Idea*, New York: Norton and Company.

Tucker, Robert C. 1972 [1961], *Philosophy and Myth in Karl Marx*, 2nd edition, Cambridge: Cambridge University Press.

Tuschling, Burkhard 1976, *Rechtsform und Produktionsverhältnisse. Zur materialistischen Theorie des Rechtsstaates*, Frankfurt am Main: Europäisches Verlagsanstalt.

Uchida, Hiroshi (ed.) 2006, *Marx for the 21st Century*, Oxon: Routledge.

Vallentyne, Peter 2012, 'Left-Libertarianism', in *Oxford Handbook of Political Philosophy*, edited by David Estlund, Oxford: Oxford University Press.

Vatter, Miguel 2005, 'Pettit and Modern Republican Political Thought', in *Nomos XLVI: Political Exclusion and Domination*, edited by Melissa S. Williams and Stephen Macedo, New York: New York University Press.

Veer, Donald van de 1973, 'Marx's View of Justice', *Philosophy and Phenomenological Research*, 33: 366–86.

Vorländer, Karl 1911, *Kant und Marx. Ein Beitrag zur Philosophie des Sozialismus*, Tübingen: J.C.B. Mohr.

Vrousalis, Nicholas 2013, 'Exploitation, Vulnerability, and Social Domination', *Philosophy and Public Affairs*, 41, 2: 131–57.

Waldron, Jeremy 1987, *'Nonsense on Stilts'. Bentham, Burke and Marx on the Rights of Man*, London: Methuen and Co.

Weber, Max 1978 [1922], *Economy and Society, Volume 1*, edited by Guenther Roth and Claus Wittich, Berkeley, CA: University of California Press.

Weber, Max 1988 [1904], 'Die Objektivität sozialwissenschaftlicher und sozialpolitischer Erkenntnis', in *Gesammelte Aufsätze zur Wissenschaftslehre*, Tübingen: J.C.B. Mohr.

Weber, Max 2005 [1922], *Wirtschaft und Gesellschaft. Grundriss der verstehenden Soziologie*, Frankfurt am Main: Melzer.

Weber, Max 2012 [1904], 'The "Objectivity" of Knowledge in Social Science and Social Policy', in *Max Weber: Collected Methodological Writings*, edited by Hans Henrik Bruun and Sam Whimster, translated by Hans Henrik Bruun, London: Routledge.

Welcker, Carl 2001 [1813], *Die letzten Gründe von Recht, Staat und Strafe*, Goldbach: Keip.

Wertheimer, Alan 1996, *Exploitation*, Princeton: Princeton University Press.

Wetherly, Paul (ed.) 1992, *Marx's Theory of History: The Contemporary Debate*, Aldershot: Avebury.

Wetherly, Paul 2005, *Marxism and the State: An Analytical Approach*, Basingstoke: Palgrave Macmillan.

Wike, Victoria S. 1982, *Kant's Antinomies of Reason: Their Origin and their Resolution*, Washington: University Press of America.

Wildt, Andreas 1986, 'Gerechtigkeit in Marx' Kapital', in *Ethik und Marx. Moralkritik und Normative Grundlagen der Marxschen Theorie*, edited by Emil Angehrn and Georg Lohmann, Königstein im Taunus: Athenäum.

Wildt, Andreas 1997, 'Paradoxien in der Marxschen Moralkritik und ihre Auflösungen', *Logos*, 4, 3, 210–42.

Wood, Allen W. 1972, 'The Marxian Critique of Justice', *Philosophy and Public Affairs*, 1, 3: 244–82.

Wood, Allen W. 1979, 'Marx on Right and Justice: A Reply to Husami', *Philosophy and Public Affairs*, 8, 3: 267–95.

Wood, Allen W. 1984, 'Justice and Class Interests', *Philosophica*, 33, 1: 9–32.

Wood, Allen W. 1990, *Hegel's Ethical Thought*, Cambridge: Cambridge University Press.

Wood, Allen W. 1995, 'What is Exploitation?', *Social Philosophy and Policy*, 12, 2: 136–58.

Wood, Allen W. 1998, 'Kant on Duties Regarding Nonrational Nature', *Proceedings of the Aristotelian Society*, Supplementary Volume, 72: 189–210.

Wood, Allen W. 1999, *Kant's Ethical Thought*, Cambridge: Cambridge University Press.

Wood, Allen W. 2004 [1981], *Karl Marx*, 2nd edition, London: Routledge.

Wood, Allen W. 2008, *Kantian Ethics*, Cambridge: Cambridge University Press.

Wood, Allen W. 2014, *The Free Development of Each*, Oxford: Oxford University Press.

Wood, Allen W. 2017, 'Marx and Kant on Capitalist Exploitation', *Kantian Review*, 22, 4: 641–59.

Wood, Ellen Meiksins 1989, 'Rational Choice Marxism: Is the Game Worth the Candle?', *New Left Review*, I/177: 41–88.

Wright, Erik Olin 1982, 'The Status of the Political in the Concept of Class Structure', *Politics and Society*, 11, 3: 321–41.

Wright, Erik Olin 1985, *Classes*, London: Verso.

Wright, Erik Olin 1995, 'What is Analytical Marxism?', in *Rational Choice Marxism*, edited by Terrell Carver and Paul Thomas, Basingstoke: Macmillan.

Wright, Erik Olin (ed.) 2005, *Approaches to Class Analysis*, Cambridge: Cambridge University Press.

Wright, Erik Olin, Andrew Levine and Elliot Sober 1992, *Reconstructing Marxism*, London: Verso.

Xiaoping, Wei 2010, 'Rethinking Historical Materialism: The New Edition of The German Ideology', *Science and Society*, 74, 4: 489–508.

Young, Gary 1978, 'Justice and Capitalist Production: Marx and Bourgeois Ideology', *Canadian Journal of Philosophy*, 8, 3: 421–55.

Young, Gary 1981, 'Doing Marx Justice', *Canadian Journal of Philosophy*, Supplementary Volume, VII: 251–68.

Index